Edwin Abbott Abbott

**Via Latina : A First Latin Book**

Including Accidence, Rules of Syntax, Exercises, Vocabularies, and Rules....

Edwin Abbott Abbott

**Via Latina : A First Latin Book**
*Including Accidence, Rules of Syntax, Exercises, Vocabularies, and Rules....*

ISBN/EAN: 9783337158644

Printed in Europe, USA, Canada, Australia, Japan

Cover: Foto ©Paul-Georg Meister /pixelio.de

More available books at **www.hansebooks.com**

# A First Latin Book,

INCLUDING

## ACCIDENCE, RULES OF SYNTAX, EXERCISES, VOCABULARIES,

AND

## RULES FOR CONSTRUING.

BY

EDWIN A. ABBOTT, D.D.,

*Head Master of the City of London School.*

SEVENTH THOUSAND.

LONDON:
SEELEY, JACKSON, AND HALLIDAY, FLEET STREET.
1882.

# PREFACE.

ALTHOUGH two or three very fair Latin "First Books" are already in existence, yet the present results of Latin teaching are not so satisfactory as to necessitate an apology for a new attempt. For a very long time the Author (in the course of a weekly entrance-examination of a most elementary kind) has been in the habit of asking those boys who profess to have learned Latin—almost all of whom are over thirteen years of age, and have learned Latin two, three, four, or five years—to construe the sentence "Oppida magna boni agricolae habent": and not one in five has been able to construe these few simple words correctly. The Examiner would have been well content with the translation "They have the great towns of the good husbandman": but almost all have succumbed to the temptation of treating "oppida" as Nominative, and have then "plunged" to the rendering "Great towns have good husbandmen"—or something worse.

One reason for these miserable results is probably that, at present (1880), a private school may be "kept" by any one with or without any degree, or other proof of the possession either of knowledge or of the power to impart knowledge: but it is also possible that many of our elementary Latin books are to some extent responsible for these failures, because they lay scarcely sufficient stress on *parsing before construing*. The Latin sentences placed before beginners are so easy that the pupil soon finds he can *construe* without the trouble of *parsing*; and he thus early contracts the fatal habit of "plunging" at the meaning instead of reasoning it out. To provide against this evil is one of the principal objects of the *Via Latina*. From the very first page the pupil is taught to parse as well as to construe, and not to construe till he has parsed; and throughout the book, parsing questions are put bearing on the Latin Exercises, and the answers are suggested by paragraph references.

In the preparation of the Exercises the *dictum* of Lord Bacon has been borne in mind that in all kinds of training we should imitate dancers, who practise at one time in heavy boots, at another in light shoes. A considerable experience of teaching has led the Author to the conclusion that a First Latin Book requires a great diversity of Exercises, some to illustrate special rules, others of a more general nature; some on points of Accidence, the Irregular Nouns and Verbs, and the like, others on difficulties of Syntax; and again, some difficult and accompanied with helps, others easy to be done without help; some to be written with preparation, others to be answered *vivâ voce*. This want he has attempted to supply in the present volume, and at the same time to combine the Exercises with an outline of the Accidence, and the principal Rules of Syntax.

As regards the arrangement of the Exercises, some departures from the usual order have been introduced, especially in the earlier introduction of the simpler uses of the Subjunctive Mood. It is not uncommon for boys, after committing the Verbs to memory, to allow the Subjunctive Mood to rust for some weeks or months before they make any use of it, and consequently to find that, when they need to use it, they no longer remember it; the consequence is that, during all this while, they remain under the impression that "amemus" means *we may love*, and "amaremus" *we might love*—statements which are very partial, and almost erroneous, expressions of the real truth. It seems better to introduce the Subjunctive earlier in simple and intelligible rules and examples, so as to impress the pupil from the first with the principle of the Sequence of Tenses.

The Author has also aimed at introducing a little more variety into the examples by teaching somewhat more of *idiom* than is usually taught in First Latin Books; and some hints on the particles have not been thought out of place. In Greek a boy is taught to pay attention to particles almost from the beginning, but in Latin they are too much neglected; and, for want of them, the language too often strikes beginners as uninteresting and lifeless.

Most of the longer sentences in the Latin Exercises have been selected from classical authors, occasionally modified: and here, as well as in the statement and explanation of several of the Rules, ample acknowledgments are due to the *Public School Grammar.* Several of them may appear at first sight somewhat difficult for beginners; but it will generally be found that the Vocabularies and the paragraph references supply all the help that is needed for a pupil who will honestly *parse before construing.* The Author has worked through most of them with a pupil ten years old, whose questions and difficulties have suggested many of the footnotes bearing on the Exercises.

The Irregular Verbs are arranged in two lists; first according to their formation, and then in alphabetical order. This repetition may appear superfluous; but the object of it is to enable the pupil to learn the Verbs according to their logical order in the first list, but afterwards to test his knowledge by repeating them when presented to him miscellaneously in the second list, which also includes a large number of the more important Compound Verbs in which boys frequently go wrong.

The Hints on Construing are intended not only as a preparation for translating a Latin author, but also as a summary of Rules for parsing the sentences in the Latin Exercises, and for translating English into Latin.

It is hoped that the Glossary of Grammatical Terms, while escaping the necessity of breaking the thread of the Accidence and Syntax by interposing continual explanations of terms, will on the other hand avoid the greater evil of suffering the pupil to use words of the meaning of which he knows nothing.

In the Public Schools and in the better class of Preparatory Schools (to the excellence of which the Author bears willing testimony) such portentous failures as were mentioned in the beginning of this Preface are (no doubt) unknown: but even there it sometimes appears as though it were very difficult to ground boys well in Latin Grammar without an inordinate waste of time, or without dwarfing the pupil's faculties by an excessive prolongation of a mechanical and monotonous word-drill. Good teachers will succeed without any books in avoiding the evil and attaining the good; but even good teachers may occasionally be helped by a book, and to them this book is offered, not as a substitute, but as a help, for good teaching.

I gratefully acknowledge much valuable help for which I am indebted to Mr. J. S. Reid, Fellow and Tutor of Caius College, Cambridge, and one of the Classical Examiners for the University of London.

# PREFACE TO THE REVISED EDITION.

This Edition contains many corrections and modifications suggested by the use of the book in teaching. All the Exercises have been worked through with the view of detecting omissions in the Vocabulary, or difficulties that required additional help. The Exercises themselves have received very few alterations, but many references to Rules have been inserted, and the deficiencies in the Vocabularies have been supplied.

My thanks are due to Mr. J. S. Phillpotts, Head Master of Bedford Grammar School, for many useful suggestions incorporated in the present Edition.

# CONTENTS.

|  | PAGE |
|---|---|
| Pronunciation | xvi |
| The Cases of Nouns | 1—4 |
| The First Declension | 6 |
| The Second Declension | 8 |
| Ablative of Instrument and Agent | 11 |
| Adjectives of the First and Second Declension | 13—16 |
| The Third Declension (Consonant Branch) | 18 |
| Adj. governing Dative; **dignus**, g. Ablative | 19 |
| The Abl. answering to *When?* and *Within what time?* | 21 |
| The Acc. answering to *How long?* or *During what time?* | 21 |
| **Multi**, *many (men)*; **multa**, *many (things)* | 23 |
| Neuter Nouns of the Third Declension (Consonant Branch) | 24 |
| Third Declension, continued (the -i Nouns) | 25 |
| Adjectives of the Third Declension | 27 |
| The Fourth Declension | 31 |
| The Fifth Declension | 33 |
| The Comparison of Adjectives; **quam**, or Ablative | 34—5 |

## CONTENTS.

|  | PAGE |
|---|---|
| Irregular Comparison | 37—8 |
| Numeral Adjectives | 39—42 |
| The Dative of Possession with est | 42 |
| **Ūnus, ullus, sōlus, ălĭus, &c.** | 43—4 |
| Pronouns and Pronominal Adjectives | 45 |
| A Verb agrees with its Nom. Case in Number and Person | 46 |
| Direct Questions | 48 |
| Demonstrative and Emphatic Pronouns | 49—50 |
| Relative and Interrogative Pronouns | 51—2 |
| The First Conjugation (Active) | 53—5 |
| The Second ,, ,, | 56—8 |
| The Third ,, ,, | 58—60 |
| The Fourth ,, ,, | 60—2 |
| The Latin and English Tenses; Apposition | 63—4 |
| A Verb agrees with the First Person, rather than the Second, and the Second rather than the Third | 65 |
| The Infinitive as a Subject or Object | 66 |
| The Imperative; the use of **nē** in Prohibition | 67 |
| The Subjunctive expressing Purpose | 67 |
| The Subjunctive expressing a Dependent Question | 69 |
| The Sequence of Tenses | 70 |
| **Quĭdem, vēro, ĕtiam, vĕl** | 70—2 |
| Verbs signifying *pleasing, obeying*, &c., take the Dative | 72 |
| Verbs of *asking, commanding, advising,* and *striving* are followed by **ut**, or **nē**, with the Subjunctive | 74 |
| Verbs of *preventing* are followed by **quōmĭnus** and the Subjunctive; **nōn est dŭbĭum quīn** | 75 |
| **Cum**, with the Subjunctive Mood | 77 |

## CONTENTS. xiii

|  | PAGE |
|---|---|
| **Vĕnio, vinco, vincio, rĕpĕrio** | 78 |
| The Verb **sum** | 79—81 |
| The Active Participles | 81 |
| The Dependent Future Interrogative; **quando** | 82 |
| The First Conjugation (Passive) | 83—6 |
| The Second      „            „ | 86—8 |
| The Third       „            „ | 88—91 |
| The Fourth      „            „ | 91—3 |
| The Passive Participle | 94 |
| An Adjective agreeing with Nouns of different Genders | 95 |
| Impersonal Use of the Passive | 96 |
| An Active Verb that governs the Dative retains the Dative in the Passive | 97 |
| The Gerundive Construction with the Dative of the Agent | 99 |
| **Capio**, Conjugation of | 100—1 |
| **Utrum—ăn; -nĕ—ăn** | 102 |
| The Prepositions | 104—9 |
| The Ablative of Manner | 106 |
| **Ăd** with the Gerund and the Gerundive | 108 |
| Verbs compounded with Prepositions | 110—1 |
| **Mĭnĭmum ăbest quĭn**, &c. | 111 |
| The Ablative Absolute | 112—4 |
| Deponent Verbs | 115—7 |
| **Oblīviscor, mĭsĕreor,** &c.; **fungor, fruor, ūtor,** &c. | 119 |
| The Accusative and Infinitive; its Tenses | 120—2 |
| **Fŏre ŭt; sē, suus** | 122—3 |
| Impersonal Verbs | 124—5 |
| **Possum, vŏlo, nōlo, mālo, fĕro** | 126—22 |

## CONTENTS.

| | PAGE |
|---|---|
| Indirect Questions after Verbs of *knowing, discovering*, &c. | 133 |
| The Verb **eo** | 135 |
| Supines; **captum īri** | 137—8 |
| The Gerund and Gerundive | 139 |
| The Verb **fio**; The Complementary Subject | 141 |
| Cases; The Accusative of Extension | 142 |
| The Locative Case | 143 |
| The Dative of Equivalence or Purpose | 144 |
| The Ablative; of *Definite Price*; of *Quality*; *Plenty* or *Want* | 145—6 |
| The Genitive of *Quality*; *Value*; *Indefinite Price*; *Plenty* or *Want*; to express "it is the *mark* of"; after Adjectives used as Nouns; after Adjectives of *knowledge, desire*, &c. | 147—8 |
| The Subjunctive used to express *result* or *consequence*; *optatively*; *hortatively*; *concessively*; in Conditional Sentences; after **qui** | 149—52 |
| **Sī quĭs; nē quĭs** | 151 |
| **Ŭt nōn**, when used for **nē** | 152 |
| **Vĕreor ŭt; nescio ăn** | 153 |
| **Quo** with Comparative; **suus, sē, ipsĕ** | 154—5 |
| **Quisquam, ălĭquĭs, quīlībet, quīdam** | 156 |

Irregular Verbs and Genders of Nouns
- Irregular Nouns . . . . . . . 157
- **Cēlo, dŏceo**; Adverbial **antĕ** and **post** 158
- Distrib. Numerals; **cum...tum** . 159—60
- **Quam qui**; Historical Infinitive . 161—2
- **Quamquam** and **quamvīs**; **jampridem** . . . . . . . . 163—4
- **Quam** with Superl.; **intĕrest, rĕfert** 166—7

## CONTENTS.

| | PAGE |
|---|---|
| Elementary Rules on Oratio Obliqua . . . . | 168—71 |
| Easy and Recapitulatory Exercises . . . . . . . . | 172—186 |

## APPENDICES.

| | |
|---|---|
| I.—Irregular Verbs in Order of Formation . . . . . | 189 |
| II.— ,, ,, ,, Alphabetical Order . . . . . | 200 |
| III.—Hints on Construing . . . . . . . . . . . | 216 |
| IV.—A Parsing Table . . . . . . . . . . . . | 224 |
| V.—A Table of Genders . . . . . . . . . . . | 226 |
| VI.—On the Latin Days of the Month . . . . . . . | 229 |
| VII.—Elementary Rules on Quantity . . . . . . . . | 230 |
| VIII.—Glossary of Grammatical Terms . . . . . . . | 232 |
| IX.—Vocabularies for the Earlier Exercises . . . . . | 240 |
| X.—Latin-English Vocabulary . . . . . . . . . | 248 |
| XI.—English-Latin Vocabulary . . . . . . . . . | 284 |

# SCHEME OF LATIN PRONUNCIATION.[1]

*Based on the nearest English Approximations.*

### VOWELS AND DIPHTHONGS.

| Latin | | | English | | |
|---|---|---|---|---|---|
| Latin | ā[2] | = | English | *a* | in f*a*ther. |
| ,, | ă | = | ,, | first *a* | in aw*a*y, or *a* in vill*a* |
| ,, | ē | = | ,, | *ai* | in p*ai*n. |
| ,, | ae | = | ,, | *ai* | in p*ai*n. |
| ,, | oe | = | ,, | *ai* | in p*ai*n. |
| ,, | ĕ | = | ,, | *e* | in m*e*n. |
| ,, | ī | = | ,, | *i* | in mach*i*ne. |
| ,, | ĭ | = | ,, | *i* | in p*i*ty. |
| ,, | ō | = | ,, | *o* | in h*o*me. |
| ,, | ŏ | = | ,, | *o* | in t*o*p. |
| ,, | ū | = | ,, | *u* | in r*u*le. |
| ,, | ŭ | = | ,, | *u* | in f*u*ll. |
| ,, | au | = | ,, | *ow* | in p*ow*er. |
| ,, | ui | = | ,, | *we*, e.g. in Lat. qui, cui. |
| ,, | eu | = | ,, | {Latin ĕ followed quickly by Latin ŭ (differs little from present pronunciation). |
| ,, | ei | = | ,, | {Latin ĕ followed quickly by Latin i (differs little from *ai* in p*ai*n). |

### CONSONANTS.

| | | | | | |
|---|---|---|---|---|---|
| Latin c, ch | = | English | *k*. | | |
| ,, g | = | ,, | *g* in *g*et. | | |
| ,, s | = | ,, | *s* in *s*in. | | |
| ,, t (rătĭo) | = | ,, | *t* in ca*t*, not *sh*, as in na*t*ion. |
| ,, j | = | ,, | *y* in *y*ard. | | |
| ,, v | = | ,, | *v*. | | |
| ,, z, ph, th | = | ,, | *z, ph, th*. | | |

Latin s between two vowels = (sometimes) English *s* in ro*s*e, *e.g.* "ro*s*a."

---

[1] Taken from the *Syllabus of Latin Pronunciation*, issued by the Professors of Latin at the Universities of Cambridge and Oxford, at the request of the Head Masters of Schools. Some modifications have been made by the suppression of all Italian standards, and of all the English standards of pronunciation that contain a vowel followed by *r*. Consequently the Latin o is represented by the English o. The Professors give the option of pronouncing v as *v* or as *w*.

[2] Syllables in Latin are either long or short. A short syllable is denoted by this mark (‿), a long one by this (‒). A few elementary rules about the *quantity*, i.e. the length or shortness of syllables, are given in Appendix VII. on Prosody.

# VIA LATINA.

## THE CASES OF NOUNS.[1]

### THE FIRST OR -A DECLENSION.

Ăquĭl-ă, *(an) eagle.* Fēmĭn-ă, *(a) woman.* Fīlĭ-ă, *(a) daughter.*
Ăqu-ă, *water.* Dextr-ă, *(a) right hand.* Pĕcūnĭ-ă, *money.*
Ămă-t, *(he) loves.* Dă-t, *(he) gives.* Lăvă-t, *(he) washes.*
Lībĕră-t, *(he) frees.* Monstră-t, *(he) points out.*
Sŭpĕră-t, *(he) overcomes.* Vŏră-t, *(he) devours.*[2]

1 English Nouns have (now) only two Cases, of which the Possessive is indicated by the affix *'s*: "*John's* book;" "the *sun's* light;" "*men's* clothes."

Latin Nouns have six Cases.

2   1. THE NOMINATIVE CASE.—When a Noun answers the question *Who?* or *What?* before a Verb (i.e. when it is the Subject of a Verb), it is put in the Nominative Case, which, in Nouns of the First Declension, is expressed by the termination -a short, -ă:

*The woman loves.*   Fēmĭn-ă ămăt.
*The eagle devours.*   Ăquĭl-ă vŏrăt.

---

[1] For an explanation of the terms Case, Noun, &c., see the Glossary of Grammatical Terms, Appendix VIII. p. 232.

[2] A vowel before t final is always short: the *quantity* of a-t (˘) will therefore not be marked for the future.

*Who* loves ?—Ans., the *woman*, **fēmĭn-ă**. *What* devours ? —Ans., the *eagle*, **ăquĭl-ă**.

In parsing Latin, the question is generally asked as follows: Why is **fēmĭnă** Nominative?—Ans., *because it is the Subject of* (or *Nominative to*) **ămăt**.

**3** 2. THE VOCATIVE CASE.—When a person or thing is addressed, the Noun expressing the person or thing is put in the Vocative Case, which, in the First Declension, is the same as the Nominative:

*O woman,* **Fēmĭn-ă**.      *O eagle,* **Ăquĭl-ă**.

Why is **fēmĭnă** (or **ăquīla**) Vocative?—Ans., *because it is a person* (or *thing*) *addressed.*

**4** 3. THE ACCUSATIVE CASE.—When a Noun answers the question *Whom?* or *What?* after *a Verb* (i.e. when it is the Direct Object of a Verb), it is put in the Accusative Case, which is expressed, in the First Declension, by the termination **-am**:

*The daughter loves the woman.*    Fĭlĭ-ă **fēmĭn-am** ămă-t.
*The woman points out the eagle.*    Fēmĭn-ă **ăquĭl-am** monstră-t.

Loves *whom?*—Ans., the *woman.*    Points out *what?*— Ans., the *eagle.*

Why is **fēmĭnam** the Accusative?—Ans., *because it is the Direct Object of* (or *Accusative governed by*) **ămăt**.

**5** *N.B.* Note here that the order of the words is not the same in a Latin and in an English sentence.

In English the Object generally follows the Verb, and the Subject generally precedes the Verb, so that the order of the words shows which is Subject and which is Object.

**5a** But in Latin the Verb generally comes at the end of the sentence; and the Nominative and Accusative must be discovered, not by the order, *but by examining the Case.*

Thus, in the last example, **-am** is the Accusative termination, and **-ă** is the Nominative termination. Therefore

**fēmĭn-ă** is the Nominative, and the Subject of **monstrăt**; and **ăquĭl-am** is the Accusative, and the Object of **monstrăt**.

**6** 4. THE GENITIVE CASE.—The Latin Genitive (besides other uses) expresses the English Possessive Case, and, in the First Declension, terminates in **-ae**:

| | |
|---|---|
| *The woman's daughter.* | **Fēmĭn-ae** fīlĭă, *or (less commonly)* fīlĭă **fēmĭn-ae**. |

As the Latin Gen. expresses many other relations besides possession, it is usual, in parsing a Gen. Noun qualifying another Noun, to say that the former is *governed by* the latter.

Why is **fēmĭnae** Genitive?—Ans., *Because it is governed by the Noun* **fīlĭă**.

In English the Possessive Case *always* precedes the Noun which it qualifies.[1] In Latin the Genitive generally precedes, but *not always*.

**7** 5. THE DATIVE CASE.—When a Noun expresses the person (or thing) (1) *to whom* a thing is *given*, or (2) *for whom* a thing is done, the Noun is put in the Dative (i.e. *Giving*) Case, which, in the First Declension, is expressed by the termination **-ae**:

| | |
|---|---|
| (1) *The daughter gives an eagle to the woman.* | Fīlĭ-a ăquĭl-am **fēmĭn-ae** dă-t. |
| (2) *The woman points out the eagle to,* or *for,* (*her*) *daughter.* | Fēmĭn-ă ăquĭl-am **fīlĭ-ae** monstra-t. |

(1) Why is **fēmĭnae** Dative?—Ans., *After a verb of Giving, or, Indirect Object of* **dat**.

In answer to the question (2) Why is **fīlĭae** Dative? it is usual to say *Dative of Advantage or Disadvantage*.

---

[1] Distinguish the English Possessive Case "sun's" from "of the sun," which is not a Case at all, but a Phrase used instead of a Case.

**8**  6. THE ABLATIVE CASE, besides (1) *sometimes* expressing *separation*, or *motion from*, i.e. *ablation*, also (2) *always* expresses the *instrument with* or *by* which an action is performed.  In the First Declension, the Ablative is denoted by -a long, -ā:

(1) *The woman frees the daugh-*   Fēmĭn-a fīlĭ-am **culpā** lībĕra-t.
*ter from blame.*
*He hastens from Capua.*          Prŏpĕră-t **Căpŭ-ā**.

(2) *The woman washes the*    Fēmĭn-ă fīlĭ-am **ăqu-ā** lăva-t.
*daughter with water.*
*The daughter gives money with*  Fīlĭ-ă pĕcūnĭ-am **dextr-ā** da-t.
*(her) right hand.*

(1) Why is **culp-ā** the Ablative?—Ans., *Ablative of Separation*.[1]

(2) Why is **ăquā** the Ablative?—Ans., *Ablative of the Means or Instrument*.

FIRST DECLENSION, SINGULAR NUMBER.

*Nom.* **Insŭl-ă**, (*an* or *the*) *island* (Subject).
*Voc.* **Insŭl-ă**, *O island*.
*Acc.* **Insŭl-am**, (*an* or *the*) *island* (Object).
*Gen.* **Insŭl-ae**, (*an* or *the*) *island's*, or *of* (*an* or *the*) *island*.
*Dat.* **Insŭl-ae**, *to* or *for* (*an* or *the*) *island*.
*Abl.* **Insŭl-ā**, *from, with,* or *by* (*an* or *the*) *island*.[1]

**9**  THE ARTICLE.—From the above form it will be seen that what is sometimes called "the Article" in English (i.e. *a* or *the*) does not exist in Latin. **Insŭl-ă** must be rendered "*an* island" or "*the* island," according to the sense.

EXERCISE I.

(*Learn Vocabulary I.*)

1. [2]Fili-ae.  2. Aquil-ā.  3. Pecuni-am.  4. [2]Femin-ă.  5. Reginam.  6. Aqu-ā.  7. [2]Puell-ae.  8. Naut-ă.[2]

---

[1] The Ablative is only *sometimes* used to express *separation*. Most frequently it cannot be so used *without a Preposition*. The particular Verbs and Adjectives of Separation, which are followed by an Ablative without a Preposition, will be given later on. But the pupil must remember that **insŭlā**, *without an accompanying Preposition*, very seldom means *from an island*.

[2] These words are capable of more than one translation. Each translation should be written down, both here and for the future.

1. *Of a sailor.* 2. *To a sailor.* 3. *Money* (object). 4. *Water* (subject). 5. *For a girl.* 6. *By water.* 7. *With money.* 8. *O sailor.*

### Exercise II.

Parse the Nouns in the following Exercise, stating in what Case each is, and why.

1. Femină naut-am aqu-ā lava-t. 2. Naut-ae sapienti-ā procell-am supera-t. 3. Naut-ae sapienti-ā procell-ae violenti-am supera-t. 4. Regină insul-am fili-ae da-t. 5. Fili-ă pecuni-am dextr-ā dat. 6. Femin-ă pecuni-am naut-ae dextr-ā da-t. 7. Femin-ae patienti-ā naut-ae violenti-am supera-t. 8. Femin-ă patienti-ā naut-am supera-t. 9. Patienti-ă, O femin-ă, violenti-am supera-t. 10. Experienti-ă sapienti-am regin-ae dat. 11. Naut-ae dextr-ă fēmin-am violenti-ā (9a) līber-a-t.[1]

[Words in brackets, thus (*her*), are not to be translated.]

1. *The queen gives an island to* (*her*) *daughter.*[2] 2. *The woman's daughter gives money to the sailor.* 3. *The sailor washes* (*his*) *daughter with* (*his*) *right hand* (5a). 4. *The sailor's violence overcomes the patience of the queen.* 5. *The woman by* (*her*) *patience overcomes the sailor's violence.* 6. *The daughter gives the queen's money to the sailor.* 7. (*Thy*) *daughter's patience, O woman, overcomes the violence of the queen.* 8. *Experience gives* (*to*) *the sailor wisdom.* 9. *The sailor's prudence delivers the daughter from the storm.*

(When this Exercise is turned into Latin, parse the Latin; and do the same with future Exercises.)

THE SINGULAR AND PLURAL OF THE FIRST DECLENSION.

There are six similar cases for the Plural of each Noun, so that the Singular and Plural of insŭl-ă are thus declined:

---

[1] The Pupil should parse this Exercise *before construing it*. He should then commit the Latin to memory so as to be able to repeat the Latin of this Exercise from his own English, or from the English when read aloud to him, before he translates the next Exercise into Latin.

[2] The Pupil should note the order of the words in the Latin Exercise above, and imitate it by putting the Verb (for the present) *at the end.*

Words that are bracketed in the English Exercises are not to be translated into Latin, e.g. *her* in the first sentence of the English Exercise II.

## FIRST DECLENSION.

|  | Singular. | Plural. |
|---|---|---|
| Nom. | Insŭl-ă, *an island.* | Insŭl-ae, *islands.* |
| Voc. | Insŭl-ă, *O island.* | Insŭl-ae, *O islands.* |
| Acc. | Insŭl-am, *an island.* | Insŭl-ās, *islands.* |
| Gen. | Insŭl-ae, *of an island.* | Insŭl-ārum, *of islands.* |
| Dat. | Insŭl-ae, *to or for an island.* | Insŭl-īs, *to or for islands.* |
| Abl. | Insŭl-ă, *from, with, or by an island.* | Insŭl-īs, *from, with, or by islands.* |

### EXERCISE III.

1. Puell-īs.[1]  2. Femin-ārum.  3. Femin-ă.[1]  4. Naut-ae.[1]
5. Violenti-ā.  6. Aquil-ae.[1]  7. Aquil-īs.[1]  8. Aquil-ās.
9. Patienti-am.  10. Naut-ārum.

1. *To women.*  2. *From blame.*  3. *Eagles* (object).  4. *By patience.*  5. *Of eagles.*  6. *O women.*  7. *To eagles.*  8. *Women* (subject).  9. *From an eagle.*  10. *To sailors.*

If a Nominative is changed from the Singular to the Plural Number, the Verb changes also:

| *The woman loves.* | Fēmĭn-ă ămă-t. |
| *The women love.* | Fēmĭn-ae ăma-nt. |
| *The eagle devours.* | Ăquĭl-a vŏră-t. |
| *The eagles devour.* | Ăquĭl-ae vŏra-nt. |

The Plural of all Verbs ending in -ă-t is formed by inserting **n** between **a** and **t**:

**Sŭpĕra-nt**, *they overcome*, **monstra-nt**, *they point out*, **da-nt**, *they give.*

### EXERCISE IV.

*A.*—Change the Singular into the Plural in the Nouns and Verbs of the following:

1. Naut-ă ama-t.  2. Regin-ă monstra-t.  3. Fili-ă lava-t.  4. Femin-ă da-t.  5. Naut-ă supera-t.  6. Puell-ă libera-t.

*B.*—Change the Plural into the Singular in the following:

1. Nautae da-nt.  2. Regin-ae supera-nt.  3. Aquil-ae vora-nt.  4. Fili-ae ama-nt.  5. Dextr-ae libera-nt.  6. Stell-ae monstra-nt.

---

[1] The words or sentences thus marked are capable of different renderings; all of which should be given.

## Exercise V.

1. Naut-ă procell-am supera-t. 2. Naut-ae procell-am supera-nt. 3. Regin-ă pecuni-am puell-ae da-t. 4. Reginae pecuni-am puell-ae dant (9a). 5. Naut-arum patienti-ă procell-as supera-t.[1] 6. Naut-ae patienti-ā procellam supera-nt. 7. Femin-ă naut-ārum fili-ās lavat. 8. Femin-ă naut-ārum fili-ās aqu-ā lava-t. 9. Patienti-ă, O naut-ae, violenti-am super-at. 10. Naut-ae, O regin-ă, patienti-ā procell-ārum violenti-am supera-nt. 11. Naut-arum dextr-ae regin-am procell-ae violenti-ā libera-nt.[2]

1. *The sailor overcomes the storm.* 2. *The sailors overcome the storm.* 3. *The women love the girl.* 4. *The woman loves the girl.* 5. *The queen gives money to the sailors.* 6. *The eagles devour the sailor.* 7. *By patience the sailor overcomes the storms.* 8. *The sailor's daughter points out the eagle.* 9. *The sailor's daughters point out the eagle to the queen with (their) right hands.* 10. *The queen's wisdom frees the woman from blame.* 11. *The daughters of the sailors wash the women with water* (5a).

## Exercise VI.

**11**   After the verb "give," *to* is often not used in English, but the Dative must be retained in Latin :

| *The queen gives the sailors money.* | Rēgīna pĕcūnĭam **nautīs** dat. |

**12**   Et, (which means *both* or *and*,) is sometimes repeated to couple together two Nouns *in the same case :*

| *Experience gives both patience and wisdom.* | Expĕrientĭă **et pătĭentĭam et săpĭentĭam** dat. |

Sometimes the former et (*both*) is omitted :

| *The stars point out the way for (both) the sailors and the women.* | Stellae vĭam **(et) nautīs et fēmĭnīs** monstrant. |

---

[1] Sŭpĕrat is Sing. agreeing with its Nom. pătĭentĭ-a, and is not affected by the Plural Number of the Genitive **nautārum**. What overcomes?—Ans., *patience*.

[2] This and all the following Latin Exercises should be carefully parsed *before being construed*, and then learned, so that the pupil can readily repeat them when the English is given.

For **fīliābus, dĕābus,** &c., see Exercise LXXXIV., p. 155, and foll.

1. Fīli-ă aqu-am naut-ae dat. 2. Sapienti-ā, o nautae, regin-ă violenti-am supera-t. 3. Regin-ă fīli-ae pecuni-am dextr-ā dat. 4. Stell-ae vi-am naut-is monstra-nt. 5. Experienti-ă naut-is sapienti-am da-t. 6. Stell-ă naut-ae fīli-ae vi-am monstra-t. 7. Regin-ae fīli-ae naut-as aqu-ā lava-nt. 8. Experienti-ā et sapienti-ā naut-ae procell-as supera-nt. 9. Regin-ă nautis et aquam et pecuni-am da-t. 10. Sapientiă regin-am īr-ā et intemperanti-ā libera-t.

1. By experience and (by) patience the sailor overcomes the storm. 2. The queen gives water both to the sailors and to the women. 3. The women give to the sailors water and money. 4. Wisdom, O sailors, gives patience to the queen. 5. The stars point out the way for the daughter of the sailor. 6. The queen's daughter washes the woman with water. 7. The patience of sailors, O daughter, overcomes the storm. 8. The sailors, by (their) patience, overcome the violence of the storm. 9. The queen's daughters give the (11) sailor water. 10. By money the woman frees (her) daughter from the violence of the sailors.

## THE SECOND OR O- DECLENSION.

This Declension is divided into three groups, in which the Nominative ends in:

(1) -ŭs          (2) -r          (3) -um

### 1.—NOUNS IN -ŭs.

| | Singular. | Plural. |
|---|---|---|
| Nom. | Dŏmĭn-ŭs, a lord.[1] | Dŏmĭn-ī, lords. |
| Voc. | Dŏmĭn-ĕ, O lord. | Dŏmĭn-ī, O lords. |
| Acc. | Dŏmĭn-um, a lord. | Dŏmĭn-ōs, lords. |
| Gen. | Dŏmĭn-ī, of a lord.[2] | Dŏmĭn-ōrum, of lords. |
| Dat. | Dŏmĭn-ō, to or for a lord. | Dŏmĭn-īs, to or for lords. |
| Abl. | Dŏmĭn-ō, by, with, or from a lord.[3] | Dŏmĭn-īs, by, with, or from lords. |

13  The Voc. Sing. of fīlĭ-ŭs, a son, and of proper names in -ĭus, contracts -ĭĕ into -ī: fīlī, O son; Mercŭrī, O

---

[1] Dŏmĭnŭs means lord in the sense of owner, master.
[2] The Gen. Sing. of nouns in -ĭus, -ium, was generally contracted into -ī; but most English books retain -ii.
13a  [3] N.B. A noun denoting a living thing is never used with by without the Latin Preposition ā or ăb. The pupil should remember that by a spear may be translated hastā, but by a lord is ā dŏmĭno.

*Mercury.* The termination -ie was avoided even in common nouns in -ius, *e.g.* nuntĭ-us, *a messenger.* The Vocatives of these words were not used at all. The Voc. of **Deus**, *God*, is the same as the Nominative.

2.—*a.* Nouns in -ĕr (gen. -rī).[1]

| | | |
|---|---|---|
| *Nom.* | **Măgistĕr**, *a master.* | **Măgistr-ī**, *masters.* |
| *Voc.* | **Măgistĕr**, *O master.* | **Măgistr-ī**, *O masters.* |
| *Acc.* | **Măgistr-um**, *a master.* | **Măgistr-ōs**, *masters.* |
| *Gen.* | **Măgistr-ī**, *of a master.* | **Măgistr-ōrum**, *of masters.* |
| *Dat.* | **Măgistr-ō**, *to or for a master.* | **Măgistr-īs**, *to or for masters.* |
| *Abl.* | **Măgistr-ō**, *by* (13a),*with, or from a master.* | **Măgistr-īs**, *by, with, or from masters.* |

2.—*b.* Nouns in -ĕr (gen. -ĕrī).[2]

| | | |
|---|---|---|
| *Nom.* | **Pŭĕr**, *a boy.* | **Pŭĕr-ī**, *boys.* |
| *Voc.* | **Pŭĕr**, *O boy.* | **Pŭĕr-ī**, *O boys.* |
| *Acc.* | **Pŭĕr-um**, *a boy.* | **Pŭĕr-ōs**, *boys.* |
| *Gen.* | **Pŭĕr-ī**, *of a boy.* | **Pŭĕr-ōrum**, *of boys.* |
| *Dat.* | **Pŭĕr-o**, *to or for a boy.* | **Pŭĕr-īs**, *to or for boys.* |
| *Abl.* | **Pŭĕr-o**, *by* (13a), *with,or from a boy.* | **Pŭĕr-īs**, *by, with, or from boys.*[2] |

**Vĭr**, *a man*, is declined like **pŭĕr**, except that I is written for ĕ: vĭr-um, vĭr-i, vĭr-o, and vĭr-i, vĭr-os, vĭr-ōrum, vĭr-is.

**Nouns** in -ri and -ĕri. The best way to remember which Nouns make -ri and which make -eri, is to remember that

14 1. The *only* Nouns declined like **pŭĕr** are **vĭr**, *man;* **gĕnĕr**, *son-in-law;* **sŏcĕr**, *father-in-law;* **vespĕr**, *evening;* **Lībĕr**, *the god of wine* (called by the Greeks *Bacchus*); also lĭbĕr-i, *children* (used only in the plural).[3]

15 [1] Nouns in -er once ended in -ĕrus, like **nŭmĕr-us**, *a number.* The Voc. pŭĕr-ĕ is found in Old Latin.

[2] Final -i, -o are always long. Also final -is, in the Dat. and Abl. Pl. of the Second Declension, is always long, and final -us in the Nom. Sing. is always short. These syllables will not therefore be always marked long or short for the future.

16 [3] The Adjective **ădulter** (used as a Noun to mean *an adulterer*) may also be included in this list; and so may Adjectives in -fer and -ger used as Nouns, *e.g.* **signifer**, *standard-bearer*, **armĭger**, *armour-bearer or squire.*

## SECOND DECLENSION.

2. All other Nouns in **ĕr** are declined like **măgister** *e.g.* ăger, căper, &c.

### 3.—Nouns in -um.

| Singular. | Plural. |
|---|---|
| *Nom.* **Regn-um**, *a kingdom* | **Regn-ă**, *kingdoms.* |
| *Voc.* **Regn-um**, *O kingdom.* | **Regn-ă**, *O kingdoms.* |
| *Acc.* **Regn-um**, *a kingdom.* | **Regn-ă**, *kingdoms.* |
| *Gen.* **Regn-ī**, *of a kingdom.* | **Regn-ōrum**, *of kingdoms.* |
| *Dat.* **Regn-ō**, *to or for a kingdom.* | **Regn-īs**, *to or for kingdoms.* |
| *Abl.* **Regn-ō**, *by, with, or from a kingdom.* | **Regn-īs**, *by, with, or from kingdoms.* |

### Exercise VII.

**Hăbĕ-t**, (*he*) *has.*  **Hăbe-nt**, (*they*) *have.*
**Terrĕ-t**, (*he*) *terrifies.*  **Terre-nt**, (*they*) *terrify.*
**Tĭmĕ-t**, (*he*) *fears.*  **Tĭme-nt**, (*they*) *fear.*

1. Hortos habent.[1] 2. Dominus filio hortum dat. 3. Dominorum filii hortum habent. 4. Filii hortum dominus servo dat. 5. Servo equum dat. 6. Filii servorum equos habent. 7. Domini equum gladio terret. 8. Nauta servos experientiā superat. 9. Servorum patientiā dominum superat. 10. Fluvius aquam habet. 11. Servi, domine, minas timent. 12. Minae, O fili (13), servos terrent.

1. *The lord has a garden.* 2. *The lord's son has gardens.* 3. *The lord's sons have gardens.* 4. *The lord gives a garden to (his) son.* 5. *The master gives the slave a horse.*[2] 6. *The slave has a sword.* 7. *The lord's sword terrifies the slave.* 8. *The slaves fear the master's sword.* 9. *The master terrifies the men with (his) sword.* 10. *The slaves overcome the man by patience.* 11. *Experience, O son, gives men patience.* 12. *The slave's patience overcomes the master's violence* (5a).

### Exercise VIII.—Nouns like măgistĕr.

An Active Verb in **-at, -ant,** or **-et, -ent,** can be made Passive by adding **-ur**; but the **ā** or **ē** of the Verb, which was shortened before **t** (**supĕră-t, terrĕ-t**), is long before **-ur**.

---

[1] Where there is no Subject to the Verb expressed, *he* or *they* must be supplied. Here **hăbent** must be translated *they have.*

[2] "The slave" here stands for "to the slave," and must be placed in the Dative Case. The pupil must be prepared for this in similar sentences where "to" is omitted after the word "give."

**sŭpĕrā-tur,** *he is (being) overcome;* **sŭpĕrant-ur,** *they are (being) overcome.*

**terrē-tur,** *he is (being) terrified;* **terrent-ur,** *they are (being) terrified.*

**17** RULE.—(1) The *instrument* is expressed by the Ablative alone; but (2) the *agent* (whether a *man* or *other animal*) requires, before the Ablative, the Preposition ā (ăb, before a vowel or h).

*The girl is terrified* (1) *with* (or    Puella (1) **hastā** (2) ā **nautā**
*by) a spear* (2) *by the sailor.*          terrētur.

1. Minister librum habet. 2. Magister agros fabris dat. 3. Aper caprum terret. 4. Minister caprum cultro terret. 5. Ager colubros habet. 6. Cancer colubros timet. 7. Cancri colubrorum violentiam timent. 8. Fabri minister Austrum timet. 9. Domini ministros arbiter sapientiā superat. 10. Pueri a colubris et ab apris terrentur. 11. Apri servorum hastis et gladiis superantur. 12. Feminas (16a) terrent.

EXERCISE IX.

CAUTION.—Distinguish between:

**Lĭbr-os,** *books.*      **Lībĕr-os,** *children.*
**Lĭbr-um,** *a book.*     **Lībĕr-um,** *Liber, the god of wine.*

A. 1. *Of snakes.* 2. *To a son-in-law.* 3. *To a crab.* 4. *To Liber.* 5. *By* (17) *goats.* 6. *Children* (Abl.). 7. *Of boys.* 8. *Of wild-boars.* 9. *Artificers* (Abl.). 10. *To books.* 11. *To children.* 12. *Attendants* (Abl.). 13. *For sons-in-law.* 14. *Of a father-in-law.* 15. *Of the South Wind.* 16. *To a field.* 17. *To a man.* 18. *To crabs.* 19. *To Liber.* 20. *Of children.* 21. *By* (17) *children.* 22. *By books.* 23. *By goats.* 24. *By wild-boars.*

B. 1. The master terrifies the servants. 2. The servant fears the master's violence. 3. The crab fears the snakes of the field. 4. The goat fears the servant's knife. 5. The umpire overcomes the lord's violence by (his) patience. 6. The artificer gives the servant a field. 7. The servant gives (his) master a knife. 8. The servants are terrified by the lord's threats. 9. The lord is overcome by the slaves.

EXERCISE X.—NOUNS LIKE **pŭĕr.**

1. Hortum puero dant. 2. Vesperum puer timet. 3. Agricolae Liberum amant. 4. Vesper virum terret. 5. Viri socer

feminam terret. 6. Virorum soceri feminae generum terrent. 7. Puerorum violentiā virorum patientiam superat. 8. Gener a socero gladio terretur. 9. Regina procellae violentiā nautarum experientiā liberatur.

1. *The boy loves Liber.* 2. *The woman's son-in-law fears the father-in-law.* 3. *The women fear the man's son-in-law.* 4. *The men's father-in-law terrifies the boys.* 5. *The woman's patience overcomes the violence of the children.* 6. *Experience gives men wisdom.* 7. *By patience children overcome the father-in-law's violence.* 8. *The wild-boars are overcome by the spears of the lords.* 9. *The queen is delivered (8) from the envy of the servants (5a).*

EXERCISE XI.—NOUNS LIKE **măgistĕr** AND **pŭĕr**.

**Nōn**, *not.*[1]  **Nĕquĕ**, *and not.*
**Lauda-t**, *praises.*  **Culpa-t**, *blames.*

1. *The lord does not blame the woman.*
2. *The lord praises the man, and does not blame the woman.*

1. Dŏmĭnus fēmĭnam **nōn** culpat.
2. Dŏmĭnus vĭrum laudat **nĕquĕ** fēmĭnam culpat.

1. Capri puerum timent. 2. Caper puerorum cultros timet. 3. Liberi minister librum non laudat. 4. Puer virum timet neque feminam amat. 5. Feminae generos culpant neque soceros laudant. 6. Colubri fabri ministros terrent. 7. Fabrorum generi arbitri patientiam culpant neque sapientiam laudant. 8. Liberi ministris caprum agricola dat. 9. Aper servos non timet neque domini hastā superatur. 10. Puella a capris non terretur.

1. *The book praises Liber.* 2. *The servants of Liber do not praise books.* 3. *The boys terrify the goats and do not fear the snakes.* 4. *The boy terrifies the goat with a knife.* 5. *The man praises (his) father-in-law's field.* 6. *The snakes terrify the artificer's son-in-law.* 7. *The man fears (his) father-in-law, and does not love (his) son-in-law.* 8. *The husbandmen give Liber a goat.* 9. *The queen is not delivered from the storm by the sailors (5a).*

---

[1] Nōn always means *not;* but *not* is not always to be translated nōn. In commands and some other sentences, nē is used, see Exercise XXXVI. But *not* may always be translated by nōn in *statements and direct questions;* and these are the only sentences with which the pupil will have to do for the present.

### Exercise XII.—Nouns in -um and -ĕr.

**20  Rule.**—Two Nominatives coupled by -et take the Verb in the Plural:

*Patience and constancy overcome violence.*   Pătĭentĭa et constantĭa vīolentĭam sŭpĕrant.

1. Agricola Liberi dona laudat neque libros amat. 2. Magister argentum ministro dat. 3. Argentum, non aurum, dominus servis dat. 4. Pueri diligentiae praemiis delectantur. 5. Puerorum praemia viri non amant. 6. Templa Liber et Neptunus habent. 7. Liberi templa argentum habent. 8. Liberi templa argentum, non libros, habent. 9. Liberi templis agricolae aurum dant. 10. Diligentiā et constantiā praemia habent. 11. Oppida muros et templa habent. 12. Horti et arva ab agricolis laudantur.

1. *The master gives the attendants gold.* 2. *The master's gifts are not praised by the boys.* 3. *The boy and the girl love rewards.* 4. *The master gives the boy the reward of diligence.* 5. *The husbandmen are delighted by the walls and temples of the town.* 6. *The temples of the town have silver and gold.* 7. *The husbandman and the sailor give gifts to the temples of the towns.* 8. *The man by (his) gifts overcomes the sailor's constancy.* 9. *The sailors praise the husbandmen's cornfields.* 10. *The lord is terrified by the storm, and does not love water.*

## ADJECTIVES

### FIRST AND SECOND DECLENSION.

#### Adjectives in -ŭs, -ă, -um.

Adjectives in Latin *agree in Number and Case* with the Nouns which they qualify:

| | | |
|---|---|---|
| *Nom. Sing.* | **Bŏnus dŏmĭnus.** | *The good lord.* |
| *Gen. Sing.* | **Bŏni dŏmĭni.** | *Of the good lord.* |
| *Nom. Plur.* | **Bŏni dŏmĭni.** | *The good lords.* |
| *Gen. Plur.* | **Bŏnōrum dŏmĭnórum.** | *Of the good lords.* |

But besides agreeing in number and case, most Latin Adjectives also have three forms to suit the three kinds of Noun-terminations represented by (1) **dŏmĭnus**, (2) **fēmĭna**, (3) **regnum**.

Nom. Sing. Bŏnus dŏmĭnus, bŏna fēmĭna, bŏnum regnum.
Gen. Sing. Bŏnī dŏmĭnī, bŏnae fēmĭnae, bŏnī regnī.
Nom. Plur. Bŏnī dŏmĭnī, bŏnae fēmĭnae, bŏna regna.
Gen. Plur. Bŏnōrum dŏmĭnōrum, bŏnārum fēmĭnārum, bŏnōrum regnōrum.

These three forms of the Adjective are called its *Genders*. (1) The form in -ŭs is called the Masculine Gender, (2) the form in -ă the Feminine, (3) the form in -um the Neuter.

**21** RULE.—Adjectives agree with their Nouns in Gender, Number, and Case.

*Singular.*     1.     *Plural.*

|  | Masc. | Fem. | Neut. | Masc. | Fem. | Neut. |
|---|---|---|---|---|---|---|
| Nom. | Bŏn-us | bŏn-ă | bŏn-um | Bŏn-ī | bŏn-ae | bŏn-ă |
| Voc. | Bŏn-ĕ | bŏn-ă | bŏn-um | Bŏn-ī | bŏn-ae | bŏn-ă |
| Acc. | Bŏn-um | bŏn-am | bŏn-um | Bŏn-ōs | bŏn-ās | bŏn-ă |
| Gen. | Bŏn-ī | bŏn-ae | bŏn-ī | Bŏn-ōrum | bŏn-ārum | bŏn-ōrum |
| Dat. | Bŏn-ō | bŏn-ae | bŏn-ō | Bŏn-īs | bŏn-īs | bŏn-īs |
| Abl. | Bŏn-ō | bŏn-ā | bŏn-ō | Bŏn-īs | bŏn-īs | bŏn-īs |

2.

|  | Masc. | Fem. | Neut. | Masc. | Fem. | Neut. |
|---|---|---|---|---|---|---|
| N.V. | Nĭgĕr | nigr-ă | nigr-um | Nigr-ī | nigr-ae | nigr-ă |
| Acc. | Nigr-um | nigr-am | nigr-um | Nigr-ōs | nigr-ās | nigr-ă |
| Gen. | Nigr-ī | nigr-ae | nigr-ī | Nigr-ōrum | nigr-ārum | nigr-ōrum |
| Dat. | Nigr-ō | nigr-ae | nigr-ō | Nigr-īs | nigr-īs | nigr-īs |
| Abl. | Nigr-ō | nigr-ā | nigr-ō | Nigr-īs | nigr-īs | nigr-īs |

**22** GENDER OF THE FIRST DECLENSION.—Nouns of the First Declension are Feminine.

*Exceptions*: **nauta**, *a sailor*, **aurīga**, *a charioteer*, and other words denoting the occupations of men, are Masculine.

**23** GENDER OF THE SECOND DECLENSION.—(1) Nouns in -ŭs and -ĕr are Masculine, (2) Nouns in -um are Neuter.

*Exceptions.*—**Dŏmus**, *house*, and **hŭmus**, *ground*, are Feminine; **pĕlăgus**, *the sea*, **vīrus**, *poison*, and **vulgus**, *the common folk*, are Neuter.[1]

---

[1] The exceptional Masculine use of **vulgus** is not to be imitated. For the other exceptions, see the Table of Genders, p. 226.

A few Nouns (together with all those which may denote either males or

## FIRST AND SECOND DECLENSION.

### SINGULAR NUMBER.

|  | Feminine. | Masculine. | Neuter. |
|---|---|---|---|
|  | *A good woman.* | *A good lord.* | *A good gift.* |
| Nom. | Bŏn-ă fēmĭn-ă | Bŏn-us dŏmĭn-us | Bŏn-um dŏn-um |
| Voc. | „ -ă  „ -ă | „ -ĕ  „ -ĕ | „ -um  „ -um |
| Acc. | „ -am „ -am | „ -um „ -um | „ -um „ -um |
| Gen. | „ -ae „ -ae | „ -i  „ -i | „ -i  „ -i |
| Dat. | „ -ae „ -ae | „ -o  „ -o | „ -o  „ -o |
| Abl. | „ -ā  „ -ā | „ -o  „ -o | „ -o  „ -o |

### PLURAL NUMBER.

|  | *Good women.* | *Good lords.* | *Good gifts.* |
|---|---|---|---|
| Nom. | Bŭn-ae femin-ae | Bŏn-i domin-i | Bŏn-a dŏn-a |
| Voc. | „ -ae „ -ae | „ -i  „ -i | „ -ă  „ -ă |
| Acc. | „ -as „ -as | „ -os „ -os | „ -ă  „ -ă |
| Gen. | „ -ārum „ -ārum | „ -ōrum „ -ōrum | „ -ōrum -ōrum |
| Dat. | „ -īs „ -īs | „ -īs „ -īs | „ -īs „ -īs |
| Abl. | „ -īs „ -īs | „ -īs „ -īs | „ -īs „ -īs |

Hitherto the terminations of the Noun and Adjective have been the same. But this is not always the case, as may be seen from the following instances:

### SINGULAR.

|  | *A great man.* | *A great charioteer (m).* | *A great sea (n).* |
|---|---|---|---|
| Nom. | Magn-us vir | Magn-us aurīg-ă | Magn-um pĕlăg-us |
| Voc. | Magn-ĕ vir | Magn-ĕ  aurīg-a | Magn-um pĕlăg-us |
| Acc. | „ -um vir -um | Magn-um aurīg-am | Magn-um pĕlăg-us |
| Gen. | „ -i  „ -i | Magn-i  aurīg-ae | „ -i  „ -i |
| Dat. | „ -o  „ -o | Magn-o  aurīg-ae | „ -o  „ -o |
| Abl. | „ -o  „ -o | Magn-o  aurīg-ā | „ -o  „ -o |

### EXERCISE XIII.

1. Vir magnus a nautā strenuo laudatur. 2. Dona parva improbi pueri culpant. 3. Naută impavidus pelagus non timet. 4. Pelagus vastum et procella magna nautas pavidos terrent. 5. Scribă strenuus docti magistri jussa non timet. 6. Aurigam probum pericula magna non terrent. 7. Nautae improbo regina dona splendida dat. 8. Nautarum proborum filii praemia magna habent. 9. Aurigae strenui patientiā nauta improbus superatur. 10. Feminam probam et nautam strenuum regina bona laudat. 11. Pericula, parve fili, viros justos non terrent. 12. Via aurigae strenuo a puellā monstratur.

---

females, *e.g.* pŏēta, *poet*, incŏla, *inhabitant*) vary between the Masc. and Fem.; these are said to be *of common Gender*, and are indicated in the Vocabularies by *c*. But incŏla, pŏēta, and the like, are so much more frequently Masc. than Fem., that they are marked *m*.

## ADJECTIVES.

(The Adjective in Latin generally, but not always, follows its Noun.)

1. *The vigorous charioteer is not terrified by dangers.* 2. *The danger of the way, and the violence of the storm, do not terrify the fearless charioteers.* 3. *The learned master gives a long letter to the honest scribe.* 4. *The daughters of the dishonest clerk fear the commands of the good queen.* 5. *The sailor's daughter fears the vast sea.* 6. *The dangers of the long way overcome the constancy of the good charioteer.* 7. *The queen by splendid gifts overcomes the constancy of the worthy sailors.* 8. *The unworthy charioteers terrify with threats the sailor's daughter.* 9. *Storms, O fearful sailor, do not terrify fearless men.* 10. *The man points out the way with (his) right hand for the honest sailor.*

### EXERCISE XIV.

**Est,** (*he, she, it*) *is.*  **Sunt,** (*they*) *are.*

*After* the Verb **est** or **sunt** the question *who?* or *what?* is answered by the NOMINATIVE.

*Britain is an island.*  Brĭtannia est **insŭla.**
*Wars are the causes of evils.*  Bella sunt mălōrum **caus-ae.**

**24** RULE.—The Verb *to be* takes the same Case after it as before it.

Why are **insŭla** and **causae** Nom.?—*Ans.*, Because the Verb **est** takes the same Case after it as before it.

*The horses are great (horses).*  Ĕqui sunt **magni** (ĕqui).
*The woman is (a) good (woman).*  Fĕmĭna est **bŏna** (fĕmĭna).

**24a** From the last examples we see that an Adjective still agrees with its Noun in Number, Gender, and Case, even when separated from the Noun by the Verb *to be*.

1. Britanniae incolae sunt nautae. 2. Nautae non sunt timidi. 3. Agri sunt lati. 4. Oppidum est magnum. 5. Puer est validus. 6. Pueri patientia magna est. 7. Aquila est alba. 8. Aquilarum alae sunt albae. 9. Oppida parva sunt. 10. Oppidorum templa sunt alta. 11. Dominus ab equis albis delectatur. 12. Femina proborum generorum filias amat.

1. *The sailor is timid.* 2. *The walls of the town are high.* 3. *The field is broad.* 4. *The towns are not great.* 5. *The experience*

*of the boy is small.* 6. *The wings of the eagle are great.*
7. *The walls of the temple are white.* 8. *The master has black horses and white goats.* 9. *The master's horses are black.* 10. *The eagle has white wings.* 11. *The timid sailor is terrified both by the unjust queen and by the vast sea.*

### Exercise XV.

#### Adjectives in -ĕr.[1]

Like the Nouns in -er, so also the Adjectives in -er are declined (1) some like **puer**, (2) others like **măgister**.

The pupil will find it the best course to commit to memory the former class, as being the fewer.

**25** 1. Declined like **puer**: asper, *rough*, līber, *free* (whence līberi, *children*), mĭser, *wretched*, prosper, *prosperous*, tĕner, *tender*.[2]

2. Declined like **măgister**: all Adjectives in -er not contained in the above list.

1 Inpigrum agricolam poeta piger timet. 2. Regina pulchra ab improbis incolis terretur. 3. Agricolae vafri tenerum puerum verbis falsis laudant. 4. Domini prosperi macros capros habent. 5. Reginae liberis libros sacros poëtae dant. 6. Et nauta miser et auriga strenuus filios aegros habent. 7. Templorum sacrorum portis rubris et muris nigris viri delectantur. 8. Morbi agricolas miseros superant. 9. Agricolae vafri filius parvae puellae caprum macrum dat. 10. Morbum taetrum nautae pavidi timent.

1. *The beautiful woman is overcome by the foul disease.* 2. *The slothful sailors fear the active husbandman.* 3. *The cunning boys give a lean goat to the miserable sailor.* 4. *The wretched sons of the sick husbandman fear the foul disease.* 5. *The foul disease terrifies the wretched sailors.* 6. *The sick women praise the sacred books with foolish words.* 7. *The vigorous husbandmen overcome by (their) wisdom the foul diseases* (5a). 8. *The cunning lord gives lean goats to the sick women.*

---

[1] As final -er is always short, it will not be marked short for the future.

**26** [2] Besides these, there are (though not contained in the following Exercises), (1) lăcer, *torn*, and (2) Adjectives derived from the Verbs fer-o and ger-o, *I bear*, viz. frūgī-fer, *fruit-bearing*; corn-ĭger, *horn-bearing*.

In the nom. sing. **prospĕrus** is more common than **prosper**.

## THE THIRD DECLENSION.

### 1. THE CONSONANT BRANCH.

In the Third Declension some Nouns have a Stem (see Glossary, Appendix VIII.) ending in a consonant, *e.g.* c in judĭc-is, judĭc-i, *of a judge, to a judge*, or m in hiĕm-is, hiĕm-i, *of winter, to winter*. This class of Nouns is called the Consonant Branch.

In the Consonant Branch of the Third Declension the Nom. Sing. endings are numerous, but -s (sometimes disguised in the shape of -x, which represents -gs, and -cs) is the most common.

#### A.—MASCULINE AND FEMININE NOUNS.

| | *Singular.* | *Plural.* |
|---|---|---|
| Nom. Voc. | [-s] | -ēs |
| Acc. | -em | -ēs |
| Gen. | -ĭs | -um |
| Dat. | -ī | -ĭbus |
| Abl. | -ĕ, rarely -ī | -ĭbus |

I. Nouns in which the Stem ends in a guttural (throat) letter, *i.e.* -c hard, or -g :

*Singular.*

| | *Leader* (m). | *Judge* (c).[1] | *Law* (f). | *Citadel* (f). |
|---|---|---|---|---|
| N.V. | Dux (Duc-s) | Judex (Judic-s) | Lex (Leg-s) | Arx (Arc-s) |
| Acc. | Dŭc-em | Judĭc-em | Lēg-em | Arc-em |
| Gen. | Dŭc-is | Judĭc-is | Lēg-is | Arc-is |
| Dat. | Dŭc-i | Judĭc-i | Lēg-i | Arc-i |
| Abl. | Dŭc-ĕ | Judĭc-ĕ | Lēg-ĕ | Arc-ĕ |

*Plural.*

| | | | | |
|---|---|---|---|---|
| N.V. | Dŭc-ēs | Judĭc-ēs | Lēg-ēs | Arc-ēs |
| Acc. | Dŭc-ēs | Judĭc-ēs | Lēg-ēs | Arc-ēs |
| Gen. | Dŭc-um | Judĭc-um | Lēg-um | Arc-ĭum |
| Dat. | Dŭc-ĭbus | Judĭc-ĭbus | Lēg-ĭbus | Arc-ĭbus |
| Abl. | Dŭc-ĭbus | Judĭc-ĭbus | Lēg-ĭbus | Arc-ĭbus |

---

[1] The abbreviation *c.* means that jūdex is of *common* gender, being mostly masculine, but sometimes feminine.

II. Nouns in which the Stem ends with a dental (tooth) letter, *i.e.* -t or -d:

*Singular.*

| | *Soldier (m).* | *Foot (m).* | *Summer (f).* |
|---|---|---|---|
| *N.V.* | Mīles (Mīlet-s)[1] | Pēs (Ped-s) | Æstās (Æstat-s) |
| *Acc.* | Mīlĭt-em | Pĕd-em | Æstāt-em |
| *Gen.* | Mīlĭt-is | Pĕd-is | Æstāt-is |
| *Dat.* | Mīlĭt-i | Pĕd-i | Æstāt-i |
| *Abl.* | Mīlĭt-ĕ | Pĕd-ĕ | Æstāt-ĕ |

*Plural.*

| | | | |
|---|---|---|---|
| *N.V.* | Mīlĭt-ēs | Pĕd-ēs | Æstāt-ēs |
| *Acc.* | Mīlĭt-ēs | Pĕd-ēs | Æstāt-ēs |
| *Gen.* | Mīlĭt-um | Pĕd-um | Æstāt-um |
| *Dat.* | Mīlĭt-ĭbus | Pĕd-ĭbus | Æstāt-ĭbus |
| *Abl.* | Mīlĭt-ĭbus | Pĕd-ĭbus | Æstāt-ĭbus |

Nox, *f.* (for noct-s) Gen. noct-is, *night*, is declined like Æstās; but the Gen. Plur. (see Par. 40) is noct-ĭum.

**27** RULE.—The Dative is used after Adjectives signifying *pleasing, displeasing, troublesome, easy, difficult,* and the like:

*Laws are not troublesome to a just judge.*    Lēges jūdĭci justo non mŏlestae sunt.

**28** RULE.—Dignus and indignus (*worthy* and *unworthy*) govern the Ablative:

*Impatience is unworthy of a leader.*    Impătientia dŭcĕ indigna est.

EXERCISE XVI.

**Laed-ĭt,** (*he*) *hurts.*    **Laed-unt,** (*they*) *hurt.*
**Laedĭt-ur,** (*he*) *is* (*being*) *hurt.*    **Laedunt-ur,** (*they*) *are* (*being*) *hurt.*

1. Leges justae regibus bonis non sunt molestae. 2. Bella militibus jucunda sunt. 3. Militum ignavia ducibus claris ingrata

---

**29** [1] The e of the true Stem (mīlĕt-) is changed into -ĭ in all except the Nom. and Voc. Cases. Similarly, the true Stem of virgo (virgŏn-) is changed into virgĭn-. But sometimes, as in jūdex above, the true Stem (jūdĭc-) is lost in the Nom. but preserved in the other Cases.

est. 4. Lapides militum miserorum pedes laedunt. 5. Comitis validi constantiā fessus eques delectatur. 6. Equites peditem acutis gladiis terrent. 7. Rege bono leges malae indignae sunt. 8. Judicum verba injusta dominis justis molesta sunt. 9. Noctes obscuras pueri parvi timent. 10. Domini arx ab agricolā laudatur. 11. Aestatis memoria militibus grata est. 12. Aurigae pes sinister spinā acuta laeditur. 13. Agricolae equi validi (24a) sunt.

1. The constancy of the strong soldiers is pleasing to the good king. 2. Slothfulness is unworthy of a great leader. 3. The husbandmen point out the citadel of the lord to (their) companions. 4. A dark night terrifies the timid boy. 5. The memory of the pleasant summer is agreeable to the miserable husbandmen. 6. The anger of the horsemen is displeasing to the foot-soldiers. 7. The companions of the horse-soldier hurt the good husbandman with many stones. 8. Good laws are worthy of a just king. 9. The feet of the weary companions are hurt by the sharp stones. 10. The queen gives just laws to the renowned leader and to the good judges.

III. Nouns in which the Stem ends with a labial (lip) letter, *i.e.* -m, -p, -b:

*Singular.*

|  | *Chief (m.).* | *Beam (f.).* | *Winter (f.).* |
|---|---|---|---|
| N.V. | Princep-s (Princip-s) | Trab-s | Hiem(p)-s [1] |
| Acc. | Princĭp-em | Trăb-em | Hiĕm-em |
| Gen. | Princĭp-is | Trăb-is | Hiĕm-is |
| Dat. | Princĭp-i | Trăb-i | Hiĕm-i |
| Abl. | Princĭp-ĕ | Trăb-ĕ | Hiĕm-ĕ |

*Plural.*

| N.V. | Princĭp-ēs | Trăb-ēs | Hiĕm-ēs |
|---|---|---|---|
| Acc. | Princĭp-ēs | Trăb-ēs | Hiĕm-ēs |
| Gen. | Princĭp-um | Trăb-um | Hiĕm-um |
| Dat. | Princĭp-ĭbus | Trăb-ĭbus | Hiĕm-ĭbus |
| Abl. | Princĭp-ĭbus | Trăb-ĭbus | Hiĕm-ĭbus |

IV. Nouns in which the stem ends with (1) a nasal (nose) letter, *i.e.* -n, or (2) -u:

---

[1] P is inserted for euphony, between m and s in the Nominative of this word, so that the right spelling is **hiemps**.

## THIRD DECLENSION.

### Singular.

| | Lion (m.). | Maiden (f.). | Crane (c.). |
|---|---|---|---|
| N.V. | Leō (Leŏ-n) | Virgō (Virgŏ-n)[1] | Grū-s |
| Acc | Leōn-em | Virgĭn-em | Grŭ-em |
| Gen. | Leōn-is | Virgĭn-is | Grŭ-is |
| Dat. | Leōn-i | Virgĭn-i | Grŭ-i |
| Abl. | Leōn-ĕ | Virgĭn-ĕ | Grŭ-ĕ |

### Plural.

| | | | |
|---|---|---|---|
| N.V. | Leōn-ēs | Virgĭn-ēs | Grŭ-ēs |
| Acc. | Leōn-ēs | Virgĭn-ēs | Grŭ-ēs |
| Gen. | Leōn-um | Virgĭn-um | Grŭ-um |
| Dat. | Leōn-ĭbus | Virgĭn-ĭbus | Grŭ-ĭbus |
| Abl. | Leōn-ĭbus | Virgĭn-ĭbus | Grŭ-ĭbus |

EXERCISE XVII.

**30** RULE.—The question *When?* or *Within what time?* is answered by the Ablative, as **hĭĕme,** *in winter,* **nocte,** *by night.*

**31** RULE.—The question *How long?* or *During what time?* is answered by the Accusative, as **multos annos,** *for,* or *during, many years.*

**Vīvit,** (*he*) *lives.*    **Vīvunt,** (*they*) *live.*

1. Multi homines aestatem hieme laudant. 2. Virgines aestate hiemem, hieme aestatem laudant. 3 Leones multas aestates et multas hiemes vivunt. 4. Principibus pavidis leo molestus est. 5. Nautae nocte magnam gruum multitudinem puellae monstrant. 6. Virgines tenerae ab improbis principum filiis minis terrentur. 7. Papiliones paucas horas, elephantes multos annos vivunt.[2] 8. Leoni fero equitis comes caprum macrum dat. 9. Templum longas trabes, portas magnas, habet.[3] 10. Templi trabs longitudinem miram habet. 11 Comites pavidi principe indigni sunt. 12. Multa poma aestate terra habet.

1. *The sailor praises land in winter, (but) blames (it) in summer.* 2. *For many hours the lion devours the tender goats.* 3. *The sailor by night points out a multitude of cranes to the maiden.* 4. *The daughters of the chiefs fear the savage lion.* 5. *A*

---

[1] **Virgo** and **hŏmo** originally kept the o throughout, and **hŏmōnes,** for **hŏmĭnes,** is actually preserved, though, of course, not to be used.

[2] Repeat **vivunt** after **păpĭlĭōnēs,** "paucas horas (vivunt)."

**32** [3] In enumerations, and in other sentences, ĕt, or some other conjunction, is often omitted where the English must insert *and, but,* &c.

*butterfly does not live for-many hours.* 6. *Unjust words are unworthy of a chief.* 7. *By the companions of the beautiful maidens the lion is frightened with a sword.* 8. *The winter is troublesome to the maidens and not agreeable to the chief.* 9. *The queen gives praise to chiefs and gold to poets.* 10. *In the night the lion devours a multitude of tender goats.*

V. Nouns in which the Stem ends with (1) a liquid, *i.e.* -l, -r, or (2) a sibilant, *i.e.* -s : [1]

*Singular.*

|  | *Consul (m.).* | *Love (m.).* | *Tree (f.).* | *Flower (m.).* |
|---|---|---|---|---|
| *N.V.* | Consul | Ămor [2] | Arbor(-ōs) [2] | Flōs [1] |
| *Acc.* | Consŭl-em | Amōr-em | Arbŏr-em | Flŏr-em |
| *Gen.* | Consŭl-is | Amōr-is | Arbŏr-is | Flŏr-is |
| *Dat.* | Consŭl-i | Amōr-i | Arbŏr-i | Flŏr-i |
| *Abl.* | Consŭl-ĕ | Amor-ĕ | Arbŏr-ĕ | Flŏr-ĕ |

*Plural.*

|  | | | | |
|---|---|---|---|---|
| *N.V.* | Consŭl-ēs | Ămōr-ēs | Arbŏr-ēs | Flŏr-ēs |
| *Acc.* | Consŭl-ēs | Amōr-ēs | Arbŏr-ēs | Flŏr-ēs |
| *Gen.* | Consŭl-um | Amōr-um | Arbŏr-um | Flŏr-um |
| *Dat.* | Consŭl-ĭbus | Amōr-ĭbus | Arbŏr-ĭbus | Flŏr-ĭbus |
| *Abl.* | Consŭl-ĭbus | Amōr-ĭbus | Arbŏr-ĭbus | Flŏr-ĭbus |

Cĭnĭs *c.*, makes cĭnĕr-em, cĭnĕr-is, cĭnĕr-i, &c.

**33** Note that **anser** differs from **păter**, as **pŭer** from **măgister**; the former retains, the latter rejects, in the other Cases, the -e of the Nom.

*Singular.*

|  | *Goose (m.).* | *Father (m.).* | *Mother (f.).* |
|---|---|---|---|
| *N.V.* | Anser | Păter(Păter-) | Māter (Măter-) |
| *Acc.* | Ansĕr-em | Patr-em | Matr-em |
| *Gen.* | Ansĕr-is | Patr-is | Matr-is |
| *Dat.* | Ansĕr-i | Patr-i | Matr-i |
| *Abl.* | Ansĕr-ĕ | Patr-ĕ | Matr-ĕ |

---

[1] (1) Many sibilant stems retain -s in the Nom. Sing., but change it to -r in the other cases: flŏs, Gen. flŏr-is (for flŏs-is), rōs, Gen. rōr-is (for rōs-is) *of dew* (2) Others have two forms of the Nom.: labŏs or labor, Gen. labŏr-is, *of labour;* and so arbŏs or arbor, Gen. arbŏr-is, *of a tree.*

[2] Final -or is short, and therefore its quantity is not marked in ămor, arbor, &c.

## THIRD DECLENSION.

*Plural.*

| | | |
|---|---|---|
| *N.V.* **Ansĕr-ēs** | **Patr-ēs** | **Matr-ēs** |
| *Acc.* **Ansĕr-ēs** | **Patr-ēs** | **Matr-ēs** |
| *Gen.* **Ansĕr-um** | **Patr-um** | **Matr-um** |
| *Dat.* **Ansĕr-ĭbus** | **Patr-ĭbus** | **Matr-ĭbus** |
| *Abl.* **Ansĕr-ĭbus** | **Patr-ĭbus** | **Matr-ĭbus**[1] |

EXERCISE XVIII.

**34** RULE.—An Adjective is sometimes used (1) in the Masculine to agree with *men* understood; (2) in the Neuter to agree with *thing* or *things* understood.

*Many (men) praise the king.* **Multi** rēgem laudant.
*The father gives (his) son many (things).* Păter fīlĭo **multa** dat.
*To err is (a) dangerous (thing).* Errāre est **pĕrīcŭlōsum**.[2]

**Sŭpĕrā-re,** *to overcome.* **Culpā-re,** *to blame.*
**Laudā-re,** *to praise.* **Ĕrat,** *(he) was,* **ĕrant,** *(they) were.*

**35** N.B.—The Adj. is often separated from its Noun by a Gen. belonging to the Noun, *e.g., the consul's clear voice,* **clāra** consulis **vox**; and sometimes by other words: **flōrĭbus sē pulchris** dēlectat, *he delights himself with beautiful flowers.*

1. Multi regem laudant neque reginam culpant. 2. Jucundum est laudāre, culpare injucundum (est). 3. Rex pauca filio dat, filiae multa (dat). 4. Puer anserem timet, patrem et matrem non timet. 5. Sepulcrum pulchrum multorum amicorum cineres habet. 6. Hiemps frigida arbores magnas et parvos flores laedit. 7. Milites magno clamore claram consulis vocem superant. 8. Pulchri florum colores virginum oculis grati sunt. 9. Anserem stultum multa terrent. 10. Femina a virgine amore magno amatur. 11. Militum clamor timoris causa est agricolis.[3] 12. Consulum jussa timoris causae erant militibus. 13. Timidos nocte (30) multa terrent.

---

**36** [1] The pupil should note that in the Consonant Branch of the Third Declension, he can form the cases of any Noun without committing them to memory, if he remembers the Nom. and Gen. Singular.
All the other cases can be formed by striking off the -is from the Gen., *e.g.* anser-, patr-, and adding -em, -i, -ĕ, -es, -um, -ĭbus. See p. 18.

**36a** [2] Here, part of a Verb is treated as a Noun, and is the Subject of **est**. See further, Exercise XXXV.

[3] Agrīcŏlis may be parsed as the "Dative of Advantage or Disadvantage." See par. 7.

1. *To overcome is pleasant for soldiers.* 2. *The consul gives many things*[1] *to the vigorous soldier.* 3. *Many praise the king, few blame (him).* 4. *A goose fears many-things, (and) terrifies few-men.*[1] 5. *The companions of the soldiers overpower the king's voice by (their) clamour.* 6. *The colour of the flowers is agreeable to the eyes of the beautiful maidens.* 7. *The broad sepulchres have the ashes of many soldiers.* 8. *The flower by (its) colour and pleasant odour delights the maidens.* 9. *The cold winters were troublesome to the timid sons of the husbandmen.* 10. *To praise the bad is unpleasing and-not just.* 11. *For-a-few hours* (31) *the soldiers overcome the sailors.*

### B.—NEUTER NOUNS OF THE CONSONANT BRANCH.

*Singular.*

| | Head (n.). | Name (n.). | Right or Law (n.). | Work (n.). |
|---|---|---|---|---|
| N.V. Acc. | Căput | Nōmen | Jūs | Ŏpus |
| Gen. | Căpĭt-is | Nōmĭn-is | Jūr-is | Ŏpĕr-ĭs |
| Dat. | Căpĭt-i | Nōmĭn-i | Jūr-i | Ŏpĕr-i |
| Abl. | Căpĭt-ĕ | Nōmĭn-ĕ | Jūr-ĕ | Ŏpĕr-ĕ |

*Plural*

| | | | | |
|---|---|---|---|---|
| N.V. Acc. | Căpĭt-ă | Nōmĭn-ă | Jūr-ă | Ŏpĕr-ă |
| Gen. | Căpĭt-um | Nōmĭn-um | Jūr-um | Ŏpĕr-um |
| Dat. | Căpĭt-ĭbus | Nōmĭn-ĭbus | Jūr-ĭbus | Ŏpĕr-ĭbus |
| Abl. | Căpĭt-ĭbus | Nōmĭn-ĭbus | Jūr-ĭbus | Ŏpĕr-ĭbus |

Note also **corpus, corpŏr-is, corpŏr-i**, &c., *a body.*

#### Exercise XIX.

**37** When two Nouns of kindred meaning are connected together in one phrase, instead of **et** between the two Nouns, **-quĕ** is added *as an extra syllable* to the *latter* of the two Nouns: *flowers and trees,* flōres **arbŏresquĕ**.

1. Fulmen arbores fruticesque et corpora hominum laedit. 2. Carmina sunt poetarum opera. 3. Jura belli agricolae timent. 4. Pueri nomen pulchrum erat. 5. Verbera judicibus consulibusque indigna sunt. 6. Equitum peditumque multitudinem vastam mercatores jure[2] timent. 7. Militum opera oppidorum incolis ingrata erant. 8. Capri capita parva,

---

**38**  [1] The words *things* and *men* (here and in other passages where they are used with *many* or *few*) should not be translated. See the Rule above.

[2] Jure is the Abl. used as an Adverb, *by right,* i.e. *rightly, naturally.*

corpora macra, pedes longos habent. 9. Multis hominibus multorum scelerum causa est aurum.¹ 10. Sidera nautis hieme grata erant. 11. Injusti judicis verba bona (erant), facta mala erant. 12. Corpori cibum, doctrinam menti Deus dat. 13. Miles ab injusto judice culpa (8) liberatur.

² 1. *The leader's head (was) small, his body was lean.* 2. *The multitude of the merchants fears the horse-soldiers and foot-soldiers.* 3. *The works of soldiers are displeasing to husband-men.* 4. *Flowers and shrubs are agreeable to the inhabitants of towns.* 5. *Boys give food and sleep (use -què) to (their) bodies, learning to (their) minds.* 6. *The names of the boys and girls are beautiful.* 7. *Unjust laws are unworthy of kings and queens.* 8. *The horse-soldiers and foot-soldiers are not terrified by the crimes of (their) leaders.* 9. *The poet's work delights the queen with (its) beautiful name.* 10. *It was (a) renowned (thing) to overcome a multitude of horse-soldiers and foot-soldiers in-war* (Abl. of instr.)

THIRD DECLENSION.

2.—NOUNS WHOSE STEM ENDS IN i.

**39** These Nouns differ from the Consonant Branch in this respect, that they make the Gen. Plur. in -ĭum; whereas, in the Consonant Branch, the Gen. Plur. mostly ends in -um.³ But the Stem i (being very variable, often dropped, and often changed into e,) frequently disappears.

---

¹ What case is hŏmĭnĭbus, and why? See Par. 7.

² For the Genders of Nouns of the Third Declension see page 226; and for Exercises on the Exceptions see Exercises LXXXIV to XCII.

**40** ³ The more advanced pupil will find that several Nouns of the Consonant Branch take -ium in the Gen. Pl. The following rules will be found useful:—

1. Nouns whose Gen. Sing. is ˘ ˘ (as dŭc-ĭs), take -um (dŭc-um).
Examples: pătr-um, sĕn-um, pĕd-um, grĕg-um, ăp-um, &c.

2. Nouns whose Gen. Sing. is ˉ ˘ (as ārc-is) take -ium.
Examples: falc-ium, urb-ium, art-ium, lit-ium, font-ium, pont-ium, mont-ium, noct-ium, &c.
Exceptions are vōc-um, lēg-um, rēg-um, jūr-um, and a few others.

## B.—1. Masculine and Feminine Nouns.

### Singular.

|  | Ship (f.) | Shower (m.) | Cloud (f.) |
|---|---|---|---|
| N.V. | Nāv-ĭs | Imber (Imbri-) | Nūb-ēs (Nubi-) |
| Acc. | Nāv-em | Imbr-em | Nūb-em |
| Gen. | Nāv-ĭs | Imbr-ĭs | Nūb-is |
| Dat. | Nāv-i | Imbr-i | Nūb-i |
| Abl. | Nāv-i or -ĕ | Imbr-i (-ĕ) [1] | Nūb-ĕ |

### Plural.

|  |  |  |  |
|---|---|---|---|
| N.V. | Nāv-ēs | Imbr-ēs | Nūb-ēs |
| Acc. | Nāv-ēs | Imbr-ēs | Nūb-ēs |
| Gen. | Nāv-ĭum | Imbr-ĭum | Nūb-ĭum |
| Dat. | Nāv-ĭbus | Imbr-ĭbus | Nūb-ĭbus |
| Abl. | Nāv-ĭbus | Imbr-ĭbus | Nūb-ĭbus |

### 2.—Neuter Nouns.

### Singular.

|  | Sea (n.) | Animal (n.) | Spur (n.) | Bone (n.) |
|---|---|---|---|---|
| N.V. Acc. | Măr-ĕ | Anĭmăl | Calcar | Ŏs [2] |
| Gen. | Măr-is | Anĭmāl-is | Calcār-is | Oss-ĭs |
| Dat. | Măr-i | Anĭmāl-i | Calcār-i | Oss-i |
| Abl. | Măr-i | Anĭmāl-i | Calcār-i | Oss-ĕ |

### Plural.

|  |  |  |  |  |
|---|---|---|---|---|
| N.V. Acc. | Marĭ-ă | Anĭmāl-ĭă | Calcār-ĭă | Oss-ă |
| Gen. | Marĭ-um | Anĭmāl-ĭum | Calcār-ĭum | Oss-ĭum |
| Dat. | Marĭ-bus | Anĭmāl-ĭbus | Calcār-ĭbus | Oss-ĭbus |
| Abl. | Marĭ-bus | Anĭmāl-ĭbus | Calcār-ĭbus | Oss-ĭbus |

**41** Nĕque or nĕc, when repeated, means *neither . . . nor.*

Consūm-it, *(he) consumes.*     Consūm-unt, *(they) consume.*

### Exercise XX.

1. Nautae validi neque imbres crebros neque maria saeva timent. 2. Imbri longo et fulmine crebro pastores terrentur. 3. Hominum sapientiā et animalium robur et maris furor superantur. 4. Navem rapidam mare avidum vorat. 5. Naves

---

**42** [1] A few Nouns in -is take only -im in the Acc., and only -i in the Abl.: sĭtis, *thirst;* tussis, *cough;* vīs, *violence;* and names of towns and rivers, *e.g.*, Tĭbĕris, *the Tiber.* The following commonly take -im. febris, *fever;* pelvis, *basin;* puppis, *poop;* restis, *rope;* turris, *tower;* sĕcūris, *axe.*

**43** Ignis makes Abl. in -i, except in poetry: and Abl. -i is always found in those Nouns that always make Acc. -im.

[2] Distinguish this word from ŏs, ōris, n., *mouth*, or *countenance*. Ănĭmal, calcar, and almost all other Neuters with Abl. in -i, are derived from Adjectives.

validas maris furor et tempestatis violentia superant.  6. Duces aurea calcaria et decora magna equitibus dant.  7. Hostium urbem dux igni ferroque consumit.  8. Nauta navi valida pelagi furorem superat.  9. Britannorum naves multis urbibus multisque gentibus notae sunt.  10. Ducum certamina prosperis civitatibus saepe causa exitii sunt.  11. Equus ignavus calcar timet.  12. Multa genera et animalium et lapidum mare habet.  13. Morbus capros totam aestatem (31) consumit.

1. *Strong horses often fear the spur.*  2. *The soldiers consume the cities with fire and sword.*  3. *Repeated lightning and a great storm terrify the merchants.*  4. *The animals of the sea are many and wonderful.*  5. *Men by (their) wisdom overcome the threats of seas and the madness of savage animals.*  6. *Both to leaders and to states strife is often the cause of destruction.*  7. *Golden spurs give great honour to horse-soldiers.*  8. *The strength of the ships overcomes both the madness of the sea and the violence of the storms.*  9. *The bones of small animals are small.*  10. *The tempest terrifies the citizens with a great cloud.*  11. *By wisdom and experience men are freed from the violence of savage animals.*  12. *He lives a few hours.*

## ADJECTIVES OF THE THIRD DECLENSION.

**44** These are declined like Nouns of the Third Declension; except that in almost all of them the Abl. Sing. is -i and not -e; and the Gen. Plur. -ĭum and not -um.

*A.*—Adjectives with Abl. Sing. in -i, and Gen. Plur. in -ĭum.

1.—ADJECTIVES OF THREE TERMINATIONS.

Ācer, *sharp.*

| | Singular. | | | Plural. | |
|---|---|---|---|---|---|
| | *M.* | *F.* | *N.* | *M. and F.* | *N.* |
| N.V. | Ācer | ācr-ĭs | ācr-ĕ | Ācr-ēs | ācr-ĭă |
| Acc. | Ācr-em | ācr-em | ācr-ĕ | Ācr-ēs | ācr-ĭă |
| Gen. | Ācr-ĭs | ācr-ĭs | ācr-ĭs | Ācr-ĭum | ācr-ĭum |
| Dat. | Ācr-i | ācr-i | ācr-i | Ācr-ĭbus | ācr-ĭbus |
| Abl. | Ācr-i | ācr-i | ācr-i | Ācr-ĭbus | ācr-ĭbus [1] |

**45** [1] Other similar Adjectives are sălūb-er, *healthy,* ălăc-er, *brisk,* ĕquester, *equestrian.* In the Nom. Masc. Sing., the forms ācr-is, sălūbr-is, ălăcr-is &c. are sometimes used, but more often in poetry than in prose.  Cĕl-er retains the ĕ in the Fem. cĕlĕr-is and in the Neut. cĕlĕr-e.

## 2.—ADJECTIVES OF TWO TERMINATIONS.

### Tristis, *sad.*

| | *Singular.* | | | *Plural.* | |
|---|---|---|---|---|---|
| | *M. and F.* | *N.* | | *M. and F.* | *N.* |
| *N.V.* | Trist-ĭs | trist-ĕ | | Trist-ēs | trist-ĭă |
| *Acc.* | Trist-em | trist-ĕ | | Trist-ēs | trist-ĭă |
| *Gen.* | Trist-ĭs | trist-ĭs | | Trist-ĭum | trist-ĭum |
| *Dat.* | Trist-ī | trist-ī | | Trist-ĭbus | trist-ĭbus |
| *Abl.* | Trist-ī | trist-ī | | Trist-ĭbus | trist-ĭbus |

## 3.—ADJECTIVES OF ONE TERMINATION.

### Felix, *happy.*

| | *Singular.* | | *Plural.* | |
|---|---|---|---|---|
| | *M., F., and N.* | | *M. and F.* | *N.* |
| *N.V.* | Fēlīx | | Fēlīc-ēs | fēlīc-ĭă |
| *Acc.* | Fēlīc-em | | Fēlīc-ēs | fēlīc-ĭă |
| *Gen.* | Fēlīc-is | | Fēlīc-ĭum | fēlīc-ĭum |
| *Dat.* | Fēlīc-ī | | Fēlīc-ĭbŭs | fēlīc-ĭbŭs |
| *Abl.* | Fēlīc-ī | | Fēlīc-ĭbŭs | fēlīc-ĭbŭs |

**46** B.—Adjectives with Abl. Sing. in -ĕ, and Gen. Plur. in -um.

These are mostly Comparatives ending in -ĭor (*m.* and *f.*), -ĭus (*n.*) : **trist-ĭor**, *sadder*, **fēlīc-ĭor**, *happier.*

| | *Singular.* | | | *Plural.* | |
|---|---|---|---|---|---|
| | *M. and F.* | *N.* | | *M. and F.* | *N.* |
| *N.V.* | Tristĭor | tristĭŭs | | Tristĭōr-ēs | tristĭōr-ă |
| *Acc.* | Tristĭōr-em | tristĭŭs | | Tristĭōr-ēs | tristĭōr-ă |
| *Gen.* | Tristĭōr-ĭs | tristĭōr-ĭs | | Tristĭōr-um | tristĭōr-um |
| *Dat.* | Tristĭōr-ī | tristĭōr-ī | | Tristĭōr-ĭbŭs | tristĭōr-ĭbus |
| *Abl.* | Tristĭōr-ĕ | tristĭōr-ĕ | | Tristĭōr-ĭbŭs | tristĭōr-ĭbus |

**47** Besides Comparatives, a few other words make the Abl. Sing. in -ĕ and the Gen. Plur. in -um. Most of them are capable of being used as Nouns : **dīvĕs**, (*a*) *rich* (*man*), **supplex**, *a suppliant*, **vĭgĭl**, *a watchman*, **princeps** *a chief*, **pauper**, *a poor man*, **superstĕs**, *a survivor.*[1]

**48** [1] A useful Rule is given (*Public School Grammar*) that :—
i. Adjectives in which the Gen. Sing. has the penult. short, make **-um** in the Gen. Pl., *e.g.* **supplex**, Gen. Sing. **supplĭcis**, Gen. Pl. **supplĭcum**.
ii. Adjectives in which the Gen. Sing. has the penult. long, make **-ium** in the Gen. Pl., *e.g.* **felix**, Gen. Sing. **fēlīcis**, Gen. Pl. **fēlīcium**.

## THIRD DECLENSION.

### 1.—Cĕlĕr ĕquus, *the swift horse.*

| | Singular. | Plural. |
|---|---|---|
| Nom. | Cĕler ĕqu-us | Cĕlĕr-ēs ĕqu-ī |
| Voc. | Cĕler ĕqu-e | Cĕlĕr-ēs ĕqu-ī |
| Acc. | Cĕlĕr-em ĕqu-um | Cĕlĕr-ēs ĕqu-ōs |
| Gen. | Cĕlĕr-is ĕqu-i | Cĕlĕr-ĭum ĕqu-ōrum [1] |
| Dat. | Cĕlĕr-ī ĕqu-o | Cĕlĕr-ĭbus ĕqu-īs |
| Abl. | Cĕlĕr-ī ĕqu-o | Cĕlĕr-ĭbus ĕqu-īs |

### 2.—Mĕlĭus dōnum, *the better gift.*

| | Singular. | Plural. |
|---|---|---|
| N.V. Acc. | Melĭŭs dōn-um | Mĕlĭor-ă dōn-ă |
| Gen. | Melĭōr-is dōn-ī | Mĕlĭōr-um dōn-ōrum |
| Dat. | Mĕlĭōr-ī dōn-ō | Mĕlĭōr-ĭbŭs dōn-īs |
| Abl. | Mĕlĭōr-ĕ dōn-ō | Mĕlĭōr-ĭbŭs dōn-īs |

### 3.—Fēlix jūdex, *a happy judge.*

**49** Note the two points of difference in the Noun and Adjective (1) Noun -ĕ, -um; Adj. -ī, -ĭum:

(1) Fēlīc-ī jūdĭc-ĕ, *by* (13a), *with, or from the happy judge.*

(2) Fēlīc-ĭum jūdĭc-um, *of happy judges.*

### Exercise XXI.

1. Mater bona meliore filio digna est. 2. Celerium equorum terga ab aurigis verberibus laeduntur. 3. Patres laeti meliora dona filiis dant. 4. Poeta sapiens regem insignem tristiore carmine delectat. 5. Rex insignis infelici morte indignus est. 6. Agricolarum vita salubris est; scribae diligentis labor non est saluber. 7. Equus acer certamen equestre amat. 8. Mercatorum divitum vitam miles fortis non amat. 9. Ira acri ducum tristium cives timidi terrentur. 10. Dulce carmen poeta insigni dignum est. 11. Puer tristis donum melius amat. 12. Principes justi fortibus militibus agros feraces dant. 13. Regina prudenti animo et audacibus consiliis seditionem superat. 14. Eques comitem culpa (8) liberat.

1. *The joyful father gives a better gift to (his) son.* 2. *The life of a soldier is not agreeable to the son of the rich merchant.*

---

**50** [1] The Gen. Pl. Cĕlĕr-um is only used when the word is used as a Noun, to signify the ancient body-guard in Rome; just as we speak of the "Blues," the "Scots Greys."

3. By (*his*) *sweet poem the good poet delights the great king.*
4. *A keen contest is pleasant to strong soldiers.* 5. *The labours of the unhappy judges were displeasing to the just king.* 6. *The keen anger of the citizens terrifies the companions of the sad leaders.* 7. *The diligent husbandman is worthy of a fruitful field.* 8. *The just judges give rewards to the charioteers of the swift horses.* 9. *The healthy life of the happy sailors was pleasing to the brave boy.* 10. *The good king is delighted by the songs of the sad poets and* (17) *by the brave boy.*[1] 11. *The master frees the boys from blame.*

## ADJECTIVES OF THE FIRST AND SECOND DECLENSION WITH NOUNS OF THE THIRD DECLENSION.

### Saevus hostis, *a cruel enemy.*

| | Singular | Plural |
|---|---|---|
| Nom. | Saevus hostĭs | Saevi hostēs |
| Voc. | Saevĕ hostĭs | Saevi hostēs |
| Acc. | Saevum hostem | Saevos hostēs |
| Gen. | Saevi hostĭs | Saevōrum hostĭum |
| Dat. | Saevo hostī | Saevīs hostĭbŭs |
| Abl. | Saevo hostĕ | Saevīs hostĭbŭs |

### Almă māter, *loving mother.*

| | Singular. | Plural. |
|---|---|---|
| N.V. | Almă māter | Almae mātrēs |
| Acc. | Almam mātrem | Almās mātrēs |
| Gen. | Almae mātrĭs | Almārum mātrum |
| Dat. | Almae mātrī | Almīs mātribŭs |
| Abl. | Almā mātrĕ | Almīs mātribŭs |

### Magnum ŏpus, *a great work.*

| | Singular. | Plural. |
|---|---|---|
| N.V. Acc. | Magnum ŏpŭs | Magnă ŏpĕra |
| Gen. | Magnī ŏpĕris | Magnōrum ŏpĕrum |
| Dat. | Magno ŏpĕrī | Magnīs ŏpĕrĭbŭs |
| Abl. | Magno ŏpĕrĕ | Magnīs ŏpĕrĭbŭs |

### EXERCISE XXII.

**Quĭs?** *What (man)? Who* (Nom.)? **Quem?** *What (man)? Whom* (Acc.)? **Quĭd?** *What (thing)? What* (Nom. and Acc.)?

1. Bonorum operum memoria forti viro dulcis erat. 2. Virgines pulchrae ducis iracundi minas timent. 3. Milites primae

---

[1] Numbers bracketed thus (17) in the Exercises refer to the Paragraphs indicated by the figures in the margin.

cohortis hostibus iracundis terga dant.¹ 4. Quis vinum vetus puero, quis seni verbera dat? 5. Benigno patri acris filiorum ira molesta erat. 6. Gladios breves, (32) longas hastas milites habent. 7. Mater alma filiarum tristium poenitentiam laudat. 8. Hostium saevorum feritas atrox cives timidos terret. 9. Senes infirmi regum minis atrocibus terrentur. 10. Tempestas atris nubibus et crebro fulmine virgines teneras terret. 11. Quis non virtutem amat? Quem non bonorum operum memoria delectat? 12. Senex probus inhonesta morte et turpi fama indignus est.

1. *Brave men fear a dishonourable reputation.* 2. *A disgraceful death terrifies strong soldiers.* 3. *Who loves vice? Who is not delighted by* (trans. *Whom delights not*) *the memory of virtue?* 4. *Who (gives) swords to weak old-men? who gives wine to boys?* 5. *The enemy* (use pl.), *by (their) savageness and cruel threats, terrify the timid hostages.* 6. *The tender maidens fear the dark-black clouds and the frequent lightning.* 7. *The memory of a good work is pleasing to all* (men). 8. *The citizens flee before the strong cohort* (trans. *give their backs to the strong cohort*). 9. *The loving mothers are delighted by the brave deeds of the bold boys.* 10. *The sad woman is worthy of a better death.* 11. *(He) is-terrified in the night.*

## THE FOURTH OR -u DECLENSION.

*Singular.*

|  | Step (m.). | Hand (f.). | Knee (n.). |
|---|---|---|---|
| N.V. | Grăd-ŭs | Măn-ŭs | Gĕn-ū |
| Acc. | Grăd-um | Măn-um | Gĕn-ū |
| Gen. | Grăd-ūs | Măn-ūs | Gĕn-ūs |
| Dat. | Grăd-ŭi | Măn-ŭi | Gĕn-ŭi |
| Abl. | Grăd-ū | Măn-ū | Gĕn-ū |

*Plural.*

|  | | | |
|---|---|---|---|
| N.V. | Grăd-ūs | Măn-ūs | Gĕn-ŭă |
| Acc. | Grăd-ūs | Măn-ūs | Gĕn-ŭă |
| Gen. | Grăd-ŭum | Măn-ŭum | Gĕn-ŭum |
| Dat. | Grăd-ĭbus | Măn-ĭbus | Gĕn-ĭbus |
| Abl. | Grăd-ĭbus | Măn-ĭbus | Gĕn-ĭbus |

51   1. The Dat. Sing. in -ŭi is sometimes contracted into -ū.

---

¹ "To *give backs* to an enemy" means "to *flee from* an enemy."

**52**  2. Some names of trees, e.g. **pīnus**, *pine-tree*, vary between the 2nd and 4th Decl. in Gen. and Abl. Singular, and in Nom. and Acc. Plural.

**53**  3. The Dat. Plur. is formed in **-ŭbus** (not **-ĭbus**) by **arcus**, m., *bow*, **artus**, m., *limb*, and **partus**, m., *birth*, so as not to be confounded with the Dat. Plur. of **arx**, f., *citadel*, **ars**, f., *art*, and **pars**, f., *part*. The Dat. in **-ŭbus** is also formed by **ăcus**, f., *needle*, **portus**, m., *harbour*, and **trĭb-us**, f., *tribe*. (See also Par. 311.)

**54**  All nouns of the Fourth Declension that have nom. **-us**, are masculine, except the names of trees, and five others (see Appendix V. p. 226); those in **-ū** are neuter.

## Exercise XXIII.

**55**  Carefully distinguish the different constructions of the Preposition **ĭn**:

**Ĭn** (foll. by Abl.) *in*:     **Ĭn** (foll. by Acc.) *into, to, towards*:

(*My*) *father is in the garden.*     Păter **ĭn horto** est.
*The leader leads the soldiers into the city.*     Dux mīlĭtes **ĭn urbem** dūcit.

1. Pinus altae fructum non habent; glandes sunt quercuum fructus. 2. Hostes magnam copiam arcuum et sagittarum comparant. 3. Imbres quercui dant aquam. 4. Scythae arcu dux vulneratur. 5. Equi albi sinistrum genu durum est. 6. Acus longa digitum mulieris vulnerat. 7. Naves longae in tuto portu ventos secundos expectant. 8. Naves longas in portus diversos tempestas agit. 9. Nautae, in portu pelagus, in pelago portum laudant. 10. Auditus visusque utilitatem quis non intelligit? 11. Romanae plebis tribubus frumentum a Caesare datur. 12. Hiemis gelu myrto perniciosum erat; pinui et quercui non erat (perniciosum). 13. Multa (34) totam noctem (31) timet (16*a*).

1. *The Scythian overcomes* (*his*) *enemy with* (*his*) *strong bow.* 2. *The diligent women have sharp needles.* 3. *Adverse winds drive the ships into safe harbours.* 4. *The frost of winter is not destructive to pines.* 5. *The ships of-war are awaiting favourable winds in the safe harbour.* 6. *Stags by their running, foxes by* (*their*) *subtlety, overcome the hunter.* 7. *The branches of the tall oaks have many acorns.* 8. *By*

*hearing and by sight men avoid destructive (things), (and) obtain useful (things).* 9. *The stag (has) long horns, the bull has short (horns).* 10. *The bull with his left horn wounds the shepherd.* 11. *He was sick for-the-whole winter* (31).

### THE FIFTH OR -E DECLENSION.

| *Day (m.).* | | *Thing (f.).* | |
| --- | --- | --- | --- |
| Singular. | Plural. | Singular. | Plural. |
| N.V. Dĭ-ēs | Dĭ-ēs | R-ēs[1] | R-ēs |
| Acc. Dĭ-em | Dĭ-ēs | R-em | R-ēs |
| Gen. Dĭ-ēi | Dĭ-ērum | R-ei[2] | R-ērum |
| Dat. Dĭ-ēi | Dĭ-ēbus | R-ei | R-ēbus |
| Abl. Dĭ-ē | Dĭ-ēbus | R-ē | R-ēbus |

**56** In the Gen. and Dat., final -ei is sometimes contracted into -ē; diē, fidē.

**57** All nouns of the Fifth Declension are Feminine, except diēs, *day,* and merīdiēs, *midday,* which are Masculine.[3]

### Exercise XXIV.

**Ăg-it,** *(he) drives,* or *leads.* **Ăg-ĭtur,** *(he) is (being) driven.*

1. Agricola spē fructuum in laborem agitur. 2. Acies densa ab hostibus in fugam agitur. 3. Magna pars exercitūs in planitiē erat. 4. Tanta vitia tam pulchra facie indigna sunt. 5. Memoria pulchrae faciēi hominibus jucunda est. 6. Mora spei inimica est. 7. Rex justus melioribus rebus dignus est. 8. Rebus adversis vir fortis in dolorem agitur. 9. Exercitus omnis in spem novam a forti duce agitur. 10. In Britanniā apricorum dierum numerus non magnus est. 11. Fluminis rapidi cursus interdum glacie superatur. 12. Rerum adversarum memoria in rebus secundis interdum jucunda est.

1. *In summer the hours of the day are many, in winter (the hours) of the night* (30). 2. *There-were many horse-soldiers and foot-soldiers* (use -quĕ) *in the line of the enemy.* 3. *The light of mid-day is (being) overcome by a dark-black cloud.* 4. *The*

---

[1] This Noun is printed thus (as also in the *Public School Grammar*) to exhibit the Case Terminations more clearly. But the true Stem of rēs is not r- but re-. See p. 239, ' *Stem.*'

[2] The quantity of r-ei varies.

[3] Diēs should not be used by the beginner in the Feminine, except poetically; to signify, not a literal *day,* but a *season,* e.g. *The evil day has come,* Atra diēs vēnit.

Diēs and rēs are the only Nouns in the Fifth Declension that are fully declined; and all (but nine) have no *Plural.*

long line of the enemy (trans. enemies) is being overcome by the fearless soldiers. 5. The memory of prosperity is sometimes unpleasing to the wretched. 6. The heat of the sun was destructive to the thin ice. 7. The memory of joyful days was pleasing to the just judge. 8. Great is the utility of hope. 9. The hostage is being driven into the citadel by the bold leader. 10. The queen shews (her) grief by (her) sad face.

## COMPARISON OF ADJECTIVES.

### I.—REGULAR.

**58** 1. **The Comparative Degree**, if regular, is formed from the Gen. Sing. by taking away -i, (alt-i, alt-) or -is (ferac-is, ferac-), and adding -ĭor: alt-ĭor, *higher*, fĕrāc-ĭor, *more fruitful*.

**59** 2. **The Superlative Degree** is formed by taking away -i or -is and adding -issĭmus: alt-issĭmus, fĕrāc-issĭmus.

| Gen. Sing. | Comparative. | Superlative. |
|---|---|---|
| Trist-ĭs, | trist-ĭor, *sadder*, | trist-issĭmŭs, *saddest*. |
| Rĕcent-ĭs, | rĕcent-ĭor, *more recent*, | rĕcent-issĭmŭs, *most recent*. |

### II.—IRREGULAR SUPERLATIVES.

#### 1. -lĭmus.

**60** 1. Six Adj. in -ĭlis, form the Compar. regularly, but the Superl. by adding -lĭmus instead of -issĭmus.

| Positive. | Comparative. | Superlative. |
|---|---|---|
| Făcĭl-is, *easy* | facĭl-ĭor | facil-lĭmus |
| Diffĭcil-ĭs, *difficult* | diffĭcĭl-ĭor | diffĭcil-lĭmus |
| Sĭmĭl-ĭs, *like* | sĭmĭl-ĭor | sĭmil-lĭmus |
| Dissĭmil-ĭs, *unlike* | dissĭmĭl-ĭor | dissĭmil-lĭmus |
| Grăcĭl-ĭs, *thin* | grăcĭl-ĭor | grăcil-lĭmus |
| Hŭmĭl-ĭs, *low* | hŭmĭl-ĭor | hŭmil-lĭmus |

The rest, fertĭl-ĭs, ūtĭl-ĭs &c., have either no Superlative or -issĭmus; fertĭl-issĭmus, ūtil-issĭmus, &c.

## 2. -rĭmus.

**61** 2. All Adj. ending in -er form the Compar. regularly, but the Superl. by *adding* -rĭmus *to the Nominative:*

| Positive. | Comparative. | Superlative. |
|---|---|---|
| Nom. Gen. | | |
| Līber, lĭbĕr-i, *free* | lībĕr-ĭor | līber-rĭmus |
| Cĕler, cĕlĕr-is, *swift* | cĕlĕr-ĭor | cĕler-rĭmus |
| Pulcher, pulchr-i, *beautiful* | pulchr-ĭor | pulcher-rĭmus |
| Ācer, acr-is, *sharp* | acr-ĭor | ācer-rĭmus |

The Adjective vĕtŭs, Gen. vĕtĕr-is, *old*, has Comp. vĕtust-ĭor, Superl. veter-rĭmus.[1]

### Quam, *than.*

**62** RULE.—Nouns coupled by **quam** (*than*) and a Comparative Adj. or Adv., are in the same case:

1. *Nom.* { Ĕqui ūtĭlĭores sunt **quam capri** (sunt).
   *Horses are more useful than goats (are).*

2. *Gen.* { Pŭdor **flăgĭtĭi**, măgis quam **errōris**, hŏmĭnem complet.
   *Shame for the crime, rather than for the error, possesses the man:* lit. *of the crime, of the error.*

3. *Dat.* { **Pŭĕro** dat mēlĭōra dona **quam pŭellae** (dat).
   *To the boy he gives better gifts than (he gives) to the girl.*

4. *Acc.* { Mālus **fōlĭa** hăbet densĭōra **quam māla** (hăbet).[2]
   *The apple-tree has leaves thicker than (it has) apples.*

**63** RULE.—When the first Noun is in the Nominative or Accusative, the second Noun is generally put in the Ablative without **quam**:

*Nothing is more lovable than virtue.*   Nĭhil est **virtūte** ămābĭlĭus.

---

[1] The Comparative vĕtĕrior is rare and archaic.
[2] Distinguish between māla, *apples*, and māla, *evils.*

*N.B.* Superlatives and Comparatives have each more meanings than one:

**64** I. **Tard-issĭmus** means (1) *slowest*, (2) *very slow.*

**65** II. **Tard-ĭor** means (1) *slower*, (2) *rather*, or *somewhat, slow,* or (3) *too slow.*

### Exercise XXV.

**66** Rule.—**Sĭmĭlis**, *like,* takes a (1) Gen. or (2) Dat.: [1]—

(1) *The boys are like* (i.e., *the likenesses of*) (*their*) *father.*   Pŭĕri **patris** sĭmĭles sunt.

(2) *All things were more like* (*to*) *a camp than* (*to*) *a city.*   Omnĭa **castris** quam **urbi** sĭmĭlĭōra ĕrant.

**67 Quĭdem,** *on the one hand; indeed.* **Autem,** *on the other hand; however; but.* Neither of these words can stand first in a clause. They must be placed after some emphatic word. See Sentence 9 below.

1. Vallis humilior erat campo. 2. Nihil est virtute pulchrius, nihil amicitiā dulcius. 3. Puer omnibus praeceptoris discipulis procerior erat. 4. Uxori vir melius donum quam sorori dat. 5. Amor patriae magis quam filiorum ducem acerrimum complet. 6. Cervus animal est celerrimum, et testudini dissimillimum.[2] 7. Hieme·dies breviores sunt noctibus. 8. Iter puellae difficilius est quam puero. 9. Turdus quidem avis tardior (65) est, aquila autem velocissima. 10. In regione aspera itinera hieme difficiliora quam aestate sunt. 11. Puer aegerrimus crura et brachia graciliora habet. 12. Puellae patris quam matris similiores erant. 13. Puellam quidem totum diem (31) culpat (16a), puerum autem laudat.

1. *Nothing is more useful to men than sight and hearing.* 2. *The husbandman's garden is more fertile than the rich king's fields.* 3. *Who is bolder than a soldier? who* (*is*) *juster than a judge?* 4. *The ass is a somewhat-foolish* (65) *animal; the dog is very sagacious.* 5. *The boy's sisters were more like* (*their*) *mother than* (*their*) *father.* 6. *The anger of the king was keener than the madness of the soldiers.* 7. *By very swift journeys*

---

[1] The Dative is rare in Cicero, but very common in later writers.
[2] Two Adjectives coupled by **ĕt** can agree with the same Noun.

*the general leads (his) soldiers into a most rugged region.* 8. *Very beautiful trees fill the very low[1] valleys of (the) most[1] fertile region.* 9. *The very brave soldiers are being driven into the city by (a) very keen and bold leader.*[1] 10. *The very[1] ailing boy has very thin legs in winter.*

IRREGULAR COMPARISON.

**68**

| Positive. | Comparative. | Superlative. |
|---|---|---|
| bŏnus, *good* | mĕlior | optĭmus |
| mălus, *bad* | pējor | pessĭmus |
| magnus, *great* | mājor | maxĭmus |
| parvus, *small* | mĭnor | mĭnĭmus |
| multi, (pl.), *many* | plūres | plūrĭmi [2] |
| nēquam, (indecl.) *worthless* | nēquior | nēquissĭmus |

**68a** Adjectives ending in -dĭcus, *-speaking*, -fĭcus, *doing*, -vŏlus, *wishing*, form the Comp. in -entĭor, the Superl. in -entissĭmus:

mălĕ-dĭcus, *ill-speaking*, -dĭcentĭor, -dĭcentissĭmus.
mūnĭ-fĭcus, *gift-making*, -fĭcentĭor, -fĭcentissĭmus.
bĕnĕ-vŏlus, *well-wishing*, -vŏlentĭor, -vŏlentissĭmus.

(These forms are really derived from Verbal forms in -ens, which will be recognised when the Verbs are mastered.)

**68b** Adjectives ending in -ēus, -ĭus, -ŭus, seldom have a Compar. or Superl. form of their own, but are compared by appending the adverbs **măgis**, *more*, **maxĭmē**, *most* : **pĭus**, *dutiful*, **măgis pĭus**, *more dutiful*, **maxĭmē pĭus**, *most dutiful*.

**69** In the following the Positive is defective, and is represented by a Noun, Adjective, or Preposition:

---

**70** [1] In Latin the Superlative is more frequently used than in English. We should say "*the brave* soldiers," "*a bold* leader." But in Latin the Superlatives must be expressed.

**71** [2] **Multum, plūs**, and **plūrĭmum** are also used in the Neut. Sing. as Nouns governing a Genitive Case.

| | | |
|---|---|---|
| *They have much* | **Multum** | |
| *more* ⎫ (*of*) *money.* | **Plūs** ⎬ pĕcūnĭae hăbent. | |
| *very much* ⎭ | **Plūrĭmum** ⎭ | |

| | | |
|---|---|---|
| [Sĕnex], *an old man* | sĕnior¹ | nātu maxĭmus, *oldest.* |
| [Jŭvĕnis], *a young man* | jūnior¹ | nātu mĭnĭmus, *youngest.* |
| [Sŭpĕrus], *upper* | sŭpĕrior | suprēmus, summus, *highest.* |
| [Infĕrus], *lower* | infĕrior | infĭmus, īmus, *lowest.* |
| [Extĕrus], *outside* | extĕrior | extrēmus, (*outermost* or *last*). |
| [prep. Intrā], *inside* | intĕrior | intĭmus, *inmost.* |
| [Postĕrus], *after, behind* | postĕrior | postrēmus, (*hindmost* or *last*). |
| [prep. Prae], *before* | prĭor | prīmus, (*foremost* or *first*). |
| [prep. Prŏpē], *near* | prŏpĭor¹ | proxĭmus, (*nearest* or *next*). |
| [prep. Ultrā], *beyond* | ultĕrĭor | ultĭmus, (*furthest* or *last*). |

**72**  Plūs, *more*, is thus declined :

*Singular : a Noun.*  
*Neuter.*

| | |
|---|---|
| *Nom. and Acc.* | Plūs |
| *Gen.* | Plūrĭs |
| *Dat.* | Plūrī |
| *Abl.* | Plūrĕ |

*Plural : an Adjective.*

| *Masc. and Fem.* | *Neut.* |
|---|---|
| Plūrēs | Plūră |
| Plūrĭum | Plūrĭum |
| Plūrĭbus | Plūrĭbus |
| Plūrĭbus | Plūrĭbus |

Măgis means *more in degree* and is used with Adjectives ; plūs, *more in quantity*, and is used with Verbs.

*Balbus is more dutiful, but Tullius delights (his) father more.*   Balbus măgis pĭus est, sed Tullius patrem plūs dēlectat.

### Exercise XXVI.

**73**  Rule.—A Superlative, in agreement with a Noun understood, is followed by the Genitive :

*The horse is the most useful (animal) of animals.*   Ĕquus ūtĭlĭssĭmum (animal) ănĭmālĭum est.

1. Alexander erat ducum praestantissimus.² 2. Optimorum virorum filii interdum pessimi sunt. 3. Quid pejus erat Balbi contione ! Quid optimae (35) Tullii contioni (66) simile habet ?³ 4. Majores natu ratio, non spes, agit. 5. Junioribus

---

¹ Nātu major and nātu minor are also used. Nātu means *by birth*, and is not declined.

² Why is dŭcum Gen. ? Ans. *governed by* dux *understood.*

³ An Adj. *e.g.* optīmae, is often separated from its Noun by an intervening Geuitive *e.g.* Tullii. (Par. 35.) Quĭd (Exercise XXII) is Acc. gov. by hăbet.

The Nom. to hăbet is *it*, i.e. *the speech of Balbus,* understood.

seniores dona dant. 6. Ducis optimi dies ultimus erat felicissimus. 7. Socrates optimus Graecorum erat. 8. Castrorum pars exterior parte intimā major erat. 9. Plus erat (71) modestiae quam sapientiae in viro benevolentissimo.¹ 10. Plurimorum facta nequissima, optima verba sunt. 11. Minima pars propioris regionis maximā parte regionis ulterioris major erat. 12. Senes priora (34) laudant, juniorum facta culpant. 13. Proximo die imperator maximam partem hostium superat. 14. Virgo a milite hasta totum diem terretur.

1. The king, (who was) worse than (his) father, has a (still) more worthless son. 2. Very old men praise former times. 3. The greater part of the outermost wall was nearest to the citadel. 4. The most benevolent of the younger (men) were inferior to (trans. as if to were than) the worst of the elder (men). 5. He gives more gifts to the worst of the sisters than to the most dutiful of the brothers. 6. The lowest part of the mountain was higher (comp. and superl. of superus) than the highest part of the citadel. 7. The younger rightly give reverence to (their) elders.' 8. The younger of the brothers was very like the elder sister. 9. Very many praise what is best (trans. best-things). 10. On the last (30) day of (his) life the old-man was most happy. 11. He is-blamed the whole day (long).

## NUMERAL ADJECTIVES.

**74** Numeral Adjectives are either (1) Cardinal, denoting *how many*, or (2) Ordinal, denoting *in what order*.² All the Ordinal Adjectives are declined like **bŏnus**; but of the Cardinal Adjectives only a few are declined.

1. **Ūnus**, *one*.

| | *Masc.* | *Fem.* | *Neut.* |
|---|---|---|---|
| Gen. Sing. | **Ūn-īus** | un-īus | un-īus |
| Dat. Sing. | **Un-i** | un-i | un-i |

In the other cases, Sing. and Plur., it is like **bonus**.

---

**75** ¹ Why is **mŏdestĭae** Gen? Ans. *governed by* **plūs**, Adj. used as Noun. Why is **săpĭentĭae** Gen.? *Because* **quam** (Par. 62) *takes the same Case after it as before it*. In translating **bĕnĕvŏlentissĭmo** add *the* or *that*.

**76** The Gen. after **pars, plūs, multum,** &c., is often called the *Partitive Genitive*.

**77** ² For the Distributive Numeral Adjectives see Exercise LXXXV. They are all declined like **bŏni, -ae, -a**: (1) **singŭli**, *one a-piece;* (2) **bīni**, *two a-piece;* (3) **terni** or **trīni**; (4) **quăterni**; (5) **quīni**; (6) **sēni**; (7) **septēni**; (8) **octōni**; (9) **nŏvēni**; (10) **dēni**; (11) **undēni**; (100) **centēni**; (101) **centēni singŭli**; (200) **dūcēni**; (300) **trēcēni**; (400) **quadringēni**; (600) **sescēni**; (1,000) **singŭla mīlia**.

**78**  2. **Dŭo,** *two.*   3. **Trēs,** *three.*

|  | Masc. | Fem. | Neut. | Masc. & Fem. | Neut. |
|---|---|---|---|---|---|
| N.V. | Dŭ-ŏ | dŭ-ae | dŭ-ŏ | Trēs | trĭă |
| Acc. | Dŭ-os[1] | dŭ-as | dŭ-ŏ | Trēs[2] | trĭă |
| Gen. | Dŭ-ōrum | dŭ-ārum | dŭ-ōrum | Trĭum | trĭum |
| Dat. | Dŭ-ōbus | dŭ-ābus | dŭ-ōbus | Trĭbus | trĭbus |
| Abl. | Dŭ-ōbus | dŭ-ābus | dŭ-ōbus | Trĭbus | trĭbus |

**Ambo,** *both,* is declined like **dŭo.**

**79**  The Cardinal Numbers, from *four* to a *hundred,* are indeclinable.

The compounds of a *hundred* are declined like **bŏnus**: *Of two hundred men,* **Dŭcentōrum** hŏmĭnum.

4. **Mĭllĕ,** *thousand.*

**80**  The two uses of **mĭllĕ** (*a*) Sing. (*b*) Plural, must be carefully distinguished:

*a.* Singular, an indeclinable *Adjective:*

**Mĭllĕ** passūs, *a thousand paces.*
**Mĭllĕ** passĭbus, *to a thousand paces, &c.*

*b.* Plural, a *Noun* of the Third Declension, having an Adjective *agreeing with it in Number and Case,* and *governing another Noun in the Genitive:*

| | |
|---|---|
| N.V. and Acc. | Multa **mīlĭa** passuum, *many thousands of paces.* |
| Gen. | Multōrum **mīlĭum** passuum, *of many thousands of paces.* |
| Dat. | Multis **mīlĭbus** passuum, *to many thousands of paces.* |
| Abl. | Multis **mīlĭbus** passuum, *by many thousands of paces.* |

---

[1] Less commonly, **dŭ-o.**
[2] Less commonly, **trīs.**

## NUMERAL ADJECTIVES.

| Arabic Symbols. | Roman Symbols. | Cardinals. | Ordinals. |
|---|---|---|---|
| 1 | I | ūnus, -a, -um | prīmus |
| 2 | II | dŭŏ, -æ, -o | sĕcundus *or* altĕr |
| 3 | III | trēs, -tria | tertĭus |
| 4 | IV | quattŭŏr (quātŭŏr) | quartus |
| 5 | V | quinquĕ | quintus |
| 6 | VI | sex | sextus |
| 7 | VII | septem | septĭmus |
| 8 | VIII | octŏ | octāvus |
| 9 | IX | nŏvem | nōnus |
| 10 | X | dĕcem | dĕcĭmus |
| 11 | XI | undĕcim | undĕcĭmus |
| 12 | XII | duŏdĕcim | duŏdĕcĭmus |
| 13 | XIII | trĕdĕcim | tertĭus dĕcĭmus |
| 14 | XIV | quattuordĕcim | quartus dĕcĭmus |
| 15 | XV | quindĕcim | quintus dĕcĭmus |
| 16 | XVI | sēdĕcim | sextus dĕcĭmus |
| 17 | XVII | septemdĕcim | septĭmus dĕcĭmus |
| 18 | XVIII | duŏdēvīgintī | duŏdēvīcēsĭmus |
| 19 | XIX | undēvīgintī | undēvīcēsĭmus |
| 20 | XX | vīgintī | vīcēsĭmus |
| 21 | XXI | ūnus et vīgintī *or* vīgintī ūnus | unus et vīcēsĭmus, *or* vīcēsĭmus prīmus |
| 22 | XXII | dŭŏ et vīgintī *or* vīgintī duo | alter et vīcēsĭmus, *or* vīcēsĭmus alter |
| 23 | XXIII | trēs et ·vīgintī *or* vīgintī trēs | tertĭus et vīcēsĭmus, *or* vīcēsĭmus tertĭus |
| 28 | XXVIII | duŏdētrīgintā | duŏdētrīcēsĭmus |
| 29 | XXIX | undētrīgintā | undētrīcēsĭmus |
| 30 | XXX | trīgintā | trīcēsĭmus |
| 40 | XL | quadrāgintā | quadrāgēsĭmus |
| 50 | L | quinquāgintā | quinquāgēsĭmus |
| 60 | LX | sexāgintā | sexāgēsĭmus |
| 70 | LXX | septŭāgintā | septŭāgēsĭmus |
| 80 | LXXX | octōgintā | octōgēsĭmus |
| 90 | XC | nōnāgintā | nōnāgēsĭmus |
| 100 | C | centum | centēsĭmus |
| 101 | CI | centum et unus *or* centum unus | centēsĭmus prīmus |
| 136 | CXXXVI | centum et trīgintā sex *or* centum, triginta sex | centēsĭmus trīcēsĭmus sextus |
| 200 | CC | dŭcentī, -æ, -ă | dŭcentēsĭmus |
| 300 | CCC | trĕcentī, -æ, -ă | trĕcentēsĭmus |

| Arabic Symbols. | Roman Symbols. | Cardinals. | Ordinals. |
|---|---|---|---|
| 400 | CCCC | quadringentī, -ae, -ă | quadringentēsĭmus |
| 500 | IƆ or D | quingentī, -ae, -ă | quingentēsĭmus |
| 600 | DC | sescentī, -ae, -ă | sexcentēsĭmus |
| 700 | DCC | septingentī, -ae, -ă | septingentēsĭmus |
| 800 | DCCC | octingentī, -ae, -ă | octingentēsĭmus |
| 900 | DCCCC | nongentī, -ae, -ă | nongentēsĭmus |
| 1,000 | CIƆ or M | mille | millēsĭmus |
| 2,000 | MM | duŏ miliă | bis millēsĭmus |
| 100,000 | CCCIƆƆƆ | centum miliă | centiēs millēsĭmus [1] |

Exercise XXVII.

**82** Rule.—The Possessor is often expressed by the Dative Case with the Verb **est, (sunt, ĕrat, ĕrant,** &c.):

*Balbus has,* or *had a book,* i.e. there was a book for Balbus.   **Balbo est,** or ĕrat, lĭber.

1. Duos consules decem tribunorum constantia superat. 2. Militi veterrimo unus solum oculus et novem digiti erant.[2] 3. In legione Romana decem cohortes erant. 4. Mensis September quondam septimus (erat), nunc nonus anni mensis est.[3] 5. Juvenis alteram et vicesimam partem patrimonii pauperibus dat. 6. Arbori centum et triginta sex poma tunc erant. 7. Agricola sedecim nuces, (32) nonaginta octo cerasa mulieri dat. 8. Centuria erat altera pars manipuli, sexta pars cohortis, legionis sexagesima (pars). 9. Legio trecentos equites habet. 10. In hostium exercitu sunt mille nongenti equites,

**83** [1] The number 500, IƆ, is multiplied by 10 as often as Ɔ is subjoined:—
$$IƆƆ = 10 \times 500 = 5,000.$$
$$IƆƆƆ = 10 \times 5,000 = 50,000.$$
In order to double IƆ, or IƆƆ, you must prefix C as many times as it is suffixed:—
$$CIƆ = 2 \times 500 = 1,000.$$
$$CCIƆƆ = 2 \times 5,000 = 10,000.$$

**84** [2] Why is **mīlĭti** Dat? Ans., *Dat of the Possessive after* **est.**

[3] **Jānŭārĭus** and **September** are Adjectives agreeing with **mensis.** The adjectival names of the months are sometimes used as Nouns, **mensis** being understood, e.g. **Februārĭi** in sentence 11. See p. 229.

peditum tria millia. 11. Januarii mensis unus dies est pars una et tricesima; Februarii, duodetricesima.[1] 12. Undetriginta verberibus miles a centurione castigatur.

1. *The general had (erant) three hundred and seven foot-soldiers. 2. The enemy had six hundred foot-soldiers, (and) two thousand horse-soldiers. 3. The husbandman gives twenty-five eggs to the wretched sailor. 4. There were on (in) the oak many thousand acorns. 5. On the sixth month of the year, in the seventh hour, there were in the city three thousand Germans. 6. The general leads into the city the twentieth legion and the third part of the thirtieth legion. 7. A century was the sixth part of a cohort; a cohort (was) the tenth part of a legion. 8. Once a legion had three thousand soldiers. 9. There were then in the legion six thousand foot-soldiers (and) three hundred horse-soldiers. 10. Once March was the first month of the year, November (was) the ninth, (and) December the tenth. 11. The old soldier had thirty-three wounds.*

## IRREGULAR ADJECTIVES.

**85** The following adjectives (most of them capable of being used as Pronouns) are declined regularly (like **bŏnus**) in the Plural, and in all cases of the Singular, except the Gen. and Dat.; but (like the Pronouns) they make the Gen. Sing in -īus (-ĭus) or -rīus, and the Dat. Sing. in -i:

| 1. -īus (-ĭus). | 2. -rīus. |
|---|---|
| **Ūnus**, *one, one only.* | **Alter**, Gen. altĕrĭus, *one (of two), the other (of two).* |
| **Ullus**, *any.*[2] | |
| **Nullus**, *no, not any, none.* | **Ūter ?** utr-īus ? *which (of the two) ?* |
| **Sōlus**, *alone.* | |
| **Tōtus**, *whole.* | **Neuter**, neutr-īus, *neither.* |

**86** **Ălĭus**, *other*, makes the Neut. Sing. in -ud. When *twice* used co-ordinately (*i.e.* so that *and, but, &c.,* might be inserted), it means, in the Sing., *one . . . another*, or, in the Plur., *some . . . others;* and **alter . . . alter** mean, similarly, *one of the two . . . the other of the two.*

---

[1] Why is **Februārīi** (mensis) Gen.? Ans. *governed by* pars *understood*. You must repeat "unus dies est pars" with **dŭŏdĕtrĭcēsĭma.**
The pupil may henceforth (with the aid of Appendix VI.) write the Latin day of the month on his exercise.

**87** [2] Ullus is only used in (1) *negative and* (2) *comparative sentences, or in* (3) *questions that expect a negative answer.*

# IRREGULAR ADJECTIVES. [Par. 88—91]

(1) *He blames one thing, (and) praises another.*    Ălĭud culpat, ălĭud laudat.

(2) *Some overcome, (but) others are overcome.*    Ălĭi sŭpĕrant, ălĭi sŭpĕrantur.

(3) *He gives one of the two sisters a pear, the other an apple.*    Altĕri sŏrōrum pīrum, altĕri pōmum dat.

**Ălius,** *other.*
*Singular.*

|      | Masc. | Fem. | Neut. |
|------|-------|------|-------|
| Nom. | Ălĭus | ălĭa | ălĭud |
| Voc. | *Wanting* | | |
| Acc. | Ălĭum | ălĭam | ălĭud |
| Gen. | Alīus | ălīus | ălīus |
| Dat. | Alĭi  | ălĭi  | ălĭi  |
| Abl. | Alĭo  | ălĭā  | ălĭo  |

**Nullus,** *no.*
*Singular.*

|      | Masc. | Fem. | Neut. |
|------|-------|------|-------|
| Nom. | Nullus | nullă | nullum |
| Voc. | [Nulle | nulla | nullum] |
| Acc. | Nullum | nullam | nullum |
| Gen. | Nullīus | nullīus | nullīus |
| Dat. | Nulli | nulli | nulli |
| Abl. | Nullo | nullā | nullo |

**88** When **ălius** is repeated *not co-ordinately* (see Par. 86), it is sometimes construed as follows:—

*Some women praise some things, others praise others.*    Mŭlĭĕres ălĭae alĭa laudant.

The Nom. of **ălīus** has ĭ, the Gen. has ī:

*One man praises one man's conduct, another man another's.*    Ălĭus ălīus mōrēs laudat.

**89** Note **alt-ĕrīus**, but **ut-rīus**; so **asp-ĕri**, but **pulch-ri**.

### EXERCISE XXVIII.

**90** Adjectives signifying *nearness, dearness, pleasantness, fitness, likeness, equality,* &c., and their opposites, govern the Dative.

1. Utri senum filia viam monstrat?[1]   2. Neutrius exercitus dux timidus erat. 3. Uni soli tot militum dux coronam dat.[2] 4. Fratrum optimorum alter alterius filium valde amat. 5. Pater alteri filiorum equum validissimum, alteri ensem dat. 6. Mulieres aliae alia clamant. 7. Milites (88) alīus agros, alīus armenta et equos laudant. 8. Mater puellis dona diversa dat; alii dat aurum, alii argentum. 9. Nemini

---

**91** [1] **Sĕnum** is *Gen., governed by* **utri.** But the Gen. after **ŭter, neuter, ūnus,** &c. and also after the Numerals generally, is often called a *Partitive Genitive,* because it implies a *part* belonging to a larger number or whole.

[2] What sort of a Gen. is **mīlĭtum**? **Sōli** agrees with **ūni,** which (85) is used as a Pronoun.

molestus erat; nullius mores culpat.[1] 10. Pater majora dona filiae quam ulli filiorum dat.[2] 11. Homo avarus est, neque (18) ulli carus.[2] 12. Utrique genti facile (34) erat belli mala vitare (36a).

1. *Which of the (two) brothers is the dearer to (their) mother?*
2. *The man is very worthless* (68), *and not dear to any of the citizens.* 3. *To one of the (two) brothers he gives blame; to the other praise.* 4. *To neither of the leaders was the cowardice of the armies pleasing.* 5. *Virtue is agreeable to one, pleasure (is agreeable) to another.* 6. *One (man's) constancy, another (man's) prudence, is praised by the leader.* 7. *To one alone of the women does the queen give praise.* 8. *He gives to (his) brother a better gift than to any* (87) *of his sisters.* 9. *Some had* (82) *shields, others had swords; (but) no one had horses.* 10. *The woman was very worthless, and* (18) *not dear to any of (her) sisters.* 11. *The butterfly lives one day.*

## PRONOUNS AND PRONOMINAL ADJECTIVES.

| 1. First Person. | | 2. Second Person. | |
|---|---|---|---|
| Singular. | Plural. | Singular. | Plural. |
| I, me, &c. | We, us, &c. | Thou, thee. &c. | Ye, you, &c. |
| *Nom.* Ĕgŏ | Nōs | *N. and V.* Tū | Vōs |
| *Acc.* Mē | Nōs | Tē | Vōs |
| *Gen.* Mĕī | Nostri[3] (-trum) | Tŭī | Vestri[3](-trum) |
| *Dat.* Mĭhī | Nōbīs | Tĭbī | Vōbīs |
| *Abl.* Mē | Nōbīs | Tē | Vōbīs |

### 3. Third Person.

To express *he, she, it,* use is made of the Adjective (1) **ĭs**, m., *that (man),* (2) **ĕa**, f., *that (woman),* (3) **ĭd**, n., *that (thing).*

---

[1] Nullius, nullo are used for nēmĭnis and nēmĭne:
From nēmo let me never see
Nēmĭnis and nēmĭne.

[2] In what sort of sentences is ullus used? Why is it used (87) here?

[3] The Genitives Plural nostrum and vestrum, are used only in such phrases as "nēmo nostrum, vestrum, *no one of us, of you;* the wisest of us; *some of us,* &c. It is then called a Partitive Genitive: see above, Par. 76, 91. Nostri, vestri are really Adjectives in Gen. Sing. agreeing with a Noun understood: mĕmor est nostri, *He is mindful of our (business)* i.e. *of us.*

|       | Singular. |       |       | Plural. |          |          |
|-------|-----------|-------|-------|---------|----------|----------|
|       | *He*      | *She* | *It*  | *They*  | *They*   | *Those*  |
| Nom.  | Ĭs        | ĕă    | ĭd    | Ei (ii) | eae      | ĕă       |
| Acc.  | Ĕum       | ĕam   | ĭd    | Ēos     | ĕas      | ĕă       |
| Gen.  | Ēius      | ēius  | ēius  | Ēōrum   | ĕārum    | ĕōrum    |
| Dat.  | Ei        | ei    | ei    | Eis (iis) | eis (iis) | eis (iis) |
| Abl.  | Ēo        | ĕā    | ĕo    | Eis (iis) | eis (iis) | eis (iis)[1] |

**94** The Gen. eius, eōrum, is often used for *his, her, their*: "lĭber eius," *his*, or *her book*; "eōrum lĭber," *their book*.

### 4. THE REFLEXIVE PRONOUN.

This Pronoun has no Nominative nor Vocative, and the Plural is the same as the Singular.

|       |        | Singular. |           |         | Plural. |
|-------|--------|-----------|-----------|---------|---------|
| Acc.  | Sē     | *himself, herself, itself*[2] | | | *themselves* |
| Gen.  | Sŭi    | *of* „ | „ | „ | „ |
| Dat.  | Sĭbĭ   | *to or for* „ | „ | „ | „ |
| Abl.  | Sē[2]  | *by* (17), *with, from* „ | „ | „ | „ |

### EXERCISE XXIX.

*I* (or *we*), *thou* (or *ye*), *he* (or *they*) are said to be respectively the First, Second, and Third *Persons*. All ordinary Nouns are said to be in the Third Person (see page 237).

The form of the Verb in Latin must be altered to suit the *Person* as well as the Number of its Subject:

| Person. | Singular. | | | Plural. | |
|---------|-----------|---|---|---------|---|
| 1st | *I love,* | (ĕgŏ) ăm-o | *We* ⎫ | (nōs) ămā-mus |
| 2nd | *Thou lovest,* | (tū) ămā-s | *Ye* ⎬ *love,* | (vōs) ămā-tis |
| 3rd | *He loves,* | (ĭs) ăma-t | *They* ⎭ | (ei) ăma-nt |

**95** RULE.—The Verb agrees with its Nominative Case in Number and Person.

All the Verbs that make the 3rd Pers. Sing. in -at (such as sŭpĕra-t, lauda-t, &c.), are changed in the same way as ămo above: but da-t has the a short, dămus, dătis.

---

[1] The quantity of the e in ei, eis is doubtful.
[2] Instead of sē there is sometimes used the emphatic form sēsē. The pupil must be prepared hereafter to find that sē is used in some instances for *he, him*. But, for the present, it will be only used for *himself, herself &c.* (never for *thyself, yourself*).

[Par. 96—98] PRONOMINAL ADJECTIVES. 47

**96** Ūnus is sometimes used in agreement with a Noun or Pronoun to mean *alone* or *only*:—

*Only Tullius loves me.*  **Ūnus** Tullius mē ămat.

1. Ego eum amo. 2. Tu eius fratrem amas.¹ 3. Nos eorum fratrem amamus. 4. Vos eius sorores amatis. 5. Dona eius mihi uni (96) grata sunt. 6. Agri agricolarum eis grati sunt. 7. Mater filium amat, ego eam laudo. 8. Matri filius poma dat, ego eum laudo. 9. Poma talia mihi grata non sunt; ego porcis eă do. 10. Tu mihi et ei dona meliora quam eis das. 11. Vos eorum dona laudatis, earum (dona) culpatis. 12. Omnes sese amant. 13. Nemo non sibi benignus est.

1. *I love her, she loves me.* 2. *Thou lovest her¹ father.* 3. *Ye love their (94) gifts.* 4. *We love them, ye love us.* 5. *They give us better gifts than (they give) to him.* 6. *His patience is pleasing to me.* 7. *Their patience is pleasing to him.* 8. *Her constancy is pleasing to them.* 9. *No one blames himself.* 10. *His folly is pleasing to thee (96) alone.*

### PRONOMINAL ADJECTIVES.

**97** The Genitives **ēius, eōrum**, are used for *his, her, their*; but the Genitives **měi, tŭi, nostri, vestri**, &c., are hardly ever used for *my, thy, our, your,* &c. For this purpose the following Pronominal Adjectives are used:

| Masc. | Fem. | Neut. | |
|---|---|---|---|
| **Měus** | měă | měum | *my, mine* |
| **Tŭus** | tŭă | tŭum | *thy, thine* |
| **Noster** | nostră | nostrum | *our, ours* |
| **Vester** | vestră | vestrum | *your, yours* |
| **Sŭus** | sŭa | sŭum | *his own, her own, its own, their own* |

**98** Eius and Sŭus. Note the difference. **Suus** may be used (for the present) where you can insert *own* in the English.

(1) *The mother loves her (own) son.*  Māter fīlium **sŭum** ămat.
(2) *Gaius and his brother love me.* (See page 328.)  Gaius et frātĕr **ēius** mē ămant.
(3) *I love her son.*  Āmo **ēius** fī'ium.

---

¹ Note the ambiguity in Latin: **eius** is used both for *her* and for *his*. In practice, of course, the ambiguity would be generally removed by the context. On the other hand, the ambiguity of the English *their* is removed by the Latin use of **eōrum** and **eārum**.

**99** Ĕgo, tū, ĭs, nōs, &c., are generally omitted as the Subjects of a Verb: ămās, *thou lovest*, ămāmus, *we love, &c.*

**99a** But if emphasis is intended to be laid on the Pronouns, they are inserted: "ĕgo tē ămo, tū mē nōn ămās."

### Exercise XXX.

**100** A question is asked by nōnne, num or -nĕ; -nĕ is added to, and emphasizes, *the first word in the Sentence*.

Do YOU blame me?    Tūnĕ mē culpās?
Do you blame ME?    Mēnĕ culpās?

**101** Nōnnĕ? (*i.e.* nōn-nĕ?) expects *yes;* num? expects *no.*[1]

Does he not blame me?    Nōnnĕ mē culpat?
He does not blame me, does he?    Num mē culpat?

**102** RULE.—Adjectives signifying *mindfulness, knowledge,* or *forgetfulness* and *ignorance,* take the Genitive.

1. Mercator sua laudat (32), aliena culpat. 2. Puer vobis carus est; nonne sororem eius amatis? 3. Non omnes semper sui memores sunt. 4. Puellae patrem non habent: omnes eis benigni sunt. 5. Nonne omnes sibi benigni sunt, aliorum immemores? 6. Amici mei Tullium valde amant, et semper eius memores sunt. 7. Soror tua, O amice, patrem suum non amat. 8. Nos sumus vestri memores; sed nemo vestrum nostri memor est.[2] 9. Mater tua non est tibi carior quam meus pater mihi.[3] 10. Laudamus aliena (34), nostra non curamus. 11. Cur non agros vestros curatis, agricolae ignavissimi? 12. Tune, O filiarum pessima, patris tui virtutem culpas? 13. Num tu, viae ignarus, viam aliis monstras? 14. Interdum sui immemor (16a) est.

1. [4] *Balbus is not mindful of us; but* (67) *we love him.* 2. *No one of us praises his folly.* 3. *The girl is dear to us; we love her*

---

[1] With cūr? *why?* quis? *who?* and other interrogatives, -nĕ, nōnne, num, are omitted: *Why does he not blame?* Cūr nōn culpat? When nonne and num are used in direct questions, they generally stand at the beginning of the Sentence.

[2] What case is vestrum, and why? Why not vestri? What case is nostri, and why? Why not nostrum? See Par. 93.

[3] MĬhĬ is Dat., *governed by* "cārus (est)" *understood.*

[4] Before doing this exercise, the pupil should read through all the sentences and ask which of the Pronominal Adjectives of the 3rd Pers., *his, her, their,* &c., can have *own* added to it. Wherever *own* can be added, sŭus is the word to be used. But of course this does not apply to Pronouns not of the 3rd Pers. (*my own, your own*), which are to be rendered mĕus, &c.

*exceedingly.* 4. Thy sister does not love her father. 5. His brothers do not love their father. 6. Ye praise the fields of others, ye do not take care of your (own) (fields). 7. Our sisters are dearer to us, O most cruel (men), than your brothers to you. 8. Do ye, (being) ignorant of the way, point-out the way to us, O most foolish (men)? 9. Why dost thou blame thy father, and dost not (18) praise his virtue? 10. The generals overcome the anger of the soldiers by their wisdom.

## 103  DEMONSTRATIVE AND EMPHATIC PRONOUNS.

1. **Illĕ**, *that (yonder);* pl. *those.*

*Singular.*

|      | Masc.  | Fem.   | Neut.  |
|------|--------|--------|--------|
| Nom. | Illĕ   | illă   | illŭd  |
| Acc. | Illum  | illam  | illŭd  |
| Gen. | Illīus | illīus | illīus |
| Dat. | Illi   | illi   | illi   |
| Abl. | Illo   | illā   | illo   |

*Plural.*

|      | Masc.   | Fem.    | Neut.   |
|------|---------|---------|---------|
| Nom. | Illi    | illae   | illă    |
| Acc. | Illos   | illas   | illă    |
| Gen. | Illōrum | illārum | illōrum |
| Dat. | Illīs   | illīs   | illīs   |
| Abl. | Illīs   | illīs   | illīs   |

2. **Istĕ**, *that (near you, or of yours),* often used contemptuously; declined like **illĕ**.

3. **Hic** (-ĭ or -ī), *this (near me);* pl. *these.*

*Singular.*

|      | Masc. | Fem.  | Neut. |
|------|-------|-------|-------|
| Nom. | Hic   | haec  | hōc   |
| Acc. | Hunc  | hanc  | hōc   |
| Gen. | Huius | huius | huius |
| Dat. | Huic  | huic  | huic  |
| Abl. | Hōc   | hāc   | hōc   |

*Plural.*

|      | Masc. | Fem.  | Neut. |
|------|-------|-------|-------|
| Nom. | Hi    | hae   | haec  |
| Acc. | Hos   | has   | haec  |
| Gen. | Hōrum | hārum | hōrum |
| Dat. | Hīs   | his   | his   |
| Abl. | Hīs   | his   | his   |

4. **Ipsĕ**, *-self, himself, herself, itself;* pl. *themselves.*

*Singular.*

|      | Masc.  | Fem.   | Neut.     |
|------|--------|--------|-----------|
| Nom. | Ipsĕ   | ipsă   | ipsum[1]  |
| Acc. | Ipsum  | ipsam  | ipsum     |
| Gen. | Ipsīus | ipsīus | ipsīus    |
| Dat. | Ipsi   | ipsi   | ipsi      |
| Abl. | Ipso   | ipsā   | ipso      |

*Plural.*

|      | Masc.   | Fem.    | Neut.   |
|------|---------|---------|---------|
| Nom. | Ipsi    | ipsae   | ipsă    |
| Acc. | Ipsos   | ipsas   | ipsă    |
| Gen. | Ipsōrum | ipsārum | ipsōrum |
| Dat. | Ipsīs   | ipsīs   | ipsīs   |
| Abl. | Ipsīs   | ipsīs   | ipsīs   |

Note that **ipsĕ** differs from **illĕ** only in the Neut. Nom. Singular.

5. **Īdem**, *the same* (declined like **Ĭs**; but **is-dem** is written **īdem**, **id-dem** is written **ĭdem**, and **m** before **-dem** is changed into **n**).

|  | *Singular.* | | | *Plural.* | | |
|---|---|---|---|---|---|---|
|  | Masc. | Fem. | Neut. | Masc. | Fem. | Neut. |
| *Nom.* | Īdem | ĕădem | ĭdem | Īidem | ĕaedem | ĕădem |
| *Acc.* | Eŭndem | ĕandem | dem | Ĕosdem | ĕasdem | ĕădem |
| *Gen.* | Eiusdem | eiusdem | eiusdem | Ĕorundem | ĕarundem | ĕorundem |
| *Dat.* | Eidem | eidem | eidem | Eisdem | eisdem | eisdem |
| *Abl.* | Ĕodem | ĕădem | ĕodem | Eisdem | eisdem | eisdem[1] |

EXERCISE XXXI.

**104** [Do not, for the future, use *thou* or *ye* in translating the Exercises, unless the language is poetical. *You* in English is commonly used of the Singular Number, and will be so used in future Exercises; it should therefore be rendered by **tu**, not by **vos**, *unless the context shows that it is Plural*].

**105** Ipsĕ is an Adj., agreeing in Gender, Number and Case with (1) a Noun or Pronoun understood; or (2) a Noun or Pronoun expressed.

(1) *(She) herself loves me.*   **Ipsa** mē ămat.
(2) *I give this to you yourself,*   Tĭbī **ipsi**, O fīlia, hōc do.
    *O daughter.*
(3) *The queen herself loves.*   Rēgīna **ipsa** ămat.

1. Non īdem labor eisdem semper jucundus est. 2. Amicus iste fratrem suum non amat. 3. Huic equum, illi canem, isti asinum pigrum agricola dat. 4. In te ipso fons est laetitiae. 5. Non īdem donum agricolis et nautis gratum est. 6. Vitiosi vitium ipsum amant. 7. Homeri et Vergilii opera vobis nota sunt; ille[2] Graecus erat, hic Romanus. 8. Eorundem agricolarum agri non semper pariter fertiles sunt. 9. Num amicorum ipsorum mores culpatis? 10. Cur huic mulieri dona meliora quam ipsi matri tuae das? 11. Vestis eadem eidem mulieri non semper grata est. 12. Alexandri et Darii nomina nota sunt omnibus: illi laudem, huic misericordiam dāmus.[2] 13. Quis centum (31) annos vivit?

1. *That gift of-yours is more pleasing to you yourself than to Balbus.* 2. *We all love the same native-land.* 3. *You, O friends, love the same (things), the same danger terrifies*

**106**   [1] For **eisdem** there is sometimes used **īsdem**.
[2] (1) **Ille**... (2) **hic**, when thus used together, mean (1) *that which is furthest, first-mentioned*...(2) *that which is nearest, last-mentioned*: hence (1) *the former*...(2) *the latter*.

*you.* 4. *This man we love, this man's conduct we praise.*
5. *The same-things are not always pleasing to the same-persons* (34). 6. *Why do you give larger gifts to this woman than to your own mother* (trans. *to your mother herself*)? 7. *The children of the same parents are not always equally beautiful.* 8. *The same vice is worse in a learned man than in an unlearned.* 9. *Do you blame us, O foolish* (man)? *In you yourself is the cause of these evils.* 10. *Do you give to yourself the best gifts?* 11. *Do you blame us the whole* (85) *day* (long) (31)?

### THE RELATIVE AND INTERROGATIVE PRONOUNS.

**107**    1. **Quī**, *which* (man, woman, thing); *who; that.*

| | Singular. | | | Plural. | | |
|---|---|---|---|---|---|---|
| | Masc. | Fem. | Neut. | Masc. | Fem | Neut. |
| *Nom.* | Quī | quae | quŏd | Quī | quae | quae |
| *Acc.* | Quem | quam | quŏd | Quōs | quās | quae |
| *Gen.* | Cuius | cuius | cuius | Quōrum | quārum | quōrum |
| *Dat.* | Cui | cui | cui | Quĭbus | quĭbus | quĭbus [1] |
| *Abl.* | Quō | quā | quō | Quĭbus | quĭbus | quĭbus [1] |

The Relative in Latin often (1) precedes its Antecedent, and sometimes (2) is placed with it like an Adjective.

(1) *He whom all love, is praised by all.*    **Quem** omnes ămant **ĭs** ab omnĭbus laudātur.
(1) *What, or that which, some praise, others blame.*    **Quŏd** ălii laudant **ĭd** ălii culpant.
(2) *The friends whom* (or *what friends*) *he has, he praises.*    **Quōs** ămīcos hăbet, laudat.[2]

**108**    RULE.—The Relative Pronoun agrees with its Antecedent in Gender, Number, and Person.[3]

*You yourself, sister, who love others, do not love me.*    Tū ipsa, sŏror, **quae** ălĭos **ămās**, mē nōn ămās.
*You, brothers, who blame me, praise Tullius, who himself praises me.*    Vōs, frātres, **qui** mē **culpātis**, Tullĭum laudātis, **qui** ipsĕ mē **laudat**.

---

**109**    [1] Quĭbus is sometimes contracted into quīs.
[2] Here the Antecedent is repeated, "quos amicos habet (eos amicos) laudat": and it may be said that **quos** agrees (like an Adj.) with the *repeated Antecedent*, but has for its Antecedent "eos amicos" *understood*.
**109a**    [3] N.B In Gender, Number, and Person—*but not necessarily in Case.*

## THE INTERROGATIVE PRONOUN. [Par. 110—113a]

**110**   2. The **Interrogative Pronoun quĭs** differs in form from the Relative Pronoun merely in the Nom. Sing. Masc. and Neuter: **quĭs?** *who?* **quĭd?** *what?* The rest of its cases are the same as those of the Relative Pronoun:

*Who gives you this?*   **Quĭs** tĭbĭ hŏc dat?
*What do you give me?*   **Quĭd** mĭhĭ dās?

**111**   The **Interrogative Adjective quī** is the same as the Relative in every case:[1]

*What has he done? What*   Quĭd fēcit?   **Quŏd** făcĭnus
*misdeed has he committed?*   commīsit?

### Exercise XXXII.

**112**   Rule.—Adjectives signifying *nearness*, e.g. **vīcīnus**, *near (to)*, **fīnĭtĭmus**, *bordering on*, **proxĭmus**, *nearest*, or *next (to)*, are followed by the Dative.

1. Qui aliis viam monstrat hunc alii jure (38) laudant. 2. Qui sibi benigniores (65) sunt, ei non semper ab amicis laudantur. 3. Te, O soror, quae haec dona mihi das, maxime laudo. 4. Quis hos milites ducit? Quod periculum eos terret? 5. Ego, O fratres, qui vobis dona optima do, nonne sum vobis carissimus? 6. Cuius verba me culpant eum non laudo. 7. Quibus rex dona dat, eos non semper amat. 8. Quae pericula patrem terrent, ea nonne filii timent? 9. Agricola arbores serit quarum fructum ipse non gustat.[2] 10. Cui patria cara est is bonus civis est. 11. Minae istae quibus agricolae timidi terrentur, militem non terrent. 12. In urbe, quae mari proxima erat, nautae plurimi erant: huc imperator suos (34) ducit. 13. Belgae, quorum agri Gallis finitimi sunt, a Caesare bello superantur.[2]

1. *You, O women, who* (108) *praise injustice (i.e. unjust things) are paying* (trans. *giving*) *the penalty of your folly.* 2. *To you, O sister, who blame your brother, (your) brother himself gives this gift.* 3. *Those whose* (113a) *conduct is depraved, you do right not to praise* (trans. *you rightly do not praise*). 4. *His mother, who loves you exceedingly, praises you too much.* 5. *Why do you err, (you) who point out the way to them?* 6. *What are you tasting, O boys? What fruit delights you?* 7. *We who overcome the nations bordering-on us, are overcome by the*

---

[1] Quĭs is sometimes an Adj., chiefly with persons: **quĭs** rex? *what king?*
[2] Note that the Relative in the Genit. precedes the Noun that governs it: "**quārum** fructum," *not* "fructum **quārum**."

nation next-to the Belgians. 8. The general leads his (men) into a plain which was nearer and larger. 9. You, O soldiers, are entering this city, which the enemy (pl.) at the same (SO) time enter. 10. Friends love those who love (their) friends. 11. Who is this (man) whose blame terrifies you?[1]

## THE VERB.

**114** Latin Verbs are divided into Four Classes called Conjugations. In the third Conjugation the Active Infinitive Present ends in -ĕre, in the rest in -re. That part of the word which comes before -re or -ĕre is called the Stem, and the last letter of the Stem distinguishes the Conjugation.

|   |   |   |   |   | Act., Inf., Pres. |
|---|---|---|---|---|---|
| 1. | First, | or | **A** | Conjugation | ămā-re, *to love* |
| 2. | Second, | „ | **E** | „ | mŏnē-re, *to advise* |
| 3. (a) | Third, | „ | Consonant | „ | rĕg-ĕre, *to rule* |
| (b) | „ | „ | **U** | „ | mĭnŭ-ĕre, *to diminish* |
| 4. | Fourth, | „ | **I** | „ | audī-re, *to hear* |

### FIRST OR A CONJUGATION.—ACTIVE VOICE.

**Ămo, ămāvī, ămātum, ămārĕ,**—*to love.* Stem : **ămā-**.

#### INDICATIVE MOOD.

##### 1. PRESENT TENSE.

Sing. 1. **Amo,** *I love, or am loving*  
2. **Am-ās,** *thou lovest, or art loving*  
3. **Am-ăt,** *he loves, or is loving.*

Plur. 1. **Am-āmŭs,** *We love, or are loving*  
2. **Am-ātĭs,** *ye love, or are loving*  
3. **Am-ant,** *they love, or are loving.*

##### 2. FUTURE-SIMPLE TENSE.

Sing. **Am-ābo,** *I shall love*  
**Am-ābĭs,** *thou wilt love*  
**Am-ābĭt,** *he will love.*

Pl. **Am-ābĭmŭs,** *We shall love*  
**Am-ābĭtĭs,** *ye will love*  
**Am-ābunt,** *they will love.*

##### 3. IMPERFECT TENSE.[2]

Sing. **Am-ābam,** *I was loving*  
**Am-ābās,** *thou wast loving*  
**Am-ābăt,** *he was loving.*

Pl. **Am-ābāmŭs,** *We were loving*  
**Am-ābātĭs,** *ye were loving*  
**Am-ābant,** *they were loving.*

---

[1] For additional elementary exercises on the Relative, see p. 186.

**115** [2] The Imperf. also means *I used-to-love, thou wast-wont-to-love, he used-to-love,* &c. It has other meanings, which must be learned by practice.

## FIRST CONJUGATION. [Par. 116—118a]

### 4. Perfect Tense.

*Sing.* **Am-āvī,** *I have loved, or I loved*
**Am-āvistī,** *thou hast loved, or thou lovedst*
**Am-āvĭt,** *he has loved, or he loved.*

*Pl.* **Am-āvĭmŭs,** *We have loved, or we loved*
**Am-āvistĭs,** *ye have loved, or ye loved*
**Am-āvērunt,** or **ăm-āvērĕ**[1] { *they have loved, or they loved.* }

### 5. Future-Perfect Tense.

*S.* **Am-āvĕro,** *I shall* }
**Am-āvĕrĭs,** *thou wilt* } *have loved.*
**Am-āvĕrĭt,** *he will* }

**Am-āvĕrĭmŭs,** *We shall* }
**Am-āvĕrĭtĭs,** *ye will* } *have loved*
**Am-āvĕrint,**[2] *they will* }

### 6. Pluperfect Tense.

*S.* **Am-āvĕram,** *I had loved*
**Am-āvĕrās,** *thou hadst loved*
**Am-āvĕrăt,** *he had loved.*

**Am-āvĕrāmŭs,** *We had loved.*
**Am-āvĕrātĭs,** *ye had loved*
**Am-āvĕrant,** *they had loved.*

## IMPERATIVE MOOD.

### Present Tense.

*S.* **Am-ā,** *Love thou.* | *P.* **Am-ātĕ,** *Love ye.*

### Future Tense.[3]

*S.* **Am-āto,** *Thou must love*
**Am-āto,** *he must love.*

*P.* **Am-ātōtĕ,** *Ye must love*
**Am-anto,** *they must love.*

## SUBJUNCTIVE MOOD.[4]

### 1. Present Tense.

**Am-em,** *I may love*
**Am-ēs,** *thou mayst love*
**Am-ĕt,** *he may love.*

**Am-ēmŭs,**[5] *We may love*
**Am-ētĭs,** *ye may love*
**Am-ent,** *they may love.*

---

[116] [1] As in English *v* is omitted in *o'er*, *ne'er*, so in Latin -vi- and -ve- are sometimes omitted *where no ambiguity would be caused*. Thus ămāvisti, ămāvĕrunt, &c. become ămasti, ămārunt, &c; but ămāvimus, ămāvēre, cannot be contracted into ămāmus, ămāre, because these contractions would be liable to be confused with the Pres. Indic. and Pres. Infin.

[2] The usual pronunciation is ămāvĕrĭs, ămāvĕrĭmus; but the i is sometimes long.

[117] [3] The Tense distinction between the Forms of the Imperative is very doubtful. The forms in -o are generally reserved for legal language: see Par. 129. *Must* is seldom expressed by the Imperative, see Par. 163, 168.

[118] [4] This Mood is sometimes called the Conjunctive. The meanings *I may love* and *I might love* are seldom attached to the Subjunctive without the accompanying conjunction ŭt (*that*).

[118a] [5] **Amēmŭs,** without a Conjunction, generally means *let us love*.

## FIRST CONJUGATION.

### 2. IMPERFECT TENSE.

| | | | |
|---|---|---|---|
| Am-ārem, | I might love | Am-ārēmŭs, | We might love |
| Am-ārēs, | thou mightst love | Am-ārētĭs, | ye might love |
| Am-ārĕt, | he might love. | Am-ārent, | they might love. |

### 3. PERFECT TENSE.

| | | | |
|---|---|---|---|
| Am-āvĕrim, | I may ⎫ have | Am-āvĕrimŭs, | We may ⎫ have |
| Am-āvĕrĭs, | thou mayst ⎬ loved. | Am-āvĕritĭs, | ye may ⎬ loved. |
| Am-āvĕrĭt, | he may ⎭ | Am-āvĕrint, | they may ⎭ |

### 4. PLUPERFECT TENSE.

| | | | |
|---|---|---|---|
| Am-āvissem, | I should ⎫ have | Am-āvissēmŭs | We should ⎫ have |
| Am-āvissēs, | thou wouldst ⎬ loved. | Am-āvissētĭs, | ye would ⎬ loved |
| Am-āvissĕt, | he would ⎭ | Am-āvissent, | they would ⎭ |

### INFINITIVE MOOD.[1]

**INFINITIVES.**

PRES. and IMPERF. } **Am-ārĕ,** to love.
PERF. and PLUPERF. } **Am-āvissĕ,** { to have loved.
FUTURE. { **Am-ātūrŭs essĕ,** { to be about to love.

**GERUND.**

Gen. **Am-andī,** of loving
Dat. **Am-andō,** for loving
Acc. **Am-andum,** the loving
Abl. **Am-andō,** by loving.

---

**SUPINES.**

**Am-ātum,**[2] to love.

**Am-ātū,**[2] in loving.

**PARTICIPLES.**

PRESENT. **Am-ans, -antis,** &c., [loving.
FUTURE. **Am-ātūrŭs (ă, um),** [about to love.

---

[1] This part of the Verb is sometimes spoken of as the *Verb Infinite*, and not as the *Infinitive Mood*.

[2] The Supines are really Nouns used *only in the Acc. and Abl.*; (1) the Supine in -um after Verbs of Motion, (2) the Supine in -u with a few Adjectives, Exercise LXXIV.

Hence **āmātum** can never be used (as **amāre** is, Par. 34) for the Subject of a Verb.

## SECOND OR E CONJUGATION.—ACTIVE VOICE.

**Mŏneo, mŏnuī, mŏnĭtum, mŏnērĕ,**—*to advise.* Stem: **mŏnē-.**

### INDICATIVE MOOD.

#### 1. Present Tense.

| | | | |
|---|---|---|---|
| **Mŏn-eo,**[1] | *I advise, or am advising* | **Mŏn-ēmŭs,** | *We advise, or are advising* |
| **Mŏn-ēs,** | *thou advisest, or art advising* | **Mŏn-ētĭs,** | *ye advise, or are advising* |
| **Mŏn-ĕt,** | *he advises, or is advising.* | **Mŏn-ent,** | *they advise, or are advising.* |

#### 2. Future-Simple Tense.

| | | | |
|---|---|---|---|
| **Mŏn-ēbo,** | *I shall advise* | **Mŏn-ēbĭmŭs,** | *We shall advise* |
| **Mŏn-ēbĭs,** | *thou wilt advise* | **Mŏn-ēbĭtĭs,** | *ye will advise* |
| **Mŏn-ēbĭt,** | *he will advise.* | **Mŏn-ēbunt,** | *they will advise.* |

#### 3. Imperfect Tense.

| | | | |
|---|---|---|---|
| **Mŏn-ēbam,** | *I was advising* | **Mŏn-ēbāmŭs,** | *We were advising* |
| **Mŏn-ēbās,** | *thou wast advising* | **Mŏn-ēbātĭs,** | *ye were advising* |
| **Mŏn-ēbăt,** | *he was advising.* | **Mŏn-ēbant,** | *they were advising.*[2] |

#### 4. Perfect Tense.

| | | | |
|---|---|---|---|
| **Mŏn-uī,** | *I have advised, or I advised* | **Mŏn-uĭmŭs,** | *We have advised, or we advised* |
| **Mŏn-uistī,** | *thou hast advised, or advisedst* | **Mŏn-uistĭs,** | *ye have advised, or ye advised* |
| **Mŏn-uĭt,** | *he has advised, or he advised.* | **Mŏn-uērunt,** *or* **-uērĕ,** | *they have advised, or they advised.* |

#### 5. Future-Perfect Tense.

| | | | |
|---|---|---|---|
| **Mŏn-uĕro,** | *I shall* } *have advised.* | **Mŏn-uĕrĭmŭs,** | *We shall* } *have advised.* |
| **Mŏn-uĕrĭs,** | *thou wilt* | **Mŏn-uĕrĭtĭs,** | *ye will* |
| **Mŏn-uĕrĭt,** | *he will* | **Mŏn-uĕrint,** | *they will* |

---

[1] The quantity of the e before o, and of u before i is not marked, because it is an invariable rule in Latin that *a vowel before another vowel is short:* see Appendix VII., p. 230.

[2] The Imperf. also means *I used-to-advise, thou wast-wont-to-advise, he used-to-advise,* &c.

## SECOND CONJUGATION.

### 6. PLUPERFECT TENSE.

Mŏn-uĕram, *I had advised*
Mŏn-uĕrās, *thou hadst advised*
Mŏn-uĕrăt, *he had advised.*

Mŏn-uĕrāmŭs, *We had advised*
Mŏn-uĕrātĭs, *ye had advised*
Mŏn-uĕrant, *they had advised.*

### IMPERATIVE MOOD.

#### PRESENT TENSE.

Mŏn-ē, *Advise thou.*  |  Mŏn-ētĕ, *Advise ye.*

#### FUTURE (see Par. 117) TENSE.

Mŏn-ēto, *Thou must advise*
Mŏn-ēto, *he must advise.*

Mŏn-ētōtĕ, *Ye must advise*
Mŏn-ento, *they must advise.*

### SUBJUNCTIVE MOOD.

#### 1. PRESENT TENSE.

Mŏn-eam, *I may advise*
Mŏn-eās, *thou mayst advise*
Mŏn-eăt, *he may advise.*

Mŏn-eāmŭs, *We may advise*[1]
Mŏn-eātĭs, *ye may advise*
Mŏn-eant, *they may advise.*

#### 2. IMPERFECT TENSE.

Mŏn-ērem, *I might advise*
Mŏn-ērēs, *thou mightst advise*
Mŏn-ērĕt, *he might advise.*

Mŏn-ērēmŭs, *We might advise*
Mŏn-ērētĭs, *ye might advise*
Mŏn-ērent, *they might advise.*

#### 3. PERFECT TENSE.

Mŏn-uĕrim, *I may* }
Mŏn-uĕrĭs, *thou mayst* } *have advised.*
Mŏn-uĕrĭt, *he may* }

Mŏn-uĕrĭmŭs, *We may* }
Mŏn-uĕrĭtĭs, *ye may* } *have advised.*
Mŏn-uĕrint, *they may* }

#### 4. PLUPERFECT TENSE.

Mŏn-uissem, *I should* }
Mŏn-uissēs, *thou wouldst* } *have advised.*
Mŏn-uissĕt, *he would* }

Mŏn-uissēmŭs, *We should* }
Mŏn-uissētĭs, *ye would* } *have advised.*
Mŏn-uissent, *they would* }

---

[1] Mŏneāmus, without a Conjunction, generally means *let us advise.*

## THIRD CONJUGATION. [Par. 120]

### INFINITIVE MOOD.

INFINITIVES.

Pres. and Imperf. } **Mŏn-ērĕ,** *to advise.*
Perf. and Pluperf. } **Mŏn-uissĕ,** {*to have advised.*
Future. { **Mŏn-ĭtūrŭs essĕ,** { *to be about to advise.*

GERUND.

*Gen.* **Mŏn-endī,** *of advising*
*Dat.* **Mŏn-endō,** *for advising*
*Acc.* **Mŏn-endum,** *the advising*
*Abl.* **Mŏn-endō,** *by advising.*

SUPINES.

**Mŏn-ĭtum,** *to advise.*
**Mŏn-ĭtū,** *in advising.*

PARTICIPLES.

Present. **Mŏn-ens, -entis,** &c., *advising.*
Future. **Mŏn-ĭtūrŭs (ă, um),** *about to advise.*

---

THIRD OR **Consonant** AND **U** CONJUGATION.—ACTIVE VOICE.

**Rĕgo, rexī, rectum, rĕgĕrĕ,**—*to rule.* Stem: **rĕg-**.

### INDICATIVE MOOD.

1. Present Tense.

**Rĕg-o,** *I rule, or am*
**Rĕg-ĭs,** *thou rulest, or art* } *ruling.*
**Rĕg-ĭt,** *he rules, or is*

**Rĕg-ĭmŭs,** *We rule, or are*
**Rĕg-ĭtĭs,** *ye rule, or are* } *ruling.*
**Rĕg-unt,** *they rule, or are*

2. Future-Simple Tense.

**Rĕg-am,** *I shall rule*
**Rĕg-ēs,** *thou wilt rule*
**Rĕg-ĕt,** *he will rule.*

**Rĕg-ēmŭs,** *We shall rule*
**Rĕg-ētĭs,** *ye will rule*
**Rĕg-ent,** *they will rule.*

3. Imperfect Tense.

**Rĕg-ēbam,** *I was ruling*
**Rĕg-ēbās,** *thou wast ruling*
**Rĕg-ēbăt,** *he was ruling.*

**Rĕg-ēbāmŭs,** *We were ruling*
**Rĕg-ēbātĭs,** *ye were ruling*
**Rĕg-ēbant,** *they were ruling.*[1]

---

[1] The Imperf. also means *I used-to-rule, thou wast-wont-to-rule, he used-to-rule,* &c.

## THIRD CONJUGATION.

### 4 PERFECT TENSE.

| | | | |
|---|---|---|---|
| Rex-ī, | I have ruled, or I ruled | Rex-ĭmŭs, | We have ruled, or we ruled |
| Rex-istī, | thou hast ruled, or thou ruledst | Rex-istĭs, | ye have ruled, or ye ruled |
| Rex-ĭt, | he has ruled, or he ruled. | Rex-ērunt, or rex-ērĕ, | they have ruled, or they ruled. |

### 5 FUTURE-PERFECT TENSE.

| | | | |
|---|---|---|---|
| Rex-ĕro, | I shall have ruled | Rex-ĕrĭmŭs, | We shall have ruled |
| Rex-ĕrĭs, | thou wilt have ruled | Rex-ĕrĭtĭs, | ye will have ruled |
| Rex-ĕrĭt, | he will have ruled. | Rex-ĕrint, | they will have ruled. |

### 6. PLUPERFECT TENSE.

| | | | |
|---|---|---|---|
| Rex-ĕram, | I had ruled | Rex-ĕrāmŭs, | We had ruled |
| Rex-ĕrās, | thou hadst ruled | Rex-ĕrātĭs, | ye had ruled |
| Rex-ĕrăt, | he had ruled. | Rex-ĕrant, | they had ruled. |

### IMPERATIVE MOOD.

#### PRESENT TENSE.

| | | | |
|---|---|---|---|
| Rĕg-ĕ, | Rule thou. | Rĕg-ĭtĕ, | Rule ye. |

#### FUTURE (see Par. 117) TENSE.

| | | | |
|---|---|---|---|
| Rĕg-ĭto, | Thou shalt or must rule | Rĕg-ĭtōtĕ, | Ye shall or must rule |
| Rĕg-ĭto, | he shall or must rule. | Rĕg-unto, | they shall or must [rule. |

### SUBJUNCTIVE MOOD.

#### 1. PRESENT TENSE.

| | | | |
|---|---|---|---|
| Rĕg-am, | I may rule | Rĕg-āmŭs, | We may rule[1] |
| Rĕg-ās, | thou mayst rule | Rĕg-ātĭs, | ye may rule |
| Rĕg-ăt, | he may rule. | Rĕg-ant, | they may rule. |

#### 2. IMPERFECT TENSE.

| | | | |
|---|---|---|---|
| Rĕg-ĕrem, | I might rule | Rĕg-ĕrēmŭs, | We might rule |
| Rĕg-ĕrēs, | thou mightst rule | Rĕg-ĕrētĭs, | ye might rule |
| Rĕg-ĕrĕt, | he might rule. | Rĕg-ĕrent, | they might rule. |

#### 3. PERFECT TENSE.

| | | | |
|---|---|---|---|
| Rex-ĕrim, | I may | Rex-ĕrĭmŭs, | We may |
| Rex-ĕrĭs, | thou mayst } have ruled | Rex-ĕrĭtĭs, | ye may } have ruled |
| Rex-ĕrĭt, | he may | Rex-ĕrint, | they may |

---

[1] Rĕgāmus, without a Conjunction, generally means let us rule.

## FOURTH CONJUGATION. [Par. 120

### 4. Pluperfect Tense.

Rex-issem, *I should* ⎫ *have*    Rex-issēmŭs, *We should* ⎫ *have*
Rex-issēs, *thou wouldst* ⎬ *ruled.*    Rex-issētĭs, *ye would* ⎬ *ruled.*
Rex-issĕt, *he would* ⎭    Rex-issent, *they would* ⎭

### INFINITIVE MOOD.

| INFINITIVES. | | | GERUND. | |
|---|---|---|---|---|
| Pres. and Imperf. | Rĕg-ĕrĕ, | *to rule.* | Gen. Rĕg-endī, | *of ruling* |
| Perf. and Pluperf. | Rex-issĕ, | { *to have ruled.* | Dat. Rĕg-endō, | *for ruling* |
| | | | Acc. Rĕg-endum, | *the ruling* |
| Future. | { Rec-tūrŭs essĕ, | { *to be about to rule.* | Abl. Rĕg-endō, | *by ruling.* |

| SUPINES. | | PARTICIPLES. | |
|---|---|---|---|
| Rec-tum, | *to rule.* | Present. Rĕg-ens, -entis, &c., [*ruling.*] | |
| Rec-tū, | *in ruling.* | Future. Rec-tūrŭs (ă, um), [*about to rule.*] | |

---

## FOURTH OR I CONJUGATION.—ACTIVE VOICE.

**Audio, audīvī, audītum, audīrĕ,**—*to hear.* Stem: **audī-**.

### INDICATIVE MOOD.

#### 1. Present Tense.

Aud-io, *I hear, or am* ⎫    Aud-īmŭs, *We hear, or are* ⎫
Aud-īs, *thou hearest, or art* ⎬ *hearing.*    Aud-ītĭs, *ye hear, or are* ⎬ *hearing*
Aud-ĭt, *he hears, or is* ⎭    Aud-iunt, *they hear, or are* ⎭

#### 2. Future-Simple Tense.

| Aud-iam, | *I shall hear* | Aud-iēmŭs, | *We shall hear* |
| Aud-iēs, | *thou wilt hear* | Aud-iētĭs, | *ye will hear* |
| Aud-iĕt, | *he will hear.* | Aud-ient, | *they will hear* |

#### 3. Imperfect Tense.

| Aud-iēbam, | *I was hearing* | Aud-iēbāmŭs, | *We were hearing* |
| Aud-iēbās, | *thou wast hearing* | Aud-iēbātĭs, | *ye were hearing* |
| Aud-iēbăt, | *he was hearing.* | Aud-iēbant, | *they were hearing.*[1] |

---

[1] The Imperf. also means, *I used-to-hear, thou wast-wont-to-hear, he used-to-hear,* &c.

## FOURTH CONJUGATION.

### 4. PERFECT TENSE.

| | | | |
|---|---|---|---|
| Aud-īvī, | I have heard, or I heard | Aud-īvĭmŭs, | We have heard, or we heard |
| Aud-īvistī, | thou hast heard, or thou heardst | Aud-ivistĭs, | ye have heard, or ye heard |
| Aud-īvīt, | he has heard, or he heard. | Aud-īvērunt, or -īvērĕ, | they have heard, or they heard. |

### 5. FUTURE-PERFECT TENSE.

Aud-īvĕro, I shall ⎫
Aud-īvĕrĭs, thou wilt ⎬ have heard.
Aud-īvĕrĭt, he will ⎭

Aud-īvĕrĭmŭs, We shall ⎫
Aud-īvĕrĭtĭs, ye will ⎬ have heard.
Aud-īvĕrint, they will ⎭

### 6. PLUPERFECT TENSE.

| | | | |
|---|---|---|---|
| Aud-īvĕram, | I had heard | Aud-īvĕrāmŭs, | We had heard |
| Aud-īvĕrās, | thou hadst heard | Aud-īvĕrātĭs, | ye had heard |
| Aud-īvĕrăt, | he had heard. | Aud-īvĕrant, | they had heard. |

### IMPERATIVE MOOD.

#### PRESENT TENSE.

| | | | |
|---|---|---|---|
| Aud-ī, | Hear thou. | Aud-ītĕ, | Hear ye. |

#### FUTURE (see Par. 117) TENSE.

| | | | |
|---|---|---|---|
| Aud-īto, | Thou must hear | Aud-ītōtĕ, | Ye must hear |
| Aud-īto, | he must hear. | Aud-iunto, | they must hear. |

### SUBJUNCTIVE MOOD.

#### 1. PRESENT TENSE.

| | | | |
|---|---|---|---|
| Aud-iam, | I may hear | Aud-iāmŭs, | We may hear [1] |
| Aud-iās, | thou mayst hear | Aud-iātĭs, | ye may hear |
| Aud-iăt, | he may hear. | Aud-iant, | they may hear. |

#### 2. IMPERFECT TENSE.

| | | | |
|---|---|---|---|
| Aud-īrem, | I might hear | Aud-īrēmŭs, | We might hear |
| Aud-īrēs, | thou mightst hear | Aud-īrētĭs, | ye might hear |
| Aud-īrĕt, | he might hear | Aud-īrent, | they might hear. |

#### 3. PERFECT TENSE.

Aud-īvĕrim, I may ⎫
Aud-īvĕrĭs, thou mayst ⎬ have heard.
Aud-īvĕrĭt, he may ⎭

Aud-īvĕrimus, We may ⎫
Aud-īvĕrĭtĭs, ye may ⎬ have heard.
Aud-īvĕrint, they may ⎭

---

[1] Audiāmus, without a Conjunction, generally means *let us hear*.

### 4. PLUPERFECT TENSE.

Audīvissem, *I should* ⎫ *have*
Aud-īvissēs, *thou wouldst* ⎬ *heard.*
Aud-īvissĕt, *he would* ⎭

Aud-īvissēmŭs, *We should* ⎫ *have*
Aud-īvissētĭs, *ye would* ⎬ *heard.*
Aud-īvissent, *they would* ⎭

### INFINITIVE MOOD

#### INFINITIVES.

Pres. and Imperf. **Aud-īrĕ,** *to hear.*
Perf. and Pluperf. **Aud-īvissĕ,** *to have heard.*
Future. **Aud-ītūrŭs essĕ,** *to be about to hear.*

#### GERUND.

*Gen.* **Aud-iendī,** *of hearing*
*Dat.* **Aud-iendō,** *for hearing*
*Acc.* **Aud-iendum,** *the hearing*
*Abl.* **Aud-iendō,** *by hearing.*

#### SUPINES.

**Aud-ītum,** *to hear.*
**Aud-ītū,** *in hearing.*

#### PARTICIPLES.

Present. **Aud-iens,** -entis, [&c., *hearing.*
Future. **Aud-ītūrŭs (ă, um),** [*about to hear.*

---

**121**  In the Fourth, (as in the First) Conjugation, the omission of **v** causes the following

#### CONTRACTED FORMS.

##### INDICATIVE.

| PERFECT. | | FUTURE PERFECT. | PLUPERFECT. |
|---|---|---|---|
| Audii | Audiimus | Audiero | Audieram |
| Audiisti (audisti) | Audiistis (audistis) | Audieris, &c. | Audieras |
| Audiit | Audiērunt | Audierit, &c. | Audierat, &c. |

##### SUBJUNCTIVE.

| PLUPERFECT. | | PERFECT. |
|---|---|---|
| Audiissem (audissem) | Audiissemus (audissemus) | Audierim |
| Audiisses (audisses) | Audiissetis (audissetis) | Audieris |
| Audiisset (audisset) | Audiissent (audissent) | Audierit, &c. |

INFINITIVE-PERFECT.

Audiisse (audisse).

## THE LATIN PERFECT.

The Latin Tenses are inferior to the English in fulness as will be seen from the following Table:

Capto, *I catch.*

|  | Simple or Indefinite. | Incomplete. | Complete. |
|---|---|---|---|
| Present. | *I catch*<br>capto | *I am catching*<br>capto | *I have caught*<br>**CAPTĀVI**[1] |
| Future. | *I shall catch*<br>captābo | *I shall be catching*<br>captābo | *I shall have caught*<br>captāvero |
| Past. | *I caught*<br>**CAPTĀVI** | *I was catching*<br>captābam | *I had caught*<br>captāveram[2] |

**122**    The Latin Perfect, captāvi, has to express two English Tenses, and though it is always called "Perfect," *i.e. complete*, it is really not always Perfect or Complete, but:

1. Sometimes *Complete Present*, captāvi, *I have caught.*
2. Sometimes *Simple Past*, captāvi, *I caught.*

[1] That this Present Complete Tense, *I have caught*, is really a Present (though the result of a past action) may be seen from such a sentence as " *I have caught* this fish," which means " *I have* (present) this fish—in my pocket, basket," &c. Until the pupil clearly understands that the English Complete Present is *a Present* and *not a Past* Tense, he will never intelligently master the rule for the Latin Sequence of Tenses.

[2] Besides these, other columns might have been added by substituting " been catching " for " caught " in the third column: *I have been catching, I shall have been catching, I had been catching*, and by substituting " about to catch " for " catching " in the second column.

These two meanings of the Latin Perf. are called (1) "the Perfect with *have*," (2) "the Perfect without *have*."

### Exercise XXXIII.

**123** Apposition.—When two Nouns (or a Noun and Pronoun) are *placed together* without a Conjunction, so that one describes the other, they are said to be *in Apposition*, and both are in the same case.

**124** When a *Noun* is in Apposition to a *Name*, the Name stands *second in English*, but *first in Latin*.

| | |
|---|---|
| *The renowned general Balbus overcomes the enemy.* | **Balbus, impĕrātor clārissĭmus** (70), hostem sŭpĕrat. |
| *I will give a book to the industrious boy Tullius.* | **Tullĭo, pŭĕro dīlĭgentissĭmo,** librum dōnābo. |

**125** "If" with English Present often refers to *Future time*, and must then be translated by Latin Fut. Simple or Fut. Perfect:

*I will give it if he asks.*     Dăbo sī **rŏgābit** (*or* -āvĕrit).

1. Sidera iter nautis monstrabant. 2. Hieme nautae aestatem laudabunt. 3. Dăbo librum ei, si rogabit.[1] 4. Nonne puellam diligentem laudabitis? 5. Qui nos culpatis, nonne vos ipsos emendatis? 6. Cur me vituperabatis (32), vos ipsos laudabatis? 7. Agricolae agrum, equum militi donabimus. 8. Judici, viro justissimo,[2] rex injustus inimicus erat. 9. Tulliae, puellae optimae, cur non praemium donas? 10. Nemo Germanorum, gentis fortissimae, tam pravos mores laudat.[3]

1. *You, O women, who praised* (108) *injustice* (34), *will rightly pay the penalty*. 2. *To you, O sister, who blamed your brother,* (*your*) *brother himself gives this gift.* 3. *Those whose morals are depraved, you were right in not praising* (trans. *you rightly did not praise*). 4. *His excellent mother* (trans. *his mother, a most excellent woman*), *who loved you exceedingly, praised you too-much.* 5. *Will you point out the way to us,* (*you*) *who your-*

---

[1] The Latin Future, after **sī**, must be translated by English Present.

[2] Lit. *the judge, a very just man*, but in English we say *the very just judge*, or, more commonly (70), *the just judge*. Why is **vīro** Dat.? Ans. *Dat. in Apposition with* **jūdĭci**. Why is **gentis** (Sent. 10) Genitive?

[3] In Apposition, write the literal English first and the idiomatic English afterwards: *e.g.* "Germanis, genti fortissimae" lit., *to the Germans, a very brave race*, i.e., *to the brave race of the Germans*. N.B.—Two Nouns in Apposition need not be of the same Number.

*selves often err?* 6. *We used to praise the conduct of the* (126) *brave centurion Tullius.* 7. *I shall not punish the boy if he improves* (125) *his conduct.* 8. *They will not err if the leader points out the way to them.*

EXERCISE XXXIV.[1]

**127** If the Subject consists of two Nouns or Pronouns, the Verb is in the Plural; but the Verb agrees with the First Person rather than the Second, and with the Second rather than the Third.

1. Si tu et frater tuus peccaveritis (125a), leges vos castigabunt. 2. Judicem, quia male judicaverat, ego et frater meus graviter culpavimus. 3. Piscator et nauta, qui iter militibus antea monstraverant, jam ipsi erraverunt. 4. Milites ferro ignique agros regis sui vastaverunt. 5. Hieme, si venti flaverint, nautae mare formidabunt. 6. Cur Tullium, hominem innocentissimum, castigavistis? 7. Agricolae stultissimi aestate calorem, hieme frigus culpaverunt. 8. Rex militibus, indignis dono (28), equos pulcherrimos donaverat. 9. Nonne vobis haec dona ego et Tullius donavimus? 10. Graeci Trojanos equo ligneo, dono pernicioso (126a) superaverunt. 11. Qui virtutem maxime simulavere, ei jam maxime erravere. 12. Quos quondam castigastis, ei iterum peccarunt.

[1] 1. *You and I have presented excellent gifts to his mother.*[2] 2. *Why did the unjust judge Tullius* (126) *chastise the innocent Balbus* (trans. *Balbus, a most innocent man*)?[3] 3. *In winter, O husbandmen, you had blamed the cold, in summer the heat.* 4. *The king had given a horse to the same soldier whom he had before blamed.* 5. *If you overcome* (trans. *shall have overcome*) *the enemy, O soldiers, all will praise you.* 6. *Did* (127b) *not you and Tullius blame the kind Balbus?* 7. *The women dreaded the sea because the winds had blown violently.* 8. *Did not you, O Greeks, present to the Trojans the destructive gift of a wooden horse* (trans. *a wooden horse, a most destructive gift*)? 9. *Why did you, who pointed out the road to others, yourselves err?* 10. *You and Balbus blamed Alexander, the most illustrious of generals.*

---

[1] For this and future Exercises the pupil must look out the words in the Latin-English and English-Latin Vocabularies at the end of the book.

127a [2] In English we say "you and I," in Latin the order is reversed, "Ego et tu."

127b [3] The English Simple Past inserts *did*, when used negatively or interrogatively: "you blamed"; but "*did* you blame?" "you *did* not blame." But all three are expressed by the Latin Perfect.

## THE INFINITIVE.

**128** The Infinitive (though not declinable like a Noun) is nevertheless used as the Subject or Direct Object of a Verb:

*To err is human.*     **Errāre** (nom.) humānum est.
*Boys like to jump.*     Pŭĕri **saltāre** (acc.) ămant.

The Infinitive, although used as Subject or Object, may itself have an Object, and may be modified by an Adverb.

*The woman desires to get wealth.*     Mŭlĭer dīvĭtĭas **părāre** optat.
*To have gained fame honourably is sweet.*     Fāmam hŏnestē **părăvisse** dulcĕ (34) est.

### Exercise XXXV.

1. Peccare facile est, mores emendare difficillimum (est). 2. Quis non divitias comparare optat? 3. Saltare dulce est puellis, senibus autem molestissimum. 4. Aestate omnes nare amamus.[1] 5. Melius est virtutem quam aurum parare. 6. Amicum amare praesentem dulce est; desiderare absentem est tristissimum.[1] 7. Peccare leve est plerisque pueris; senibus peccavisse est acerbissimum. 8. Pericula superare saepe durum est; superasse semper dulcissimum est.

1. *It is easier to blame than to praise.* 2. *To whom is it not pleasant to swim in summer?* 3. *It is sad for an old man to have sinned.* 4. *To all it is most pleasant to have overcome dangers by wise counsels.* 5. *Most men desire to get gold and silver.* 6. *You and I love to walk by night; Tullius and his* (98, 2) *brother love to walk by day.* 7. *It is very easy to swim; it is very difficult to swim well.* 8. *To have erred is sad; to err is sadder.*

## THE IMPERATIVE MOOD, PROHIBITIONS.

**129** The word for *not* in commands is **nē**. But this is seldom used with the Present Imperative except in Poetry, and seldom with (what is sometimes called) the Future Imperative, *except in legal forms.* Consequently, for the negative Imperative—

---

[1] **Omnes** agrees with "**nos**" *understood.*
[2] **Absentem** agrees with "**ămīcum**" *understood.*

RULE.—Use **nē** with the Perfect Subjunctive of the Second Person, and with the Present Subjunctive of other Persons.[1]

*Singular.*

| | |
|---|---|
| *Do not love.* | Nē ămāvĕris. |
| *Let him not love.* | Nē ămet. |

*Plural.*

| | |
|---|---|
| *Do not love.* | Nē ămāvĕrĭtis. |
| *Let them not love.* | Nē ăment. |

The First and Third Persons Plural of the Subjunctive can be used, with or without **nē**, in an Imperative sense:

| | |
|---|---|
| *Let us (not) love.* | (Nĕ) ămēmus. |
| *Let him amend his conduct.* | Ēmendet mōres. |

### EXERCISE XXXVI.

1. Emendate mores vestros. 2. Obtempera, O puer, patri. 3. Ne sontes poenam vitent. 4. Ne castigaveritis insontem; ne mortuum culpaveritis. 5. Huic magistratui omnes cives obtemperanto. 6. Amemus amicos, inimicos ne vituperemus. 7. Praeceptor discipulos verberibus paucis castigato. 8. Regem, si injustus est, ne tu laudaveris. 9. Virgines Vestales ignem curanto. 10. Judicem justum laudā; injustum culpā, sed ne vituperaveris.

1. *Let us love absent friends.* 2. *Let us prepare arms; let not the enemy overcome us.* 3. *Take-care-of his children, O friends; do not blame the dead.* 4. *Do not appease the gods, O foolish (men), with victims; appease them with pious deeds.* 5. *Let (legal) ten maidens carry the image of Diana.* 6. *Let us praise virtue, let us not punish the good.* 7. *Tullius is guilty; let him not avoid punishment.* 8. *Let us not blame those-who-are-worthy* (i.e. *the worthy*) *of* (28) *praise* (5a).

### THE SUBJUNCTIVE MOOD.—I.

*(Expressing purpose.)*

130   The Subjunctive Mood (besides other uses which will be hereafter mentioned) is used when a Verb is *subjoined* to another Verb, in order to express purpose.

---

[1] The Subjunctive, when not subjoined to some principal Verb, is sometimes called the Conjunctive: and some use the term Conjunctive in all instances instead of Subjunctive. For the method of expressing a prohibition by nōli with the Infinitive, see Par. 169.

**131** In such cases, *that* or *in order that* is expressed by **ŭt**; *that . . . not*, by **nē**.

**132** The Tenses of the Subjunctive are:

(1) *Present, after* (a) *Pres.* (*whether Simple or Complete*); *after* (b) *Future Indic.*; *and after* (c) *Imperative*.

(2) *Past, after Past Tenses*:

| | | | | |
|---|---|---|---|---|
| 1. (a) *I punish, or have punished*[1] <br> (b) *I shall punish* <br> (c) *Punish* | *the boy that he may amend his conduct.* | (a) **Castīgo**, or **Castīgāvi** <br> (b) **Castīgābo** <br> (c) **Castīgā** | puĕrum ut mōres **ēmendet**. |
| 2. (a) *I punished* <br> (b) *I was punishing* <br> (c) *I had punished* | *the boy that he might amend his conduct.* | (a) **Castīgāvi** <br> (b) **Castīgābam** <br> (c) **Castīgāvĕram** | puĕrum ut mōres **ēmendāret**. |

**133** CAUTION.—The precise meaning of the ambiguous word **castīgāvi** cannot be ascertained until we see whether it is followed by the Present or Imperf. Subj. If it is followed by the Present, it must be rendered *I have punished*; if by the Imperf., *I punished*.

EXERCISE XXXVII.

1. Nauta sidera servabit ne ex itinere erret. 2. Urbem rex aedificabat ut in eā quattuor millia civium habitarent. 3. Nostri terram vastaverunt ut hostes ad pugnam provocent. 3a. Nostri terram vastaverunt ut hostes ad pugnam provocarent. 4. Agricola agros araverat ut segetem sibi pararet. 5. Parate arma, cives, ut hostem propulsetis. 6. Cives arma celeriter paraverant ne milites urbem expugnarent. 7. Castigavi te ut mores emendes. 8. Senex in horto ambulavit ut floribus so (35) pulcherrimis delectaret. 9. Rex judicem injustum capite multavit ut ceteri judices rectō judicent.[2] 10. Balbum praemio decoravi ut litteras amet; Tullium heri (*adv.*) casti-

---

[1] *I have punished* is really a (complete) Present Tense : Par. 122, note.
[2] See **căput** in Vocab.: **căpĭte** may be parsed as *Abl. of Instr.*, as it is here used to denote *the punishment of death*.

gavi ne iterum peccaret. 11. Germanos, gentem ferocissimam (126a), armis propulsate, ne fines vestros vastent. 12. Aliis equos aliis arma donemus (118), ne viam hostibus monstrent.

1. *Let us lay-waste the lands of the enemy that they may not fight a second time.* 2. *The citizens will point out the way for us that we may not err.* 3. *We pointed out the way for the beautiful maiden* (124) *Tullia that she might not err.* 4. *Our (men) will build for you, O Tullius* (13), *a great house, that your friends may dwell in it.* 5. *Let us build a temple and prepare victims that we appease Jupiter.* 6. *We have prepared arms that we may repulse the enemy.* 7. *We chastised the boy that he might improve his* (98) *conduct.* 8. *He had preserved the letter of (his) sister that you might not blame her.* 9. *Why do you not walk in the garden that you may delight yourselves with the scent of the beautiful flowers* (5a)? 10. *He was hastening into the garden that he might show the flowers to his friends.*

### THE SUBJUNCTIVE MOOD.—II.

(*Expressing a Dependent Question.*)

Hitherto the Subjunctive in Latin has been expressed by the English *may* or *might;* we now come to idioms where the ordinary English *Indicative* has to be expressed by the Latin Subjunctive.

**134** 1. A DIRECT OR INDEPENDENT QUESTION is a question in the words of the speaker:

*Does he love me?* Num mē āmat?
*Does he not love me?* Nōnne mē āmat?

**135** 2. AN INDIRECT OR DEPENDENT QUESTION is one that is the Subject or Object of a Verb (called the Principal Verb):

*I will ask* { *whether he loves me.* *whether he does not love me.* } Interrŏgābo { num mē **āmet**. nōnnĕ mē **āmet**.

**136** RULE.—An Indirect or Dependent Question is expressed in Latin by the Subjunctive.

The Tense, in an Indirect Question, depends on the Tense of the Principal Verb; and the rule is, as above

(132), that *Present Tenses of the Subjunctive follow Present Tenses of the Indicative, and Past Tenses of the Subjunctive follow Past Tenses of the Indicative.*

1. *Ask* ⎫ (a) *whether they love,* **Interrŏgā** ⎫(a) num mē
   *I ask* ⎬     *or are loving me.* **Interrŏgo**  ⎬    ăment.
   *I will ask* ⎪ (b) *whether they loved* **Interrŏgābo** ⎬(b) num mē
   *I have asked*⎭    *me* [1]             **Interrŏgāvi,** ămāvĕrint.[2]

2. ⎧ (a) *whether they loved,* or *were lov-* **Interrŏgābam** ⎫(a) num mē
   *I was asking* ⎨         *ing me.* **Interrŏgāvi**        ⎬    ămārent.
   *I asked*      ⎪ (b) *whether they* **Interrŏgāveram**    ⎪(b) num mē
   *I had asked*  ⎩     *had loved me.*                      ⎭    ămāvissent.[2]

**137**  (1) If the Tense of the Principal Verb is either Imperative, or Indic. Pres., Fut., or "Perf. with *have*"—the Tense of the Dependent Verb is Pres. Subj., or Perf. Subjunctive.

**138**  (2) If the Tense of the Principal Verb is Indic. Imperf., Pluperf., or "Perf. without *have*" (*i.e.* Simple Past)—the Tense of the Dependent Verb is Imperf. Subj., or Pluperf. Subjunctive.

Exercise XXXVIII.

**139 and 139a**  **Quĭdem** (67) *on the one hand*, is often followed by the enclitic **vēro**, *however, but yet* (to be distinguished from **vērē**, *truthfully*). **Equĭdem**, a form of **quĭdem**, is often used with the First Person in the Nom. to mean *I on the one hand*, i.e. *I at all events, I for my part.*

A. 1. Hodie quidem pareāmus (118a) arma; cras vero hostem propulsemus. 2. Tu quidem me interrogas quid fecerim; ego vero nihil respondeo. 3. Balbo quidem omnia monstravi; tibi autem nihil. 4. Quaero cur fratrum alterum quidem laudes, alterum autem culpes. 5. Equidem hoc affirmo, tu vero unus (96) negas. 6. Interrogat cur mihi quidem multa des, Tullio autem nihil.

---

[1] A common error is to write "āmārent," in 1. *b.*, "because the English is not *have loved*, but *loved:*" but the Latin Perf. Subj. (like the Latin Perf. Indic.) represents *loved*, as well as *have loved*.

**139b**  [2] Do not translate the Latin Subjunctive in a Dependent *Question* by *may, might, could, should*, &c.; in a Dependent *Question*, it must be translated by the English Indicative.

**140** Quisquĕ, quaequĕ, quodquĕ (*pron. form* quicquĕ), *each*, often follows a Superl. (with a Sing. Verb) to denote *all* :

*All the worst men deny this.*　　Pessĭmus quisquĕ hŏc nĕgat.
*This is denied by all the best*　　Hŏc ab optĭmō quōquĕ ci
*citizens.*　　vĭum nĕgātur.

B. 1. Interrogabimus num miles fidem servaverit.¹ 2. Equidem rogo nonne puer vera narraverit; tu vero nihil affirmas. 3. Regina interrogavit num fabri aedes aedificavissent (*or* aedificâssent). 4. Renuntiate mihi, O exploratores, num hostis in eo loco insidias paret. 5. Miles centurionibus non renuntiavit num hostes proelium pararent (*were preparing*). 6. Valde dubito num nuntius vera narraverit. 7. Sapientissimus quisque nostrum (93) dubitabat num milites vera narrarent. 8. Nonne rogabis puerum num ita peccaverit? 9. Explorabamus num hostes huc properarent. 10. Ne dubitemus, O amici, num hostes arma parent. 11. Si nobis renuntiabitis quo in loco hostes insidias parent, fortissimum quemque civium convocabimus ut eos propulsemus. 12. Rogavit patrem num domum (139b) pararet ut nos in ea habitaremus.

1. *I for my part will ask whether the enemy laid-waste our territories; but the messenger will not relate the truth* (i.e. *true things*). 2. *He asked whether the enemy took the city by storm.*² 3. *Bring-back-word to me, O friend, whether the enemy is hastening hither.* 4. *Will you not ask all* (140) *the bravest of our-men whether they prepared arms?* 5. *Call-together the citizens that the enemy may not lay-waste our lands.* 6. *I had asked your father whether he had built a home that your brothers might dwell in it.* 7. *I doubt whether the enemy has laid waste these lands.* 8. *Let us explore whether the enemy is hastening hither.* 9. *You were asking the boy whether he had thus sinned.* 10. *They asked whether he had not* (135) *called-together the citizens.*

---

140a　¹ Note that in this and similar sentences (where the Perf. Subj. follows the Pres. or Fut. Indic.) there is often an ambiguity  It may mean " whether the soldier *kept his word*," or " whether the soldier *has kept his word*." Both translations should be given.

140b　² Here, for *took*, may be read *had taken;* and therefore *the Pluperf. Subj. may be used.* N.B.—Whenever, after a Past Tense of the Principal Verb, the English Simple Past, e.g. *took*, may be replaced by the English Complete Past, e.g. *had taken*, the Pluperf. Subj. may be used in Latin. The Imperf. Subj. might mean *was taking*.

## SECOND CONJUGATION.

### Exercise XXXIX.

**141** *Not even* is **nē...quǐdem**: but **nē** *must be separated from* **quǐdem** *by the word which* even *modifies*:
(1) *Not even you will deny this.*   **Nē tū quǐdem** hōc nĕgābis.¹
(2) *Not even the smallest tree.*   **Nē** mĭnĭma **quǐdem** arbor.¹

**141a** The Latin for *even* (without a negative) is **vĕl**, or **ĕtĭam**, coming before the word emphasized.

*This is clear even to the blind,*   Haec **ĕtĭam** caecis ăperta;
*easy even for boys.*                haec **vĕl** pŭeris făcĭlĭa.²

**142** Rule.—Some Verbs signifying (1) *pleasing, obeying, helping*, (2) *displeasing, disobeying*, and *harming*, take the Dative.

1. Dolere inutile est. 2. Graviter dolebam quod (*conj.*) tu, O fili, părentibus tuis non pāres. 3. Pueri patribus pārento. 4. Leges justae bonis civibus placebunt. 5. Milites ducem timebant, qui plurimos eorum (91) minis et suppliciis crudelissimis terruerat. 6. Nunc quidem monemus; mox vero, verberibus nisi pārebis, te coercebimus. 7. Ne tu, senex benevolentissime, pessimum exemplum pueris (129) praebueris. 8. Epaminondas exemplum optimum omnibus imperatoribus praebuit. 9. Cui non avium cantus placet, cum ne cithara quidem movebit. 10. Cur puellam eam minis terretis, quam nemo docuit, cui nemo exemplum bonum praebuit? 11. Senioribus ne displicueris; patri matrique obtempera. 12. Alexander, victor clarissimus, Poro, Indorum regi, veniam dedit.³

1. *To teach is more useful than to weep.* 2. *Why did you not set a better example to your son?* 3. *Do not terrify this girl with threats.* 4. *If you obey your parents, your children will obey you.* 5. *Not even the most costly banquets will please the sick* (*men*). 6. *Do not displease your mother, O boys; obey* (*your*) *elders, who advise you well.* 7. *You, who terrify others, yourself fear all things.* 8. *He does not obey even his own* (141, 2)

---

**142** ¹ N.B.—(*a*) In this phrase alone it is allowable to use **nē** with the Indicative Mood. (*b*) **Quǐdem**, without **nē**, never means *even*. (*c*) In translating **nē ... quǐdem**, be careful to put *even* before the word that precedes **quǐdem**: *not even you, not even the smallest.*

**142d** ² **Sunt**, (or **est**), is often omitted where the omission causes no ambiguity.

³ Why is **Pōro** Dat.? Why is **rēgi**? See Par. 123.

*father.* 9. *Those whom you were advising were wiser and better than those whom you had not advised.* 10. *You are destroying, O soldiers, a most prosperous city with fire and sword.*

### Exercise XL.

The Perfects of some Verbs of the 2nd Conj. end in -vi instead of -ui: but the parts of Verb *after* u and i are always the same, e.g. dēleo, dēlēvi:

*Perf.* mŏnu- / dēlēv- } -i, -isti, -it, &c.

*Pluperf.* mŏnu- / dēlēv- } -ĕram, -ĕras, -ĕrat, &c.

*2nd. Fut.* mŏnu- / dēlēv- } -ĕro, -ĕris, -ĕrit, &c.

1. Interrogabo civem nonne legibus pareat. 2. Interrogavi regis filium cur non melius exemplum ceteris militibus praeberet. 3. Coerce linguam istam ne forte tibi noceat. 4. Sapientes corpus exercebunt ut mentem sanam habeant. 5. Renuntia ei num milites ejus agricolas nostros terruerint. 6. Interrogavi fortissimum quemque (140) militum nonne hostes urbem jam delevissent. 7. Num dulce est olim multa habuisse, nunc habere nihil? 8. Qui legibus parebit eum leges non terrebunt. 9. Ne tu invidiam timueris; sed virtute malevolos, invidos modestia coerce. 10. Plurimum pecuniae eidem mulieri donavit quam antea minis terruerat.[1] 11. Barbari tantam urbem habent quantam ipsi non habemus.[2] 12. Dux tantum pecuniae donabat militibus quantum rogaverunt. 13. Interrogabo adulescentem cur hesterna nocte tam crudelibus minis fratrem meum terruerit.

1. *Do not restrain a young-man too much lest he obey you, (but) not virtue.* 2. *Why did you not restrain the young-men (127b) that they might obey their parents?* 3. *Since not even punishment terrified him, certainly threats will not terrify him.* 4. *Why do you not obey him to whom you owe so-much?* 5. *Ask whether the young-man whose* (113a) *death is now known to us was older than my brother.* 6. *I did not terrify the boy with threats, lest (the) work should become-distasteful to him.* 7. *I asked the brave centurion Tullius whether the arrow had hurt him.* 8. *Let us give rewards to all* (140) *the bravest (trans. each most*

---

[1] Why is pĕcūniae Gen.? See Par. 71, and add tantum and quantum as taking Partitive Genitives.

[2] *So great a city as we ourselves have not,* i.e. *a greater city than we have.*

*brave*) *of the soldiers that they may set an example to the rest.*
9. *Do you now terrify with threats her to whom you gave so large a sum* (trans. *so-much*) *of money?* 10. *The unjust king Balbus had* (86) *one* (*man's*) *silver, another* (*man's*) *lands, another* (*man's*) *cattle.*

### Exercise XLI.

Several Verbs that are followed by the Infinitive in English may be regarded as implying a purpose, and hence :

**143** Rule.—Verbs of *asking, commanding, advising,* and *striving,* are followed by **ŭt** or **nē** with the Subjunctive.[1]

| | |
|---|---|
| *Take care to teach him,* i.e. *in order that you may teach him.* | Cūrā **ŭt** eum **dŏcĕās.** |
| *He asked me not to hasten.* | Rŏgāvit mē **nē prŏpĕrārem.** |

**143a** N.B.—As the translation of English *to* by the Latin Inf. is one of the commonest errors of beginners, it is well to recollect that the English Infinitive is *never to be rendered by the Latin Infinitive except where* (128) *it is the Subject or Object of a Verb.*

1. Imperavit agricolis imperator ut frumentum compararent. 2. Curate ut prima vigilia adventum hostium expectetis. 3. Admonuit nos senex ut parentibus nostris semper pareremus. 4. Rogabo adulescentem ut junioribus exemplum melius praebeat. 5. Ne optimus quidem praeceptorum omnia docebit. 6. Sapientissimus quisque curabit ut linguam coerceat. 7. Quoties imperavi tibi ut mores emendes! 8. Cave ne viam aliis monstres, ipse tamen erres. 9. Orabat explorator, homo mendacissimus (126a), ut sibi veniam darem. 10. Quantum cuique debetis, tantum curate ut detis. 11. Imperavit dux militibus ne mercatorem detinerent.

1. *Give-orders to the soldiers to prepare their arms.* 2. *He gave-orders to the spies not to show these-things to the king.* 3. *Our parents advised us to await the arrival of friends.* 4. *Tullius asked me to teach his* (98) *children.* 5. *I beg you to grant*

---
[1] This Rule is sometimes remembered by the following rhyme:
"With *ask, command, advise,* and *strive,*
By ut translate Infinitive."

## THIRD CONJUGATION.

*pardon to the wicked Balbus.* 6. *Have you not again and again advised that fellow* (iste) *to restrain his tongue?* 7. *If you teach* (125), *take care to teach well.* 8. *Take care that you do not displease those whom you are bound* (debeo) *to please.*[1] 9. *On the fourth day we gave-orders to him to call-together three thousand* (80b) *soldiers.*

### THIRD CONJUGATION.

**144** Verbs of *preventing* are followed by **quo-minus** (*by-which-the-less*) and the Subjunctive.

*I have hindered the man from speaking,* lit. *by-which-the-less he may speak.*    Hŏmĭnem prŏhĭbŭi **quōmĭnus dīcat.**

**145** The words **nōn est dŭbĭum quīn,** *it is not doubtful but that,* i.e. *there is no doubt that,* are followed by the Latin Subjunctive, (though the English is Indicative):

*There is no doubt that he said this* (N.B. not *may have said*).    Nōn dūbĭum est **quīn** haec **dixĕrit.**

As regards the Tense of the Subjunctive, the Rule of the Sequence of Tenses must be observed. *Like follows like:* (see Par. 137).

*There was no doubt that he feared* (N.B. not *would fear*).    Nōn dūbĭum ĕrat **quīn** timeret.[2]

### Exercise XLII.

**146** Et sometimes means *even* or *also*:

"*Good morning.*"    "*Good morning to you too.*"    "Salvē," (lit. "*Be well.*")    "Salvē **et** tu."

1. Aut discite aut discedite : sors tertia hic nulla est. 2. Nostri, si urbem fortiter defendent, hostem facile vincent. 3. Si tu scribes, ego legam. 4. Prohibui istum quominus vincat. 5. Multa dicere facilius est quam multa discere. 6. Non

---

[1] What is the government of *whom?*

145a    [2] Probably the *doubt* is regarded as a kind of *prevention;* but instead of **quōmĭnus,** there is used an old form of quo, viz. **quī,** followed by ne, the two words **quī-ne** being contracted into **quīn.**

145b    As regards the Tense to be used after "**nōn dūbĭum erat quīn,**" the Pluperf. should be used when (but only when) *had* is, or could be, inserted in the English: *there was no doubt that the woman* (had) *killed him,* "nōn ĕrat dūbĭum quīn mūlĭer eum interfēcisset."

dubium est quin hostes aciem jam instruant: instruite et (146) vestram, centuriones. 7. Liberi Deos quotidie orabant ut pater tuto (adv.) viveret.[1] 8. Caesar materiam parabat ut Rhenum ponte jungeret. 9. Num vera dicis? Matremne terruisti? Nonne igitur rubes? 10. Scribamus diligenter, ne nos praeceptor culpet. 11. Hastas in terra figite, milites. 12. Non dubium erat quin cives urbem fortiter defenderent.

1. *I advise you to depart.* 2. *There is no doubt that the wise learn daily.* 3. *They asked us to fix our spears in the earth.* 4. *If you read* (125), *(my) friends,* (99a) *I will write.* 5. *It is often more useful to learn than to speak.* 6. *We shall conquer the enemy, if you* (99), *O citizens, defend your city.* 7. *The leader will take care to draw up the line-of-battle.* 8. *Say what-is-true* (trans. *true-things*), *my friends;· let us not feign what-is-false* (i.e. *false-things*). 9. *There was no doubt that the boys wrote carefully.* 10. *I will hinder that-fellow from conquering.*

EXERCISE XLIII.

(Vinco, vincio, fingo, figo.)

**147** Almost all Superlatives, and many Positives, in -us, -a, -um, make Adverbs in -ē, e.g. **cĕlerrĭmē, dĭfĭcillĭmē**, tardē.

**148** Almost all Comparatives in -ĭor use the Neut. in -ĭus as an Adverb: **tardĭus**, *more (rather, too) slowly*; **dīligentĭus**, *more (rather, too) diligently.*

**149** The Adverbs, like the Adjectives (64), have more than one meaning: thus, **tardĭus**, besides meaning (1) *more slowly*, may also mean (2) *rather slowly*, or (3) *too slowly*.

1. Mettum, Albanum imperatorem, equi distraxerunt. 2. Non dubium est quin Caesar multa milia Gallorum vicerit. 3. Quis dubitabat quin centurio, homo crudelissimus, captivos vinxisset? 4. Caesar Rhenum ponte junxit, (32) aciem summa celeritate instruxit. 5. Si celerrime scribes, amici tui fortasse difficillime legent. 6. Interrogabo hominem num has litteras scripserit. 7. Interrogavi patrem nonne dilexisset duos liberorum, ceteros neglexisset. 8. Nonne commeatus collegisti? Nonne equites peditesque contraxisti? 9. Non dubium erat quin errores alios correxisset, alios neglexisset. 10. Falsane finxistis, o perfidissimorum obsidum filii? 11. Centurio militem interrogabat cur hastam in terra fixisset. 12. Mene interrogas, mi fili, cur hoc dixerim?[2]

---

[1] Quŏtīdĭē is more correctly spelt cottīdĭē or cŏtīdĭē.
[2] Mī is the irregular Vocative Masc. Sing. of mĕus.

1. *Do not feign what-is-false* (i.e. *false-things*), *my son.* 2. *I will ask him whether (his) leader bridged the river.* 3. *Do not write the letter too-quickly* (149) *lest your friends read it with-very-great-difficulty* (use adverb). 4. *There is no doubt that he wrote this letter.* 5. *There was no doubt that the general had collected supplies, (and) had drawn (his) army together.* 6. *Take care, my friend, to correct those errors of-yours; do not* (5a) *neglect even* (141) *one (error).* 7. *Have you asked the centurion why the soldiers fixed their spears in the earth?* 8. *There was no doubt that the hostages had feigned what-was-false.* 9. *Ask the centurion why he bound the captives.* 10. *I hindered the boy from exulting; but there was no doubt that he had conquered.*

### Exercise XLIV.

**151** Rule.—**Cum**, *when*, if followed by the Imperfect or Pluperfect, generally requires the Subjunctive Mood.[1]

1. Interrogabo num puer versus heri didicerit. 2. Hostes, cum tuba cecinisset, in campum descenderunt. 3. Statui puerum corrigere ut diligenter disceret. 4. Dux, cum exercitum collegisset, in Galliam contendit. 5. Orabunt imperatorem milites ut aciem instruat. 6. Non dubium est quin hostes jam in urbem irruperint, aedificia igni absumant, omnia clamore et caede turbent. 7. Quod (*trans. as if* quod vere hoc) cum intelligerem, statim interrogabam nuntium cur haec non antea dixisset. 8. Correxi errores eius ne amicis suis temeritate sua graviter noceret. 9. Interrogabat imperator nonne jussa sua neglexissem, num murum fortiter defendissem?

1. *When I heard this* (i.e. *which things when I had understood*), *I determined to obey* (142) *the general.* 2. *Correct these errors, my* (151) *son, lest they injure your friends.* 3. *When he had collected supplies, the general closed the gates of the city.* 4. *What do you say, (my) friends? Do you ask me why I neglected this task?* 5. *There was no doubt that traitors had closed the gates of the two citadels.* 6. *Who hindered the citizens from defending the wall?* 7. *When the trumpet sounded* (i.e. *had sounded*), *not even the most cowardly of the soldiers neglected the signal.* 8. *At-the-time-when my friend* (152) *was hastening into the city, I was walking in the garden.*

151a [1] With these Tenses, **cum** generally implies not simply *at-the-time-when*, but *because* (or at least some logical connection), and "**Cum** *causal*" is followed by the Subjunctive."

**152** But when **cum** simply means *at-the-time-when*, it may be followed by the Indicative Imperfect or Pluperfect.

## FOURTH CONJUGATION.

### Exercise XLV.

1. Dum vos dormitis, hostes castra muniunt. 2. Audistisne clamorem hostium qui, jam vino pleni, captivum male custodiunt?[1] 3. Qui bene servit patriae, ei (*dat.*) cives libenter servient. 4. Non dubium est quin te pater optime erudiverit (9a). 5. Qui (107, 1) bene corpus tuum vestiisti, bene nutriisti, nonne tu etiam mentem tuam simili cura erudies?[2] 6. Cives legibus obediunto. 7. Mors mihi spiritum, non vitam finiet. 8. Interrogo te cur hesterna nocte captivum tam male custodiveris. 9. Non dubium erat quin hostes castra diligenter muniissent. 10. Audite alios (*others*) ut alii te audiant. 11. Ne tu punieris puellam: patrem eius puniamus, qui poena dignus est. 12. Mater rogavit me ne puellam punirem.

1. *Do you sleep, O foolish (men), while the enemy are bursting into the city?* 2. *There is no doubt that the soldiers guarded the captive badly.* 3. *Why did you not train the boy better that he might obey (his) elders.* 4. *I ask you why you punished the innocent child Tulliola* (124). 5. *Let us ask the judge not to punish the boy, who is undeserving of punishment.* 6. *You who nourished your children's bodies with so-great care, will you not, O my friends, train also their minds?* 7. *We who had never obeyed our parents* (108), *punished our children because they did not obey us.* 8. *Train your mind that you may learn very-many (things).* 9. *When we had fortified our camp, the enemy descended into the plain* (5a). 10. *Have you asked the boy whether he has lost his books?*

### Exercise XLVI.

(Vĕnio, rĕpĕrio.)

1. Imperator cum tandem nostros vicisset, plurimos gravissima catena vinxit. 2. Serius (149) venistis: comites enim vestri hesterna nocte venerunt. 3. Interrogas cur aurum non reppereris: non repperisti, quia in hac terra aurum non est. 4. Non dubium erat quin serius venissent; sed rex eis veniam dedit. 5. Si forte cras venies, fortasse quod amisisti reperies. 6. Quamdiu dux ille vixit, nostri (34) vicerunt. 7. Archimedes multa et mira invenit.[3] 8. Inter-

---

152a [1] Vino may be parsed, for the present, as *Abl. of Instr.*: but see Par. 275.
[2] Though **nōnne** and **num** generally stand first in a Direct Question, they are sometimes preceded by the Clause containing the Relative Pronoun: see Exercise XXXIII, Sentence 5.

153 [3] In English we do not translate **ĕt** coming between **multus** and another co-ordinate Adjective, *e.g.* "multa et pulchra," *many beautiful things.*

rogavi centurionem cur captivos tam gravi catena vinxisset
9. Jam omnia parabam ut venirem. 10. Ne tu huc veneris:
nam, si venies, non facile discedes.

1. *Why, O most cruel of men, did you bind with so heavy a chain the innocent* (126) *Balbus?* 2. *The woman came rather-late, but the king granted her pardon.* 3. *We conquered those who lived in that plain.* 4. *There is no doubt that they did not find gold in this land.* 5. *I asked why they came* (145b), *but no-one heard me.* 6. *I found yesterday night* (30) *what* (i.e. *that which*) *I had lost.* 7. *Will he not tell me why he came here?* 8. *Hast thou come at-length, O best of sons?*

## THE VERB Sum, *I am.*

### Sum, fŭī, fŭtŭrŭs, essĕ,—*to be.*

#### INDICATIVE MOOD.

##### 1. PRESENT TENSE.

| | | | | | |
|---|---|---|---|---|---|
| *Sing.* | **Sum,** | *I am* | *Plur.* | **Sŭmŭs,** | *We are* |
| | **Es,** | *thou art* | | **Estĭs,** | *ye are* |
| | **Est,** | *he is.* | | **Sunt,** | *they are.* |

##### 2. FUTURE-SIMPLE TENSE.

| | | | | | |
|---|---|---|---|---|---|
| *Sing.* | **Ĕro,** | *I shall be* | *Plur.* | **Ĕrĭmŭs,** | *We shall be* |
| | **Ĕrĭs,** | *thou wilt be* | | **Ĕrĭtĭs,** | *ye will be* |
| | **Ĕrĭt,** | *he will be.* | | **Erunt,** | *they will be.* |

##### 3. IMPERFECT TENSE.

| | | | | | |
|---|---|---|---|---|---|
| *Sing.* | **Ĕram,** | *I was* | *Plur.* | **Ĕrāmŭs,** | *We were* |
| | **Ĕrās,** | *thou wast* | | **Ĕrātĭs,** | *ye were* |
| | **Ĕrăt,** | *he was.* | | **Ĕrant,** | *they were.* |

##### 4. PERFECT TENSE.

| | | | | | |
|---|---|---|---|---|---|
| *Sing.* | **Fuī,** | *I have been,* or *I was* | *P.* | **Fuĭmŭs,** | *We have been,* or *we were* |
| | **Fuistī,** | *thou hast been,* or *thou wast* | | **Fuistĭs,** | *ye have been,* or *ye were* |
| | **Fuĭt,** | *he has been,* or *he was.* | | **Fuērunt** or **fuērĕ** | *they have been,* or *they were.* |

### 5. Future-Perfect Tense.

S. **Fuĕro,** *I shall have been*　　P. **Fuĕrĭmŭs,** *We shall have been*
　**Fuĕrĭs,** *thou wilt have been*　　　**Fuĕrĭtĭs,** *ye will have been*
　**Fuĕrĭt,** *he will have been.*　　　　**Fuĕrint,** *they will have been.*

### 6. Pluperfect Tense.

S. **Fuĕram,** *I had been*　　　P. **Fuĕrāmŭs,** *We had been*
　**Fuĕrās,** *thou hadst been*　　　**Fuĕrātĭs,** *ye had been*
　**Fuĕrăt,** *he had been.*　　　　**Fuĕrant,** *they had been.*

## IMPERATIVE MOOD.

### 1. Present Tense.

*Sing.* **Ĕs,**　*Be thou.*　　　| *Plur.* **Estĕ,**　*Be ye.*

### 2. Future Tense.

*Sing.* **Estō,** *Thou shalt or must be*　　*Plur.* **Estōtĕ,** *Ye shall or must be*
　　　**Estō,** *he shall or must be, or let him be.*　　　**Sunto,** *they shall or must be, or let them be.*

## SUBJUNCTIVE MOOD.

### 1. Present Tense.

*Sing.* **Sim,**　*I may be*　　*Plur.* **Sīmŭs,**　*We may be*[1]
　**Sīs,**　*thou mayst be*　　　**Sītĭs,**　*ye may be*
　**Sĭt,**　*he may be.*　　　　**Sint,**　*they may be.*

### 2. Imperfect Tense.

*Sing.* **Essem** or **fŏrem,** } *I might be*　　P. **Essēmŭs** or **fŏrēmŭs,** } *We might be*
　**Essēs** or **fŏrēs,** } *thou mightst be*　　**Essētĭs** or **fŏrētĭs,** } *ye might be*
　**Essĕt** or **fŏrĕt,** } *he might be.*　　**Essent** or **fŏrent,** } *they might be.*

### 3. Perfect Tense.

S. **Fuĕrim,** *I may have been*　　**Fuĕrĭmŭs,** *We may have been*
　**Fuĕrĭs,** *thou mayst have been*　　**Fuĕrĭtĭs,** *ye may have been*
　**Fuĕrĭt,** *he may have been.*　　**Fuĕrint,** *they may have been.*

### 4. Pluperfect Tense.

S. **Fuissem,** *I should* } *have been*　　**Fuissēmŭs,** *We should* } *have been*
　**Fuissēs,** *thou wouldst*　　　**Fuissētĭs,** *ye would*
　**Fuissĕt,** *he would*　　　**Fuissent,** *they would*

---

[1] **Sīmus,** without a Conjunction, generally means *let us be.*

## INFINITIVE MOOD.

| | | |
|---|---|---|
| Infinitive Present, and Imperfect, | } Essĕ, | to be. |
| Infinitive Perfect, and Pluperfect, | } Fuissĕ, | to have been. |
| Infinitive Future, | Fŭtūrŭs essĕ, or fŏrĕ, | to be about to be. |
| Participle Future, | Fŭtūrŭs, -a, -um, | about to be. |

### Exercise XLVII.

1. Nos Angli sumus, vos estis Galli, ille Germanus est. 2. Fuit Troja; fuere Mycenae; tu, Roma, etiam nunc es. 3. Nisi ego dux vester (125) ero, victores non eritis. 4. Amici eius quondam divites fuerant: tum vero erant pauperrimi. 5. Dictorum eius, O pueri, este semper memores. 6. Judices justi sunto. 7. Gratus esto, puer, si amicos benignos habere optas. 8. Ne fueris, O soror, eis molesta qui tibi benevolentissimi semper fuerunt. 9. Contentus ero, O judices, si vos justi fueritis.¹ 10. Interrogavit num judices justi essent. 11. Cura, rex magne, ut sis munificentior (68a). 12. Ego et tu laetissimi sumus. 13. Prudentes este ut benefici sitis.

1. *You and I have been (127) very poor.* 2. *We (99a) were in the city; he and his brother were in the field.* 3. *Had you not been ungrateful, sister, to those who were formerly most benevolent to you?* 4. *If you are (i.e. shall have been) joyful, I shall be most joyful.* 5. *Take care not to be troublesome to the benevolent.* 6. *I asked the boy whether he was younger than his [own] brother.* 7. *There is no doubt that Tullius was very ungrateful.* 8. *Be brave, O soldiers, that ye may be fortunate.* 9. *You will be happy, (my) friends, if you are (125) always contented.* 10. *There was no doubt that Tullius had formerly been very rich, but was now very poor.*

## THE ACTIVE PARTICIPLES.

**154** The Participle is partly like an Adjective, in that it agrees with a Noun or Pronoun, and partly like a Verb, in that it may govern an Object.²

| | |
|---|---|
| *The citizen slew the king (when he was, or who was) about to destroy the city with fire.* | Civis rēgem urbem jam igni **absumptūrum** interfēcit. |
| *The darts were troublesome to our men (while they were, or who were) waiting for help.* | Tēla nostris mŏlesta ĕrant auxĭlium **expectantĭbus**. |

---

¹ Not *if you shall have been just* (125). But **optas** (Sent. 7) is Present, because it refers to Present time.

² The Participle must often be translated by a Conjunction *when, while,* &c., or by the Relative Pronoun.

## THE DEPENDENT FUTURE INTERROGATIVE.

**155** It has been shown above (Par. 136) how to turn a Direct Question in the Past or Present Tenses into an Indirect Question, by changing the Indicative Tenses into corresponding Subjunctive Tenses. But, as there is no Subjunctive Future, we cannot thus turn a Direct Question in the Future, *Will he come?* "Num veniet?" into an Indirect Question, *I ask whether he will come.*

For this purpose we employ a form compounded of the Verb **sum**, and the Participle in **-rus**: **ventūrus sum**, *I am about to come;* **ventūrae sunt**, *they* (fem.) *are about to come;* **ventūrus fuerās**, *you had been about to come*, &c.

Hence *Will she come?* or *Is she about to come?* becomes, when changed into an Indirect Question:

| | | | |
|---|---|---|---|
| *Ask* <br> *I ask* <br> *I will ask* <br> *I have asked* } | *whether the woman is about to come.* | **Interrŏgā** <br> **Interrŏgo** <br> **Interrŏgābo** <br> **Interrŏgāvi** | } **num mŭlier ventūra sit.** |
| *I was asking* <br> *I asked* <br> *I had asked* } | *whether the woman was about to come* | **Interrŏgābam** <br> **Interrŏgāvi** <br> **Interrŏgāvĕram** | } **num mŭlier ventūra esset.** |

### Exercise XLVIII.

**156** The Latin for *when* in *questions*, whether dependent or independent, is not **cum** but **quando**.

*When will he come?*      **Quando** vĕniet?
*Let us inquire when he will come.*      Quaerāmus **quando** ventūrus sit.

1. Interrogavi puellam num matri obeditura esset. 2. Filium, parentes nutriturum (154a), cur culpas? 3. Obsidibus, haec audientibus, non placuit in urbem venire.[1] 4. Interrogate sorores vestras quando patri obediturae sint. 5. Hostibus, jam urbem intrantibus, nox molesta erat. 6. Tibi, O puella, graviter erraturae, pauca dicam. 7. Arbori, fructum jam praebiturae, frigus nocuit. 8. Praeceptori, optime docenti, discipulorum stultitia multum displicuit. 9. Nonne audis patris tui

---

[1] The Subj. of **plăcuit** is **venīre**, see Par. 128. Parse **obsĭdĭbus**; see Par. 142

verba, te culpantis, te in meliora revocantis? 10. Ecce, veniunt gladiatores, principem salutaturi. 11. Non erat dubium quin pauca dictura esset. 12. Vitione potius quam virtuti obtemperaturus es?

1. *The speech of the general was troublesome to our men, (since they were) not then expecting an attack. 2. You, (being) yourself about-to-err, blame your brother (who is) erring. 3. You, who are destined soon to ask help* (trans. *you, soon about-to-ask help*) *in-vain, now despise your friends (who are) affording help. 4. You ought to hear the voice of your friends (who are) chiding you (and) recalling you to the path of virtue. 5. There was no doubt that his daughter was on the point of coming,* i.e. *about-to-come. 6. Why, O pupils, did you displease your teacher, (though he was) teaching you most-excellently? 7. When we heard this, we resolved to obey the general* (trans. (it) *pleased us, hearing these things, to obey,* &c.). *8. When will you obey your friends (who are) giving you many gifts and about-to-give you more (gifts)? 9. Let us ask his sisters whether they are going to obey* (i.e. *about-to-obey*) (*their*) *father. 10. The frost destroyed very many vines (when they were) just* (jam) *about-to-put-forth (their) fruit.*

## FIRST OR A CONJUGATION.—PASSIVE VOICE.

Ămŏr, ămātŭs sum, ămārī,—*to be loved.*

### INDICATIVE MOOD.

#### 1. Present Tense.

| | | | |
|---|---|---|---|
| **Am-ŏr,** | *I am loved* | **Am-āmŭr,** | *We are loved* |
| **Am-āris** or **ăm-ārĕ,** | } *thou art loved* | **Am-āmĭnī,** | *ye are loved* |
| **Am-ātŭr,** | *he is loved.* | **Am-antŭr,** | *they are loved.*[1] |

#### 2. Future-Simple Tense.

| | | | |
|---|---|---|---|
| **Am-ābŏr,** | *I shall be loved* | **Am-ābĭmŭr,** | *We shall be loved* |
| **Am-ābĕris** or **ămābĕrĕ,** | } *thou wilt be loved* | **Am-ābĭmĭnī,** | *ye will be loved* |
| **Am-ābĭtŭr,** | *he will be loved.* | **Am-ābuntŭr,** | *they will be loved.* |

---

[1] Cicero rarely uses **ămāre** for **ămāris**. It is liable to be confused with the Imper. Passive, as well as with the Pres. Inf. Active.

## PASSIVE VOICE.

### 3. IMPERFECT TENSE.

| | | | |
|---|---|---|---|
| **Am-ābăr,** | I was being loved (115) | **Am-ābāmŭr,** | We were being loved |
| **Am-ābārĭs** or **ăm-ābārĕ** | thou wast being loved | **Am-ābāmĭnī,** | ye were being loved |
| **Am-ābātŭr,** | he was being loved. | **Am-ābantŭr,** | they were being loved. |

### 4. PERFECT TENSE.

| | | | |
|---|---|---|---|
| **Am-ātŭs sum** or **fuī,** | I have been loved, or was loved | **Am-ātī sŭmŭs** or **fuĭmŭs,** | We have been loved, or were loved |
| **Am-ātŭs ĕs** or **fuistī,** | thou hast been loved, or wast loved | **Am-ātī estĭs** or **fuistĭs,** | ye have been loved, or were loved |
| **Am-ātŭs est** or **fuĭt,** | he has been loved, or was loved. | **Am-ātī sunt, fuērunt,** or **fuērĕ,** | they have been loved, or were loved[1] |

### 5. FUTURE-PERFECT TENSE.

| | | | |
|---|---|---|---|
| **Am-ātŭs ĕro** or **fuĕro,** | I shall have been loved | **Am-ātī ĕrĭmŭs** or **fuĕrĭmŭs,** | We shall have been loved |
| **Am-ātŭs ĕrĭs** or **fuĕrĭs,** | thou wilt have been loved | **Am-ātī ĕrĭtĭs** or **fuĕritĭs,** | ye will have been loved |
| **Am-ātŭs ĕrĭt** or **fuĕrit,** | he will have been loved. | **Am-ātī ĕrunt** or **fuĕrint,** | they will have been loved. |

### 6. PLUPERFECT TENSE.

| | | | |
|---|---|---|---|
| **Am-ātŭs ĕram** or **fuĕram,** | I had been loved | **Am-ātī ĕrāmŭs** or **fuĕrāmŭs,** | We had been loved |
| **Am-ātŭs ĕrās** or **fuĕrās,** | thou hadst been loved | **Am-ātī ĕrātĭs** or **fuĕrātĭs,** | ye had been loved |
| **Am-ātŭs ĕrăt** or **fuĕrăt,** | he had been loved. | **Am-ātī ĕrant** or **fuĕrant,** | they had been loved. |

### IMPERATIVE MOOD.

#### PRESENT TENSE.

| | | | |
|---|---|---|---|
| **Am-ārĕ,** | Be thou loved. | **Am-āmĭnī,** | Be ye loved. |

---

**157** [1] The Latin Perfect Passive may sometimes be translated by *is, are*: *The man is slain*, hŏmo interfectus est. Hence, when *is, are* imply that an action is completed, translate by the Latin Perfect.

# FIRST CONJUGATION.

### FUTURE (see Par. 117) TENSE.

| | | | |
|---|---|---|---|
| Am-ātŏr, | Thou must be loved | Am-antŏr, | They must be loved. |
| Am-ātŏr, | he must be loved. | | |

## SUBJUNCTIVE MOOD.

### 1. PRESENT TENSE.

| | | | |
|---|---|---|---|
| Am-ĕr, | I may be loved | Am-ēmŭr, | We may be loved |
| Am-ērĭs or ăm-ērĕ, | thou mayst be loved | Am-ēmĭnī, | ye may be loved |
| Am-ētŭr, | he may be loved. | Am-entŭr, | they may be loved. |

### 2. IMPERFECT TENSE.

| | | | |
|---|---|---|---|
| Am-ārĕr, | I might be loved | Am-ārēmŭr, | We might be loved |
| Am-ārērĭs or ăm-ārērĕ, | thou mightst be loved | Am-ārēmĭnī, | ye might be loved |
| Am-ārētŭr, | he might be loved. | Am-ārentŭr, | they might be loved. |

### 3. PERFECT TENSE.

| | | | |
|---|---|---|---|
| Am-ātŭs sim or fuĕrim, | I may have been loved | Am-ātī sīmŭs or fuĕrimŭs, | We may have been loved |
| Am-ātŭs sis or fuĕrĭs, | thou mayst have been loved | Am-ātī sītĭs or fuĕritĭs, | ye may have been loved |
| Am-ātŭs sĭt or fuĕrĭt, | he may have been loved. | Am-ātī sint or fuĕrint, | they may have been loved. |

### 4. PLUPERFECT TENSE.

| | | | |
|---|---|---|---|
| Am-ātŭs essem or fuissem, | I should have been loved | Am-ātī essēmŭs or fuissēmŭs, | We should have been loved |
| Am-ātŭs essēs or fuissēs, | thou wouldst have been loved | Am-ātī essētĭs or fuissētĭs, | ye would have been loved |
| Am-ātŭs essĕt or fuissĕt, | he would have been loved. | Am-ātī essent or fuissent, | they would have been loved. |

## INFINITIVE MOOD.

| | | |
|---|---|---|
| PRES. and IMP. | Am-ārī, | to be loved |
| PERF. and PLUP. | Am-ātŭs (-a, -um) essĕ or fuissĕ, | to have been loved |
| FUTURE. | Am-ātum īrī (not declined), | to be about to be loved.[1] |

---

[1] For an explanation of ămātum īri, see Exercise LXXIV.

## PARTICIPLES

PERFECT. **Am-ātŭs (-a, -um),** *loved or having been loved.*
GERUNDIVE. **Am-andŭs (-a, -um),** *meet to be loved.*

## SECOND OR E CONJUGATION.—PASSIVE VOICE.

**Mŏneŏr, mŏnĭtŭs sum, mŏnērī**—*to be advised.*

### INDICATIVE MOOD.

#### 1. PRESENT TENSE.

| | | | |
|---|---|---|---|
| **Mŏn-eŏr,** | *I am advised* | **Mŏn-ēmŭr,** | *We are advised* |
| **Mŏn-ērĭs,** | { *thou art advised* | **Mŏn-ēmĭnī,** | *ye are advised* |
| **Mŏn-ētŭr,** | *he is advised.* | **Mŏn-entŭr,** | *they are advised.* |

#### 2. FUTURE-SIMPLE TENSE.

| | | | |
|---|---|---|---|
| **Mŏn-ēbŏr,** | { *I shall be advised* | **Mŏn-ēbĭmŭr,** | { *We shall be advised* |
| **Mŏn-ēbĕrĭs** or **mŏn-ēbĕrĕ,** | { *thou wilt be advised* | **Mŏn-ēbĭmĭnī,** | { *ye will be advised* |
| **Mŏn-ēbĭtŭr** | { *he will be advised.* | **Mŏn-ēbuntŭr,** | { *they will be advised.* |

#### 3. IMPERFECT TENSE.

| | | | |
|---|---|---|---|
| **Mŏn-ēbăr,** | { *I was being advised* (115) | **Mŏn-ēbāmŭr,** | { *We were being advised* |
| **Mŏn-ēbārĭs** or **mŏn-ēbārĕ,** | { *thou wast being advised* | **Mŏn-ēbāmĭnī,** | { *ye were being advised* |
| **Mŏn-ēbātŭr,** | { *he was being advised.* | **Mŏn-ēbantŭr,** | { *they were being advised.* |

#### 4. PERFECT TENSE.

| | | | |
|---|---|---|---|
| **Mŏn-ĭtŭs sum** or **fuī,** | { *I have been advised,* or *was advised* | **Mŏn-ĭtī sŭmŭs** or **fuīmŭs,** | { *We have been advised,* or *were advised* |
| **Mŏn-ĭtŭs ĕs** or **fuistī,** | { *thou hast been advised,* or *wast advised* | **Mŏn-ĭtī estĭs** or **fuistĭs,** | { *ye have been advised,* or *were advised* |
| **Mŏn-ĭtŭs est** or **fŭĭt,** | { *he has been advised,* or *was advised.* | **Mŏn-ĭtī sunt, fuērunt,** or **fuērĕ,** | { *they have been advised,* or *were advised.* |

## SECOND CONJUGATION.

### 5. Future-Perfect Tense.

| | | | |
|---|---|---|---|
| Mŏn-ĭtŭs ĕro or fuĕro, | I shall have been advised | Mŏn-ĭtī ĕrĭmŭs or fuĕrĭmŭs, | We shall have been advised |
| Mŏn-ĭtŭs ĕrĭs or fuĕrĭs, | thou wilt have been advised | Mŏn-ĭtī ĕrĭtĭs or fuĕrĭtĭs, | ye will have been advised |
| Mŏn-ĭtŭs ĕrĭt or fuĕrĭt, | he will have been advised. | Mŏn-ĭtī ĕrunt or fuĕrint, | they will have been advised. |

### 6. Pluperfect Tense.

| | | | |
|---|---|---|---|
| Mŏn-ĭtŭs ĕram or fuĕram, | I had been advised | Mŏn-ĭtī ĕrāmŭs or fuĕrāmŭs, | We had been advised |
| Mŏn-ĭtŭs ĕrās or fuĕrās, | thou hadst been advised | Mŏn-ĭtī ĕrātĭs or fuĕrātĭs, | ye had been advised |
| Mŏn-ĭtŭs ĕrăt or fuĕrăt, | he had been advised. | Mŏn-ĭtī ĕrant or fuĕrant, | they had been advised. |

### IMPERATIVE MOOD.

#### Present Tense.

| | | | |
|---|---|---|---|
| Mŏn-ērĕ, | Be thou advised. | Mŏn-ēmĭnī, | Be ye advised |

#### Future (see Par. 117) Tense.

| | | | |
|---|---|---|---|
| Mŏn-ētŏr, | Thou must be advised | Mŏn-entŏr, | They must be advised. |
| Mŏn-ētŏr, | he must be advised. | | |

### SUBJUNCTIVE MOOD.

#### 1. Present Tense.

| | | | |
|---|---|---|---|
| Mŏn-eăr, | I may be advised | Mŏn-eāmŭr, | We may be advised |
| Mŏn-eārĭs or mŏn-eārĕ, | thou mayst be advised | Mŏn-eāmĭnī, | ye may be advised. |
| Mŏn-eātŭr, | he may be advised. | Mŏn-eantŭr, | they may be advised. |

#### 2. Imperfect Tense.

| | | | |
|---|---|---|---|
| Mŏn-ērĕr, | I might be advised | Mŏn-ērēmŭr, | We might be advised |
| Mŏn-ērērĭs or mŏn-ērērĕ, | thou mightst be advised | Mŏn-ērēmĭnī, | ye might be advised |
| Mŏn-ērētŭr, | he might be advised | Mŏn-ērentŭr, | they might be advised. |

## PASSIVE VOICE.

### 3. Perfect Tense.

| | | | |
|---|---|---|---|
| Mŏn-ĭtŭs sim or fuĕrim, | I may have been advised | Mŏn-ĭtī sīmŭs or fuĕrimŭs, | We may have been advised |
| Mŏn-ĭtŭs sīs or fuĕrīs, | thou mayst have been advised | Mŏn-ĭtī sītĭs or fuĕritĭs, | ye may have been advised |
| Mŏn-ĭtŭs sĭt or fuĕrĭt, | he may have been advised | Mŏn-ĭtī sint or fuĕrint, | they may have been advised. |

### 4. Pluperfect Tense.

| | | | |
|---|---|---|---|
| Mŏn-ĭtŭs essem or fuissem, | I should have been advised | Mŏn-ĭtī essēmŭs or fuissēmŭs, | We should have been advised |
| Mŏn-ĭtŭs essēs, or fuissēs, | thou wouldst have been advised | Mŏn-ĭtī essētĭs or fuissētĭs, | ye would have been advised |
| Mŏn-ĭtŭs essĕt or fuissĕt, | he would have been advised. | Mŏn-ĭtī essent or fuissent, | they would have been advised. |

### INFINITIVE MOOD.

Pres. and Imp.    **Mŏn-ērī,**                      *to be advised.*
Perf. and Plup.    **Mŏn-ĭtŭs (-a, -um) essĕ** *or* **fuissĕ,** *to have been ad-*
                                                                       [*vised.*
Future.             **Mŏn-ĭtum īrī** (not declined),    *to be about to*
                                                                                      [*be advised.*

Perfect.      **Mŏn-ĭtŭs (-a, -um),** *advised, or having been advised.*
Gerundive.   **Mŏn-endŭs (-a, -um),** *meet to be advised.*

## THIRD OR Consonant AND U CONJUGATION.—PASSIVE VOICE.

**Rĕgŏr, rectŭs sum, rĕgī,**—*to be ruled.*

### INDICATIVE MOOD.

#### 1. Present Tense.

| | | | |
|---|---|---|---|
| Rĕg-ŏr, | I am ruled | Rĕg-ĭmŭr, | We are ruled |
| Rĕg-ĕrĭs, | thou art ruled | Rĕg-ĭmĭnī, | ye are ruled |
| Rĕg-ĭtŭr, | he is ruled. | Rĕg-untŭr, | they are ruled. |

## THIRD CONJUGATION.

### 2. Future-Simple Tense.

| | | | |
|---|---|---|---|
| Rĕg-ăr, | I shall be ruled | Rĕg-ēmŭr, | We shall be ruled |
| Rĕg-ērĭs or rĕg-ērĕ, | thou wilt be ruled | Rĕg-ēmĭnī, | ye will be ruled |
| Rĕg-ētŭr, | he will be ruled. | Rĕg-entŭr, | they will be ruled. |

### 3. Imperfect Tense.

| | | | |
|---|---|---|---|
| Rĕg-ēbăr, | I was being ruled (115) | Rĕg-ēbāmŭr, | We were being ruled |
| Rĕg-ēbārĭs or rĕg-ēbārĕ, | thou wast being ruled | Rĕg-ēbāmĭnī, | ye were being ruled |
| Rĕg-ēbātŭr, | he was being ruled. | Rĕg-ēbantŭr, | they were being ruled. |

### 4. Perfect Tense.

| | | | |
|---|---|---|---|
| Rec-tŭs sum or fŭī, | I have been ruled, or was ruled | Rec-tī sŭmŭs or fuĭmŭs, | We have been ruled, or were ruled |
| Rec-tŭs ĕs or fuistī, | thou hast been ruled, or wast ruled | Rec-tī estĭs or fuistĭs, | ye have been ruled, or were ruled |
| Rectŭs est or fŭit, | he has been ruled, or was ruled. | Rec-tī sunt, fuērunt, or fuērĕ, | they have been ruled, or were ruled. |

### 5. Future-Perfect Tense.

| | | | |
|---|---|---|---|
| Rec-tŭs ĕro or fuĕro, | I shall have been ruled | Rec-tī ĕrĭmŭs or fuĕrĭmŭs, | We shall have been ruled |
| Rec-tŭs ĕrĭs or fuĕrĭs, | thou wilt have been ruled | Rec-tī ĕrĭtĭs or fuĕritĭs, | ye will have been ruled |
| Rec-tŭs ĕrĭt or fuĕrĭt, | he will have been ruled. | Rec-tī ĕrunt or fuĕrint, | they will have been ruled. |

### 6. Pluperfect Tense.

| | | | |
|---|---|---|---|
| Rec-tŭs ĕram or fuĕram, | I had been ruled | Rec-tī ĕrāmŭs or fuĕrāmŭs, | We had been ruled |
| Rec-tŭs ĕrās or fuĕrās, | thou hadst been ruled | Rec-tī ĕrātĭs or fuĕrātĭs, | ye had been ruled |
| Rec-tŭs ĕrăt or fuĕrăt, | he had been ruled. | Rec-tī ĕrant or fuĕrant, | they had been ruled. |

### IMPERATIVE MOOD.

#### Present Tense.

| | | | |
|---|---|---|---|
| Rĕg-ĕrĕ, | Be thou ruled. | Rĕg-ĭmĭnī, | Be ye ruled. |

## PASSIVE VOICE. [Par. 157

### FUTURE (see Par. 117) TENSE.

Rĕg-ĭtŏr, { *Thou must be ruled*
Rĕg-ĭtŏr, { *he must be ruled.*
Rĕg-untŏr, *They must be ruled.*

### SUBJUNCTIVE MOOD.

#### 1. PRESENT TENSE.

Rĕg-ăr, *I may be ruled*
Rĕg-ārĭs or reg-ārĕ, } *thou mayst be ruled*
Rĕg-ātŭr, *he may be ruled.*
Rĕg-āmŭr, *We may be ruled*
Rĕg-āmĭnī, *ye may be ruled*
Rĕg-antŭr, *they may be ruled.*

#### 2. IMPERFECT TENSE.

Rĕg-ĕrĕr, *I might be ruled*
Rĕg-ĕrērĭs or reg-ĕrērĕ, } *thou mightst be ruled*
Rĕg-ĕrētŭr, *he might be ruled.*
Rĕg-ĕrēmŭr, *We might be ruled*
Rĕg-ĕrēmĭnī, *ye might be ruled*
Rĕg-ĕrentŭr, *they might be ruled.*

#### 3. PERFECT TENSE.

Rec-tŭs sim or fuĕrim, } *I may have been ruled*
Rec-tŭs sīs or fuĕrĭs, } *thou mayst have been ruled*
Rec-tŭs sit or fuĕrĭt, } *he may have been ruled.*
Rec-tī sīmŭs or fuĕrimŭs, } *We may have been ruled*
Rec-tī sītĭs or fuĕrītĭs, } *ye may have been ruled*
Rec-tī sint or fuĕrint, } *they may have been ruled.*

#### 4. PLUPERFECT TENSE.

Rec-tŭs essem or fuissem, } *I should have been ruled*
Rec-tŭs essēs or fuissēs, } *thou wouldst have been ruled*
Rec-tŭs essĕt or fuissĕt, } *he would have been ruled.*
Rec-tī essēmŭs or fuissēmŭs, } *We should have been ruled*
Rec-tī essētĭs or fuissētĭs, } *ye would have been ruled*
Rec-tī essent or fuissent, } *they would have been ruled.*

### INFINITIVE MOOD.

PRES. and IMP.    Rĕg-ī,                           *to be ruled.*
PERF and PLUP.   Rec-tŭs (-a, -um) essĕ or fuissĕ, *to have been ruled*
FUTURE.              Rec-tum īrī (not declined),    *to be about to be*
                                                                   [*ruled.*

## FOURTH CONJUGATION.

### PARTICIPLES

PERFECT.     Rec-tŭs (-a, -um),     *ruled* or *having been ruled.*
GERUNDIVE.     Rĕg-endŭs (-a, -um),     *meet to be ruled.*

## FOURTH OR I CONJUGATION.—PASSIVE VOICE.

Audiŏr, audītŭs sum, audīrī,—*to be heard.*

### INDICATIVE MOOD.

#### 1. PRESENT TENSE.

| | | | |
|---|---|---|---|
| Aud-iŏr, | *I am heard* | Aud-imŭr, | *We are heard* |
| Aud-īrĭs, | *thou art heard* | Aud-īmĭnī, | *ye are heard* |
| Aud-ītŭr, | *he is heard* | Aud-iuntŭr, | *they are heard.* |

#### 2. FUTURE-SIMPLE TENSE.

| | | | |
|---|---|---|---|
| Aud-iăr, | *I shall be heard* | Aud-iēmŭr, | *We shall be heard* |
| Aud-iērĭs *or* aud-iērĕ, | *thou wilt be heard* | Aud-iēmĭnī, | *ye will be heard* |
| Aud-iētŭr, | *he will be heard.* | Aud-ientŭr, | *they will be heard.* |

#### 3. IMPERFECT TENSE.

| | | | |
|---|---|---|---|
| Aud-iēbăr, | *I was being heard* (115) | Aud-iēbāmŭr, | *We were being heard* |
| Aud-iēbārĭs *or* aud-iēbārĕ, | *thou wast being heard* | Aud-iēbāmĭnī, | *ye were being heard* |
| Aud-iēbātŭr, | *he was being heard.* | Aud-iēbantŭr, | *they were being heard.* |

#### 4. PERFECT TENSE.

| | | | |
|---|---|---|---|
| Aud-ītŭs sum *or* fuī, | *I have been heard, or was heard* | Aud-ītī sŭmŭs *or* fuĭmŭs, | *We have been heard, or were heard* |
| Aud-ītŭs es *or* fuistī, | *thou hast been heard, or wast heard* | Aud-ītī estĭs *or* fuistĭs, | *ye have been heard, or were heard* |
| Aud-ītŭs est *or* fuĭt, | *he has been heard, or was heard.* | Aud-ītī sunt, fuērunt, *or* fuērĕ, | *they have been heard, or were heard.* |

## PASSIVE VOICE.

### 5. FUTURE-PERFECT TENSE.

Aud-ītŭs ĕro or fuĕro, } I shall have been heard
Aud-ītŭs ĕrĭs or fuĕrĭs, } thou wilt have been heard
Aud-ītŭs ĕrĭt or fuĕrĭt, } he will have been heard

Aud-ītī ĕrĭmŭs or fuĕrimŭs, } We shall have been heard
Aud-ītī ĕrĭtĭs or fuĕritĭs, } ye will have been heard
Aud-ītī ĕrunt or fuĕrint, } they will have been heard.

### 6. PLUPERFECT TENSE.

Aud-ītŭs ĕram or fuĕram, } I had been heard
Aud-ītŭs ĕrās or fuĕrās, } thou hadst been heard
Aud-ītŭs ĕrăt or fuĕrăt, } he had been heard.

Aud-ītī-ĕrāmŭs or fuĕrāmŭs, } We had been heard
Aud-ītī ĕrātĭs or fuĕrātĭs, } ye had been heard
Aud-ītī ĕrant or fuĕrant, } they had been heard.

## IMPERATIVE MOOD.

### PRESENT TENSE.

Aud-īrĕ, *Be thou heard.* | Aud-īmĭnī, *Be ye heard.*

### FUTURE (see Par. 117) TENSE.

Aud-ītŏr, *Thou must be heard.*
Aud-ītŏr, *he must be heard.*
Aud-iuntŏr, *They must be heard.*

## SUBJUNCTIVE MOOD.

### 1. PRESENT TENSE.

Aud-iăr { *I may be heard*
Aud-iārĭs or aud-iārĕ, { *thou mayst be heard*
Aud-iātŭr, { *he may be heard.*

Aud-iāmŭr, *We may be heard*
Aud-iāmĭnī, *ye may be heard*
Aud-iantŭr, *they may be heard.*

### 2. IMPERFECT TENSE.

Aud-īrĕr, { *I might be heard*
Aud-īrērĭs or aud-īrērĕ, { *thou mightst be heard*
Aud-īrētŭr, { *he might be heard.*

Aud-īrēmŭr, *We might be heard*
Aud-īrēmĭnī, *ye might be heard*
Aud-īrentŭr, *they might be heard.*

## FOURTH CONJUGATION.

### 3. PERFECT TENSE.

Aud-ītŭs sim or fuĕrim, — *I may have been heard*
Aud-ītŭs sīs or fuĕrīs, — *thou mayst have been heard*
Aud-ītŭs sĭt or fuĕrĭt, — *he may have been heard.*

Aud-ītī sīmŭs or fuĕrĭmŭs, — *We may have been heard*
Aud-ītī sītĭs or fuĕrĭtĭs, — *ye may have been heard*
Aud-ītī sint or fuĕrint, — *they may have been heard.*

### 4. PLUPERFECT TENSE.

Aud-ītŭs essem or fuissem, — *I should have been heard*
Aud-ītŭs essēs or fuissēs, — *thou wouldst have been heard*
Aud-ītŭs essĕt or fuissĕt, — *he would have been heard*

Aud-ītī essēmŭs or fuissēmŭs, — *We should have been heard*
Aud-ītī essētĭs or fuissētĭs, — *ye would have been heard*
Aud-ītī essent or fuissent, — *they would have been heard.*

### INFINITIVE MOOD.

PRES. and IMP.    Aud-īrī,    *to be heard.*
PERF. and PLUP.    Aud-ītŭs (-a, -um) essĕ or fuissĕ, *to have been heard.*
FUTURE.    Aud-ītum īrī (not declined), *to be about to be [heard.*

### PARTICIPLES.

PERFECT.    Aud-ītŭs (-a, -um), *heard or having been heard.*
GERUNDIVE.    Aud-iendŭs (-a, -um), *meet to be heard.*

### EXERCISE XLIX.

**57a**    If two Subjects are connected by Disjunctive Conjunctions, *e.g.* vĕl, *or (if you please), or (rather),* aut *or (else),* the Verb generally agrees with the latter of the two.

*What man or what monster committed this crime?*    Qui hŏmo, vĕl quae bēlŭa hōc făcĭnus **commīsit?**
*Either you or Tullius said this.*    Aut tū aut Tullius haec **dixit.**

1. Equus ab aurīga domabitur (32), mox aurīgam dorso portabit.
2. Cura ut Tullia, puella pulcherrima, floribus a matre ornetur.
3. Si urbem incendent, quomodo in tanto incendio servabimini?
4. Interrogavi civem quomodo urbs servaretur.
5. Curavit sacerdos ut hae divitiae in aedem Jovis portarentur.
6. Si animum recreabis, nihil obstabit quominus saneris.
7. Cura ut a medico saneris, qui te facillime sanabit, si

tu ei obtemperabis. 8. Agri tui qui nunquam antea vastabantur, jam vastabuntur, nisi nobis iter monstraveris. 9. Curabit dux ut a me servemini nisi jussa mea neglexeritis. 10. Portae urbis omni cura firmantor ne ab hostibus subito[1] superemur. 11. Curate ne, impetum non expectantes, ab hoste superemini. 12. Nisi a medico sanabere (125), num tibi aurum argentumque utilia erunt?

1. *The land of the Germans, which was never* (115) *wont-to-be laid-waste before, was laid waste by our men.* 2. *While we are being overcome by disease, our allies are being overcome by the enemy.* 3. *The leader took care that the citizens should be preserved.* 4. *Take care that the gates of the city are strongly-guarded,* (trans. *strengthened with a guard*), *that our men may not be overcome by the enemy.* 5. *What enemy, or* (*rather*) *what danger* (111) *prevented this wealth from being carried* (use quōmĭnus, see Par. 144) *into the temple?* 6. *Our men, not expecting an attack, were being overcome by the enemy.* 7. *We shall be cured* (17) *by this medicine if we obey the physician's precepts.* 8. *How will you be preserved,* (*my*) *friends, in this great* (trans. *so-great*) *conflagration?* 9. *The priests were-taking-pains that the temple should be adorned by the servants with very-many flowers.* 10. *Let us take-care that the gates of the city are* (143) *strongly-guarded*

## PARTICIPLES AND PARTICIPIAL TENSES.

**158** The Participle Passive agrees with its Noun in Number and Gender.

| | |
|---|---|
| *The enemy, having been overcome, are fleeing,* i.e. *have been overcome and are fleeing.* | Hostes **sŭpĕrāti** fŭgiŭnt. |
| *They burn the city* (*when it had been*) *taken,* i.e. *they take and burn the city.* | Urbem **captam** incendunt. |

**159** *N.B.*—Note how the English *and* can be expressed by the Latin Passive Participle.

**159a** The Perfect, Future Perfect, and Pluperfect Tenses of **ămor**, both in the Indicative and in the Subjunctive, are not really independent Tenses of **ămor**, but rather Tenses

**160** [1] Sŭbĭto is an Adv. Adj. in -us, -a, -um, and -er, -a, -um, mostly make Adv. in -ē; but there are exceptions: tūto, *safely;* cĭto, *quickly;* &c.

of the Verb **sum** joined to forms of the Passive Participle
ămātus *which must agree with some Noun or Pronoun:*

| | |
|---|---|
| *The town is taken.* | Oppĭdum **captum** est. |
| *The girls will have been adorned.* | Puellae **ornātae** fuĕrint. |

### Exercise L.

**161** If two or more Subjects are (1) animate beings of different genders, their Adjective or Participle is Masculine; (2) if inanimate, generally Neuter Plural.

| | |
|---|---|
| (1) *His father and mother have been slain.* | Păter eius et māter **interfecti** sunt. |
| (2) *Anger and avarice were more powerful than authority.* | Ira et ăvărĭtĭa impĕrio **pŏtentĭōra** ĕrant. |

1. Interroga num pater meus et mater a Tullio servati sint (9a).
2. Imperator, cum hostium equites jam turbati fuissent, pedites facile fugavit. 3. Oppidum ipsum ab hoste expugnatum est, sed arx virtute ducis nostri est servata. 4. Si equites superati fuerint (125a), quomodo pedites servabuntur? 5. Cur tanto auri pondere ornatae estis, mulieres stultissimae? 6. Murus et porta a sacerdote centum aureis statuis, ducentis argenteis, ornata fuerant. 7. Hostis, tandem superatus, ab imperatore nostro fugatus est. 8. Agri pauperrimorum agricolarum a crudelissimis hostibus ferro atque igni vastati sunt. 9. Hostes superati sunt, urbes quinquaginta expugnatae, segetes omnes vastatae (32). 10. Non dubium erat quin iter hostibus a proditore monstratum fuisset.

1. *Have the wall and the gate been stormed by the enemy* (101)?
2. *Ask whether the wall and the gate have been preserved by the citizens.* 3. *The town is stormed* (i.e. *has been stormed*): *our men are overcome.* 4. *The bridge, having been preserved by the husbandmen, had been pointed out to us by the spy.* 5. *There was no doubt that two hundred ships of war had been preserved by the enemy.* 6. *The shower was troublesome to the enemy* (*who were*) *now put-to-flight.* 7. *Did you not owe everything* (trans. *all things*) *to Tullius, by whom your very life had been preserved?* 8. *Having been praised by all the best citizens* (140), *will you and your sister,* (150) *my* (*dear*) *Tullius, commit this great* (i.e. *so great*) *crime* (101)?

## THE IMPERSONAL PASSIVE. [Par. 162—165

### SECOND CONJUGATION.

#### Exercise LI.

**162** The Passive is sometimes used impersonally in Latin where we use the Active:

*All laughed*, lit. *it was laughed by all.*     **Rīdēbātur** ăb omnĭbus.

*The enemy had fought bravely*, lit. *it had been fought bravely by the enemy*     **Pugnātum ĕrat** ācrĭter ăb hostĭbus.

**163** The Neuter of the Passive Participle in **-ndus** (commonly called the Gerundive) is very frequently used in this impersonal way, *the Agent being expressed by the Dative*:

*I must fight*, lit. *it is meet to be fought to*, or *for, me.*     **Pugnandum** est **mĭhi.**[1]

*Ought you not to remain?*     Nōnne **tĭbi mănendum** est?

1. Cura ne periculo terrearis. 2. Justorum judicum animi neque minis neque a rege ipso movebuntur. 3. Cives, ab imperatore territi, in sua quisque domo manserunt.[2] 4. Quid obstabat vobis quominus a praeceptore doceremini? 5. Magister curavit ut omnia vere a servis suis responderentur. 6. Non dubium est quin puer optime doceatur. 7. Curate ut corpora puerorum bene exerceantur. 8. Agricola fluctibus terrebatur, quos nauta ridebat. 9. Cum haec tanta (trans. *this great*) tempestas impenderet, flebatur ab agricolis, a nautis ridebatur. 10. Imperatori, captivos interroganti nonne cruciatus timerent, a regina nostra fortissime responsum est. 11. Nobis flendum est, vobis et hostibus exultandum. 12. Hostes jam superatos, et in urbem fugientes, equitatus noster paene delevit.

1. There is no doubt that two-hundred cities were utterly-destroyed by the cruel general Balbus (124). 2. We must fight bravely that the enemy may not (131) take the city by-storm. 3. Fighting

---

**164** [1] If the Verb *e.g.* **pāreo** governs a Dat., "pārendum est nōbīs" would be ambiguous, meaning either *obedience must be paid to us*, or *by us*. This ambiguity is avoided by using **ā** with the Abl. to express the Agent:
*We must obey the magistrate.* Mgistrātūi ā nōbīs pārendum est.

**165** [2] **Quisquē** is Nom. Sing. in Apposition to **cīves.** Note that in this phrase, *they came, returned, each to his* &c., **sŭus** *always precedes* **quisquē.**

*was kept up briskly* (trans. *it-was-fought briskly*) *by the Germans, that our men, terrified by the multitude of the darts, might retire into the city.* 4. *There is no doubt that the master will exercise* (155) *the bodies of the slaves.* 5. *Why must you weep? Ought* (163) *not you* (101) *rather to fight that your fields may not be laid waste by the enemy?* 6. *There is no doubt that answer-was-made most-bravely by our leader.* 7. *I took care that the city might be filled with-soldiers that you might not be terrified by the danger.* 8. *We ought not to be terrified in this great danger* (trans. *this so-great danger*). 9. *Our men, when-they-could scarcely sustain the charge of the enemy* (trans. *scarcely sustaining*) *and* (*were*) *almost fleeing, were recalled by the voice of* (*their*) *brave* (70) *leader.* 10. *What tyrant, or* (157a) *what* (111) *danger, will prevent* (144) *us from remaining in our city?*

THIRD CONJUGATION.

EXERCISE LII.

66 *I am on the point of conquering.*   In ĕo sum ŭt vincam.
*I was on the point of conquering.*   In ĕo ĕram ŭt vincĕrem.

RULE.—When an Active Verb governing a Dative is turned into the Passive, it retains the Dative but is used impersonally. Thus, *all obey you,* omnes tĭbĭ pārēbunt; but :

67 *You will be obeyed by all,* i.e.   **Tĭbi** ăb omnĭbus **pārēbĭtur**
*it will be obeyed to you by all.*     (not tū pārēbĕris).

1. Qui non, puer, regitur, is, senex, non bene reget.[1] 2. Nisi te ipsum (125a) viceris, hostes a te inutiliter vincentur. 3. Cura ne falsa a te fingantur. 4. Curabant senes ut a filiis suis recte viveretur. 5. Cum nostri in eo essent ut urbem intrarent, subito portae clausae sunt. 6. Non dubium est quin exercitus, fortiter pugnans, ab hostibus oppressus sit. 7. Cavendum est ne ab hostibus contemnamini. 8. Interrogavisti nonne conjuratio alteri consuli a tribus testibus detecta esset. 9. Rhenus fluvius a Cæsare ponte eo tempore jungebatur. 10. Castra a duobus milibus militum, viris acerrimis, defendentur. 11. Liber ille a liberis meis summa diligentia scribitur. 12. Quid obstat quominus agri colantur, quoniam mox hostes in fugam vertentur? 13. Tune agros colis qui, quotiens colentur, totiens ab hostibus vastabuntur?

---

[1] **Puer** is Nom., in Apposition with **qui,** *he who, when* (or *as*) *a boy,* &c.

1. *The town will be defended bravely by the citizens.* 2. *Take care that the gates are shut and that the city is guarded* (trans. strengthened with a guard). 3. *If the river* (125) *is bridged by the enemy, you will be in great danger, citizens.* 4. *Do you* (tu), *the partner* [1] *of our plans, give-orders that the conspiracy shall be disclosed* (pres. subjunct.)? 5. *I asked my children whether the books were being written by them.* 6. *There was no doubt that the fields, formerly laid-waste by the enemy, were now being cultivated.* 7. *If you, (when) a boy, obey your parents, you will be obeyed, when old, by your children* (trans. it-will-be-obeyed to you (when) an old-man). 8. *Our men are on the point of putting the enemy to flight.* 9. *The enemy were on the point of being put to flight by our men.* 10. *If the conspiracy is disclosed* (125) *to-morrow, the city will be preserved by you.*

### Exercise LIII.

1. Cur non auxilium mittere statuistis? 2. Interrogandum est nobis num epistola a puero scripta sit. 3. Interrogandum erat mulieri quando epistolae a pueris scriptae essent. 4. Non erat dubium quin duci (142) nostro placuisset legatos mittere. 5. Cum jam agri diligentissime culti fuissent, subito segetes omnes imbribus absumptae sunt. 6. Quid obstabat quominus oppidum defenderetur? 7. Urbem hanc, a duobus millibus civium defensam, decem milia hostium obsederunt. 8. Quare vos, quingenti viri, ab hostibus ducentis victi estis? 9. Interrogavi nonne a sene pueri semper dilecti essent, nonne memoria eius ab illis etiam tum coleretur. 10. Fabula, si a poeta docte scripta fuerit, omnibus placebit. 11. Cum jam naves plurimae ab imperatore collectae essent, exploratores ad Britanniam quinto die missi sunt. 12. Jam acies instructa erat, jam pedites ad proelium parati (142 *d*); cum subito legati ab hostibus pacem petituri missi sunt.

1. *There is no doubt that the letter was written by his sister.* 2. *What prevented the fields from being cultivated?* 3. *When the enemy had now been conquered, the husbandmen determined to cultivate the fields.* 4. *There was no doubt that the old man's memory had been cherished* (lit. *cultivated*) *by those whom he had taught.* 5. *Let us ask the poet why he did not compose* (lit. *write*) *a better story.* 6. *The king asked the general why he had not himself drawn up the line-of-battle with greater care* (lit. *more-diligently*). 7. *Our ambassadors were sent a-second-time into the city to seek for peace* (lit. about-to-

---

[1] In what case should *partner* be? See Par. 123.

seek). 8. *The spears of the soldiers, fixed in the earth, shewed the camp of the enemy.* 9. *Which of the two* (85) *daughters was especially loved* (dīlĭgo) *by* (her) *father?* 10. *If he violates* (125) *this law, let him* (129a) *be driven into exile.*

## FOURTH CONJUGATION.

When the Gerundive is used as an Adjective, it still takes the Dative of the Agent; (if (164) there is no ambiguity:)

| | | | |
|---|---|---|---|
| *The boys* } *are (fit) to be punish-* | Pueri } | sunt **mĭhĭ** pūniend | -i. |
| *girls* } *ed by me.* | Puellae } | | -ae. |
| *I must learn this.* | Haec **mĭhĭ** discenda sunt. | | |

### EXERCISE LIV.

1. Audiendi sunt nobis exploratores; nam hostium urbes clam muniuntur. 2. Quid obstat quominus extra urbem corpus sepeliatur? 3. Curandum erat legatis ut bellum pace finiretur. 4. Interrogabo Numidam num leones in Africa reperiantur. 5. Puniēris, nisi cito veneris. 6. Cur tam deformibus vestibus vestiebamini? 7. Patri a quo nutrimini, vestimini, educamini, nonne parebitis? 8. Mortui extra (*see Vocab.* extrā) urbem sepeliuntur. 9. Tertia nocte a nostris dormiebatur, ab hostibus castra muniebantur. 10. Ab eo vinciere qui nuper a te ipso vinciebatur.

1. *There is no doubt that lions are found in Africa.* 2. *Will you not obey, O most ungrateful boy, the father by whom you were clothed, nourished, (and) educated?* 3. *Let us take care that war may be terminated by peace.* 4. *The spies of the enemy must be punished by us.* 5. *What prevents the camp from being fortified by our men* (144)? 6. *The dead used-to-be-buried by the ancients outside the city.* 7. *On the fourth day, my son, you will be heard by the judges.* 8. *You were being patiently heard by all: why did* (127b) *you not yourself* (105) *hear me?*

### EXERCISE LV.

1. Hae urbes nobis muniendae sunt. 2. Cum corpora mortuorum sepulta essent, arcem optime munitam hostes nobis tradiderunt. 3. Reperti sunt leones quinque: de (*about*) tigribus nihil auditum (est). 4. Nisi melius vestita fuerit (125a), mulier frigus vix tolerabit. 5. Nutriendus est nobis pauperrimus ille puer qui a patre ipso non nutritus est. 6. Cur tandem, O puellae, matris immemores estis? Nonne estis ab illa nutritae? Nonne (142d) vestitae? Nonne summa diligentia[1] educatae? 7. Ego, si finitum fuerit bellum, in

---

[1] **Diligentiā** is *Abl. of Manner:* see Exercise LXXIX.

Italiam veniam. 8. Tria milia captivorum, a nostris vincti,[1] clam evaserunt. 9. Qui a patre tuo nutritus es, nonne tu patrem, jam senem, ipse nutries? 10. Non dubium erat quin castra hostium clam diligentissime munita essent.

1. *I asked whether the bodies of the dead had been buried.* 2. *Will (it) not please you to nourish those by whom you yourselves have been nourished?* 3. *There is no doubt that very many lions have been found in Africa.* 4. *These who have been bound by you, O soldiers, have secretly escaped.* 5. *The story which had been beautifully written by the poet did not please the king.* 6. *Take-care that you are clothed with a thick garment, that the cold may not* (131) *hurt you.* 7. *She was heard by the same judges by whom his sisters had already been heard.* 8. *What have you found, my friend, which has not already been found out by others* (5a) *?* [2]

## THIRD CONJUGATION IN I.

**Căpĭo, cēpi, captum, căpĕrĕ,**—*to take.*
(stem: **căp-**, or **căpĭ-**.)

When the First Pers. Sing. Pres. Indic. of the Third Conjugation ends in **-ĭo**, it (1) drops the ĭ before ĭ and ĕ,[3] but (2) retains it otherwise, *e.g.* before a, o, ē, and u.

Thus (1) **căp-ĭmus, căp-ĕre, căp-ĕ.**

But (2) **căpi-am, căpi-o, căpi-ēs, căpi-unt.**

### I. ACTIVE VOICE.

#### INDICATIVE MOOD.

*Pres.* **Căpi-o, căp-ĭs, căp-ĭt, căp-ĭmus, căp-ĭtis, căpĭ-unt.**
*Fut.* **Căpi-am, căpi-ēs, căpi-et, căpi-emus, căpi-etis, căpi-ent.**
*Imperf.* **Căpi-ēbam, căpi-ēbas, căpi-ēbat, căpi-ēbamus, căpi-ēbatis, căpĭ-ēbant**

Regular Tenses.
{ *Perf.* **Cēp-i, Cēp-isti,** &c.
{ *Pluperf.* **Cēp-ĕram, Cēp-ĕrasti,** &c.
{ *Future Perf.* **Cēp-ĕro, Cēp-ĕris,** &c.

---

[1] **Vincti** is Masc. Nom. agreeing with a Masc. Nom., *men* or *captives*, implied in **milia**.

[2] For easy Exercises on the Regular Verbs, see pp. 173—175.

[3] The only exception is the 3rd Pers. Sing. of the Fut. Indic. **căpi-ĕt**, which follows the form of the other persons, **căpi-ēs, căpi-ēmus,** &c.

## THIRD CONJUGATION IN -I.

### IMPERATIVE MOOD.

*Pres.* căp-ĕ,   căp-ĭte,
*Fut.* căp-ĭto, căp-ĭto, căp-ĭtōte, căpĭ-unto,

### SUBJUNCTIVE MOOD.

*Pres.* Căpĭ-am, căpĭ-as, căpĭ-at, căpĭ-amus, căpĭ-atis, căpĭ-ant,
*Imperf.* Căp-ĕrem, căp-ĕres, căp-ĕret, căp-ĕremus, căp-ĕretis, căp-ĕrent,

Regular Tenses. { *Perf.* Cēp-ĕrim, cēp-ĕris, &c.
{ *Pluperf.* Cēp-issem, cēp-isses, &c.

### INFINITIVE MOOD.     PARTICIPLES.

*Pres.* **Căp-ĕre,**   *Perf.* Cēp-isse   *Pres.* **Căpiens,**   *Fut.* Capturus.

GERUND.           SUPINES.
**Capi-endi.**    Captum, captu.

### II. PASSIVE VOICE.

*(Only the Present and Present-Derived Tenses are given below.)*

### INDICATIVE MOOD.

*Pres.* Căpĭ-or, căp-ĕris, căp-ĭtur, căp-ĭmur, căp-ĭmini, căpi-untur.
*Fut.* Căpĭ-ar, căpĭ-ēris (-ērĕ), căpĭ-ētur, căpĭ-ēmur, căpĭ-ēmini, căpĭ-entur.
*Imperf.* Căpĭ-ēbar, căpĭ-ēbaris (-bārĕ), căpĭ-ēbatur, &c.

### IMPERATIVE MOOD.

*Pres.* Căp-ĕre, căp-ĭmini.
*Fut.* Căpĭ-tor, căpĭ-untor.

### SUBJUNCTIVE MOOD.

*Pres.* **Căpĭ-ar,** căpĭ-āris, căpĭ-ātur, &c.
*Imperf.* **Căp-ĕrer,** capĕr-ēris, capĕr-ētur, &c.

### INFINITIVE MOOD.

**Căp-i.**

## Exercise LVI.

**169** A prohibition is often expressed by the Imperative Sing. nōlī or Plur. **nōlīte,** *be unwilling :*

*Do not flee,* i.e. be unwilling to flee. **Nōlī,** or **nōlīte,** fŭgĕre.

**170** The Ablative of the Gerund is used instrumentally:

*Water hollows the rock by falling.*   Ăqua saxum căvat **cădendo.**

1. Cape pira quoniam cupis, sed noli piro meae quatiendo nocere. 2. Si haec scripseris, mox cupies non scripsisse. 3. Interrogavit num, haec facientes, recte et sapienter faceremus. 4. Accipe trecentos denarios, si dederit; ducentos ne acceperis. 5. Curate ut versus vestri Nasonem sapiant. 6. Nolite fugere, O milites; fodiendum est, non fugiendum, ut castra muniamus. 7. Si quaeris monumentum, circumspice.[1] 8. Noli, O judex, injusta facere : nonne te oravit rex ut justitiam semper respiceres? 9. Miles, jam telum conjecturus, hostem jacentem aspexit. 10. Interrogavi qualia animalia multiplices fetus parerent.[2]

1. *Have-regard-to virtue; do not have-regard-to the commands of a tyrant.*[3] 2. *There was no doubt that he received five hundred denarii, and was* (155) *about-to-receive two thousand denarii.* 3. *When the youth beheld his father, he cast away his dart.* 4. *Flee, O friends; do not look round.* 5. *The leaders asked what we desired to do.* 6. *What prevents his verses from savouring-of Maro* (see *Maro* in Vocabulary)? 7. *What* (i.e. that which) *they did, they took care* (143) *to do well.* 8. *You will make your discourse accurate by writing, learned by reading.*

## Exercise LVII.

**171** *Whether . . . or,* in (*a*) Independent, as well as in (*b*) Dependent Questions, can be expressed by (1) **utrum . . . ăn;** (2) **-ně . . . ăn:**

(*a* 1) *Is this true or false?*   **Utrum** haec vēra **ăn** falsa sunt?
(*a* 2) *Was he white or black?*   Albusně **ăn** āter ĕrat?

---

[1] These words are inscribed on the tomb of Sir Christopher Wren in St. Paul's ; **quaeris** refers to present, not (125) to future time.

[2] From what two Verbs may **parerent** come, the quantity being left unmarked? What Case does each govern?

[3] Note that *have-regard-to* is one Verb in Latin governing an *Accusative Case.*

| | |
|---|---|
| (*b* 1) *We must enquire whether this is true or false.* | Quaerendum est **utrum** haec vēra sint **ăn** falsa. |
| (*b* 2) *It is uncertain whether he was black or white.* | Incertum est albusnĕ **ăn** āter fuĕrit.[1] |

**172** *Or not* in Interrogatives may be rendered by **annōn** or **necnĕ**:

*Ask whether he will come or not.* Quaerĕ utrum ventūrus sit **necnĕ** (or **annōn**).

**173** N.B. (1) **Aut** and **vĕl** (157*a*) are not to be used in Dependent or Independent Questions.

**174** (2) When *whether* is not followed by *or*, **num** (135) is generally used instead of **utrum**.

**175** (3) The Rule (136) for Sequence of Tenses *always holds*.

1. Praeceptor dubitabat tune an Tullius rem melius gereret.[2] 2. Dux, cum jam proelii, vel potius caedis, finem fecisset, urbem incenderat. 3. Aut pugnandum est aut cedendum, milites. 4. Hunc vicum barbari oppidum vel urbem appellavere. 5. Milites cum jam spolia vel praedam rapuissent cupierunt urbem incendere. 6. Latona dicitur uno partu Apollinem et Dianam peperisse.[3] 7. Quaerendum est utrum regina an filius eius bellum acrius gesturus sit. 8. Arma nobis capienda sunt nĕ (*not* -nĕ) tyrannus, vel tyranni milites, bona nostra diripiant. 9. Haec cum imperator aspexit, constituit aut aciem statim instruere aut clam nocte discedere. 10. Cum pedites nostri fugissent, naves tempestate quassae fuissent, urbes ab hostibus direptae, statim magna pars nostrorum pacem petere cupiebat. 11. Quaerendum est per (*by means of*) exploratores utrum urbs ab hostibus incensa sit necne.

---

**176** [1] Both in Independent and Dependent Questions (c) **ăn** is sometimes used without **utrum** or -**nĕ** preceding; and in Dependent Questions (d) -**nĕ** is sometimes used for *or*, without a preceding particle.

*It is uncertain whether he was the son or grandson of Tullius.* Filius nĕpōsne fuerit Tullii incertum est.

**176***a* [2] The disjunctive **ăn** disjoins **tū** from **Tullius** and causes **gĕrĕret** to agree with **Tullius**; **tū** may be parsed as "the subject of **gĕrĕres** understood:" see Par. 157*a*.

**177** [3] **Dīcĭtur**, with a Personal Subject, should generally be rendered in English impersonally, *it is said that Latona*, &c.

1. *Who doubted whether you or your brother had made these verses?* 2. *We must either depart or learn.* 3. *Let us make an end of this war or (rather) insurrection.* 4. *The general ordered the soldiers to hurl their darts against* (in gov. acc.) *the enemy.* 5. *Either we shall carry on this war prosperously or we shall be driven into exile.* 6. *There was no doubt that the queen, or (rather) her son, had waged that war very-prosperously.* 7. *It was doubtful whether the general had seen the horse-soldiers, or (whether) ignorant of their arrival, he had drawn up the line-of-battle.* 8. *Let us ask whether the men will come on the third or fourth day.* 9. *It is uncertain whether the city has been stormed or not.* 10. *Who doubts whether the queen will* (155) *carry on the war in winter* (5a)*?*

## PREPOSITIONS.

**178** 1. The following Prepositions take the Ablative, and no other Case:

**A, ăb** (before a vowel), *by, from.*
**Absquĕ** (rare), *without.*
**Clam**, *secretly, without the knowledge of.*[1]
**Cōram**, *in the presence of.*
**Cum**, *with.*
**Dē**, *down from, from, concerning.*

**Ē, (ex** before a vowel), *out of.*
**Pălam**, *openly, in the presence of.*[2]
**Prae**, *before, in comparison with,* (with a negative *because of.*)[3]
**Prō**, *before, for, on behalf of, instead of, in return for.*
**Sĭne**, *without.*
**Tĕnus** (after its Case), *as far as.*[4]

These Prepositions are sometimes committed to memory in the following rhyme:

Ā, or ăb, and **ex** or ē
Cum, pălam, cōram, clam and dē
Tĕnus, sĭne, prō, and **prae**
Always govern the Ablative.

---

[1] **Clam** is used by the Comic Authors with the Accusative.
[2] **Pălam** is used as a Preposition only after Cicero, and mostly by poets.
[3] **Prae** is rarely used by Cicero to mean *because of* except with **non, vix,** &c.: *I am not able to speak for sorrow*, **Prae** maerōre lŏqui nōn possum.
[4] **Tĕnus** governs the Abl. Sing.; but with a Plural Noun, more often takes the Genitive, Alpium tĕnus, *as far as the Alps:* but the Gen. Pl. construction is not found in the prose of Cicero.

### Exercise LVIII.

**179** Rule.—Cum is affixed to tē, mē, sē, nōbīs, vōbīs, quō, quĭbus: mēcum, (*not* cum mē) nōbīscum, quōcum, &c.

1. Puer inde a pueritia cum matre vixerat, quae ab Italia ad Graeciam se receperat. 2. Pecuniam mihi reddidit quam ipse a fratre meo, proximo anno, coram patre meo acceperat. 3. Irruperunt clam imperatore milites cum gladiis, cum scutis; qui (*see* 'qui') cum me vehementissime increpuissent, equidem cum constantia respondi. 4. Tu quidem Rheno tenus regnabis, filius autem tecum regnabit. 5. Alpium tenus omnes gentes vicerat. 6. Verbo tenus te adjuvabit, re ipsa nihil faciet.[1] 7. Ira sine viribus inutilissima est. 8. Pro obsidibus causam egit Tullius; cui (*i.e.* et ei, *see* Par. 298, I) pro tantis eius laboribus gratias Allobroges egerunt. 9. Palam populo sine misericordia jugulatus est. 10. Tibi, O amice, prae omnibus amicis beate, ego, hominum miserrimus, prae lacrimis vix scribo. 11. Nos pro patria pugnantes dejecistis de Capitolio (32), jam ex urbe ejicitis. 12. Multis de[2] causis cupio tecum de hac re deliberare.

1. *In-the-presence-of his father the youth deliberated with me concerning this matter.* 2. *Let us return thanks to the worthy Balbus, who pleaded our cause with* (181) *zeal before the king.* 3. *There was no doubt that he had conquered all Asia as-far-as Taurus.* 4. *From a boy he had lived in Greece.* 5. *Since the general forbids (us), let us fight for (our) country without his knowledge.* 6. *He was slain by the soldiers in-the-sight-of the people.* 7. *From Italy I shall retire to Greece, and my son will travel with me.* 8. *Tullius, who pleaded for us, replied to these charges with indignation.* 9. *I scarcely write for tears: having been driven out-of (my) native-land into exile.* 10. *What will anger without wisdom effect for us?*

**180** PREPOSITIONS TAKING THE ACCUSATIVE OR ABLATIVE.

| ABLATIVE. | | ACCUSATIVE. | |
|---|---|---|---|
| Ĭn, | meaning *rest in* | Ĭn, | meaning *into, to, towards* |
| Sŭb, | ,, *rest under* | Sŭb, | ,, *motion from below*,[3] |
| Sŭper, | ,, *concerning.* | Sŭper, | ,, *above, over, upon.*[4] |

[1] Dē is Adverbial Abl.; see Par. 182.

[2] '*From many reasons*,' i.e. '*for many reasons.*'

[3] The form sŭbter (hardly, if at all, found, except in poets and late prose writers), meaning *extension under*, generally takes the Acc. but sometimes the Abl. in poetry.

[4] Sŭper, meaning *above*, also takes the Abl. in poetry, and in Caesar.

## Exercise LIX.

**181** RULE.—The *Manner* of an action may be expressed (1) by the Abl. of a Noun, *with an Adjective attached to it;* (2) by the Abl. following **cum**.

*He spoke with,* or *in, anger; I replied with the greatest firmness.*   Ille quĭdem **cum** īra lŏcūtus est; ĕgŏ vēro **summā constantiā** respondi.

*N.B.* The Abl. *without an Adj.* or *Prep.* is used to denote *Instrument*, but not *Manner*.

**182** Some exceptional Ablatives of Nouns are used (without Adjectives) adverbially, *e.g.* **jūre**, *rightly;* **ordĭne**, *in order;* **spĕcĭē**, *in appearance;* **rē** *or* **rē ipsā**, in *fact,* &c. They may be parsed as *Adverbial Ablatives*.

1. In Italia paulisper manserat, mox in Galliam contendit. 2. In eo loco a Samnitium imperatore Romani sub jugum missi sunt. 3. Sub oculis patris ipsius filii ambo interfecti sunt. 4. Sub oculos nobis[1] duae columbae venerunt. 5. Equites sub jactu teli nondum erant; pedites jam sub ictum venerant. 6. Super navem turrem exstruxeramus. 7. Super hac re cuperam vobiscum deliberare. 8. Vulnus super vulnus centurio fortissimus acceperat. 9. Judaea, provincia turbulenta, sub Pontio Pilato tum erat. 10. In ore omnium Persarum tunc erat Alexandri humanitas. 11. Nioba dicitur a Sophocle, poeta Atheniensi, in saxum ab Apolline mutata esse. 12. Dux aliquid de stipendio equitum dempsit.

1. *The wisdom of Socrates was the talk* (trans. *was in the mouth*) *of all the Athenians.* 2. *There is no doubt that he will deliberate with you about this matter.* 3. *Why, O foolish man, did you send the Romans under the yoke, (since you were) soon about-to-pay the penalty of (your) deed by death?* 4. *If this comes under your notice* (trans. *eyes*), *do not neglect (it).* 5. *Above the wall let us erect a very high tower, that our men may not be under fire.* 6. *By-this-time two cohorts of our men had come under the fire of the enemy.* 7. *It is said that Daphne was changed* (trans. *Daphne is said to have been changed*) *into a laurel by Apollo.* 8. *How-long did you remain in Italy, and what do you say of* (i.e. *concerning*) *that country?* 9. *The Romans, who subtracted a part from his*

---

[1] Lit. *for us under eyes,* i.e. *under our eyes.* Why is **nōbīs** Dat.? See Par. 7.

kingdom, presented to him, (in return) for this (part), a new province. 10. There is no doubt that the brave centurion Balbus received wound on wound.

### PREPOSITIONS TAKING THE ACCUSATIVE ALONE.

| | | | |
|---|---|---|---|
| Ăd, | to. | Juxtā, | near, hard by, next to. |
| Adversŭs, | towards, against. | | |
| Antĕ, | before. | Ŏb, | in front of (rare), on account of. |
| Ăpŭd, | at, near, among, in the house of, in the presence of, in the pages of. | Pĕnĕs, | in the hands of. |
| | | Pĕr, | through. |
| | | Post, | after.[1] |
| | | Praetĕr, | besides, beyond. |
| Circā, circum, | around. | Prŏpĕ, | near. |
| Circĭtĕr, | about. | Proptĕr, | close to, on account of. |
| Cis & citrā, | on this side of. | | |
| Contrā, | against, contrary to. | Sĕcundum, | following, in accordance with. |
| Ergā, | towards (only of the feelings). | Suprā, | above. |
| | | Trans, | across. |
| Extrā, | outside of. | Ultrā, | on the farther side of. |
| Infrā, | below. | | |
| Intĕr, | between, among. | Versŭs, | towards (in the direction of).[2] |
| Intrā, | inside of, within. | | |

The various meanings of the Prepositions (only a few of which have been given above) must be learned by practice. But some help may be gained by remembering that most Prepositions can be used to denote some THOUGHT, such as that of *cause, obstacle, superiority*, &c., besides denoting relations of PLACE and TIME. Thus ŏb meant originally (1) *in front of*, but it means more commonly (2) *on account of;* pĕr means (1) *through*, of SPACE, but it also means (2) *throughout* or *during*, of TIME, and (3) *through*, of MEANS, or *owing to*, of CAUSE; antĕ means (1) *before*, of TIME, " before

---

[1] Pŏnĕ, an old form of post, is used as an adverb by Virgil, but is rarely used as a Preposition except by ante-classical and post-classical authors.
[2] Versus usually follows the name of the place to which motion is directed: *in the direction of Ambracia*, Ambrăciam versus. Sometimes ad is inserted before the name of the place: ad Ōceănum versus. Versus and adversus have old forms versum and adversum.

"AD" WITH THE GERUNDIVE. [Par. 186—188

daybreak;" (2) *before*, of PLACE, "*before* the gates;" (3) *before*, of ESTIMATION, "He loved Balbus *before*, or *above*, the rest."

### EXERCISE LX.

**186** Ăd, *to* or *towards*, is used to denote *purpose*, with the Acc. of (1) the Gerund, or (2) if the Verb is used *transitively* in English, the Acc. of the *Gerundive Adjective*.

(1) *This will be useful to drink-(ing).*[1]    Hoc ăd bĭbendum ūtĭlĕ ĕrit.

*I am prepared to fight(ing).*    Ăd pugnandum părātus sum.

(2) *This is useful for cultivating the fields*, i.e. *towards the fields being hereafter cultivated.*    Hōc est ăd agros cŏlendos ūtĭlĕ (*not* ăd agros cŏlendum).

1. Postquam ad multam noctem pugnatum est, ad castra uterque exercitus revertit.[2] 2. Qui apud me manserant, ii apud judices rei facti sunt.[3] 3. Apud antiquos (sic apud Ciceronem scriptum est) mos erat ante lucem surgere, negotia ante voluptatem ponere. 4. Post paucos dies videbo te cum manibus tuis post tergum vinctis ad carcerem reductum. 5. Citra Alpes erat Gallia Cisalpina; ultra Alpes, Gallia Transalpina. 6. Phaethon, Phoebi filius, quum per aethera patris sui equos paulisper egisset, de curru dejectus est. 7. Ob oculos mihi mors est; hanc poenam superbiae meae jure do.[4] 8. Hoc contra jus fasque est, trans Euphratem exercitum tuum in pace trajicere.[5] 9. Interfecti sunt hostium supra viginti milia.[6] 10. Hoc est infra tuam dignitatem. 11. Tela haec ad eminus (*adv.*) feriendum sunt utilissima. 12. Vallis ad pugnandum nostro equitatui parum apta erat.[7]

---

**187**   [1] In Old English *to* was followed by a Gerund resembling the form *drinking*, not by an Infinitive.

**188**   [2] Trans. "after the battle *had* gone on," and remember that **postquam** *with the Latin Perfect* (not Pluperfect) represents the English *had*.
   Also distinguish carefully between the Conjunction **postquam,** *when* or *after (that)*, and the Preposition **post.**
   [3] Look out rĕus.
   [4] Why is jūrĕ Abl.? See Par. 182.
   [5] "Trajicere . . . . exercitum" is in Apposition to hōc.
   [6] Hostium is Gen. governed by mīlia. The Nom. to interfecti sunt is hostes *understood*, or some other Masc. Nom. implied from the context.
   [7] Equĭtātui is *Dat. of Advantage*, see Par. 7.

1. *Among the ancients it was the custom to rise before dawn and to dine in the evening* (30). 2. *Why have you led your army across the Euphrates?* 3. *In-the-pages-of Cicero we read many (things) (that are) truly, all (things) tastefully expressed* (i.e. *said*). 4. *When he had been accused in-the-presence-of the judges he was led to prison.* 5. *Bread is useful even for quenching thirst.* 6. *This water is not fit to drink.* 7. *Why do you do these things against the law of-man and of-God?* 8. *It is right to place business before pleasure.* 9. *Have not these things come under your notice* (i.e. *eyes*)? 10. *During* (per) *two nights, in this great* (i.e. *so-great*) *storm, death was before our eyes.*

## Exercise LXI.

**Intĕr se** (expressing all reciprocal relations) means *among themselves; together; with, between,* or *from, one another.*

| | |
|---|---|
| *Cicero's children are very loving among one another.* | Cīcĕrōnis pŭĕri ămant **intĕr se**. |
| *These things do not agree together,* or *disagree from one another.* | Haec **intĕr sē** rĕpugnant, *or* contrāria sunt. |

1. Imperatori, penes quem est imperium, jam adversus Gallos bellum moventi, debes parere. 2. Inter urbem et campum fossa erat, per quam amnis quondam fluxerat. 3. Tullius, quem praeter modum stultissimus quisque laudat (140) neminem praeter sese amat.[1] 4. "Qui per alium facit, facit per se." 5. Per tres annos vitam in insula quadam propter Siciliam egit. 6. Quaedam propter sese expetenda sunt. 7. Hoc inter sese disputant philosophi: sed inter disputationes et facta quantum (*adv.*) interest! 8. Centurio noster, qui hanc ob causam extra teli jactum suos retinebat, cum extra culpam esset (151 *a*), non punitus est. 9. Quando hanc tantam eius benevolentiam erga te agnosces? 10. Nonne quaerendum est nobis quomodo hae sententiae inter sese contrariae sint? 11. Via una praeter fluminis ripam erat; altera inter duos altissimos montes; tertia per silvam ad urbem ducebat.

1. *He who loves no one besides himself is himself loved by no one* (92). 2. *Virtue is to-be-sought on-account-of itself.*[2] 3. *How*

---

[1] Which is the Principal Verb? The Antecedent of **quem**? The subject of **laudat**? See *Hints on Construing*, Appendix III., p. 216.

[2] *To-be-sought*, i.e. *meet-to-be-sought.*

*great a-difference-is* (there) *between hopes and deeds!* 4. *The general took-care to keep his soldiers out of shot.* 5. *One road* (led) *beside the walls of the city, the other* (86) *led through a small wood, across a stream.* 6. *The judgment is in your hands : When* (156) *will you judge ?* 7. *Why do you beyond measure praise the foolish* (126) *Tullius ?* 8. *Labienus will hasten in-the-direction of the Rhine.* 9. *When will you send our cavalry against the enemy, who are now fighting amongst one another ?* 10. *I ask you, my friends, how virtue and vice are contrary* (161) *to one another.* 11. *For this cause we prepared an ambush in a wood, which was near* (prŏpĕ) *the town.*

### VERBS COMPOUNDED WITH PREPOSITIONS.

**190** FORMATION.—(1) The Present Tenses of Verbs compounded of a Preposition and a Verb usually change **a** or **e** of the Verb into **i**: thus, from **făcĭo** we have **dēfĭcĭo sufficĭo**, (*i.e.* sub-fĭcĭo), **confĭcĭo**, (*i.e.* cum-fĭcĭo), &c., and from **lĕgo** we have **dēlĭgo, collĭgo**, (*i.e.* con-lĭgo or cum-lĭgo), &c.[1] But the perfects remain unchanged: **dē-fēci, suf-fēci, de-lēgi, collēgi**, &c.[2]

**191** (2) The Verb **prōd-est**, *it is profitable*, retains **d** before all forms of **sum** beginning with a vowel, but drops it before all beginning with a consonant.

Prōd-est;   prōd-ĕrat;   prōd-ĕrit;   prōd-esse.
Prō-sum;   prō-fuit;   prō-fuĕrat;   prō-fuĕrit.

**192** CONSTRUCTION.—Verbs compounded with Prepositions mostly either (1) take a Dative of the Indirect Object, or, (2) they repeat the Preposition with the Case proper to the Preposition.

(1) *He took a ring from me.*    Ānŭlum **mĭhi dētraxit**.

(2) *He took a ring from my finger.*    Ānŭlum **dē dĭgĭto** mĕo **dētraxit**.

---

[1] But there are exceptions: *e.g.* **intellĕgo** (not intellĭgo) is the correct form.

**193** [2] Three compounds of -**lĕgo** make the Perf. in -**lexi**, (1) **dīlĭgo,** *love;* (2) **neglĕgo,** *neglect;* (3) **intellĕgo,** *understand.*

The Compounds of **sum**, e.g. ădest, ĭnest, intĕrest, &c., all take a Dative:

*Help me, Jupiter!*      Adĕs **mĭhi**, Juppĭter.

Note the following use of **ăbest**:

*I am, or shall be, within a very little of falling,* lit. *very little is absent by-which-not* (145a) *I fall.*
     Mĭnĭmum **ăbest**, *or* **ăbĕrit**, quīn cădam.

*I was within a very little of falling.*
     Mĭnĭmum **āfuit** (*not* **abfuit**) quīn cădĕrem.

Exercise LXII.

1. Non prodest tibi flere. 2. Non dubium est quin tributum victis impositum sit (9a). 3. Nostri urbi murum circumdederunt. 4. Cur non ei gladium eripuisti? 5. Alexander ipse his proeliis interfuit. 6. Minimum afuit quin urbs ab hostibus caperetur. 7. Romani Armeniam stultissimo illi regi detrahent. 8. Interrogabo cur huic tam forti equiti equum detraxerit (9a). 9. Non dubium erat quin frumentum civibus deesset. 10. Hoc (*Nom.*) cum militibus nostris summum terrorem injecisset, imperator Tullium decimae legioni praefecit. 11. Ob hanc causam frumentum exercitui defuturum erat. 12. Tu, qui me isti hodie postponis, cras antepones. 13. Oro te ne tales condiciones victae genti imponas.

1. *There was no doubt that the enemy had surrounded their camp with a ditch* (i.e. *set-round the camp a ditch*). 2. *The camp was within a very little of being taken by the enemy.* 3. *I asked the leader how-much* (*of*) *tribute* (71) *he was about-to-impose-on the conquered city.* 4. *That old soldier has taken-part-in twenty-two battles.* 5. *You are within a little of committing a very-great wickedness.* 6. *Why did you snatch-from me the last hope I had* (trans. *the hope which I had last,* '*last* to agree with '*which*')? 7. *These words of the general displeased the king: who withdrew from him a large part of the army.* 8. *I will ask him why he imposed-on us these hard* (trans. *these so hard*) *conditions.* 9. *By-this-time all hope was gone* (i.e. *was absent*) *from us.* 10. *Conquered* (pass. part. agrees with '*Balbus*') *by this great calamity, Balbus was within a very little of surrendering the city.*

## THE ABLATIVE ABSOLUTE.

**196** There is no regular Perfect Participle *Active* in Latin, so as to express the English *having killed*. Latin has therefore to use the *Passive* Participle in the Ablative, thus:

*The barbarians, the citizens having been killed (by them) set the city on fire* i.e. *the barbarians, having killed the citizens, set the city on fire.*

Barbări, **cīvĭbus interfectis**, urbem incendērunt.

The Noun and Participle thus expressing *some circumstance in connection with the principal Verb*, are put in the Ablative (which is the ordinary Case to express *manner* and *circumstance*, as well as *instrument*, see Par. 181); and this Ablative is called the Ablative Absolute.

The Ablative Absolute cannot always be rendered by the English Active, *e.g.*

*The citizens having been slain, the city was set on fire.*

**Cīvĭbus interfectis**, urbs incensa est.

### Exercise LXIII.

1. Caesar, Rheno trajecto, constituit in Galliam se recipere.[1]
2. Hostes, castris relictis, in suos fines subito se receperunt.
3. Brutus, filiis suis a se ipso interfectis, culpam non effugit.
4. Hieme barbari, missis legatis, pacem ab imperatore petiverunt.
5. Imperator, direpto a barbaris templo, statuit urbem eorum incendere.
6. Iis auditis nostri clamorem tollunt, et trajecto amne impetum in hostem faciunt.
7. Tarquinio ex urbe expulso, consules imperium susceperunt.
8. Imperator, re feliciter gesta, tributum victae genti imposuerat.
9. Exposito exercitu Caesar equitatum ante se mittit.
10. Non dubium est quin, cognito hostium adventu, terror ingens nostros invasurus sit.

---

[1] In this exercise the Ablative Absolute should be translated in two ways, 1st, literally, *the Rhine having been crossed (by him)*, and 2nd, according to the English idiom, *having crossed the Rhine* or *when he had crossed the Rhine*. In subsequent Exercises the second or true English translation may suffice.

## ABLATIVE ABSOLUTE.

1. *The enemy having made a charge* (i.e. *a charge having been made by the enemy*), *our men for-a-short-time retreated.*
2. *Having disembarked (his) cavalry, Caesar gave-orders-to (his) foot-soldiers to leap down into the water,* i.e. *the cavalry having been disembarked, Caesar gave, &c.*
3. *There is no doubt that our leader, having ascertained the number of the enemy, will quickly retire.*
4. *Having carried on the war most-prosperously, the general was praised by all (his) countrymen.*
5. *The city having been plundered, the citizens determined to declare war against the barbarians.*
6. *After slaying the three hundred hostages* (i.e. *the three hundred hostages having been slain*) *the barbarians had no hope of peace.*
7. *The general, having imposed this heavy tribute* (trans. *this so-great tribute having been imposed*) *on the conquered nation, restored to them the cities he had taken.*[1]
8. *Codrus, king* (123) *of the Athenians, having been slain, those who were besieging Athens retired in-haste* (181).

### ABLATIVE ABSOLUTE (*continued*).

The Ablative Absolute is also used (1) with Active Present Participles, and (2) with a few Nouns or Adjectives.

(1) *When the sun sets,* lit. *the sun setting, lions leave their caves.*   **Sōle occĭdente,** leōnes antra linquunt (p. 207).

(2) *While Tullius was king,* lit. *Tullius being king.*   **Tulliō rēge.**
*While I am alive,* i.e. *I being alive.*   **Mē vīvo** (adj.).
*In my judgment,* i.e. *while I am judge.*   **Mē jūdĭce.**

N.B.—When the Noun with which the Participle agrees can be made the *Subject or Object* of a Verb, *the Ablative Absolute must not be used.* Thus, *While the general was leading on his men, he was transfixed by an arrow*, must not be rendered "Impĕrātōre mīlĭtes dūcente (ĭs) săgittā transfixus est," but "Impĕrātor, mīlĭtes dūcens, săgittā transfixus est," or else "Impĕrātōrem, mīlĭtes dūcentem, săgittā transfixit."

---

[1] Note that the Relative, when omitted in English, must be inserted in Latin: *the cities (which) he had taken.*

| | |
|---|---|
| *Dionysius having been banished, (he) taught boys.*[1] | **Dĭŏnȳsius**, ex urbe **pulsus**, pŭĕros docebat (*not*, **Dĭŏnȳsĭo pulso**.) |
| *Having at last found the boy, Tullius sent him back to his (the boy's) friends.* | **Pŭĕrum** tandem rĕpertum Tullius ad ămīcos eius rĕmīsit (*not*, **Pŭĕro** rĕperto ... T. **eum** remīsit.) |

### Exercise LXIV.

1  Hostes, me duce, facillime vincetis.  2. Trecentos obsidum, quos in armis cepimus, vinctos statim interfecimus.  3. Filia, matre nequiquam misericordiam implorante, jugulata est.  4. Mulier, nequiquam misericordiam implorans, coram rege jugulata est.  5. Tullius, reclamante optimo quoque civium, in exilium pulsus est.  6. Trajecto fluvio, Suevorum fines intrabimus; a quibus, me judice, nobis acerrime resistetur (167).  7. Gaio haec dicente, omnes tacebant; itaque Tullius, nullo reclamante, ab exilio revocatus est.  8. Caesare et Bibulo consulibus, hoc templum prope viam Latinam aedificatum est.  9. Non igitur dubium est quin Alpibus trajectis Hannibal in Italiam descensurus sit.  10. Itaque, his compertis, consentientibus civibus, magistratus omnia ad resistendum (186) paraverunt.

1. *By your own judgment* (i.e. *you yourself being judge*) *your brother has conducted this war unsuccessfully.*  2. *The barbarians, having immediately slain the hostages, determined to stir up a war against us.*  3. *The daughter was led before the king, while the mother in vain protested* (i.e. *the mother in vain protesting*).  4. *The general having been pierced with an arrow, the enemy determined to deliver him to us* (198).  5. *The bridge having been broken-down, we determined to withdraw from Germany into Gaul.*  6. *During-the-reign-of Tarquin, great buildings were erected in the city.*  7. *There is no doubt that our general, having ascertained the arrival of the enemy, will immediately retire.*  8. *The excellent Tullius* (126) *was recalled to his country, on the fourth day, no one* (92) *protesting (against it).*

---

[1] The *he* is very often (though incorrectly) inserted even in modern English; but it must be omitted in Latin.

## Exercise LXIV.*

(*Recapitulatory.*)

1. In eo eramus ut vinceremur. 2. Curate ne ab hostibus opprimamini. 3. Si urbem ipsi incenderitis, nemo vestrum servabitur. 4. Murus et arx ab equitibus capta sunt. 5. Et ego et tu ab optimo quoque civium laudati sumus. 6. Urbem captam Balbus, dux crudelissimus, incenderat. 7. Ne tu injustos, Tulli optime, laudaveris. 8. Quod scelus commisit? Quid morte dignum fecit? 9. Num tu, puer jam duodecim annos (31), natus octo vel novem horas dormis? 10. Interrogastine num in oppido mulier mansura sit? 11. Balbum, plura fortasse dicturum, hastae equitum transfixerunt. 12. Quid huic arbori, fructum jam praebiturae, tantum (*adv.*) nocuit? 13. Huius tantae calamitatis vel memoria nobis semper erit ingratissima. 14. Interrogate quando ventura sit (32)? num in animo habeat biduum in oppido manere? 15. De Tullio valde dubito num vitio potius quam virtuti obtemperaturus sit. 16. Balbus, homo parum (*adv.*) contentus, aliena laudat, sua semper culpat. 17. Cur tibi, nostri immemori, tot dona damus? 18. Ab optimo quoque civium responsum est. 19. Nobis (192) pro patria pugnantibus homo ignavissimus ob ignaviam suam spem ultimam eripuit. 20. Minimum afuit quin urbi fossam circumdaremus. 21. Non est dubium quin Balbus decimae legioni praefectus fuerit.

## DEPONENT VERBS.

A few Verbs (called Deponent) have a Past Participle with Active meaning. These Verbs, though having an *Active meaning*, yet have a *Passive form* in all the Tenses and in the Past Participle, as **hortor**, *I exhort*, **hortābor**, *I will exhort*, **hortātus**, *having exhorted*.

Besides the Passive forms, every Deponent Verb has also the Active forms of the *Participles, Supines, and Gerunds:* **hortans, hortaturus**, *exhorting, about to exhort, &c.*

The Deponent Gerundive, *e.g.* **hortandus**, *meet to be exhorted*, is used like the Gerundive of an ordinary Verb.[1]

---

[1] The Past Participles of a few Deponent Verbs are sometimes used Passively, as, **ădeptŭs**, *having been obtained*, from **ădĭpiscor**.

# DEPONENT VERBS. [Par. 201

## DEPONENT

I. Hortŏr, hortātŭs sum, hortārī, *exhort*, like ămŏr.
II. Věreŏr, věrĭtŭs sum, věrērī, *fear*, like mŏneŏr.

| | | I. | | | II. | |
|---|---|---|---|---|---|---|
| **Indicative Mood.** | *Present.* | Hort-ŏr, | *I exhort, or am exhorting.* | Věr-eŏr, | *I fear, or am fearing.* |
| | | Hort-ārĭs (ārĕ), &c. | *thou exhortest.* &c. | Věr-ērĭs (ērĕ), &c. | *thou fearest.* &c. |
| | *Future Simple.* | Hort-ābŏr, | *I shall exhort.* | Věr-ēbŏr, | *I shall fear.* |
| | *Imperfect.* | Hort-ābăr, | *I was exhorting.* | Věr-ēbăr, | *I was fearing.* |
| | *Perfect.* | Hort-ātŭs sum, | *I have exhorted, or I exhorted.* | Věr-ĭtŭs sum, | *I have feared, or I feared.* |
| | *Fut. Perfect.* | Hort-ātŭs ěro, | *I shall have exhorted.* | Věr-ĭtŭs ěro, | *I shall have feared.* |
| | *Pluperfect.* | Hort-ātŭs ěram, | *I had exhorted.* | Věr-ĭtŭs ěram, | *I had feared.* |
| **Subjunctive Mood.** | *Present.* | Hort-ér, | *I may exhort.* | Věr-eăr, | *I may fear.* |
| | *Imperfect.* | Hort-ārĕr, | *I might exhort.* | Věr-ērĕr, | *I might fear.* |
| | *Perfect.* | Hort-ātŭs sim, | *I may have exhorted.* | Věr-ĭtŭs sim, | *I may have feared.* |
| | *Pluperfect.* | Hort-ātŭs essem | *I should have exhorted.* | Věr-ĭtŭs essem, | *I should have feared,* |
| **Imperative.** | *Present.* | Hort-ārĕ, | *Exhort thou.* | Věr-ērĕ, | *Fear thou.* |
| | *Future.* | Hort-ātŏr, | *thou shalt, or must exhort.* | Věr-ētŏr, | *thou shalt, or must fear.* |
| **Infinitive.** | *Pres. & Imperf.* | Hort-ārī, | *to exhort.* | Věr-ērī, | *to fear.* |
| | *Perf. & Plup.* | Hort-ātŭs esse, | *to have exhorted.* | Věr-ĭtŭs esse, | *to have feared.* |
| | *Future.* | Hort-ātūrus esse, | *to be about to exhort.* | Věr-ĭtūrus esse, | *to be about to fear.* |
| **Participles.** | *Present.* | Hort-ans, | *exhorting.* | Věr-ens, | *fearing.* |
| | *Future.* | Hort-ātūrus, | *about to exhort.* | Věr-ĭtūrŭs, | *about to fear.* |
| | *Perfect.* | Hort-ātŭs, | *having exhorted.* | Věr-ĭtŭs, | *having feared.* |
| | *Gerundive.* | Hort-andŭs | *meet to be exhorted.* | Věr-endŭs, | *meet to be feared.* |
| **Supines.** | | Hort-ātum, | *to exhort.* | Věr-ĭtum, | *to fear.* |
| | | Hort-ātū, | *to be exhorted.* | Věr-ĭtu, | *to be feared.* |
| **Gerund.** | | Hort-andi, &c. | *of exhorting.* &c. | Věr-endi, &c. | *of fearing.* &c. |

## VERBS.

III. Lŏquŏr, lŏcūtŭs sum, lŏquī, *speak*, like rĕgŏr.
IV. Partiŏr, partītŭs sum, partīrī, *divide*, like audiō.

### III.

**Indicative Mood.**

| | | |
|---|---|---|
| *Present.* | Lŏqu-ŏr, | { *I speak, or am speaking.* |
| | Lŏqu-ĕrĭs (ĕrĕ), &c. | } *thou speakest.* &c. |
| *Fut. Simple.* | Lŏqu-ăr, | *I shall speak.* |
| *Imperfect.* | Lŏqu-ēbăr, | *I was speaking.* |
| *Perfect.* | Lŏcū-tŭs sum, | } *I have spoken, or I spoke.* |
| *Fut. Perfect.* | Lŏcū-tŭs ĕro, | } *I shall have spoken* |
| *Pluperfect.* | Lŏcū-tŭs ĕram, | } *I had spoken.* |

**Subjunctive Mood.**

| | | |
|---|---|---|
| *Present.* | Lŏqu-ăr, | *I may speak.* |
| *Imperfect.* | Lŏqu-ĕrĕr, | *I might speak.* |
| *Perfect.* | Lŏcū-tŭs sim, | } *I may have spoken.* |
| *Pluperfect.* | Lŏcū-tŭs essem, | } *I should have spoken.* |

**Imperative.**

| | | |
|---|---|---|
| *Present.* | Lŏqu-ĕrĕ, | *speak thou.* |
| *Future.* | Lŏqu-ĭtŏr, | { *thou shalt, or must speak.* |

**Infinitive.**

| | | |
|---|---|---|
| *Pres. & Imp.* | Lŏqu-ī, | *to speak.* |
| *Perf. & Plup.* | Lŏcū-tŭs essĕ, | } *to have spoken.* |
| *Future.* | Lŏcū-tŭrŭs essĕ, | } *to be about to speak.* |

**Participles.**

| | | |
|---|---|---|
| *Present.* | Lŏqu-ens, | *speaking.* |
| *Future.* | Lŏcu-tūrŭs, | *about to speak.* |
| *Perfect.* | Lŏcu-tŭs, | *having spoken.* |
| *Gerundive.* | Lŏqu-endŭs | *meet to be spoken* |

| | | |
|---|---|---|
| Supines. | Lŏcu-tum, | *to speak.* |
| | Lŏcu-tū, | *to be spoken.* |
| Gerund. | Lŏqu-endi, &c. | *of speaking.* &c. |

### IV.

**Indicative Mood.**

| | | |
|---|---|---|
| *Present.* | Part-iŏr, | { *I divide, or am dividing.* |
| | Part-īrĭs (īrĕ), &c. | } *thou dividest.* &c. |
| | Part-iăr, | *I shall divide.* |
| | Part-iēbăr, | *I was dividing.* |
| | Part-ītŭs sum, | } *I have divided, or I divided.* |
| | Part-ītŭs ĕro. | } *I shall have divided.* |
| | Part-ītŭs ĕram, | } *I had divided.* |

**Subjunctive Mood.**

| | | |
|---|---|---|
| | Part-iăr, | *I may divide.* |
| | Part-irĕr, | *I might divide.* |
| | Part-ītŭs sim, | } *I may have divided.* |
| | Part-ītŭs essem, | } *I should have divided.* |

**Imperative.**

| | | |
|---|---|---|
| | Part-īrĕ, | *Divide thou.* |
| | Part-ītŏr, | { *thou shalt, or must divide.* |

**Infinitive.**

| | | |
|---|---|---|
| | Part-īrī, | *to divide.* |
| | Part-ītŭs essĕ, | } *to have divided.* |
| | Part-ītūrŭs essĕ, | } *to be about to divide.* |

**Participles.**

| | | |
|---|---|---|
| | Part-iens, | *dividing.* |
| | Part-itūrŭs, | *about to divide.* |
| | Part-ītŭs, | *having divided.* |
| | Part-iendŭs, | *meet to be divided* |

| | | |
|---|---|---|
| | Part-ītum, | *to divide.* |
| | Part-ītū, | *to be divided.* |
| | Part-iendi, &c. | *of dividing.* &c. |

## Exercise LXV.

**202** The Participle can be used (like the Adjective, Par. 34) to agree with *men* understood : **victis parcĕ**, *spare the conquered ;* **fŭgĭentes** sĕquĕre, *follow those-who-are fleeing.*[1]

1. Non dubium est quin regina filias suas hortata sit (9*a*). 2. Ne mentitus sis, mi fili. 3. Interrogabam puerum cur asini vocem imitaretur. 4. Pygmalion, diu imaginem contemplatus, tandem eam spirantem mirabatur. 5. Conatus parva, homo ignavissimus minora perficiebat. 6. Non dubium est quin miranda perfecturus sis, nisi tyranni exemplum imitaberis. 7. Hortandus est tibi frater ne pessimi istius amici exemplum imitetur.[2] 8. Deos veneramini, imitamini parentes. 9. Diu dolum meditatus tandem servis suis imperavit ut armati gladiis Tullium nocte sequerentur. 10. O divinam illam vitam voluptatem (202) aspernantium, sequentium virtutem![3]

1. *Virtue is to be followed for its own sake* (i.e. *on account of itself*). 2. *Having imitated the bad from (his) boyhood, the boy made himself very like* (66) *the bad.* 3. *The life of those-who-follow* (trans. *those-following*) *virtue is most happy.* 4. *Attempt great things, that you may at-least accomplish small things.* 5. *Having long contemplated the stars, the philosopher did not see the well at* (ad) *his feet.* 6. *Why, O ye traitors, do ye meditate plots? How-often shall I entreat you not to* (143) *lie-in-wait-for the consul?* 7. *In-vain do you venerate the gods, most deceitful of men, (while) meditating snares for the innocent* (7). 8. *Ah! the happy life of those-who-scorn wealth and do not* (18) *suffer poverty.*

**203**   RULE.—**Oblīviscor, rĕmĭniscor, rĕcordor, mĭsĕreor,** commonly govern the Genitive.[4]

---

[1] Note that "iis victis" would mean "them, *since* they are conquered," and "eos fugientes," "them, *while*, or *since*, they are fleeing;" and generally a Latin Participle, *in agreement with a Noun or Pronoun*, may be rendered by an English Conjunction (154*a*).

[2] When an ordinary and a Pronominal Adjective both agree with the same Noun the Pronominal Adjective generally comes between the ordinary Adjective and the Noun: *That distinguished man,* clārissimus illĕ vir.

[3] The Accusative is commonly used with O in *exclamation* (not in *address*), and may be called the *Exclamatory Accusative.*

[4] These Verbs were once reflexive, *I forget-myself, remember-myself, pity-myself of,* &c. Compare the French "se plaindre," *to pity,* and in Old English, *I remember myself of.*

Distinguish between (1) **mĭsĕror, -āri,** *I shew-pity-to,* which governs an Acc., and (2) **mĭsĕreor, -ēri,** *I feel-pity-for,* which governs a Genitive.

**207** Rule.—**Fungor, fruor, ūtor, vescor, pŏtior,** govern the Ablative.[1]

### Exercise LXVI.

1. Non dubium est quin mulier oratione liberrima usa sit (9a). 2. Interrogabam barbaros num pane vescerentur, nonne ferarum pellibus pro vestitu uterentur. 3. Miserere Balbi, viri justissimi, quem nemo adhuc miseratus est. 4. Recordare uxoris tuae; ne liberorum oblitus sis, in te uno spem ponentium. 5. Vastandi sunt agri gentis illius crudelissimae quae nihil veneratur, nullius miseretur. 6. Regno potitus, promissorum statim oblitus est. 7. Qui magistratibus functi erant, eos, capta urbe summo honore affecimus. 8. Dum vita fruimini, nolite (169) virtutis oblivisci. 9. Sagacitate canum ad nostram utilitatem utimur. 10. Cur nullius ipse miseritus, nostra misericordia frui cupis?

1. *To remember past evils is sometimes pleasant.* 2. *There is no doubt that very-many enjoy the memory of past evils.* 3. *You should eat* (i.e. *it-is-to-be-eaten*) *that you may live; you should not live that you may eat.* 4. *Let us use the opportunity which the enemy have afforded us.* 5. *If you do not* (i.e. *unless you shall*) *show pity to the conquered, beware lest you yourselves suffer the same fate* [trans. *same* (*things*).] 6. *Having suffered adversity, the woman will peculiarly* [i.e. *before* (ante) *others*] *enjoy prosperity.* 7. *I will ask whether he discharges his duty well or* (171) *ill.* 8. *Do not forget,* (as) *an old-man, those precepts which you learned* (as) *a boy.*[2]

### Exercise LXVII.

1. Nisi res adversas experiemur patientiam non discemus. 2. Loquere pauca, multa disce. 3. Parentes et verendi et amandi sunt. 4. Plurima pollicentibus ne tu credideris.[3] 5. Forte leo et asinus et vulpes, partituri praedam, de partibus sortiebantur.[4] 6. Dux noster, cives captae urbis clementer allocutus, pavorem omnium minuit. 7. Nocte proficiscamur ne hostis nos videat. 8. Nonne scelus fatemini? Fatendum est, si poenam effugere cupitis. 9. Quid tibi videtur? Qui pro

---

[1] These Verbs were also once reflexive, *e.g.* **fruor,** *I enjoy myself with;* **vescor,** *I feed myself with;* **ūtor,** *I employ myself with.*

[2] *Old-man* is in *Apposition* with *you* the Subject of *forget.*

[3] **Pollicentibus** is *not* Abl.; see Par. 202.

[4] **Vulpēs** is feminine; why therefore is **partitūri** masc.; See Par. 161.
N.B. Latin inserts **et** *between each pair of a list of Nouns or omits* **et** *between each; English inserts it only before the last*
*The lion, the ass, and the fox.*   Lĕo, (et) ăsĭnus, (et) vulpēs.

patria moritur nonne is laude dignus est?[1] 10. Cohorti jam ex urbe proficiscenti sex aquilae, omen optimum,[2] visae sunt (*appeared*). 11. Non dubium erat quin mulier fame et siti mortua esset. 12. Adepti libertatem, nonne contenti eritis nisi et (146) imperium adipiscemini?

1. *Did not pain seem the greatest of evils* (73) *to the disciples of Epicurus?* 2. *Take care to obtain liberty.* 3. *Having confessed this, do you dare to remain in the city?* 4. *The general made every preparation* (i.e. *prepared all things*) *that he might set-out on the next day.* 5. *The woman was within a very little* (194) *of dying of* (Lat. Abl.) *hunger and thirst.* 6. *When-they-had-conversed* (154a) *together* (189) *they determined to set-out at night.* 7. *Do not draw-lots about the booty, O soldiers, since-you-are* (i.e. *being*) *about-to-obtain a greater booty by fighting.* 8. *Trust one-who-has-experienced* (202) (*it*): *he-who promises much* (i.e. *many things*) *performs little* (i.e. *few things*). 9. *I asked the rich Balbus when* (156) *he was going to enjoy* (i.e. *was about-to-enjoy*) *the riches which he had* (subjunctive) *obtained.* 10. *What prevented you from confessing the truth* (i.e. *true things*)?

### THE ACCUSATIVE AND INFINITIVE (ACTIVE).

**208** 1. OBJECT-CLAUSES.—When a Principal Sentence, *e.g. he is mistaken*, becomes the Object of a Verb, *e.g. believe, declare, &c.*, there are two ways of expressing the change in English *but only one in Latin, viz., the Accusative and Infinitive:*

*I declare* (1) *that he is mistaken.*  Dīco **ĕum errāre.**
*I declare* (2) *him to be mistaken.*

Here **errāre** is "the Infinitive depending on **dīco**"; and **ĕum** is "the Subject of the Infinitive **errāre**," (*i.e.* **ĕum** is so related to **errāre** that, *if* **errāre** were in the Indicative, **ĕum**, or rather **ĭs**, *would be* its Subject or Nominative).

**209** 2. SUBJECT-CLAUSES.—The same construction, viz., Accusative and Infinitive, is used in Subject-Clauses: *That-he-is-in-error, is certain*, (or, *It is certain that he is in error*),

---

[1] What is the antecedent (Par. 107) of **qui**?
[2] The punctuation shews that **ōmen** is not Nom. after **sunt**: what Case is it then (123)?

Certum est **ēum errāre**; *That I should go into exile pleased them*, (or, *It pleased them that I should go into exile*), Plăcŭit eis **mē** In exsĭlium **īre**.

**210** THE TENSE IN SUBJECT AND OBJECT-CLAUSES.—After a Past Tense of the Principal Verb, the Tense of the English Indicative e.g. *is* (208, 1) is changed, but the Tense of the English Infinitive e.g. *to be* (208, 2) *remains unchanged*: and the Latin Infinitive also *remains unchanged*: *I declared* (1) *that he* WAS *mistaken; I declared* (2) *him* TO BE *mistaken*: dixi **ēum errāre**.[1]

**211**

| OBJECT-CLAUSE. | PRINCIPAL SENTENCE. | |
|---|---|---|
| *Tullius said that* | *Tullius said,* | Tullius dixit |
| (1) | (1) | (1) |
| (a) *he conquered* | "*I conquer*" | sē **vincĕre** |
| (b) *he was conquering* | "*I am conquering*" | |
| (2) | (2) | (2) |
| { *he conquered,* *had conquered,* or, *had been conquering* | "*I conquered*" "*I was conquering*" "*I had conquered*" "*I had been conquering*" "*I have conquered*" | sē **vīcisse** |
| (3) | (3) | (3) |
| *he should conquer* *he was about to conquer* | "*I shall conquer*" "*I am about to conquer*" | sē **victūrum esse**[2] |

### EXERCISE LXVII, A.

1. Tullia dicit se tibi haec pollicenti creditūram esse.[3]  2. Clamaverunt obsides se meliore fato dignos esse.  3. Responderunt virgines nunquam se tantae virtutis oblituras esse.  4. Negavit magister discipulos corpora satis exercuisse.  5. Placetne tibi tot cives uni tyranno parere?  6. Respondit puer se nescire quot sorores haberet.  7. Fatendum est te promisisse multa, pauca perficere.  8. Scribunt mihi se duos menses in Italia mansisse, jam in Graeciam profecturos esse.

---

[1] Dixi **ēum errāvisse** would have meant, *I declared him to have been*, or *that he had been, mistaken*.

[2] In accordance with Par. 24, **esse** takes the same case after it as before it; and therefore, since **sē** is the Accusative, **victūrum** is also Accusative.

[3] Hitherto **sē** has been used only for *himself, themselves*, &c.: but in Object-Clauses it must often be rendered by *he, they*, &c.

(Write out the Subject and Object-Clauses in the above Exercise as Principal Sentences: 1. Ego tibi... credam. 2. Meliore fato digni sumus, &c.; see 218*a*).

1. *It is certain that no dangers will terrify him.* 2. *He said that he feared* (210) *these dangers.*[1] 3. *The boy writes that he had always exercised* (his) *body.* 4. *My sister says that she will not depart from the city.* 5. *Have you heard that the barbarians set the city on fire?* 6. *Do not* (169) *say that you did this.* 7. *He said that he should bind the captives.* 8. *He did-not-know that they had escaped in the night.*

## THE ACCUSATIVE AND INFINITIVE (PASSIVE).

**212** As the Latin Passive has no Future Infinitive (except the Supine **īrī**, (248)), the Latin employs a periphrasis:

*Tullius said that he should be conquered.*    Tullius dixit **fŏre,** *or* **fŭtūrum esse, ut vincerētur,** i.e. *that it would come to pass that he would be conquered.*

**213**

| Object-Clause. | Principal Sentence. | Tullius dixit |
|---|---|---|
| (1) *he was being conquered* | (1) "*I am being conquered*" | (1) **sē vinci** |
| (2) (*a*) (*b*) *he was conquered* (*c*) (*d*) *he had been conquered* | (2) (*a*) "*I am conquered*"[3] (*b*) "*I was conquered*" (*c*) "*I had been conquered*" (*d*) "*I have been conquered*" | (2) (*a*)(*b*) **sē victum esse**[2] (*c*)(*d*) **sē victum fuisse**[2] |
| (3) *he should be conquered he was about to be conquered* | (3) "*I shall be conquered*" "*I am about to be conquered*" | (3) **fŏre,** *or* **fŭtūrum esse ut vincerētur** |

[1] Wherever *he, she,* &c., in a Subordinate Clause, stand for some Noun or Pronoun which is the Nominative to the Principal Verb, they must be rendered by **sē**.

**214** [2] The **esse** or **fŭisse** is sometimes omitted (as also in the Active Inf.): and care is then required to distinguish the Inf. from the Participle.

**215** Some Compound Tenses are occasionally supplied in Latin by the phrase "in eo sum ut" (Par. 166). *Tullius said that he was* or *had been (on the point of) being conquered,* Tullius dixit se **in eo esse,** *or* **fuisse, ut vincĕrētur.**

**216** [3] "I am *loved*" would imply that the action continued, and would be rendered "**sē ămāri;**" but "I am *conquered*" implies that the *action* is

**Par. 217—218a**] IN SUBJECT AND OBJECT CLAUSES. 123

N.B.—The Tense of the Latin Infinitive in the *third* column above, is the same as that of the English Verb in the *second* column, where it is used *as a Principal Verb.*

**217** RULE.—*The Latin Inf. in a Subject or Object-Clause is of the same Tense as the English Verb would be, if it were made a Principal Verb in the words of the speaker.*

EXERCISE LXVIII.

**218** RULE.—Use sē, suus, &c. (not ĕum, eius, &c.) when the Pronoun (in a Subordinate Clause, see page 328) stands for the Subject of the Principal Verb:

*Tullius said that he* (i.e. *Tullius*)   Tullius dixit sē errāre.
*was mistaken.*

*I said that he was mistaken.*   Dixi ĕum errāre.

1. Quis nescit solem luna majorem esse? 2. Dixit se in animo habere ad patriam reverti. 3. Dixit se in animo habuisse ex Italia proficisci; sed tempestatem obstitisse. 4. Mulieres clamaverunt nunquam se ad oppidum libenter reversuras esse. 5. Balbum certiorem fecimus nos ad Italiam venisse. ibi paulisper manere, inde ad Graeciam venturos (214). 6. Tullius clamavit quondam se sontem fuisse, nunc vero venia dignum esse. 7. Interrogavi num captivos vinxisset: respondit nondum se vinxisse, cras autem vincturum esse. 8. Certum erat urbem ab ipsis civibus incensam esse. 9. Compertum erat hostium (91) trecentos prope a castris nostris abesse. 10. Certum est nunquam fore ut urbs a te capiatur. 11. Negavere hostes futurum esse ut nobis urbem intrantibus resisteretur (167). 12. Respondimus legatos a nobis quoque ad hostem mitti.[1]

---

*past*, and only the *result* is *present*. The pupil must carefully distinguish between *the two meanings of the ambiguous English Passive*, e.g. (1) "the house *is burned*, incensa est;" (2) "the house is *guarded*," custōdītur.

218a  [1] The pupil (before proceeding to the English-Latin Exercise) should write out the Subject and Object Clauses in the Latin Exercise, as Principal Sentences, and in the words of the speakers. Thus, (1) sol lunā major est. (2) Ego in animo habeo, &c. (3) Ego in animo habui (*or* habueram) ex Italia, &c. (4) Nunquam nos revertemur, &c.

In the English-Latin Exercise, (before being turned into Latin) the Subject and Object Clauses may be similarly turned into Principal Sentences. (1) *Four hundred of the enemy are hastening*, &c. (2) *Some of the citizens say one thing, others another.* (3) *I had purposed to set out for Greece, but now I purpose*, &c. Then use the Rule in Par. 217.

1. It had been ascertained that four hundred of the enemy were hastening to the city. 2. He answered that some (86) of the citizens said one thing, others another. 3. He said that he had formerly purposed to set-out for (i.e. to) Greece, but (139a) that now he purposed to remain in Italy. 4. It is certain that the women will never remain in Greece. 5. Who does-not-know that Italy is larger than Sicily? 6. We did-not-know that the hostages had been immediately bound. 7. I informed his brother that we had the horse, and that we should sell it to-morrow. 8. It was ascertained by our spies that three thousand of the enemy had set-out from the camp by night. 9. They said that we (212) should be conquered by the Scythians. 10. Who does-not-know that Tarquin was sent into exile by Brutus? 11. I for-my-part (139) still hope; but Tullius says that the river will be crossed before the third day. 12. When will you confess that you (168) (164) alone (96) must pay the penalty of this folly?

## IMPERSONAL VERBS.

**219** 1. Impersonal Verbs denoting *feeling* require the Accusative of the Person and the Genitive of the Cause [1]:

| | | | |
|---|---|---|---|
| Mĭsĕret | | | pity |
| Pĭget | | | am vexed at |
| Poenĭtet | me tuae stultītiae. | I | repent of | your folly. |
| Pŭdet | | | am ashamed of |
| Taedet | | | am weary of |

**220** 2. Others require an Accusative of the Person, and an Infinitive, or Nominative, for the Subject:

| | | | | |
|---|---|---|---|---|
| Dĕcet | mē | dīlĭgentia. | Industry | becomes |
| Dēdĕcet | | hōc făcĕre. | To do this | or / misbecomes | me. |

**221** 3. Others require a Dative of the Person and an Infinitive for the Subject.

| | | | |
|---|---|---|---|
| Lĭbet | mĭhī hōc făcĕre. | It pleases me (suits my fancy) | to do this.[2] |
| Lĭcet | | It is lawful for me | |

---

[1] So in Old English, *it repents me of*, *it pitied him of*, &c.

**221a** [2] Plăcet is used somewhat similarly with a subject-clause, "plăcŭit lēgātos mitti," *it pleased them*, i.e. they resolved, that ambassadors should be sent; but being personally used, it is not classed among Impersonal Verbs.

## IMPERSONAL VERBS.

**222**    4. The verbs ŏportet, *it behoves*, and līquet, *it is clear*, take an Accusative and Infinitive as their Subject-Clause.[1]

*It is clear that the man has been slain.*    Līquet hŏmĭnem interfectum esse.

**223**    Note that ŏportet (or dēbeo, *I owe*) *is never followed by the Perfect Infinitive*.

*You ought to come*, lit., *it behoves you to come.*    Ŏportet tē (*or* dēbēs) vĕnīre.

*You ought to have come*, lit., *it behoved you to come.*    Ŏportuit tē (*or* dēbuisti) vĕnīre.

**224**    5. Several Verbs relating to the weather are used impersonally, as in English: plŭit, *it rains*, &c.

**225**    All the above Verbs (except those in Class 5) are of the 2nd conjugation: dĕcēre, dĕcēbit, dĕcēbat, dĕcuit, dĕcuĕrat, dĕcuisset, &c.

**226**    Besides the Perfects in -ŭit, there are also in use pertaesum est (for taedŭit); mĭsĕrĭtum est; pĭgĭtum est; pŭdĭtum est; lĭcĭtum est; lĭbĭtum est (which is found in Cicero perhaps to the exclusion of lĭbŭit).

### Exercise LXIX.

1. Senem stultitiae suae poenitebit.[2]   2. Quando mulieres suspicionis suae pudebit?   3. Non dubium est quin pedites huius tam longi itineris taedeat.   4. Licebit hosti nocte ex urbe proficisci.   5. Oportuit te ei mulieri veniam dare.   6. Nonne licebat nobis isti praedam eripere?   7. Interrogavi latronem nonne se tot scelerum puderet, nonne latrociniorum jam pertaesum esset.   8. Nonne judicem dedecebat inepte loqui?   9. Aliquando te tuae tam ineptae jactationis poenitebit.[3]   10. De hac re libitum est mihi plura scribere.

---

**227**   [1] Ŏpŏrtet and licet are also followed by the Subjunctive with ŭt omitted; ŏpŏrtet (ŭt) virtūtem ămes, *it is right that you should love virtue.* The insertion of the ŭt is post-classical, or rare.

**227a**   [2] As the *implied Subject* of the sentence is sĕnex, "the old man will repent," sŭus is here used and not eius, see Par. 218.

**228**   [3] Tam is often used between a pronominal and ordinary Adjective in the sense of *very*.

11. Interrogabo mulierem nonne se jam jactationis suae taedeat. 12. Liquebat hostes per dolum atque insidias pacem petere. 13. Licet omnes (227) fremant; consilium meum non muto.

1. *When will it-be-lawful for us to set-out from the city?* 2. *There is no doubt that the citizens are-ashamed of their* (227a) *boasting.* 3. *Ask, dear son, whether the women repented of their suspicion.* 4. *Does it befit an orator to be-angry without cause?* 5. *You ought to know at-least these-things which it misbecomes even* (141a) *a boy to-be-ignorant-of.* 6. *I asked the magistrate whether it-was-lawful to bury the dead within the city.* 7. *It-is-clear that his brothers were treacherously slain.* 8. *Let* (227) *them murmur to one another* (189) *that I am guilty; I-for-my-part* (139) *know that I am innocent.* 9. *When will you confess that you ought to* (223) *have led those two hundred soldiers with you?* 10. *It was uncertain whether the woman was weary of the journey or desired to return to her father.* 11. *Balbus declared that his slaves ought to have snatched the booty from the robbers.*

## IRREGULAR VERBS.

**229**  1. **Possum, pŏtuī, possĕ,**—*to be able; can.*[1]

| Indicative. | Subjunctive. | Indicative. | Subjunctive. |
|---|---|---|---|
| 1. *Present.* | | 3. *Imperfect.* | |
| **Pos-sum** | **Pos-sim** | **Pŏt-ĕram** | **Pos-sem** |
| **Pŏt-ĕs** | **Pos-sīs** | **Pŏt-ĕrās** | **Pos-sēs** |
| **Pŏt-est** | **Pos-sĭt** | **Pŏt-ĕrăt** | **Pos-sĕt** |
| **Pos-sŭmŭs** | **Pos-sīmŭs** | **Pŏt-ĕrāmŭs** | **Pos-sēmŭs** |
| **Pŏt-estĭs** | **Pos-sītĭs** | **Pŏt-ĕrātĭs** | **Pos-sētĭs** |
| **Pos-sunt** | **Pos-sint** | **Pŏt-ĕrant** | **Pos-sent** |
| 2. *Future-Simple.* | | 4. *Perfect.* | |
| **Pŏt-ĕro** | (wanting.) | **Pŏt-uī** | **Pŏt-uĕrim** |
| **Pŏt-ĕrĭs** | | **Pŏt-uistī** | **Pŏt-uĕrĭs** |
| **Pŏt-ĕrĭt** | | **Pŏt-uĭt** | **Pŏt-uĕrĭt** |
| **Pŏt-ĕrīmŭs** | | **Pŏt-uĭmŭs** | **Pŏt-uĕrĭmŭs** |
| **Pŏt-ĕrītĭs** | | **Pŏt-uistĭs** | **Pŏt-uĕritĭs** |
| **Pŏt-ĕrunt** | | **Pŏt-uērunt(ērĕ)** | **Pŏt-uĕrint** |

**230** [1] **Pos-sum** is compounded of **potis-sum**, *I-am-able*, which passes into **pŏte-sum** and thence to **pos-sum**. The Tenses may be obtained by putting **pot-** before the different parts of the Verb **sum** and (1) striking out f after t, *e.g.* pot-(f)ui; (2) changing t into s before s, *e.g.* pos-sum (not pot-sum); (3) contracting pot-esse and pot-essem into posse and possem.

| INDICATIVE. | SUBJUNCTIVE. | INDICATIVE. | SUBJUNCTIVE. |
|---|---|---|---|
| 5. *Future-Perfect.* | | 6. *Pluperfect.* | |
| Pŏt-uĕro | (wanting) | Pŏt-uĕram | Pŏt-uissem |
| Pŏt-uĕrĭs | | Pŏt-uĕrās | Pŏt-uissēs |
| Pŏt-uĕrĭt | | Pŏt-uĕrăt | Pŏt-uissĕt |
| Pŏt-uĕrĭmŭs | | Pŏt-uĕrāmŭs | Pŏt-uissēmŭs |
| Pŏt-uĕrĭtĭs | | Pŏt-uĕrātĭs | Pŏt-uissētĭs |
| Pŏt-uĕrint | | Pŏt-uĕrant | Pŏt-uissent |

INFINITIVE.

*Pres. and Imp.*—**Possĕ.** *Perf. and Plup.*—**Pŏtuissĕ.** *Future* —wanting. (Participle **pŏtens**, used only as Adjective, *powerful.*)

**231** As **possum** has no Participle in **-rus**, it cannot form the Periphrastic Tense of the Subjunctive (Par. 155) used to represent the Future in an Indirect Sentence. Hence, in this and other Verbs which have not the Participle in **-rus**, a Periphrasis (see Par. 212) is used:

*I will ask whether he will be able to help me.*   Interrŏgābo num **fŭtūrum sit ut possit** mĭhī subvĕnīre, i.e. *whether it-will-come-to-pass that he may be able.*

EXERCISE LXX.

**232** **Pŏtui** (and sometimes **pŏtĕram**) is sometimes followed, like **ŏportuit** above, by a Present Inf. where the English *could* requires the Perfect Infinitive :

*You could have come.*   Pŏtuisti (*or* pŏtĕras) **vĕnīre.**

1. Veniam si potero; cura tu ut venire possis. 2. Poteras patri tuo parere, sed beneficiorum eius plerumque immemor eras. 3. Interrogavi nonne possent trecenti nostrorum, cum mille equitibus sociorum, duobus milibus hostium resistere. 4. Non possumus justius quam a te gubernari. 5. Nonne potuistis melius scribere? Frater vester optime scribere poterat (*used to be able*). 6. Nihil honestius Epaminondae dari potuit quam mors clarissima. 7. Quis dubitat quin urbs

a nostris (34) expugnari potuerit ? 8. Interrogavi agricolam nonne potuisset quolibet tempore fundum suum vendere.[1] 9. Valde dubito num futurum sit ut possis voluptatis illecebris resistere. 10. Miserum est olim potuisse, nunc non posse, amicis subvenire.

1. *There is no doubt that you can help me, O friends. 2. I asked our men whether they could resist three thousand of the enemy.[2] 3. Will you not be able to come, boys, if we ask you? 4. You could have written better, but you neglected the matter. 5. That you may be able to help others, acquire riches. 6. The enemy bridged the river that they might be able at any time (quilibet) to invade our territories. 7. Do you believe that you will be able to resist these great enticements? 8. Those who cannot be first, can generally be before (prior) the last.*

2. **Vŏlo, vŏluī, vellĕ,**—*I am willing, wish.*
3. **Nōlo, nōluī, nollĕ,**—*I am unwilling, do not wish.* [3]
4. **Mālo, māluī, mallĕ,**—*I prefer, would rather, had rather.*[3]

INDICATIVE MOOD.

1 *Present.*

| Vŏlo | Nōlo | Mālo |
|---|---|---|
| Vīs | Nōn vīs | Māvīs |
| Vult | Nōn vult | Māvult |
| Vŏlŭmŭs | Nōlŭmŭs | Mālŭmŭs |
| Vultis | Nōn vultĭs | Māvultĭs |
| Vŏlunt | Nōlunt | Mālunt |

2. *Future-Simple.*[4]

| Vŏl-am | Nōl-am | Māl-am |
|---|---|---|
| Vŏl-ēs, &c. | Nōl-ēs, &c. | Māl-ēs, &c. |

3. *Imperfect.*[4]

| Vŏl-ēbam | Nōl-ēbam | Māl-ēbam |
|---|---|---|
| Vŏl-ēbās, &c. | Nōl-ēbās, &c. | Māl-ēbās, &c. |

---

232a [1] Where **suus** cannot possibly refer to the Subject of the Principal Verb, it may be used to refer to the Subject of the Subordinate Verb.

233 [2] For *can* may be substituted *am, is, are able;* and for *could, was,* or *were able;* and this will often help the pupil to determine the Tense and Mood of **possum** into which *can* should be translated.

234 [3] Nōlo is for nĕ-vŏlo, and mālo for ma- (*i.e.* măgis or măge) -vŏlo. The dropping of the **v** is illustrated by the forms sīs (for **si vīs,** *if you please*) and (**sultis for si vultis**).

[4] These Tenses are declined like the corresponding Tenses of **rĕgo.**

## VOLO, NOLO, MALO.

### 4. *Perfect.*[1]

| | | |
|---|---|---|
| Vŏl-uī | Nōl-uī | Māl-uī |
| Vŏl-uistī, &c. | Nōl-uistī, &c. | Māl-uistī, &c. |

### 5. *Future-Perfect.*[1]

| | | |
|---|---|---|
| Vŏl-uĕro | Nōl-uĕro | Māl-uĕro |
| Vŏl-uĕrĭs, &c. | Nōl-uĕrĭs, &c. | Māl-uĕrĭs, &c. |

### 6. *Pluperfect.*[1]

| | | |
|---|---|---|
| Vŏl-ueram | Nōl-uĕram | Māl-uĕrām |
| Vŏl-uĕrās, &c. | Nōl-uĕrās, &c. | Māl-uĕrās, &c. |

## SUBJUNCTIVE MOOD.

### 1. *Present.*

| | | |
|---|---|---|
| Vĕl-im | Nōl-im | Māl-im |
| Vĕl-īs | Nōl-īs | Māl-īs |
| Vĕl-ĭt | Nōl-ĭt | Māl-ĭt |
| Vĕl-īmŭs | Nōl-īmŭs | Māl-īmŭs |
| Vĕl-ītĭs | Nōl-ītĭs | Māl-ītĭs |
| Vĕl-int | Nōl-int | Māl-int |

### 2. *Imperfect.*

| | | |
|---|---|---|
| Vel-lem | Nol-lem | Mal-lem |
| Vel-lēs | Nol-lēs | Mal-lēs |
| Vel-lĕt | Nol-lĕt | Mal-lĕt |
| Vel-lēmŭs | Nol-lēmŭs | Mal-lēmŭs |
| Vel-lētĭs | Nol-lētĭs | Mal-lētĭs |
| Vel-lent | Nol-lent | Mal-lent |

### 3. *Perfect.*[1]

| | | |
|---|---|---|
| Vŏl-uĕrim | Nōl-uĕrim | Māl-uĕrim |
| Vŏl-uĕrĭs, &c. | Nōl-uĕrĭs, &c. | Māl-uĕrĭs, &c. |

### 4. *Pluperfect.*[1]

| | | |
|---|---|---|
| Vŏl-uissem | Nōl-uissem | Māl-uissem |
| Vŏl-uissēs, &c. | Nōl-uissēs, &c. | Māl-uissēs, &c. |

---

[1] These Tenses are declined like the corresponding Tenses of mŏnĕo.

## IMPERATIVE MOOD.

|  | Present. |  |
|---|---|---|
| (Wanting.) | Nōl-ī.<br>Nōl-īte. | (Wanting.) |
|  | Future. |  |
|  | Nōl-ītō.<br>Nōl-ītō.<br>Nōl-ītōte.<br>Nōl-untō. |  |

## INFINITIVE MOOD

|  | Present. |  |
|---|---|---|
| Vel-lĕ. | Nol-lĕ. | Mal-lĕ. |
|  | Perfect. |  |
| Vŏl-uissĕ. | Nōl-uissĕ. | Māl-uissĕ. |
|  | Present Participle. |  |
| Vŏl-ens. | Nōl-ens. | (Wanting.) |
|  | Gerunds and Supines. |  |
| (Wanting.) | (Wanting.) | (Wanting.) |

### EXERCISE LXXI.

**Mālo,** (being a contraction of **măgis—vŏlo,** *I wish rather*), is naturally followed by **quam** *than*, coupling Infinitives or Nouns (62) in the same Case.

*We had rather fight than yield.* Pugnāre **quam** cĕdĕre **mālŭmus.**

1. Idem velle atque idem nolle—ea demum est vera amicitia.[1]
2. Imperator cum nollet mihi obesse, interrogavit fratrem meum num vellem clam ex urbe excedere. 3. Non dubium est quin malis hic (*adv.*) manere; sed excedendum tibi erit. 4. Mane nunc, si vis; sed si cras voles excedere, non tibi

---

[1] The Nom. to **est** is the sentence **Idem ... nolle. Idem** (not **Idem**, Par. 103) is Acc. Neut. governed by **velle.** Instead of **ea** we ought strictly to have **id,** *i.e. that* (*thing*), Nom. in Apposition to the sentence **Idem ... nolle.** But **id** is "attracted" into the gender of **ămīcītĭa.**

licebit. 5. Quid vultis, ignavissimi? Semper fugere quam mori maluistis. 6. Hoc vel voluisse mox tibi inhonestum videbitur.[1] 7. Curate, judices, ut justa non solum dicatis sed etiam velitis. 8. Nolebam reum vinciri; sed, si praetor ita voluerit, vinciendus erit. 9. Nunc quidem puer non vult discere; sed non dubium est quin futurum sit ut mox discere malit quam ludere.[2] 10. Interrogavi (133) fratrem eius num ludere quam discere maluerit. 11. Quam turpe est fallere! Nolite mentiri, ne multa, quae non vultis, pati cogamini. 12. Roganti mihi ut cenaret mecum, respondit se nolle foris cenare.[3] 13. Nonne disciplinam quam fugam (62) mavis.

1. *What do you wish, citizens? Do you prefer six hundred kings to* (quam) *one?* 2. *Why, O friend, would you not* (i.e. *were you unwilling to*) *obey the excellent Tullius?* 3. *There is no doubt that he was unwilling to resist the citizens.* 4. *When, if-not* (nisi) *now, will they be willing to take up* (i.e., *to prepare*) *arms that they may preserve the city?* 5. *I have no doubt, (my) friend, that you prefer death to* (quam) *slavery.* 6. *I asked them whether they wished to be slaves* (i.e., *to serve*); *but they* (illi autem) *replied that they preferred* (217) *to pay tribute rather than die.* 7. *To wish-for things-useful, is a great part of a happy life.* 8. *I asked his friends to help him; but they were unwilling to sustain an idle man.* 9. *Which* (85) *of you* (93) *two prefers to dine out of doors?* 10. *I am ashamed of having even* (141a) *wished-for this.*

Fĕro, tŭli, ferrĕ, lātum, *I bear, endure, bring.*

Fĕro, in the Present-derived Tenses, is conjugated like rĕgo, except that, after fer- :

(1) e final is dropped, and also e before r.[4]

fer-(e), Imperat.; fer-(e)res, Imperf. Subj.

(2) i is dropped before s or t.

fer-(i)s, fer-(i)t, Indic. Pres.

---

[1] The Subject of vĭdēbĭtur is a Clause. Hōc is Acc. governed by vŏluisse.

[2] Not lūdĕrĕ māllt. The Latins do not like to have a prose sentence ending in ⏑ ‑ ⏑ ‑, because it is the regular end of a hexameter verse. They would prefer "rĕdīrĕ stătim vŏlēbant" to "stătim rĕdīrĕ vŏlēbant."

[3] Where is the Dat. naturally governed by respondit? Fŏris is an Adverb.

[4] The -e final is similarly dropped in the Imperative Sing. of dīco, dūco, and făcio: dīc, dūc, făc.

The Perfect-derived tenses are formed, in the Active, regularly from **tŭli** (root toll-o, *I bear*), and, in the Passive, from **lātus** (another form of the same root).

## I. ACTIVE VOICE.

### IRREGULAR TENSES.

*Indic. Present.* **Fĕr-o, fer-s, fer-t, fĕr-ĭmus, fĕr-tis, fĕr-unt.**
*Imperative Pres.* **Fer, fer-tĕ.** *Fut.* **Fer-to, fert-o, fer-tōtĕ, fĕr-unto.**
*Subjunct. Imperf.* **Fer-rem, fer-res, fer-ret, fer-rēmus, fer-rētis, fer-rent.**
*Infinitive Pres.* **Fer-re.**

### REGULAR TENSES.

*Indicative Fut. Simple.* **Fĕr-am.** *Imperf.* **Fĕr-ēbam.** *Perf.* **Tŭli.**
*Fut. Perf.* **Tŭl-ero.** *Pluperf.* **Tŭl-eram.**
*Subjunctive Pres.* **Fĕr-am.** *Perf.* **Tŭl-ĕrim.** *Pluperf.* **Tŭl-issem.**
*Infinitive Perf.* **Tŭ-lisse.** *Fut.* **Lātūrŭs esse.**
*Participle Pres.* **Fĕrens.** *Fut.* **Lātūrus.**
*Supines.* **Lātum, lātu.**
*Gerund.* **Fĕrendi, &c.**

## II. PASSIVE VOICE.

### IRREGULAR TENSES.

*Indicative Pres.* **Fĕr-or, fer-ris, fer-tur, fĕr-ĭmur, fĕr-ĭmĭni, fĕr-untur.**
*Imperative Pres.* **[Fer-re]**,[1] **fĕr-ĭmĭni.** *Fut.* **Fer-tor, fer-tor, fĕr-untor.**
*Subjunctive Imperf.* **Fer-rer, fer-rēris, fer-rētur, fer-rēmur, fer-rēmini, fer-rentur.**
*Infinitive Pres.* **Fer-ri.**

---

[1] There is no instance of this form occurring in Latin literature.

REGULAR TENSES.

*Indicative Fut. Simple.* **Fĕr-ar.** *Imperf.* **Fĕr-ēbar.** *Perf.* **Lātus sum.**
*Fut. Perf.* **Lātus ĕro.** *Pluperf.* **Lātus essem.**
*Subjunctive Pres.* **Fĕr-ar.** *Perf.* **Lātus sim.** *Pluperf.* **Lātus essem.**
*Infinitive Perf.* **Lātus esse.** *Fut.* **Lātum īri.**
*Participle Perf.* **Lātus.**
*Gerundive.* **Fĕr-endus.**

**238** The following compounds of **fero** are noteworthy for the changes of the prefix:

> Af-fĕro (ad-fĕro) af-ferrĕ, at-tŭli, ad-lātum.
> Au-fĕro (ab-fĕro) au-ferrĕ, abs-tŭli, ab-lātum.
> Ef-fĕro (ex-fĕro) ef-ferrĕ, ex-tŭli, ē-lātum.
> In-fĕro (in-fĕro) in-ferrĕ, in-tŭli, il-lātum.
> Of-fĕro (ob-fĕro) ob-ferrĕ, ob-tŭli, ob-lātum.
> Rĕ-fero (rĕ-fĕro) rĕ-ferrĕ, { rĕ-tŭli / ret-tŭli } rēlātum.

INDIRECT QUESTIONS.

**239** The construction of the Indirect Question (Par. 136) is used with Interrogative Pronouns and Conjunctions, not only after Verbs of *asking*, but also after any Verbs that take a question as their Subject or Object. Thus the Direct Question "Quĭd fēcisti ?" *What did you do?* becomes:

| *It is uncertain* | | | | |
|---|---|---|---|---|
| *Tell me* | } *what you did.* | Incertum est | } | quĭd fēcĕris.[2] |
| *I shall ascertain* | | Dīc mĭhī | | |
| *I know* | | Cognoscam | | |
| | | Cognōvi[1] | | |

**240**
**240a**

[1] Cognōvi and nōvi, (Perf.) mean *I have ascertained*, and hence *I know*.
[2] Why quĭd, not quŏd? Ans. *because it is the construction of the Indirect Question.* This constr. is used with intĕrest and rēfert (329); *it matters not what he said*, non rēfert quĭd dixĕrit.

After all these Verbs, there holds the law of the SEQUENCE of TENSES (Par. 136).

### EXERCISE LXXII.

1. Respondete, milites fortissimi, quomodo laturi sitis hanc tantam contumeliam hostium vel ad vallum vestrum equitantium (154a). 2. Ferebamus convicia eius, feremus maledicta; laudem eius perferre omnino non poteramus.[1] 3. Nonne reperire potes quis hanc rogationem ad populum tulerit?[2] 4. Non dubium est quin Ariovisto, regi potentissimo, bellum illaturi simus. 5. Nonne miles es? Nonne vallum fers et arma? 6. Interrogavi nonne milites essent? cur tandem arma ferrent nisi ut hostibus resisterent.[3] 7. Comperistine quot nostrorum in hoc tam (228) funesto proelio ceciderint? 8. De provinciis ad Patres consules rettulerunt; de legatis nihil relatum est. 9. Cognoscam per nuntium num legem a Graccho rogatam Patres aegre tulerint. 10. Cognoscere voluimus num hae tot tantaeque calamitates a fratre eius patientius perferrentur. 11. Quid obstat quominus, occasione oblata, res ad senatum referatur? 12. Spem mihi (192), quam unam habui, tu tua temeritate abstulisti. 13. Tu qui toties promisisti, (152a) nonne jam perficies?

1. *I have never been able to ascertain why the matter was referred to the senate.* 2. *Tell* (237) *me, friend, why you took away from* (192) *me the last hope* (i.e. *the hope which last*) *I had.* 3. *Do not tell them how-many insults you endured, nor how many you are about to endure; for they will not believe you.* 4. *The consuls had referred the subject of the prisoners* (trans. *had referred concerning the prisoners*) *to the senate.* 5. *The matter was referred to the senate: nevertheless you who* (108) *referred* (*it*), *now deny that you referred* (*it*). 6. *Tell me, Tullius* (13), *when* (156) *you will bring help to me.* 7. *I asked the soldier why he bore arms except to* (143a) *fight against the enemies of* (*his*) *country.* 8. *We could not* (i.e. *were-not-able to*) *ascertain how-many captives our-men had taken.* 9. *You who patiently endured so many great* (i.e. *so-many and so-great*) *calamities, will you not* (see sent. 13, above, and Par.

---

[1] (a) **Omnīno nōn** means *altogether not*, i.e. *not at all, certainly not*;
(b) **nōn omnīno** means *not altogether, not quite.*
[2] Why **quis**, not **qui**?
[3] Repeat **interrogāvi** before **cūr**; look out **tandem**.

152a) *endure this very* (228) *slight loss?* 10. *There is no doubt that the enemy will soon offer us an opportunity* (5a).

## 6. Ĕo, īvī, īrĕ, ĭtum—*I go.*

| INDICATIVE. | SUBJUNCTIVE. | INDICATIVE. | | SUBJUNCTIVE. | |
|---|---|---|---|---|---|
| *1. Present.* | | *4. Perfect.* | | | |
| Ĕ-o | E-am | Ĭ-vī *or* | I-ī | Ĭ-vĕrim *or* | I-ĕrim |
| Ī-s | E-ās | Ĭ-vistī | &c. | Ĭ-vĕrĭs | &c. |
| Ĭ-t | E-ăt | Ĭ-vĭt | &c. | Ĭ-vĕrĭt | &c. |
| Ĭ-mŭs | E-āmŭs | Ĭ-vĭmŭs | &c. | Ĭ-vĕrimŭs | &c. |
| Ĭ-tis | E-ātĭs | Ĭ-vistīs | &c. | Ĭ-vĕritĭs | &c. |
| E-unt | E-ant | Ĭ-vērunt | &c. | Ĭ-vĕrint | &c. |
|  |  | *or* I-vērĕ |  |  |  |
| *2. Future-Simple.* | | *5. Future-Perfect.* | | | |
| Ĭ-bo | Ĭ-tūrŭs sim | Ĭ-vĕro *or* Ĭ-ĕro | | (wanting) | |
| Ĭ-bĭs | Ĭ-tŭrŭs sīs | Ĭ-vĕrĭs | &c. | | |
| Ĭ-bĭt | Ĭ-tŭrŭs-sīt | I-vĕrĭt | &c. | | |
| Ĭ-bĭmŭs | Ĭ-tūrī sīmŭs | Ĭ-vĕrimŭs | &c. | | |
| Ĭ-bĭtĭs | Ĭ-tūrī sītĭs | Ĭ-vĕritĭs | &c. | | |
| Ī-bunt | Ĭ-tūrī sint | Ĭ-vĕrint | &c. | | |
| *3. Imperfect.* | | *6. Pluperfect.* | | | |
| I-bam | Ī-rem | Ĭ-vĕram *or* | | Ĭ-vissem, I-issem, | |
| Ĭ-bās | Ī-rēs | I-ĕram | | *or* I-ssem | |
| Ĭ-băt | Ī-rĕt | Ĭ-vĕrās | &c. | Ĭ-vissēs | &c. |
| Ĭ-bāmŭs | Ī-rēmŭs | Ĭ-vĕrăt | &c. | Ĭ-vissēt | &c. |
| Ĭ-bātĭs | I-rētis | Ĭ-vĕrāmŭs | &c. | Ĭ-vissēmŭs | &c. |
| Ĭ-bant | Ĭ-rent | Ĭ-vĕrātĭs | &c. | Ĭ-vissētĭs | &c. |
|  |  | Ĭ-vĕrant | &c. | Ĭ-vissent | &c. |

## EO AND ITS COMPOUNDS. [Par. 242—245

| | IMPERATIVE. | | PARTICIPLES. |
|---|---|---|---|
| Present. | Ĭ | Present. | Ĭ-ens (Gen. ĕ-untĭs) |
| | Ĭ-tĕ | Future. | Ĭ-tūrŭs (ă, um) |
| Future. | Ĭ-to | | |
| | Ĭ-to | | GERUND. |
| | Ĭ-tōtĕ | Gen. | Ĕ-undi, &c. |
| | Ĕ-unto | | |
| | | | SUPINE. |
| | INFINITIVE. | | Ĭ-tum |
| Pres. and Imp. | Ĭ-rĕ | | |
| Perf. and Plup. | Ĭ-vissĕ, Ĭ-issĕ, or issĕ | | |
| Future. | Ĭ-tūrus essĕ | | |

**242** The Passive of ĕo is only used impersonally, e.g. ītur, it is gone, i.e. they go: see Par. 247.

**243** 1. The compounds of ĕo are conjugated in the same way, except that those which take an Accusative in the Active, have the full Passive Voice. Thus from in-ĕo and praeter-ĕo come the Pass. Participle ĭn-ĭtus and praetĕr-ĭtus, and the Gerundives, ĭn-ĕundus and praetĕr-ĕundus.

**244** 2. The compounds of ĕo generally omit v in the Perf. and Perfect-derived Tenses: rĕd-ii, trans-iĕrim, praeter-iĕram, &c.

**245** 3. The Dative is not governed by these compounds, except by sŭb-eo (rarely), and prae-eo.

### EXERCISE LXXIII.

1. Cum jam mulieres liberique flumen auctum imbribus transiissent, curavit imperator ut senes transirent. 2. Peribit iste, nisi celeriter (125) redieris. 3. Cum ad ripam rediissem, alios transituros, alios jam transeuntes inveni. 4. Ibam forte ad forum cum subito Tullius me adiit. 5. I, decus nostrum, i pater patriae, ut mox triumphaturus redeas. 6. Praei jusjurandum mihi, pontifex. 7. Pudet me abiisse; redire statim volo. 8. Unus tantum (adv.) exiens ab hostibus captus est: ceteri, cum jam exeuntes fraudem intellexissent, subito redierunt. 9. Flumen quod heri transiistis, jam glacie plenum omnino (241) non transibitis. 10. Quid obstat quominus

redeas aditurus Apollinem? 11. Apollo aditus respondit mortem homini decimo die esse obeundam. 12. Praeterita (34) redire nequeunt.

1. *There is no doubt that he met death with* (181) *fortitude.* 2. *Having passed over the river* (196) *they began-to-wish* (imperf.) *immediately to return* (redeo) (236). 3. *If you begin the battle without cavalry, you will not be able to resist the greater forces of the enemy.* 4. *Alas! when, O citizens, will you return to the city whence you now go-forth exulting?* 5. *There is no doubt that we must return to the city with speed.* 6. *Returning to the city I met Balbus himself returning.* 7. *Tullius besought me to go to the city with him.* 8. *The river which you crossed in-the-morning cannot be crossed now, since-it-is-swollen* (i.e., *being-increased*) *by showers* (236) (5a). 9. *Are you ignorant that death must be met by all?* 10. *The battle having now begun* (i.e., *having-been begun*) *the general gave-orders-to the sixth legion to* (143) *charge the enemy.*

## THE SUPINES.

1. The Supine in -u is a Verbal Noun of the Fourth Declension, used only in the Ablative, and mostly after Adjectives signifying *good* or *evil*, *pleasant* or *unpleasant*, *fitness* or *unfitness*, &c., as "ămārum **gustātu**," *bitter in the tasting*, i.e., *bitter to the taste.*

2. The Supine in **-um** is a Verbal Noun used only in the Accusative after Verbs of Motion without the Preposition ăd. It can take an object after it, which the Supine in -u cannot do:

*He came to play.*      Vēnit **lūsum.**
*He went to see the city.*      Īvit **vīsum** urbem.

3. Besides the form with **fŏre** mentioned in Par. 212, the Supine in **-um** is used after the Pres. Inf. Passive of eo, *I go*, to supply the missing Future Passive Infinitive:

*He said that the city would be taken.*      Dixit **īri captum** urbem.[1]

---

[1] The words are arranged in this order to show the construction; but *in practice*, Iri *follows the Supine.*

The literal rendering of this is, *He said that-there-was-a-going* (īri being used impersonally) *to take* (**captum** being the Supine after the Verb of Motion) *the city* (**urbem** being Accusative after **captum**). So:

*He said that we should be sent to the prison.*   Dixit nōs ăd carcĕrem **ductum** īri. (*Parse* **nōs**).

Exercise LXXIV.

**249**   Names of Towns and small Islands are put in the Accusative (without a Preposition) after Verbs of Motion; and so are the Nouns **dŏmum** and **rūs**.

1. Dictu difficile est uter horum peccaverit (9*a*). 2. Venimus Romam spectatum ludos.[1] 3 Audierat pater non datum iri uxorem filio suo. 4. Inde Delum navigant consulturi Apollinem; qui respondit frustra se consuli, (32) urbem captum iri. 5. Nonne hoc nefas visu est? Nonne etiam dictu turpissimum? 6. Mittendi sunt Athenas legati pacem petituri. 7. Non dubium est quin qui urbem speculatum venerunt, re infecta redierint. 8. Diversas ob causas juvenes philosophum adierunt; alii quidem jocatum venerunt, alii autem ad discendum parati. 9. I tu consultum Jovem, equidem Delphos ibo Apollinem consulturus. 10. Interrogate nautas utrum Carthaginem an ad Italiam navigent.

1. *The ambassadors who have been sent to seek-for peace have returned without-accomplishing anything.* 2. *The citizens sent the prophet in vain to Delos; for Apollo predicted that the captives would be slain by the enemy.* 3. *We have come here* (i.e. *hither*) *to fight, not to talk.* 4. *I asked the physician whether the herb was bitter or* (171) *sweet to taste.* 5. *When will you return home, my son?* 6. *The youth* (*monstrous to relate!*) *set-out-for the country from the city intending-to slay* (trans. *about-to slay*) *his own father.* 7. *Having set the city on fire, the general gave orders to his men to set-out-for Carthage* (196). 8. *I asked the young man to come to dine with* (see '*with*') *me, but he answered that he must-go to Athens on that day.*

---

[1] What are the two pronunciations, and consequently the two meanings of "venimus"? Why is **uxōrem** (in Sent. 3) Accusative (248)?

## THE GERUND.

**250** 1. When an English Transitive Verbal, e.g. *writing*, is the Nominative to a Verb, or the Accusative governed by a Verb, it is expressed (Par. 128) by the Latin Infinitive:

| | |
|---|---|
| *Writing letters is easy.* | Făcĭle est ĕpistŏlas **scrībĕre**. |
| *I prefer writing letters.* | Mālo ĕpistŏlas **scrībĕre**. |

**251** 2. But when the Transitive Verbal is preceded by *of, for, to, towards, during, in, by,* &c., the former Object of the Verbal *writing* is now made the Object of the Preposition *of, for,* &c., and the Latin Gerundive *Adjective* **scrībendus**, *meet-to-be-written,* is used in agreement with its former Object:

| | |
|---|---|
| *The art of writing letters,* i.e *of letters meet-to-be-written.* | Ars ĕpistŏlārum **scrībendārum.** |
| *Let us pay attention to making a bridge,* i.e. *to a bridge meet-to-be-made.* | Dēmus ŏpĕram ponti **făcĭendo**. |
| *During the building of a city* i.e. *during a city meet-to-be-built.*[1] | Inter urbem **aedĭfĭcandam**. |
| *In making a bridge,* i.e. *in a-bridge-meet-to-be-built.* | In ponte **făcĭendo**. |
| *Choiceness of expression is increased by reading orators and poets.* | Lŏquendi ĕlĕgantia augētur **lĕgendis ōratōrĭbus** et **pŏētis**.[2] |

**252** 3. If the Verbal (1) is Intransitively used, or (2) requires a Dative Case in Latin, the Latin Gerundive *Noun* is used, governing a Dative if necessary:

| | |
|---|---|
| (1a) *The art of writing.* | Ars **scrībendi**. |
| (1b) *We are born for acting.* | Nāti sūmus ad **ăgendum**. |
| (2) *I am desirous of pleasing friends.* | Stŭdĭōsus sum **plăcendi** āmīcis. |

---

[1] With the English Verbal, we may *generally* either insert or omit the ... *of: in (the) building (of) a city,* but the Latin construction is the same in either case. The English *meet-to-be-built, made,* &c., is an inadequate rendering of the Latin Gerundive, which has no exact English equivalent.

[2] The use of the Gerundive Adjective to express the *Ablative of the Instrument,* is rare.

**253**    4. The impersonal Gerundive (163) may govern any case except the Accusative :

We must do our duty.     Fungendum est **offĭcio**.
We must obey the laws.     Pārendum est **lēgĭbus**.
We must not forget benefits.     Non est oblīviscendum **bĕnĕfĭciōrum**.

Exercise LXXV.

**254**    Rule.—To turn into Latin a Transitive English Verbal preceded by a Preposition, place the Object in the Case demanded by the English Preposition, and make the Gerundive agree with it.[1]

1. Barbari legatos causa petendae pacis miserunt. 2. Quid vultis, legati? Nonne ad pacem petendam parati estis? 3. Tunc quidem ab inimicis nostris ridebatur ; nunc nobis ridendum est. 4. Si vis scribere, si scribendi causa huc venis, cur non scribendo operam das? 5. Rogavit me ut venandi causa equos plures colligerem. 6. Traditum est Fabium Maximum rem Romanam cunctando restituisse. 7. Mors est omnibus (168) obeunda : nec nos flendo (170) morti moram afferemus. 8. Quis nescit mentem nutriri legendo, disputando acui? 9. Duc (237) nos citius, centurio ; utendum est occasione ab hoste nobis data.[2] 10. Vita et utenda est et fruenda.[2]

1. *They-live for the sake of eating ; in-eating they consume their lives.* 2. *Do* (237) *something, my son ; we are born to act* (i.e. *for acting*), *not to consume the fruits of the earth.* 3. *For the sake of discharging duty towards his friends, Tullius neglected his children.*[2] 4. *By punishing and by pardoning, not by forgetting, will you improve the bad.* 5. (*We*) *must obey* (*our*) *elders ; we must pity the poor.* 6. *The conspirators had conceived the hope* (trans. *had come into the hope*) *of slaying the consul.* 7. *He pays attention to writing verses.* 8. *Have you come to Athens to hear philosophers, or* (171) *for the sake of breeding dogs?* 9. *Even in* (in) *leading a cohort there is some art* (i.e. *something of art*); *either* (157a) *lead better, Marcus, or-else do not lead.*

**255**    [1] Of course in such sentences as *I will take-care-of the making of the bridge*, the "Case demanded by the English Preposition" is the Acc., because *take-care-of* is really a Transitive Verb, cūrāre.

**256**    [2] The Verbs fungor, fruor, ūtor, vescor, pŏtior (207) may be used either in the Impersonal or in the Personal Construction, *i.e.* either governing the Abl. or agreeing with a Noun.

## THE IMPERSONAL INFINITIVE, &c.

**257** (1) *He is persuaded.*     Persuāsum est (167) ei.[1]
(2) (*It*) *is certain that he is persuaded.*     Certum est ei persuāsum esse.
(3) *He says he is persuaded.*     Dīcit sibī persuāsum esse.

**258**    2. The Verb **fīo**, *I am made, I become,* is used as the Passive of **făcio**. In its Present and Present-derived Tenses it is conjugated like the Active of **audio**, except that **fīr-** is always written **fĭer-**; and the Infinitive is **fĭĕri** (not **fīrĕ** nor **fĭĕre**). The Perfect-derived Tenses are formed regularly from the Passive Participle **factus**.

**259**    3. Incomplete Transitive Verbs, *e.g. make, esteem, call,* &c. (which require, besides the Primary Object, a Complementary Noun or Adjective to complete the meaning) have the Complementary Object in the same case as the Primary Object.

*We will make you leader*     Te dŭcem făciēmus.

**260**    4. In the Passive, these Verbs take the Complementary Subject in the same Case as the Subject.

*Balbus was made leader*     Balbus dux factus est.
*He said that Balbus was made leader*     Dixit Balbum dŭcem factum esse.

### Exercise LXXVI.

1. Mulieres ob incolumitatem filiorum suorum gavisae sunt. 2. Histrio omnia fit: heri rex fiebat, cras fiet servus. 3. Quis nescit Palladis imaginem a Phidia factam esse? 4. Quid obstabat quominus mercator fieres? scio enim tibi in omnibus rebus a patre indultum esse. 5. Constat legibus obtemperatum esse, ab eis qui in leges jurati sunt. 6. Interrogavit cur nos, crudelitatem nostram jactare soliti, regem cenatum occidere noluissemus. 7. Scribit se philosophum fieri et ob hanc causam velle Athenas venire philosophos auditurum. 8. Constat paucos hostium resistere ausos esse (32), nemini

---

**261**   [1] Persuādētur ei would mean *it is being persuaded to him*, i.e. *he is being persuaded.*

a nobis parsum (214). 9. Breves esse cupientes, o poëtae, obscuri fitis. 10. Admonete socios vestros ne arma contra patriam moveant.

1. There was no doubt that the cruel Tullia had rejoiced on-account-of the death of her own son. 2. You, who lately became a praetor, will soon become a consul. 3. I know that you have always been too-much indulged (257) by your father. 4. It is certain that the laws are not always obeyed. 5. What prevented you from becoming consul? 6. Having themselves been accustomed to spare no one, the barbarians declared that no one was spared. 7. Is it not well-known that Cincinnatus from (ex) a ploughman was made a consul? 8. The scout brought-word that a hundred of our men had been slain, (and) two hundred had been spared.

## THE ACCUSATIVE OF EXTENT.

**262** The Accusative expresses extent (a) of *space*, and (b) of *time*; and therefore answers to the questions (1) *How far? high? long? deep? broad?* (2) *For*, or *during, how long a time?* and (313) sometimes (3) *How long ago?*

(1) *The ditch is ten feet broad.*   Fossa decem **pedes** est lāta.
(2) *He sleeps all the night.*   Tōtam **noctem** dormit.
(3) *He died two years ago.*   Abhinc **biennium** ŏbiit.

**263** ACCUSATIVE AND ABLATIVE OF TIME.—Distinguish between the Accusative of *extent of time (how long?)*, and (3) the Ablative (Par. 30) of the *point of time* or *season (when?)*[1]

*He cannot sleep in the night.*   **Nocte** dormīre nōn pŏtest.

### EXERCISE LXXVII.

1. Tiberius Caesar tredecim annos principatum obtinuit. 2. Quis nescit Platonem octoginta unum annos vixisse, Socratem anno septuagesimo veneno interfectum esse? 3. Decimo die post captam urbem,[2] fossam decem pedes altam arci

---

**263a** [1] The Ablative also answers to the question: *Within what time? We shall know everything in (the next) three days*, Omnia **his trĭbus diēbus**, *or* **hoc trĭduo**, comperta hăbēbĭmus: see Par. 30.

**264** [2] Note this idiom *after the city taken*, i.e. *after the taking of the city*; so **ante urbem condĭtam**, *before the foundation of the city*.

circumdedimus. 4. Pericles, cum quadraginta annos Atheniensibus praefuisset, morbo correptus est. 5. Cum jam viginti milia passuum iter fecissemus, nuntiant exploratores bidui iter hostes abesse. 6. His auditis, imperator aggerem ducentos pedes latum, triginta altum, exstruere statuit. 7. Non erat dubium quin hostes castra tria tantum milia passuum ab urbe posuissent. 8. Decima hora per exploratores compertum est hostes habere in animo nocte castra oppugnare. 9. Tullius, senex impigerrimus, jam sex et sexaginta annos natus, dicit se tribus bis mensibus Athenas navigaturum, esse. 10. Quis non meminit Trojam, decem annos obsessam, per Ulyssis dolos esse captam ? 11. Tullius, pŏēta praeclarissimus, dictitabat nunquam se plus agere quam cum nihil ageret. 12. Dicitur urbs abhinc centum annos floruisse.

1. *Do you not remember that Plato lived eighty-one years?* 2. *When we had advanced forty days' journey it was found that the enemy were distant twenty-four miles.* 3. *I asked the workmen to build a wall thirty-five feet high.* 4. *Having crossed the river we shall-have-to-journey for two-days through an uncultivated district.* 5. *For three-days our men resisted three thousand of the enemy.* 6. *When Balbus was sixty-three years old, he was struck by lightning and died* (trans. *having been struck . . . . he died*) *in the third month of (his) sixty-fourth year.* 7. *Within the-next three hours we shall take the city which has resisted our army for three-years.* 8. *Caesar writes that the territories of the Helvetii extend two hundred and forty miles in* (in *with Acc.*) *length.*

## THE LOCATIVE CASE.

**265** With the names of Towns and small Islands (and with hŭm-i, *on the ground;* dŏm-i, *at home;* bell-i,[1] *in the wars;* mīlĭtiae, *in the wars;* rūr-i, *in the country*), the question *Where?* is answered by the old Locative Case, thus:

|  | Singular. | Plural. |
|---|---|---|
| First declension | Rŏm-ae | Athēn-īs |
| Second „ | Cŏrinth-i | Coriŏl-īs |
| Third „ | Carthăgĭn-ĕ [2] | Cŭr-ĭbus |

**265a** With the names of Towns and small Islands (and also with dŏmo and rūre) the question *Whence?* is always answered by the Ablative.

---

**266**  [1] Mīlĭtiae and belli are seldom used *except with* dŏmi.
**267**  [2] The older form Carthăgĭn-i is only to be used where the Acc. is in -im, as Neăpŏl-im, Neăpŏl-i. Rŏm-ae, is a contraction for Rŏm-āī.

144 THE DATIVE OF PURPOSE. [Par. 268—272

**268**   Rule.—The Dative is sometimes used to denote a purpose, especially with the Verbs **sum** and **do**.

*He imputed it to me as a fault,*     Id mihī **vĭtio** dĕdit, *or* vertit.
   lit., *gave for a fault.*
*This will be (for) a proof to*        Hōc ĕrit mihī **dŏcŭmento**.
   *me.*

### Exercise LXXVIII.

1. Num vitam rusticam crimini esse putas? 2. Pater meus litteris Epheso datis,[1] scribit se mihi libros hos dono daturum. 3. Hostemne oras ut te adjuvet? Num vis omnibus esse derisui? 4. Conjurati, Athenis capti, epistolam concremaverunt ne forte sociis suis, qui Corinthi tum erant, periculo foret. 5. Si domi manseris, ipse tibi dedecori eris; si ruri (id quod pater suadet) vitam ages, nunquam te facti poenitebit.[2] 6. Cur vitio mihi res domi militiaeque honestissime gestas dedisti? 7. Nobis, qui tum Romae vitam agebamus, Tullii crudelitas odio erat. 8. Eniti debes ut, non[3] solum tibi ipsi, sed amicis omnibus qui Carthagine nunc sunt, adjumento esse possis. 9. Dum forte Neapoli moror, audiebam pullos sacros in aquam conjectos esse, quam rem Romani omnes religioni habuerunt.[4] 10. Vobis qui Delphis vivitis, quique (*not from* quisque, 37) Apollinem veneramini, nonne turpissimum videtur Apollinis responsa simul quaestui simul derisui habere?[5] 11. Audistine Cannis infeliciter pugnatum esse? Occĭdimus; actum est de exercitu. 12. I Roma.

1. *There-is no doubt that, if you remain longer at Corinth, you will be a disgrace to your friends.* 2. *Let his life be an example to you, that you may know that life in-the-country is often happier than in the city.* 3. *I asked him not to impute to me as a fault the-fact-that* (quod, *i.e., because*) *I had departed from Carthage in-order-to live at Rome.* 4. *You will remain three months at Rome, your brother at Athens, we at Samos; soon we shall all go to Gaul, thence we shall sail to Rhodes.* 5. *When Socrates had been put-to-death at Athens—which* (270) *was a disgrace to the Athenians—his friend Glaucus betook himself to Cyprus; thence after two months he set out for Asia.* 6. *I like to live at Rome; that-fellow (likes to live) in Campania;*

**269** [1] *i.e.* "dated *from* Ephesus," (not "*at* Ephesus," which would be Ĕphĕsi): see Par. 265a.
**270** [2] Note this use of **Id quŏd**, *that which*, i.e. *as, your father recommends:* Id may be parsed as *Nom.* in *Apposition to the sentence* "rūri vitam ages."
**271** [3] Not **nē**, because the **nōn** goes with **sōlum**.
**272** [4] **Dum** is mostly used with the *Present*, though the Principal Verb is in the *Past:* "dum haec gĕruntur, hostes terga dăbant."
[5] **Vōbīs** is Dat. governed by **vĭdētur**.

*you, who are a laughing-stock to all the best-men* (140), *are setting out from Athens that you may live at Capua.* 7. *That great man was not more-renowned in-war than in-the-arts-of peace* (trans. at home). 8. *There is no doubt that you remember* (memini, Appendix II., page 216) *when* (156) *the Romans were defeated by Hannibal at Cannae* (239).

## THE ABLATIVE.

**273** 1. Since the Ablative denotes the *means* or *instrument*, it can express the *definite price*, by means of which anything is bought.

*The fish was bought for a denarius,* i.e. *with a denarius.*   Piscis dēnārio emptus est.

**274** 2. It can also express the *measure*, by *means* of which one thing *exceeds*, or *falls short of*, another.

*The sun is* (*by*) *many times larger than the moon.*   Sōl **multis partĭbus** mājor est quam luna.[1]

**275** 3. It can express that, by *means* of which anything is *filled*.

*The river is full of water,* i.e. *filled with water.*   Amnis plēnus **ăquā** est.[2]

**276** 4. It can also express any *circumstance, in* which, or *with* which, something occurs; and hence it can express, (*a*) *manner,* or (*b*) *quality.*[3] But in such cases the Noun must have an Adj. agreeing with it.

(*a*) MANNER, *He answered in haste.*   Respondit **summā cĕlĕrĭtāte,** or cum cĕlĕrĭtāte.
(*b*) QUALITY. *Tullius was a man of ability.*   Tullius ingĕnio **haud parvo,** or **magno,** ĕrat.

---

**277** [1] Hence "*much* better," "*little* better," should be rendered "multo paulo, mēlior," not multum.
**278** [2] But in the best writers plēnus more often takes the Genitive.
[3] Under this head comes the Rule (Par. 28) that **dignus, indignus, frētus, contentus,** &c., take the Ablative; but the Ablative after these words requires no Adjective agreeing with it.

**279**  5. The Ablative is also used after Verbs and Adjectives implying *need, deprivation, emptiness, freedom from,* &c.

*I am free from cares.*  Văcuus sum **cūris**.
*I have need of money.*  Ŏpus est mĭhĭ **argento**.

**280**  RULE.—After Verbs of *promising* and *hoping*, the English Present Infinitive is expressed by the Latin Future Infinitive.

*I promise to come,* or *that I will come.*  Prōmitto, *or*, pollĭceor, **mē ventūrum esse.**
*I hope to see her to-morrow.*  Spēro **mē** crās eam **vīsūrum esse.**

### EXERCISE LXXIX.

1. Ne mille quidem talentis virtutem emere poteris. 2. Multo sanguine ea victoria nobis stetit. 3. Duabus unciis procerior eras quam frater tuus. 4. Fossae aqua plenae erant, urbs frumento abundabat; sed omnes armis egebamus. 5. Compertum est nostros ab hostibus commeatu interclusos esse. 6. Magno timore sum, sed spero mox fore ut puer convalescat.[1] 7. Centurioni, viro summa probitate, promittenti se venturum, nonne tu credes? 8. Omitte timorem, mi fili; nam, quo fortius ei resistes, eo facilius tibi cedet.[2] 9. Divitiis facile carebis; nemo facile virtute caret. 10. Opus est auxilio tuo; miliens promisisti te venturum esse; omissis jam excusationibus, fac venias (*see* 'facio'). 11. Balbus (multo felicior quam frater) ante urbem captam mortem obierat. 12. Quod ne asse (*see* 'as') quidem emere volumus, id asse carum est.

1. There is no need of excuses; promise to help us. 2. There is no doubt that that victory cost us much blood. 3. We (can) easily do-without flesh, but (sed) we need water. 4. Tullius, a man of approved excellence, had promised to come to see us. 5. Are you much taller than your brothers? 6. The more patiently he bore these insults, the more-steadily he was loved by the citizens. 7. I will ask the general whether he has cut off the enemy from supplies. 8. He answered in-anger (276)

---

[1] Verbs ending in **-sco** commonly have the sense of *beginning* an action or state, and are called *Inceptives*. Inceptives rarely have a Fut. Part. in **-rus**, and consequently require, even in the Active, the use of the periphrasis forĕ ut, like possum (Par. 231).

[2] Quo .... eo, lit. *by how much* .... *by so much*, i.e. *the more bravely .... the more easily.* Why is quo Abl.? See Par. 274.

*that there was no need of an axe.* 9. *He is a man of little ability, yet by his perseverance he conquered very many rivals.* 10. *What prevents us from carrying on the war much more successfully, Tullius being now* (jam) *our leader* (197) (5a)?

## THE GENITIVE.

The Genitive is used in the following constructions:

**282**    1. (*a*) *Descriptively*, and (*b*) to express *quality*, as in English.

(*a*) *A fleet of two hundred vessels.*    Classis **dŭcentārum nāvium.**

(*b*) *He is a man of ability.*    Vir est **magni ingĕnii.**

In such instances, the Genitive Noun must always be accompanied by an Adjective.

**283**    2. To express (*a*) *estimation*, and (*b*) *indefinite price.*

(*a*) Rule.—**Magni, plūris, plūrĭmi, parvi, mĭnōris, mĭnĭmi, tanti, quanti,** and **nĭhĭli,** are used after Verbs of *estimation*, such as **pendo** (I *hang, weigh, value*), **făcĭo, aestĭmo.**

**284**    (*b*) Rule.—**Tanti, quanti, plūris, mĭnōris** (but **magno, parvo, plūrĭmo,** &c.) are used after Verbs of *selling* and *buying.*

(*a*) *I do not count you worth a straw.*    **Nōn flocci tē făcĭo.**

(*b*) *At what price was the corn bought? For a large sum.*    **Quanti** frūmentum emptum est? **Magno.**[1]

**285**    3. To express *plenty* or *want* (but this is more often expressed by the Ablative).

The pupil must learn by practice what words generally take the Genitive and what the Ablative: for example, **indĭgeo** generally takes the Genitive, and **ĕgeo** the Ablative.

**286**    [1] The distinction between the Genitive and Ablative appears to be this: the Gen. is used when the price is stated *indefinitely* and regarded as a *quality*, the Abl. when it is stated *definitely* and regarded as the *instrument* whereby the purchase is effected.

**287** 4. After Adjectives of *knowledge* and *ignorance,* such as **conscĭus,** *conscious of,* **nescĭus,** *ignorant of,* **insuētus,** *unaccustomed to,* &c.

*He is ignorant of manners, but very learned in the law.*
**Mōrum** impĕrītus est, **jūris** autem perītissĭmus.

*He informed me of his plan,* i.e., *he made me more certain of his plan.*
**Consĭlii sui** mē certiōrem fēcit.

**288** 5. After Present Participles and Adjectives that have the force of Nouns, such as **ăvĭdus, pŏtens, insŏlens, cŭpĭdus,** &c.

*Patient* (i.e. *an endurer*) *of cold.*
Pātiens **frīgŏris.**

*He was an extreme lover of his country.*
Patrĭae ĕrat **ămantissĭmus.**

**289** 6. After a suppressed Noun, such as *nature, mark, duty, lot, part,* &c.

*It is (the mark) of a wise man not to be easily disturbed.*
**Săpientis** est nōn făcĭle perturbāri.

*It is (the duty) of a young man to respect his elders.*
**Ădŭlescentis** est mājōres nātu vĕrēri.

*It is not (the luck) of every one to do this.*
Nōn **cuiusvīs** est hōc făcĕre.

**290** 7. After a suppressed Noun, such as *charge, cause,* &c., with Verbs of *accusing, acquitting, convicting,* &c.

*Having been accused (on the charge) of theft, Balbus was condemned to death.*
Balbus (crīmĭne) **furti** accusātus, căpĭtis damnātus est.[1]

Exercise LXXX.

1. Non cuiusvis est summos honores assequi. 2. Haruspices aut stultitiae aut vanitatis recte condemnamus. 3. Quanti praedium emptum est? Magno: sed equidem id parvi aestimo.

---

**290**a [1] The Genitive is not habitually used to denote the *punishment,* but only the *charge.* But it is used of the *punishment* in the phrases, "**capĭtĭs, dupli, quadrupli,** &c., (multā) condemnāre," *to condemn (in the fine) of death, two-fold, four-fold,* &c.

4. Tardi ingenii est nihil nisi omnibus nota[1] perspicere.
5. Themistocles, providi animi vir, persuasit Atheniensibus ut classem centum navium compararent. 6. Majestatis accusati, alii in metalla, alii ad bestias, alii capitis damnati sunt.
7. Quaerebam mecum quare apud hanc gentem parum (*adv.*) virium veritas haberet. 8. Rhodum aut aliquo (*adv.*) terrarum hinc migrandum est. 9. Omnium regionum, id temporis,[2] Gallia et frugum et metallorum fertilissima esse videbatur.
10. Stultorum est doctrinae cupidos contemnere. 11. Barbaros, insuetos laboris, disciplinae insolentes, rudes rei militaris, facile vicimus. 12. Tempori cedere a plerisque, sed non a Catone, sapientis est habitum.

1. *The Christians, having been accused of treason before* (apud) *the proconsul, were condemned to the mines.* 2. *Where* (292a) *in-the-world shall we find a-second-man so fond of learning, so patient of labour?* 3. *Balbus, a man of incredible perfidy, was found guilty of bribery.* 4. *I value the farm at-a-great-price; but it was sold for-a-small price.* 5. *I asked why the farm had been sold for more than* (quam) *the house.* 6. *It is not like a philosopher* (i.e. *the mark of a philosopher*) *to be disturbed by trifles.* 7. *It is not the lot of everybody to persuade those-who-listen* (202). 8. *His brother was acquitted of theft; but Balbus himself, a man free from all fault, was condemned to death.* 9. *It requires* (i.e. *it is the part of*) *a great leader to effect this task; for effecting* (186) *which, Tullius has too-little ability.* 10. *Whither in-the world are you migrating from Athens?*

SOME USES OF THE SUBJUNCTIVE.

**291** I. The Subjunctive Mood is used in its proper Subjunctive use when it is *subjoined* to a Principal Verb, to express (132) *purpose* or *indirect question*. But it is also *subjoined* to express (1) *result*, and (2) *reason*: (for **cum** causal with Subjunctive, see Par. 151a).

---

**292** [1] **Nōta** is Neut. Pl. Acc., used as a Noun, governed by **perspĭcis** understood: *to perceive nothing unless* (*you perceive*) *things-known to all*. The phrase **nīl nīsi** is often used thus with the force of *except*.

[2] Here **Id** is the Accusative of Duration (262); but instead of **tempus**, there is the Partitive Genitive **tempŏris**.

**292a** The Partitive Gen. often follows (*a*) Neut. Pronouns, *e.g.* "quicquĭd, *or* sī quid cĭbi hăbŭimus," *whatever food*, or *all the food. we had*; and also (*b*) Adverbs, *e.g.* **ălĭquo terrārum**, lit. *some-whither of lands*, i.e. *to some place or other in the world;* **ŭbĭ terrārum?** *where in the world?*

(1) *The fighting was so brisk that many were slain on both sides; among whom it happened that the leader himself fell.*

Tam ācrĭter pugnātum est ut multi utrimque **interfĭcĕrentur**; inter quos accĭdit ut dux ipse **occĭdĕret**.

(2) *The Athenians condemned Socrates to death because he had (said they) corrupted the youth.*

Ăthēnienses Sōcrătem căpĭtis damnāvērunt quod jŭventūtem **corrūpisset**.[1]

**293** II. Besides its uses in the above *subjoined* clauses, the Subjunctive (or, as it is sometimes called, the Conjunctive Mood) is also used independently, as follows:

(1) *Hortatively*, i.e. *exhorting*: **ămēmus**, *let us love*.[2]

(2) *Concessively*, i.e. *granting* for the sake of argument:

*Grant that you expel nature, yet she will continually return.*    Nātūram **expellas**; usquĕ tămen rĕcurret.

(3) *Optatively*, i.e. *wishing*: **pĕreas**! *may you perish!*

(4) *Conditionally*, i.e. expressing a statement made subject to the fulfilment of a *condition*.

*I should like to come (i.e. if it could be allowed, &c.).*    **Vĕlim** vĕnīre.

III. The Subjunctive is used (1) after **si**, *if*, to express a *condition*, and also (2) to express a *consequence*.[3]

*If he came, (then) he would conquer.*    Si (1) **vĕniat**, (2) **vincat**.

The *if-clause* is called the Protasis (see p. 238); the Consequent, or *then-clause*, is called the Apodosis (see p. 233).

---

[1] The Subjunctive implies that the reason influences the mind of others, not the mind of the writer. **Corrūpĕrat** would have implied that the writer believed the charge: *because he had (as a fact) corrupted the youth*.

[2] This usage is ordinarily placed under the Imperative.

[3] **Si** with the Indic. Pres. or Perf. (less frequently Imperf. or Pluperf.) is used in conditions *which are assumed to be true*, and is often equivalent to *when* or *since*.

**294** RULE.—After **sī, nē, num,** use **quĭs** for *any one,* **quando** for *at any time,* ("**sī ălĭquis**" would mean *if some one;* "**sī ălĭquando**," *if at some time*).

**295** The Tenses of the Subjunctive in Conditional Sentences vary with the nature of the condition.

The *Past Tenses* of the Subjunctive are naturally employed to express conditions (1 *a*) *impossible* or (1 *b*) *regarded as impossible.*

The *Present* expresses (2 *a*) conditions *possible* or (2 *b*) though really impossible, *graphically regarded as possible.*

(1 *a*) *If I had received anything (which I have not done) I would have given it.* — Si quid **accēpissem, dĕdissem** (**dărem** *would mean 'I should now be giving'*).

(1 *b*) *Should I receive, or, if I received anything (which there is no reason for thinking likely) I would give it.* — Si quid **accīpĕrem, dărem.**

(2 *a*) *Should I receive, or, if I received, anything (which is possible) I would give it.* — Si quid **accĭpĭam, dem,** i.e. *imagine me receiving something.*

(2 *b*) *Imagine Plato come to life again; believe me, you would blush while saying this.* — Si **rĕvīvīscat** Plăto; crĕdĕ mĭhī, haec dīcens **rūbĕas,** i.e. *I see you blushing.*

N.B.—*The Tense is the same* in the Protasis and Apodosis.

EXERCISE LXXXI.

**296** RULE.—**Ut . . . . non** is *not* to be changed into **nē** when the Subjunctive expresses Consequence.

*So vigorous was the charge that they could not resist.* — Tantus ērat impĕtus **ŭt** rĕsistere **nōn** possent.

1. Bonorum exempla imitemur, malorum caveamus.[1] 2. Peream nisi haec vere dico. 3. Plures cecidissent ni nox proelio intervenisset. 4. Si semper optima videre et facere possemus, haud sane praeceptore nobis opus foret. 5. Si quis gladium a te insaniens poscat, nonne dare peccatum sit?

---

**297** [1] Note that, where in English we say "*those* of the bad," the Latin either (1) repeats the Noun, "mălōrum exempla," or (2), as above, leaves the Noun to be understood; but in no case inserts **ea.**

6. Si vir bonus hanc vim habeat ut verbo inimicos interficere possit, hac vi profecto (*adv.*) non utatur (295, 2 *b*). 7. At si Marco Crasso dares hanc vim ut digitorum percussione divitissimum quemque interficeret (32), divitias ipse acciperet, in foro (mihi crede) prae gaudio saltaret. 8. Cave ne quis tibi, epistola mea usus, ignaro noceat. 9. Num quis tam amens est ut filiis suis invideat? 10. Tanta vi hostes in urbem irruperunt ut nostri, tanta multitudine oppressi, in arcem se recipere non possent.

1. *By-chance it happened that a few of our-men had been slain by the arrows of the enemy.*[1] 2. *If the excellent Tullius had promised to* (280) *help a friend, he would have kept his word.* 3. *If any one asked* (295, 2a) *you whence you come, you would reply that you come from Carthage.* 4. *It cannot be* (fĭĕri) *that a just man would wish to use an unjust power.*[1] 5. *If by some* (quĭdam) *magic art, Balbus were able to assume the form of any animal* (he-pleased), *he would choose a fish, that he might* (131) *not be compelled to speak.* 6. *The general was so greedy of fame as to envy* (i.e. *that he envied*) *even his own centurions.* 7. *How are you-getting-on* (i.e. *what are you doing*, quid ăgis) *at Athens, my son?* 8. *Write to me how you are getting-on at Corinth.*

### THE SUBJUNCTIVE (*continued*).

**298** Qui takes the Indicative (I.) when it is used for a Demonstrative Pronoun with a Coordinate Conjunction such as *and, but,* &c.[2]; but (II.) it takes the Subjunctive when used for a Demonstrative with a Subordinate Conjunction denoting (1) *purpose*, (2) *consequence*, (3) *cause*, &c.

| | |
|---|---|
| I. *At length we reached the enemy; who* (i.e. *but they*) *immediately fled.* | Tandem ventum ĕrat ad hostes; qui stătim terga **dăbant.** |
| II. (1) *We sent ambassadors to* (Lat. *who should* i.e. *that they should*) *ask for peace.* | Mīsĭmus lēgā'os **qui** (i.e. **ut ĕi**) pācem **pĕtĕrent.** |
| (2) *There were some that* (i.e. *such that they*) *blamed you.* | Ĕrant **qui** (i.e. ălĭqui tāles ut) te culpārent. |

**299** [1] See the use of **accĭdit** in the first example in page 150, above. The Subjunctive is used after Verbs of *happening, coming to pass,* &c. as if they implied a *result* consequent on something preceding.

**299a** [2] **Qui** is sometimes used for the Demonstrative without a Conjunction, *e.g.* in the idiom "tū, **cuius ĕs săpientiae** (282*b*), non errābis," *you* (*of such wisdom are you, i.e. such is your wisdom*) *will not err.*

| | |
|---|---|
| (3) *I congratulate you because you have such a son.* | Grātŭlor tĭbĭ **quī** (*i.e.* **quod tu**) tālem fīlium hăbeās. |

**300** After the antecedent **nēmo**, or **quīs**, you must not write **quī nōn**, nor **quō** (old form **quī**) **nōn**, but **quīn** (this applies to all Genders.)

| | |
|---|---|
| (2 *a*) *Who is there* (or, *there is no one*) *that does not hate you?* | Quĭs est (*or*, Nēmo est) **quīn** tē ōdĕrit? |
| *There was no day but Tullius walked with me,* lit. *on-which-not T. walked with me.* | Dies ĕrat nullus **quīn** (*i.e.* quo nōn) Tullius mēcum ambŭlāret. |

**301** **Vĕrĕor** means *I am anxiously on the watch.* Hence, when it is translated *I fear,* the English requires (1) the insertion of a negative if the Latin omits it, and (2) the omission of a negative if the Latin inserts it.

| | |
|---|---|
| (1) *I fear he will not come.* | Vĕreor (*or* tĭmeo) **ŭt** vĕniat, lit. *I am anxiously watching that he may come.* |
| (2) *I feared he would come.* | Vĕrĭtus sum (*or* tīmui) **nē** vĕnīret, lit. *I anxiously watched that he might not come.* |

N.B.—After *fear*, translate the English Future by the Latin Subjunctive.

**302** **Nescĭo ăn.** Before **ăn**, **utrum** is always implied, if not expressed. Hence in Direct Questions **ăn** is used to introduce an *alternative* to which the speaker is driven, "(Utrum hōc fătēris) ăn hōc nĕgās?" (*Whether do you confess this) Or must I suppose that you actually deny this?* Similarly, in Indirect Questions, **nescĭo ăn** introduces an *alternative and more probable supposition;* thus, "Nescĭo (utrum ventūrus sit) ăn nōn ventūrus sit," means, *I do not know (whether he will come), or whether, as is more probable, he will not come,* i.e., *I rather think he will not come.* Consequently, with **nescĭo ăn** (as with **vĕrĕor**) a negative must be inserted or omitted in Latin, in a manner exactly contrary to the English idiom.

| | |
|---|---|
| *I do not know whether he will come.* | Nescio ăn **nōn** ventūrus sit, i.e. *I rather think he will not come.* |
| *I do not know whether he will not come.* | Nescio ăn ventūrus sit,[1] i.e. *I rather think he will come.* |

### Exercise LXXXII.

**303** Rule.—With a Comparative Adverb, purpose is expressed by **quo**, *i.e.* **ut ĕo** (Par. 277):

| | |
|---|---|
| *In order that he might swim more quickly.* | **Quo** (*i.e.* **ut ĕo**) cĕlĕrius nāret. |

1. Mittamus legatos qui pacem petant. 2. Quotusquisque est qui tibi faveat! Sunt qui te oderint; nemo fere est quin tibi invideat. 3. Omnes laudabant victorem qui tot milia civium incolumes servasset, toties hostem sub jugum misisset. 4. Quis est quin sibi consulat, alienis sua anteponat? 5. Dies fere nullus erat quin (*i.e.* quo non) rus tecum irem. 6. Fossam castris circumdedimus quo (*i.e.* ut eo) facilius hostibus resisteremus. 7. Vereor ne optimus quisque civium nos deserat. 8. Nescio an res mihi non bene successura sit; sed id agam ut tibi subveniam. 9. Nescio an mulieres venturae sint; sed, si aberunt, equidem tibi subveniam. 10. Pavor ceperat milites ne praeda sibi criperetur. 11. Lege quādam cavebatur ne quis, ob causam orandam, pecuniam donumve (*see* -ve) acciperet. 12. Cave ne aeger neve hieme naviges. 13. Non tu is (*see Vocab.* '*is*') es qui mentiaris.[2]

1. *They sent ambassadors to* (qui) *ask for peace.* 2. *I am not the man* (is qui) *to use this opportunity.*[2] 3. *There was no one but wished to help him.* 4. *I feared that all the best of the citizens would set out for the country.* 5. *All praise you for* (298, 3) (qui) *having conquered so many thousands of the enemy.* 6. *Even if it were possible,*[3] *I should not wish to do this.* 7. *I fear that the enemy, having now crossed the river, will not make* (fĕrio) *peace.* 8. *There were some who answered that not even an assassin must be delivered-over against the laws.* 9. *How-few* (quŏtus-quisque *with sing.*) *are there*

---

[1] These differences between the English and Latin idioms are sometimes expressed in the lines:—
With **vĕreor** and **nescio**
For English *yes*, put Latin *no*.

**303a** [2] Note that, after "nōn ĕgo īs sum, tū īs ĕs, īs est, qui," the Relative agrees, *in Person*, with the Subject of the Verb *to be*, not with **Is**.

**304** [3] *It is possible*, i.e. *it is able to be done*, "fĭeri pŏtest," not **pŏtest** alone, except in the phrases "ut pŏtest," "si pŏtest," and these mostly in colloquial Latin. The pupil should use **pŏtest** to mean *it is able*, not *it is possible*. See Vocab. "*even.*"

*who are unwilling to use an opportunity of obtaining wealth!*
10. *There is no one in this city who will not prefer his-interests* (i.e. *his-things*, 34) *to mine.*

## Sē, ipsĕ, &c.

It has been said above (Par. 218, and see page 328) that **sē, suus,** &c. (and not **eum, eius**) are used when they refer (in a Subordinate Clause) to the Subject of the Principal Verb. But there are exceptions to this Rule.

I. Sometimes an apparently Subordinate Sentence (*e.g.* one introduced by *because*) is really equivalent to a Co-ordinate Sentence introduced by *for*.

| | |
|---|---|
| *Marcius returned safe because I had spared him.* | Marcius salvus rĕdiit quod ei pĕpercĕram.[1] |

This is really equivalent to the two Co-ordinate Sentences, *Marcius returned safe : for I had spared him,* "Marcius salvus rĕdiit; nam ei pĕpercĕram:" and **ei** is therefore used, because **rĕdiit** is regarded, not as a Principal, but as a Co-ordinate Verb.

But if the *because-clause* be more closely connected with what precedes, and if some notion of *thought he, said he*, be introduced, so as to make the latter part appear, *not a historical fact*, but rather dependent upon *what Marcius thought, said,* &c.—then **sĭbĭ** must be used.

| | |
|---|---|
| *Marcius returned me thanks because (said he) I had spared him.* | Marcius grātias ēgit mĭhĭ quod sĭbĭ pĕpercissem.[1] |

II. Occasionally **suus** is used of different persons in the same sentence. In such cases the *sense* must determine the translation.

| | |
|---|---|
| *The Veneti sent an ambassador to Caesar (commanding that) if he wished to receive back his own men, he should send their hostages back for them.* | Vĕnĕti lēgātum ad Caesărem mīsērunt: " Si vellet **suos** rĕcĭpere, obsĭdes **sĭbĭ** rĕ-mittĕret."[2] |

---

[1] Note also that the Indicative **pĕpercĕram** is changed into the Subjunctive **pĕpercissem** (293*a*).

[2] The construction of **rĕmittĕret** is explained more fully in the rules on Exercise XCIII.: here, **rĕmittĕret** may be parsed as Subjunctive after **impĕrāvērunt ut**, which is *implied* in **mīsērunt**, *they sent* (*with orders that*).

**307** III. Ambiguity in English is sometimes avoided by the distinction between *him* and *himself:* but in Latin both these pronouns are sometimes rendered by **sē**, so that the meaning of **sē** has to be determined by *the sense of the whole passage:*

| | |
|---|---|
| *The captive besought the conqueror to spare him.* | Captīvus victōrem obsecrāvit ut sĭbĭ parcĕret. |
| *The father commanded the son to restrain himself.* | Păter fīlio impĕrāvit ut **sē** coercēret. |

**308** IV. Ambiguity is sometimes removed in Latin (1) by adding **ipsĕ** to the Subject of the Subordinate Verb, to which **se** refers:

| | |
|---|---|
| (1) *Nature impels a child to love itself.* | Nātūra mŏvet infantem ut **se ipsĕ** dīlĭgat. |

(2) by placing **ipsĕ** in antithesis with **sē**, using **ipsĕ** to refer to the Principal Subject and **sē** to refer to the Subordinate Subject:

| | |
|---|---|
| *Caesar asked (his soldiers) why they distrusted their own valour or his diligence.* | Caesar quaesīvit (ex mīlĭtĭbus) cur de **suā** virtūte aut de **ipsĭus** dīlĭgentia despērārent. |

### Exercise LXXXIII.

**309** Rule.—**Quisquam**, and **ullus**, *any*, are used in negative and comparative sentences, and in interrogative sentences that expect the answer *No.*

**Quisquam** is used for the English *no one* and *nothing* when *and* precedes: *and no one* **nĕc quisquam**; *and nothing*, **nĕc quidquam**. Similarly, *and never*, **neque unquam**, &c.

**310** Distinguish between **quisquam** and **quisquĕ**, *each one;* **quisquĭs**, *whoever;* **quīlĭbet** and **quīvīs**, *any one you like;* **quīdam**, *a certain (person);* **ălĭquĭs**, *some one.*[1]

---

[1] **Quĭdam** means *a certain person (whom I could mention by name, if I desired)*, **ălĭquĭs** *some one (who exists, but it matters not who precisely it is)*. Note that **quisquĭs** is the only one of these words that has a Relative force.

## GENDERS OF NOUNS.

1. Venator orabat comites ne se ante oculos suos perire sinerent. 2. Pertimuerunt ne ab ipsis desciscerct et cum suis in gratiam rediret. 3. Quaesivit imperator cur milites sibi totiens antea obtemperassent, jam obtemperare nollent. 4. Tum vero rex circumstantes obsecrat ut suae quisque saluti consulant, ipsum morientem neglegant.[1] 5. Quodam tempore natus sum; aliquo tempore mihi moriendum erit. 6. Non cuivis contingit optimo cuique suorum civium placere. 7. Si quis in scena saltat, ei non quivis motus sed certus quidam (motus) datur. 8. Inest etiam superbis falsa quaedam modestiae species. 9. Interrogavi nonne major natu esset quam quisquam ex fratribus suis. 10. Dixerit aliquis (*some one may be inclined to say*) inutilem fuisse hanc victoriam; sed eiusmodi dicta (quae cuilibet prompta sunt), flocci non facio. 11. Neapoli profectura subito obiit (265*a*).

1. *I hope that the city will soon be captured, and that no one* (i.e. *nor any one*) *of the enemy will escape.* 2. *They believed that the boy had departed from them and returned to his (friends.)* 3. *The general besought the soldiers to trust in their own valour and in his wisdom.* 4. *When I asked* (i.e. *to me asking*) *who* (240*a*) *would* (i.e. *wished to*) *carry the letter, one*[2] *of my brother's servants replied that he would do it.* 5. *Some-one may say* (see Sent. 10 above) *that death is an eternal sleep: but, even among* (apud) *the ancients, most of the philosophers believed that there is something after death.* 6. *It is lawful to the actor to utter not any words he-likes, but certain fixed words.* 7. *Sometimes it is a kind-of virtue* (see '*kind*') *even to abstain from vice.* 8. *Can any one* (294) *deny that we must beware lest any one of the spies should hear this?*

### EXERCISES ON THE GENDERS OF THE NOUNS AND IRREGULAR VERBS.

**Dea, -ae,** f. *goddess,* makes Dat. Pl. **deābus** in classical authors: and **fīliābus** is found in inscriptions and legal forms.

**Bōs,** c. *ox* or *cow,* Gen. **bŏvis,** has Dat. and Abl. Pl. **bōbus** and **būbus.**

**Vīs,** f. sing. *force, violence,* has Gen. and Dat. Sing. wanting, and is declined Nom. **vīs,** Acc. **vim,** Abl. **vī.**

**Vīres,** f. pl. *strength* (Pl. of **vīs,** but not meaning *violence*), is formed regularly, **vīrĭum, vīrĭbus, vīres.**

---

[1] What case is **quisquĕ**? See the word in the Vocabulary.
[2] Trans. *a certain one;* not **ūnus,** which would mean *one only.*

Jŭppĭtĕr makes Jŏvem, Jŏvis, Jŏvi, Jŏve.

Dŏmŭs is formed partly from the Second and partly from the Fourth Declension. The Gen. and Dat., Sing. and Pl., are of the Fourth, dŏmūs, dŏmui, domŭum, dŏmĭbus, and also the Abl. Pl. dŏmĭbus; the rest are of the Second.[1]

Jūs-jūrandum, *oath* (which has no Plural), and rēspublĭca, *state*, are not irregular, but simply words compounded of Nouns and Adjectives agreeing with them, Gen. jūris-jūrandi, rĕipublĭcæ, &c.

### Exercise LXXXIV.

**312**  Rule.—Cēlo, dŏceo, and some other Verbs take two Accusatives in the Active, and one in the Passive:

| | |
|---|---|
| *Mercury taught Cupid letters.* | Mercŭrius **Cŭpīdĭnem littĕras** dŏcuit. |
| *My son must be taught letters.* | Fīlius meus **littĕras** est dŏcendus. |

**313**  Rule.—Antĕ, post (placed *Adverbially* between the Noun and Adj. of time), and sometimes (216) ăbhinc, *ago*, are used with the Abl. of *Measure* (274), to denote an interval before or after.

| | |
|---|---|
| *He died a very few days before.* | Hŏmo **perpaucis** antĕ **diēbus** ŏbiit. |
| *Many years afterwards, he returned home.* | **Multis** post **annis**, dŏmum rĕdiit. |
| *They perished two years ago.* | Abhinc **biennio** pĕriĕrunt. |

1. Non dubium est quin solverit quod pro fratre spopondit. 2. Rogavi imperatorem utrum civitatem omnem an paucos procerum jure-jurando obstrinxisset. 3. Quibus domibus milites pepercerant eas cives ipsi incenderunt. 4. Quod frater tuus me non celavit, id cur tu occuluisti? 5. Num, te jubente, consul secures sumpsit posuitque? 6. Nolo exorsa (*see* exordior) vel potius fere detexta, postea, jam senex, retexere. 7. Tullius, primis annis, puer, equis bubusque

---

**313a**  [1] The Gen. and Acc. Pl. dŏmōrum and dŏmūs are sometimes found. The forms are sometimes remembered by the lines:—
  Si dēclīnāre dŏmus vīs
    Tolle (i.e. *take away*) -mĕ, -mŭ, -mī, et -mīs.
The form dŏmi, *at home*, is the Locative Case, see Par. 265.

alendis; mox juvenis, rei-publicae operam dedit.[1] 8. Si quid mihi humanitus (*adv.*) accidisset, liberi mei defensore caruissent (295, 1a). 9. Quotusquisque didicit quomodo vivendum sit! 10. Filiorum eius alteri Tullia nupsit; alteri soror eius, perpaucis post mensibus. 11. Fertur Venus[2] filium suum Mercurio literas docendum tradidisse. 12. Homo stultissimus filio, qui natu maximus est, grandem pecuniam testamento (*abl. instr.*) legat; filiabus nihil legat.

1. *The worthless Balbus was-unwilling to support the parents who had supported him from boyhood.* 2. *I asked the husbandman when* (i.e. *at what time*) *he had sown* (*his*) *corn* (*pl.*). 3. *There is no doubt that the soldiers distrusted the general.* 4. *I asked Tullius why he was going-to-leave so-large a sum-of-money to his three daughters.* 5. *Did you, a few days afterwards, promise your daughter* (*in-marriage*) *to that-fellow?* 6. *Do you, who elected me consul, now hope, O citizens, to wrest the consulate from-me* (mihi) *by violence* (152a)? 7. *At-first our men were driven-back; (but) soon a-second-time advancing they drove the enemy down from the hill.* 8. *Why have you pledged-yourself to pay so large a sum-of-money?* 9. *Because you are bankrupt, do not* (ne) *on that account make false promises.* 10. *Are-you-ignorant of the way in which* (i.e. *in-what-way*) *Brutus drove-out Tarquin?*

### Exercise LXXXV.

**314** 1. The Distributive Numerals (for which see Par. 77) are used, (1) where the same number applies to *each* of a class; (2) where the Noun with which the Numeral agrees is Singular in meaning, though Plural in form, *e.g.* **littĕrae, castra** (so that the Noun implies a *group*, e.g. **littĕrae**, *a group of alphabetical letters*); (3) in poetry.[3]

(1) *The men will be contented with two or at all events three denarii a-piece.*  Hōmĭnes **bīnis,** aut certo **ternis** dēnāriis contenti ĕrunt.

---

[1] **Dat** governs **ĕquis** as well as **rei-publicae**.

**315** [2] Note the Latin idiom. *It is reported that Venus did,* &c., is never to be rendered "fertur **Vĕnĕrem** fecisse," &c., but always *Venus is reported to have done,* &c., "fertur **Vĕnus** fēcisse," &c. A similar construction is used with **dīcĭtur**, see Par. 177.

**316** [3] Because, in poetry, number is regarded not as a precise collection of units, but as a *group*, a "brace," "dozen," "score," "hundred," &c., which may belong to any number of persons *a-piece*, so that a kind of distribution is implied. Thus any hero may carry his "couple" of darts, and any giant may have his "hundred hands"; and hence Virgil speaks of "**bīna hastīlia,**" in the hand of Æneas, and "**centēnae mănūs**" belonging to a giant.

(2) *At that time I used to write one, two, three, four, sometimes five letters a day.*

Eo tempŏre **singŭlis** diēbus **ūnas, bīnas, trīnas, quăternas,** interdum ětiam **quīnas littĕras** scrībēbam.[1]

**317.** 2. **Cum ... tum,** used like **ět ... ět,** sometimes mean *not only, but also:* see sentence 7 below.

(*Look out* allĭcio, diffindo, ĭnūro, oblĭno.)

1. Quam messem senex severat filius eius messuit. 2. Hostes fusos fugatosque tanta vi nostri colle depulerunt ut ne equites quidem in arcem se recipere possent. 3. Vita eius tot tantisque flagitiis oblīta fuerat ut turpitudinis nŏtam non sibi soli sed toti generi et nomini suo inussisset. 4. Nonne apud Plinium, in Naturali Historia, legistis piscibus non supra quaternas pinnas esse, quibusdam binas, aliquibus nullas?[2] 5. Hujus urbis portas aurum vestrum, non virtus, diffĭdit.[3] 6. Inter occulta et sepulta non multum interest. 7. Allexerunt audientium animos, cum oratoris eloquentia, tum jurisjurandi commemoratio, et hostium jam accedentium minae. 8. Incertum est utrum militibus singulos an binos denarios dederit, an denique alios pecunia alios promissis ad seditionem impulerit. 9. Qui cum (i.e. *Now when he*) decemvir legibus scribendis[4] delectus esset, statim intellexit Licinius rem non jam neglegendam esse. 10. Tanta erat hostium multitudo ut ne trina quidem castra eis sufficerent.

1. *To (his) two daughters, whom he loved to a remarkable-degree* (unice), *he left ten thousand denarii a-piece.* 2. (*His*) *sons he entirely neglected, except one, the youngest, to whom he left all-the-money-that* (quantum pecuniae) *he had collected.* 3. *The soldiers he allured, by promising to some six, to others seven, denarii a-piece.* 4. *The daughter did not marry that (man) to whom her father had promised-her-in-marriage.* 5. *Having drawn the water, the girl returned to the well to draw (some) again.*[5] 6. *At the command of the emperor the consul laid-aside the fasces, which he had assumed a very-few days before.* 7. *I*

---

[1] Note that, with Pl. Nouns of Sing. meaning, the forms **ūni, trīni** are used, instead of the ordinary distributives, **singŭli, terni.**

[2] For a list of the distributive numerals, see Par. 77.

[3] It was a proverb of Philip of Macedon that any city could be taken, to the gates of which a mule laden with gold, *i.e.* a bribe, could make its way.

[4] This dative (for "ad leges scribendas") is rare, except in *official appellations;* and it is not to be imitated.

[5] Remember that the Eng. Infinitive is never to be rendered by the Latin Inf. unless it is the Subject or Object of a Verb: see Par. 217.

*fear that something* (301) *amiss has befallen the excellent Tullius.* 8. *My son, what you have sown, that you will reap.*

### Exercise LXXXVI.

319  *He is too cruel to be loved by any one.*   Crūdēlior est quam qui (or ut) a quoquam amētur.
*He is the same as he always was.*   Īdem est ac (or qui) semper fuit.

(*Look out* accumbo, cōgo, comprěhendo, dēposco, nanciscor, rěgěro, părio, excŭtio.)

1. Proserpina, ut flores aspexit, "Accedite," inquit, "comites."[1] 2. Crudelior erat rex quam ut cuiquam indulgeret vel ignosceret. 3. Sperasne ceteros poenas daturos, tibi uni indultum iri?[2] 4. Centurioni militibus increpanti vox haesit; nam meminerat et sibi uxorem liberosque domi manere.[3] 5. Praetor eadem, quae antea, respondit, lege sanctum fuisse ne quis mortuum intra urbem sepeliret. 6. Homo cum inter cenandum obdormiisset, subito tanto strepitu stertuit ut qui una (*adv.*) accubuerant omnes risum tollerent. 7. Mulier cum tres liberos uno partu peperisset, solitum praemium a regina depoposcit. 8. Exuta veste piscator se in undam mersit; mox anulum nactus regerit. 9. Tum Balbus, quem facinorum quae coactus commiserat jam poenituerat, rem omnem consuli pandit. 10. Continuo, excusso sopore, pater latronem comprensurus exsiluit foras.

1. *When* (*she*) *had approached the meadow the flowers attracted the maiden's eyes.* 2. (*His*) *voice failed* (desum) *him when he attempted* (i.e. *attempting*) *to ask the tyrant what he wished to do.* 3. *Having shaken off sleep, our men leaped out of their beds.* 4. *We went yesterday to Rome to see a picture painted by the celebrated painter Tullius.* 5. *If he had revealed the* (295, 1a) *matter of-his-own-accord he would have-been-spared* (167) *by the conquerors.* 6. *It had been enacted that no one should possess more than two hundred acres, but the sons of Tullius possessed three hundred acres a-piece.* 7. *There is no doubt that you compelled the man to bind himself by an oath.* 8. *Those who remained in Corinth were all taken and slain.* 9. *When will you go from Rome* (265a)?

---

[1] Inquit always comes after the first emphatic word of a speech, see page 215. For ŭt with the Indicative, see the Latin Vocabulary.
[2] Esse is omitted after dātūros, a very common omission (211).
[3] Centŭriōni is *Dat. of Disadvantage;* sibī, *Dat. of Advantage;* for ĕt see Par. 146.

## Exercise LXXXVII.

**321** The Historical Infinitive is used for the Indicative (always in the Present, and more commonly Active than Passive), when a writer is describing a number of actions so confused together that the times and persons are not easily defined; so that the *Infinitive*, i.e. the *Infinite* or *Indefinite* form of the Verb is naturally preferred. The consequent indefiniteness is somewhat similar to that which arises from the omission of **sum**; and this Infinitive is often found in a sentence in which **sum** is actually omitted.

| | |
|---|---|
| *Horses and men, friends and foes were mingled together; all was chance*, lit. *chance ruled all things.* | Ĕqui, vĭri, hostes, cīves permixti; fors omnia **rĕgĕre**. |

**322** A Dative of *Purpose* (besides the Dat. of Possession or Reception) is used after **sum** and **do** (268):

| | |
|---|---|
| *He gave me the book (to serve) for a gift.* | Lĭbrum mĭhi **dōno** dĕdit. |
| *This will be (for) a help to me.* | Hōc ĕrit mĭhi **adjūmento**. |

A similar Dat. is sometimes used after **dūco, hăbĕo**, &c., meaning *consider*:

| | |
|---|---|
| *This was considered (for) a great insult.* | Hōc magnae **contŭmēlĭae** hăbĭtum est. |

(*Look out* allĭcĭo, anquīro, excŏlo, torreo.)

1. Foeda inde colluvies; pars cedere, alii insequi; hi fugere, illi resistere ac propulsare; nihil consilio agi. 2. Campus, frumentis optime excultus, decem milia passuum in latitudinem, tria in longitudinem patebat. 3. Consenserant Patres; uni Catoni aliter visum est. 4. Virgines alias (88) alii flores allexere; huic rosae, illi violae curae¹ erant: una Proserpina liliis sinum replebat. 5. Fertur Ceres famem longam papavere imprudens solvisse, quod, intratura senis domum, forte collegerat. 6. Nostri per apertas portas irruĕre; ibi clamorem tollere, caede atque incendio omnia miscere. 7. Cur non ante confessus es te peccavisse quam res ipsa anquisita est? 8. Credo fore ut mox judices timeas, quamquam nunc

---
¹ Cūrae is Dative; rŏsae and vĭŏlae Nominative.

quidem negas quidquam de te compertum esse. 9. Quid?
Errorem tuum, nisi tibi ipsi nocuerit, nonne vis corrigere?
10. Ulmos vitibus amictas quis non rubetis (*not from* rŭbeo),
sole tostis anteponit?

1. *The false witnesses had not deceived* (fallo) *the judge, who favoured neither of us.* 2. *The fields, scorched by the sun, have not produced (their) usual fruits.* 3. *The maiden whom your brother has demanded in* (in *with acc.*) *marriage, her father has not promised-in-marriage.* 4. *The two armies, which consisted of four legions (each), filled the whole (of the) valley.* 5. *There is no doubt that he collected a great sum-of-money.* 6. *When he had plunged into the sea, he saw nothing but stones.* 7. *When all had agreed, Balbus alone resisted the proposal* (i.e. *plan*). 8. *She did not confess her fault until* (ante ... quam) *the king bound her by an oath.*

Exercise LXXXVIII.

(1) **Quamquam**, *although*, mostly takes the Indicative;
(2) **quamvīs**, *however much*, always the Subjunctive (in Prose). (3) But **quamvīs** is sometimes used as an Adverb:
"ālĭge quamvīs **multa**,"[1] *choose however many*, i.e. *as many as you please*.

(*Look out* pando, prōgigno, reor, sarcio, scindo.)

1. Scissa veste, crine passo, virgo ad caelum supplices manus protendebat. 2. Hic, quamvis male sevisset, sperabat se bene messurum esse. 3. Romani, quamquam hostem fuderant, tamen insequi fugientes nequibant. 4. Vestem sartam quidem, si necesse erit. patiar; turpem vero et maculis foedatam non patiar. 5. Legimus, apud Vergilium, Famam extremam prolem a Tellure progenitam. 6. Difficile est dictu cur hic tantus imperator tam imbellem gentem non facile perdomuerit. 7. His minis perterritus, saepsit se tyrannus militibus; tremere et exalbescere vel amicis adeuntibus; adeo (*adv.*) ut, ob metum tonsoris, se ipsum radere, coactus formidine, discerct. 8. Hanc occasionem delendae urbis minime spernendam esse ratus, Balbus regem ad necandos fame captivos

---

[1] **Quamvis** is used once with the Indicative by Cicero, but this use is not to be imitated. **Quamquam** is used with the Subjunctive (1) in general statements, mostly in the Second Person (called the *Gnomic Subjunctive*), "*Although you may forgive a man, it is difficult to improve him*," "Quamquam **ignoscas**, diffĭcĭle est ēmendāre," (2) in statements expressing, not *fact*, but the *thought* of the writer.

impulit, jure-jurando se obstringens ita demum rem-publicam salvam fore.[1] 9. Itane mentieris? Nec nosti (*see* nosco), prout seres, ita te messurum esse ? 10. Jure falluntur ei qui divitiis, non virtute, homines metiuntur.

1. *It is one-thing* (34) *to dine, another-thing to stuff one's stomach with food.* 2. *Did you envy that-vile* (iste) *tyrant, hedged-round with soldiers, who measured dangers by his own fear?* 3. *There is no doubt that, as-boys, we learned many-things which as-old men we shall forget.* 4. *Having routed the enemy, why did you not pursue the fugitives* (i.e. *those fleeing*)? 5. *Thinking that this opportunity was not to be neglected, the general ordered his-soldiers to charge.* 6. *After you had bound yourself by an oath to spare us, did you then impel the king to* (ad) *slay us?* 7. *The disciples of Epicurus, measuring* (i.e. *having-measured*) *all things by pleasure, were unable to estimate virtue at a sufficiently high value* (283). 8. *You who spurned her while--she-lived* (i.e. *living*), *will you spurn* (*her*) (*now-that-she-is-*) *about-to-die?*

Exercise LXXXIX.

**324** **Jampridem** and **jamdudum** change the Latin Present into the English Complete Present (Perfect with *have*), and the Latin Imperfect into the English Pluperfect: "**Jamdūdum** opto, *or* optābam," *I have been,* or *had been,* long *desiring.*

(*Look out* dīgĕro, expergiscor, lābor, quĕror.)

1. Ceres, diu secum questa, tandem his verbis Tonantem allocuta est. 2. Aut non erat paciscendum, aut, si pactus es, standum est promissis. 3. Nec fefellit opinionem eventus ; tanta enim vi milites in castra irruperunt ut ducem ipsum in lecto nondum experrectum caperent. 4. Jampridem colonum admonebam ut pirum fructu gravatam et jam lapsuram fulciret. 5. Circa amnem, piscium (278) omnis generis plenum, armenta pinguia pascebantur. 6. Quamvis multa dedecora in se admisisset, non dubium erat quin semper promissis stetisset. 7. Flores inter se dissimillimi, arte quadam in serto digesti, quis nescit quantum oblectationis afferant?[2] 8. Num imperatorem incusas quod unius et alterius (*see* 'alter') salutem ob incolumitatem totius exercitus neglexerit?

**325** [1] **Dēmum** adds emphasis to the word before it, and is often equivalent to *only :* tum dēmum, *only then, then and not till then.*
[2] **Flōres** is Nom. to **affĕrant.**

1. *Awake at-last, or sleep for ever* (in aeternum) *slaves*. 2. *If you had not made-this-bargain, citizens, the city would not have been delivered-over by the enemy*. 3. *It is reported that* (315) *Paris fed sheep round Mount Ida* (i.e. Ida the mountain).¹ 4. *Our men, shut* (in) *on-one-side by the enemy, on-the-other by a river and by mountains, were cut-off-from* (their) *supplies*. 5. *It is* (the part) *of an orator not-only* (317) *to arrange* (his) *facts, but-also to explain* (them) *clearly* (when) *arranged*.² 6. *You have caused me as-much sorrow as* (you caused) *yourself joy*. 7. *When I asked* (i.e. to me asking) *why she had complained she replied that her daughter had been torn-away from* (de) *her embrace*. 8. *This great man, whom neither threats had terrified nor gifts had tamed, succumbed at-last to Fortune*.

### Exercise XC.

1. Apud antiquos cor (non cerebrum) visum est sapientiae esse sedes. 2. Nostri, cum ad collem confugissent, biduum ibi hostibus resistebant. 3. Nostris famem longam vix sustentantibus allatum est magnum gregem nuper ab hostibus in castra compulsum esse. 4. Fasces illos severos et secures sanguineas nemo plebis non formidabat. 5. Post tertium mensem, quum in eam vallem descendissemus quam nuntius indicaverat, nihil repperimus nisi tabescentia cadavera eorum quos pestis absumpserat. 6. Hoc sermone perterriti, suam quisque (165) domum conjurati dilapsi sunt. 7. Nescisne Taurum montem, inter Asiam et Syriam interjacentem, a Livio cardinem quendam appellatum esse? 8. Hunc panem ne furi quidem invidere possim. 9. Jure dictitabat Menenius plerosque, ventre (197) pleno, humaniores esse. 10. Hinc orta est inter senatorium et equestrem ordinem summa discordia; quorum alter Caesari, alter Pompeio favebat.

1. *Seest thou not, O Brutus, thine axes polluted and thy fasces dyed with the blood of thy sons?* 2. *Having broken the two hinges, the robbers tore-away the gate*. 3. *Contented with a little* (exiguus) *bread, this great philosopher demanded no more* (i.e. did not demand more-things). 4. *Your sheep were lying under a beech-tree, which* (was) *struck with lightning* (and) *fell*. 5. *By his pleasant discourse this witty poet delighted both old-men and young*. 6. *Near a very high hill was a narrow valley*

---

¹ In Latin the name of the individual precedes the name of the class.
² Avoid the repetition of Pronouns in Latin: trans. *facts not only to arrange, but also,* (when) *arranged, to explain;* making (*facts*) the Obj. both of *arrange* and of *explain*.

*watered by a small stream* (amnis). 7. (*Fair*)-*shone the ground* (hŭmus) *painted with many kinds of beautiful flowers.* 8. *I have been long hoping that the city will be taken in two months.*

### Exercise XCI.

**327** **Quam**, *as far as*, is sometimes put briefly for "quam pŏtŭit, pŏtĕris," &c.: *he prepared as sumptuous a dinner as he could*, "cēnam **quam** (pŏtuit) ŏpĭmam părāvit." This construction, with the Positive degree, is rare, and not to be imitated: but *with the Superlative it is common*:

| | |
|---|---|
| *He hastened with as long marches as possible.* | **Quam** (pŏtuit) **maxĭmis** ĭtĭnĕrĭbus contendit. |
| *Take care to come as often as you can.* (Lat. *shall be able.*) | Cūrā ŭt **quam** (pŏtĕris) **saepissĭmē** vĕnias. |

1. O sortem (206) infelicissimam! Quibus pelagus pepercerat, eos fere in portu perire![1] 2. Specum quendam, in ipso montis vertice, pumice exeso structum, anus haec incolere ferebatur. 3. Hic inter frutices viridissimos amnis parvus de gelido fonte defluens quam gratissimos latices nobis suppeditabat. 4. Tales sonos si quis e lyra elicere velit, Phoebeo pollice opus sit. 5. Nondum venenatum calicem reus exhauserat, cum accurrit nuntius clamans regem mortuum esse. 6. Tuas messes, ut aiunt, ussisti; tua vineta cecīdisti. 7. Aggerem illum altissimum decem diebus nostri exstruxerant. 8. Balbone credis? Peribis hercle, nisi anguem illum in herba latentem quam celerrime extimueris. 9. Has urbes Philippus ille magni aestimabat tamquam compedes ipsas Graeciae.[2] 10. Vergilius scribit Tartarearum portarum postes adamantinos ne a caelicolis quidem exscindi posse.

1. *The open-sea* (pĕlăgus) *is not to-be-tried by us in this small ship.* 2. *Let us hope that the harvest will be as great as possible.* 3. *The general surrounded the town with a mound thirty feet high.* 4. *We have four fingers and one thumb* (314). 5. *Did you see the snake which the eagle had carried off?*

---

**328** [1] Trans. *to think that they should perish!* and parse as *Exclamatory Infinitive.*

[2] **Compēdes** is Acc. governed by **aestĭmāret** understood: "tam quam (aestimaret)" *as much as* (*he would value*) *the fetters*, &c. The meaning is that certain fortresses in Greece enabled their owner to keep the whole country in subjection, as fetters enable a jailor to keep a prisoner.

6. *Horace says that* (uego) *he cannot free himself from the pleasing fetter of love.* 7. *There is no doubt that the goat injured that beautiful tree as much as possible with (his) destructive tooth.* 8. *Are you not ashamed* (see Vocab. 'ashamed'), *soldiers, of having yielded to enemies so few (in-numbers)?* 9. *As-long-as you are* (125) *in debt, you will never be able to be contented with your lot.*

### Exercise XCII.

With intĕrest and rēfert, to express *it concerns you, me, himself* (not *him*), the forms meā, tuā, nostrā, suā, &c., are used.

These Verbs are qualified by the Adverbs nihil, multum, tantum, quantum, quid, and also by magni, parvi, plūris, mĭnōris, tanti, as well as by ordinary Adverbs such as maxĭmē.

| | |
|---|---|
| *What does it matter to me in what manner you compel me?* | Quĭd meā rēfert quā rātiōne mē (240) cōgātis? |

Intĕrest, *it concerns*, is used with the Gen. of the person or thing concerned; (but rēfert is rarely thus used). Both are followed by the Acc. and Inf., or by ŭt (or nē) with the Subjunctive.

| | |
|---|---|
| *It concerns the State and us that you should be well.* | Ĕt rei-publĭcae ĕt nostrā intĕrest tē vălēre. |
| *It is important for you to come.* | Tuā intĕrest ŭt vĕniās. |

Ŭtĭnam, *would that!* or *O that!* is used to signify a wish, (1) with the Pres. Subjunctive for a *possible*, (2) the Imperf. or Pluperf. Subjunctive for an *impossible* wish.

| | |
|---|---|
| *O that the past might return!* | Ŭtĭnam praetĕrĭta rĕdīrent! |
| *O that he might arrive to-day!* | Ŭtĭnam hŏdiē advĕniat! |

1. A recta conscientia ne transversum quidem unguem discesseris.[1] 2. Interrogavi colonum num domi sedens murmur maris exaudire posset. 3. Respondit fulmen ibi decem ante annis de caelo cecidisse.[2] 4. Non nostri moris est ebur et aurum ad Deum colendum adhibere.[3] 5. Quis tumidum guttur

---

[1] Why is unguem the Acc. (262)? Nē affects (129) the translation of discessĕris.
[2] Parse annis: Par. 313.
[3] Parse mōrĭs: Par. 289.

in Alpibus miratur? 6. Qui humana carne vescebantur apud Graecos Anthropophagi nominati sunt. 7. Utinam ex hoc fonte nunquam pestis in totam rempublicam defluat! 8. Eligendum erat inter duo itinera, quorum alterum per montes altissimos ducebat, alterum trans angustum pontem, quo nuper amnem junxeramus. 9. Dicebat homo sponte sua se venisse; sed frons ipsa testabatur eum adesse invitum. 10. Multum interest rei familiaris tuae te quam celerrime venire. 11. Utinam fur pecuniâ multaretur, neve verbera passus esset! 12. Minoris refert qualibus in aedibus vivas (240), si modo Romae vivis. 13. Aere alieno quondam oppressus, ne nunc quidem se omnino liberavit.

1. *The fellow had not-yet vomited-forth against me the venom of his enry.* 2. *He who had not feared even lashes and tortures, now hearing* (abl. abs.) *the words of the judge, trembled from-head to-foot* (toto corpore). 3. *It is reported that the raven, whereas* (cum, *with* subjunct.) *he ought to have brought* (223) *a golden cup to Apollo, lied, feigning that a long snake had caused him delay.* 4. *The centurion, his eye having been struck out* (effodio), *was no longer fit for performing military service* (stipendia merēre, lit. *to earn pay*). 5. *They spoke with-every-appearance-of-truth* (trans. *with a most true forehead*); *but, in my judgment, they were lying.* 6. *There is no doubt that from this source many evils flowed into our country.* 7. *There was no doubt that he had been scourged before he was sent* (i.e. *had been sent*) *into exile* (145*b*). 8. *O-that you would not depart even a hair's breadth from the precepts of your father!* 9. *He thought to himself* (i.e., *with himself*) *how important it was for Balbus that he himself should return home* (Acc. and Pres. Inf.). 10. *What does it matter whether these birds are fed or not?*

## ELEMENTARY RULES FOR ORATIO OBLIQUA.

**331** Speech reported in the First Person ("*I* fear," said Balbus, "*I am* mistaken") is called Oratio Recta, or, *Direct Speech;* speech reported in the Third Person (Balbus said that "*He* feared *he* was mistaken") is called Oratio Obliqua, or *Indirect Speech.*

In passing from English O. R. to O. O. almost the only change is in the Personal Pronouns and Tenses, as above, *I* into *he, am* into *was:*

| Speech in First Person. | Speech in Third Person. |
|---|---|
| "*I know*," said *Balbus*, "*that you will help me. What is lost can be regained. The cities that have been taken before we came here, can be recovered. Take courage therefore. Why do you delay? Is not the enemy now but a little way off? Are we not prepared to fight? Do not desert me. Trust in your own right-hands and in my diligence.*" | Balbus said that "*He knew that they would help him. What had been lost could be regained. The cities that had been taken before they came there, could be recovered. They should therefore take courage. Why did they delay? Was not the enemy now but a little way off? Were they not prepared to fight? They should (or let them) not desert him. They should trust in their own right hands and in his diligence.*"[1] |

But in Latin there are changes in the Moods, besides other changes, as follows:

**332** 1. (a) *Principal Verbs in the Indicative* are changed into Infinitives, and their Subjects into Accusatives. (b) **Inquit** is changed into **dixit** or some other Verb.

| Oratio Recta. | Oratio Obliqua. |
|---|---|
| "*I know*," said *Balbus*, | Balbus said that "*He knew*" |
| Tum Balbus "scio" inquit (320) | Balbus dixit "**Sē scīre**" |

**333** 2. **Ĕgo** and **nōs** are changed into **sē**; **vōs** into **eos**.

| that you will help me. | that they would help him. |
|---|---|
| vos mihī adfuturos. | eos sibī adfūtūros. |

**334** 3. *Indicatives after Relatives and after Non-co-ordinate Conjunctions*, are changed into Subjunctives.[2]

| The cities that have been taken before we came here, can be recovered. | The cities that had been taken before they came there, could be recovered. |
|---|---|
| Quae urbes captae sunt, antequam hūc vēnīmus, rĕcŭpĕrāri possunt. | Quae urbes captae **fŭissent**, antĕquam illūc **vēnissent**, posse rĕcŭpĕrāri. |

---

[1] Before the pupil writes Latin he should practise turning English speech of the First Person into speech of the Third Person.

**334a** [2] (1) Co-ordinate Conjunctions are **sĕd, autem, tămen, et, -que, nam, enim, ĭtaque, ĭgĭtur**, &c. (2) Non-co-ordinate or Subordinate Conj. are **ŭt, quŏd, quĭa, cum, dōnĕc, antĕquam, postquam, sī, quamquam**, &c.

When the Relative, *e.g.* **quos**, can be replaced by a Demonstrative and a Coordinate Conjunction, (**et eos**), it is *sometimes* followed by an Infinitive. But for the beginner this construction will not be necessary.

**335**   4. *Imperatives* are changed into Subjunctives.

| | |
|---|---|
| *Take courage therefore.* | (*He begged that*) *They should therefore take courage.* |
| Ērĭgĭte ĭgĭtur ănĭmos. | **Ērĭgĕrent** ĭgĭtur ănĭmos. |

**336**   5. Questions asked in the *Second Person* are rendered by the Subjunctive in the Third Person (*being really Indirect Questions*).

| | |
|---|---|
| *Why do you delay?* | (*He asked*) *Why did they delay?* |
| Cūr mŏrāmĭni? | Cūr mŏrārentur? |

**337**   6. Questions asked in the *First* and *Third Person* are rendered by the Accusative and Infinitive.

| | |
|---|---|
| *Is not the enemy now but a little way off? Are we not prepared to fight?* | *Was not the enemy now but a little way off? Were they not prepared to fight?* |
| Nonne hostis prŏpĕ jam ăbest? Nonne ad pugnandum părāti sŭmus? | Nonne **hostem** prŏpĕ jam **ăbesse?** Nonne **sē** ad pugnandum părātos **esse?** [1] |

**338**   7. (*a*) **Sē, sĭbĭ**, &c., are used for the Person speaking; (*b*) but where **sē, suus**, &c., are needed to express the Person addressed, **ipse** is used for the Person speaking.

| | |
|---|---|
| (*a*) *Do not desert me.* | (*a*) *They should not desert him.* |
| Nōlīte me dēsĕrĕre. | Nollent **sē** dēsĕrĕre. |
| (*b*) *Trust in your own right hands and in my diligence.*" | (*b*) *They should trust in their own right hands and in his diligence.*" |
| Spem in vestris dextris et in meā dīlĭgentiā pōnĭte." | Spem in **suis** dextris et in **ipsius** dīlĭgentiā pōnĕrent." |

EXERCISE XCIII.

*To be turned into Latin Oratio Obliqua.*

A. His auditis, Tullius, ad amicos conversus, "Cur" inquit (332 *b*) "moramini? Neque enim ego volo amicis exitium ferre neque vos jam potestis morituro prodesse. Hostes jam

---

[1] These questions are really partly questions, partly passionate statements: *The enemy is but a little way off, is he not? We are prepared to fight, are we not?* Hence, they are expressed by the Accusative and Infinitive.

prope absunt; mox aderunt. Urbs capietur. Fugite igitur. Quod facere potui, feci; nihil praeter mortem mihi jam restat. Quae vobiscum auferre potestis, ea auferte. Num respondetis vos hic mansuros? Antequam vos inter cohortes conscripsi promisistis vos (338*b*) mihi obtemperaturos, nec fidem fefellistis. Satis virtuti datum est: jam saluti consulite. At cur nos hic tempus inani colloquio terimus? Equidem,[1] quoniam necesse est, moriar. Vos (335) vivite et valete, et curate ut mortem meam ulciscamini."

(*B. is already in* O. O.; *C. must be turned into* O. O.)

B. *Balbus having now departed from the senate-house, the consul addressed the senators (i.e. the fathers) to this effect:* "*Why did they (336) hesitate? Let them choose, if it was necessary, between a glorious death and an inglorious servitude. But he was persuaded that this was not necessary. Victory, not death, awaited them, if, without fear, they consulted-the-interest-of the country. Not even the lowest of the citizens now favoured the conspirators. Already they were praised by all the best of the citizens, soon they would be praised by all. Why therefore did they sit there hesitating, since both Fortune and Necessity taught them that they ought not now to deliberate but to act? When they had made a beginning, the citizens would to a man (ad unum) approve their plans. He would say no more, for there was need not of words but of deeds."*

C. *Tullius now turned to the soldiers of the tenth legion.* "*Why,*" *said he* (332*b*), "*do you fear the multitude of the enemy?*[2] *We indeed have only three thousand, the enemy ten thousand; but three free citizens can easily resist ten slaves. The victories that the enemy has lately gained have been gained by treachery and guile; but in this plain, treachery will avail nothing (nullo modo). Be of good cheer therefore, since Mars will give the palm to the more worthy army. If only you can repel the first assault of (their) cavalry, the infantry will speedily turn their backs. Trust in your own valour and in my skill (i.e. plans). What avail ten thousand sheep against one wolf? But why do I waste time in speaking? The enemy is-at-hand, the contest-is-to-be-waged (i.e. it-is-to-be-striven) not with tongues but with swords.*"

---

339   [1] **Equidem** being (139) almost always used with the *first person*, should be changed into **quidem** when attached to sē.

  [2] In turning this into O. O., **inquit** must *not* be used. You may either translate *Tullius having turned to* .... *spoke to this effect,* '*Why did they fear,*' &c., or omit the Verb of speaking and leave it to be understood: *Tullius now turned* .... *legion,* '*Why did they fear?*' &c.

# EASY AND RECAPITULATORY EXERCISES.

## I.—ON THE NOUNS, ADJECTIVES, AND PRONOUNS.[1]

(*The only Verbs required are those given in paragraphs* 1—112.)

### Exercise I.

1. Probo scribae.  2. Fabri (9*a*) pigri.  3. Molesto pediti.  4. Pavidorum nautarum.  5. Jucundā insulā.  6.  7. Temporum prosperorum.  8. Stultis principibus.  9. Parvi papilionis.  10. Ossium magnorum.  11. Ab indigno comite.  12. Insigni labore.  13. Meliorum judicum.  14. Scytha perniciosus.  15. Itineris longi.  16. Planitici vastae.  17. Velocium equitum.  18. Vigilum tribunorum.  19. Regionum pulchrarum.  20. Morum antiquorum.  21. A benigno nauta.

1. *From the good leader.  2. To the wretched sailor.  3. Of frequent lightnings.  4. Of the poor girl.  5. To great hope.  6. Of the left horn.  7. To the wise charioteer.  8. Of the active inhabitants.  9. Of the black teeth.  10. By the difficult journey.  11. To the short bows.  12. Of the third tribe.  13. To the lean face.  14. O angry poet.  15. Of the stern leaders.  16. Of beautiful fountains.  17. To the useful bow.  18. Of high citadels.  19. By the enemy's camp.  20. To a few soldiers.  21. Of the second cohort.  22. By (13a) the king.  23. By great hope.  24. Of long days.*

### Exercise II.

1. Maximus ille vir.  2. Pulcherrimarum urbium muri.  3. Optimorum poetarum dulcia carmina.  4. Majorum oppidorum arces.  5. Difficillimorum et maximorum operum.  6. Principum munificentissimorum jussa.  7. Harum tam miserarum calamitatum.  8. Pessima haec exempla.  9. Pulcherrimorum florum color.  10. Imbri tristi et pernicioso.  11. Quercus nigerrimae glandes paucae.  12. Ultimi illius diei memoria.  13. Morborum taetriorum multitudo.  14. Aurigae maxime strenuo dona (95) damus.  15. Quis te pessimo hoc rege liberat?  16. Quis haec ei dat?

---

[1] These exercises may be heard *vivâ voce*, and the sentences are numbered that the pupil may be rapidly called to translate any sentence at the teacher's discretion.

## ON THE REGULAR VERBS.

1.[1] *To this very wise girl. 2. The two brothers of the same woman. 3. The largest part of the outer wall. 4. Of very slender legs. 5. The girl loves his two brothers: which-of-the two do you love most* (maxime)? *6. The very-old soldier loves older wine. 7. The very contemptible* (superl. of humilis) *memory of that most unhappy day. 8. With which of these two cities? 9. To the same woman he gives three apples. 10. To Tullia alone he gives three hundred cherries. 11. To the other sea. 12. Of the same camp. 13. To one-man's spurs, to another-man's sword. 14. Of the younger soldiers. 15. By this most troublesome thirst. 16. By the older* (61) *soldier.*

### Exercise III.

1. Hic vi, ille sapientia, hostes superat. 2. Multos pericula minima terrent. 3. Alterius constantiam, alterius diligentiam laudamus. 4. Piscator tria milia piscium habet. 5. Nequissimorum puerorum versus non laudo. 6. Tussi febrique medicus te liberat. 7. Plura tibi quam nobis dat. 8. Pejor est iste pessimo meorum comitum. 9. Agricola optimus meliore fato dignus erat. 10. Nulli suorum carior erat quam sibi. 11. Haec tibi uni jucunda sunt.

1. *Which of these two journeys do you praise? 2. To this very-tender maiden alone he gives a hundred oxen. 3. The boy is smaller than the largest of the men. 4. Wisdom frees him from anger. 5. To you he gives more gifts than to himself. 6. The memory of that very keen contest was more bitter to you than to him. 7. This was more agreeable to you than to any of his companions. 8. By patience he delivers himself from fever. 9. What poet is wiser than Homer? what poem better than his poems? 10. The former is wiser than the latter.*

## II.—ON THE REGULAR VERBS.

### Exercise IV.—First Conjugation.

1. Castigaberis. 2. Agros vastavisti. 3. Laudatus est. 4. Pugnabunt. 5. Ne erraveritis. 6. Vastate agros. 7. Pugnaverant. 8. Ut aedificet urbem. 9. Vulnerata est. 10. Vituperabimini. 11. Ambulaveratis. 12. Cantavissetis. 13. Ut cantarent. ·14. Cantemus. 15. Dubitate. 16. Servemus urbem. 17. Ambulaveritis. 18. Oppidum aedificatum erat. 19. Ut servaremur. 20. Ut laudarere. 21. Canta.

---

[1] On the position of the Pronoun Adjective between an ordinary Adjective and Noun, see Vocabulary, *this*.

1. *You will sing.* 2. *He will have been wounded.* 3. *Ye must build* (imper.). 4. *The city had been built.* 5. *Let us praise them.* 6. *The fields have been laid waste.* 7. *You will be chastised.* 8. *That he might be wounded.* 9. *That we might sing.* 10. *Do not doubt, O friend.* 11. *We shall have preserved the city.* 12. *I should have carried.* 13. *They would have been blamed.* 14. *Ye will not be loved.* 15. *That ye may take-care.* 16. *We shall have been preserved.* 17. *You had sung, O daughter.* 18. *Sing, O daughter.* 19. *Ye were being preserved.* 20. *Ye will be wounded.*

### Exercise V.—Second Conjugation.

1. Puer valebat. 2. Terrebamini. 3. Timebere. 4. Territus fuerat. 5. Ut exerceres corpus. 6. Monuissem te. 7. Ut monereris. 8. Doce puerum. 9. Ne timueris. 10. Exercueris. 11. Filia monita fuisset. 12. Ut terreare. 13. Valuistis. 14. Exercetor. 15. Exerceamus corpora. 16. Ne territa sis, O mulier. 17. Docebimur. 18. Terrebare. 19. Terres puerum. 20. Terremur. 21. Terruistis.

1. *We had been terrified.* 2. *That he may fear.* 3. *Ye will be taught.* 4. *He was being advised.* 5. *We should have feared.* 6. *That they might exercise (their) bodies.* 7. *Ye have been advised, O citizens.* 8. *You will be terrified, O friend.* 9. *You have terrified us.* 10. *That you might be advised.* 11. *Let us terrify the enemy.* 12. *I used-to-have* (115) *a book.* 13. *You had taught us.* 14. *Do not teach him.* 15. *He will have terrified you.* 16. *You will have been terrified, O friends.* 17. *Exercise (your) bodies.* 18. *Ye would have taught him.* 19. *The soldiers terrified the woman.*

### Exercise VI.—Third Conjugation.

1. Duxeratis. 2. Contraxisti. 3. Quid homo dixerat? 4. Ut instruantur milites. 5. Ut instrueret aciem. 6. Scribes epistolam. 7. Hoc spem nostram minuerat. 8. Gloriam eius minuemus. 9. Agger structus fuerat. 10. Flumen ponte junxissemus. 11. Milites ducentur. 12. Ut ducare. 13. Libri scripti sunt. 14. Ut duceremini. 15. Quis legionem ducebat. 16. Ne nos duxeris. 17. Haec tibi dixissemus. 18. Dicamus vera (Par. 34). 19. Duceris. 20. Ducĕris.

1. *That they might rule.* 2. *You will be led.* 3. *He would have said these-things.* 4. *You have piled up a mound, soldiers.* 5. *She has been led.* 6. *The mound has been piled up.* 7. *Be ye drawn-up, soldiers.* 8. *He had drawn together-foot-*

*soldiers.* 9. *What will you say, friends?* 10. *His glory has been diminished.* 11. *That we may bridge the river.* 12. *The river would have been bridged.* 13. *You were being drawn-up, soldiers.* 14. *Do not say this.* 15. *Let us pile-up a mound.* 16. *You had written a letter, my brother.* 17. *Do not write these letters, friends.* 18. *I shall be led.* 19. *They are being drawn up.* 20. *They would have been led.* 21. *Our hopes were diminished.* 22. *They will write.*

### Exercise VII.—Fourth Conjugation.

1. Dormiisti. 2. Puniti erant. 3. Urbs munietur. 4. Opus finitum est. 5. Ut erudiremini. 6. Nutriebantur. 7. Ut vestias puerum. 8. Opus finieris. 9. Custodiverat obsides. 10. Obsides custodiuntor. 11. Urbes custoditae fuissent. 12. Erudientur pueri. 13. Ut opus finiatur. 14. Custodiere milites captivum. 15. A magistro erudiemur. 16. Dormiamus. 17. Erudiebamini. 18. Erudientur. 19. Ne puerum erudiveris. 20. Ut erudiremini. 22. Erudieris.

1. *We had slept.* 2. *You will sleep.* 3. *That you may be punished, O citizens.* 4. *The girl had been clothed.* 5. *The boy will be guarded.* 6. *The camp would have been fortified.* 7. *That the boy might be instructed.* 8. *Let us guard the leader.* 9. *We shall clothe the boy.* 10. *The boy was being instructed.* 11. *That the tasks may be ended.* 12. *The boys must be instructed* (imper.). 13. *Nourish the boys.* 14. *We shall fortify the city.* 15. *That you may fortify the city, soldiers.* 16. *That you might sleep.* 17. *You were being instructed, boys.* 18. *You will have instructed the boys, most learned master.* 19. *The boys will have been instructed.* 20. *The boys will sleep.* 22. *They used-to-sleep* (115). 23. *You slept, boys.*

## III.—GENERAL EXERCISES.

### Exercise VIII.

(*Exercises* VIII. *to* XI. *refer to Par.* 1—129; *see also page* 186.)

1. Bidui iter fecēre. 2. Multi hoc negant. 3. Quantum pecuniae habes? 4. Et ego et tu hoc negamus. 5. Errare humanum est. 6. Multa eis dedimus. 7. Fato meliore digna est. 8. Puer matri est simillimus. 9. Plura tibi quam mihi dederunt. 10. Nonne equus est animalium utilissimum? 11. Utri plura dedisti? Neutri: eadem ambobus dedi.

1. *I will give a book to one of you.* 2. *Many of the children gave us flowers.* 3. *You and I have erred.* 4. *The girl is more like her father than her mother.* 5. *Let us hasten by night.* 6. *The soldiers are most worthy of punishment.* 7. *We led the army into the nearest city.* 8. *This work is not very easy.* 9. *The words of the unjust sailor are very base.* 10. *A hundred brave (men) are better than two hundred cowardly (men).* 11. *He was more worthy of punishment than you.*

### Exercise IX.

1. Uter fontium major est? 2. Decem millia passuum iter fecimus. 3. Tullius, rex crudelissimus, veniam Balbo dedit. 4. Nocte hostes castra nostra invaserunt. 5. Decem his diebus trecentos elephantos ad exercitum mittemus. 6. Equites peditesque plurimos habemus. 7. Regum fortium vitae nos delectant. 8. Hoc opus facilius est quam illud. 9. Et mihi et tibi felicium supplicum verba jucunda sunt. 10. Nullius dona, quam fratris tui mihi jucundiora sunt.

1. *What have you done worthy of praise?* 2. *He is worse than his brother.* 3. *The keenest soldiers fought most bravely.* 4. *You journeyed for (i.e. made a journey of) two-days in a very rough country.* 5. *Neither of the fountains had very sweet water.* 6. *Which of the two girls loves her father more?* 7. *He is more like you than me.* 8. *Where is the book you gave me?* 9. *Do not say many-things.* 10. *All love themselves.* 11. *Do you say this?*

### Exercise X.

1. Pueri ludere amant. 2. Ne plura rogaveris. 3. Milites in campum ducamus. 4. Si venti flaverint, in portu manebimus. 5. Multas noctes in urbe mansimus. 6. Dicamus vera. 7. Senex septuagesimo altero anno uxorem tertiam duxit. 8. Senum memoria infirmior quam juvenum est. 9. Pejor morte est infamia. 10. Verba eius isti molesta sunt.

1. *Very many say this.* 2. *You say the same.* 3. *He wounded me with a spear.* 4. *Let us walk six days.* 5. *His words are more pleasant to you than to any of your brothers.* 6. *The brave Balbus was leader of the whole* (totus) *army.* 7. *Both to you and to me he gave the same gifts.* 8. *No poet blames his own poems.* 9. *If he comes by night, we will depart in three hours.* 10. *To one of his two sons he gave a thousand oxen, to the other two thousand sheep.* 11. *Do not sleep, boy.*

## GENERAL EXERCISES.

### Exercise XI.

(*Exercises* XI. *to* XIX. *refer to Par.* 1—295.)

1. Clam parentibus huc venisti. 2. Ne tu quidem idem dedecus bis in te admittes. 3. Nostri ab hostibus superati sunt. 4. Quid obstat quominus patri tuo pareas? 5. Plura dicturum duae sagittae transfixerunt. 6. Interrogavi matrem num huc ventura esset. 7. Hostes urbem captam incendunt. 8. Non dubium est quin aurum in ea regione reppereris. 9. Captivos vinctos centurio ad imperatorem duxerat. 10. Quot dies hostibus resistebatis? 11. Tune times?

1. *There is no doubt that he pardoned the accused* (*man*). 2. *Cultivate learning that you may not be unlearned.* 3. *Not even Tullius will spare this city.* 4. *Let us ask her on what day she will come.* 5. *What prevented you from pleasing his father?* 6. *I will do my best to pardon him.* 7. *They took and burned the city* (Par. 159). 8. *The leaders gave orders-to their men not to resist the enemy.* 9. *There was no doubt that the city had been taken by the tenth legion.* 10. *She was killed by poison, without-the-knowledge-of the king.*

### Exercise XII.

1. Extra urbem decem horas pugnatum est. 2. In eo eram ut Balbum vincerem. 3. Saepe me interrogavisti utrum Romanus sim an Atheniensis. 4. Civibus pro patria fortiter pugnandum est. 5. Aut vincendum est aut serviendum. 6. Oravi ducem ut captis parceret. 7. Interrogate hominem num coram judice hoc dixerit. 8. Reo, haec neganti, mendacium graviter nocuit. 9. Dux suis imperavit ne acie cederent. 10. Ne tibi quidem rex ignoscet, si a Tullio stabis. 11. Quis nescit urbem incendi?

1. *He was silent for two hours in-the-presence-of the judge.* 2. *He had reigned ten years as-far-as the Alps.* 3. *He was on the point of conquering.* 4. *The king asked us whether we were husbandmen or sailors.* 5. *There is no doubt that the cold hurt the beautiful pine-tree.* 6. *He asked me whether the centurion was worthy of this great* (see Vocab. *great*) *reward.* 7. *I advised the soldier to answer the leader with these words.* 8. *We must make-haste that we may not come late.* 9. *When the general had heard this, he ordered the line-of-battle to retire.* 10. *Answer-was-made to the king in these words.*

## EASY AND RECAPITULATORY EXERCISES.

### EXERCISE XIII.

1. What is pleasant to some is troublesome to others. 2. He built a house twenty feet high. 3. I asked him, O citizens, to come by night. 4. I asked which of you two said these-things. 5. Did you say this to deceive us? 6. It is very difficult to make very long marches in winter. 7. The excellent physician Balbus gave you medicine to cure you. 8. The girl is even now more beautiful than her sister. 9. There is no doubt that he gave you more gifts than me. 10. By the fruitful harvest the hearts of the husbandmen were delighted. 11. He asked why the goats were larger than most of the sheep.

### EXERCISE XIV.

1. Come here in haste, my son. 2. Is he very poor? 3. When were the Gauls conquered by Caesar? 4. Do you call me a citizen? 5. There is no doubt that he was created consul by the citizens. 6. At last the enemy, overcome by our men, fled to the camp. 7. Each of the two brothers pleased (placeo) himself alone. 8. Do not set-out from the city by night. 9. She is about-to-return to Asia. 10. The head of Hasdrubal was thrown into the camp. 11. You slept the whole night.

### EXERCISE XV.

1. He sent a letter to his friend. 2. Give that woman the same book you gave me. 3. Do not declare war, O king. 4. When will you quench your thirst? 5. Have you ever used a golden axe? 6. I shall have given you, my son, three hundred denarii. 7. What you say, is true. 8. What is more faithful than a faithful dog? 9. There is no doubt that every good man resisted this law. 10. You will be no longer foolish but base, if, even now, you please yourself alone. 11. Do not stay.

### EXERCISE XVI.

1. Some stood here, others there. 2. The disease did not hurt even one of the sheep. 3. On the fifth day you came to Egypt. 4. Being-about-to-set-out for Europe we shall send two messengers to Alexander. 5. You and I will pay attention to philosophy. 6. Who took the city (of) Corinth? 7. Mummius, who took Corinth, was very poor. 8. He came a-second-time into the forum. 9. What prevented him from walking in his brother's garden? 10. Ajax slew himself with the sword which he had received from Hector. 11. He is free from cares.

## Exercise XVII.

1. *This work is finished.* 2. *My son and I sent messengers to you.* 3. *My brother and sister are very happy.* 4. *There is no doubt that it is pleasant to conquer.* 5. *We ought to command* (164); *you ought to obey.* 6. *The city is being built; a great part of it is built already.* 7. *The small town (of) Corioli was taken* (agrees with 'town') *by Marcius, who was thence called Coriolanus.* 8. *Balbus and Tullius besought me to pardon both (of) them.* 9. *You praised both, you pleased neither.* 10. *Nothing prevents you from building a new bridge.*

## Exercise XVIII.

1. Spem mihi ultimam eripuisti. 2. Sole orto, in campum descensum est. 3. Hoc ad agros colendos erat utilissimum. 4. Romae biennium habitavimus. 5. Huic genti quis tributum imponere ausus est? 6. Capta urbe, arcem incendimus. 7. Nonne vis fateri quantum te tuae stultitiae pudeat? 8. Quando ibis Corinthum? 9. Hodie Arpinum eo, cras Romae manebo. 10. E malevolo, fis malevolentior; mox fies malevolentissimus. 11. Ego et frater hic (*adv.*) manemus.

1. *Are you not weary of idleness?* 2. *He built walls twenty-five feet high.* 3. *Dionysius, driven from Syracuse, taught boys.* 4. *Why do you not confess that you repent of your wickedness?* 5. *He says that this ditch is twenty feet deep.* 6. *When will you come to see me?* 7. *No one pities the conquered.* 8. *He could have helped me, but he would not.* 9. *I can no longer bear these great insults.* 10. *I hear that he is becoming weaker.* 11. *Will you go to Rome or remain in Corinth?*

## Exercise XIX.

1. Utrum duos an tres menses vis Carthagine manere? 2. Non facile istum tuli querentem de seditione. 3. Nostine quo velit ire? 4. Tot scelera fassus, num putas nos posse tui misereri? 5. Negavit se sui tanti flagitii poenitere. 6. Postquam ab hostibus clamatum est, nostri, Balbo hortante, e silvis erupere. 7. Aliorum oblitus num speras alios tui non oblituros esse? 8. Oportuit te non isti sed patri tuo placere. 9. Quantum pecuniae tibi pater ad emendos flores dedit? 10. Negari non potest ambos semper eadem voluisse, eadem noluisse. 11. Licuit tibi esse felici; sed noluisti mihi parere. 12. Operam dabat libris scribendis.

## EASY AND RECAPITULATORY EXERCISES.

1. To live in Rome seemed to me more pleasant than to live at Gaoii. 2. Have you already, O foolish girls, forgotten these most easy verses? 3. Who ordered the fourth tribe to be-present? 4. Having suffered so many evils, you ought to pity others. 5. The two boys, horrible to relate! attempted to murder their own father. 6. In three days you will become richer than his brother if your ship returns to Corinth. 7. You might have dined with (183) your kind host; but you would dine at home. 8. I have come here to see-to the building of a bridge. 9. Who does-not-know that water, by often falling, hollows even the hardest stone?

### EXERCISE XX.

(*Exercises XX. to XXIX. refer to the whole of the book.*)

1. Barbari erant proceris corporibus, promisso capillo. 2. Non opus est mihi tanta pecunia. 3. Virtutem maximi aestimate. 4. Die quarto aggerem jam decem pedes altum exstruxerant. 5. His condicionibus pax ab utroque duce facta est. 6. Respondit se non assis me facere. 7. Certum erat fundum grandi pecunia emptum fuisse. 8. Patriae amantissimus erat, patientissimus periculorum, suis contentus, alienarum divitiarum nunquam cupidus. 9. Respondit se nolle sua pretio emere. 10. Tu, cuius (299a) es sapientiae, intelleges quid his respondere oporteat. 11. Non est moris nostri quos praesentes laudavimus eos absentes condemnare.

1. He was acquitted of bribery. 2. Why did you, O judges, condemn the innocent Balbus to death? 3. He was endowed with a (see 'a') wonderful art of persuading. 4. By this road you will never come to Athens. 5. He sent a messenger to ask which of his two brothers lived at Gabii. 6. The girl replied that she was descended from royal parents. 7. Do you think that it is the mark of a philosopher to envy the wealth of-others? 8. He was learned in the law, and very brave, but greedy of wealth. 9. Are you certain of this thing? 10. My barns are full of corn; I have much money at home.

### EXERCISE XXI.

1. Nescio an mulier Carthagine ventura sit. 2. Misi qui praedium magno pretio emat. 3. Vereor ut puer virtutem pluris quam voluptatem aestimet. 4. Si auxilium poposcisses, abhinc biduum misissem. 5. Nescisne inepti esse nunquam ridere? 6. Quis Thracum more velit bibere? 7. Non cuiusvis est multa bene facere. 8. Si illuc ibis, vereor ne

serpentis morsu pereas. 9. Num quis audeat negare consules bene de republica meritos esse? 10. Duabus unciis procerior est quam quisquam nostrum.

1. *If any one had given me the book I would have read (it).* 2. *I feared he would be weary of the journey.* 3. *My father advises Balbus to consult his own interests.* 4. *It makes a great difference whether you live at Rome or at Carthage.* 5. *Whatever he had, he gave to all the poorest of the citizens.* 6. *I have long been desirous of hearing Tullius.* 7. *He came from the city to the country as speedily as possible.* 8. *Ask your brother who sang this song.* 9. *The elder of the two brothers died before the capture of the city* (i.e. *before the city having been captured*). 10. *He is a man of wisdom.*

[Exercise XXII.[1]

1. Crudelior erat quam ut cuiquam parceret. 2. Quidquid armorum habuimus, id omne tradendum erat. 3. Quamvis errorem feceris, licebit tibi meliora facere. 4. Idem es qui semper fuisti. 5. Cuilibet licuisset mentiri nisi hunc testem produxisses. 6. Quid refert utrum haec vera sint annon? 7. Nostine plerisque piscibus pinnas binas esse? 8. Tantae multitudini trinis castris opus erat. 9. Si quis tibi Achillis arma promitteret se daturum esse, quid tandem faceres? 10. Balbus moriens fratrem admonuit ut se ipse servaret. 11. Mira quadam arte erat suadendi. 12. Fallacior est quam cui credas. 13. Haec, sive vera sunt sive falsa, nullo modo me movent.

1. *Whatever you wish to say must be said at once.* 2. *It matters little whether we die to-day or to-morrow.* 3. *There is a certain pleasure in recollecting calamities.* 4. *What would you have replied if he had promised to give you money?* 5. *He is too deceitful for you to converse with.* 6. *He hastened to Athens by the most rapid marches possible.* 7. *He was on the point of dying on the fourth day before the taking of the city.* 8. *He is better than any of his brothers.* 9. *Two-days ago, we sent messengers to ascertain what prevented Balbus from coming to Corinth.* 10. *Ask him to come to see me as quickly as possible.*

---

[1] In this and the following Exercises, some idioms are introduced that are not given in the previous part of the book: but they will be found explained in the Vocabularies.

## Exercise XXIII.

1. Promisit se Gades venturum. 2. Erant qui dicerent urbem nunquam captum iri. 3. Misit imperator centurionem qui captivos deposceret. 4. Non adhuc compertum habeo quis hunc tantum virum rhetoricam docuerit. 5. Aggerem exstruxit quo facilius hostem prohiberet. 6. Nemini pepercit, nullius miseritus est. 7. Cur tam parvo fune uteris? 8. Turpior erat quam quocum colloqucreris. 9. Dies fere nullus est quin eam querentem audiam. 10. Spero fore ut urbs decem his diebus capiatur. 11. Interrogavit utrum haec caedes abhinc biennium an triennium facta sit. 12. Respondit iste se tuas excusationes parvi aestimare.

1. *It is said that you burned this temple, Tullius.* 2. *Do not pardon that wicked soldier.* 3. *The brave general Balbus opposed four thousand Scythians.* 4. *Having gained possession of our gold, O Persians, do you now wish to despoil us of our liberty?* 5. *In the battle of Cannae there fell many thousand Roman knights.* 6. *Arioristus was answered in these words by Caesar.* 7. *Our men, under Labienus, laid waste the greatest part of the province, as far as the Alps.* 8. *Who was there that did not hate you, a man devoid of all kindness and courtesy?* 9. *Not even the older men were spared by the conquerors.* 10. *They threatened the man with death that they might the more easily ascertain the truth.*

## Exercise XXIV.

1. Cur me morbum fratris mei celasti? 2. Hoc te moneo ne quem, clam patre tuo, domi accipias. 3. Diceris, mi fili, ipse hunc pontem rescidisse. 4. Non dubium est quin in certamen eloquentiae ambo venerint. 5. Obsecravit ducem mater ne sibi filiam eriperet. 6. Nonne licuit tibi, divitiis his carenti, consulem (*see* licet *in Vocab.*) fieri? 7. Ego me Phidiam esse mallem quam vel optimum fabrum tignarium. 8. Illud permagni referre arbitror ut domestica cura te liberem. 9. Alii alibi steterunt; erant qui ne stare quidem possent sed humi occumberent. 10. Leonidas cum trecentis se multis milibus Persarum opposuit. 11. Alii capi; alii cadere; plurimi vulnera accipere. 12. In eo proelio trecenta milia hostium interfecti sunt.

1. *Who founded the city of Carthage?* 2. *He was asked his opinion by Tullius, but answered nothing.* 3. *By this time the wall* (murus) *and the citadel had been taken by our men.* 4. *Do you suppose that two hundred can resist two*

*thousand?* 5. *I do not know whether she will agree with you.*
6. *The consul was the first who was asked his opinion.* 7. *There is no doubt that he bought the horse at a very high price.* 8. *I was informed of his arrival the-day-before he came to Corioli.*
9. *Will any one promise to go with him?* 10. *I fear that we shall arrive at Athens (too) late unless we hasten by forced marches.*

## Exercise XXV.

1. Quis nescit nos omnes famae atque fortunarum expertes esse?
2. Decimo anno post conditam urbem in exsilium pulsus est.
3. Fac ut quam celerrime in Italiam ad amicos redeas.
4. Adulatores, turbam levissimam, dux contemnebat. 5. Interrogavit num crederem se tantum dedecus in se admittere potuisse. 6. Non est cur fugias, hominum turpissime. 7. Non dubium est quin tibi pater nimis indulserit. 8. Utra harum dearum Vulcano nupsit? 9. Tandem ei persuasit pater ut mulierem in matrimonium duceret. 10. Quis non huius tanti philosophi audiendi studiosus erit? 11. Speraveram fore ut frigus mitesceret. 12. Aurum, argentum, ferrum, utilia illa quidem omnia; sed non pariter utilia.[1]

1. *The boy had concealed* (celo) *the fact from his father by a falsehood.* 2. *Having burnt the village, the cohort set out for the nearest river* (amnis). 3. *You ought to have consulted the interests of each of your two sisters.* 4. *After he had conquered the Scythians, the general sent ambassadors to offer peace.* 5. *I am very desirous of hearing this story, if it is not troublesome to you.* 6. *Having accused others of bribery, he was himself condemned on the same charge.* 7. *If you ever come to Gabii, I hope you will stay with me for a few days.*
8. *There were some who said that it mattered little what Tullius decided.* 9. *There is no doubt that all the best of the citizens resisted this law.* 10. *This field was valued at a high rate, but bought by me for a small price.*

## Exercise XXVI.

1. Nunc quod agitur agamus; agitur autem liberine vivamus[2] an obeamus. 2. Quis negat Socratem parentem philosophiae jure dici posse? 3. Vir ille maximus cum a ceteris scriptoribus

---

[1] The redundant **illē** (sometimes **Is**) is commonly found before **quidem** when a concession is made, but immediately qualified, 'Tuus dolor humanus is **quidem**, sed tamen moderandus,' *Yours is a grief natural to man, I admit, but one which should be modified.*"

[2] Not here *whether we live*, but *whether we are to live*.

tum a Xenophonte laudatus est. 4. Si qui capti sunt, omnes ad unum interfecti. 5. Et mea et tua interest ut huic legi resistamus. 6. Vereor ne ex hoc fonte magna pestis in rempublicam fluxura sit. 7. Nunc quidem valetudini tribuamus aliquid, cras autem rei-publicae. 8. Non tibi tantus dolor est quantus isti. 9. Victis hostibus, Caesar ab urbibus quinque trecenos obsides poposcit. 10. Credisne hanc perfidiam ei profuturam esse?

1. *In Xenophon we read a good deal (i.e. many things) about the illustrious general Agesilaus. 2. It concerns the whole country that Catiline should perish. 3. Having bound yourselves by an oath, do you now say that you did not promise to help him? 4. It is said that Labienus was at that time in command of thirty thousand soldiers. 5. It is said that Venus, the most beautiful of the goddesses, married Vulcan. 6. In the reign of Tullius the learned poet Balbus wrote very good poems. 7. I asked him why he did not do-his-duty to (trans. satisfy) his country. 8. Do not teach young boys philosophy.*[1] *9. I do not care a farthing for any of you. 10. Ask the boy whether Cyrus conquered the Scythians.*

## Exercise XXVII.

1. Nunquam in dicendo irascor. An tibi irasci videor si quid acrius dico, permovendorum judicum causa? 2. Constat Labienum dimidio exercitus a Caesare praefectum esse. 3. In summo monte casa quaedam erat; quo inter venandum rex ventitabat. 4. Philoctetes, Lemni relictus, multis post annis Trojam a Neoptolemo reductus esse fertur. 5. Contigit tibi quod haud scio an nemini.[2] 6. Quaeritur suamne propter dignitatem an propter fructus aliquos virtus expetenda sit. 7. Caesar Aeduis quadringentos obsides imperaverat. 8. Non jam stulti eritis, sed turpissimi, si diutius ab illo stabitis. 9. Milites in verba imperatoris jurarunt. 10. Poma haec utilia quidem sunt, sed amariora gustatu. 11. Dixit se plura facturum fuisse, nisi sibi persuasum fuisset judicem neutri favere. 12. Milites pugnam poposcerunt, quibus imperator "Cunctando," inquit, "rem restituemus."

1. *He was answered by Tullius, but not even Tullius could excuse the deed. 2. Before he bound the captives he compelled them to swear not to escape. 3. Do you doubt, O citizens, what is*

---

[1] For "young" write "younger," and remember never to use "juvenis" as an Adjective.

[2] Supply "contigerit." The antecedent of "quod" is "id," nom. to "contigit."

*to be done?* 4. *Tell me, (my) boy, for how much he sold this farm.* 5. *For the same price as Tullius sold it to me.* 6. *We should have written much better verses if time had not failed us.* 7. *Have you not sworn to obey this law?* 8. *Homer and Virgil are read by all; the latter imitated the former.* 9. *The work, I say* (see say), *is quite finished.* 10. *The boys used no longer to be taught music by their father.*

### Exercise XXVIII.

1. Medio in foro, coram rege ipso, a plebe turbatum est. 2. Terra marique diversis casibus jam multos annos pugnatum erat. 3. Te duce, vel ignavissimi nostrum tubam canentem libenter audient. 4. Post Corinthum captam magna praeda Romam a Mummio missa est. 5. Non ante venit nobis auxilio quam quinquiens misissemus. 6. Satis erat tibi semel ignoscere; quoniam bis peccavisti, non iterum es excusandus. 7. Corinthum, tribus his diebus, veniet tui visendi causa. 8. Apud Romanos arma in majore honore quam pacis artes habebantur. 9. Multa terra marique passus tandem se in Italiam contulit. 10. Aurum plurimis et viris et civitatibus plurimarum miseriarum causa est. 11. Haec urbs, gentis devictae caput, quam celerrime delenda est. 12. Tullia, regina miserrima, fertur veneno fuisse interfecta.

1. *After he had remained two months in the country he set out for the city.* 2. *Two cohorts came as a reinforcement for the besieged citizens.* 3. *You ought not to have promised to come before the third day.* 4. *She replied that she was born of noble but very poor parents.* 5. *This field cost me more than that meadow.* 6. *In the middle of the night we rose up terrified by the sound of robbers.* 7. *Having taken the city the enemy slew the citizens, and no one was spared.* 8. *You ought to have sent messengers three or four times to the city.* 9. *I have no need of excuse, for I am worthy of praise.* 10. *It is said that the Cyclopes had only one eye in the middle of their forehead.*

### Exercise XXIX.

1. Auctore Balbo, carissimo amicorum, juvenis ex Italia cessit. 2. Puella multo quam frater peritior erat canendi. 3. Responderunt homines pauperrimi non jam pares se esse solvendo. 4. Admonendus es foederis; cuius tu jam fere oblitus es. 5. Dic mihi Tulliaene an sorori eius promiseris te anulum daturum esse. 6. Nisi te itineris taeduisset, jampridem domum perventum fuisset. 7. Olim lupus, cuius in faucibus os inhaeserat, mercede conduxit gruem qui id

extraheret. 8. Senex filios convocatos hortatur, ut fascem frangant. 9. Quod quum nequirent facere, singulis singulas virgas distribuit. 10. Quibus facillime fractis ita pueros docuit quam firma res esset concordia.

1. *Pallas was worshipped by the Athenians with the highest honours.* 2. *It is reported that the girl died of grief* (trans. *on account of grief*). 3. *By my advice you will set out for Corinth in the spring.* 4. *Who says that Jupiter did not marry Juno?* 5. *Can any one deny that you poured poison into my cup?* 6. *In my judgment, it is less disgraceful to dance in the middle of the forum than to lie.* 7. *The speech was too long for you to learn in three days.* 8. *It is said that the Druids were in great honour among the Britons.* 9. *Did you come here hoping to see her?* 10. *The foolish Balbus replied that he had once been more learned than any of his brothers.*

## ADDITIONAL EXERCISES ON THE RELATIVE PRONOUN.

(Following Exercise XXXII., p. 53.)

### Exercise XXXII. A.

1. *Do you blame him who is praised by your brother?* 2. *Many-things are troublesome to him who loves pleasure very greatly.* 3. *No one loves Tullia, who was always unmindful of others and ignorant of pity.* 4. *Do you who chastise the unjust, praise unjust-things?* 5. *The Belgians, who were bordering on our land, were very troublesome to us.* 6. *He is always mindful of his sister, who is both very good and very beautiful.* 7. *We do not always love most-of-all those to whom we give the largest gifts.* 8. *The fruits you give me are not good.* 9. *The queen is overcome by pity, of which* (trans. *of which thing*) *they are ignorant.* 10. *His son takes-care-of the pigs, of which he has very-many* (trans. *which he has very-many*).

### Exercise XXXII. B.

1. *Who is that-fellow whose threats terrify you?* 2. *For-the-whole-of that winter* (31), *which was very cold, the husbandmen were ignorant of the cause of the disease.* 3. *To us, who give many gifts to the poor, your words are disagreeable.* 4. *To the butterfly, who lives* (only) *a few hours, life is very pleasant.* 5. *Our line of battle, which was very long, is-being-overcome by the enemy.* 6. *Those whom virtue delights, vices do not*

*delight.* 7. *Few of those who praise you blame me.* 8. *Who terrifies him? What does the man fear?* 9. *What do you avoid? What deed terrifies you?* 10. *What you love I do not love.*

### Exercise XXXII. C.

1. *Do you, O sisters, who blame Tullius, praise his brother?* 2. *To what woman are you giving this?* 3. *These fountains, which were in his garden, were very agreeable to us during that whole summer.* 4. *The frost, which was destructive to the tall tree, was more pleasing than heat to the strong soldier.* 5. *This delay, which is unworthy of you and your brother, is destructive to the army.* 6. *Whose threats terrify you?* 7. *During-the-whole-of this year, you, who blame the vices of Tullius, are praising the-same-things in Balbus.* 8. *I praise the same-things as* (i.e. *which*) *you* (*praise*). 9. *The same woman who praises herself blames her friends.* 10. *Of those* (34) *who were in the garden ten* (*were*) *boys, four were old-men.*

# APPENDIX I.

## IRREGULAR VERBS
## IN THE ORDER OF THEIR FORMATION.[1]

When a Compound Verb is formed from a Simple Verb and a Preposition or other Prefix, the **a** or **e** of the Simple Verb is changed, in the Compound Verb, into:

|   | PRESENT. | PERFECT. | SUPINE. |   |
|---|---|---|---|---|
|   | **i** | **ē** or **ĭ** | **a, e,** or **u** |   |
| Ăgo | rĕdĭgo | rĕdēgi | rĕdactum | *reduce* |
| Cădo | occĭdo | occĭdi | occāsum | *die* |
| Răpio | ĕrĭpio | ĕrĭpui | ēreptum | *snatch* |
| Făcio | conficio | confēci | confectum | *finish* |
| Sălio | prŏsĭlio | prŏsĭlui | prōsultum | *spring forth* |
| Făteor | confĭteor |   | confessus | *confess* |
| Tĕneo | sustĭneo | sustĭnui | sustentum | *sustain* |
| Lĕgo | ēlĭgo | ēlēgi | ēlectum | *elect*[2] |
| Ĕgeo | indĭgeo | indĭgui | — | *need* |

In the following lists all the Compounds of the above Simple Verbs, and of **scando, [pleo], tango, [specio], cedo, caedo, jacio, emo,** &c., will not be given, as they follow the forms of the Simple Verbs.

Note that when the Simple Verb has a reduplicated Perfect of three syllables, **pĕpŭli, cĕcĭdi, tĕtĭgi, cĕcĭni,** the Perfect of the Compound Verb often rejects a syllable, **ex-pŭli, con-cĭdi, con-tĭgi, con-cĭnui,** &c.: but there are exceptions to this rule, viz. the compounds of **disco, posco, -dĕre,** and sometimes of **curro.**

---

[1] The order of the *Public School Grammar* is adopted in this list.
[2] But note that three compounds of **lĕgo,** viz., **neglĕgo, intellĕgo,** and **dīligo,** make the perfects **neglexi, intellexi, dilexi.**

## IRREGULAR VERBS

### FIRST CONJUGATION.[1]

| | | | |
|---|---|---|---|
| Dăre | dĕdi | dătum | *give, put* |
| Stāre | stĕti | [stătum][2] | *stand* |
| Iŭv-āre | iūvi | iūtum | *help* |
| Lăv-āre[3] | lāvi | lōtum | *wash* |
| Frĭc-āre | frĭcui | frictum | *rub* |
| Sĕc-āre | sĕcui | sectum | *cut* |
| Crĕp-āre | crĕpui | crĕpĭtum | *creak, prattle* |
| Cŭb-āre | cŭbui | cŭbĭtum | *lie down* |
| Dŏm-āre | dŏmui | dŏmĭtum | *tame* |
| Sŏn-āre | sŏnui | sŏnĭtum | *sound* |
| Tŏn-āre | tŏnui | tŏnĭtum | *thunder* |
| Vĕt-āre | vĕtui | vĕtĭtum | *forbid* |
| Plĭc-āre | plĭcāvi (-ui) | plĭcĭtum (-ātum) | *fold* |
| Mĭc-āre | mĭcui (-āvi) | [-mĭcātum] | *glitter* |

### SECOND CONJUGATION.

| | | | |
|---|---|---|---|
| Mord-ēre | mŏmordi | morsum | *bite* |
| Pend-ēre | pĕpendi | — | *hang* |
| Spond-ēre | spŏpondi | sponsum | *contract* |
| Tond-ēre | tŏtondi | tonsum | *shear* |
| Căv-ēre | cāvi | cautum | *beware* |
| Făv-ēre | fāvi | fautum | *favour* |
| Fŏv-ēre | fōvi | fōtum | *cherish* |
| Mŏv-ēre | mōvi | mōtum | *move* |

---

[1] Verbs that may be omitted by beginners are marked thus *.

[2] A bracket denotes that the form, although correct according to the rules of the language, seldom or never occurs in Latin literature. This is the case with many Supines commonly given in Latin Grammars. In many cases, a Participle is found where there is no Supine. Thus **haesum** is not found, but **haesūrus** is; there is no **cărĭtum**, but there is **cărĭtūrus**; no **quĭtum**, but **quĭtus**; no **fŭgĭtum**, but **fŭgĭtūrus**. The Supine is in fact a comparatively rare form in all verbs, and it is to be regretted that usage has selected it as a typical part of a Latin Verb to be committed to memory. The Perf. Passive Participle would be preferable.

Note also that the Fut. Participle often does not follow the Supine, *e.g.* **sectum** but **sĕcātūrus**, **sŏnĭtum** but **sŏnātūrus**, &c.

[3] In classical prose, *sup.* **lăvātum**, *perf. part.* **lautus**.

## IN ORDER OF FORMATION.

| | | | |
|---|---|---|---|
| Vŏv-ēre | vŏvi | vŏtum | *vow* |
| Păv-ēre | păvi | — | *quake* |
| | | | |
| Sĕd-ēre | sĕdi | sessum | *sit* |
| Vĭd-ēre | vĭdi | vīsum | *see* |
| | | | |
| Prand-ēre | prandi | pransum | *dine* |
| | | | |
| Cōnīv-ēre | [cōnīvi or -nixi] | — | *blink* |
| Strīd-ēre | strīdi | — | *creak* |
| Ferv-ēre | ferbui or fervi | — | *boil* |
| | | | |
| Dĕl-ēre | dĕlēvi | dĕlētum | *blot out* |
| Fl-ēre | flēvi | flētum | *weep* |
| N-ēre | nēvi | nētum | *spin* |
| [-Plēre] | [-plēvi] | [-plētum] | *fill* |
| *Vi-ēre | [viēvi] | viētum | *bind with twigs* |
| Ci-ēre | cīvi | cĭtum | *stir up*[1] |
| -Ŏlēre | [-ŏlēvi] | [ŏlĭtum] | *grow,* &c. |
| [Su-ēre] | suevi | suetum | *be wont* |
| | | | |
| Arc-ēre | arcui | — | *ward off* |
| Coerc-ēre | coercui | coercĭtum | *restrain* |
| Exerc-ēre | exercui | exercĭtum | *exercise* |
| Căr-ēre | cărui | [cărĭtum] | *be without, be in want of* |
| Dĕb-ēre | dēbui | dēbĭtum | *owe*[2] |
| Dŏl-ēre | dŏlui | [dŏlĭtum] | *grieve* |
| Hăb-ēre | hăbui | hăbĭtum | *have* |
| Jăc-ēre | jăcui | [jăcĭtum] | *lie* |
| Lĭc-ēre | lĭcui | lĭcĭtum | *be bid for* |
| Mĕr-ēre | mĕrui | mĕrĭtum | *deserve, earn* |
| Mŏn-ēre | mŏnui | mŏnĭtum | *advise* |
| Nŏc-ēre | nŏcui | nŏcĭtum | *hurt* |
| Păr-ēre | părui | [părĭtum] | *appear, obey* |
| Plăc-ēre | plăcui | plăcĭtum | *please* |
| Praeb-ēre | praebui | praebĭtum | *afford* |
| Terr-ēre | terrui | terrĭtum | *affright* |
| Tăc-ēre | tăcui | tăcĭtum | *be silent* |
| Văl-ēre | vălui | [vălĭtum] | *be strong, be well* |
| | | | |
| Dŏc-ēre | dŏcui | dŏctum | *teach* |
| Misc-ēre | miscui | { mistum / mixtum } | *mingle* |

[1] The primitive form is **cio, cīre** (found in the compounds **accio, excio**).
[2] This is properly a compound of **hăbeo**; but some of the less obvious compounds of verbs are included in this list.

# IRREGULAR VERBS

| | | | |
|---|---|---|---|
| Tĕn-ēre | tĕnui | tentum | *hold* |
| Torr-ēre | torrui | tostum | *scorch* |
| | | | |
| Cens-ēre | censui | censum | *value, vote* |
| | | | |
| Ĕg-ēre | ĕgui | — | *want* |
| *[-Mĭn-ēre] | [-mĭnui] | — | *jut* |
| Ŏl-ēre | ŏlui | — | *smell* |
| Sorb-ēre | sorbui | — | *suck up* |
| Stŭd-ēre | stŭdui | — | *study*[1] |
| | | | |
| Aug-ēre | auxi | auctum | *increase* (trans.) |
| Indulg-ēre | indulsi | indultum | *indulge* |
| Mulg-ēre | mulsi | [mulctum] | *milk* |
| Torqu-ēre | torsi | tortum | *twist* |
| Lūg-ēre | luxi | — | *mourn* |
| | | | |
| Mulcēre | mulsi | mulsum | *soothe* |
| Tergēre | tersi | -tersum | *wipe* |
| Ardēre | arsi | arsum | *take fire* |
| Rīdēre | rīsi | rīsum | *laugh* |
| Suādēre | suāsi | suāsum | *persuade* |
| Iŭbēre | iussi | iussum | *command* |
| Mănēre | mansi | mansum | *remain* |
| Haerēre | haesi | [haesum] | *stick* |
| | | | |
| Algēre | alsi | — | *be cold* |
| Fulgēre | fulsi | — | *glitter* |
| *Turg-ēre | tursi | — | *swell* |
| Urg-ēre | ursi | — | *urge* |
| *Frīgēre | [-frixi] | — | *be cold* |
| Lūcēre | luxi | — | *shine* |
| Aud-ēre | ausus sum | — | *dare* |
| Gaud-ēre | gāvīsus sum | — | *rejoice* |
| Sŏl-ēre | sŏlĭtus sum | — | *be wont* |
| | | | |
| Lĭc-ēri | lĭcĭtus | — | *bid for* |
| Mĕr-ēri | mĕrĭtus | — | *deserve* |
| Mĭser-ēri | mĭsĕrĭtus | — | *pity* |
| Tu-ēri | tuĭtus | — | *view, protect* |
| Vĕr-ēri | vĕrĭtus | — | *fear, respect* |
| R-ēri | rătus | — | *think* |
| Făt-ēri | fassus | — | *confess* |
| Mĕd-ēri | — | — | *heal* |

[1] Several Verbs that have an Adjective in Ĭdus reject the Supine, *e.g.* **stŭpeo, ăveo, flōreo**; and some that have no such Adjective, as **lăteo**.

## IN ORDER OF FORMATION.

### FOURTH CONJUGATION.

| | | | |
|---|---|---|---|
| Sĕpĕl-īre | sĕpĕlīvi | sĕpultum | *bury* |
| Īre (eo) | īvi | ītum | *go* |
| Quīre (queo) | quīvi | quĭtum | *be able* |
| | | | |
| Săl-īre | sălui | (saltum) | *leap, dance* |
| Ăpĕr-īre | ăpĕrui | ăpertum | *open* |
| Ŏpĕr-īre | ŏpĕrui | ŏpertum | *cover* |
| | | | |
| Compĕr-ire | compĕri | compertum | *find* |
| Repĕr-īre | reppĕri | rĕpertum | *discover* |
| | | | |
| Vĕn-īre | vēni | ventum | *come* |
| | | | |
| Ămĭc-īre | ămixi & -ĭcui | ămictum | *clothe* |
| Farc-īre | farsi | fartum | *stuff* |
| Fulc-īre | fulsi | fultum | *prop* |
| Sanc-īre | sanxi | sanctum | *consecrate* |
| Sarc-īre | sarsi | sartum | *mend* |
| Vinc-īre | vinxi | vinctum | *bind* |
| Saep-īre | saepsi | saeptum | *hedge in* |
| Haur-īre | hausi | haustum | *drain* |
| *Rauc-īre [1] | — | — | *be hoarse* |
| | | | |
| Sent-īre | sensi | sensum | *feel* [2] |
| | | | |
| Expĕr-īri | | expertus | *experience* |
| Oppĕr-īri | | oppertus | *wait for* |
| Ŏr-īri | | ortus | *arise* |
| | | | |
| Assent-īri | | assensus | *agree* |
| Mĕt-īri | | mensus | *measure* |
| Ord-īri | | orsus | *begin* |

### THIRD CONJUGATION.

| | | | |
|---|---|---|---|
| Disc-ĕre [3] | dĭdĭci | — | *learn* |
| Posc-ĕre | pŏposci | — | *demand* |
| Pa-n-g-ĕre [4] | pĕpĭgi | pactum | *fasten, covenant* |

---

[1] There are also found rausūrus and ir-rausĕrit; *denotes rare occurrence.

[2] Some Verbs, such as gestio, *I am eager*, and others which express only passions, *e.g.* singultio, *I sob*, have neither Perfect nor Supine.

[3] Compounds of Verbs with Reduplicated Perfect drop Reduplication, except those of disco, posco, sisto, -dĕre, and sometimes of curro.

[4] The n in this and following Verbs is not a part of the root. The forms pĕpĭgi, pactum, are reserved for the metaph. meaning, *covenant*; for the lit. meaning, the forms in use are pēgi or panxi, and panctum.

# IRREGULAR VERBS

| | | | |
|---|---|---|---|
| Pu-*n*-g-ĕre | pŭpŭgi | punctum | *prick* |
| Ta-*n*-g-ĕre | tĕtĭgi | tactum | *touch* |
| Sist-ĕre | [-stĭti¹] | [-stĭtum¹] | *stop* |
| [-d-ĕre¹] | [-dĭdi] | [-dĭtum] | *put, give* |
| Tend-ĕre | tĕtendi | { tensum *and* tentum } | *stretch* |
| Căn-ĕre | cĕcĭni | cantum | *sing* |
| Păr-ĕre | pĕpĕri | partum | *bring forth* |
| Toll-ĕre | sustŭli | sublātum | *take up* |
| | | | |
| Parc-ĕre | pĕperci | parsum | *spare* |
| Căd-ĕre | cĕcĭdi | cāsum | *fall* |
| Caed-ĕre | cĕcīdi | caesum | *cut, beat, kill* |
| Pend-ĕre | pĕpendi | pensum | *weigh* |
| Tu-n-d-ĕre | (tŭtŭdi) | tūsum | *thump, pound* |
| Curr-ĕre | cŭcurri | cursum | *run* |
| Fall-ĕre | fĕfelli | falsum | *deceive* |
| Pell-ĕre | pĕpŭli | pulsum | *drive* |
| [-Cell-ĕre]¹ | [cĕcŭli] | [-culsum¹] | *push* |
| | | | |
| Făc-ĕre (*i*-o) | fēci | factum | *make, do* |
| Jăc-ĕre (*i*-o) | jēci | jactum | *throw* |
| Li-*n*-qu-ĕre | līqui | [-lictum] | *leave* |
| Vi-*n*-c-ĕre | vīci | victum | *conquer* |
| Ăg-ĕre | ēgi | actum | *do* |
| Fra-*n*-g-ĕre | frēgi | fractum | *break* |
| Lĕg-ĕre | lĕgi (-lexi)² | lectum | *read, choose* |
| Căp-ĕre (*i*-o) | cēpi | captum | *take* |
| Ru-*m*-p-ĕre | rūpi | ruptum | *break* |
| Ĕm-ĕre | ēmi | emptum | *buy, take* |
| *Scăb-ĕre | scābi | — | *scratch* |
| | | | |
| Ĕd-ĕre | ēdi | ēsum | *eat* |
| Fŏd-ĕre (*i*-o) | fōdi | fossum | *dig* |
| Fu-*n*-d-ĕre | fūdi | fūsum | *pour* |
| | | | |
| Fŭg-ĕre (*i*-o) | fūgī | [fŭgĭtum] | *fly* |
| | | | |
| Bĭb-ĕre | bĭbi | bĭbĭtum | *drink* |
| | | | |
| Īc-ĕre | īci³ | ictum | *strike* |

---

¹ Only found in Compounds.
² The form -**lexi** is found only in **dī-lĭgo, neg-lĕgo, intel-lĕgo**.
³ This form is non-classical.

## IN ORDER OF FORMATION.

| | | | |
|---|---|---|---|
| Fi-*n*-d-ĕre | fĭdi | fissum | *cleave* |
| Sci-*n*-d-ĕre | scĭdi | scissum | *cut* |
| | | | |
| Vert-ĕre | verti | versum | *turn* |
| [-Cend-ĕre] | [-cendi] | [-censum] | *set alight* |
| Cūd-ĕre | cūdi | cūsum | *hammer* |
| [-Fend-ĕre] | [-fendi] | [-fensum] | *strike* |
| Mand-ĕre | mandi | mansum | *chew* |
| Pand-ĕre | pandi | passum | *spread* |
| Prehend-ĕre | prehendi | prehensum | *take, grasp* |
| Scand-ĕre | -scandi | -scansum | *climb* |
| Sīd-ĕre | sīdi¹ | — | *settle* |
| Lamb-ĕre | [lambi]² | [lambĭtum] | *lick* |
| Verr-ĕre | verri | versum | *sweep* |
| Vell-ĕre | { velli / vulsi }³ | vulsum | *rend, pluck* |
| *Psall-ĕre | psalli | — | *play (chords)* |
| Vīs-ĕre | vīsi | — | *visit* |
| Fīdere | fīsus sum | — | *trust* |
| | | | |
| Compesc-ĕre | compescui | — | *restrain* |
| Răp-ĕre (*i*-o) | rapui | raptum | *seize* |
| Ăl-ĕre | ălui | altum | *nourish* |
| Cŏl-ĕre | cŏlui | cultum | *till* |
| Consŭl-ĕre | consŭlui | consultum | *consult* |
| Occŭl-ĕre | occŭlui | occultum | *hide* |
| Sĕr-ĕre | sĕrui | sertum | *join together* |
| *Pins-ĕre | pinsui | pistum⁴ | *pound* |
| Tex-ĕre | texui | textum | *weave* |
| *Deps-ĕre | depsui | — | *knead, tan* |
| | | | |
| Stert-ĕre | stĕrtui | — | *snore* |
| Strĕp-ĕre | strĕpui | strĕpĭtum | *rattle* |
| [-Cu*m*b-ĕre] | cŭbui | cŭbĭtum | *lie down* |
| Frĕm-ĕre | frĕmui | [frĕmĭtum]⁵ | *roar* |
| Gĕm-ĕre | gĕmui | [gĕmĭtum]⁵ | *groan* |
| Tĕm-ĕre | trĕmui | [trĕmĭtum]⁵ | *tremble* |
| Vŏm-ĕre | vŏmui | vŏmĭtum | *vomit* |
| Gign-ĕre | gĕnui | gĕnĭtum | *beget* |
| Pŏn-ĕre | pŏsui | pŏsĭtum | *place* |
| Mŏl-ĕre | mŏlui | mŏlĭtum | *grind* |

¹ More commonly, sēdi, from sĕdeo.
² The Perf. and Sup. are only found in Priscian.
³ Vulsi is the rarer of the two forms.
⁴ There are also pinsi, pinsum, and pinsĭtum.
⁵ These forms are found in Priscian only, who does not assign them to any authors.

# IRREGULAR VERBS

| | | | |
|---|---|---|---|
| Velle (vŏlo) | vŏlui | — | *wish* |
| Nolle (nōlo) | nōlui | — | *wish not* |
| Malle (mālo) | mālui | — | *wish rather* |
| | | | |
| Mĕt-ĕre | messui | messum | *mow, reap* |
| *Frend-ĕre | [frendui][1] | fressum | *gnash, bruise* |
| | | | |
| Lĭn-ĕre | lēvi | lĭtum | *smear* |
| Sĭn-ĕre | sīvi | sĭtum | *allow* |
| Cern-ĕre | [crēvi] | [-crētum] | *sift* |
| Spern-ĕre | sprēvi | sprētum | *spurn* |
| Stern-ĕre | strāvi | strātum | *strew* |
| Sĕr-ĕre | sēvi | sătum | *sow* |
| Cresc-ĕre | crēvi | crētum | *grow* |
| Quiesc-ĕre | quiēvi | [quiētum] | *rest* |
| Suesc-ĕre | suēvi | [suētum] | *be wont* |
| (G)nosc-ĕre[2] | (g)nōvi | (g)nōtum | *know* |
| Pasc-ĕre | pāvi | pastum | *feed* |
| Cŭp-ĕre (i-o) | cŭpīvi | cŭpītum | *desire* |
| Pĕt-ĕre | pĕtīvi | petītum | *demand* |
| Quaer-ĕre | quaesīvi | quaesītum | *seek* |
| *Rŭd-ĕre | [rŭdīvi][3] | [rŭdītum] | *bray* |
| Săp-ĕre (i-o) | sapĭi (-īvi)[4] | — | *savour* |
| Tĕr-ĕre | trīvi | trītum | *rub, bruise* |
| Arcess-ĕre | arcessīvi | arcessītum | *fetch* |
| Incess-ĕre | incessīvi | incessītum | *attack* |
| Căpess-ĕre | căpessīvi | căpessītum | *take in hand* |
| Făcess-ĕre | făcessīvi | făcessītum | *cause* |
| Lăcess-ĕre | lăcessīvi | lăcessītum | *provoke* |
| | | | |
| Dīc-ĕre | dixi | dictum | *say* |
| Dūc-ĕre | duxi | ductum | *lead* |
| [-Lăc-ĕre (i-o)][5] | [-lexi] | [-lectum] | *entice* |
| [-Spĕc-ĕre (i-o)][6] | [-spexi] | [-spectum] | *espy* |
| Cŏqu-ĕre | coxi | çoctum | *cook* |
| Cing-ĕre | cinxi | cinctum | *surround* |
| Fing-ĕre | finxi | fictum | *fashion* |
| *Flīg-ĕre | flixi | flictum | *smite* |

---

[1] Frendui is not found; **frendēre** is found.

[2] **Nosco** has dropt g which reappears in **agnōsco, agnōvi, agnĭtum; cognosco, cognōvi, cognĭtum; ignosco, ignōvi**: Adj. **ignōtus.**

[3] Rŭdīvi is only in Apuleius; rŭdītum, nowhere.

[4] But dēsĭpio, dēsĭpui. Augustine has săpui.

[5] Compare **al-lĭcio, il-lĭcio, pel-lĭcio, pro-lĭcio,** which make -lexi, -lectum. But **ēlĭcio** makes **ēlĭcui, ēlĭcĭtum.**

[6] Compare (circum- con- de- di- in- per- pro- re-)-spĭcio -spexi -spectum. So **aspĭcio, suspĭcio.**

## IN ORDER OF FORMATION. 197

| | | | |
|---|---|---|---|
| Frīg-ĕre | frixi | frictum | *roast, fry* |
| Jung-ĕre | junxi | junctum | *join* |
| *Ling-ĕre | [-linxi] | [-linctum] | *lick* |
| *Mung-ĕre | [-munxi] | [-munctum] | *wipe* |
| Ping-ĕre | pinxi | pictum | *paint* |
| Plang-ĕre | planxi | planctum | *beat* |
| Rĕg-ĕre [1] | rexi | rectum | *rule* |
| String-ĕre | strinxi | strictum | *bind* |
| Sūg-ĕre | suxi | suctum | *suck* |
| Tĕg-ĕre | texi | tectum | *cover* |
| *Stingu-ĕre | [-stinxi] | [-stinctum] | — |
| Tingu-ĕre | tinxi | tinctum | *stain* |
| Ungu-ĕre | unxi | unctum | *anoint* |
| Ningu-ĕre | ninxi | — | *snow* |
| Ang-ĕre | [anxi] | [anctum] [2] | *squeeze* |
| *[Clang-ĕre] | — | — | *rattle* |
| Trăh-ĕre | traxi | tractum | *draw* |
| Vĕh-ĕre | vexi | vectum | *carry* |
| Vīv-ĕre | vixi | victum | *live* |
| Stru-ĕre | struxi | structum | *pile* |
| Fīg-ĕre | fixi | fixum | *fix* |
| Flu-ĕre | fluxi | fluxum | *flow* |
| Merg-ĕre | mersi | mersum | *drown* |
| Sparg-ĕre [3] | sparsi | sparsum | *sprinkle* |
| Terg-ĕre | tersi | tersum | *wipe* |
| | | | |
| Flect-ĕre | flexi | flexum | *bend* |
| Nect-ĕre | { nexi / nexui } | nexum | *twine* |
| Pect-ĕre | pexi | pexum | *comb* |
| Plect-ĕre | — | [-plexum] | { *plait* / *smite* } |
| Mitt-ĕre | misi | missum | *send* |
| Quăt-ĕre (*i-o*) [4] | — | quassum | *shake* |
| Cēd-ĕre | cessi | cessum | *yield* |
| Claud-ĕre | clausi | clausum | *shut* |
| Dīvĭd-ĕre | dīvīsi | dīvīsum | *divide* |
| Laed-ĕre | laesi | laesum | *hurt* |
| Lūd-ĕre | lūsi | lūsum | *play* |

---

[1] Compare **arrĭgo, corrĭgo, dīrĭgo; (e- per-)-rĭgo -rexi -rectum.** Also **pergo, perrexi, perrectum; surgo,** *rise,* **surrexi, surrectum,** with its compounds: (as **con- ex- in- re-)-surg -surrexi -surrectum.**

[2] Priscian mentions these forms, but no authorities for them.

[3] Compare **conspergo, dispergo; (ad- in- re-)-spergo -spersi -spersum.**

[4] Compare (**con- dis- ex- in- per-)-cŭtio -cussi -cussum.** So **rĕpercŭtio.**

# IRREGULAR VERBS

| | | | |
|---|---|---|---|
| Plaud-ĕre | plausi | plausum | *clap hands* |
| Rād-ĕre | rāsi | rāsum | *shave* |
| Rōd-ĕre | rōsi | rōsum | *gnaw* |
| Trūd-ĕre | trūsi | trūsum | *thrust* |
| Vād-ĕre | [-vāsi] | [-vāsum] | *go* |
| | | | |
| Carp-ĕro | carpsi | carptum | *pluck* |
| *Clĕp-ĕre | clepsi | cleptum | *steal* |
| ⎰ Rĕp-ĕre | repsi | [reptum] | *creep* |
| ⎱ Serp-ĕre | serpsi | [serptum] | *crawl* |
| ⎰ Scalp-ĕre | scalpsi | scalptum | *scratch* |
| ⎱ Sculp-ĕre | sculpsi | sculptum | *grave* |
| *Glūb-ĕre | [glupsi] | [gluptum] | *peel* |
| Nūb-ĕre | nupsi | nuptum | *wed* |
| Scrīb-ĕre | scripsi | scriptum | *write* |
| | | | |
| Cōm-ĕre | compsi | comptum | *dress hair* |
| Dēm-ĕre | dempsi | demptum | *take away* |
| Prōm-ĕre | prompsi | promptum | *take forth* |
| Sūm-ĕre | sumpsi | sumptum | *take up* |
| Temn-ĕre | tempsi | temptum | *despise* |
| | | | |
| Prĕm-ĕre [1] | pressi | pressum | *press* |
| | | | |
| Gĕr-ĕre | gessi | gestum | *carry on* |
| Ūr-ĕre | ussi | ustum | *burn* |
| | | | |
| Ăcu-ĕre | ăcui | ăcūtum | *sharpen* |
| Argu-ĕre | argui | argūtum | *prove* |
| Exu-ĕre | exui | exūtum | *put off* |
| Indu-ĕre | indui | indūtum | *put on* |
| Imbu-ĕre | imbui | imbūtum | *tinge* |
| Lu-ĕre | lui | — [2] | *atone* |
| Mĭnu-ĕre | mĭnui | mĭnūtum | *lessen* |
| Nu-ĕre | nui | — [2] | *nod* |
| Spu-ĕre | spui | spūtum | *spit* |
| Stătu-ĕre | stătui | stătūtum | *set up* |
| Sternu-ĕre | sternui | [sternūtum] | *sneeze* |
| Su-ĕre | sui | sūtum | *sew* |
| Trĭbu-ĕre | trĭbui | trĭbūtum | *assign, pay* |
| Solv-ĕre | solvi | sŏlūtum | *loose, pay* |
| Volv-ĕre | volvi | vŏlūtum | *roll* |

---

[1] Compare **imprĭmo, supprĭmo**; (com- de- ex- op- re-)-prĭmo -pressi -**pressum.**

[2] No Supine is found; but the fut. part. luĭtūrus points to luĭtum as Supine; and **abnuĭtūrus** to nuĭtum for nuo.

## IN ORDER OF FORMATION.

| | | | |
|---|---|---|---|
| Ru-ĕre | rui | rūtum (rŭĭtum) | rush |
| *Batu-ĕre | batui | — | beat |
| *-Gru-ĕre | -grui | — | cry like a crane |
| Mĕtu-ĕre | mĕtui | — | fear |
| Plu-ĕre | plui or plŭvi | — | rain |
| | | | |
| Fung-i | functus | | perform |
| Nīt-i | nīsus (nixus) | | strive |
| Plect-i | [-plexus] | | twine |
| Păt-i (i-or) | passus | | suffer |
| Ūti | ūsus | | use |
| Grăd-i (i-or) | gressus | | step |
| Lāb-i | lapsus | | glide, fall |
| Mŏr-i (i-or) | mortuus | | die |
| Quĕr-i | questus | | complain |
| Fru-i | fruĭtus | | enjoy |
| Lŏqu-i | locūtus | | speak |
| Sĕqu-i | secūtus | | follow |
| Ăpisc-i | aptus | | obtain |
| [-Mĕnisc-i][1] | [-mentus] | | have in mind |
| Expergisc-i | experrectus | | wake up |
| Fătisc-i | fessus | | be weary |
| (g)nasc-i | (g)nātus | | be born |
| Īrasc-i | īrātus | | be angry |
| Nancisc-i | nactus or nanctus | | find |
| Oblīvisc-i | oblītus | | forget |
| Păcisc-i | pactus | | bargain |
| Prŏficisc-i | prŏfectus | | set out |
| Ulcisc-i | ultus | | avenge |
| Vesc-i | — | | feed |
| Līqu-i | — | | melt |
| *Ring-i | — | | grin |

---

[1] Compare com-mīniscor, -mentus, 3; rĕ-mīniscor, 3.

# APPENDIX II.

## IRREGULAR VERBS,

### WITH MANY OF THEIR MORE IMPORTANT COMPOUNDS.

*(Alphabetically arranged.[1])*

| | | | | |
|---|---|---|---|---|
| Abdo | -ĕre | abdĭdi | abdĭtum | *hide* |
| Ăbĭgo | -ĕre | ăbēgi | ăbactum | *drive away* |
| Ăbŏleo | -ēre | ăbŏlēvi | ăbŏlĭtum | *destroy* |
| Abrĭpĭo | -ĕre | abrĭpui | abreptum | *snatch away* |
| Accendo | -ĕre | accendi | accensum | *set on fire* |
| Accumbo | -ĕre | accŭbui | accŭbitum | *recline at table* |
| Accurro | -ĕre | accŭcurri *and* accurri | accursum | *run up* |
| Acquīro | -ĕre | acquīsīvi | acquīsĭtum | *acquire* |
| Addo | -ĕre | addĭdi | addĭtum | *add* |
| Ădeo | -īre | ădii | ădĭtum | *go to* |
| Ădĭmo | -ĕre | ădēmi | ădemptum | *take away* |
| Adjŭvo | -āre | adjūvi | adjūtum | *help* |
| Ădŏleo | -ēre | ădŏlŭi | ădultum | *to honour in worship* |
| Ădŏlesco | -ĕre | ădŏlēvi | ădultum | *grow up* |
| Agnosco | -ĕre | agnōvi | agnĭtum | *recognize* |
| Ăgo | -ĕre | ēgi | actum | *do, act, drive* |
| Algeo | -ēre | alsi | — | *be cold* |
| Allĭcio | -ĕre | allexi | allectum | *entice* |
| Ălo | -ĕre | ălui | altum [2] | *feed, nourish* |
| Ămĭcio | -īre | [ămĭcui & -ixi] | ămictum | *clothe* |
| Ămitto | -ĕre | āmīsi | āmissum | *lose* |
| Amplector | -i | amplexus (sum) | — | *embrace* |
| Ango | -ĕre | — | — | *squeeze* |
| Anquīro | -ĕre | anquīsīvi | anquīsĭtum | *examine into* |
| Antecello | -ĕre | — | — | *surpass* |
| Ăpĕrio | -īre | ăpĕrui | ăpertum | *open* |
| Appello [3] | -ĕre | appŭli | appulsum | *put into shore* |

---

[1] The object of this list is to test the memory of the pupil. Looking at the first column, and covering the other columns with his hand, he can repeat the Perfects and Supines without having the guidance which is necessarily furnished by the grouping in List I.

[2] **Ălĭtum** was introduced in the post-Augustan age, possibly to distinguish it from the adj. **altus** *high*.

[3] Distinguish this word from **appello, appellāre, -āvi, -ātum,** *call*.

## IRREGULAR VERBS, WITH COMPOUNDS.

| | | | | |
|---|---|---|---|---|
| Applĭco | -āre | applĭcui and applĭcāvi | applĭcĭtum and applĭcātum | apply |
| Arcesso | -ĕre | arcessīvi | arcessītum | send for |
| Ardeo | -ēre | arsi | arsum (neut.) | take fire |
| Arguo | -ĕre | argui | argūtum | prove |
| Ascendo | -ĕre | ascendi | ascensum | ascend |
| Attendo | -ĕre | attendi | attentum | attend |
| Audeo | -ēre | ausus sum | — | dare |
| Aufŭgio | -ĕre | aufūgi | — | flee away |
| Aufĕro | -erre | abstŭli | ablatum | carry away |
| Augeo | -ēre | auxi | auctum | increase |
| Bĭbo | -ĕre | bĭbi | — | drink |
| Cădo | -ĕre | cĕcĭdi | cāsum | fall |
| Caedo | -ĕre | cĕcĭdi | caesum | cut, beat, kill |
| Căno | -ĕre | cĕcĭni | cantum | sing |
| Căpesso | -ĕre | căpessīvi | căpessītum | seize, take hold of |
| Căpio | -ĕre | cēpi | captum | take |
| Carpo | -ĕre | carpsi | carptum | pluck |
| Căveo | -ēre | cāvi | cautum | beware |
| Cēdo | -ĕre | cessi | cessum | yield |
| Censeo | -ēre | censui | censum | vote |
| Cerno [1] | -ĕre | — | — | discern |
| Cieo | ciēre | [cīvi | cĭtum] | stir up |
| Cio | cīre | [cīvi | cĭtum] | stir up |
| Cingo | -ĕre | cinxi | cinctum | surround |
| Circumcīdo | -ĕre | circumcīdi | circumcīsum | clip |
| Clango | -ĕre | — | — | resound |
| Claudo [2] | -ĕre | clausi | clausum | shut |
| Cŏ-ĕmo | -ĕre | cŏ-ēmi | cŏ-emptum | buy up |
| [Coepio] | -isse | coeptus (sum) | used with Pass. Inf. | begin |
| Cognosco | -ĕre | cognōvi | cognĭtum | find out, know |
| Cōgo | -ĕre | cŏēgi | cŏactum | compel |
| Collĭgo | -ĕre | collēgi | collectum | collect |
| Cŏlo | -ĕre | cŏlui | cultum | till |
| Cōmo | -ĕre | compsi | comptum | adorn |
| Compello [3] | -ĕre | compŭli | compulsum | drive together |
| Compĕrio | -īre | compĕri | compertum | ascertain |
| Compesco | -ĕre | compescui | — | restrain |
| Compleo | -ēre | complēvi | complētum | fill |
| Comprĕ-hendo } or Comprendo | -ĕre | comprehendi | comprehensum | seize |
| Comprendo | -ĕre | comprendi | comprensum | seize |

[1] The Perfect and Supine crēvi and crētum are rarely used in this sense.
[2] The compounds of claudo are similar, except that they change au into u, e.g. circumclūdo, conclūdo, &c.
[3] Distinguish this from compellāre, accost.

# IRREGULAR VERBS,

| | | | | |
|---|---|---|---|---|
| Concīdo | -ĕre | concīdi | concīsum | *cut in pieces* |
| Concĭdo | -ĕre | concĭdi | — | *fall in a heap* |
| Concĭno | -ĕre | concĭnui | — | *play together, harmonize* |
| Concurro | -ĕre | concurri | concursum | *run together* |
| Concŭtio | -ĕre | concussi | concussum | *shake together* |
| Condo | -ĕre | condĭdi | condĭtum | *found* |
| Confīdo | -ĕre | confīsus (sum) | — | *confide* |
| Conjĭcio | -ĕre | conjēci | conjectum | *throw* |
| Cōnīveo | -ēre | [cōnīvi & -ixi] | — | *wink* |
| Conscendo | -ĕre | conscendi | conscensum | *go up* |
| Consentio | -īre | consensi | consensum | *agree* |
| Consĕro | -ĕre | consēvi | consĭtum | *sow, plant* |
| Consĕro | -ĕre | consĕrui | consertum | *put close together* |
| Consīdo | -ĕre | consēdi | consessum | *sit down* |
| Conspergo | -ĕre | conspersi | conspersum | *sprinkle* |
| Consŭlo | -ĕre | consŭlui | consultum | *consult* |
| Contingo | -ĕre | contĭgi | contactum | *touch, happen* |
| Convello | -ĕre | convelli | convulsum | *tear up* |
| Converto | -ĕre | converti | conversum | *turn towards* |
| Cŏquo | -ĕre | coxi | coctum | *cook* |
| Crēdo | -ĕre | crēdĭdi | credĭtum | *believe* |
| Crĕpo | -āre | crĕpui | crĕpĭtum | *creak* |
| Cresco | -ĕre | crēvi | [crētum] | *grow* |
| Cŭbo | -āre | cŭbui | cŭbĭtum | *lie down* |
| [-cumbo | -ĕre | -cŭbui | -cŭbĭtum | *lie down*] |
| Cūdo | -ĕre | cūdi | cūsum | *fashion* |
| Cŭpio | cupĕre | cŭpīvi | cŭpītum | *covet, desire* |
| Curro | -ĕre | cŭcurri | cursum | *run* |
| [-cŭtio[1] | -ĕre | -cussi | -cussum | *shake*] |
| Dēcerno | -ĕre | dēcrēvi | dēcretum | *decree* |
| Dēcĭdo | -ĕre | dēcĭdi | — | *fall down* |
| Dēcīdo | -ĕre | dēcīdi | dēcīsum | *decide* |
| Dēcurro | -ĕre | dēcŭcurri and dēcurri | dēcursum | *run a course* |
| Dēdisco | -ĕre | dēdĭdĭci | — | *unlearn* |
| Dēfendo | -ĕre | dēfendi | dēfensum | *defend* |
| Dēgo | -ĕre | — | — | *live* |
| Dēleo | -ēre | dēlēvi | dēlētum | *blot out* |
| Dēmo | -ĕre | dempsi | demptum | *take away* |
| Dēpello | -ĕre | dēpŭli | dēpulsum | *drive down* |
| Dēpendeo | -ēre | — | — | *hang down* (intr.) |
| Dēpendo | -ĕre | dēpendi | dēpensum | *pay down* |
| Dēposco | -ĕre | dēpoposci | — | *demand* |
| Descendo | -ĕre | descendi | descensum | *descend* |
| Dēsĭno | -ĕre | dēsĭi [-ivi] | [dēsĭtum] | *cease* |

---

[1] A form of **quătio** only found in the compounds **concŭtio, percŭtio**, &c.

| | | | | |
|---|---|---|---|---|
| Despondeo | -ēre | despondi [-spopondi] | desponsum | *pledge* |
| Dētergeo | -ēre | dētersi | dētersum | *wipe away* |
| Dēvincio | -īre | dēvinxi | dēvinctum | *bind down* |
| Dīco | -ĕre | dixi | dictum | *say* |
| Diffīdo | -ĕre | diffīsus (sum) | — | *distrust* |
| Diffindo | -ĕre | diffĭdi | diffissum | *cleave asunder* |
| Dīgĕro | -ĕre | dīgessi | dīgestum | *set apart* |
| Dignosco | -ĕre | — | — | *distinguish* |
| Dīlĭgo | -ĕre | dīlexi | dīlectum | *love* |
| Dīlūcesco | -ĕre | dīluxi | — | *dawn* |
| Dīmētior | -īri | dīmensus (sum) | — | *measure out* |
| Dīmĭco | -āre | dīmĭcāvi & ui | dīmĭcātum | *fight* |
| Dĭrĭmo | -ĕre | dīrĕmi | dīremptum | *break off, or up* |
| Dĭrĭpio | -ĕre | dīrĭpui | dīreptum | *tear asunder* |
| Dīrumpo | -ĕre | dīrūpi | dīruptum | *burst asunder* |
| Discĕdo | -ĕre | discessi | discessum | *depart* |
| Discindo | -ĕre | discĭdi | discissum | *rend asunder* |
| Disco | -ĕre | dĭdĭci | — | *learn* |
| Discumbo | -ĕre | discŭbui | discŭbĭtum | *recline (at dinner)* |
| Discurro | -ere | discurri | discursum | *run in different directions* |
| Discŭtio | -ĕre | discussi | discussum | *shake asunder* |
| Disjĭcio | -ĕre | disjēci | disjectum | *cast asunder* |
| Dispergo | -ĕre | dispersi | dispersum | *scatter apart* |
| Dissentio | -īre | dissensi | dissensum | *disagree with* |
| Dissĕro | -ĕre | dissĕrui | [dissertum] | *set forth distinctly, discourse* |
| Dissĭdeo | -ēre | dissēdi | dissessum | *be at variance with* |
| Dissĭlio | -īre | dissĭlui | dissultum | *leap apart* |
| Dissolvo | -ĕre | dissolvi | dissolūtum | *dissolve* |
| Dissuādeo | -ēre | dissuāsi | dissuāsum | *dissuade* |
| Distinguo | -ĕre | distinxi | distinctum | *discriminate* |
| Disto | -āre | — | — | *be distant* |
| Distrăho | -ĕre | distraxi | distractum | *draw apart* |
| Dīvello | -ĕre | dīvelli | dīvulsum | *rend asunder* |
| Dīvĭdo | -ĕre | dīvīsi | dīvīsum | *divide* |
| Do | dăre | dĕdi | dătum | *give* |
| Dŏceo | -ēre | dŏcui | doctum | *teach* |
| Dŏmo | -āre | dŏmui | dŏmĭtum | *tame* |
| Dūco | -ĕre | duxi | ductum | *lead* |
| Ēdisco | -ĕre | ēdĭdĭci | — | *learn off* |
| Ĕdo | ĕdĕre & esse | ĕdi | ēsum | *eat* |
| Ēdo | -ĕre | ēdĭdi | ēdĭtum | *give out* |
| Effervesco | -ĕre | efferbui | — | *effervesce* |

## IRREGULAR VERBS,

| | | | | |
|---|---|---|---|---|
| Effulgeo | -ēre[1] | effulsi | effulsum | *shine forth* |
| Effundo | -ĕre | effūdi | effūsum | *pour forth* |
| Ēlĭcio | -ĕre | ēlĭcui | ēlĭcĭtum | *entice forth* |
| Elīdo | -ĕre | elīsi | elīsum | *knock out* |
| Ēlĭgo | -ĕre | ēlēgi | ēlectum | *choose out* |
| Ēmentior | -īri | ēmentitus (sum) | — | *lie outright* |
| Ēmĭco | -āre | ēmĭcŭi | ēmĭcatum | *flash out* |
| Ĕmo | -ĕre | ēmi | emptum | *buy, take* |
| Ĕnĕco | -āre | ĕnĕcui [ĕnĕcavi] | ĕnectum [ĕnĕcātum][2] | *kill* |
| Ēnĭteo | -ēre | ēnĭtui | — | *shine out* |
| Ēnītor | -i | ēnīsus (enixus) | — | *strive hard* |
| Eo | īre | īvi | ītum | *go* |
| Ēvello | -ĕre | ĕvelli | ĕvulsum | *tear out* |
| Ēvŏmo | -ĕre | ĕvŏmui | ĕvŏmĭtum | *vomit forth* |
| Excēdo | -ĕre | excessi | excessum | *retire from* |
| Excello | -ĕre | excellui | [excelsum] | *excel* |
| Excerpo | -ĕre | excerpsi | excerptum | *pick out* |
| Excīdo | -ĕre | excīdi | excīsum | *hew out* |
| Excĭdo | -ere | excĭdi | — | *fall out* |
| Excŏlo | -ĕre | excŏlui | excultum | *cultivate carefully* |
| Excŭbo | -āre | excŭbŭi | excŭbĭtum | *lie out of doors* |
| Excūdo | -ĕre | excūdi | excūsum | *hammer out* |
| Excurro | -ĕre | excŭcurri | excursum | *run out* |
| Excŭtio | -ĕre | excussi | excussum | *shake out* |
| Exĕdo | -ĕre | exēdi | exēsum | *gnaw out* |
| Exĭmo | -ĕre | exēmi | exemptum | *take out* |
| Exŏlesco | -ĕre | exŏlēvi | exŏlētum | *grow out of date* |
| Expello | -ĕre | expŭli | expulsum | *expel* |
| Expergis- cor | -i | experrectus (sum) | — | *awake oneself* |
| Expĕrior | -īri | expertus sum | — | *test* |
| Expĕto | -ĕre | expĕtīvi | expĕtītum | *seek out* |
| Expleo | -ēre | explēvi | explētum | *fill up* |
| Explĭco | -āre | explicāvi (-ui) | explĭcātum, (-itum) | *unfold* |
| Explōdo | -ĕre | explōsi | explōsum | *hiss off the stage* |
| Expōno | -ĕre | expŏsui | expŏsitum | *set forth* |
| Exposco | -ĕre | expŏposci | — | *demand earnestly* |
| Exprĭmo | -ĕre | expressi | expressum | *squeeze out* |
| Exquīro | -ĕre | exquīsivi | exquīsĭtum | *search out* |
| Exscindo | -ĕre | exscĭdi | exscissum | *extirpate* |
| Exsĕco | -āre | exsĕcui | exsectum | *cut out* |
| Exsĕro | -ĕre | exsĕrui | exsertum | *protrude* |

---

[1] So in Virgil. Perhaps the verb should be **effulgo, 3**.
[2] The forms in -āvi, -ātum, are less classical; but note that **nĕco** is of the first conj., and regular.

## WITH COMPOUNDS. 205

| | | | | |
|---|---|---|---|---|
| Exsĭlio | -īre | exsĭlui | exsultum | *leap forth* |
| Exsisto | -ĕre | exstĭti | [exstĭtum] | *come forth, arise* |
| Exsolvo | -ĕre | exsŏlui | exsŏlūtum | *unloose* |
| Exstinguo | -ĕre | exstinxi | exstinctum | *extinguish* |
| Exsto | -āre | exstĭti | — | *project, be extant* |
| Exstrŭo | -ĕre | exstruxi | exstructum | *heap up* |
| Exsurgo | -ĕre | exsurrexi | exsurrectum | *rise up, recover* |
| Extendo | -ĕre | extendi | extentum (-tensum) | *stretch out* |
| Exuo | -ĕre | exŭi | exūtum | *put off* |
| Făcesso | -ĕre | făcessīvi | făcessītum | *accomplish* |
| Făcio | făcĕre | fēci | factum | *do, make* |
| Fallo | -ĕre | fĕfelli | falsum | *deceive* |
| Farcio | -īre | farsi | fartum | *stuff* |
| Făteor | -ēri | fassus (sum) | — | *confess* |
| Făveo | -ēre | făvi | fautum | *favour* |
| Fĕrio [1] | -īre | — | — | *strike* |
| Fĕro | ferre | tŭli | lātum | *bear* |
| Ferveo & vo | -ēre -ĕre | fervi *and* -bui | — | *boil* |
| Fīdo | -ĕre | fīsus sum | — | *trust* |
| Fīgo | -ĕre | fixi | fixum | *fix* |
| Findo | -ĕre | fĭdi | fissum | *cleave* |
| Fingo | -ĕre | finxi | fictum | *fashion* |
| Fīo | fĭĕri | factus sum | — | *be made, become* |
| Flecto | -ĕre | flexi | flexum | *bend* |
| Fleo | -ēre | flēvi | flētum | *weep* |
| Flīgo | -ĕre | flixi | flictum | *dash* |
| Fluo | -ĕre | fluxi | [fluxum] | *flow* |
| Fŏdio | fŏdĕre | fōdi | fossum | *dig* |
| Fŏveo | -ēre | fŏvi | fōtum | *cherish* |
| Frango | -ĕre | frēgi | fractum | *break* |
| Frĕmo | -ĕre | frĕmui | [frĕmītum] | *mutter, murmur* |
| Frendo | -ĕre | — | fressum & frēsum | *gnash* |
| Frĭco | -āre | frĭcui | frictum | *rub* |
| Frīgeo | -ēre | frixi | — | *be cold* |
| Frīgo | -ĕre | frixi | frictum | *roast* |
| Fŭgio | fŭgĕre | fūgi | [fŭgĭtum] | *flee* |
| Fulcio | -īre | fulsi | fultum | *prop* |
| Fulgeo | -ēre | fulsi | — | *glitter* |
| Fundo | -ĕre | fūdi | fūsum | *pour, rout* |
| Fŭro [2] | -ĕre | [fŭrui] | — | *be mad* |
| Gaudeo | -ēre | gāvīsus sum | — | *rejoice* |
| Gĕmo | -ĕre | gĕmui | gĕmĭtum | *groan* |
| Gĕro | -ĕre | gessi | gestum | *carry on* |

[1] The perfect forms **percussi, percussum**, are supplied from **percŭtio**.
[2] The perfect form generally supplied instead of **fŭrui, insānīvi**.

| | | | | |
|---|---|---|---|---|
| Gigno | -ĕre | gĕnui | gĕnĭtum | *produce* |
| Grădior | -i | gressus (sum) | — | *step* |
| Hāereo | -ēre | haesi | haesum | *stick* |
| Haurio | -īre | hausi | haustum | *drain* |
| Ico | -ĕre | ici | ictum | *strike* |
| Ignosco | -ĕre | ignōvi | ignōtum | *pardon* |
| Illĭno | -ĕre | illēvi | illĭtum | *smear* |
| Illūcesco | -ĕre | illuxi | — | *dawn* |
| Illūdo | -ĕre | illūsi | illūsum | *make game of* |
| Imbuo | -ĕre | imbui | imbūtum | *tinge* |
| Immisceo | -ēre | immiscui | immixtum(-mistum) | *intermix* |
| Impendeo | -ēre | — | — | *impend* |
| Impendo | -ĕre | impendi | impensum | *expend* |
| Impingo | -ĕre | impēgi | impactum | *thrust against* |
| Impleo | -ēre | implēvi | implētum | *fill* |
| Incēdo | -ĕre | incessi | incessum | *step* |
| Incendo | -ĕre | incendi | incensum | *set on fire* |
| Incesso | -ĕre | incessīvi | — | *assail* |
| Incĭdo | -ĕre | incĭdi | [incāsum] | *fall, light on* |
| Incīdo | -ĕre | incīdi | incīsum | *cut into, engrave* |
| Incingo | -ĕre | incinxi | incinctum | *gird* |
| Inclūdo | -ĕre | inclūsi | inclūsum | *shut in* |
| Incŏlo | -ĕre | incŏlui | incultum | *inhabit* |
| Incŭbo | -āre | incŭbui | incŭbĭtum | *brood over* |
| Incumbo | -ĕre | incŭbui | incŭbĭtum | *lean on, bend one's mind to* |
| Incurro | -ĕre | incurri[-cŭcurri] | incursum | *run towards, meet* |
| Incŭtio | -ĕre | incussi | incussum | *strike against* |
| Indĭgeo | -ēre | indĭgui | — | *need* |
| Indo | -ĕre | indĭdi | indĭtum | *put in, apply* |
| Indulgeo | -ēre | indulsi | indultum | *indulge* |
| Induo | -ĕre | indui | indūtum | *put on* |
| Ineo | -īre | ĭnĭi | ĭnĭtum | *enter* |
| Influo | -ĕre | influxi | [influxum] | *flow into* |
| Insĕro | -ĕre | insēvi | insĭtum | *sow in* |
| Insĕro | -ĕre | insĕrui | insertum | *put in, mingle* |
| Insisto | -ĕre | instĭti | — | *stand on, persevere* |
| Insto | -āre | instĭti | [instātum] | *press on* |
| Insurgo | -ĕre | insurrexi | insurrectum | *rise up, or to* |
| Intellĕgo | -ĕre | intellexi | intellectum | *understand* |
| Intendo | -ĕre | intendi | intentum, or -sum | *stretch, direct* |
| Intercēdo | -ĕre | intercessi | intercessum | *intervene, interpose* |
| Intĕreo | -īre | intĕrĭi | intĕrĭtum | *perish* |
| Interĭmo | -ĕre | intĕrēmi | interemptum | *destroy* |
| Interlĭno | -ĕre | interlēvi | interlĭtum | *smear, falsify by erasures* |
| Internosco | -ĕre | internōvi | — | *distinguish* |

## WITH COMPOUNDS.

| | | | | |
|---|---|---|---|---|
| Intŏno | -āre | intŏnui | intŏnitum | *thunder* |
| Intorqueo | -ēre | intorsi | intortum | *twist, hurl* |
| Intueor | -ērī | intuĭtus (sum) | — | *look on, regard* |
| Invĭdeo | -ēre | invīdi | invīsum | *envy* |
| Jăcio | -ĕre | jēci | jactum | *throw* |
| Jŭbeo | -ēre | jussi | jussum | *command* |
| Jungo | -ĕre | junxi | junctum | *join* |
| Jŭvo | -āre | jūvi | jūtum | *help* |
| Lābor | -i | lapsus (sum) | — | *glide* |
| Lăcesso | -ĕre | lăcessīvi | lăcessītum | *provoke* |
| Laedo | -ĕre | lacsi | laesum | *hurt* |
| Lambo | -ĕre | lambi | — | *lick* |
| Lăvo | -āre[1] | lāvi | lăvātum / lautum, lōtum | } *wash* |
| Lĕgo | -ĕre | lēgi | lectum | *read, choose* |
| Lĭbet | -ēre | lĭbĭtum est | — | *it pleases, suits* |
| Lingo | -ĕre | linxi | linctum | *lick* |
| Līno | -ĕre | līvi and lēvi | lĭtum | *smear* |
| Linquo | -ĕre | līqui | [lictum] | *leave* |
| Lūceo | -ēre | luxi | — | *shine* |
| Lūdo | -ĕre | lūsi | lūsum | *play* |
| Lūgeo | -ēre | luxi | — | *mourn* |
| Luo | -ĕre | lui | luĭtum | *wash, atone* |
| Mālo | malle | mālui | — | *prefer* |
| Mando | -ĕre | mandi | mansum | *chew* |
| Măneo | -ēre | mansi | mansum | *remain* |
| Mĕdeor | -ērī | — | — | *heal* |
| ——— | mĕmĭn-isse | mĕmĭni | — | *remember* |
| Mergo | -ĕre | mersi | mersum | *drown* |
| Mētior[3] | -īrī | mensus (sum) | — | *measure* |
| Mĕto | -ĕre | messui | messum | *mow, reap* |
| Mĕtuo | -ĕre | mĕtui | — | *fear* |
| Mĭco | -āre | mĭcui | — | *glitter* |
| Mĭnuo | -ĕre | mĭnui | mĭnūtum | *lessen* |
| Misceo | -ĕre | miscui | mistum *or* mixtum | *mix* |
| Mĭsĕreor | -ērī | mĭsĕrĭtus (sum) | — | *pity* |
| Mitto | -ĕre | mīsi | missum | *send* |
| Mŏlo | -ĕre | mŏlui | mŏlĭtum | *grind* |
| Mordeo | -ēre | mŏmordi | morsum | *bite* |
| Mŏrĭor | -i | mortŭus (sum) | — | *die* |
| Mŏveo | -ēre | mōvi | mōtum | *move* |
| Mulceo | -ēre | mulsi | mulsum | *soothe* |

[1] There is an ante-classical and poetical form lăvĕre.
[2] The form lĭbuit is perhaps not found in Cicero.
[3] Distinguish this from mentior, mentīri, mentītus, *lie*.

## IRREGULAR VERBS.

| | | | | |
|---|---|---|---|---|
| Mulgeo | -ēre | mulsi | mulctum | *milk* |
| Nanciscor | -i | nactus, nanctus (sum) | — | *obtain* |
| Nascor | -i | nătus (sum) | — | *be born* |
| Necto | -ĕre | nexui & nexi | nexum | *tie, bind* |
| Neglĕgo | -ĕre | neglexi | neglectum | *neglect* |
| Neo | nēre | nēvi | nētum | *spin* |
| Ningo | -ĕre | ninxi | — | *snow* |
| Nĭteo | -ēre | — | — | *shine* |
| Nītor | -i | nīsus *and* nixus | — | *strive* |
| Nŏlo | nolle | nōlui | — | *be unwilling* |
| Nosco [1] | -ĕre | nōvi | nōtum | *come to know* |
| Nūbo | -ĕre | nupsi | nuptum | *be married* |
| Ŏbeo | -īre | ŏbĭi *and* īvi | — | *go towards, down* |
| Oblĭno | -ĕre | oblēvi | oblĭtum | *besmear* |
| Oblīviscor | -i | oblītus (sum) | — | *forget* |
| Obrēpo | -ĕre | obrepsi | obreptum | *creep up to* |
| Obrŭo | -ĕre | obrui | obrŭtum | *overwhelm* |
| Obsĭdeo | -ēre | obsēdi | obsessum | *besiege* |
| Obsisto | -ĕre | obstĭti | [obstĭtum] | *oppose* |
| Obsŏlesco | -ĕre | obsŏlēvi | obsŏlētum | *wear out* |
| Obsto | -āre | obstĭti | obstātum | *stand in the way of* |
| Obstringo | -ĕre | obstrinxi | obstrictum | *bind (by oath)* |
| Obtĕro | -ĕre | obtrīvi | obtrītum | *trample underfoot* |
| Occīdo | -ĕre | occīdi | occīsum | *slay* |
| Occĭdo | -ĕre | occĭdi | occāsum | *fall, die* |
| Occŭlo | -ĕre | occŭlui | occultum | *hide* |
| Occurro | -ĕre | occurri | occursum | *meet, resist* |
| —— | ōdisse | ōdi | [ōsum] | *hate* |
| Offendo | -ĕre | offendi | offensum | *knock against* |
| Offero | -erre | obtŭli | oblātum | *offer* |
| Ŏmitto | -ĕre | ŏmīsi | ŏmissum | *pass over* |
| Ŏpĕrio | -īre | ŏpĕrui | ŏpertum | *cover* |
| Oppōno | -ĕre | oppŏsui | oppŏsĭtum | *put in the way* |
| Opprĭmo | -ĕre | oppressi | oppressum | *press down, overpower* |
| Ordior | -īri | orsus (sum) | — | *commence* |
| Orior | -īri | ortus (sum) | — | *arise* |
| Păciscor | -i | pactus (sum) | — | *bargain* |
| Pando | -ĕre | pandi | passum & pansum | *expand, spread* |
| Pango | -ĕre | pĕpĭgi / pēgi / panxi | pactum / panctum | *frame, fasten* |
| Parco | -ĕre | pĕperci | parsum | *spare* |

[1] **Nosco** means, *I make acquaintance with;* **nōvi** means, *I have made the acquaintance of,* i.e. *I know.*

## WITH COMPOUNDS.

| | | | | |
|---|---|---|---|---|
| Păriŏ [1] | -ĕre | pĕpĕri | partum | *bring forth* |
| Pasco | -ĕre | pāvi | pastum | *feed* |
| Păveo | -ēre | pāvi | — | *fear* |
| Pecto | -ĕre | pexui *and* pexi | pexum | *comb* |
| Pello | -ĕre | pĕpŭli | pulsum | *drive away* |
| Pellĭcio | -ĕre | pellexi | pellectum | *allure* |
| Pendeo | -ēre | pĕpendi | — | *hang* (*intr.*) |
| Pendo | -ĕre | pĕpendi | pensum | *hang, weigh* (*tr.*) |
| Pĕrăgo | -ĕre | perēgi | peractum | *complete* |
| Percello | -ĕre | percŭli | perculsum | *strike* (*with terror*) |
| Pĕrcŭtio | -ĕre | percussi | percussum | *strike* |
| Perdo | -ĕre | perdĭdi | perdĭtum | *lose, destroy* |
| Pergo | -gĕre | perrexi | perrectum | *continue* |
| Pĕrĭmo | -ĕre | perēmi | peremptum | *make away with* |
| Perlĕgo | -ĕre | perlēgi | perlectum | *read through* |
| Perpĕtiŏr | -i | perpessus (sum) | — | *endure* |
| Persto | -āre | perstĭti | perstātum | *persevere* |
| Pĕto | -ĕre | pĕtivi & pĕtii | pĕtītum | *seek* |
| Pingo | -ĕre | pinxi | pictum | *paint* |
| Pinso | -ĕre | pinsi & pinsui | pinsum | *pound* |
| Plango | -ĕre | planxi | planctum | *beat* |
| Plaudo | -ĕre | plausi | plausum | *clap hands* |
| Plecto | -ĕre | — | — | *lash* |
| Plecto | -ĕre | plexui, plexi | plexum | *plait* |
| [Pleo | plēre | plēvi | plētum | *fill*] |
| Plico | -āre | plĭcuī | plīcatum & plĭcĭtum | *fold* |
| Plŭo | -ĕre | plŭit *and* plūvit | — | *rain* |
| Pōno | -ĕre | pŏsui | pŏsĭtum | *place* |
| Posco | -ĕre | pŏposci | — | *demand* |
| Possum [2] | posse | pŏtui | — | *be able* |
| Pōto | -āre | pŏtāvi | pŏtātum & pŏtum | *drink* |
| Praecăveo | -ēre | praecāvi | praecautum | *take precautions* |
| Praecello | -ĕre | — | — | *excel* |
| Praecīdo | -ĕre | praecīdi | praecīsum | *cut off, abridge* |
| Praecĭno | -ĕre | praecĭnui | praecentum | *play before, foretell* |
| Praecurro [3] | -ĕre | praecŭcurri | praecursum | *precede* |
| Praedīco [4] | -ĕre | praedixi | praedictum | *predict* |
| Praeeo | -īre | praeĭi, *or* -īvi | praeĭtum | *go before, dictate* |
| Praesto | -āre | praestĭti | praestātum [-ĭtum] | *excel, answer for* |

---

[1] Distinguish this from **pāreo, pārēre, pārui, pārĭtum,** *obey*.
[2] Distinguish this from the forms of the regular Verb **pŏtior,** *I gain possession of*.
[3] Note that here, and in **excurro,** the longer form of the Perfect is the more common.
[4] Distinguish this from **praedĭco, praedĭcāre, praedĭcavi, praedĭcātum,** *proclaim*.

P

# IRREGULAR VERBS,

| | | | | |
|---|---|---|---|---|
| Praetexo | -ĕre | praetexui | praetextum | *border, pretend* |
| Prandeo | -ēre | prandi | pransum | *lunch, dine* |
| Prĕhendo | -ĕre | prĕhendi | prensum | *seize, grasp* |
| Prĕmo | -ĕre | pressi | pressum | *press* |
| Prōcumbo | -ĕre | prōcŭbui | prōcŭbĭtum | *fall (on one's knees, wounded, &c.)* |
| Prōdeo | -īre | prōdĭi | prōdĭtum | *go forth* |
| Prōdo | -ĕre | prōdĭdi | prōdĭtum | *betray* |
| Prōfĭciscor | -i | prŏfectus (sum) | — | *set out* |
| Prōfīteor | -ēri | prŏfessus (sum) | — | *avow* |
| Prōfundo | -ĕre | prōfūdi | prōfūsum | *pour forth* |
| Prōmo | -ĕre | prompsi | promptum | *take forth* |
| Prōmŏveo | -ēre | prōmōvi | prōmōtum | *move forward* |
| Prōpello | -ĕre | prōpŭli | prōpulsum | *drive before one* |
| Proscribo | -ĕre | proscripsi | proscriptum | *publish, proscribe* |
| Prōvĭdeo | -ēre | prōvīdi | prōvisum | *foresee, provide* |
| Psallo | -ĕre | psalli | — | *play on harp* |
| Pungo | -ĕre | pŭpŭgi | punctum | *prick* |
| Quaero | -ĕre | quaesīvi | quaesītum | *seek* |
| Quătio | quătĕre | | quassum | *shake* |
| Queo | quīre | quīvi | quĭtum | *be able* |
| Quĕror | -i | questus (sum) | — | *complain* |
| Quiesco | -ĕre | quiēvi | quiētum | *rest* |
| Rādo | -ĕre | rāsi | rāsum | *scrape* |
| Răpio | răpĕre | răpui | raptum | *seize* |
| Rĕcĭdo | -ĕre | reccĭdi [1] | rĕcāsum | *fall back, relapse* |
| Rĕcīdo | -ĕre | rĕcīdi | rĕcīsum | *lop, retrench* |
| Rĕcumbo | -ĕre | recŭbui | — | *lie down* |
| Reclūdo | -ĕre | reclūsi | reclūsum | *disclose* |
| Reddo | -ĕre | reddĭdi | reddĭtum | *restore, render* |
| Rĕdeo | -īre | rĕdĭi | rĕdĭtum | *return* |
| Rĕdigo | -ĕre | rĕdēgi | rĕdactum | *bring back, reduce* |
| Rĕdĭmo | -ĕre | rĕdēmi | rĕdemptum | *buy back, buy up* |
| Rĕfello | -ĕre | rĕfelli | — | *refute* |
| Rĕfercio | -īre | rĕfersi | rĕfertum | *cram* |
| Rĕfīgo | -ĕre | rĕfīxi | rĕfīxum | *unfasten* |
| Rĕdŏleo | -ĕre | rĕdŏlui | — | *smell of* |
| Refrīgesco | -ĕre | refrixi | — | *grow cool, flag* |
| Refringo | -ĕre | rĕfrēgi | refractum | *break open, destroy* |
| Rĕgero | -ĕre | rĕgessi | rĕgestum | *cast back* |
| Rĕlĕgo [2] | -ĕre | rĕlēgi | rĕlectum | *gather up, go through again* |
| Rĕmaneo | -ēre | rĕmansi | — | *stay behind* |

---

[1] Other verbs that lengthen compound re- in the perfect, are, rettŭli and reppĕri.
[2] Distinguish this from rĕlēgo, -āre, -āvi, -ātum, *banish*.

## WITH COMPOUNDS.

| | | | | |
|---|---|---|---|---|
| Rĕor | -ēri | rătus (sum) | — | *think, suppose* |
| Rĕpello | -ĕre | reppŭli | rĕpulsum | *drive back* |
| Rĕpendo | -ĕre | rĕpendi | rĕpensum | *pay back* |
| Rĕpĕrio | -ire | reppĕri | rĕpertum | *discover* |
| Rēpo | -ĕre | repsi | reptum | *creep* |
| Rĕquiro | -ĕre | rĕquīsīvi | rĕquīsītum | *seek again* |
| Rescindo | -ĕre | rescĭdi | rescissum | *break open, down, rescind* |
| Rĕsĕco | -āre | rĕsĕcui | rĕsectum | *prune* |
| Rĕsĭdeo | -ĕre | rĕsēdi | rĕsessum | *remain behind* |
| Rĕsīdo | -ĕre | rĕsēdi | — | *sit down, settle* |
| Rĕsĭpisco | -ĕre | rĕsĭpīvi and ui | — | *recover one's senses* |
| Rĕsisto | -ĕre | restĭti | — | *halt, resist* |
| Respergo | -ĕre | respersi | respersum | *besprinkle* |
| Respicio | -ĕre | respexi | respectum | *have regard to* |
| Respondeo | -ēre | respondi | responsum | *answer* |
| Restinguo[1] | -ĕre | restinxi | restinctum | *quench* |
| Resto | -āre | restĭti | — | *remain, hold out* |
| Rĕtexo | -ĕre | retexui | rĕtextum | *unweave* |
| Rĕtundo | -ĕre | rĕtŭdi & rettŭdi | rĕtūsum | *blunt* |
| Rĕvello | -ĕre | rĕvelli | rĕvulsum | *tear away* |
| Rĕverto[2] | -ĕre | rĕverti | rĕversum | *return* |
| Rīdeo | -ēre | rīsi | rīsum | *laugh* |
| Rōdo | -ĕre | rōsi | rōsum | *gnaw* |
| Rŭdo | -ĕre | [rŭdīvi] | [rŭdītum] | *bray* |
| Rumpo | -ĕre | rūpi | ruptum | *break* |
| Ruo | ruĕre | rui | ruĭtum [rŭtum][3] | *rush, fall* |
| Saepio | -īre | sacpsi | saeptum | *hedge in* |
| Sălio | -īre | sălui | [saltum] | *leap* |
| Sălio | -īre | — | salītum | *salt* |
| Sancio | -īre | sanxi [-īvi] | sanctum [-ītum] | *render sacred, enact* |
| Săpio | -ĕre | săpīvi and -ii | — | *savour of, have taste, or wisdom* |
| Sarcio | -īre | sarsi | sartum | *patch* |
| Scăbo | -ĕre | scābi | — | *scratch* |
| Scalpo | -ĕre | scalpsi | scalptum | *scratch* |
| Scando | -ĕre | — | — | *climb* |
| Scindo | -ĕre | scĭdi | scissum | *cut, tear* |

---

[1] The obsolete **stinguo** is only found (in Present forms) in Lucretius and quotations of Priscian.

[2] In the Present and Present-derived Tenses rĕvertĭtur is more common; in the Perfect and Perfect-derived Tenses rĕverti, rĕvertĕram, &c.: but the best authors use the Dep. Participle rĕversus.

[3] The Fut. Part. ruĭtūrus points to sup. ruĭtum; but in an old legal word "rūta," *things dug up (on an estate),* the vowel was long. In the compounds obrŭtus, ērŭtus and surrŭtus the vowel was short.

# IRREGULAR VERBS.

| | | | | |
|---|---|---|---|---|
| Scisco | -ĕre | scīvi | scītum | *decree* |
| Scrībo | -ĕre | scripsi | scriptum | *write* |
| Sculpo | -ĕre | sculpsi | sculptum | *engrave* |
| Sĕco | -āre | sĕcui | sectum | *cut* |
| Sĕdeo | -ēre | sēdi | sessum | *sit* |
| Sentio | -īre | sensi | sensum | *feel* |
| Sĕpĕlio | -īre | sĕpĕlīvi | sĕpultum | *bury* |
| Sĕro | -ĕre | sĕrui | sertum | *join together* |
| Sĕro | -ĕre | sēvi | sătum | *sow* |
| Serpo | -ĕre | serpsi | serptum | *crawl* |
| Sīdo | -ĕre | sīdi | — | *sit down* |
| Singultio | -īre | singultīvi | — | *sob* |
| Sĭno | -ĕre | sīvi | sĭtum | *allow* |
| Sisto | -ĕre | — | — | *stop, make stand* |
| Sŏleo | -ēre | sŏlĭtus sum | — | *be accustomed* |
| Solvo | -ĕre | solvi | sŏlūtum | *loosen* |
| Sŏno¹ | -āre | sŏnui | sŏnĭtum | *sound* |
| Sorbeo | -ēre | sorbui [sorpsi] | — | *suck up* |
| Spargo | -ĕre | sparsi | sparsum | *sprinkle* |
| [Spĕcio | -ĕre | spexi | spectum] | *espy* |
| Sperno | -ĕre | sprēvi | sprētum | *despise* |
| Spondeo | -ēre | spŏpondi | sponsum | *pledge, promise* |
| Stătuo | -ĕre | stătui | stătūtum | *set up* |
| Sterno | -ĕre | strāvi | strātum | *strew* |
| Sterto | -ĕre | stertui | — | *snore* |
| Sto | stāre | stĕti | stătum | *stand* |
| Strĕpo | -ĕre | strĕpui | [strĕpĭtum] | *roar* |
| Strīdeo & Strīdo | -ēre & -ĕre | } strīdi | — | *creak, hiss, whizz* |
| Stringo | -ĕre | strinxi | strictum | *tie* |
| Struo | -ĕre | struxi | structum | *build, pile* |
| Suādeo | -ēre | suāsi | suasum | *advise, persuade* |
| Sŭbĕo | -īre | sŭbĭi | sŭbĭtum | *go under, spring up* |
| Sŭbĭgo | -ĕre | sŭbēgi | subactum | *bring under, subduc* |
| Subnecto | -ĕre | subnexui | subnexum | *tie under* |
| Subruo, *see* surruo. | | | | |
| Subsīdo | -ĕre | subsēdi | subsessum | *sink down* |
| Subvĕnio | -īre | subvēni | subventum | *help* |
| Subverto | -ĕro | subverti | subversum | *subvert* |
| Succēdo | -ĕre | successi | successum | *approach, follow* |
| Succendo | -ĕre | succendi | succensum | *set on fire* |
| Succurro | -ĕre | succurri | succursum | *help* |
| Suesco | -ĕre | suēvi | suētum | *be accustomed* |
| Suffĕro | -erre | sustŭli | sublātum | *endure* |

¹ Note **insŏnui** and **consŏnui**, but **rĕsŏnāvi**.

## WITH COMPOUNDS.

| | | | | |
|---|---|---|---|---|
| Suffundo | -ĕre | suffūdi | suffūsum | *suffuse* |
| Suggĕro | -ĕre | suggessi | suggestum | *supply, subjoin* |
| Sūgo | -ĕre | suxi | suctum | *suck* |
| Summŏveo | -ēre | summŏvi | summōtum | *thrust off* |
| Sūmo | -ĕre | sumpsi | sumptum | *take* |
| Suo | -ĕre | — | sūtum | *sew* |
| Suppĕto | -ĕre | suppĕtīvi | suppĕtītum | *be in store, suffice* |
| Suppleo | -ēre | supplēvi | supplētum | *fill up* |
| Suppōno | -ĕre | suppŏsui | suppŏsītum | *substitute, counterfeit* |
| Supprĭmo | -ĕre | suppressi | suppressum | *check, conceal* |
| Surgo | -ĕre | surrexi | surrectum | *arise* |
| Surrĕpo | -ere | surrepsi | surreptum | *creep up to* |
| Surrĭgo [1] | -ĕre | surrexi | surrectum | *raise* |
| Surrĭpio | -ĕre | surrĭpui | surreptum | *snatch by stealth* |
| Surruo | -ĕre | surrui | surrŭtum | *undermine* |
| Suspendo | -ĕre | suspendi | suspensum | *suspend* |
| Suspĭcio | -ĕre | suspexi | suspectum | *look up to* |
| Tango | -ĕre | tĕtĭgi | tactum | *touch* |
| Tĕgo | -ĕre | texi | tectum | *cover* |
| Temno | -ĕre | — | — | *despise* |
| Tendo | -ĕre | tĕtendi | [tentum & tensum][2] | *stretch* |
| Tĕneo | -ēre | tĕnui | [tentum] | *hold* |
| Tergeo & tergo | -ēre -ĕre | tersi | tersum | *wipe* |
| Tĕro | -ĕre | trīvi | trītum | *rub* |
| Texo | -ĕre | texui | textum | *weave* |
| Tinguo | -ĕre | tinxi | tinctum | *dye* |
| Tollo | -ĕre | sustŭli [3] | sublātum [3] | *take up* |
| Tondeo | -ēre | tŏtondi | tonsum | *shave* |
| Tŏno | -āre | tŏnui | tŏnĭtum | *thunder* |
| Torqueo | -ēre | torsi | tortum | *twist* |
| Torreo | -ēre | torrui | tostum | *roast* |
| Trādo | -ĕre | trādĭdi | trādĭtum | *hand over* |
| Trăho | -ĕre | traxi | tractum | *draw* |
| Transeo | -īre | transĭi *and* -īvi | transĭtum | *pass over* |
| Transĭgo | -ĕre | transēgi | transactum | *transact* |
| Transĭlio | -īre | transĭlui [-īvi] [4] | — | *leap across* |
| Trĕmo | -ĕre | trĕmui | — | *tremble* |
| Trĭbuo | -ĕre | trĭbui | trĭbūtum | *assign* |
| Trūdo | -ĕre | trūsi | trūsum | *thrust* |

[1] This is the uncontracted form of **surgo** used transitively.

[2] These Supine forms have probably no existence, and are merely inferred from the Pass. Part. **tentus** and **tensus**.

[3] These forms do not properly belong to **tollo**, but are assigned to it, as it has no perfect and supine: see note on **fūro** above.

[4] Livy uses -ui; Plautus and Pliny, -ivi.

## DEFECTIVE VERBS.

| | | | | |
|---|---|---|---|---|
| Tŭcor[tuor]-ĕri | | tuĭtus *and* tūtus (sum) | — | *regard, guard* |
| Tundo | -ĕre | tŭtŭdi | tūsum & tunsum | *thump* |
| Turgeo | -ēre | tursi | — | *swell* |
| Ulciscor | -i | ultus (sum) | — | *avenge myself on* |
| Unguo | -ĕre | unxi | unctum | *anoint* |
| Urgeo | -ēre | ursi | — | *urge* |
| Ūro | -ĕre | ussi | ustum | *burn* |
| Ūtor | -i | ūsus (sum) | — | *use* |
| Vādo | -ĕre | [vāsi] | [vasum] | *go* |
| Vĕho | -ĕre | vexi | vectum | *carry* |
| Vello | -ĕre | velli *and* vulsi | vulsum | *rend* |
| Vēneo | -īre | vēnii | — | *be sold* |
| Vĕnio | -īre | vēni | ventum | *come* |
| Vergo | -ĕre | [versi] | — | *bend* |
| Verro | -ĕre | verri | versum | *sweep* |
| Verto | -ĕre | verti | versum | *turn* |
| Vĕto | -āre | vĕtui | vĕtĭtum | *forbid* |
| Vĭdeo | -ēre | vīdi | vīsum | *see* |
| Vincio | -īre | vinxi | vinctum | *bind* |
| Vinco | -ĕre | vīci | victum | *conquer* |
| Vīso | -ĕre | visi | — | *visit* |
| Vīvo | -ĕre | vixi | victum | *live* |
| Vŏlo | velle | vŏlui | — | *wish* |
| Volvo | -ĕre | volvi | vŏlūtum | *roll* |
| Vŏmo | -ĕre | vŏmui | vŏmĭtum | *vomit* |
| Vŏveo | -ēre | vōvi | vōtum | *vow* |

## DEFECTIVE VERBS.

The Defective Verbs **coepī**, *begin*, **mĕmĭnī**, *remember*, and **ōdī**, *hate*, have no Tenses except those derived from the Perfect. Thus *I remembered* is **mĕmĭnĕram**; *that they may remember*, or *let them remember*, **mĕmĭnĕrint**; *I shall remember*, **mĕmĭnĕro**; and the same of **ōdī**.

### INDICATIVE.

| | (1) | (2) | (3) |
|---|---|---|---|
| *Perfect.* | Coepī | Mĕmĭni | Ŏdi |
| *Fut.-Perf.* | Coepĕro | Mĕmĭnĕro | Ŏdĕro |
| *Pluperf.* | Coepĕram | Mĕmĭnĕram | Ŏdĕram |

## DEFECTIVE VERBS.

### Subjunctive.

| | | | |
|---|---|---|---|
| *Perfect.* | Coepĕrim | Mĕmĭnĕrim | Ŏdĕrim |
| *Pluperf.* | Coepissem | Mĕmĭnissem | Ŏdissem |

### Imperative.

| | | | |
|---|---|---|---|
| *Future.* | (wanting) | Mĕmento | (wanting) |
| | | Mĕmentōte | |

### Infinitive.

| | | | |
|---|---|---|---|
| *Perfect.* | Coepissĕ | Mĕmĭnissĕ | Ŏdissĕ |

### Participle.

| | | | |
|---|---|---|---|
| *Future.* | Coeptūrŭs | (wanting) | Ŏsūrŭs |

### 4. Aio, *I say* :—

| Indicative. | Subjunctive. | Indicative. | Subjunctive. |
|---|---|---|---|
| *Present.* | | *Imperfect.* | |
| S. Aio | — | S. Aiĕbam | — |
| Aïs | Aiās | Aiĕbās | — |
| Aït | Aiāt | Aiĕbāt | — |
| P. — | — | P. Aiĕbāmŭs | — |
| — | — | Aiĕbātĭs | — |
| Aiunt | Aiant | Aiĕbant | — |

Present Participle.

### 5. Inquam, *say I* :—

#### Indicative.

| *Present.* | *Imperfect.* | *Future.* | *Perfect.* |
|---|---|---|---|
| Inquam | — | — | Inquĭi |
| Inquĭs | — | Inquĭēs | Inquistī |
| Inquĭt | Inquiĕbāt[1] | Inquĭĕt | — |
| Inquĭmŭs | — | | |
| Inquĭtĭs | — | | |
| Inquĭunt | | | |

#### Imperative.

| *Present.* | *Future.* |
|---|---|
| Inquĕ | 2 *Pers.* Inquĭto. |

*N.B.*—**Inquam** is always used after the first emphatic word in a speech, and is almost always separated from its Nominative.

| Then Balbus said, "This I deny." | Tum Balbus, "Haec," inquit, "nĕgo." |
|---|---|

---

[1] But this form is found without the e.

# APPENDIX III.

## HINTS ON CONSTRUING.

Take as an example:

> Terra tribus scopulis vastum procurrit in aequor
> Trinacris, a positu nomen adepta loci.

### I.—QUESTIONS ON THE SENTENCE.

1. The first question is, *Which is the Principal Verb?* Ans., **procurrit**—*runs forth.*

2. *What is the Subject of the Principal Verb?* Ans., **Terra**, *a land.*

3. (a) *Is the Principal Verb Intransitive; or has it (b) a Direct Object? (c) an Indirect Object?*
Ans., It is Intransitive.

4. (a) *Is there any Noun in Apposition with the Subject? (b) Is there any Adjective or Participle in agreement with the Subject, or is there any Genitive Case dependent on it?*
Ans., (a) **Trinacris** (*i.e.* **trin-acris**, *three-promontoried*) is sometimes a Noun (a name of Sicily), sometimes an Adjective, and may be regarded either as in Apposition to **terra**, or as agreeing with it; (b) **Adepta**, from **adipiscor**, is a Participle agreeing with **terra**, meaning *having obtained.*

---

[1] Bear in mind that *two Adjectives* (unless connected by a Conjunction) rarely agree with the same Noun: *many serious sorrows*, multi **et** graves dolores (153). But an *Adjective and Participle* may agree with the same Noun, without a Conjunction.

5. *Is there any Adjective or Participle in agreement with the Object, or is there any Genitive Case dependent on it?*

6. The next question is to ask, *Are there any Adverbial Clauses attached to the Principal Verb?* i.e. any Clauses answering to the question (*a*) *How?* (*b*) *When?* (*c*) *Where?* (*d*) *Whence?* (*e*) *Why*, &c.

Ans. *How?* **tribus scopulis**, *with three rocks;* (*c*) *Where?* or *Whither?* **vastum in aequor**, *into the vast sea.*

7. Coming to **adepta**, repeat the above questions. Is it Transitive? Has it an Object? Adverbial Clauses, &c.?

Ans. (3) (*b*). The Object is **nomen**, *the name;* (5) **loci**, *of the place*, is Gen. depending on **nomen** (or **positu**); (6) *Whence?* Ans., **a positu**, *from its position*.[1]

8. No further questions are required for this sentence: but instead of the Participle **adepta**, a prose author might have written **quod**, or **quia adepta fuerat**, *because it had obtained*, and the Conjunction **quod** or **quia** would have introduced a Subordinate Sentence.

Therefore it must be borne in mind that the answer to the question (6) *How? When? Why?* &c., may be conveyed by a Subordinate Sentence introduced by a Conjunction, *because, though, when, in order that*, &c.: and this Subordinate Sentence must be taken to pieces in the same way as the Principal Sentence.

*N.B.*—A Subordinate Sentence may sometimes be the Subject or Object of the Principal Verb, *e.g.* "incertum est (*or* nescio) num locus a positu nomen adeptus fuerit," *it is uncertain whether the place obtained its name from its position:* here **est** (or **nescio**) is the Principal Verb, and has for its Subject (or Object) "num.... fuerit."

---

[1] Possibly, **loci** may be transposed, as is sometimes done in poetry, and may be dependent on **positu**: *from the position of the place.*

## II.—RULES FOR THE CASES.

In order to answer the question *What Case?* it is not enough, for example, to say that "**loci** is Genitive because it means *of the place;* " the pupil must say "Genitive Case, governed by **nomen** (or **positu**)." In other words, the pupil *must give the Rule.*

The Rules for the Cases are as follows :—

### 1. Nominative.

1. *The Subject of a Verb.*
2. *In Apposition* to another Nominative.
3. *The Complementary Nominative* (Par. 260).
4. *By connection,* i.e. because it is connected with another Nom. by some Conjunction, **quam, vel, et,** &c.

### 2. Accusative.

1. *The Subject of an Infinitive* (Par. 208, 209).

2. *The Object of a Verb.*

This includes the Accusative (often called *Cognate Accusative*) found after some Intransitive Verbs, when the Verb and Noun are of kindred, *i.e. Cognate* meaning, *e.g.* "ludo **ludum**," *I play a game;* "eo **viam**," *I go my way.*

3. *Governed by a Preposition* (Par. 183).

4. *In Apposition* to another Accusative (Par. 123).

\* 5. *The Accusative of Respect* (or *the Accusative of the Part affected*).

This is more common in poetry than in prose, especially with Passive Participles : "tectus cālīgĭnĕ **vultum**," *covered with darkness as to his features.*

6. *The Accusative of Extension* of (*a*) time or (*b*) space (Par. 262).

---

\* This mark denotes a construction more common in poetry than in prose.

7. The *Accusative of Place Whither* (towns and small islands, Par. 249).

8. The *Exclamatory Accusative:* "**me** miserum!" *wretch that I am!* "O sortem infelicem," *O, unhappy fate!* (206).

9. The *Double Accusative* (after Verbs of *asking, teaching, and concealing*): Par. 312.

10. The (a) *Primary* and (b) *Complementary* Accusative: see Par. 259.

| | |
|---|---|
| *We thought you a second Cato.* | Alterum **te Catonem** putabamus. |
| *They will create you king.* | **Te regem** creabunt. |

Here the person (**te**) is (a) the *Primary* Object of the Verb, and requires (b) a *Complementary* Accusative, **Catonem** or **regem**, to make the meaning complete.[1]

*11. An *Adverbial Accusative* is sometimes formed from the Neuter of an Adjective, especially in poetry: "**torva** tuens," *looking grimly;* "**dulce** ridentem Lalagen," *Lalage sweetly laughing.*

### 3. The Dative.

1. *Of the Remote Object:* after Verbs of *giving, pleasing, helping, obeying,* and their opposites (Par. 142); also after *Verbs Compounded of Prepositions* (Par. 192); after many Adjectives signifying *nearness, pleasantness, fitness, likeness, equality,* &c., and their opposites (Pars. 27, 90, 112).

*2. *Of Advantage or Disadvantage* (sometimes called "Commodi et Incommodi"):

| | |
|---|---|
| *Thou sowest for thyself.* | **Tibi** seris. |
| *We desire office for thee.* | **Tibi** honores optamus. |

This construction should be rarely employed by beginners in Latin Prose.

---

[1] In the *Public School Grammar* this is called the Oblique Double Accusative with Factitive Verb.

3. *Of Purpose* (Par. 268): often accompanied by the *Dat. of Advantage* or *Disadvantage*, or some other Dative:

He came for a help to us.   Venit **auxilio** (*Dat. of P.*) **nobis** (*Dat. of Advantage*).
He gave this for a present to me.   Hoc mihi (*Dat. of Recipient.*) dono (*Dat. of P.*) dedit.

4. *Of the Recipient used for the Agent*, found only with Perfect Passive, Passive Participles, especially Gerundives (Par. 168), and Verbals in -**bilis**.[1]

I have now made up my mind.   **Mihi** jam consilium captum est.

### 4. THE ABLATIVE (Par. 273—280).

1. *Governed by a Preposition* (Par. 178).
This includes the Ablative *of the Agent* with **a** or **ab**.

2. *Of the Instrument* (Par. 8).

3. *Of the Measure of Excess or Defect* (Par. 274).

4. *Of Definite Price* (Par. 273).

5. *Of Manner* (Par. 276).

This requires an Adjective joined to the Noun (Par. 181), except with a few Adverbial Ablatives: **nomine**, *in name;* **re**, or **re ipsa**, *in fact;* **verbo**, *in word;* **specie**, *in appearance;* **jure**, *rightly;* neque **injuria**, *and not unnaturally;* recte atque **ordine**, *in due course;* **via** atque **ratione**, *methodically;* **vi**, *forcibly;* **dolo**, *craftily*.

6. *Of Quality.*
This also requires an Adjective (Par. 281).

7. *Of the Point of Time* (Par. 30, 263).

8. *Of Comparison* (Par. 63).

9. *Absolute* (Par. 196).

---

[1] The poets use this Construction with Tenses not derived from the Perfect.
I am scarce heard by any.   Vix audior ulli.—*Ovid*.

10. Used with **dignus, indignus, fretus** (Par. 28, 278).[1]

11. Object of **fungor, fruor, utor, potior** (Par. 207).

12. (a) *Of Plenty and Want;* (b) with "opus est," "usus est"; see Par. 279.

13. *Of the Place Where* (with towns and small islands in the Third Declension, and in the Plural of the First and Second Declension); see Par. 265.

\* 14. *A Poetic Local Ablative,* where Prose writers would insert the Preposition **in**.

15. *Of the Place Whence* (of all towns and small islands); see Par. 265.

\* 16. *Of Separation* (after a few words, mostly legal, "abdico me **magistratu**," *I resign my office;* "moveo te **senatu**," *I expel you from the senate*").

Most of the Verbs (Par. 8) which allow an *Abl. of Separation* in Poetry require or allow a Preposition in Prose.

17. *Of Origin*, after **natus, ortus, genitus, satus, cretus.**

## 5. THE GENITIVE.

Genitives may be divided into two large classes, those in which the Gen. can be readily replaced (i.) by a Subject; (ii.) by an Object. The former are called *Subjective;* the latter, *Objective*.

Thus "injuriae **Æduorum**" may mean (i.) "wrongs inflicted *by the Ædui*" (*i.e.* "the Ædui wronged some one"), a *Subjective* Genitive; but it may mean (ii.) "wrongs inflicted *on the Ædui*" (*i.e.* "some one wronged the Ædui"), an *Objective* Genitive.

---

[1] The Abl. after the Verbal Adjectives **contentus, fretus, onustus**, is really an Abl. of the Instrument.

(i.) THE SUBJECTIVE GENITIVE (Par. 281—292).

1. *The Possessive* Genitive.

The Noun governing this Genitive is often omitted (Par. 289) in such phrases as *it is the mark of, characteristic of,* &c.

2. *The Descriptive* or *Adjectival* Genitive; see Par. 282.

This may be illustrated by the English descriptive Adjective formed out of a Noun, *sun-light* (i.e. *sun's light*), *a pine forest,* &c. So in Latin: "**lauri** nemus," *a laurel grove;*" nomen **regis**," *the name of king* (or *the royal name*); virtus **constantiae**, *the virtue of constancy.*

3. *Of the charge,* after Verbs of accusing and condemning.

This is really governed by some Noun understood, as **crimine, nomine, causa,** &c.: see Par. 290.

4. *Of Quality* (Par. 282), *Value, or Indefinite Price* (Par. 283).

5. *The Partitive Genitive* (Par. 91).

*6. A Genitive, in Poetry, often follows a Neuter (mostly Plural) used instead of a Noun: "secreta **silvarum**," *the secret place of the woods.*

7. After some Verbs and Adjectives of *plenty* and *want* (285).[1]

(ii.) THE OBJECTIVE GENITIVE.

8. *Governed by a Noun.*

This Gen. must be rendered by different English Prepositions: **auri** fames, *hunger for gold;* **militiae** vacatio, *exemption from military service;* remedium **irae**, *remedy against anger;* incitamenta **periculi,** *incitements to peril;* quies **laborum,** *rest* from *evils.* (In writing Latin avoid this construction where it is ambiguous: obsequium **coelibis,**

---

[1] This is said (*Pub. Sch. Gr.* p. 420) to be a Partitive Genitive, and it would therefore fall under the head of Subjective, not Objective Genitives.

*respect* to *a bachelor;* praestantia **animarum** reliquarum, *superiority* to *other souls.*)

9. With *Verbal Adjectives and Present Participles used as Nouns* (Par. 288).

10. *With Adjectives of knowledge and ignorance, and some Adjectives of desire* (Par. 287).

11. *With Impersonal Verbs* (as the Impersonal Object): see Par. 219.

12. *With Verbs of remembering and forgetting:* Par. 203.

13. An apparent Genitive, more properly called *the Locative Case in* -i, is used in the Second Declension to represent *Place Where*, of towns and small islands, and with a few other Nouns (Par. 265.)

### 6. All Cases.

N.B.—A Noun may be in any Case by (1) *Connection*, *i.e.* through being connected with some other Noun by a Conjunction, *e.g.* **quam, vel, et**; or by (2) *Apposition.*

# APPENDIX IV.

## PARSING TABLE.

The following Table shows how the different parts of speech should be parsed.

The pupil is intended to use the Table, principally to show him how to parse *viva-voce*; but he may occasionally make similar Parsing Tables for himself in order to fill up the columns in writing.

"Rogāvērant cives ut urbs, incendio fērē delēta, a nostris restituĕrētur."

| | ACCIDENCE. | | | | | | | | | SYNTAX. |
|---|---|---|---|---|---|---|---|---|---|---|
| Verb ... | Pres. Ind. 1st Pers. | Pres. Inf. and Conjugation. | Perf. Ind. 1st Pers. | Supine. | Voice. | Mood. | Tense. | Number. | Person. | Agrees with what Nom.? Has what Object? Principal? or how dependent?[1] |
| Noun or Pronoun. | Nom. Sing. | — | Decl. | Gender. | Number. | Case. | [Person.] | — | — | Why that Case? |
| Adjective ... | Nom. S. of all Gend. | Gen. Sing. | Decl. | Gender. | Number. | Case. | [Comp. Superl.] | — | — | Agrees with what Noun or Pronoun? |
| Participle ... | Pres. Ind. 1st Pers. | Pres. Inf. and Conjugation. | Perf. Ind. 1st Pers. | Supine. | Voice. | Tense. | Gender. | Number. | Case. | Agrees with what Noun or Pronoun? |
| Preposition ... | — | — | — | — | — | — | — | — | — | Governs what Noun or Pronoun? |
| Adverb ... | — | — | — | — | — | — | — | — | — | Modifies what Verb? |
| Conjunction ... | — | — | — | — | — | — | — | — | — | Joins what? |

[1] (1) The Verb must have a Subject, which should always be stated in the Syntax; (2) it may be (*a*) Intransitive, or have (*b*) a Direct Object, or (*c*) an Indirect Object; (3) it may be (*a*) Principal, or (*b*) Coordinate, or (*c*) Subordinate to another Verb; or, if Inf., (*d*) Subject or Object of some Verb, or Partial Object or Subject.

# PARSING TABLE.

| Word | Root | Ending | Decl. | Gender | Voice/Num | Case/Mood | Tense | Number | Person | Notes |
|---|---|---|---|---|---|---|---|---|---|---|
| "Rogaverant." Verb. | rogo | -are 1st | — | — | Act. | Indic. | Pluperf. | Pl. | 3rd | Agrees with Nom. "cives," has for its Obj. the sentence "ut urbs...restituerotur." |
| "Cives." Noun. | civis | civis | 3rd | Masc. | Pl. | Nom. | — | Pl. | — | To the Verb "rogaverant." |
| "Ut." Conjunction. | — | — | — | — | — | — | — | — | — | Joins "rogaverant" with "restitueretur." |
| "Urbs." Noun. | urbs | urbis | 3rd | Fem. | Sing. | Nom. | — | Sing. | — | To the Verb "restitueretur." |
| "Incendio." Noun. | incendium | -i | 2nd | Neut. | Sing. | Abl. | — | — | — | Abl. of Instrument. |
| "fere." Adverb. | — | — | — | — | — | — | — | — | — | Modifies "deleta." |
| "deleta." Participle. | deleo | -ere 2nd | — | -tum | Passive | Perf. | Fem. | Sing. | Nom. | Agrees with "urbs." |
| "a." Preposition. | — | — | — | — | — | — | — | — | — | Governs the Abl. "nostris (hominibus)." |
| "nostris." Pronoun Adj. | noster, -ra, -rum | nostri, -ae, -i | 2nd | Masc. | Pl. | Abl. | no Compar. | no Superl. | — | Agrees with "hominibus" understood, which is Abl. of the Agent, governed by "a." |
| "restituerotur." Verb. | restituo | -ere 3rd | -i | -tum | Pass. | Subj. | Imperf. | Sing. | 3rd | (1) Agrees with its Nom. "urbs"; (2) subordinate to "rogaverant," Subjunctive after "ut." RULE. Verbs signifying ask, command, &c. take "ut" with the Subjunctive. |

# APPENDIX V.

## LATIN GENDERS.

*Fem. Nouns are in* **black type**; *Neut., in* CAPITALS; *Masculine in* ordinary type; (f. *means sometimes fem.*; m., *sometimes masc.*).

### I.—BY TERMINATIONS.

#### FIRST DECLENSION.

FEMININE.[1]

#### SECOND DECLENSION.

*Masculine endings* -er, -ir, -us.   *Neuter endings* -UM.

*Exceptions* { alvus, cŏlus (m.), dŏmus, hŭmus, vannus; arctus,† ătŏmus,† carbăsus,† diălectus,† phărus,† PĔLĂGUS,† VĪRUS, VULGUS.

#### THIRD DECLENSION.

*Masculine Terminations.*

-er, -or, -os.
-es *increasing in the Genitive.*
-o (*when not* -do, -go, -io).

*Principal Exceptions.*

| | | |
|---|---|---|
| -er] | **linter** | CĂDĀVER |
|  | ĬTER | PĂPĀVER[2] |
|  | ŪBER | VĒR |
|  | VERBER |  |
| -or] | **arbor** | ÆQUOR |
|  | COR | MARMOR |
| -os] | **cōs** | **dōs** |
|  | ŎS | ŌS |
|  | CHAOS† | ĔPOS† |
| -es] | **compēs** | **mercēs** |
|  | **mergēs** | **quiēs** |
|  | **rĕquiēs** | **sĕgĕs** |
|  | **tĕgĕs** | ÆS |
| -o] | **căro** | ĒCHO† |

---

[1] Excepting names of men and men's occupations, and national names, such as Scȳtha, *a Scythian*, pŏēta, *a poet* &c.; for which see "Genders by Meaning" below. Add also the Greek-derived words cŏmēta *m.*, and plănēta *m.*

[2] Also some other names of vegetable products, as ĂCER, CĬCER, PĪPĔR, SĪLER, SĬSER, TŬBER, &c.

† This sign denotes a Greek derivation.

# TABLE OF GENDERS.

*Feminine Terminations.*

**-do, -go, -io, -as, -is, -aus, x.**
**-es,** *not increasing in the Genitive.*
**-s,** *preceded by a consonant.*
**-ūs** (*long*) *in words of more than one syllable.*

*Principal Exceptions.*

| | | | |
|---|---|---|---|
| **-do]** | cardo | cupīdo (f.) | ordo |
| **-go]** | harpăgo | līgo | margo |
| **-io]** | *concrete nouns, such as* păpīlio. | | |
| | pŭgio | ūnio | |
| **-as]** | as | ĕlĕphās† | văs |
| | vās | fās | nĕfās |
| **-is]** | amnis | anguis | axis | cassis (-is) |
| | caulis | cĭnis | collis | clūnis |
| | crīnis | cŭcŭmis | ensis | fascis |
| | fīnis (f.) | follis | fūnis | fustis |
| | ignis | lăpis | mensis | orbis |
| | pānis | piscis | postis | pulvis |
| | sanguis | torris | unguis | vectis |
| | vermis | | | |
| **-x]** | ăpex | cŭlex | cŏdex | cortex (f.) |
| | frŭtex | grex | lătex | mūrex |
| | pollex | sīlex (f.) | thŏrax | vertex |
| **-es]** | ăcīnăcēs | | | |
| **ns, -ps, &c.]** | bĭdens (f.) | dens | fons | hydrops |
| | mons | pons | rŭdens (f.) | |

*Neuter Terminations.*

**-c, -a, -t, -e, -l, -n.**
**-ar, -ur, -ŭs** (*short*).
**-ūs** (*long*) *in monosyllable.*

*Principal Exceptions.*

| | | |
|---|---|---|
| **-l]** | sāl | sŏl |
| **-n]** | liĕn | pectĕn |
| | rēn | splēn |
| **-ur]** | fūr | furfŭr |
| | turtŭr | vultŭr |
| **-ŭs]** | lĕpŭs | **pĕcŭs (udis)** |
| **-ūs]** | **grūs** m.} | **sūs** (m.) |
| | mūs | |

† This sign denotes a Greek derivation.

#### FOURTH DECLENSION.

##### MASCULINE.

*Except* ăcus, īdus (pl.), **mănus, portĭcus, trĭbus.**

##### FIFTH DECLENSION.

##### FEMININE.

*Except* dĭēs (*f. in Poets*), mĕrīdĭēs.

### II.—GENDERS REGULATED BY MEANING.

#### *A.*—MASCULINE.

Names of (1) men, (2) men's occupations, (3) months, (4) winds, (5) mountains, (6) rivers, (7) peoples.[1] The exceptions arise from the terminations, such as :—

Exceptions
{
(5) **Aetna, Hybla, Īda**; **Calpē, Cyllēnē, Rhŏdŏpē**; **Alpēs** (pl.); PĒLĬON *and Plurals implying ranges* (JŬGA) such as GARGĂRĂ, ISMĂRĂ, &c.; SŌRACTĒ.
(6) **Allia,** *and others in* -ă, **Lēthē, Styx.**
}

#### *B.*—FEMININE.

Names of (1) women, (2) plants, (3) countries, (4) islands, (5) cities.[2]

Exceptions
{
(2) *Nouns of Decl.* 2, *in* -us *and* -er, *e.g.* ăcanthus, ŏleaster; *Nouns in* -UM, *e.g.* ĂPIUM; *Nouns of* 3*rd Decl. in* -ER, *e.g.* ĂCER, CĬCER, PĂPĀVER, PĪPER, SĬLER, SĬSER, *and* SŪBER; *also* RŌBUR *and* TŪS.
*The following are common:* bălănus, cўtĭsus, lōtus, rūbus, spīnus.
(3) *Masc. Decl.* 2, Pontus; *Neut. Nouns. in* -UM.
(5) *Masc.* (*a*) *all Plurals in* -i, *e.g.* Cŏrĭŏli; *also* (*b*) Cănōpus and Orchŏmĕnus; (*c*) *Nouns in* -as, -ant, *e.g.* Acrăgas, -antis; (*d*) *several in* -o, -on, *e.g.* Hippo, -ōnis; (*e*) *a few in* -us, -unt-, *e.g.* Pessīnus, -untis. *Neut.* (*a*) Nouns in -UM, -ON, -A (pl.) of *Decl.* 2 ; (*b*) most in -E, -UR, -OS of *Decl.* 3.
}

---

[1] These names may be regarded as adjectives agreeing with (1) and, (2) hŏmo, (3) mensis, (4) ventus, (5) mons, (6) flŭvĭus, (7) pŏpŭlus.

[2] These names may be regarded as adjectives agreeing with (1) mŭlier, (2) planta, (3) terra, (4) insŭla, (5) urbs.

# APPENDIX VI.
## RULE FOR TURNING THE DAYS OF THE MONTH FROM ENGLISH INTO LATIN.

In Latin the day of the month is reckoned not as in English, from the first day of the month but from (1) the *Nones*, *i.e.* the 5th or 7th of the current month; (2) the *Ides*, *i.e.* the 13th or 15th of the current month; (3) the *Kalends*, *i.e.* the first day of the next month.

The Latin terms are—

(1) **Nōnae, -ārum** (f.), *i.e. nine days* before the Ides.[1]

(2) **Īdūs, -ŭum** (f.), *i.e.* the *dividing* days of the month, falling about the middle.[2]

(3) **Kălendae, -ārum** (f.), *i.e.* the *calling* days (Old Latin calāre, *proclaim*), the day when the order of the days of the month was *proclaimed* to the people, the first day.

There is *in every month* an interval of 8 days between the Nones and the Ides. The Nones are on the 5th, and the Ides on the 13th, in every month, except March, July, October and May; in which four months the Nones are on the 7th and the Ides on the 15th.

This is sometimes remembered from the rhyme:—

"In March, July, October, May,
The Nones are on the seventh day."

I. When the day falls *between the first* and the *Nones*, or *between the Nones* and the *Ides*, the rule is (since the Romans reckoned inclusively) *Add one to the Nones or Ides and subtract the day.*

Thus, if the day be 4 March, add 1 to the Nones of March; $7 + 1 = 8$, subtract 4, the result is 4. This is written "antĕ diem quartum Nōnas Martias."[3]

If the day be 11 April, add 1 to the Ides of April; $13 + 1 = 14$; subtract 11, the result is 3. This is written "antĕ diem tertium Idus Apriles."[3]

II. When the day falls *after the Ides*, the rule is (since here we are reckoning not from the last day of the month but from the day after that), *Add two to the total number of days in the month, and subtracting the day from the result, reckon from the Kalends of next month.*

Thus if the day be 20 January, add 2 to 31, and from 33 subtract 20, the result is 13 days before the Kalends of *February*: and this is written thus "ante diem tertium dĕcĭmum Kălendas Februārias."[3]

III. If the day is (*a*) *on*, or (*b*) *the day before*, the Nones, Ides or Kalends, it is expressed by (*a*) the Abl., or (*b*) Pridie, followed by the Acc.: (*a*) 7th *of May*, "Nōnis Maiis"; (*b*) 12th *of June*, "Prīdiē Idus Jūnias"; 30th *of June*, "Prīdiē Kălendas Quintīles"; 4th *of August*, Prīdiē Nōnas Sextīles.

IV. Note that Adjectives, (and not Nouns in the Genitive) are used in each case. The Adjectives are, ("antĕ diem—Kălendas, Nōnas, Īdus) Jānuārias, Februārias, Martias, Apriles, Maias, Jūnias, Quintīles, Sextīles, Septembres, Octōbres, Nŏvembres, Decembres."

---

[1] We should say "*eight* days before": but the Romans reckoned inclusively.

[2] This is the derivation commonly given from an Etruscan word **iduāre**, *divide*: but more probably from Sanscr. indh-, idh-, *kindle, enlighten*, (indu, *moon*) from being the days of *light*, the days of the full moon.

[3] A rarer form is "tertio, quarto, tertio décimo die antĕ," &c. The common construction cannot be explained except as a confusion.

# APPENDIX VII.

## ELEMENTARY RULES ON THE QUANTITY OF SYLLABLES

*As a Guide to Pronunciation.*

### I.—GENERAL RULES.

1. Diphthongs (**aēs**, *brass*) and contracted syllables (**quīs** for **quĭbus**) are long.

2. A vowel before another vowel (**monĕo**) is short.

3. A vowel naturally short (*e.g.* the **a** in **căno**, *I sing*), when placed before two consonants (*e.g.* in **cantus**, *song*), is said to be *long by position*, and is long for the purposes of verse-making; but it is *pronounced* in the same way as the **a** in **cano**, so that *length by position does not affect pronunciation*.

### II.—FINAL SYLLABLES.

1. Final -**ā** is *long*: exceptions; Nom., Voc., and Acc. cases; also **ĭtă**, **quĭă**.[1]

2. Final -**ĕ** is *short:* exceptions: (1) Adverbs in -**ē** derived from Adj. in -**us**, -**a**, -**um**, as **maximē**, (save **bĕnĕ**, **mălĕ**, **sŭpernĕ**); (2) Abl. Sing. of 5th Decl.; (3) 2nd Pers. Sing. Imper. of 2nd Conj.; (4) **nē**, **mē**, **tē**, **sē**.

3. Final -**ī** is *long;* but -**i** is mostly *short* in **mĭhĭ**, **tĭbĭ**, **ŭbĭ**, **ĭbĭ**, **sĭbĭ**, always in **nĭsĭ**.

4. Final -**ō** is *long;* but mostly *short* in **ĕgŏ**, **mŏdŏ** (adv.) only.

5. Final -**ū** is *long*.

6. A vowel before -**c** is *long*; exceptions, **nĕc**, **dōnĕc**, **făc**.

7. A vowel is *short* before final -**b**, -**d**, -**l**, -**n**, -**r**, and **t**.[2]

---

[1] None but the more important exceptions are given to every rule.

[2] The quantities of syllables not final must be learned by experience; but the quantity of one word often helps the pupil to that of many derived words. For example, the short **ŏ** in **mŏneo** determines the quantity in **admŏneo**, **commŏneo**, **mŏnĭtus**, -**us**, **mŏnitor**, -**ōris**, **monumentum**, -**i**, &c.: exceptions, **dŭcis**, *of a leader*, **dūco**, *I lead;* **sēdēs**, *a seat;* **sĕdeo**, *I sit*.

## QUANTITY OF SYLLABLES. 231

8. **-ās** and **-ēs** are *long*: but nouns in **-es**, increasing the Genit., are short, *e.g.* **mīlĕs, mīlĭtis**; and **ĕs** (*thou art*) is *short*, both in **sum** and in its compounds.

9. **-ĭs** is *short*: exceptions (*a*) Plural Cases, *e.g.* **insŭlīs, dŏmĭnīs, nōbīs**; (*b*) second Pers. Sing. Pres. Indic., of fourth Conj., **audīs**; (*c*) **sīs** (Pres. Subj. of **sum**) and **vīs** (Pres. Indic. of **vŏlo**), and their compounds, as well as **velīs, mālīs, nōlīs**; (*d*) **vīs**, *violence.*

10. **-ōs** is *long*: exception, **ŏs** (Gen. **ossis**).

11. **-ŭs** is *short*: exceptions; (*a*) Gen. Sing., and Nom. and Acc. Pl., of Fourth Decl.; (*b*) nouns in **-us** which increase in the Gen. with a long penult, **virtūs, -ūtis**.

N.B.—It will be seen that (by Rules 7 and 9) many of the commonest monosyllables are short; **ŏb, sŭb, ăd, ăt, ĕt, ĭd, ĭn, ăn, vĕl, pĕr, tĕr, vĭr**; also **ĭs**, and **quĭs**.

But although (according to Rule II. 2) **-quĕ, -vĕ,** and **-nĕ?** are short, **nē** *lest* is long, and so are the pronouns **mē, tē, se.** Also **cūr?** *why?* is long.

# APPENDIX VIII.

## ETYMOLOGICAL GLOSSARY OF GRAMMATICAL TERMS.

Ablative (Case) [L. *ab*, "from;" *latus*, "carried"]. The Case denoting, among other things, *ablation*, or *carrying away from* (8, 273).

Absolute (Construction) [L. *ab*, "from;" *solut-*, "loosed"]. A construction in which a Noun, Participle, &c., is supposed to be used apart, *i.e. loosed from*, its ordinary Grammatical adjuncts. But the *Abl. Absolute* is really an *Abl. of circumstance* (196).

Abstract (Noun) [L. *abs*, "from;" *tract-*, "drawn"]. The name of an *abstraction*, *i.e.* of something considered by itself, apart from (*drawn away from*) the circumstances in which it exists.

Accent [L. *ad*, "to;" *cantus*, "song"]. Perhaps originally a sing-*song*, or modulation of the voice, added *to* a syllable. Now used of stress laid on a syllable.

Accidence [L. *accident-*, "befall"]. That part of grammar which treats of the changes that *befall* words. (1); Quintilian I. 5, 41, "frequentissime in verbo quia plurima huic *accidunt.*"

Accusative (Case). 2. Probably a Latin mistake. The Greek original meant (1) *cause*, (2) *accusation*. The Latins took it in sense (2) instead of (1). The Latin name for the Direct Objective Inflexion. Possibly the Romans regarded the object as confronted with the agent, like an *accused* person with the prosecutor.

Active (Voice). The form of a Verb that usually denotes *acting* or doing.

Adjective [L. *ad*, "to;" *jact-*, "cast or put"]. A word *put to* a Noun.

Adverb [L. *ad*, "to;" *verb-*, "word" or "Verb"]. A word generally joined *to* a Verb.

Adversative [L. *adversus*, "opposite"]. An epithet applied to Conjunctions that (like "but") express *opposition*.

Affix [L. *ad*, "to;" *fix-*, "fixed"]. A syllable or letter *fixed* to the end of a word.

Agreement. The change made in the inflections of words so that they may suit or *agree* with one another.

Alphabet [Gr. *alpha*, *beta*; "a," "b"]. The list of letters, so called from the names

## OF GRAMMATICAL TERMS.

of the first two letters in Greek.

Anacolouthon [Gr. *a*-, "not;" *acolouthon*, "following"]. A break in the Grammatical sequence, or *following*.

Anomaly. A Greek-formed word meaning "unevenness," "irregularity."

Antecedent [L. *ante*, "before;" *cedent-*, "going"]. (*a*) That part of a sentence which expresses a condition. So called because the condition must go *before* its consequence. (*b*) Also used for the Noun that *goes before* a Relative Pronoun (107).

Apodosis [Gr. *apo-dosis*, "a paying back"]. A Greek name for the "Consequent," or "Then-Clause," in a Conditional Sentence (293). The Consequence was regarded as a sort of *debt*, to be *paid* in return for the fulfilment of the Condition.

Appellative [L. *appella*, "call to"]. A name for the *Vocative* or *calling* use of a noun.

Apposition [L. *ad*, "near;" *posit-*, "placed"]. The *placing* of one noun in the same case with another noun or pronoun, to express some quality, or circumstance, of the latter (123).

Asyndeton [from Greek "not bound together."] The placing of words together without a Conjunction: see Par. 32.

Attribute [L. *attribut-*, "assigned"]. An Adj. *assigned* to qualify a Noun.

Cardinal (Numbers) [L. *cardin-*, "hinge"]. That on which anything *hinges* or turns: hence, "important." A name given to those more *important* forms of Numeral Adjectives from which the Ordinal forms are derived.

Case [L. *casus*, "falling"]. The Latin translation of the Greek term for the forms of a Noun. The subjective form was regarded as "erect," and the other forms as more or less *falling* away from it. Hence "oblique," "decline,' &c.

Clause [L. *claus-*, "enclosed"]. A general term for a part of a Sentence, whether it be a Phrase or a Subordinate Sentence.

Cognate (Object) [L. *co-*, "together;" (*g*)*nat-* "born"]. The name given to an object that denotes something *akin* to (*born together* with) the action denoted by the Verb.

Common (Noun). A name that is *common* to a class and not *peculiar* or *proper* to an individual.

Comparative (Degree). The form of an Adjective denoting that a quality exists in a greater degree in some one thing than in some other with which it is *compared*.

Complementary [L. *comple-* "fill up"]. That which completes, or *fills up*.

Complete (State). A name given to an action (whether Past, Present, or Future) that was, is, or will be *complete*.

Complex (Sentence) [L. *con-* "together;" *plic-*, "fold"]. A sentence that is *folded together*, or involved by containing one or more Subordinate sentences.

Compound (Sentence) [L. *con*, or *com*, "together;" *pon-*, "place"]. A sentence made up of a number of Co-ordinate sentences *placed together*.

Concord. The name given to syntactical *agreement* between words, *e.g.* between Verb and Subject.

Conjugation [*con*, "together;" *jugatio*, "joining"]. A number of Verbs *joined* together in one class.[1]

Conjunction [L. *con*, "together;" *junct-*, "joined"]. A word that *joins together* two sentences expressed or implied.

Consequent. The name given to that part of a Sentence which expresses the *consequence* of the fulfilment of a *condition*. See *Antecedent*.

Consecutive. The name sometimes given to a clause introd. by "ut" *so that*, expressing *result*, or *consequence*, of an *action*.

Consonant [L. *con*, "together;" *sonant-*, "sounding"]. Letters (such as *p*) that can only be *sounded together with* a vowel.

Coordinate [L. *co-*, "with;" *ordin-*, "rank"]. The name given to a Sentence that *ranks with* the Principal Sentence (334*a*): see Note following the Glossary.

Correlatives. Words that are *related together* or mutually related, *e.g.*, "either," "or;" "both," "and;" "when," "then."

Dative [L. *dativus*,[2] "that which has arisen from giving"]. The Latin name for the Indirect Objective case used after Verbs of *giving*, &c. (192)

Declension. The bending or *declension* of the Oblique (see *Oblique* below) cases from the Subjective form, which was regarded as "erect."

Defective (Verbs) [L. *deficio*, "I fail"]. Verbs that are *deficient* in some of their forms: see p. 215.

Degree (of comparison) [L. *gradus*, Fr. *degré*, "step"]. The forms expressing the *steps* or *degrees* in which a quality can be expressed by an Adjective.

Dependent (Sentence). Sometimes used for Subordinate. But generally applied to *Subordinate* sentences that are the Subjects or Objects of Verbs (208, 239).

Deponent (Verbs) [L. *deponens*, "laying *aside*"]. Verbs that retain an Active meaning, while *laying aside* Active forms : Par. 199.

Diæresis [Gr. *diairesis*, "separation"]. The mark placed over one of two vowels to show that each is to be

---

[1] Hence to *conjugate* a Verb is to repeat the inflections belonging to the class or *conjugation*. But the Romans used *decline* and not *conjugate* in this sense (Madvig).

[2] Termination -*ivus* in Latin, when added to Participles, denotes *that which has arisen from*, *e.g.* "captivus," *that which has arisen from* "*capture*."

pronounced *separately*, *e.g.* in "aërial."

Diphthong [Gr. *di*, "twice;" *phthongos*, "sound"]. *Two* vowel sounds pronounced as one.

Direct (Object). The Noun that denotes what is regarded as the *direct object* of the action of a Verb.

Ellipsis [Gr. *elleipsis*, "omission"]. The *omission* of words (said to be "understood" *i.e.* implied) in a Sentence.

Enclitics [Gr. "lean on"]. Words that cannot stand without *leaning on*, and being attached to, the words before them, *e.g.* -quĕ, -vĕ, -nĕ.

Epithet [Gr. *epithetos*, "placed to"]. An Adjective *placed to* a Noun to describe some quality of the person or thing denoted by the Noun.

Final [L. *finis*, "end"]. A *final* clause expresses an *end* or *purpose;* and "ut" *final* ("in order that") is distinguished from "ut" *consecutive* ("so that") (296).

Finite (Verb). A name given to those parts of the Verb which are *defined* by Number and Person, as distinct from the *Infinitive* or *Infinite*.

Frequentative (Verb). A Verb that expresses a *frequently* repeated action, *e.g.* "ventito," *I often come.*

Gender [L. *genus*, Fr. *genre*, "breed," or "class"]. Forms to denote *class*ification according to sex.

Genitive (Case) [L. *genitiv-*, "generating"]. The Case denoting *generation*, origination, possession (282).[1]

Gerund [L. *gero*, "I carry on"]. Part of the Verb denoting the *carrying on* of the action of the Verb. The *Gerundive* is Adjectival, the *Gerund* is a Noun (163, 170, 251).

Gutturals [L. *guttur*, "throat"]. *Throat* letters, *k*, and hard *g*.

Historic Infinitive. The Infinitive used for the Indicative, as is sometimes the case in rapid *historical* narrative: see Par. 320.

Idiom [Gr. *idioma*, "peculiarity"]. A mode of expression *peculiar* to a language.

Imperative (Mood). [L. *impera-*, "command"]. The *commanding* Mood (129).

Impersonal (Verbs). Verbs not used with a *Personal* Subject : see Par. 219.

Indicative (Mood). [L. *indica-*, "point out"]. The Mood that *points out* or *indicates* an action, &c., as a past, present, or future existence.

Indirect (Object). The Noun or Pron. denoting the person or thing regarded as not directly but only *indirectly* influenced by the action of the Verb (192).

Infinitive (Mood) [L. *in*, "not;" *finit-*, "limited"]. A Mood *not limited* by any definition of Person or Number.

Inflection. [L. *inflecto*, "I

---

[1] The Latin "genitivus" is a mistranslation of the Greek *genike*, which meant the *generic* case *i.e.* the case that denoted the *genus* or *class*. For example "life," "What *class* of life?" " *Man's* life."

bend"]. The *bending* of a word from the simple form, by means of varying the termination. See *Oblique*.

Interjection [L. *inter-ject-*, "thrown between"]. An utterance *thrown in between* words, to express emotion.

Intransitive (Verb). [L. *in*, "not"; *transitiv-*, "passing across"]. A Verb whose action is not supposed to *pass across* to any Object.

Labials [L. *labium*, "lip"]. *Lip*-letters: *f, v, p, b, m, hw* and *w*.

Linguals [Latin *lingua*, "the tongue"]. Letters whose sounds are produced by the *tongue: sh, s* in pleasure.

Locative (Case) [L. *locus*, "place"]. A case expressing *place* (Par. 265).

Liquids. Letters of a flowing, *liquid* sound, as *l, r*.

Monosyllable [Gr. *mono*, "only"]. A word of *only one* syllable.

Mood [L. *mod-*, "manner"]. The form of a Verb expressing the *manner* of action.

Mutes [L. *mut-*, "dumb"]. Letters that are *dumb* without the aid of a vowel: *k, g, t, d, p, b.*

Nasal [L. *nas-*, "nose"]. Consonants sounded through the *nose; n, m.*

Neuter (Gender). [L. *neuter*, "neither"]. That Gender which is *neither* Masc. nor Feminine.

Nominative (Case) [L. *nomina-*, "to name"]. A Latin term for the Subject, because the Subject was regarded as a person or thing *named*.

Noun [L. *nomen*, Fr. *nom*, "name"]. The *name* of anything.

Object. The word, or group of words, denoting that which is regarded as the *object* or mark aimed at by the action of Verbs or the motion of Prepositions.

Oblique (Case). A name given to all Cases but the Subjective. By the Greeks the Subjective form of a Noun was regarded as *erect*, and all the other forms as *fallings* or *oblique* deviations from the Subjective.

Oblique (Speech). Speech reported, not *directly* in the First Person with the exact words of the speaker, but *indirectly* or *obliquely* in the Third Person.

Ordinal (Adjective) [L. *ordin-*, "order"]. An Adjective, that answers to the question "in what *order*."

Palatals. Letters whose sounds are produced by the *palate: ch, j*.

Participle [L. *particip-*, "participating"]. A form of a Verb *participating* in a Verb and an Adjective.

Particle. A "little part": a name given to the four undeclined "*parts* of speech," Adverb, Conjunction, Interjection and Preposition.

Partitive (Genitive). A Genitive implying *partition* (91).

Passive (Voice). A form of the Verb expressing *passiveness* rather than *activeness*.

Perfect (Tense) [L. *perfect-*, "complete"]. The Name

## OF GRAMMATICAL TERMS.

for the Latin Tense that has to represent (1) our Indef. Past, (2) our Complete Present.

Period [Gr. *peri*, "round"; *od-*, "path"]. (1) The full, *rounded path* of a complex sentence, (2) a mark at the end of a sentence.

Person [L. *per*, "through"; *son-*, "sound;" hence, *persona* "a mask *through* which an actor *sounds;*" "an actor's *part* in a play"]. The *part played* in conversation, (1) speaking; (2) spoken to; (3) spoken of.

Phrase [Gr. *phrasis*, a "saying"]. A group of words not expressing a statement, question, or command.

Pluperfect (Tense) [L. *plu-*, "more;" *perfect-*, "complete"]. A *more than complete* Tense. The Latin equivalent of our Complete Past (121).

Plural (Number) [L. *plu-*, "more"]. The form denoting *more* than one.

Polysyllable [Gr. *poly*, "many"]. A word of *many* syllables.

Positive. The simple form of an Adjective; so-called because it expresses a quality not comparatively, but *positively*.

Possessive [L. *possess-*, "possessed"]. The name given to the use or case of a Noun denoting *possession*.

Predicate [L. "*praedica-*," "proclaim," "state"]. A word or group of words making a *statement* about a Subject.

Prefix [L. *prae*, "before;" *fix-*, "fixed"]. A letter, syllable, or word *fixed before* another word.

Preposition [L. *prae*, "before;" *posit-*, "placed"]. A Word (not a Verb) generally *placed before* a Noun or Pronoun as its Object. N.B. A Preposition and its Object make up an Adverbial Phrase.

Pronoun [L. *pro*, "for;" L. *nomen*, "noun"]. A word used *for* a *Noun*.

Proper (Noun). [L. *propri-*, F. *propre*; "peculiar"]. A name that is *peculiar* or *proper* to the individual, not *common* to a class.

Prose [L. *prosa*, for *prorsa*, for *pro-versa*,[1] *i.e.* "turned forward"]. Writing that does not *turn* like *verses* but runs *straight on*. Hence, the *straightforward* arrangement of prose.

Prosody [Gr. *prosodia*, a "song"]. Hence, that part of Grammar which treats of verse, whether intended to be sung or not.

Protasis [Gr. *pro*, "before;" *tasis*, "stretching"]. Literally, *stretching before*. Hence, in a sentence, the Antecedent or Condition. See *Apodosis*.

Punctuation [L. *punctum*, "point"]. Dividing a sentence by means of *points* representing the pauses.

Quantity. The *quantity* of time necessary to pronounce a syllable.

---

[1] Compare our *e'er, o'er* for *ever, over*.

**Reduplication.** The *reduplicating* or *redoubling* of a syllable, mostly found (but with some change) in a few Latin Perfects, *e.g.* "tendo," "te-tendi."

**Reflexive (Pronoun)** [*reflexus*, "bent back"]. A Pronoun which is as it were *bent back* on the Subject, so that the Pronoun and the Subject denote the same person or thing.

**Relative (Pronoun)** [L. *re*, "back;" *lat-*, "carried"]. A name given to *qui*, *quae*, &c., when used not Interrogatively to carry one forward, but to *carry* one *back* to the Antecedent.

**Root.** A word that gives birth to a group of kindred words, as a *root* to branches.

**Sentence** [L. *Sententia*, a "meaning"]. A group of words of *meaning* so complete as to express a statement, question, or command.

**Sibilant** L. [*sibila-*, hiss]. *Hissing* letters : *s, z, sh*.

**Stem.** That part of a word which remains the same when the word is inflected.

N.B.—The True Stem of a word is sometimes concealed by changes, *e.g.* the "o" which is part of the True Stem of "dominus" is lost in almost all the Cases. Hence the Stem of "dominus" as printed in Par. 12 appears to be "domin-." This false Stem, which is obtained by clipping the True Stem of its final vowel, is sometimes called the Clipt Stem. (Par. 55, note 1.)

**Subject** [L. *subject-*, "placed under"]. That which is *placed under* one's thoughts, as the basis for speech. Hence, the Subject of a Verb is that about which the Verb makes a statement (127).

**Subjunctive (Mood)** [L. *subjunct-*, "subjoined"]. A Mood expressing a purpose, condition, &c., *subjoined* to some statement, question, or answer.

**Subordinate (Sentence)** [L. *sub*, "beneath;" *ordin-*, "rank"]. See Note p. 239.

**Substantive (Noun)** [L. *substantia*, "substance"]. A name given to Nouns, perhaps as being the *substance* or *ground standing beneath* the Adjective. It is from a Greek term, applied not to Nouns but to the *Substantive Verb*, "to be."

**Suffix** [L. *sub*, "beneath;" *fix-*, "fixed"]. Same as *Affix*.

**Supine.** A name given to two very rarely used Noun forms of the Verb used only in the Accusative and Ablative. Its origin is unknown, but it may at least serve to remind the pupil that these forms are the laziest and most *supine* of all the parts of the Verb : see Par. 246, 247.

**Superlative (degree)** [L. *super*, "above;" *lat-*, "carried"]. An Adjectival form denoting the expression of a quality in a degree *carried above* other degrees.

**Syllable** [Gr. *syn*, "together;" *lab-*, "take"]. A group of letters *taken together* so as to form one sound.

**Syntax** [Gr. *syn*, "together;"

*taxis*, "arranging"]. The *arrangement* of words *together* in a sentence.

Temporal (Clause) [L. *tempus*, "time"]. An Adverbial Clause introduced by a Conjunction of *time*.

Tense [L. *tempus*, Fr. *temps*, "time"]. The forms of a Verb indicating the *time* of an action.

Transitive [L. *trans*, "across;" *it*-, "going"]. A Verb that has an Object, so called because the action of the Verb is regarded as passing or *going across* to the Object.

Verb [L. *verb*-, "word"]. The chief *word* in a sentence.

Vocative [L. *voca*-, "call"]. The use, or Case, of a Noun when the person or thing is *called to*.

Vowels [L. *vocalis*, "having voice"]. The letters that *have a voice* or are sounded (not as the "consonants but) by themselves: *a, e, i, o, u*.

NOTE ON SUBORDINATE SENTENCES.

Subordinate Sentences are those which express some (1) **Noun**, (2) **Adjective**, or (3) **Adverb** in another Sentence called the Principal Sentence.[1]

(1) (**Noun**) { (*a*) (Subject.) " WHEN *he-will-come* is uncertain."
{ (*b*) (Object.) "I say THAT *he-will-come*."

(2) (**Adjective**.) "The battle *that-was-fought* at Cannæ was gained by Hannibal."

(3) (**Adverb**.) (*a*) (When?) " WHEN *he-had-heard-this* he departed"; (*b*) (Why?) "I will strive THAT *you-may-succeed*"; (*c*) (How?) "He behaved so gently THAT *he-surprised-everybody*"; (*d*) (Where?) " WHERE *the-Turk's-horse-goes*, nothing grows."

For a list of the Principal Subordinate and Coordinate Conjunctions see Par. 334*a*.

---

[1] A Subordinate Sentence (called also a Subordinate Clause) is sometimes defined as one that is "constructively dependent" on another Sentence. If this definition were adopted, a sentence in the Subjunctive preceded by "antequam" would be Subordinate, while the same sentence in the Indicative, preceded by "antequam," would not be Subordinate.

# APPENDIX IX.

## VOCABULARIES.

### LIST OF ABBREVIATIONS.

adj. = adjective
adv. = adverb
c. = common gender
conj. = conjunction
f. = feminine
gen. = genitive
indec. = indeclinable
inter. = interrogative

m. = masculine
n. = neuter
pl. = plural
prep. = preposition
pron. = pronoun
sing. = singular
v. = verb

### EXERCISE I.

ăqua, f. *water*
ăquĭla, f. *eagle*
fīlĭa, f. *daughter*
insŭla, f. *island*
nauta, m. *sailor*
pĕcūnĭa, f. *money*
pŭella, f. *girl*
rēgīna, f. *queen*

### EXERCISES II.—VI.

constantia, f. *constancy*
culpa, f. *blame, fault*
dextra, f. *right hand*
expĕrĭentĭa, f. *experience*
fēmĭna, f. *woman*
intempĕrantĭa, f. *intempcrance*
īra, f. *anger*
pătĭentĭa, f. *patience*
patrĭa, -ae, f. *native land*
prŏcella, f. *storm*
prūdentĭa, f. *prudence*
săpĭentĭa, f. *wisdom*
stella, f. *star*

vĭŏlentĭa, f. *violence*
ămat, v. *loves*
dăt, v. *gives*
lăvat, v. *washes*
lĭbĕrat, v. *frees, delivers*
monstrat, v. *points out, shews*
sŭpĕrat, v. *overcomes*
vŏrat, v. *devours*
ĕt . . . ĕt, conj. *both . . . and*

### EXERCISE VII.

dŏmĭnus, m. *lord, owner*
ĕquus, m. *horse*
fīlĭus, m. *son*
flŭvĭus, m. *river*
glădĭus, m. *sword*
hortus, m. *garden*
măgister, m. *master* (mostly *teacher*)
mĭna, f. *threat*
mĭnister, m. *servant, attendant*
servus, m. *slave*
hăbet, v. *has*
tĭmet, v. *fears*
terret, v. *terrifies, frightens*

## VOCABULARIES.

### EXERCISES VIII.—XI.

āger, *m. field*
agrĭcŏla, *m. husbandman*
ăper, *m. boar*
arbĭter, *m. umpire*
Auster, *m. south wind*
cancer, *m. crab*
căper, *m. goat*
cŏlŭber, *m. snake*
culter, *m. knife*
făber, *m. artificer, workman*
gĕner, *m. son-in-law*
hasta, -ae, *f. spear*
invĭdĭa, -ae, *f. envy*
līber, *m. book*
Liber, *m. Liber, the god of wine*
lībĕri, *m. pl. children*
pŭer, *m. boy*
sŏcer, *m. father-in-law*
vesper, *m. evening*
vĭr, *m. man, hero*
culpat, *v. blames*
laudat, *v. praises*
nĕque, *or* nĕc, *conj. and not, neither*
nŏn, *adv. not*
ā (ăb *before vowels or* h), *prep. by*
sŭpĕrantur, terrentur, *see* p. 11

### EXERCISE XII.

argentum, *n. silver*
arvum, *n. cornfield*
aurum, *n. gold*
dīlĭgentĭa, *f. diligence*
dōnum, *n. gift*
mūrus, *m. wall*
Neptūnus, *m. Neptune*
oppĭdum, *n. town*
porta, -ae, *f. gate*
praemĭum, *n. reward*
terra, *f. land*
templum, *n. temple*
dēlectat, *v. delights, charms*

### EXERCISE XIII.

aurīga, *m. charioteer*
bŏnus, -a, -um, *good*
dīrus, -a, -um, *terrible*
doctus, -a, -um, *learned*
ĕpistŭla, -ae, *f. letter*
impăvĭdus, -a, -um, *fearless*
imprŏbus, -a, -um, *dishonest*
injustus, -a, -um, *unjust*
jussum, *n. command*
justus, -a, -um, *just*
magnus, -a, -um, *great, large*
parvus, -a, -um, *little, small*
păvĭdus, -a, -um, *fearful*
pĕlăgus, *n. sea*
pĕrīcŭlum, *n. danger*
prŏbus, -a, -um, *honest*
scrība, *m. scribe, clerk*
splendĭdus, -a, -um, *splendid*
strēnŭus, -a, -um, *vigorous*
tĭmĭdus, -a, -um, *timid*
vastus, -a, -um, *vast*
vĭa, *f. way*

### EXERCISES XIV. AND XV.

aeger, -gra, -grum, *sick, ailing*
āla, *f. wing*
albus, -a, -um, *white*
altus, -a, -um, *high, tall*
Brĭtannĭa, *f. Britain*
falsus, -a, -um, *false*
impĭger, -gra, -grum, *active*
incŏla, *m. inhabitant*
lātus, -a, um, *broad*
măcer, -cra, -crum, *lean*
miser, -era, -crum, *wretched*
morbus, *m. disease*
nĭger, -gra, -grum, *black*
pĭger, -gra, -grum, *slothful*
pŏēta, -ae, *m. poet*
prosper, -pĕra, -pĕrum, *prosperous*
pulcher, -chra, -chrum, *beautiful*
rŭber, -bra, -brum, *red*
săcer, -cra, -crum, *sacred*

R

stultĭtia, -ae, *f. folly*
stultus, -a, -um, *foolish*
taeter, -tra, -trum, *foul*
văfer, -fra, -frum, *cunning*
vălĭdus, -a, -um, *strong*
verbum, -i, *n. word*
est, *v.* (*he*) *is;* (*there*) *is*
sunt, *v.* (*they*) *are;* (*there*) *are*

### Exercise XVI.

ăcūtus, -a, -um, *sharp*
aestās, aestatis, *f. summer*
arx, arcis, *f. citadel*
bellum, -i, *n. war*
clārus, -a, -um, *renowned*
cŏmĕs, cŏmĭtis, *m. companion*
dignus, -a, -um, *worthy* (*g. abl.*)
dux, dŭcis, *m. leader*
ĕquĕs, ĕquĭtis, *m. horse-soldier*
fessus, -a, -um, *weary*
grātus, -a, -um, *pleasing*
ignāvia, -ae, *f. sloth, cowardice*
impĕrātor, -ōris, *m. general*
indignus, -a, -um, *unworthy*
ingrātus, -a, -um, *displeasing*
injustus, -a, -um, *unjust*
jucundus, -a, -um, *agreeable*
jūdex, jūdĭcis, *m. judge*
lăpĭs, -ĭdis, *m. stone*
lēx, lēgis, *f. law*
mălus, -a, -um, *bad*
mĕmŏrĭa, *f. memory, recollection*
mīlĕs, mīlĭtis, *m. soldier*
mŏlestus, -a, -um, *troublesome*
nox, noctis, *f. night*
obscūrus, -a, -um, *dark*
pĕdĕs, pĕdĭtis, *m. foot-soldier*
pēs, pĕdis, *m. foot*
rēx, rēgis, *m. king*
sĭnister, -tra, -trum, *left*
spīna, -ae, *f. thorn*
verbum, -i, *n. word*
dēlectat, *v.* (*he*) *delights*
laedit, *v. hurts*

### Exercise XVII.

annus, -i, *m. year*
ĕlĕphās, elephantis, *m. elephant*
fĕrus, -a, -um, *savage*
grus, grŭis, *c. crane*
hiemps, hĭĕmis, *f. winter*
hŏmo, hŏmĭnis, *m. human being*
hōra, -ae, *f. hour*
lĕo, lĕōnis, *m. lion*
longĭtūdo, -tūdĭnis, *f. length*
longus, -a, -um, *long*
mīrus, -a, -um, *wonderful*
multĭtūdo, -tūdĭnis, *f. multitude*
multus, -a, -um, *many, much*
păpīlĭo, păpīlĭōnis, *m. butterfly*
pōmum, -i, *n. fruit*
princeps, princĭpis, *m. chief*
terra, -ae *f. land*
trabs, trăbis, *f. beam*
virgo, virgĭnis, *f. maiden*
vīvit, -unt, *v.* (*he*) *lives,* (*they*) *live*

### Exercise XVIII.

ămīcus, -i *m. friend*
ămor, ămoris, *m. love*
anser, ansĕris, *m. goose*
arbor, arbŏris, *f. tree*
causa, -ae, *f. cause*
cĭnis, cĭnĕris, *m. ashes*
clāmor, clāmōris, *m. clamour*
clārus, -a, -um, *clear, bright, renowned*
cŏlor, cŏlōris, *m. colour*
consul, consŭlis, *m. consul*
flōs, flōris, *m. flower,*
frāter, -tris, *m. brother*
frīgĭdus, -a, -um, *cold* [*able*
injūcundus, -a, -um, *disagree-*
jussum, -i, *n. command*
māter, mātris, *f. mother*
ŏcŭlus, -i, *m. eye*
păter, patris, *m. father*
paucus, -a, -um, (*mostly pl.*) *few*
sĕpulcrum, -i, *n. sepulchre*
tĭmor, tĭmōris, *m. fear*
vōx, vōcis, *f. voice*

## Exercise XIX.

căput, căpĭtis, *n. head*
carmen, carmĭnis, *n. poem, song*
cībus, -i, *m. food*
corpus, corpŏris, *n. body*
Dĕus, -i, *m. God*
doctrīna, -ae, *f. learning*
factum, -i, *n. deed*
frūtex, frŭtĭcis, *m. shrub*
fulmen, fulmĭnis, *n. lightning (that strikes)*
jūs, jūris, *n. right or law*
longus, -a, -um, *long* [*chant*
mercātor, mercatōris, *m. mer-*
nōmen, nŏmĭnis, *n. name*
mens, mentis, *f. mind, understanding*
ŏpus, ŏpĕris, *n. work*
pŏēta, -ae, *m. poet*
scĕlus, scĕlĕris, *n. crime*
sīdus, sīdĕris, *n. star*
verber, verbĕris, *n. lash, stripe*
-quĕ, *conj. and*
ĕrat, *v. (he) was; there (was)*
ĕrant, *v. (they) were; (there) were*

gens, gentis, *f. nation*
gĕnus, gĕneris, *n. kind, race*
hostis, hostis, *m. enemy; oft. pl. in Lat. where Eng. is sing.;* hostīum castra, *the camp of the enemy*
ignāvus, -a, -um, *slothful*
ignis, ignis, *abl.*, -i, *m. fire*
imber, imbris, *abl.*, -i, *m. shower*
măre, măris, *n. sea*
nāvis, nāvis, *f. ship*
notūs, -a, -um, *known*
nūbēs, nūbis, *f. cloud*
ōs, ōris, *n. mouth, countenance*
ŏs, ossis, *n. bone*
pastor, pastōris, *m. shepherd*
răpĭdus, -a, -um, *rapid*
rōbur, robŏris, *n. strength*
saevus, -a, -um, *cruel, fierce*
tempestās, -tātis, *f. tempest*
tōtus, -a, -um, *whole*
urbs, urbis, *f. city*
nĕque .. nĕque, *conj. neither ... nor*
saepĕ, *adv. often*
consŭmit, *v. (he) consumes*

## Exercise XX.

ănĭmal, ănĭmālis, *n. animal*
ăvĭdus, -a, -um, *greedy*
aurĕus, -a, -um, *golden*
Brĭtannus, -i, *m. adj. used as noun, a Briton*
calcar, calcāris, *n. spur*
certāmen, certāmĭnis, *n. contest, strife*
cīvis, cīvis, *m. citizen*
cīvĭtas, cīvĭtātis, *f. state, country, citizenship*
crēber, -bra, -brum, *repeated, frequent*
dĕcus, dĕcŏris, *n. honour*
exĭtĭum, -i, *n. destruction*
ferrum, -i, *n. iron, sword* [*rage*
fŭror, fŭrōris, *m. madness,*

## Exercise XXI.

ācer, *m.* ācris, *f.* ācre, *n. keen*
ănĭmus, -i, *m. mind*
audāx, *gen.* audācis, *bold*
cĕlĕr, *m.* cĕlĕris, *f.* celĕrĕ, *n. swift*
consĭlĭum, -i, *n. plan* [*gent*
dīlĭgens, *gen.* dīlĭgentis, *diligent*
dīvĕs, *gen.* dīvĭtis, *rich*
dulcis, *m. & f.* dulce, *n. sweet*
ĕquester, *m.* -tris, *f.* -tre, *n. equestrian*
fĕrāx, *gen.* ferācis, *fruitful*
fēlīx, *gen.* fēlīcis, *happy*
fortis, *m. & f.*, forte, *n. brave*
infēlīx, *gen.* infēlīcis, *unhappy*
insignis, *m. & f.* insigne, *n. distinguished, illustrious*

244 VOCABULARIES.

lăbor, lăbōris, *m. labour*
laetĭtĭa, -ae, *f. joy*
laetus, -a, -um, *joyful*
mĕlĭor, *m. & f.* mĕlĭus, *n. better*
mors, mortis, *f. death*
prūdens, *gen.* prūdentis, *prudent*
sălūber, *m.* -bris, *f.* -bre, *n. healthful*
săpĭens, *gen.* săpĭentis, *wise*
sēdĭtĭo, sēdĭtĭōnis, *f. sedition*
tergum, -i, *n. back*
tristis, *m. & f.* triste, *n. sad*
tristĭor, *m. & f.* tristĭus, *n. sadder*
verber, -ĕris, *n. lash, stripe*
vestis, -is, *f. garment*
vīta, -ae, *f. life*

EXERCISE XXII.

'almus, -a, -um, *loving*
ătrōx, *gen.* ătrōcis, *stern, gloomy*
ăter, -tra, -trum, *dark, black*
bĕnignus, -a, -um, *kind*
brĕvis, *m. & f.*, brĕve, *n. short*
cŏhors, cŏhortis, *f. a cohort, the tenth part of a Roman legion*
fāma, -ae, *f. reputation, fame*
fĕrĭtās, fĕrĭtātis, *f. savageness*
hasta, -ae, *f. spear*
infirmus, -a, -um, *weak*
inhŏnestus, -a, -um, *dishonourable*
īrācundus, -a, -um, *angry*
omnis, *m. & f.* omne, *n. all, the whole*
poenĭtentĭa, -ae, *f. penitence*
prīmus, -a, -um, *first*
sĕnex, sĕnis, *m. old man*
tĕner, -ĕra, -ĕrum, *tender*
turpis, *m. & f.* turpe, *n. disgraceful, base*
vĕtus, *gen.* vĕtĕris, *old*

vīnum, -i, *n. wine*
virtūs, virtūtis, *f. virtue*
vĭtĭum, -i, *n. vice*
quem, *pron. acc. m. whom?*
quis, *pron. nom. m. who?*

EXERCISE XXIII.

ăcŭs, -ūs, *f. needle*[1]
adversus, -a -um, *adverse*
arcus, -ūs, *bow*
audītus, -ūs, *hearing*
Caesar, -ăris. *m. Caesar*
cervus, -i, *m. stag*
cōpĭa, -ae, *f. plenty*
cornū, -ūs, *n. horn*
cursus, -ūs, *m. running, course*
dĭgĭtus, -i, *m. finger* [*ferent*
dīversus, -a, -um, *diverse, different*
dūrus, -a, -um, *hard*
fructus, -ūs, *m. fruit*
frūmentum, *n. corn*
gĕlū, -ūs, *n. frost*
gĕnū, -ūs, *n. knee*
glans, glandis, *f. acorn*
mŭlĭer, mŭlĭĕris, *f. woman*
myrtus, -i *or* -ūs, *f. myrtle*
pernĭcĭōsus, -a, -um, *destructive*
pīnus, -ūs, *or* -i, *f. pine-tree*
plebs, plēbis, *f. the common people*
portus, -ūs, *m. harbour*
quercus, -ūs, *f. oak*
rāmus, -i, m. *branch*
Rōmānus, -a, -um, *Roman*
săgitta, -ae, *f. arrow* [*perous*
sĕcundus, -a, um, *second, prosperous*
sĭnister, -tra, -trum, *left*
Scytha, -ae, *m. a Scythian*
sollertĭa, -ae, *f. skill, subtlety*
taurus, -i, *m. bull*
trĭbus, -ūs, *f. tribe*

---

[1] For the future, the quantity of the Nom. of the Fourth Decl. will not be marked. The pupil must bear in mind that the Nom. Sing. of the Fourth Decl. is to be pronounced short, diff. from the Gen. Sing. and Nom. and Acc. Pl. which are long.

## VOCABULARIES. 245

tūtus, -a, -um, *safe*
ūtīlis, *m. & f.* ūtīle, *n. useful*
ūtīlĭtās, ūtīlĭtātis, *f. utility*
vēnātor, vēnātōris, *m. hunter*
ventus, -i, *m. wind*
vīsus, -ūs, *sight*
vulpēs, vulpis, *f. fox*
dătur (*not* dātur) *v. is given*
ăgĭt, *v. drives*
compărat (-ant), *v. obtains* (-*ain*)
expectat, (-ant), *v. awaits* (-*ait*)
intellĕgit, *v. understands*
vītat, (-ant) *v. avoids* (-*oid*)
vulnĕrat (-ant), *v. wounds* (-*nd*)
nāvēs longae, *long ships, i.e. ships of war*

### Exercise XXIV.

ăcĭēs, -ĭēi, *f. line (of battle*
ăprīcus, -a, -um, *sunny*
călor, calōris, *m. heat*
densus, -a, -um, *dense, close*
dĭēs, dĭēi, *f. day*
dŏlor, dolōris, *m. grief*
exercĭtus, -ūs, *m. army*
făcĭēs, -ĭēi, *f. face*
flumen, -ĭnis, *n. river*
fŭga, -ae, *f. flight*
glăcĭēs, -ĭēi, *f. ice*
ĭnĭmīcus, -a, -um, *hostile*
lūx, lūcis, *f. light*
mŏra, -ae, *f. delay*
mĕrīdĭēs, -ĭēi, *f. mid-day*
nŏvus, -a, -um, *new*
nŭmĕrus, -i, *m. number*
pars, partis, *f. part*
plānĭtĭēs, -ĭēi, *f. level ground*
rēs, rei, *f. thing;* rēs adversae, *adverse things, i.e. adversity;* rēs sēcundae, *prosperity*
sōl, sōlis, *m. sun*
spēs, -ĕi, *f. hope*

tantus, -a, -um, *so great*
tĕnuis, *m. & f.* tenue, *n. thin*
ăgĭtur, *v. (he) is (being) driven*
interdum, *adv. sometimes*
tam, *adv. so*

### Exercise XXV.[1]

ămīcĭtĭā, -ae, *f. friendship*
ăsĭnus, *m. ass*
asper, -ĕra, -ĕrum, *rough, rugged*
ăvis, *f. bird*
brăchium, -i, *n. arm*
campus, -i, *m. a plain*
cănis, is, *m. dog*
crūs, crūris, *n. leg*
diffĭcĭlis, -e, *difficult*
discĭpŭlus, -i, *m. pupil*
dissĭmĭlis, -e, *unlike*
fertĭlis, -e, *fertile*
grăcĭlis, -e, *slender*
hŭmĭlis, -e, *low, low-minded*
ĭter, ĭtĭnĕris, *n. journey*
nĭhĭl, *indecl. n. nothing*
pătrĭa, -ae, *f. native land*
praeceptor, -ōris, *m. teacher*
prŏcērus, -a, -um, *tall*
regĭo, -iōnis, *region, district*
săgax, săgācis, *sagacious*
sĭmĭlis, -e, *like*
sŏror, ŏris, *f. sister*
tardus, -a, -um, *slow*
testūdo, -ĭnis, *f. tortoise*
turdus, -i, *m. thrush*
uxor, ōris, *f. wife*
vallis, -is, *f. valley*
vēlōx, -ōcis, *swift*
virtūs, -ūtis, *virtue, valour*
autem, *conj. in the second place, however, but,* (never comes after a stop)
măgis, *adv. more*

---

[1] The pupil must not expect to find the Comparative or Superlative forms of Adjectives in this Vocabulary. In looking out the meaning of **hŭmĭlĭor**, for example, he will only find **hŭmĭlis**, the Positive

246  VOCABULARIES

quam, *conj. than*
quĭdem, *conj. in the first place, indeed*
complet, *v. fills*
dūcit, *v. leads*

### Exercise XXVI.[1]

Ălexander, -dri, *m. Alexander*
Balbus, -i, *m. Balbus*
bĕnĕvŏlus, -a, -um, *well-wishing, benevolent*
castra, -ōrum, *n. pl. camp*
contĭo, -iōnis, *f. speech*
Graecus, -a, -um, *Greek*
maxĭmē, *adv. very greatly, most*
mons, -ntis, *m. mountain*
nātus, -ūs, *m. (used only in Abl. nātu, by birth)*
pĭus, -a, -um, *dutiful*
praestans, -antis, *excellent*
rătĭo, -iōnis, *f. reason*
rĕvĕrentia, ae, *f. reverence*
Sŏcrătēs, -is, *m. Socrates*
tempus, -ŏris, *n. time*
Tullius, -i, *m. Tullius*
quĭd, *pron. (nom. and acc.) n. what?*

### Exercise XXVII.

antīquus, -a, -um, *ancient*
centŭrĭa, -ae, *f. century* [2]
centŭrio, -iōnis, *m. a centurion*
cĕrăsum, -i, *n. cherry*
Dĕcember, *gen. -bris, adj. of December*
Germānus, -a, -um, *German*
Jānŭārĭus, -a, -um, *adj. of January*
jŭvĕnis, -is, *m. young man*
lĕgio, -iōnis, *f. legion*

mănĭpŭlus, -i, *m. maniple* [2]
Martĭus, -ĭa, -ium, *of March*
mensis, -is, *m. month*
nux, nŭcis, *f. nut*
ōvum, -i, *n. egg*
patrimōnium, *n. patrimony*
pauper, -ĕris, *poor*
pōmum, -i, *n. fruit*
Septĕmber, *gen. -bris, adj. of September*
trĭbūnus, -i, *m. tribune*
nunc, *adv. now*
quondam, *adv. formerly, once*
sōlum, *adv. alone*
tum, *adv. then, during that period*
tunc, *adv. then, at that moment*
castīgātur *v. (he) is chastised*


### Exercise XXVIII.

armentum, -i, *n. herd*
ăvārus, -a, -um, *greedy*
cārus, -a, -um, *dear*
cŏrōna, -ae, *f. crown*
ensis, -is, *m. sword*
laus, laudis, *f. praise*
mălum, -i, *n. evil*
mōres, mōrum, *m. pl. conduct*
mōs, mōris, *m. custom*
nēmo, *gen. nullīus, dat. nēmĭni, acc. nēmĭnem, abl. nullo, no one*
scūtum, -i, *n. shield*
tot, *indecl. adj. so many*
ŭterquĕ, utraquĕ, utrumquĕ, *adj. either, both*
valdē, *adv. strongly, exceedingly*
vŏluptās, -tātis, *f. pleasure*
clāmant, *v. (they) cry out*
vītāre, *v. to avoid*

---

[1] The irregular Comparatives and Superlatives given in the text are intended to be learned there, and are consequently not repeated here.

[2] These terms are explained in a sentence of Exercise XXVII.

## VOCABULARIES.

### EXERCISES XXIX. AND XXX.

aliēnus, -a, -um, *another's*
crūdēlis, *m. & f.* -e, *n. cruel*
ignārus, -a, -um, *ignorant*
immĕmor, *gen.* -ŏris, *adj. unmindful*
mĕmor, *gen.* -ŏris, *mindful*
-nĕ? *enclitic, asks a question (emphasizing the word to which it is attached)*
nōnnĕ, *interrog. adv.* (expects the answer ' *Yes* ')
num? *interrog. adv.* (expects the answer ' *No* ')
porcus, -i, *m. pig*
sĕd, *conj. but (on the other hand); but yet; but still*
tālis, -e, *adj. such*
cūrat, *v. (he) takes-care-of*

### EXERCISES XXXI. AND XXXII.

Belga, -ae, *m. a Belgian*
Dārīus, -i, *m. Darius*
doctus, -a, -um, *learned*
fīnītīmus, -a, -um, *bordering on*
fons, fontis, *m. fountain, source*
Gallus, -i, *a Gaul*
Hŏmērus, -i, *m. Homer*
hūc, *adv. hither*
indoctus, -a, -um, *unlearned*
jūre, *rightly,* see Par. 58
maxĭmē, *adv. very greatly, especially, most of all*
mĭsĕrĭcordĭa, -ae, *f. pity*
nĭmĭs, *adv. too much*
nōmen, -ĭnis, *n. name*
părĭter, *adv. equally*
părens, -rentis, *c. parent*
patrĭa, -ae, *f. native land*

poena, -ae, *f.* (mostly pl.) *penalty*
prāvus, -a, -um, *depraved*
proxĭmus, *see Par.* 69
semper, *adv. always*
sŭi, -ōrum, *m. pl.* (*adj. used as noun*) *his* (*own*) *men*
vestis, -is, *f. garment*
Virgĭlĭus, -i, (*more correctly* Vergĭlĭus) *m. Virgil*
vĭtĭōsus, -a, -um, *full-of-vice*
errat, *v.* (*he*) *errs*
gustat, *v.* (*he*) *tastes*
intrat, *v.* (*he*) *enters*
laedit, *v.* (*he*) *hurts*
sĕrit, *v.* (*he*) *sows, plants*
do poenas, *I pay the penalty*

### EXERCISE XXXIII.[1]

[The Conjugation of a Verb is denoted by the figure placed after it.]

Castīgo, -āvi, -ātum, 1, *punish, chastise*
culpo, -āvi, -ātum, 1, *blame*
**do, dĕdi, dătum, dăre**, 1, *give*[2]
dōno, -āvi, -ātum, 1, *present*
ēgrĕgĭus, -a, -um, *excellent*
ēmendo, -āvi, -ātum, 1, *improve*
erro, -āvi, -ātum, 1, *err*
inĭmīcus, -a, -um, *unfriendly*
laudo, -āvi, -ātum, 1, *praise*
monstro, -āvi, -ātum, 1, *show, point out*
optĭmus, -a, -um, *very good*
rŏgo, -āvi, -ātum, 1, *ask*
saepĕ, *adv. often*
sī, *conj. if*
Tullĭa, -iae, f. *Tullia*
vĭtŭpĕro, -āvi, -ātum, 1, *revile*

---

[1] Henceforth words must be looked out in the Vocabularies, pp. 248-327.
[2] This Verb is irregular.

# APPENDIX X.

# VOCABULARY—I.

## LATIN INTO ENGLISH.

### LIST OF ABBREVIATIONS.

| | | | | |
|---|---|---|---|---|
| *abl.* | = ablative | | *indef.* | = indefinite |
| *acc.* | = accusative | | *interj.* | = interjection |
| *adj.* | = adjective | | *inter.* | = interrogative |
| *adv.* | = adverb | | *m.* | = masculine |
| *c.* | = common gender | | *n.* | = neuter |
| *comp.* | = comparative | | *num.* | = numeral |
| *conj.* | = conjunction | | *p.* | = page |
| *dat.* | = dative | | *part.* | = participle |
| *def.* | = defective | | *pass.* | = passive |
| *dep.* | = deponent | | *pl.* | = plural |
| *f.* | = feminine | | *prep.* | = preposition |
| *g. gen., dat.,* | = governs the gen., | | *pron.* | = pronoun |
| *abl., &c.* | dat., abl., &c. | | *rel.* | = relative |
| *gen.* | = genitive | | *sing.* | = singular |
| *impers.* | = impersonal verb | | *sup.* | = superlative |
| *indec.* | = indeclinable | | *v.* | = verb |

1, 2, 3, 4, indicate the Conjugation of a Verb.

**Ab** (ā, abs), *prep.* with *abl. from, by*
ăbĕo, -ii *or* -ivi, -itum, -ire, 4, *to go away*
ăbhinc, *adv.* (216) (313) *ago* (*with acc. or abl.*)
abjĭcĭo, -jēci, -jectum, 3, *cast away*
absens, -entis, *absent*
abstŭli, *see* aufĕro
absum, afui, abesse, *I am absent;*
 mĭnĭmum ăbest quīn pĕream, *I am almost perishing,* Par. 195;
 ăbest quinquĕ milĭa passŭum, *he is five miles off;* prŏpĕ ăbest ā nōbīs, *he is close to us* [*the forms* abfui, abfūtūrus, &c., *for* afui, afūtūrus, &c., *are incorrect*]
absūmo, -mpsi, -mptum, 3, *consume, destroy*
absurdus, -a, -um, *adj. absurd*
ăbundo, -āvi, -ātum, 1, *abound*
ăbūtor, -ūsus, 3, *v. dep. misuse, use*

ac, *a form of* atque
accēdo, -essi, -essum, 3, *approach*
accĭdo, -ĭdi *(no sup.)* 3, *n. v. to happen (of ill fortune)* [*take*
accĭpĭo, -cēpi, -ceptum, 3, *receive,*
accumbo, -cŭbŭi, -cŭbĭtum, 3, *recline (at dinner)*
accurro, -cŭcurri & -curri, -cursum, 3, *run up,* or *towards*
accūso, -āvi, -ātum, 1, *accuse (g. gen. of the charge)*
ācer, -cris, -cre, *keen, sharp, active*
ăcerbus, -a, -um, *bitter, painful*
Achillēs, -is, m. *Achilles*
ăcĭes, -iēi, f. *line (of battle)*
ăcŭo, -ui, -ūtum, 3, *I sharpen*
ăcus, -ûs, f. *needle*
ăcūtŭs, -a, -um, *sharp*
ăd, *prep. (g. acc.) to, at, near, towards, for* (185, 186)
ădămantĭnus, -a, -um, *adamantine*
ădĕo, *adv. so, to such an extent*
ădĕo, -ivi or -ii, -ĭtum, 4, *go to, come to, visit, consult (g. acc.)*
ădeptus, *see* ădĭpiscor
ădhĭbĕo, -ŭi, -ĭtum, 2, *apply*
ădhūc, *adv. as yet*
ădĭpiscor, -eptus, 3, *acquire. obtain*
adjūmentum, -i, n. *assistance*
adjŭvo, -jūvi, -jūtum, 1, *assist*
admīror, -ātus, 1, *wonder at, admire*
admitto, -mīsi, -missum, 3, *to admit;* admīsit in se (acc) sceĭus, *he gave crime entrance into himself,* i.e. *committed a crime*
admŏneo, -ui, -ĭtum, 2, *warn ; remind,* (eum eius rei)
ădŏlescens, *see* ădŭlescens
adsum, affŭi, ădesse, *I am present, stand by, side with*
ădūlātĭo, -iōnis, f. *flattery*
adūlātor, -ōris, m. *flatterer*
ădūlescens, -ntis, m. *young men*
advĕnĭo, -vēni, -ventum, 4, *arrive*
adventus, -ûs, m. *arrival*
adversus, -a, -um, *adverse ;* res adversae, *adversity*

adversŭs or -um, *prep. (g. acc.) towards, against*
aedēs, -is, f. *sing. temple :* pl. *house*
aedĭfĭcĭum, -ii, n. *building*
aedĭfĭco, -āvi, -ātum, 1. *build*
Aedŭi, -ōrum, m. pl. *the Aedui, a Gallic tribe*
aeger, -gra, -grum, *sick ;* aegrē fĕro hoc, *I bear this ill,* i.e. *I resent this*
Aegyptus, -i, f. *Egypt* [*just*
aequus, -a, -um, *adj. level, even,*
āĕr, ăĕris. m. *the air*
aes. aeris, n. *brass, money ;* aes aliēnum, *debt*
aestas, -ātis, f. *summer*
aestĭmo, -āvi, -ātum, 1, *I value ; with* magni, plūris, &c. (283)
aetas, -ātis, f. *age, time of life*
aeternus, -a, -um, *adj. eternal*
aether, -ĕris, m. *the upper air, heaven*
affĕro, attŭli, allātum, afferre. *I bring to, cause ;* (impers.) allatum est, *word was brought*
afflīcĭo, -fēci, fectum, 3, *treat;* aff. te hŏnōre, voluptāte, supplĭcĭo, metu. *I treat you with honour, pleasure, &c.* i.e. *I honour you, cause you pleasure, visit you with punishment, &c.*
affirmo, -āvi, -ātum, 1. *assert*
afflīgo, -ixi, -ictum, 3, *I cast down, prostrate*
Africa, -ae, f. *Africa*
ăger, -gri, m. *field, lands*
agger, -ĕris, m. *a mound*
agnosco, -nōvi, -uĭtum. 3. *recognize*
ăgo, -ēgi, -actum, 3, *drive, lead, act, do :* id ăgo ut, *I am doing my best to ;* grātiās ăgĕre, *to return thanks;* causam a., *plead a cause ;* vītam a., *lead a life ;* nihil a., *do nothing :* actum est de nobis, *it is all over with us ;* hoc ăgĭtur. *this is being done,* i.e. *this is the point,* or *question*

agrĭcŏla, -ae, *m. husbandman*
aīo, *v. def say, see* p. 215 ; ut aiunt, *as they say,* i.e. *as the proverb goes*
āla, -ae, *f. wing*
Albānus, -a, -um, *Alban*
albus, -a, -um, *white*
Alcĭbĭădes, -is, *m. Alcibiades*
Ălexander, -dri, *m. Alexander (the Great)* [*time*
ălias, *adv. at one time, at another*
ălĭbi, *adv. at one place, at another place;* ălii a. stant, *some stand in one place, others in another*
aliēnus, -a, -um, *another's;* ălĭēna suis antĕpōnit, *he places the interests of others above his own;* aes ălĭēnum, *debt;* in aerē ă'iēno esse, *to be in debt* [*place*
ălĭo, *adv. to one place, to another*
ălĭquando, *adv. sometimes, at some time or other*
ălĭquis, -quae, -quid, *pron. some one, something, decl. like* quis
ălĭquo, *adv. somewhither;* ălĭquo terrārum, (*part. gen.*) *to some place in the world*
ălĭter, *adv. otherwise, differently*
ălius, -a, -ud, *irr. adj. one of any number, one another. See* Par. 86
allātum, *see* affero
allĭcĭo, -lexi, -lectum, 3, *allure*
Allŏbrŏges, -um, *m. the Allobroges*
allŏquor, -lŏcūtus, 3, *dep. speak to, accost (g. acc.)*
almus, -a, -um, *loving*
ălo, ălŭi, altum, 3, *nourish, rear*
Alpēs, -ium, *f. pl. the Alps.*
alter, -tĕra, -tĕrum, (*gen.* -erīus, *dat.* -eri), *one of two, second, the other;* unus et a. *one or two;* vīcēsĭmus a., *twenty-first*
altus, -a, -um, *high, deep*
ămābĭlis, -e, *adj. lovely* [Par. 288
ămans, -ntis, *adj. loving,* (*g. gen.*)
ămārus, -a, -um, *bitter*
ambo, -ae, -o, *both. See* Par. 77

ambŭlo, -āvi, -ātum, *I walk*
āmens, -ntis, *senseless, mad*
amĭcĭo, -ĭcŭi *or* -ixi, -ictum, 4, *cover, clothe*
ămĭcĭtĭa, -ae, *f. friendship*
ămīcus, -i, *m. friend*
ămo, -āvi, -ātum, 1, *love*
ămor, -ōris, *m. love*
āmitto, -mīsi, -missum, 3, *lose*
amnis, -is, *m. river*
ăn, *or (in dep. quest., see* Par. 171); (*also in direct quest., an alternative being understood*), An nōs prōdēs? i.e. (*you will be faithful, will you not?*) *Or will you actually betray us?* (171, 302)
Angli, -ōrum, *m. pl. Englishmen*
anguis, -is, *m. snake*
angustus, -a, -um, *adj. narrow*
ănĭmadverto, -i, -sum, 3, *observe*
ănĭmăl, -ălis, *n. animal.*
ănĭmus, -i, *m. mind, soul, courage*
annōn, *see* Par. 172
annus, -i, *m. year* [*vestigate*
anquīro, -quīsīvi, -quīsītum, 3, *in-*
anser, -ĕris, *m. goose*
antĕ, *prep. (g. acc.) before,* (183); *adv.* paucis ante annis, *a few years before;* N.B.—*distinguish the prep. from the conj.* ante... quam, *or* antequam ; anteā, *adv. before those things, beforehand*
antĕpōno, -pŏsui, -pŏsĭtum, 3, *prefer (g. acc. and dat.)* (192)
antĕquam, *conj. before, until*
Anthrŏpŏphăgi, -ōrum, *m. pl. man-eaters, cannibals*
antīquus, -a, -um, *ancient*
ānŭlus (*not* annŭlus), -i, *m. ring*
ănŭs, -ūs, *f. old woman*
aper, -pri, *m. wild boar*
ăpĕrio, ăpĕrŭi, ăpertum, 4, *open*
ăpertus, -a, -um, *open, clear*
Apollo, -ĭnis, *m. Apollo*
appello, -āvi, -ātum, 1, *call*
aprīcus, -a, -um, *sunny*
ăpŭd, *prep. g. acc. See* Par. 183

aptus, -a, -um, *fit*
aqua, -ae, *f. water*
aquila, -ae, *f. an eagle*
arbiter, -tri, *m. umpire*
arbitror, -atus, 1, (*v. dep.*) *consider, judge*
arbor, -ōris, *f. tree*
Archimēdēs, -is, *m. Archimedes*
arci, *see* arx
arcus, -ūs, *m. bow*
ardĕo, arsi, -sum, 2, *v. intr., I burn, am on fire*
ardūus, -a, -um, *adj. lofty, steep, difficult*
argenteus, -a, -um, *silver*
argentum, -i, *n. silver ; money*
Ariovistus, -i, *m. Ariovistus*
arma, -ōrum, *n. pl. arms*
Armĕnia, -ae, *f. Armenia*
armentum, -i, *n. herd*
armo, -āvi, -ātum, 1, *arm, equip*
aro, -āvi, -ātum, 1, *plough*
Arpīnum, -i, *n. Arpinum, the birth-place of Cicero*
ars, artis, *f. art, handicraft*
arvum, -i, *n. corn-field*
arx, arcis, *f. citadel*
as, assis, *m. the smallest Roman coin ; it may be translated a far-thing (used in the genit. of indef. price ; see Ex. LXXX.)*
Asia, -ae, *f. Asia (mostly Ā)*
asinus, -i, *m. ass*
asper, -ĕra, -ĕrum, *rough, rugged*
aspernor, -ātus, 1, *v. dep. reject, despise*
aspicio, -spexi, -spectum, 3, *look at*
assĕquor, -secutus, 3, *attain*
at, *conj. but (more abrupt than* sed)
ater, atra, atrum, *black, gloomy*
Athēnae, -ārum, *f. pl. Athens*
Athēniensis, -e, *Athenian*
atque (or ac, *but not before vowels*). *conj. and further, and ; often used to couple words of similar meaning, e.g.* socii atque amici, honestissimus atque ornatissimus

atrox, -ōcis, *stern, gloomy*
auctor, -ōris, *m. adviser, author :* Tullio auctōre, *at the advice of Tullius* (197)
auctōrĭtās, -ātis, *f. authority*
auctumnus, -i, *m. autumn*
audactĕr, *adv. boldly, daringly*
audāx, -ācis, *bold*
audĕo, ausus sum, audēre, 2, *to dare, venture*
audio, -īvi, -ītum, 4, *hear*
audītus, -us, *m. hearing*
aufĕro, abstŭli, ablātum aufern̄, *I carry away, take away*
augeo, auxi, auctum, 2, *augment*
Augustus, -i, *m. Augustus, the first emperor of Rome*
aurĕus, -a, -um, *golden*
aurīga, -ae, *m. charioteer*
auris, -is, *f. an ear*
aurum, -i, *n. gold*
ausus, *see* audeo
Auster, -tri, *m. South wind* [173]
aut...aut, *either...or else* (157a,
autem, *conj. but, in the second place (placed after the first word of the clause to which it belongs) ; see* quidem (67)
auxilium, -ii, *n. help, aid*
avārus, -a, -um, *avaricious, greedy*
avidus, -a, -um, *greedy*
avis, -is, *f. bird*
avus, -i, *m. a grandfather*

**Bǎbylōn**, -ōnis, *f. Babylon*
balaena, -ae, *f. a whale*
Balbus, -i, *m. Balbus*
barbarus, -a, -um, *barbarian*
beātē, *adv. happily*
beātus, -a -um, *adj. happy*
Belga, -ae, *m. a Belgian*
bellĭcōsus, -a, -um, *adj. warlike*
bello, -āvi, -ātum, 1, *I wage war*
bellum, -i, *n. war*
belŭa, -ae, *f. a great beast*
bĕnĕ, *adv. well*
bĕnĕfĭcĭum, -ii, *n. benefit*

běněfĭcus, -a, -um, *beneficent*
běněvŏlentĭa, -ae, *f. benevolence*
běněvŏlus, -a, -um, *well-wishing, benevolent. See Par. 68a*
běnignē, *adv. kindly*
běnignus, -a, -um, *kind*
bestĭa, -ae, *f. a beast;* damnāri ad bestĭas, *to be condemned to be exposed to the beasts (in the amphitheatre)*
bĭbo, bĭbi, bĭbĭtum, 3, *I drink*
Bĭbŭlus, -i, *m. Bibulus*
bĭdŭum, -i, *n. two days;* bĭdui īter, *two days' journey*
biennium, -i, *n. two years*
bīni, -ae, -a, *two apiece* (314)
bĭs, *adv. twice*
blandĭor, -ītus, with *dat.* 4, *v. dep. I flatter, win upon*
bŏna, -ōrum, *n. pl. goods, blessings*
bŏnus, -a, -um, *adj. good* [311
bōs, bŏvis, *c. ox, cow, see* Par.
bracchium, -i, *n. arm*
brěvis, -e, *short, brief*
Brĭtannĭa, -ae, *f. Britain*
Brĭtannus, -i, *m. a Briton*
Brūtus, -i, *m. Brutus*
būbus, *see* bōs

Cădāver, -ĕris, *n. corpse*
cădo, cěcĭdi, cāsum, 3, *I fall;* N.B. *distinguish this from* cěcīdi
caecus, -a, -um, *adj. blind*
caedēs, -is, *f. slaughter*
caedo, cecīdī, caesum, 3, *strike, cut down, slay;* N.B. *distinguish this from* cěcĭdi
caelestis, -e, *celestial*
caelĭcŏlae, -ārum, *m. pl. lit. heaven-dwellers,* i.e. *gods*
caelum, -i, *n. heaven*
Caesar, -ăris, *m. Caesar*
călămĭtas, -ātis, *f. calamity*
calcăr, -āris, *n. spur*
călix, -ĭcis, *m. cup*
călor, ōris, *m. heat*
Cămillus, -i, *m. Camillus*

Campānĭa, -ae, *f. Campania*
campus, -i, *m. plain*
cancer, -cri, *m. crab*
cănis, -is, *c. dog*
Cannae, -ārum, *f. pl. Cannae, a village where Hannibal defeated the Romans*
căno, cěcĭni, cantum, 3, *sing;* tŭbā cěcĭnit, *the trumpet sounded*
canto, -āvi, -atum, 1, *I sing*
cantus, -ūs, *m. song*
căper, -pri, *m. goat*
căpillus, -i, *m. hair (pl. once in Cicero, but in poetry often)*
căpio, cēpi, captum, 3, *take* [ive
captīvus (*or* captus) -a, -um, *capt-*
Căpŭa, -ae, *f. Capua, the most luxurious city in Italy*
căpŭt, -ĭtis, *n. head;* gentis căput, *the capital city of the nation;* căpĭte multo, *I punish with death;* căpĭtis damno, *I condemn to death (Ex. LXXX.)*
carcer, -ĕris, *m. prison*
cardo, -ĭnis, *m. hinge*
căreo, -ui, 2, *I am without (g. abl.);* făcĭle c. vīno, *I easily do without wine*
carmĕn, -ĭnis, *n. song*
căro, carnis, *f. flesh* [ginian
Carthăgĭnĭensis, -e, *adj. Cartha-*
Carthāgo, ĭnis, *f. Carthage*
cārus, -a, -um, *dear*
căsa, -ae *f. cottage*
cāsĕus, -i, *m. cheese*
castīgo, -āvi, -ātum, 1, *chastise punish*
castră, -ōrum, *n. pl. camp*
cāsus, -ūs, *m. chance, accident;* dīversis cāsibus, *with varied fortunes*
cătēna, -ae, *f. chain*
Cătĭlīna, -ae, *m. Catiline*
Căto, -ōnis, *m. Cato*
causa, -ae, *f. cause;* audiendi causā, *for the sake of hearing;* causam ēgit, *he pleaded a cause*

căvĕo, căvi, cautum, 2, *beware, beware of* (*g. acc.*); căvē nē făcĭas, *take care not to do*; căvēbātur, *precautions were taken*
cĕcĭdi, *see* cădo *and* caedo
cĕdo, cessi, cessum, 3, *yield*; c. tĭbĭ, *I yield to you*; c. ăcĭē *or* ex ăcĭē, *I retire from the battle*
cĕler, -ĕris, -ĕre, *swift*; cĕlĕrĭter, *adv. swiftly* (61)
cĕlĕrĭtas, -tātis, *f. speed*
cēlo, -āvi, -ātum, 1, *conceal*, (*g. two acc.*). *See Par.* 312
celsus, -a, -um, *adj. lofty, tall*
cēna, -ae, *f. dinner*; cēno, -āvi, -ātum, 1, *dine* (*perf. also* cēnātus sum); cenātus, *having dined*
centum, *see Par.* 81
centŭrĭa, -ae, *f. a* (*military*) *century* (*see Ex.* XXVII., *sent.* 8)
centŭrĭo, -ĭōnis, *m. centurion* (*the officer of a century*)
cĕrăsum, -i, *n. cherry*
cĕrăsus, -i, *f. the cherry-tree*
cĕrĕbrum, -i, *n. brain*
Cĕrēs, Cĕrĕris, *f. Ceres*
certāmen, -ĭnis, *n. contest, strife*; in certāmen hŏnōris vēnērunt, *they entered into a competition for distinction*
cerno, 3, *I see, discern*
certus, -a, -um, *adj. certain*; certĭōrem te fēci, *I informed you* (*foll. by Gen., or Object Infinitive*); *fixed*, certum ŏpus, *a fixed task*
cervus, -i, *m. stag*
[cēter], -ĕra, -ĕrum, *adj. the rest, the rest of* (*see Eng. Latin Vocab., of*); *pl.* cētĕri, *the others*
cĭbus, -i, *m. food*
Cĭcĕro, -ōnis, *m. Cicero*
cĭnis, cĭnĕris, *m. ashes*
cingo, -nxi, -nctum, 3, *I surround*
circā, circum, *prep.* (*g. acc.*) *around*
circĭter, *prep.* with *acc. about*
circumdo, -dăre, -dĕdi, -dătum, 1, (1) *to put round* (*acc. and dat.*); (2) *to surround* (*acc. and abl.*)
circumspĭcio, -spexi, -spectum, 3, *look round*
circumsto, -stĕti, -stāre, *stand round*; (part. *as noun*) circumstantes, -ium, *by-standers* [*of*
cis, citrā, *prep.* (*g. acc.*) *on this side*
Cisalpīnus, -a, -um, *on this side of the Alps, Cisalpine*
cĭthăra, -ae, *f. lute*
cĭto, *adv. quickly*; cĭtius, *more quickly*
cīvīlis, -e, *adj. belonging to a citizen, civil*
cīvis, -is, *m. citizen*
cīvĭtas, -tātis, *f. state, citizenship*; dōnant ĕum cīvĭtātē, *they present him with the citizenship*
clādēs, -is, *f. slaughter*
clam, *adv. secretly*; *prep.* (*g. abl.*) *without the knowledge of*
clāmo, -āvi, -ātum, 1, *cry out, shout*
clāmor, -ōris, *m. clamour, shout*
claudo, -si, -sum, 3, *shut*
clārus, -a, -um, *clear, renowned*
classis, -is, *f. a fleet*
clēmenter, *adv. gently, mercifully*
coactus, *see* cōgo
coelestis, *see* caelestis.
coelum, *see* caelum
coena, *see* cēna
coeno, *see* cēno
cŏĕo, -ĭvi *or* -ĭi, ĭtum, 4, *join together* (*v. intrans.*)
cŏercĕo, -ŭi, -ĭtum, 2, *restrain*
cōgĭto, -āvi, -ātum, 1, *I think, meditate*
cognosco, -nōvi, -nĭtum, 3, *learn, ascertain*
cōgo, cŏēgi, cŏactum, 3 *compel*
cŏhors, -rtis, *f. cohort, a tenth part of the legion*
cŏhortor, -ātus, 1, *v. dep. encourage*
collĭgo, -ēgi, -ectum, 3, *collect*

collis, -is, m., *hill*
collŏquĭum, -i, n. *conversation*
collŏquor, -cūtus, 3, v. dep. *I converse*
collŭvĭes, (acc. -em, abl. -ē) f. *medley, confusion*
cŏlo, cŏlŭi, cultum, 3, *cultivate, worship, cherish*
cŏlōnĭa, -ae, f. *a colony*
cŏlōnus, -i, m. *farmer*
cŏlor, -ōris, m. *colour*
cŏlumba, -ae, f. *dove*
cŏlŭber, -bri, m. *snake*
cŏmĕs, -ĭtis, m. *companion* [pany
cŏmĭtor, -ātus, 1, v. dep. *I accompany*
commĕātus, -ūs, m. *provisions, supplies*
commĕmŏrātĭo, -ĭōnis, f. *commemoration, mention*
commīlĭto, -ōnis, m. *fellow-soldier*
commĭnus, adv. *hand to hand*
committo, -mīsi, -missum, 3, *commit; c.* proelium, *join* (lit. *send together*) *battle*
compăro, -āvi, -ātum, 1, *get together, obtain*
compello, -pŭli, -pulsum, 3, *drive together*
compĕrĭo, -pĕri, -pertum, 4, *find, ascertain;* compertum hăbeo, *I have (it) ascertained (with acc. and inf.)*
compĕs, -pĕdis, f. *fetter*
compleo, -ēvi, -ētum, 2, *fill*
comprĕhendo (or comprendo), -di, -sum, 3, *I seize* [retire
concēdo, -essi, -essum, 3, *yield,*
concordĭa, -ae, f. *concord*
concrĕmo, -āvi, -ātum, 1, *burn up*
condemno, -āvi, -ātum, 1, *condemn*
condĭcĭo, -ĭōnis, (*less correctly* condĭtĭo), f. *condition;* (*in pl.*) *terms (of peace,* &c.)
condūco, -xi, -ctum, 3, *hire*
condo, -dĭdi, -dĭtum, 3, *found;* post condĭtam urbem, *after the foundation of the city*

confĕro, -tŭli, collātum, conferre, 3, *irr. I bring together, betake;* se contŭlit rūs, *he betook himself to the country*
confessus, *see* confĭtĕor
confĭcĭo, -fēci, -fectum, 3, *I finish, accomplish*
confīdo, -īsus ·sum, 3, g. dat. *I trust*
confĭtĕor, -fessus, 2, *confess*
confŭgĭo, -fūgi, 3, *I flee for refuge*
conjĭcĭo, -jēci, -jectum, 3, *hurl*
conjūrātĭo, -ōnis, f. *a conspiracy*
conjūrātus, -i, m. *conspirator*
cōnor, -ātus, 1. v. dep. *attempt*
conscendo, -di, -sum, 3, *mount, go on board (ship)*
conscĭentĭa, ae, f. *conscience*
conscrībo, -scripsi, -scriptum, 3, *enrol (soldiers)*
consentĭo, -nsi, -nsum, 4, *agree*
conservo, -āvi, -ātum, 1, *I preserve, maintain*
consĭlĭum, ii, n. *plan, purpose, wisdom*
constanter, adv. *steadily, firmly*
constantĭa, -ae, f. *constancy, firmness*
constat, -stĭtit, 1, *impers. v. it is agreed, well-known* &c.
constĭtŭo, -ŭi, -ūtum, 3, *determine*
consuētūdo, -ĭnis, f. *habit*
consul, -ŭlis, m. *consul;* Gaio et Balbo consŭlĭbus, *Gaius and Balbus being consuls*
consŭlātus, -ūs, m. *office of consul, consulate*
consŭlo, -lŭi, -ltum, 3, *consult;* c. tibi, *I c. your interests;* c. te, *I consult you*
consumo, -mpsi, -mptum, 3, *consume, waste away*
contemno, -mpsi, -mptum, 3, *despise*
contemplor, -ātus, 1, v. dep. *contemplate*
contendo, -di, -sum, *or* -tum, 3 *gaze at, hasten* (278)

contentus. -a, -um (*g. abl.*) *contented* (278)
contĭnĕo, -ŭi, -entum, 2, *I hold together*
contingo, -tĭgi, 3, *befall*; contĭgit mĭhĭ, *it was my good luck*
contĭnŭo, *adv. forthwith*; *N.B. not continually*
contĭo, -ĭōnis, *f. speech, harangue*
contrā, *prep.* (*g. acc.*) *against*
contrăho, -axi, -actum, 3, *draw together*
contrărius, a, -um, *contrary* (189)
contŭmēlĭa, -ae, *f. an insult*
convălesco, -vălŭi, 3, *recover from illness*
convĕnĭo, -vēni, -ventum, 4, *I assemble*
converto, -verti, -versum, 3, *turn round*; conversus, *being turned* i.e. *turning* (*himself*)
convīcĭum, -i, *n. reviling, abuse*
convŏco, -āvi, -atum, 1, *call together*
cŏpĭa, -ae, *f. plenty*; cŏpĭae, -ārum, *f. pl. forces*
cŏr, cordis, *n. the heart*
cōram, *prep.* (*g. abl.*) *in presence of*
Cŏrinthus, -i, *f. Corinth*
Cornēlĭa, -ae, *f. Cornelia*
cornū, -ūs, *n. a horn*
cŏrōna, -ae, *f. a crown*
corpus, -ŏris, *n. body*
corrĭgo, -exi, -ectum, 3, *correct*
corrĭpĭo, -rĭpŭi, -reptum, 3, *snatch away*; morbo correptus est, *he was carried off by disease*
cottĭdĭe, *see* quŏtĭdĭē
crās, *adv. to-morrow*
Crassus, -i, *m. Crassus, a miserly millionaire of the times of Cicero*
creātor, -ōris, *m. creator* [*peated*
crēber, - bra, -brum, *frequent, re-*
crēdĭbĭlis, -e, *adj. credible* [*dat.*]
crēdo, -dĭdi, -dĭtum, 3, *believe* (*g.*)
crĕo, -āvi, -ātum, 1, *I create, make*
Crēta, -ae, *f. Crete*

crīmen, -ĭnis, *n. charge, accusation*
crīnis, -is, *m. hair*
crŭcĭātus, -ūs, *m. torture*
crūdēlis, -e, *cruel*
crūdēlĭtas, -ātis, *f. cruelty*
crūs, crūris, *n. leg*
culpa, -ae, *f. blame, fault*; *see* extrā
culpo, -āvi, -atum, 1, *blame*
culter, -tri, *m. knife*
cum, *prep.* (*g. abl.*) *with*
cum, (*sometimes wrongly spelt* quum) *conj. when*, (Par. 151) *since*; cum . . . tum *not only . . . but also*; N.B. — cum *is never interrogative*: *see* quando
Cūmae, -ārum, *f. pl. Cumæ,* (*a city*)
cunctor, -atus, 1 (*r. dep.*) *delay*
cunctus, -a, -um, *adj. all* (*together*)
cŭpĭdĭtas, -ātis, *f. desire, passion*
cŭpĭdus, -a, -um, *fond of* (*g. gen.*)
cŭpĭo, -īvi and -ĭi, -ītum, 3, *desire*
cūr, *adv. why?* (*also conj. in dep. sent.*); nōn est cūr tĭmĕas, *there is not* (*any reason*) *why you should fear*
cūra, -ae, *f. care*
cūro, -āvi, -ātum, 1, *take care*; cūrā ut, *or* nē, ĕās *take care to*, *or not to, go*
curro, cŭcurri, cursum, 3, *run*
currus, -ūs, *m. chariot*
cursus, -ūs, *m. running, course*
custōdĭo, -īvi *or* -ĭi, -ītum, 4, *guard*
custos, custōdis, *m. a guardian*
Cyprus, -i, *f. Cyprus*

**Damno**, -āvi, -atum, 1, *condemn*
Dărĭus, -i, *m. Darius*
dē, *prep.* (*g. abl.*) *down from, from, concerning*
dĕa, -ae, *f. a goddess* (*dat. and abl. pl.* dĕābus) *see* Par. 311
dēbĕo, -ŭi, -ītum, 2, *owe*: dēbŭi dāre, *I ought to have given* (223)
dēbĭlis, -e, *adj. feeble*
dĕcem, *see* Par. 81

December, -bris, -bre, *of December.*
See Appendix VI., p. 229
dĕcemvir, -viri, *m. decemvir, one of ten commissioners*
dĕcĕt, dĕcŭit, dĕcērĕ, 2, *impers. v. it becomes, befits,* Par. 220.
dĕcĭmus, -a, -um, Par. 81.
dĕcĭpĭo, -cēpi, -ceptum, 3, *I deceive*
dĕcŏro, -āvi, ātum, 1, *honour, distinguish*
dĕcus, -ŏris, *n. ornament, honour, glory; Horace addresses his patron as "my guardian and glory* (dĕcus)"
dēdĕcĕt, dĕcŭit, dĕcērĕ, 2, *impers. v. it misbecomes*
dēdĕcus, -ŏris, n. *disgrace, baseness*
dēfendo, -di, -sum, 3, *defend*
dēfensor, -ōris, *a defender*
dēflăgro, -āvi, -ātum, 1, *to be burnt down*
dēfluo, -fluxi, 3, *flow down*
dēformis, -e, *ugly*
dējĭcio, -jēci, -jectum, 3, *cast down*
dēlecto, -āvi, -ātum, 1, *delight*
dēlectus, -ūs, *m. a levy* [out
dēlĕo, -ēvi, -ētum, 2, *destroy, blot*
dēlībĕro, -āvi, -ātum, 1, *deliberate*
dēlĭgo, -lēgi, -lectum, *choose*
Dēlŏs, -i, *f. the isle of Delos, the seat of an oracle of Apollo*
Delphi, -ōrum, *m. pl. Delphi, the city containing the principal oracle of Apollo*
dēmo, dempsi, demptum, 3, *subtract*
Dēmosthĕnēs, -is, *m. Demosthenes*
dēmum, *adv. indeed;* id dēmum, *that, and nothing else;* tum dēmum, *then, and not till then*
dēnārius, -ii, *m. a denarius, a Roman coin worth about 9d.*
dēnĭquĕ (*adv.*) *finally, in short*
densus, -a, -um, *dense, close*
dens, -ntis, *m. tooth*
dĕpello, -pŭli, -pulsum, 3, *drive down*

dēplōro, -āvi, -ātum, 1, *lament over, deplore*
dēposco, -poposci, 3, *demand*
dērīsŭs, -ūs, *m. laughing-stock*
descendo, -scendi, -scensum, 3, *come, or go, down*
descisco, -scīvi, -scītum, 3, *revolt*
dēsĕro, -rui, -rtum, 3, *I abandon*
dēsīdĕro, -āvi, -ātum, 1, *long for* (*what is absent*)
dēsum, -fui, -esse, (*dat.*) *be wanting to, fall short, fail*
dĕtĕgo, -xi, -ctum, 3, *reveal, disclose*
dēterrĕo, -ŭi, -ĭtum, 2, *frighten*
dĕtexo, -texŭi, -textum, 3, *finish weaving, finish*
detĭneo, -ui, 2, *detain, keep back*
dētrăho, -traxi, -tractum, *take away, withdraw*
Dĕus, -i, *m.* God
dēvinco, -vīci, -victum, 3, *subdue*
dextra, -ae, *f. right hand*
Diāna, -ae, *f. Diana*
dīco, -xi, -ctum, 3, *say, speak;* dīcĭtur Tullius, &c., *it is said that Tullius,* &c. (Par 177)
dictĭto, -āvi, -ātum, 1, *say often*
dictum, -i, *a saying*
dĭes, -ēī, *m. (f. in poets) day*
diffĭcĭlis, -e, *difficult* (60) [trust
diffīdo, -fīsus sum, 3, (*g. dat.*) *distrust*
diffindo, -fīdi, -fissum, 3, *cleave asunder*
dīgĕro, -gessi, -gestum, 3, *arrange*
dĭgĭtus, -i, *m. finger* [authority
dignĭtas, -ātis, *f. dignity, worth,*
dignus, -a, -um, *worthy (g. abl.)*
dīlābor, -lapsus, 3, *slip away in different directions*
dīlĭgens, -ntis, *adj. diligent, careful*
dīlĭgenter, *adv. carefully*
diligentia, -ae, *f. diligence*
dīlĭgentissĭmē, *adv. most carefully*
dīlĭgo, -exi, -ectum, 3, *love, esteem*
dīmĭco, -āvi, -ātum, 1, *fight (a battle)*

dīmĭdĭum, -i, n. *half*
dīmitto, -īsi, -issum, 3, *I let go, dismiss*
Dĭŏnÿsĭus, -ii, m. *Dionysius, a tyrant of Syracuse*
dīrĭpĭo, -rĭpŭi, -reptum, 3, *plunder*
discēdo, -cessi, -cessum, 3, *depart*
discĭplīna, -ae, f. *discipline*
discĭpŭlus, -i, m. *pupil*
disco, dĭdĭci, 3, *learn*
discordĭa, -ae, f. *discord*
displĭcĕo, -ŭi, -ĭtum, (g. dat.) 2, *displease*
dispŭto, -āvi, -ātum, 1, *discuss*
dispŭtātio, -ōnis, f. *discussion*
dissĭmĭlis, -e, adj. *unlike; g. gen. or dat. (see Par. 66, 60)*
distrăho, -traxi, -tractum, 3, *draw asunder*
distrĭbuo, -ŭi, -ūtum, 3, *distribute*
diū, adv. *long, for a long time*
diūtius, adv. *longer*
dīversus, -a, -um, *diverse, different*
dīvĕs, -ĭtis, *rich* [*parate*
dīvīdo, -vīsi, -vīsum, 3, *divide, se-*
dīvīnus, -a, -um, *divine*
dīvĭtĭae, -ārum, f. pl. *riches*
do, dĕdi, dătum, dăre, 1, *give;* do litteras, *I date a letter*
dŏcĕo, -ŭi, -ctum, 2, *I teach (g. two acc.) See Par. 312*
doctē, adv. *learnedly, skilfully*
doctrīna, -ae, f. *learning*
doctus, -a, -um, *learned*
dŏlĕo, -ŭi, 2, *grieve*
dŏlor, -ōris, m. *pain, grief*
dŏlus, -i, m. *craft, treachery;* per dŏlum, *treacherously*
dŏmestĭcus, -a, -um, *domestic*
dŏmĭcĭlĭum, -ii, n. *an abode*
dŏmĭna, -ae, f. *mistress*
dŏmĭnātus, -ūs, m. *rule, sovereignty*
dŏmĭnus, -i, m. *master, owner*
dŏmo, -ŭi, -ĭtum, 1, *tame, subdue*
dŏmus, -i, f. *house, home;* dŏmi, *at home;* dŏmum, *homeward,* Pars. 249, 265

dōno, -avi, -ātum, 1, *present, g. acc. and dat. like* do; *or else acc. and abl.;* dōno ĕum ĕquo, *I present him with a horse*
dōnum, -i, n. *gift*
dormĭo, -īvi *or* ĭi, -ītum, 4, *sleep*
dorsum, -i, n. *back*
dŭbĭto, -āvi, -ātum, 1, *doubt*
dŭbĭus, -a, -um, adj. *doubtful;* nōn dŭbĭum est quīn, *it is not doubtful that,* i.e., *there is no doubt that (foll. by Subjunct.)*
dŭcenti, -ae, -a, *see Par. 81* [(237)
dūco, -xi, -ctum, 3, *lead, marry*
dulcis, -e, *sweet, delightful*
dum, conj. *(Par. 272) while*
dūrus, -a, -um, *hard*
dux, dŭcis, c. *leader, general*

Ē, ex, prep. (g. abl.) *out of, from :* ex imprŏbo, fīs imprŏbĭor, *from bad, you are becoming worse*
ĕbur, ĕbŭris, n. *ivory*
eccĕ, interject. *lo! behold!*
ĕdo, ēdi, ēsum, 3, *eat*
ēdŭco, -āvi, -atum, 1, *educate*
ēdūco, -xi, -ctum, 3, *I lead out*
effĕro, extŭli, ēlātum, efferrĕ, 3, irr. v. *I carry out*
efflōresco, -flōrŭi, 3, *blossom*
effŏdio, -fōdi, -fossum, 3, *scoop out, strike out*
effŭgio, -fūgi, 3, *escape (g. acc.)*
ĕgĕo, -ŭi, 2, *to need (g. abl.)*
ĕgo, *see Par. 90*
ĕgrĕgĭus, -a, -um, adj. *excellent, eminent*
eiusmŏdi, *see* mŏdus
ējĭcĭo, -jĕci, -jectum, 3, *cast out*
ēlĕgans, -antis, adj. *elegant, exquisite*
ēlĕgantia, -ae, f. *tastefulness*
ēlĕphas, ĕlĕphantis, m. *(also* ĕlĕphantus, -i, m.*) elephant*
ēlĭcĭo, -lĭcui, -lĭcĭtum, 3, *draw forth*
ēlĭgo, -lēgi, -lectum, 3, *choose*
ēlŏquens, -entis, adj. *eloquent*

s

ēlŏquentĭa, -ae, f. eloquence
ēmendo, -āvi, -ātum, 1, improve
ēmigro, -āvi, -ātum, 1, I depart from
ēmīnus, at a distance [military term opp. to commīnus (cum, mănus), hand to hand]
ĕmo, ĕmi, emptum, 3, I buy
ēnarro, -āvi, -ātum, 1, I relate
ĕnim, conj. for (differs from nam in never standing first in a clause)
ēnītor, -Isus or ixus, 3, v. dep. strive hard
ensis, -is, m. sword
eo, adv. abl. of ĭs, by so much; (with compar.) eo mĕlius (by) so much the better; in eo (166)
ĕo, īvi, ĭtum, īre, go, Par. 241
ĕpistŏla, -ae, f. letter, epistle (perhaps better, ĕpistŭla)
Ĕpămīnondas, -ae, m. Epaminondas, a Theban patriot and general
Ĕphĕsus, -i, f. Ephesus
ĕquĕs, -ĭtis, m. horse soldier
ĕquester, -tris, -e, equestrian
ĕquĭdem (Par. 139) for my part
equĭto, -āvi, -ātum, 1, ride
ĕquĭtātus, -ūs, m. cavalry
ĕquus, -i, m. a horse
ergā, prep. (g. acc.) towards (only of the feelings) Par. 183
ērĭpio, -rĭpui, -reptum, 3, snatch away (g. acc. and dat., 192)
erro, -āvi, -ātum, 1, err, wander
error, -ōris, m. error, fault
ērŭdĭo, -īvi or -ĭi, -ītum, 4, train up, educate
ērŭdītus, -a, -um, adj. trained, educated
ērumpo, -rūpi, -ruptum, 3, burst, rush forth
ĕt, conj. and; et...et, both...and; even, (see Par. 12, 32, 153)
ĕtĭam, conj. also, even (141); (mostly before the word it modifies); nōn sōlum...sed ĕtĭam, not only ...but also

Euphrātēs, -is, m. the Euphrates
Eurīpĭdēs, -is, m. Euripides
Eurōpa, -ae, f. Europe
ēvādo, -vāsi, -vāsum, escape
ēvĕnĭo, -vĕni, -ventum, 4, to happen
ēventŭs -ūs, m., event, result
ex or ĕ, prep. with abl. out of, from; ex ĭtĭnĕre, on a journey
exalbesco, -albui, 3, turn pale
exaudio, -īvi, -ītum, 4, catch the sound of (g. acc.)
excēdo, -essi, -essum, 3, I depart from
exclāmo, -āvi, -ātum, 1, I cry out
excŏlo, -cŏlŭi, -cultum, 3, I cultivate carefully; agri exculti frūmento, lit. fields richly cultivated with corn, i.e. fields with rich corn-crops
excūsātĭo, -iōnis, f., excuse
excūso, -āvi, -ātum, 1, to excuse
excŭtĭo, -cussi, -cussum, 3, shake off
exemplum, -i, n. example
exĕdo, -ēdi, -ēsum, 3, eat out, gnaw away; exēsus pūmex, weather-hollowed rock
exĕo, -īvi or ĭi, -ītum, 4, I go out
exercĕo, -ŭi, -ĭtum, 2, exercise
exercĭtus, -ūs, m. army
exhaurio, -hausi, -haustum, 4, drain off, drink off
exĭgŭus, -a, -um, scanty, little
exĭlĭum, see exsĭlium
exĭtĭum, -ii, n. destruction
exordĭor, -orsus, 4, (v. dep.), begin a web; hence exorsa, -ōrum, n. pl. a beginning
expecto, -āvi, -atum, 1, await
expello, -pŭli, -pulsum, 3, I drive out [awakened
expergiscor, experrectus, 3, I am
expĕrĭentĭa, -ae, f. experience
expĕrĭor, -pertus, 4, dep. try, experience

expers, -rtis, *destitute of* (*g. gen.*)
expĕto, -īvi, -ītum, 3, *seek out*
explōrātor, -ōris, *m. spy, scout*
explōro, -āvi, -ātum, 1, *investigate*
expōno, -pōsui, -pōsĭtum, 3, *put forth, disembark*
expugno, -āvi, ātum, 1, *take by storm* [*destroy*
exscindo, -scĭdi, -scissum, 3, *rend,*
exsĭlio, -sĭlui, -sultum, 4, *leap forth*
exsĭlium, -i, *n. exile*
exstrŭo, -xi, -ctum, 3, *build up*
extĭmesco, -tĭmŭi, 3, *take alarm at* (*acc.*)
extrā, *prep.* (*g. acc.*) *outside of;* extrā culpam, *free from blame*
extrăho, -traxi, -tractum, 3, *draw out*
extrēmus, -a, -um, *last,* Par. 69
exulto, -āvi, -ātum, 1, *exult*
exŭo, -ŭi, -ūtum, 3, *strip off*

Făber, -bri, *m. workman, artificer*
Fābĭus, -ii, *m.* Quintus Fabius Maximus, *called* Cunctātor, *because by "delaying action" he restored success to Rome in the Second Punic War*
făbŭla, -ae, *f. story, fable*
făcĭes, -ēi, *f. face*
făcĭlĕ, *adv. easily;* comp. făcĭlius
făcĭlis, -e, *adj. easy* (60) [*crime*
făcĭnus, -ŏris, *n. daring deed,*
făcĭo, fēci, factum, făcĕrĕ, 3, *make, do;* făc (ut) vĕnĭas, *cause that you,* i.e. *take care to, come;* (*with* assis, flocci) *I value* (284)
factum, -i, *n. deed*
fallāx, -ācis, *deceitful*
fallo, fĕfelli, falsum, 3, *deceive;* fidem fĕfellit, *he broke his word;* non f. ŏpīnĭōnem, *it did not deceive our expectation*
falsus, -a, -um, *false*
fāma, -ae, *f. fame, reputation;* Fāma, *the goddess Fame*
fămĭlĭāris, -e, *belonging to the household;* rēs f. *one's property, estate*
fămēs, -is, *f. hunger*
fās, *n.* indecl. *divine law, heaven's will;* contrā jūs fāsque, *against human and divine law*
fascis, -is, *m. bundle, faggot;* fascēs, *the rods carried before consuls*
fătĕor, fassus, 2, *dep. confess*
fātum, -i, *n. fate*
faux, -cis, *f. jaw*
făveo, fāvi, fautum, 2, *favour* (*g. dat.*)
febris, -is, *f.* (-im *or* -em, -ī *or* -ĕ), *fever*
fēlīcĭtĕr, *adv. luckily, prosperously*
fēlīx, -īcis, *happy, fortunate*
fēmĭna, -ae, *f. a woman*
fĕra, -ae, *f. a wild beast*
fĕrax, -ācis, *fruitful*
fĕrē, *adv. almost, commonly;* nēmo fĕrē, *hardly anyone*
fĕrĭtas, -ātis, *f. savageness* [*peace*
fĕrĭo, 4, *strike;* f. pācem, *I make*
fĕro, tŭli, lātum, ferre, *bear, carry, endure;* fertur Gaius dixisse, *it is reported that Gaius said*
fĕrōx, -ōcis, *adj. fierce, spirited*
ferrum, -i, *n. iron, sword*
fertĭlis, -e, *fertile*
fĕrus, -a, -um, *savage, wild*
fessus, -a, -um, *weary*
fētus, -ūs, *m. offspring*
fīcus, -ūs, *f. a fig*
fīdēlis, -e, *adj. faithful*
fīdes, -ĕi, *f. faith;* servo fīdem, *I keep my word*
fīdo, fīsus sum. fīdere, 3, (*g. dat.* or *abl.*) *I trust*
fīdus, -a, -um, *adj. faithful*
fīgo, fixi, fixum, 3, *fix*
fīlĭa, -ae, *f. a daughter*
fīlĭus, -ii, *m. a son*
fingo, finxi, fictum, 3, *feign*
fīnĭo, -īvi, -ii, -ītum, 4, *I end*
fīnis, -is, *m. end, boundary* (*pl. territories*)

s 2

fīnītĭmus, -a, -um, *bordering on*
fīo, factus sum, fĭĕrī, 3, *v. irr. to become, be made* (258)
firmo, -āvi, -ātum, 1, *strengthen*
firmus, -a, -um, *adj. strong*
Flaccus, -i, *m. the surname of Quintus Horatius Flaccus, commonly called Horace*
flăgĭtĭum, -i, *n. disgraceful crime*
fleo, flēvi, flētum, 2, *weep*
flo, flāvi, flātum, 1, *blow*
floccus, -i, *m. the down of wool; hence* nōn flocci făcĭo, *I do not value at a feather* (284)
flōrens, -ntis, *adj. flourishing*
flōrĕo, -ŭi, 2, *I bloom, flourish*
flōs, flōris, *m. flower*
fluctūs, -ūs, *m. wave, billow*
flūmen, -ĭnis, *n. current, river*
fluo, -xi, 3, *flow (fut. part. act.* fluxūrus)
flŭvĭus, -ii, *m. a river*
fŏdĭo, fōdi, fossum, fŏdĕre, 3, *dig*
foedo, -āvi, -ātum, 1, *defile*
foedus, -ĕris, *n. treaty*
foedus, -a, -um, *foul, shameful*
fons, -ntis, *m. fountain, source*
fŏrĕ, *fut. inf. of* sum (Par. 212); fŏrem, fŏret, &c. *see* sum
fŏras, *adv. (motion) out of doors;* fŏrīs, *adv. (rest) out of doors*
fŏrēs, -um, *f. pl. doors*
formīdo, -āvi, -ātūm, 1, *dread*
formīdo, -ĭnis, *f. terror*
fortassĕ, *adv. perhaps (mostly refers to the future, unlike* fortĕ *below)*
fortĕ, *adv. by chance, once upon a time, never refers to the Fut., except in the phrases,* sī fortĕ, nĭsĭ fortĕ, nē fortĕ
fortis, -e, *brave, strong;* -tissĭmĕ, *adv. very bravely;* -tĭter, *adv. bravely*
fortūna, -ae, *f. fortune;* fortūnae nostrae pĕnĕs tē sunt, *our fortunes are in your hands*

fŏrum, -i, *n. market-place, forum*
fossa, -ae, *f. ditch*
frango, frēgi, fractum, 3, *break*
frāter, -tris, *m. brother*
fraus, fraudis, *f. deceit, mischief*
frĕmo, -ŭi, ĭtum, 3, *murmur*
frīgĭdus, -a, -um, *cold*
frīgus, -ŏris, *n. cold*
frons, -ndis, *f. foliage*
frons, -ntis, *f. the forehead, brow*
fructus, -ūs, *m. fruit, advantage*
frūges, -um, *f. pl. fruits, a crop*
fruor, fruĭtus *or* fructus, 3, *dep. enjoy* (207, 256)
frūmentum, -i, *n. corn (mostly harvested);* frūmenta, -orum, *corn (mostly in the fields)*
frustrā, *adv. in vain*
frŭtex, -ĭcis, *m. shrub*
fŭga, -ae, *f. flight*
fŭgĭo, fūgi, 3, *flee*
fŭgo, -āvi, -ātum, 1, *put to flight*
fulcio, fulsi, fultum, 4, *prop up*
fulgeo, fulsi, fulsum, 2, *I shine*
fulgur, -ūris, *n. lightning (that shines); in poets used for* fulmen
fulmen, -ĭnis, *n. lightning (that strikes)* [rout
fundo, fūdi, fūsum, 3, *pour, scatter*
fundus, -i, *m. farm*
fūnestus, -a, -um, *fatal, deadly*
fungor, functus, 3, *v. dep. I discharge* (207)
fūnis, -is, *m. rope*
fūnus, -ĕris, *n. a funeral*
fūr, fūris, *m. thief*
fŭror, -ōris, *m. madness, rage*

**Gādes, -ĭum,** *f. pl. Cadiz*
Gaius, *gen.* Gai, *m. (less correctly* Caius, Caii) *Gaius, a Roman praenomen or fore-name*
Gallĭa, -ae, *f. Gaul*
Gallus, -i, *m. a Gaul*
gaudĕo, gāvīsus sum, gaudēre, 2, *I rejoice*
gaudĭum, -i, *n. joy*

gĕlĭdus, -a, -um, *ice-cold*
gĕlū, -ūs, *n. frost*
gĕner, -ĕri, *m. son-in-law*
gens, gentis, *f. nation*
gĕnū, -ūs, *n. knee*
gĕnus, -ĕris, *n. kind, race*
Germanus, -a, -um, *German*
gĕro, gessi, gestum, 3, *carry on;* rem bĕnĕ gero, *I succeed;* bellum gĕro, *I wage war*
glăcies, -ēi, *f. ice*
glădĭātor, -ōris, *m. gladiator*
glădĭus, -ii, *m. a sword*
glans, -ndis, *f. acorn*
Gracchus, -i, *m. Gracchus, the name of two brothers, both of whom brought forward Agrarian laws in Rome*
grăcĭlis, -e, *slender,* 60
Graecĭa, -ae, *f. Greece* [*Greek*
Graecus, -a, -um, *adj. Grecian,*
grāmen, -ĭnis, *n. grass*
grandis, -e, *large*
grānum, -i, *n. a grain*
grātĭa, -ae, *f. favour,* in grātĭam rĕdīre, *to be restored to favour;* (*abl. sing.*) *for the sake of;* grātĭas ăgĕre, *to return thanks*
grātus, -a, -um, *pleasing, grateful*
grăvis, -e, *heavy, severe*
grăvĭter, *adv. heavily, severely, seriously;* hōc g. tŭli, *I was vexed at this*
grăvo, -āvi, -ātum, 1, *weigh down*
grex, grĕgis, *m. flock*
grus, grŭis, *c. crane*
gŭberno, -āvi, -ātum, 1, *govern*
gusto, -āvi, -ātum, 1, *taste*
guttur, -ŭris, *n. throat*

**Hăbĕo, -ŭi, -ĭtum,** 2, *have;* hăbĕo ĭn ănĭmo, *I purpose*
hăbĭto, -āvi, -ātum, 1, *dwell*
haerĕo, haesi, haesum, 2, *stick fast;* (*of the voice*) *falter*

Hannĭbal, -ălis, *m. Hannibal*
hăruspex, -ĭcis, *m. soothsayer*
hasta, -ae, *f. spear*
haud, *adv. not* (*rarely with verbs and adj. except* haud scīo ăn, haud dŭbĭum est, &c.) [*land*)
Helvĕtĭa, -ae, *f. Helvetia* (*Switzer-*
Helvĕtĭus, -a, -um, *adj. Helvetian*
herba, -ae, *f. herb*
hercle! (*an oath used as an exclamation*) *by Hercules, certainly*
hĕri, *adv. yesterday*
hesternus, -a, -um, *of yesterday*
hīberna, -ōrum, *n. pl. winter quarters;* hībernus, -a, -um, *adj. of winter, wintry*
hic, *pron. see Par.* 103; hic...ille, *the latter... the former, one... another;* trĭbus hīs mensĭbus, *within the next three months*
hic, *adv. here*
bĭemps, hĭĕmis, *f. winter*
hĭlăris, -e, *adj. cheerful*
hinc, *adv. hence, from this place*
histŏrĭa, -ae, *f. history;* Nātūrālis h. *the Natural History of Pliny*
histrĭo, -ōnis, *actor*
hŏdĭē, *adv. to-day*
Hŏmērus, -i, *m. Homer*
hŏmo, -ĭnis, *m. man* [1]
hŏnestus, -a, -um, *honourable* (*this word never means "honest"*)
hŏnor, -ōris, *m. an honour, office;* in hŏnōre est, *it is held in honour*
hōra, -ae, *f. hour*
hordeum, -i, *n. barley*
Hŏrātĭus, -ii, *Horace*
hortor, -ātus, 1, *v. dep. exhort*
hortus, -i, *m. a garden*
hostĭa, -ae, *f. a victim*
hostis, -is, *m. the enemy*
hūc, *adv. hither; often, though not perhaps with strict correctness, rendered in modern English, "here"*

---

[1] Hŏmo means *a human being,* and is occasionally (but very rarely) used of women: vir means *a good* or *brave man.*

hūmānĭtās, -ātis, *f. courtesy, kindness*

hūmānĭtŭs, *adv. after the manner of men; (hence used of misfortunes)* ălĭquid ei h. accĭdit, *he died*

hūmānus, -a, -um, *adj. human, gentle, courteous*

hŭmĭlis, -e, *low, low-minded* (60)

hŭmus, -i, *f. ground;* hŭmi, *on the ground*

I, *imperative of* ĕo

ĭbi, *adv. there*

ictus, -ūs, *m. a blow;* sub ictum venīre, *to come within striking distance*

ĭgĭtur, *conj. therefore, then; differs from* ĭtăquĕ *in not standing first in a clause (in the best authors)*

ignārus, -a, -um, *ignorant;* tĭbi ignāro prōfui, *I helped you without your being aware of it*

ignāvē, *adv. indolently*

ignāvĭa, -ae, *f. sloth, cowardice*

ignāvus, -a, -um, *slothful, cowardly*

ignĕus, -a, -um, *adj. fiery*

ignis, -is, *m. fire, abl.* ignī *(except in poets)*

ignōrātĭo, -ōnis, *f. ignorance*

ignosco, -nōvi, -nōtum, 3, *(g. dat.) pardon*

illātūri, *see* Infĕro

illĕ, (103) Alexander ille, *the great, well-known, &c., Alexander*

illĕcĕbrae, -ārum, *f. pl. allurements*

illūc, *adv. thither*

īmāgo, -ĭnis, *f. image, likeness*

imbellis, -e, *unwarlike*

imber, -ris, *m. (Abl.* -i), *shower*

īmĭtor, -atus, 1, *v. dep. imitate*

immĕmor, *gen.* -ōris, *unmindful*

immortālis, -e, *adj. immortal*

immortālĭtās, -ātis, *f. immortality*

impār, *gen.* -ăris, *unequal*

impăvĭdus, -a, -um, *fearless*

impello, -pŭli, -pu'sum, 3, *impel*

impendĕo, (*no Perf. or Sup.*) 2, *impend*

impĕrātor, -ōris, *m. general*

impĕrītus, -a, -um, (*g. gen.*) *unskilful in*

impĕrĭum, -ĭi, *n. command, empire*

impĕro, -āvi, -ātum, 1, (*g. dat.*) *give orders to;* i. tĭbi frūmentum, *I exact corn from you; foll. by* ut (143)

impĕtus, -ūs, *m. attack, onset*

impĭger, -gra, -grum, *active*

implōro, -āvi, -ātum, 1, *implore*

impōno, -pŏsui, -posĭtum, 3, *impose (a task, tribute, &c.) on,* Par. 192

improbus, -a, -um, *adj. dishonest, wicked, bad*

imprūdens, -ntis, *ignorant;* i. fēci, *I did it ignorantly*

imprūdentĭa, -ae, *f. ignorance, imprudence*

ĭn, *prep. (g. acc.) into, towards; (g. abl.) in*

ĭnānis, -e, *idle, empty* [tion

incendĭum, -i, *n. a fire, conflagra-*

incendo, -di, -sum, 3, *set fire to, burn*

incertus, -a, -um, *adj. uncertain*

incĭpĭo, -cēpi, -ceptum, 3, *begin*

incŏla, -ae, *m. inhabitant*

incŏlo, -ui, -ultum, 3, *inhabit*

incŏlŭmis, -e, *safe*

incŏlŭmĭtās, -ātis, *f. safety*

increpo, -crĕpŭi, -crĕpĭtum, 1, *reproach*

incūso, -āvi, -ātum, 1, *I accuse, find fault with*

indĕ, *adv. thence, thereupon;* indĕ ā pŭĕrĭtĭā, *even from boyhood*

Indi, -ōrum, *m. pl. Indians*

indĭco, -āvi, -ātum, 1, *point out*

indignus, -a, -um, *unworthy*

indoctus, -a, -um, *unlearned*

indulgĕo, -si, -tum, 2, (*g. dat.*) *indulge*

industrĭus, -a, -um, *adj. industrious, busy*
ĭnĕo, -īvi *or* -ĭi, -ĭtum, 4, *go into, enter, begin*
ĭneptē, *adv.* (ĭn-aptē, *unfitly*), *foolishly, without tact*
ĭneptus, -a, -um, *silly*
īners, -tis, *adj. helpless, sluggish*
infāmĭa, -ae, *f. infamy*
infāmis, -e, *adj. infamous*
infectus, -a, -um, *unaccomplished;* rē infectā, (*abl. abs.*) *the affair being unaccomplished,* i.e. *with nothing done* (Par. 197)
infēlīcĭter, *adv. unluckily;* pugnātum est i. *we have been defeated*
infēlīx, -īcis, *unfortunate, unhappy*
infĕrĭor, -ĭus, *comp.* of ĭnfĕrus, *adj. lower, inferior*
infĕro, intŭlī, illātum, inferrĕ, 3, *v. irr.;* bellum i. tĭbi, *I declare war against you*
infīnītus, -a, -um, *adj. unbounded, infinite*
infirmĭtās, -ātis, *f. weakness*
infirmus, -a, -um, *infirm, weak*
infrā, *prep.* (*g. acc.*) *below*
ingens, -ntis, *huge, great*
ingĕnĭum, -i, *n. disposition*
ingratus, -a, -um, *displeasing, ungrateful*
ingrĕdĭor, -gressus sum, 3, *v. dep. enter*
ĭnhaerĕo, -haesi, -haesum, 2, *stick fast*
ĭnhōnestus, -a, -um, *dishonourable*
ĭnĭmīcĭtĭa, -ae, *f. enmity*
ĭnĭmīcus, -a, -um, *unfriendly, hostile;* ĭnĭmīcus, -i, *m. a private enemy; opp. to* hostis, *an enemy of the state*
ĭnĭtĭum, -i, *n. a beginning*
injĭcĭo, -jēci, -jectum, 3, *cast* (*fear, &c.*) *into, inspire*
injūcundus, -a, -um, *disagreeable*
injustē, *adv. unjustly*

injustus, -a, -um, *unjust*
innŏcens, -ntis, *innocent*
innŭmĕrus, -a, -um, *adj. innumerable*
ĭnops, -ŏpis, *destitute*
inquăm, inquit, *see Defective Verbs, Appendix II.*, p. 215
insānĭo, -īvi, -ītum, 4, *I am mad*
insĕquor, -sĕcūtus, 3, *follow after, pursue*
insĭdĭae, -arum, *f. snares, an ambush;* per insĭdĭas, *insidiously*
insignis, -e, *distinguished, noted*
insŏlens, -ntis, (*g. gen.*) *unaccustomed to*
instĭtŭo, -ui, -ŭtum, 3, *I appoint, institute*
instrūmentum, -i, *n. an instrument*
instrŭo, -xi, -ctum, 3, *arrange, draw up*
insuētus, -a, -um, *untrained to* (*g. gen.*)
insŭla, -ae, *f. island*
insum, -fui, -esse, *v. irr.* (*g. dat.*) *I am in*
intellĕgo, -lexi, -lectum, 3, *understand, hear, perceive* (*less correctly* intellĭgo)
intĕr, *prep.* (*g. acc.*) *between, among;* inter vēnandum, *during hunting;* haec inter sē rĕpugnant, *these things are inconsistent with one another*
interclūdo, -ūsi, -ūsum, 3, *I cut off;* i. hostes comneātu, *I cut off the enemy from supplies*
interdum, *adv. sometimes*
intĕrĕo, -ivi *or* -ĭi, -ĭtum, 4, *perish*
intĕrest, -fŭit, -esse, (*v. impers.*) *it makes a difference, it concerns,* Par. 329
interfĭcĭo, -fēci, -fectum, 3, *slay*
intĕrĭtus, -ūs, *m. destruction*
interjăcĕo, -jacui, 2, *lie between*
interrŏgo, -āvi, -ātum, 1, *ask, question*

intersum, -fŭi, -esse, (*g. dat.*) *I am among, I take part in*
intervĕnio, -vēni, -ventum, 4, *interrupt,* (*g. dat.*) (192)
intrā, *prep.* (*g. acc.*) *inside, within*
intro, -āvi, -ātum, 1, *enter*
intrŏĕo, -īvi *or* -ĭi, -ĭtum, 4, *go into, enter*
intŭĕor, -ĭtus -sum, 2, *v. dep. look upon, into*
ĭnūro, -ussi, -ustum, 3, *brana*
inūtilis, -e, *useless*
inūtĭlĭter, *adv. uselessly, in vain*
invādo, -vāsi, -vāsum, 3, *attack*
invĕnio, -vēni, -ventum, -ae, 4, *light on, find, find out* [*dat.*
invĭdĕo, -vīdi, -vīsum, 2, *envy, g.*
invĭdĭa, -ae, *f. envy, ill-will*
invĭdus, -a, -um, *envious*
invītus, -a, -um, *unwilling ;* (*used as adj. but with adv. force*) invītus fēci, *I did it unwillingly*
ipsĕ, *see* Par. 105, 308
īra, -ae, *f. anger*
īrācundus, -a, -um, *angry*
īrascor, īrātus, 3, *v. dep. I am angry*
irrumpo, -rūpi, -ruptum, 3, *burst into, rush into*
irrŭo, -rŭi, 3, *rush in*
ĭs, ĕa, ĭd, *see* p. 46 ; nōn ĭs sum qui mentiar, *I am not the man to lie,* 303*a*
istĕ, -a, -ud, *pron. adj. that of yours* ; iste, *that fellow*
istūc, *adv. thither, where you are*
ĭtă, *in that way, thus, so*
Ĭtălĭa, -ae, *f. Italy*
ĭtăque, *and so, thereupon* ; ĭtăquĕ, (*differing from* ĭgĭtur), *stands first in a clause*
ĭter, ĭtĭnĕris, *n. journey, road, way;* ex ĭtĭnĕrĕ, *on a journey*
ĭtĕrum, *adv. a second time, again*

**Jăcĕo, -ŭi,** 2, *lie (on the ground)*
jăcĭo, jēci, jactum, 3, *I throw*

jactātĭo, -ĭōnis, *f. boasting*
jacto, -āvi, -ātum, 1, *boast*
jactŭs, -ūs, *m. cast, shot, fire ;* intrā tēli jactum, *within shot ;* sŭb jactu, *under fire*
jam, *adv.* (1) *already* ; (2) *by this time ;* cum jam *often means "just when," or "at last when"* ; non jam, *no longer*
jamdūdum *or* jamprīdem, *adv. this long while* ; j. cŭpĭo, *I have been this long while desiring* (324)
Jānŭārius, -ia, -ium, *of January*
jŏcor, -ātus, 1, (*v. dep.*) *jest*
Jŏvis, *see* Juppiter
jŭbĕo, jussi, jussum, 2, *I order,* (*g. acc. and inf.*) *bid*
jūcundus, -a, -um, *agreeable*
Jūdaea, -ae, *f. Judaea*
jūdex, -ĭcis, *m. judge ;* mē judice, *in my judgment,* lit. *I being a judge* (Par. 197)
jūdĭcĭum, -i, *n. judgment*
jūdĭco, -āvi, -ātum, 1, *judge*
jŭgŭlo, -āvi, -ātum, 1, *cut the throat of, butcher*
jŭgum, -i, *n. yoke ; to be "sent under the yoke" was the sign of defeat*
jungo, -nxi, -nctum, 3, *join ;* ponte jungĕre, *to bridge over*
jūnĭor, -oris, *younger*
Jŭno, -ōnis, *f. Juno, a goddess*
Jūppiter, Jŏvis, *m. Jupiter*
jūro, -āvi, ātum *or* jurātus sum, 1, *I swear* ; j. in lēgem, *I swear (obedience) to a law* ; j. in verba eius, *in accordance with his words*
jūs, jūris, *n. right, law* ; jūrĕ, (*adv. abl.*) *by right, rightly* (182)
jusjūrandum, jūrisjūrandi, *n. an oath*
jussum, -i, *n. command*
justē, *adv. justly* ; justĭus, *more justly*
justĭtia, -ae, *justice*
justus, -a, -um, *just*
jŭvĕnis, -is, *m. young man*

jŭventūs, -ūtis, *f. youth*
juxtā, *prep. (g. acc.) near, hard by, next to*

**Lăbĭēnus, -i,** *m. Labienus*
lăbor, -ōris, *m. labour*
lābor, lapsus, 3, *v. dep. I glide, pass away, fall*
lăc, lactis, *n. milk* [or *Sparta*
Lăcĕdaemon, -ŏnis, *f. Lacedaemon*
Lăcĕdaemŏnii, -ōrum, *m. the Lacedaemonians*
lăcrĭma, -ae, *f. a tear*
lăcus, -ūs, *m. a lake*
laedo, laesi, -sum, 3, *hurt (g. acc.)*
laetĭtĭa, -ae, *f. joy*
laetus, -a, -um, *joyful*
lăpis, -ĭdis, *m. stone*
lăpĭdĕus, -a, -um, *adj. of stone*
lātē, *adv. widely, wide*
lătĕo, -ui, 2, *lie hid, lurk*
lătex, -ĭcis, *m. water*
Lătīnus, -a, -um, *Latin*
lātĭtūdo, -inis, *f. breadth*
Lătōna, -ae, *f. Latona, mother of Apollo and Diana*
latro, -ōnis, *m. a robber*
latrōcĭnium, -i, *n. robbery*
lātūrus, *fut. part. of* fĕro
lātus, -a, -um, *wide, broad*
laudo, -āvi, -ātum, 1, *praise*
laus, laudis, *f. praise*
lăvo, -lāvi, lavātum, 1, *wash*[1]
lectus, -i, *m. bed*
lēgātus, -i, *m. ambassador, lieutenant*
lĕgĭo, -iōnis, *f. legion, from* 4,000 *to* 6,000 *men*
lĕgo, lēgi, lectum, 3, *gather, read*
lēgo, -āvi, -ātum, 1, *bequeath*
Lemnos, -i, *f. the isle of Lemnos*
lĕo, leŏnis, *m. lion*
Lĕōnĭdas, -ae, *m. Leonidas*
lĕpus, -ŏris, *m. a hare*
Lesbos, -i, *f. Lesbos*
lĕvis, -e, *light, fickle, empty*

lex, lēgis, *f. law*
lĭbenter, *adv. willingly*
lĭber, -bri, *m. book*
līber, -ĕra, -ĕrum, *free;* līberrima ōrātio, *very frank speech* (61)
Līber, -ĕri, *m. Liber, the god of wine*
lĭbĕrē, *adv. freely*
lĭbĕri, -ōrum, *m. pl. children*
lĭbĕro, -āvi, -ātum, 1, *I free, deliver (g. abl. of thing)*
lībertas, -ātis, *f. freedom, liberty*
libet (lĭbuit *and*) lĭbĭtum est, 2, *v. impers. (g. dat.) it pleases*
Lĭbya, -ae, *f. Africa*
lĭcet, lĭcŭit *and* lĭcĭtum est, lĭcēre, 2, *v. impers. (g. dat.) it is lawful, allowed; (used with Inf.; or with Subjunct. with* ut *omitted*) licet omnes frĕmant, *let them all murmur;* N.B. *after* licet mihi esse, *the Adj. may either be dat.* (Par. 24), *or attracted into the Acc., to agree with me "understood,"* licet mĭhī (mē) esse bĕātum
Lĭcīnĭus, -i, *m., Licinius*
lictor, -ōris, *m. a lictor*
lignĕus, -a, -um, *wooden*
līlĭum, -i, *n., lily*
lingua, -ae, *f. tongue, language*
līquet, līquēre, 2, *v. impers.* (Par. 222) *it is clear, evident*
littĕra, -ae, *f. a letter of the alphabet*
littĕrae, -ārum, *f. pl. letters, learning, also an epistle, letter*
lītus, -ōris, *n. a shore*
Līvĭus, -i, *m. Titus Livius the historian, commonly called Livy*
lŏcus, -i, *m. a place*
longē, *adv. far, far off* [tance
longinquĭtās, -ātis, *f. length, distance*
longinquus, -a, -um, *adj. long, distant*

---

[1] Also **lautum** and **lōtum**; this verb is never intransitive.

longĭtūdo, -dĭnis, f. length [far
longĭus, adv. comp. farther, too
longus, -a, -um, long; nāvcs
   longae, ships of war
lŏquor, lŏcūtus, 3, dep. speak
lūcescit (illuxit), lūcescĕre, 3, v.
   impers. it becomes light
lūdo, -si, -sum, 3, I play
lūdus, -i, m. play, game
lūna, -ae, f. the moon
lŭpus, -i, m. wolf
luscĭnĭa, -ae, f. nightingale
lux, lūcis, f. light, dawn
lyra, -ae, f. lyre

**Măcĕdo, -ŏnis,** m. a Macedonian
măcer, -cra, -crum, lean
măcŭla, -ae, f., spot
măgis, adv. (sup. maxĭmē), rather,
   in a higher degree, more
măgister, -tri, m. master, teacher
măgistrātus, -ūs, m. magistrate,
   magistracy
magnĭfĭcus, -a, -um, adj. magni-
   ficent; (for superl. see Par. 68a)
magnŏpĕre, adv. greatly, earnestly
magnus, -a, -um, great, large
mājestas, -ātis, f. lit. "sovereignty";
   condemnāri mājestātis, to be
   found guilty (on the charge) of
   (impairing) sovereignty, i.e. of
   treason (290)
mājor, -ōris, Par. 68
mājōres, -um, m. pl. ancestors
mălĕ, adv. comp. pējus, sup. pessĭ-
   mē, badly, ill
mălĕdictum, -i, n. slander, curse
mălĕvŏlus, -a, -um, ill-wishing,
   malevolent (superl., Par. 68a)
mălo, mălui, mallē, irr. v. I am
   more willing, I prefer, I had
   rather (p. 130)
mălum, -i, n. an apple
mălum, -i, n. evil
mălus, -i, f. an apple tree
mălus, -a, -um, bad, evil [mission
mandātum, -i, n. a charge, com-

mănĕo, -nsi, -nsum, 2, remain
mănĭfestus, -a, -um, evident, manifest
mănĭpŭlus, -i, m. a maniple
mansi, see mănĕo
mănus, -ūs, f. a hand
Mărăthon, -ōnis, f. Marathon
Marcus, -i, m., Marcus; see Crassus
măre, -is, n. sea (see terra)
margărīta, -ae, f. a pearl
mărīnus, -a, -um, adj. of the sea
marmor, -ŏris, n. marble
Martius, -a, -um, of March, p. 229
māter, -tris, f. mother
mātĕria, -ae, f. materials, timber
mātrĭmōnium, -ii, n. matrimony,
   duxit eam in mātrĭmōnium, he
   married her (always of man
   marrying women, see nūbo)
mātūrus, -a, -um, ripe
maxĭmē, adv. very greatly, especially
maxĭmus, -a, -um, see Par. 68
Maxĭmus, -i, m. Maximus, "the
   greatest"; see Făbĭus
mĕdĭcīna, -ae, f. medicine
mĕdĭcus, -i, m. physician
mĕdĭtor, -ātus, 1, v. dep. meditate
   on, study
mĕdius, -a, -um, middle (of);
   inĕdios in hostes, into the midst
   of the enemy
mĕlior, neut. -ius, see Par. 68
mĕmĭni, v. def.; see p. 215
mĕmor, -ŏris, mindful (g. gen.)
mĕmŏrābĭlis, -e, adj. memorable
mĕmōrĭa, -ae, f. memory, recollection
mendācium, -i, n. lie, falsehood
mendax, -ācis, adj. lying, deceitful
Mĕnēnĭus, -ii, m. Menenius Agrippa,
   author of the fable of the Belly
   and the Other Members
mens, mentis, f. mind
mensĭs, -is, m. month
mentior, -ītus, 4, (v. dep.) tell a lie
mercātor, -ōris, m. merchant
mercēs, -cēdis, f. pay, wage, reward

Mercŭrĭus, -i, m. *Mercury*
měrěo (*also* mĕrĕor, mĕrĭtus, 2, *v. dep.*) -ŭi, -ĭtum, 2, *I deserve;* dē patrĭā bĕnē mĕrĭtus est, *he has deserved well of his country*
mergo, mersi, mersum, 3, *plunge*
mĕrīdĭes, m. *mid-day*
messis, -is, f. *harvest*
mĕtallum, -i, n. *a metal;* mĕtalla, -ōrum, n. pl. *mines;* damnāri in m. *to be condemned to the mines.*
mētĭor, mensus, 4, (*v. dep.*) *measure*
mĕto, messŭi, messum, 3, *reap*
Mettus, -i, m. *Mettus, an Alban, torn in pieces by Tullus Hostilius*
mĕtŭo, -ŭi, -ūtum, 3, *I fear*
mĕtus, -ūs, m. *fear*
mĕus, -a, -um, *pronom. adj. my, mine*
mi, *masc. voc. of* mĕus [*part*
migro, -āvi, -ātum, 1. *migrate,* de-
mīlĕs, mīlĭtis, m. *soldier*
mīlia, (80) n. pl. (*sometimes for* mīlia passuum, *see* passus)
mīlĭtāris, -e, *military;* rēs m. *military affairs,* i.e. *warfare*
mīlĭtĭae, *adv. in war*
millĭens, *a thousand times*
mille, milia, *see* Par. 80
mīna, -ae, f. *threat*
mĭnĭmē, *adv. by no means, in the least degree;* mĭnĭmus,-a,-um(68)
mĭnister, -tri, m. *a servant*
mĭnor, *see* Par 68
mĭnŭo, -ŭi, -ūtum, 3, *diminish*
mīrandus, -a, -um, *wonderful*
mīror, -ātus, 1, (*v. dep.*) *wonder at, admire*
mīrus, -a, -um, *wonderful*
miscĕo, miscui, mixtum, 2, *mix, throw into confusion*
mĭser, -ĕra, -ĕrum, *wretched*
mĭsĕrĕor, -sertus *or* -sĕrĭtus, 2, *dep. pity* (g. gen.) (203)
mĭsĕret, mĭsĕrĭtum est, 2, v. impers., *see* Par. 219
mĭsĕrĭa,-ae, f. *misery*

mĭsĕrĭcordĭa, f. *pity* [(g. acc.)
mĭsĕror, -atus, 1, *show pity to*
mĭtesco, 3, *become mild*
mītis, -e, adj. *mild*
mitto, mīsi, missum, 3, *send*
mŏdestĭa, -ae, f. *modesty*
mŏdo, *adv. only;* sī, *or* dum, mŏdo, *if, or* prŏvided, *only;* mŏdo nunc, *only just now*
mŏdus, -i, m. *measure, manner:* praeter mŏdum, *beyond measure;* nullo modo, *in no way;* eiusmodi, *of that kind*
moenĭa, -ium, n. pl. *fortifications*
mŏlestus, -a, -um, *troublesome*
mollĭo, -īvi *or* -ĭi, -ītum, 4, *soften*
mollis, -e, adj. *soft, mellow*
mŏnĕo, -ŭi, -ĭtum, 2, *advise, warn*
mons, -ntis, m. *mountain*
monstro, -āvi, -ātum, 1, *show, point out*
mŏnŭmentum, -i, n. *monument*
mŏra, -ae, f. *delay*
morbus, -i, m. *disease*
mŏrĭor, mortŭus, 3, v. dep. *die (fut. part.* mŏrĭtūrus, *about to die*)
mŏror, mŏrātus, 1 (*v. dep.*) *delay*
mors, -tis, f. *death*
morsūs, -ūs, m. *bite*
mortālis, -e, adj. *mortal*
mortŭus, -a, -um, *dead*
mōs, mōris, m. *manner, custom:* mōres, -um, pl. *conduct, morals:* nōn nostri mōris est, *it is not (characteristic of) our custom*
mōtŭs, -ūs, m. *motion, movement*
mŏvĕo, mōvi, mōtum, 2, *move, affect;* bellum, *or* arma, mŏveo, *I stir up or commence war*
mox, *adv. soon*
mŭ'ĭer. -ĕris. f. *woman, wife*
multĭplex, -plicis, *manifold;* m. fetus, *many young ones at a time*
multĭtūdo, -ĭnis, f. *multitude*
multo, -āvi, -ātum, 1, *punish (with death, fine,* &c.)
multus, -a, -um, *much, many;*

multa nox, *a late (hour of) night;* multum *adv.,* multum interest, *it makes a great difference;* multo (*adv. with compar.*) (*by*) *much;* multo felicior, (*by*) *much more happy*
Mummius, -ii, *m. Mummius, the destroyer of Corinth*
mundus, -i, *m. the universe*
munificus, -a, -um, (68a) *liberal*
munimentum, -i, *n. a fortification*
munio, -ivi *or* -ii, -itum, 4, *fortify*
munus, -eris, *n. a gift, duty, function*
murmur, -uris, *n. murmur*
murus, -i, *m. wall*
muto, -avi, -atum, 1, *change*
Mycenae, -arum, *f. pl. Mycenae, the chief city of Greece in the Trojan times*
myrtus, -i *and* -us, *f. myrtle*

Nactus, *see* nanciscor
nam, *conj. for; differs from* enim *in standing first in a clause*
nanciscor, nactus *and* nanctus, *inf.* nancisci, 3, *obtain* (*v. dep.*)
narro, -avi, -atum, 1, *relate*
nascor, natus, 3, *v. dep. I am born* N.B. nascor *means " I am being born";* decem annos natus est, *he is ten years old*
Naso, -onis, *m. Publius Ovidius Naso, commonly called Ovid*
natu, *adv. abl. by birth*
natura, -ae, *f. nature*
naturalis, *see* historia
natus, -a, -um, *part. and adj. born, aged;* viginti annos n., *twenty years old*
nauta, -ae, *m. a sailor*
navalis, -e, *adj. naval*
navigo, -avi, -atum, 1, *sail*
navis, -is, *f. ship*
-ne, *enclitic, asks a question* (100)
ne, *conj. that not, lest* (131); ne quis, *that no one* (294); (*with perf. subj.*) (*do*) *not* (129)
Neapolis, -is, *f.* (*acc.* -im), *Naples*
nec, *see* neque
necessarius, -a, -um, *adj. necessary*
necesse, *adv. necessarily;* (*used as adj.*) necesse est, *it is necessary,* (*foll. by acc. and inf. or* ut)
neco, necavi, necatum, 1, *kill*
nefandus, -a, -um, *unspeakable, monstrous*
nefas, *n. indecl. wickedness;* n. dictu, *monstrous to relate!*
neglego, -exi, -ectum, 3, *neglect*
nego, -avi, -atum, 1, *I deny*
negotium, -i, *n. business*
nemo, nullius, *m. nobody, no one* Par. 92; n. non gaudebat, *there was no one that did not rejoice*
Neoptolemus, -i, *m. Neoptolemus*
Neptunus, -i, *m. Neptune*
nequam, *indecl. adj. comp.* nequior, *sup.* nequissimus, *worthless*
neque, *or* nec, *conj. and not;* when repeated, *neither...nor*
nequeo, -ivi *or* -ii, -itum, -ire, 4, *I am unable, cannot; imperf.* nequibam; *fut indic.* nequibo; *pres. part.* nequiens, *gen.* nequeuntis
nequiquam, *adv. in vain*
nequissimus, *see* nequam
Nero, -onis, *m. Nero*
nescio, -ivi *or* -ii, -itum, 4, *I am ignorant of, do not know;* nescio an venturus sit, *i.e.* nescio (utrum afuturus sit) an (potius) venturus sit, *I do not know whether he will be absent or whether he will rather come,* i.e. *I think he will come,* Par. 302
neuter, -tra, -trum, *adj.* (*gen. sing.* -ius, *dat.* -i), *neither of two, see* Par. 85
neve, *adv. or not, nor; or (after neg.)* ne affirmaveris neve nega veris, *say neither* 'yes' *nor* 'no'
nidus, -i, *m. a nest*

nĭger, -gra, -grum, *black*
nĭhil, *or* nĭl, *n. indecl. nothing;* (*from* nihĭlum) nĭhĭli te făcio, *I esteem you of no account;* nĭhĭlo mĭnŭs, *none the less* (277)
Nīlus, -i, *m. the Nile, a river in Egypt*
nī, *conj. a form of* nĭsĭ
nĭmĭs, *adv. too, too much*
Nĭŏba, -ae, *f. Niobe*
nĭsĭ, *conj. if...not, unless* (*has the same constr. as* sī, 125, 293-5); *after* nĭhil *and* quĭd, nĭsĭ *means "but" or "except," and has the same constr. as* quam (62)
nītor, nīsus *and* nixŭs, 3, *strive* (143)
nix, nĭvis, *f. snow*
no, nāvi, nātum, 1, *swim*
nōbĭlis, -e, *adj. distinguished, noble*
nŏcĕo, -ŭi, -ĭtum, 2, (*g. dat.*) *hurt*
nōlo, nōlŭi, nolle, *v. irreg. I am unwilling, I do not wish;* nōli vĕnīre, *do not come;* īdem nolle, *to dislike the same thing,* p. 128
nōmen, -ĭnis, *n. name*
nōmĭno, -āvi, -ātum, 1, *name*
nōn, *adv. not*
nondum, *adv. not yet*
nōnne? *interr. adv. expects the answer "yes"; sometimes a conj. whether,* Par. 135
nonnullus, -a, -um, *adj. some*
nosco, nōvi, nōtum, 3, *I gain knowledge of; hence perf.* nōvi, *I have gained knowledge of;* i.e. *I know*
noster, -stra, -strum, *pronom. adj. our, ours;* nostri *often means "our men;"* nostri *is also gen. of* nōs (93), *and* nostrum *part. gen.*
nosti *for* nōvisti, *see* nosco
nōta, -ae, *f. mark, stigma*
nōtus, -a, -um, *known*
nŏvus, -a, -um, *adj. new*

nox, noctis, *f. night* [*jurious*
noxĭus, -a, -um, *adj. hurtful, in-*
nūbēs, -is, *f. cloud*
nūbo, nupsi, nuptum, 3, *she marries* (*g. dat.*); *not used of men marrying; see* mātrĭmōnium
nullus, -a, -um, *adj. no, none; gen. sing.* -ĭus, *dat.* -ī, (85)
num? *interr. adv. expects the answer "no"; (sometimes conj.) whether,* Par. 135
nŭmĕro, -āvi, -ātum, 1, *I count*
nŭmĕrus, -i, *m. number*
Nŭmĭda, -ae, *m. a Numidian*
nunc, *adv. now, at the present time*
nunquam, *adv. never*
nuntĭo, -āvi, -ātum, 1, *bring word*
nuntĭus, -i, *m. messenger*
nūper, *adv. lately*
nūtrĭo, -īvi *and* -ĭi, -ītum, 4, *nourish*
nux, nŭcis, *f. nut*

**Ŏb,** *prep.* (*g. acc.*) *on account of, in front of*
obdormio, -īvi, -ītum, 4, *fall asleep*
ŏbēdĭo, -īvi *and* -ĭi, -ītum, 4, (*g. dat.*) *obey*
ŏbĕo, -īvi *or* -ĭi, -ītum, 4, *I meet,* esp. *meet death, I die*
oblātus, *see* offĕro
oblectātĭo, -ĭōnis, *f. delight*
oblĭno, -lēvi, -lĭtum, *besmear, defile*
oblīviscor, -lītus, 3, *dep. forget* (*g. gen.*) 203
obscūro, -āvi, -ātum, 1, *darken,*
obscūrus, -a, -um, *obscure, dark*
obsĕcro, -āvi, -ātum, 1, *beseech* (*foll. by* ut) [*respect*
observo, -āvi, -ātum, 1, *I observe,*
obses, -ĭdis, *m. hostage*
obsĭdĕo, -sēdi, -sessum, 2, *blockade, besiege*
obsĭdĭo, -ōnis, *f. a siege, blockade*
obsto, -stĭti, -stĭtum, 1, *oppose, prevent* (*g. dat.*); *nothing prevents your coming,* nĭhil obstat (tĭbi) quōmĭnus vĕnias

obstringo, -strinxi, -strictum, 3, *bind (by oath)*
obsum, obfui *or* offui, ŏbesse, *v. irreg. (g. dat.) I am in the way, am hurtful to, injure*
obtempĕro, -āvi, -ātum, 1, *comply with, obey (g. dat.)*
obtĭneo, -tĭnui, 2, *keep, hold*
occāsĭo, -ōnis, *f. opportunity*
occĭdens, -tis, *m. the west, the setting (sun)*
occĭdo, -cĭdi, -cāsum, 3, *fall;* occĭdit spēs nostra, *our hope has perished;* occĭdĭmus, *we are undone*
occīdo, -cīdi, -cīsum, 3, *slay, kill*
occŭpo, -āvi, -ātum, 1, *seize upon*
occŭlo, -cŭlŭi, -cultum, 3, *hide*
occumbo, -cŭbŭi, -cŭbĭtum, 3, *fall down*
ōcĕănus, -i, *m. the ocean*
ŏcŭlus, -i, *m. eye*
ōdi, ōdisse, *v. dep. haste; see* p. 215;
ŏdĭum, -ii, *n. hatred;* hic mihi ŏdio (268) est, *this man is hateful to me* (lit. *for hatred)*
ŏdor, -ōris, *m. a smell, scent*
offĕro, obtŭli, oblātum, offerre, 3, *v. irreg. I present*
ōlim, *adv. formerly*
ōmen, -ĭnis, *n. an omen* [*drop*
ōmitto, -mīsi, -missum, 3, *omit,*
omnīno, *adv. altogether;* (the position *alters the meaning*) o. nōn bŏnus, *not at all good;* 2, nōn o. bŏnus, *not altogether good*
omnis, -e, *all, the whole; (not "every," except in the pl.)*
ŏnus, -ĕris, *n. a load, burden*
ŏpĕra, -ae, *f. pains, labour;* hīs ŏperam do, *I pay attention to these things* [*tion*
ŏpīnĭo, -ōnis, *f. opinion, expecta-*
ŏportet, -ŭit, 2, *v. impers. it behoves, is necessary;* ŏportŭit tē tăcēre, *you ought to have been silent* (Par. 223)

oppĭdum, -i, *n. town*
oppōno, -ŏsŭi, -ĭtum, 3, *I set against;* oppōno me tibi, *I oppose you* (192) [*power*
opprĭmo, -pressi, -pressum, 3, *overoppugno, -āvi, -ātum, 1, *assault*
optĭmus, (68) *best, excellent;* optĭmē, *adv. excellently* [*sire*
opto, -āvi, -ātum, 1, *I wish, de-*
ŏpŭlentus, -a, -um, *adj. wealthy*
ŏpus, -ĕris, *n. work;* opus est (*g. abl.*) *there is need of*
ōra, -ae, *f. the coast*
ōrācŭlum, -i, *n. an oracle*
ōrāre causam, *to plead a cause*
ōrātĭo, -ōnis, *f. an oration, speech*
ōrātor, -ōris, *m. an orator*
ordĭor, -orsus, 4, *v. dep. I begin*
ordo, -ĭnis, *m. rank, order;* ordĭnem equestrem, *the order of the knights*
ŏrĭor, ortus, ŏrīri, 3, *v. dep. rise*
orno, -āvi, -ātum, 1, *adorn*
oro, -āvi, -ātum, 1, *entreat, pray;* ōrāre causam, *to plead a cause*
ortus, *see* orior
ōs, ōris, *n. mouth;* in ore omnium est, *it is the talk of everybody*
ŏs, ossis, *n. bone*
ōvum, -i, *n. egg*

**Păciscor, pactus,** 3, (*v. dep.*), *make an agreement*
paenĕ, *adv. almost*
pălam, (*adv. and prep. g. abl.*) *publicly, in the presence of*
Pallăs, -ădis, *f. Pallas Athene, not to be confounded with Minerva*
pallĭum, -ii, *n. a cloak*
pando, pandi, passum, 3, *lay open;* passo crīne, *with dishevelled hair*
pānis, -is, *m. bread*
păpāver, -ĕris, *n. poppy*
păpĭlĭo, -ōnis, *m. butterfly*
par, păris, *equal;* non est solvendo par, *he is not equal to paying,* i.e. *he is insolvent*

părātus, -a, -um, *adj. prepared*, p. ad pugnandum, *p. to fight*
parco, pĕperci, parcĭtum *or* parsum, 3, (*g. dat.*) *spare;* paucis parsum est, *few were spared*
părens, -ntis, *c. parent*
pārĕo, -ŭi, -ĭtum, 2, (*g. dat.*) *obey*
părĭo, pĕpĕri, partum, 3, (*g. acc.*) *bring forth, give birth to*
părĭter, *adv. equally*
păro, -āvi, -ātum, 1, *prepare, get*
pars, -tis, *f. part*
parsum, *see* parco
partĭor, -ītus, 4, *dep. share, divide*
partus, -ūs, *m. birth*
părum, *adv. too little; used for "not"; (used as a noun g. part. gen.)* p. virium, *too little strength*
parvus, -a, -um, *small, little*
pasco, pāvi, pastum, 3, *feed;* ŏves pascebantur, *sheep were grazing*
passus, -ūs, *m. a pace (about 5 feet);* mille passūs, *a mile*
pastor, -ōris, *m. shepherd*
pătĕo, -ŭi, 2, *extend; it extends for ten miles,* pătet in *foll. by acc.*
păter, -tris, *m. father*
pătĭens, -ntis, (*g. gen.*) *patient (of)*
pătĭenter, *adv. patiently*
pătĭor, passus, 3, *endure, suffer*
Pătres, -um, *m. pl. Fathers, a name given to the Roman Senators*
pătrĭa, -ae, *f. a native land, country*
pătrĭmōnĭum, -ii, *n. patrimony*
paulisper, *adv. for a short time*
paucus, -a, -um (*mostly pl.*) *few*
pauper, -ĕris, *poor*
paupertas, -ātis, *f. poverty*
păvĭdus, -a, -um, *fearful*
păvo, -ōnis, *m. peacock*
păvor, -ōris, *m. terror, trembling*
pax, pācis, *f. peace*
peccātum, -i, *n. fault*
pecco, -avi, -atum, 1, *err, sin*
pĕcūnĭa, -ae, *f. money, sum of money*
pĕdes, -ĭtis, *m. foot-soldier*
pĕdĭtātus, -ūs, *m. infantry*

pejor, *see* Par. 68
pĕlăgus, -i, *n. sea*
pellis, -is, *f. skin (of animals)*
pello, pĕpŭli, pulsum, 3, *drive*
pendo (page 209) *hang, weigh, value* (283)
pĕnĕs, *prep.* (*g. acc.*) *in the hands of*
penna, -ae, *f. feather, wing; (of fishes) fin*
pĕr, *prep.* (*g.acc.*) *through, by means of;* per dŏlum, *treacherously*
percĭpĭo, -cēpi, -ceptum, 3, *perceive*
percussĭo, -ōnis, *f. striking;* p. dĭgĭtōrum, *the snapping of one's fingers*
perdo, -dĭdi, -dĭtum, 3, *destroy*
perdŏmo, -ŭi, ĭtum, 1, *thoroughly tame, subdue*
pĕrĕo, -ĭi *or* -īvi, ĭtum, 4, *perish*
perfectus, -a, -um, *adj. finished, perfect*
perfĕro, -tŭli, -lātum, -ferre, *v. irr. endure*
perfĭcĭo, -fēci, -fectum, 3, *perform*
perfĭdĭa, -ae, f. *perfidy*
perfĭdus, -a, -um, *perfidious, treacherous*
Pĕrĭcles, -is, *m. Pericles*
pĕrīcŭlum, -i, *n. danger* [*gen.*]
pĕrītus, -a, -um, *adj. skilful in (g.*
per'ĕgo, -lēgi, -lectum, 3, *I read through*
permagnus, -a, -um, *very great*
permŏvĕo, -mōvi, -mōtum, 2, *rouse, stir*
permulti, -ae, -a, *very many*
pernĭcĭōsus, -a, -um, *destructive*
perpĕtŭus, -a, -um, *adj. continual*
perrumpo, -rūpi, -ruptum, 3, *burst through*
Persă, -ae, *m. a Persian*
persaepĕ, *adv. very often*
perspĭcĭo, -spexi, -spectum, 3, *see through, discern*
persuādĕo, -āsi, -āsum, 2, (*g. dat.*) *persuade* (143); persuāsum est mihi, *I am persuaded*

pertaesum, *see* taedet
perterreo, -ēre, -ŭi, -ĭtum, 2, *alarm*
pertĭmesco, -tĭmŭi, 3, *become fearful*
pervĕnĭo, -vēni, -ventum, 4, *arrive*
perversus, -a, -um, *wilful, perverse*
pēs, pĕdis, *m. foot*
pessĭmus, *see* Par. 68
pestis, -is, *f. plague*
pĕto, -īvi & -ĭi, ītum, 3, *seek*
Phăëthon, -ontis, *m. Phaëthon, a son of Apollo the Sun-god*
Phĭdĭās, -ae, *m. Phidias, an Athenian sculptor* (1st *decl.*)
Phĭlippus, -i, *m. Philip* (*of Macedonia*)
Phĭloctētēs, -ae, *m. Philoctetes*
phĭlŏsŏphĭa, -ae, *f. philosophy*
phĭlŏsŏphus, -i, *m. philosopher*
Phoebus, -i, *m. Phoebus Apollo, the Sun-god;* Phoebēus -a, -um, *adj. belonging to Phoebus Apollo*
pĭger, -gra, -grum, *slothful*
pĭgĕt, pĭguit *and* pĭgĭtum est, pĭgēre, 2, *v. impers. it vexes*
pingo, -nxi, -pictum, 3, *I paint, embroider*
pinguis, -e, *fat*
pinna, *see* penna
pīnus, -ūs *and* -i, *f. pine-tree*
pĭrum, -i, *n. a pear*
pĭrus, -i, *f. a pear-tree*
piscātor, -ōris, *m. fisherman*
piscis, -is, *m. a fish*
plăcĕo, -ŭi, -ĭtum, 2, *g. dat. please;* plăcuit, *or* plăcĭtum est, nobis venīre, *to come pleased us*, i.e., *we resolved to come*
plăcet, -uit *or* -ĭtum est, -ēre, 2, *v. impers. it pleases*
plăcĭdus, -a, -um, *adj. quiet*
plānē, *adv. altogether*
plānĭtĭes, -ĭĕi, *f. level space*
planta, -ae, *f. a sprout, plant*
Plăto, -ōnis, *m. Plato*
plebs, plēbis, *f. the common people*
plēnus, -a, -um, *full, g. gen. or abl.;* vīno plēnus, *filled with wine*, i.e. *intoxicated*
plērique, plēraeque, plēraque, *most*
plērumque, *adv. for the most part*
Plīnĭus, -ii, *m. Pliny*
plŭit, plŭit *or* plūvit, pluĕre, 3 *v. impers. it rains*
plūrĭmus, *see* Par. 68
plūs, -ūris, *more;* (neut. pl. *often used as noun*) *he spoke no more*, nec plūra dixit, *see* Par. 72
poenĭtentia, -ae, *f. penitence*
poena, -ae, *f. penalty;* dăre poenas (pl.) culpae, *to pay the penalty of a fault*
poenĭtet, -ĭtŭit, -ĭtēre, 2, *v. impers. it repents* (*me*), *see* Par. 219
pŏēta, -ae, *m. poet*
pollex, -ĭc's, *m. thumb* (*with which the lyre was twanged*)
pollĭcĕor, -ĭtus, 2, *promise* (280)
Pompēius, -ēĭi, *m. Pompey, the rival of Caesar*
pōmum, -i, *n. fruit*
pondus, -ĕris, *n. weight*
pōnĕ, *prep.* (*g. acc.*) *behind*
pōno, pŏsŭi, pŏsĭtum, 3, *place, lay aside*
pons, -ntis, *m. a bridge*
pontĭfex, -ĭcis, *m. a high priest*
Pontĭus (Pīlātus), -i, *m. Pontius Pilate*
porcus, -i, *m. pig*
porta, -ae, *f. a gate*
porto, -āvi, -ātum, 1, *carry*
portus, -ūs, *m. harbour*
Pōrus, -i, *an Indian king conquered by Alexander the Great*
posco, poposci, 3, *demand*
possum, pŏtŭi, posse, *v. irreg. I am able, can* (*see* pp. 126, 127)
post, *prep.* (*g. acc.*) *after; adv.* (313) multis post annis, *many years afterwards* (N.B. *never used like the conj.* postquam)
posteā, *adv. afterwards*

**PRO** VOCABULARY. 273

pŏstis, -is, m. *door-post*
postpōno, -pōsui, -pŏsĭtum, 3, *place after (g. acc. and dat.)*
postquam, *conj. when, after*
postrēmus, *see Par. 69*
postŭlo, -āvi, -ātum, 1, *I demand*
pŏtens, -entis, *adj. powerful*
pŏtentĭa, -ae, *f. power*
pŏtestas, -ātis, *f. power, authority*
pŏtĭor, -ītus, 4, *v. dep. (g. abl.) I make myself master of, obtain*
pŏtius...quam, *rather...than;* vel pŏtius, *or rather (used when a writer slightly corrects his own statement)*
prae, *prep. (g. abl.) before, in comparison with, by reason of, see Par. 178*
praebĕo, -ŭi, -ĭtum, 2, *I exhibit, afford:* p. exemplum, *set an example;* p. fructum, *put forth fruit*
praeceptor, -ōris, *m. teacher*
praeceptum, -i, *n. precept, instruction, lesson* [*famous*
praeclārus, -a, -um, *renowned,*
praeda, -ae, *f. booty*
praedĭum, -i, *n. farm*
praeĕo, -īvi *or* -ĭi, -ĭtum, 4, *I go before;* p. verba, *dictate words*
praefero, -tŭli, -lātum, *prefer*
praefĭcio, -fēci, -fectum, 3, *set in command over (acc. and dat.)*
praemitto, -mīsi, -missum, 3, *I send on before*
praemĭum, -i, *n. reward*
praesens, -entis, *present;* praesentem ĕum laudāvi, *I praised him in his presence*
praesĭdium, -i, *n. guard, garrison*
praestans, -antis, *excellent*
praesum, -fŭi, -esse, *v. irreg. (g. dat.) I am before, at the head of* [*yond*
praetĕr, *prep. (g. acc.) beside, be-*
praetĕrĕo, -īvi *or* -ĭi, -ĭtum, 4, *v. irreg. pass by*

praetĕrĭtus, -a, -um, *past*
praetor, -ōris, *m. the praetor*
praevĕnĭo, -vēni, -ventum, 4, *anticipate*
prāvus, -a, um, *perverse, depraved*
prĕmo, -essi, -essum, 3, *I press*
prĕtium, -i, *n. price, reward*
prīmārĭus, -a, -um, *adj. first rate, eminent*
prīmo, *adv. at first*
prīmus, -a, -um, *first* (71)
princeps, -ĭpis, *adj.* and *noun, first in rank, chief, emperor*
princĭpātūs, -ūs, *m. sovereignty*
prior, -ōris, *superior, before* (71) *g. abl.*
pristĭnus, -a, -um, *adj. former, olden*
prius, *adv. sooner, before*
priusquam, *conj. until, before, sooner than* [*behalf of*
pro, *prep. (g. abl.) before, for, on*
prŏbē, *adv. rightly, properly*
prŏbĭtas, -ātis, *f. honesty, integrity*
prŏbus, -a, -um, *honest, upright*
prŏcella, -ae, *f. storm*
prŏcĕrēs, -um, *m. pl. nobles*
prŏcērus, -a, -um, *tall*
prŏdĭtor, -ōris, *m. traitor*
prŏdo, -dĭdi, -dĭtum, 3, *I hand down*
prōduco, -xi, -ctum, 3, *bring forward*
proelium, -i, *n. battle*
prŏfecto, *adv. assuredly, indeed*
prŏfĕro, -tŭli, -lātum, -ferre, *v. irreg. extend*
prŏfĭciscor, -fectus, 3, *dep. set out*
prŏfundus, -a, -um, *adj. deep*
prōgigno, -gĕnŭi, -gĕnĭtum, 3, *bring forth, give birth to*
prōgrĕdĭor, -gressus, 3, *v. dep. advance*
prŏhĭbĕo, -ŭi, -ĭtum, 2, *hinder, prohibit, keep off*
prōlēs, -is, *f. offspring*
prōmissum, -i, *n. a promise*

T

prōmissus, -a, -um, *hanging down, long (of hair)*
prōmitto, -mīsi, -missum, 3, *promise;* p. mē ventūrum, *I promise to come (never* p. vĕnīre) (280)
promptus, -a, -um, *ready*
prŏpĕ, *prep. (g. acc.) near*
prŏpĕ, *adv. near at hand, nearly;* p. ăbest a nōbīs, *he is close to us*
prŏpĕro, -āvi, -ātum, 1, *hasten*
prŏpinquus, -a, -um, *adj. near*
proptĕr, *prep. (g. acc.) on account of;* more rarely, *near* (183)
prōpulso, -avi, -atum, 1, *repel*
Prōserpĭna, -ae, *f. Proserpine*
prosper, -pĕra, -pĕrum, *prosperous*
prōsum, -fŭi, prodesse, *(g. dat.) I am of use;* non prōdest hōc dīcĕre, *it is of no use to say this* (191)
prōtendo, -tendi, -tensum *or* -tentum, 3, *extend*
prout, *conj. according as*
prōvĭdĕo, -vīdi, -vīsum, 2, *I foresee, provide*
prōvidus, -a, -um, *provident, foreseeing*
prōvincĭa, -ae, *f. a section of the Roman Empire called a "province"*
prōvŏco, -āvi, -ātum, 1, *challenge, provoke*
proxĭmus, -a, -um, *nearest, next, last* (Par. 69)
prūdens, -ntis, *prudent*
prūdentĭa, -ae, *f. knowledge, prudence*
pūblĭcus, -a, -um, *public*
pŭdet, -ŭit, *or* pŭdītum, -ĕre, 2, *v. impers. it shames* (Par. 219)
pŭella, -ae, *f. girl*
pŭer, -ĕri, *m. boy*
pŭerĭtia, -ae, *f. boyhood*
pugna, -ae, *f. battle*
pugno, -āvi, -ātum, 1, *fight*
pulcher, -chra, -chrum, *beautiful*
pulli, -ōrum, *m. pl. chickens*

pūmex, -ĭcis, *m. pumice-rock*
Pūnĭcus, -a, -um, *Carthaginian*
pūnĭo, -īvi *and* -ĭi, -ītum, 4, *punish*
pŭto, -āvi, -ātum, 1, *I think*
putresco, 3, *putrefy*
Pygmălĭon, -ōnis, *m. Pygmalion*
Pythăgŏras, -ae, *m. Pythagoras*

**Quadringenti**, see Par. 81
quaero, quaesīvi, quaesītum, 3, *seek, ask;* quaerēbam mēcum, *I was enquiring with myself; I asked him why, &c.*, quaesīvi, ăb, ē, *or* dē, eo cūr, &c.
quaestŭs, -ūs, *m. gain, profit*
quālis, -e, *pron. adj. of what sort? what sort of? of which sort? as*
quam, *conj. or adv. than* (62) *(aft. comp.);* how,quam turpe est! *how base it is! as,* nōn tam valĭdus est quam frāter eius, *he is not so strong as his brother;* quam cĕlerrimē, *as quickly as possible* (327); quam qui, *or* ut (319)
quamdĭu, *conj. as long as*
quamquam, *conj. although (mostly with indic.)* (323)
quamvīs, *conj. however much, although (with subjunctive)* (323)
quando? *interr. adv. when? also used in dependent questions* (156)
quantus, -a, -um, *adj. how great a;* tantus...quantus, *so great a...as; (used as a Noun)* quantum pĕcūnĭae, *as much (of) money;* adv. *how much;* quantum interest, *how great a difference is there!* quanti? *at how great a price?* see Par. 283, 284
quārē? *interr. adv. and conj. why? on what account?*
quartus, see Par. 81
quăsī, *adv. as if, just as*
quăterni, -ae, -a, *four a-piece* (314)
quătĭo, *no perf.,* quassum, 3, *shake, toss*
quattuor, see Par. 81

**-que,** *conj. and ; used to combine two words of similar meaning into one phrase,* sĕnātus pŏpŭlusquĕ (37)

**quercus, -ûs,** *f. an oak* [plain

**quĕror, questus,** 3 (*v. dep.*) *com-*

**qui,** *rel. pron.* (107) ; *often precedes (never follows)* cum, *and must then be rendered demonstratively :* quod cum intellexissem, *when I perceived this ;* qui *after* quam (319) ; qui *foll. by subjunct.* (298) ; īdem qui (319) ; *see also* quo

**quĭă,** *conj. because*

**quīdam, quaedam, quoddam,** *pron. adj.* (*neut. pron.* quiddam), *a certain* (310a) ; cardo quĭdam, *a kind of hinge ; see Eng. Vocab.* "A"

**quĭdem,** *conj. or adv.* (67, 139) *on the one hand, it is true, indeed ;* quĭdem...autem (*or* vĕro *or* sĕd), *on the one hand...but on the other hand ;* nē...quĭdem, *not even* (141) ; q. *sometimes merely emphasizes a word,* e.g. nunc quĭdem rīdes, "Now *you laugh (but soon you will weep)*"

**quid** (*or* quic) quam, *see* quisquam

**quilibet, quaelibet, quodlibet** (*pron. adj.*) *any you please ;* quolibet tempore, *at any time he pleases* (*pron. neut.* quidlibet)

**quīn** (*i.e.* quī nōn, *or* quō nōn) *conj. that not,* (*with subj.*) (145, 300) nēmo est quīn rīdeat, *there is no one that does not laugh ; see also* obstat *and* dūbium, *with which it means* "*but that*"

**quinquĕ,** *see* Par. 81 ; **quinquĭens,** *adv. five times ;* **quintus,** *see* Par. 81

**quĭs, quae, quĭd,** *who? see Par.*110, 111 ; (*after* sī, nĕ, num) *any one*

**quisnam, quaenam, quidnam?** *emphatic inter. pron. who? which? what?*

**quisquam, quaequam, quodquam** (*pron. neut.* quicquam) *anyone* (*used in neg. and compar. sentences, and in questions that expect the answer* "*no*") (309)

**quisquĕ, quaequĕ, quodquĕ,** (*pron. neut.* quidquĕ *or* quicquĕ) *each, every ;* fortissĭmus quisquĕ, *each bravest man, i.e. all the bravest men ;* sŭam quisquĕ dŏmum rĕdĭērunt, *they returned, each to his own home* (*where* quisquĕ *is not nom. to r., but in Apposition to the nom. to* r.) (140, 310)

**quisquis, quaequae, quodquod** (*adj.*), *whoever ;* (*pron. neut.*) quidquid *or* quicquid, *whatever ;* quidquid ămīcōrum, *whatever* (*of*) *friends* (*part. gen.*)

**quīvīs, quaevis, quodvīs** (*pronom. neut.* quidvīs) *any you like ;* nōn cuiusvis est, *it is not every one's luck* (310)

**quō,** *adv.* (*rel.* and *interr.*) *whither*

**quo,** *conj.* and *adv.* (1) quo cĭtĭus, ĕo mēlĭus, *by how much the quicker, by so much the better ;* (2) (*with compar.*) *in order that* (303) ; quōcum (179)

**quŏd,** *conj. because, that* (*sometimes foll. by subjunct.,* 293a)

**quōmĭnus,** *conj. that not,* Par. 144 ; quid obstat q. vĕnĭas? *what prevents you from coming?*

**quōmŏdo?** *in what manner? how?* (*also used in dependent quest.*)

**quondam,** *adv. formerly*

**quŏniam,** *conj. since*

**quŏquĕ,** *see* quisquĕ

**quŏquĕ,** *conj. also, too ;* (*always after the word it modifies*)

**quŏt,** *indecl. adj. how many*

**quŏtīdĭē** (*more correctly spelt* cottīdĭē), *adv. every day*

**quŏtiens,** *adv. how many times ;* quŏtiens...tŏtiens, *as many times as...so many times*

quŏtus, -a, -um ? *what (in number)?* hōra est ? *what o'clock is it?*
quŏtusquisque, *pron.* q. est qui vĕlit ! *how few there are who wish !* (*sometimes in two words, e.g.* quŏtus ēnim quisque)
quum, *an incorrect form of* cum

**Rādo, rāsi, rāsum,** 3, *shave*
Rădīx, -īcis, *f. root*
răpāx, -ācis, *adj. rapacious*
răpĭdus, -a, -um, *rapid*
răpĭo, -ŭi, raptum, -ĕre, 3, *seize*
rārŏ, *adv. seldom, rarely*
rārus, -a, -um, *adj. rare*
rătĭo, -iōnis, *f. reason*
rătus, -a, -um, *thinking*; see reŏr
rĕcĭpĭo, -cēpi, -ceptum, 3, *take back*; sē rĕcĭpĭunt in castra, *they retreat to the camp*
rĕcĭto, -āvi, -ātum, 1, *I read aloud*
rĕclāmo, -āvi, -ātum, 1, *cry shame, protest*
rĕcordor, -ātus, 1, *call to mind* (*gen.*, *but more often acc.*)
rĕcrĕo, -āvi, -ātum, 1, *refresh*
rectĕ, *adv. rightly*
rectus, -a, -um, *adj. straight, right*
rĕcŭpĕro, -āvi, -ātum, 1, *recover, get back* [*fuse*
rĕcūso, -āvi, -ātum, 1, *object, re-*
reddo, reddĭdi, reddĭtum, 3, *restore, render*
rĕdĕo, -ĭi, -ĭtum, 4, *return*
rĕdūco, -duxi, -ductum, 3, *bring back*
rĕfĕro, rĕtŭlī *or* rettŭlī, rĕlātum, 3, *v. irreg. I bring back, report, relate, reply*; *sometimes means "refer;"* dē hāc rē ad Patres rĕlātum est, *a reference was made to the Senate on this point*
rĕfert (*or* rē-fert) *it matters, is of importance* (*conjugated like* fĕro, *but impersonal*); illud magni rĕferre reor, *I think that is of great importance* (329)

rĕgĕro, -gessi, -gestum, 3, *cast up, or back*
rēgīna, -ae, *f. a queen*
rĕgĭo, -ōnis, *f. region, district*
regno, -āvi, -ātum, 1, *reign*
regnum, -i, *n. a kingdom*
rĕgo, -xi, -ctum, 3, *I rule*
Rēgŭlus, -i, *m. Regulus*
rĕlĭgĭo, -ōnis, *f. religious scruple*, ĭd rĕlĭgĭōnī hăbĕo, *I consider this sacrilege,* lit. *for a religious scruple* (268) [*poets,* rellĭgio]
rĕnuntio, -āvi, -ātum, 1, *bring back word*
rĕlinquo, -līqui, -lictum, 3, *leave, quit*
rĕmĭniscor, 3, *I remember* (203)
rĕnŏvo, -āvi, -ātum, 1, *make new again, restore*
rĕor, rătus, rēri, (*v. dep.*) *suppose, think*
rĕpĕrio, reppĕri, rĕpertum, 4, *find* (*after search*); see invĕnĭo
rĕplĕo, -plēvi, -plētum, 2, *fill up*
rēs, rĕi, *f. thing*; rem bĕnē gĕro, *I succeed*; rēs Rōmānā, *the affairs* (*or fortunes*) *of Rome*; r. mīlĭtāris, *military matters*; r. fămĭlĭāris, *one's household affairs, property*; r. frūmentārĭa, *forage*; rē ipsa, *or* rē, *in fact* (*adv. abl.*)
rescindo, -scĭdi, -scissum, 3, *tear open,* or *down*; *break down (a bridge)*
rĕsisto, -stĭti, -stĭtum, 3, (*g. dat.*) *resist*; mĭhī rĕsistĭtur, *I am being resisted* [*gard*
respĭcio, -spexi, -spectum, 3, *re-*
respondĕo, -di, -sum, 2, *answer*
responsum, -i, *n. answer*
rēs-publica, rĕi-publicae, *f., the republic, the country, politics*
restĭtŭo, -ŭi, -ūtum, 3, *restore*
resto, -stĭti, 1, *remain*; spēs ūnă restat, *one hope remains*
rēte, -is, *n. a net*
rĕtexo, -texŭi, -textum, 3, *unweave*

rĕtĭneo, -tĭnui, -tentum, 2, *keep back*
rĕus, -i, *m. the accused, defendant;* rĕus factus sum, *I was accused*
rĕvŏco, -āvi, -ātum, 1, *recall*
rĕverto, -ti, -sum, 3, *turn back, return* (in the Pres. and Pres. derived tenses the Act form is rare: use rĕvertor)
rĕvertor, -versus, 3, *v. dep. I turn back, return*
rex, rēgis, *m. king*
Rhēnus, -i, *m. the Rhine*
rhētŏrĭca, -ae, *f. rhetoric*
Rhŏdănus, -i, *m. the Rhone*
Rhŏdus, -i, *f. Rhodes*
rĭdeo, rīsi, rīsum, 2, *laugh; laugh at* (g. acc.)
rīpa, -ae, *f. bank, shore*
rīsŭs, ūs, *laughter, a laugh*
rŏbur, -oris, *n. strength*
rŏgātĭo, -iōnis, *f.* (see rŏgo) *a bill proposed to the people;* ferre rŏgātĭōnem, *to bring forward a bill*
rŏgo, -āvi, -ātum, 1, *ask;* (used of asking the people whether they will pass a bill) hence rŏgāre lēgem, *to bring forward a bill*
Rōma, -ae, *f. Rome*
Rōmānus, -a, -um, *Roman*
Rōmŭlus, -i, *m. Romulus*
rŏsa, -ae, *f. a rose*
rŭbeo, -ni, 2, *blush*
rŭber, -bra, -brum, *red*
rŭbēta, -ōrum, *n. pl. bramble-beds;* rŭbus, -i, *m. bramble*
rŭdis, -e, *raw, ignorant* (g. gen.)
rūpēs, -is, *f. a rock*
rūs, rūris, *n. country;* rūri (Par. 265) *in the country*
rustĭcus, -a, -um, *rustic*

**Săcer, -cra, -crum,** *sacred*
săcerdōs, -ōtis, *m. priest*
saepĕ, *adv. often*
saepĕnŭmĕro, *adv. oftentimes*

saepio, saepsi, saeptum, 4, *hedge in, fence round*
saepissĭmē, *adv. very often*
saevus, -a, -um, *cruel, fierce*
săgācĭtās, -ātis, *f. keen scent, sagacity;* săgax, -ācis, *sagacious*
săgitta, -ae, *f. an arrow*
salto, -āvi, -ātum, 1, *dance*
salūber, -bris, -bre, *healthful*
sălūs, -ūtis, *f. safety*
sălūto, -āvi, -ātum, 1, *salute*
salvĕo, -ēre, 2, *I am well;* salvē, *be well,* i.e. *good morning!*
salvus, -a, -um, *adj. safe*
Samnītes, -ium, *m. pl. the Samnites*
sancĭo, sanxi, sanctum, 4, *enact:* sancio nē quīs absit, *I enact that no one shall be absent*
sānē, *adv.* (lit. *soberly, in sober earnest*) *certainly*
sanguis, -ĭnis, *m. blood*
sāno, -āvi, -ātum, 1, *heal*
sānus, -a, -um, *healthy*
săpĭens, -ntis, *wise;* săpĭenter, *adv. wisely*
săpĭentĭa, -ae, *f. wisdom*
săpĭo, -ĭvi and -ĭi, 3, *savour of* (g. acc.); *am wise*
sarcio, sarsi, sartum, 4, *patch, mend*
sătis, *adv. enough, sufficiently:* (used as a noun) sătis patriae dătum est, *enough has been given to the claims of your country*
saxum, -i, *n. rock*
scĕlus, -ĕris, *n. crime*
scēna, -ae, *f. the stage of a theatre*
scĭentĭa, -ae, *f. knowledge*
scindo, scĭdi, scissum, 3, *rend, tear*
scĭo, -ĭi or -ĭvi, -ītum, 4, *I know*
Scīpĭo, -ōnis, *m. Scipio*
scrība, -ae, *m. scribe, clerk*
scrībo, -psi, -ptum, 3, *write:* s. lēges, *I draw up laws*
scriptor, -ōris, *m. a writer, author*
scūtum, -i, *n. shield*
Scўtha, -ae, *m. a Scythian*

sē, see Par. 94, 218, 305, 306; sē-cum, see Par. 179.
sĕcundus, -a, -um, *second, prosperous;* sĕcundum, *prep. (g. acc.) following, in accordance with*
sĕcūris, -is, *f. (acc.* -im), *axe; the axes and rods* (fasces) *were the signs of the consul's office*
sĕd, *conj. but (on the other hand);* non sōlum...sed ĕtiam, *not only... but also*
sĕdĕo, sēdi, sessum, 2, *I sit*
sēdēs, -is, *f. seat, abode*
sēdĭtĭŏ, -ĭonis, *f. rebellion, sedition*
sĕgĕs, sĕgĕtis, *f. cornfield, harvest*
segnĭtĭes, -ēi, *f. slothfulness*
sĕmĕl, *adv. once (for all)*
semper, *adv. always, ever*
senātōrĭus, -a, -um, *senatorial*
sĕnātus, -ūs, *m. the senate*
sĕnectūs, -ūtis, *f. old age*
sĕnex, sĕnis, *m. old man*
sĕnior, *see* Par. 69
sensus, -ūs, *m. a sense*
sententĭa, -ae, *f. opinion*
sentĭo, -si, -sum, 4, *feel, perceive*
sĕpĕlĭo, sĕpĕlīvi *and* -ĭi, sĕpultum, 4, *bury*
September,-bris,-bre, *of September; see* Par. 84; septuāgēsimus (81)
sĕquor, sĕcūtus, 3, *v. dep. follow*
sĕrēnus, -a, -um, *adj. clear*
sermo, -ōnis, *m. a discourse*
sĕro, sēvi, sătum, 3, *plant, sow*
sēro, *late;* sērĭus, *too late*
serpens, -ntis, *f. serpent*
sertum, -i, *n. garland*
sōrus, -a, -um, *late*
servĭo, -ii, -ītum, 4, *I am a slave to, I serve (g. dat.)*
servĭtūs, -ūtis, *f. slavery*
servo, -āvi, -ātum, 1, *watch, preserve; s.* fĭdem, *I keep my word*
servus, -i, *m, slave*
sēsē, *an emphatic form of* sē
seu, *conj. whether;* seu...seu, *whether...or; (not used like* utrum an...*in dep. sentences*)
sĕvĕrus, -a, -um, *adj. severe*
sī, *conj. if* (125); sī quĭs, sī quī, *if any man, any men* (294); *with pres. and imperf. subj.* (295)
sic, *adv. thus, so*
Sĭcĭlĭa, -ae, *f. Sicily*
sīdus, -ĕris, *n. star*
signum, -i, *n. a sign, signal*
silentĭum, -ii, *n. silence*
silva, -ae, *f. a wood* [66, 60
sĭmĭlis, -e, *(g. gen.* or *dat.) like,*
sĭmŭl, *adv. at the same time;* simul ...simul, *at once...and*
sĭmŭlāc, *adv. as soon as*
sĭmŭlācrum, -i, *n. an image, statue*
sĭmŭlātĭo, -ōnis, *f. a pretence*
sĭmŭlo, -āvi, -ātum, 1, *pretend*
sĭne, *prep. (g. abl.) without*
singŭli, -ae, -a, *one a-piece, one by one* (77, 314)
sĭnister, -tra, -trum, *left*
sĭno, sīvi, sĭtum, 3, *suffer*
sĭnŭs, -ūs, *m. a fold (of the garment, especially about the breast); pocket*
sĭtis, -is, *f. (acc.* -im) *thirst;* sĭtī mŏri, *to die of* (lit. *with*) *thirst*
sīve, *conj. whether;* sīve...sīve, *whether...or, (not used like* utrum...an *in Dependent Questions*);* sīve lŏquor, sīve tăcĕo, patri nōn plăcĕo, *whether I speak or hold my tongue, I cannot please my father.*
sŏcer, -ĕri, *m. father-in-law*
sŏcĭus, -i, *m. a partner, ally, companion*
Sōcrătēs, -is, *m. Socrates*
sōl, sōlis, *m. sun*
sŏlĕo, -ĭtus sum, -ēre, 2, *v. n. I am accustomed*
sŏlĭtus, -a, -um, *customary*
Sŏlōn, -ōnis, *m. Solon*
sollertĭa, -ae, *f. skill, subtlety*
sŏlum, -i, *n. ground, soil*

sōlum, *adv. only, alone*
sōlus, -a, -um, *adj. gen. sing.* -īus, *dat.* -i, *alone*
solvo, solvi, sŏlūtum, 3, *I loosen, pay ;* s. fāmem, *I break my fast ;* impar solvendo sum, *I am not equal to paying,* i.e. *insolvent*
somnus, -i, m. *sleep*
sŏnĭtus, -ūs, m. *a sound, noise*
sons, sontis, *guilty*
sŏnus, -i, m., *sound*
Sŏphŏclēs, -is, m. *Sophocles*
sŏpor, -ōris, m. *slumber*
sŏror, -ōris, f. *sister*
sors, -tis, f. *lot, fate*
sortior, sortītus, 4, *dep. draw lots*
Sparta, -ae, f. *Sparta*
spěcĭēs, -ēi, f. *appearance* (182)
specto, -āvi, -ātum, 1, *look at*
spěcŭlor, -ātus, 1, v. dep. *I spy out*
spěcus, -ūs, m. *cave*
sperno, sprēvi, sprētum, 3, *despise*
spēro, -āvi, -ātum, 1, *I hope*
spēs, -ēi, f. *hope*
spīro, -āvi, -ātum, 1, *breathe*
spīrĭtus, -ūs, m. *breath*
splendĭdus, -a, -um, *splendid, bright*
splendor, -ōris, m. *brightness*
spŏlia, -ōrum, n. pl. *spoils*
spondĕo, spŏpondi, sponsum, 2, *pledge, promise to pay, betroth*
spontĕ (*adv. phrase*) meā, tuā, &c., *of my, your, &c., own accord*
stătim, *adv. immediately*
stătĭo, -ōnis, f. *a post, station*
stătua, -ae, f. *statue*
stătŭo, -ŭi, -ūtum, 3, *determine*
stella, -ae, f. *a star*
sterto, -tui, 3, *snore*
stīpendium, -ii, n. (*military*) *pay*
sto, stĕti, stătum, 1, *I stand, abide by* (*with abl.* or *in and abl.*) stāre prōmissis, *to abide by one's promises ;* ā Tullio stāre, *to side with Tullius ;* magno prētio stat, *it costs a great price*
strēnŭē, *adv. vigorously*

strēnŭus, -a, -um, *vigorous* (68*b*)
strepĭtŭs, -ūs, m. *noise, din*
struo, -xi, -ctum, 3, *pile up, construct*
stŭdĕo, -ŭi, 2, *I am eager, zealous*
stŭdĭōsus, -a, -um, *adj. zealous, eager after* (*g. gen.*)
stŭdĭum, -ii, n. *zeal, a pursuit, study*
stultĭtĭa, -ae, f. *folly*
stultus, -a, -um, *foolish*
suādĕo, -āsi, -āsum, 2, (*g. dat.*) *advise, persuade*
suāvis, -e, *adj. sweet, delightful*
sŭb, *prep.* (*g. abl.* or *acc.*) *up to, under ;* (*of time*) *about* (180)
subĕo, -ĭi, -ĭtum (243), *go up to*
sŭbĭto, *adv. suddenly*
sŭbĭtus, -a, -um, *sudden*
subsĕquor, -cūtus, 3, *follow up*
subsum, *no perf.*, v. *irreg. I am under, amongst* [*dat.*) *help*
subvĕnio, -vēni, -ventum, 4, (*g.*)
succēdo, -cessi, -cessum, 3, *follow, turn out ;* res mĭhĭ bĕnĕ successit, *the matter turned out well for me*
Suēvi, -orum, *the Suevi*
suffĭcio, -fēci, -fectum, 3, *suffice* (*g. dat.*)
sum, *I am,* p. 79, Par. 268, 142*d*
sūmo, sumpsi, sumptum, 3, *take, assume*
summus, -a, -um, (69) *highest, utmost ;* summā cĕlĕrĭtātĕ, *with all speed ;* summus mons, *the highest part of the mountain*
sŭper, *prep.* (*g. acc.* or *abl.*) *over, upon, concerning* (180)
sŭperbĭa, -ae, f. *pride*
sŭperbus, -a, -um, *proud*
sŭpĕro, -āvi, -ātum, 1, *overcome*
sŭpersum, -fui, -esse, v. *irreg. I remain over, survive* (*g. dat.*)
sŭpĕrus, -a, -um, *adj. upper* (69)
suppĕdĭto, -āvi, -ātum, 1, *supply*
supplex, -ĭcis, *adj. suppliant* (47, 48)
supplĭcĭum, -ii, n. *punishment*
suprā, *prep.* (*g. acc.*) *above*

suprēmus, -a, -um, *superl. of sŭpĕrus, highest; (of time) last*
surgo, surrexi, surrectum, 3, *rise*
suscĭpĭo, -cēpi, -ceptum, 3, *undertake*
suspĭcĭo, -ĭōnis, *f. suspicion*
sustento, 1, *sustain*
sŭus, -a, -um, (98 and p. 328); suis impĕrat, *he orders his (men)* (34)
Sȳria, -ae, *f. Syria*

**Tăbernācŭlum, -i,** *n. tent*
tābesco, -ui, 3, *I decay*
tăcĕo, -ŭi, -ĭtum, 2, *I am silent*
taedĕt, -dŭit *or* pertaesum est, *v. impers. it disgusts, wearies* (219)
taeter, -tra, -trum, *foul*
tălentum, -i, *n. a talent,* i.e. *a sum of money, about* £240
tālis, -e, *of that sort, such*
tam, *adv. so, to such a degree, such;* tam prāvi mōres, *such depraved conduct;* very, hōc tam longum ĭter, *this very long journey* (228)
tămen, *conj. yet, however*
tamquam, *conj. just as;* tē t. thēsaurum hăbĕo, *I consider you as a treasure;* t. sī consul esset, *just as if he were consul*
tandem, *at last;* cur (or quid) tandem? *why indeed? pray why?*
tantum, *adv. (so much and no more, hence) only;* nōmĭnĕ tantum mĭhĭ nōtus est, *he is known to me by name and no more;* ūnus tantum, *only one*
tantus, -a, -um, *so great* (a)*; (as a noun)* tantum pĕcūnĭae, *so much (of) money;* (*often used, after a Pron., for "great"*) haec tanta călămĭtās, *this great calamity;* tanti, see Par. 283, 284; tantum...quantum, *as much...as*
tārdus, -a, -um, *slow*
Tarquĭnĭus, -i, *m. Tarquin*
Tartărĕus, -a, -um, *Tartarean, belonging to Tartarus, the region of the punishment of the wicked dead*
Taurus, -i, *m. Mount Taurus*
taurus, -i, *m. a bull*
tĕgo, -xi, -ctum, 3, *I cover*
tellūs, -ūris, *f. earth, the goddess Earth*
tēlum, -i, *n. dart, missile* [ness
tĕmĕrĭtās, -ātis, *f. recklessness, rash-*
tempestās, -ātis, *f. tempest*
templum, -i, *n. temple*
tempus, -ŏris, *n. time;* tempŏri cēdĕre, *to yield to circumstances*
tĕnĕo, -ŭi, tentum, 2, *I hold, retain*
tĕner, -ĕra, -ĕrum, *tender, soft*
tĕnŭis, -e, *thin*
tĕnŭs, *prep. (g. abl.) as far as; follows its case);* verbo tĕnus, *so far as words go*
tergum, -i, *n. back;* terga dant mĭhĭ, *they flee before me*
terni, -ae, -a, *three a-piece* (314)
tĕro, trīvi, trītum, 3 *rub, waste;* tempus tĕrĭmus, *we are wasting time*
terra, -ae, *f. the earth, land;* terrā mărīque, *by sea and land (adverbial local abl.)*
terrĕo, -ŭi, -ĭtum, 2, *terrify, frighten*
terror, -ōris, *m. terror, alarm*
tertius, -a, -um, *see* Par. 81
testāmentum, -i, *n. will, testament*
testis, -is, *m. witness*
testor, -ātus, 1, *testify*
Thĕmistŏclēs, -is, *m. Themistocles*
Thrāx, Thrācis, *m. a Thracian;* Thrācum est, *it is the mark of,* i.e. *like, Thracians*
Tĭbĕrĭus, -ii, *m. Tiberius, the name of the second Roman emperor, Tiberius Caesar*
tignārĭus, -a -um, *having to do with beams;* făber t. *builder, carpenter*
tigris, -is, *or* -ĭdis, *c. a tiger, tigress*

tĭmĕo, -ŭi, 2, *fear*
tĭmĭdus, -a, -um, *adj. timid*
tĭmor, -ōris, *m. fear*
tŏlĕro, -āvi, -ātum, 1, *endure*
tollo, sustuli, sublatum, 3, *raise, take away;* tollunt rīsum, clāmōrem, &c. *they raise a laugh, shout, &c.*
Tŏnans, -ntis, *m. the Thunderer, a name of Jupiter*
tŏnat, -ŭit, -āre, 1, *v. impers. it thunders*
tonsor, -ōris, *m. barber*
torrĕo, torrui, tostum, 2, *parch, roast*
tot, *indecl. adj. so many;* hae tot cǎlǎmĭtātes, *these numerous calamities*
tŏtiens, *adv. so many times*
tōtus, -a, -um, *adj. whole, all* (85)
trabs, trăbis, *f. beam*
tracto, -āvi, -ātum, 1, *I handle, deal with*
trādo, -dĭdi, -dĭtum, 3, *deliver;* tradĭtum est, *it has been handed down*
tradūco, -xi, -ctum, 3, *I lead across*
trăho, -axi, -actum, 3, *I draw, drag*
trajĭcĭo, (*also spelt* trāĭcĭo) *same as* transjĭcĭo; (1) *throw across, carry across,* trājĭcĭo exercitum, *I lead an army across;* (2) *carry myself across,* i.e. *cross,* trājĭcĭo flūmen, *I cross a stream*
tranquillus, -a, -um, *adj. calm*
trans, *prep. g. acc. across*
Transalpīnus, -a, -um, *beyond the Alps* [*over*
transĕo, -ii, -ĭtum, 4, (241) *cross*
transfīgo, -ĭxi, -ĭxum, 3, *transfix*
transjĭcĭo, *see* trajĭcĭo
transversus, -a, -um, *turned across;* t. dĭgĭtus *or* unguis, *a finger's, or nail's breadth* [*piece*
trĕcēni, -ae, -a, *three hundred a-*
trĕcenti, -ae, -a, *three hundred*

trĕmo, trĕmui, tremĭtum, 3, *tremble*
trēs, tria, *see* Par. 68
trĭbūnus, -i, *m. tribune*
trĭbŭo, -ŭi, -ūtum, 3, *give, assign*
trĭbus, -ūs, *f. tribe*
trĭbūtum, -i, *n. tribute*
triennium, -i, *n. three years*
trīni, -ae, -a, *three* (*used with nouns like* littĕrae) (318)
tristis, -e, *sad*
trĭumpho, -āvi, -ātum, 1, *enjoy a triumph,* i.e. *a triumphal procession granted by the Romans to distinguished generals*
Trŏja, -ae, *f. Troy*
Trŏjānus, -a, -um, *Trojan*
tū, *see* p. 45
tŭba, -ae, *f. trumpet*
tŭĕor, tŭĭtus, 2, *v. dep. gaze on, guard, protect*
Tullia, -iae, *f. Tullia*
Tullius, -i, *m. Tullius*
tum, *adv. and conj. then during that time;* cum...tum, *not only ...but also* (317)
tŭmĭdus, -a, -um, *swelling, swollen*
tunc, *adv. then, at that time*
turba, -ae, *f. crowd*
turbo, -āvi, -ātum, 1, *disturb, throw into confusion;* turbātum est, *a riot was made*
turbŭlentus, -a, -um, *turbulent*
turdus, -i, *m. thrush*
turpis, -e, *base, disgraceful*
turpĭtūdo, -ĭnis, *f. disgrace*
turris, -is, *f. tower*
tussīs, -is, *f.* (*acc.* -im, *abl.* -i,) *cough*
tuto, *adv. safely;* -us, -a, -um, *safe*
tŭus, -a, -um, *pron. adj. thy, thine*
tyrannus, -i, *m. despot, tyrant*

Ŭbi, *adv. where*
ulciscor, ultŭs, 3 (*v. dep.*) *avenge*
ullus, -a, -um, *adj.* (*gen. sing.* -ĭus, *dat. sing.* -ī), *any* (85, 87, 309)
ulmus, -i, *f. elm*

ultĭmus, -a, -um, see Par. 69
ultrā, *prep. g. acc. on the farther side of, beyond*
Ŭlyssēs, -is, *m. Ulysses*
uncĭa, -ae, *f. inch*
unda, -ae, *water*
unguis, -is, *m. nail*
unquam, *adv. at any time, ever*
ūnā, *at the same time or place; together*
ūnĭcē, *adv. singularly*
ūnus, -a, -um, *adj.* (74), *one; in tē ūno, in you alone* (96); spēs quam ūnam hăbŭi, *the only hope I had;* omnes ăd ūnum, *all to a man*
urbs, urbis, *f. city*
uro, ussi, ustum, 3, *burn*
ŭt, *conj. that, in order that; often rendered by Eng. " to "* (Par. 143); ut non (*when to be used for nē*) Par. 296; (*with indic.,* "*when,*" "*as*")
ŭter, -ră, -rum (*gen.* -rīus, *dat.* -rī), *which of two?* u. hōrum, *which of these two* (85)? ŭterquĕ, utrăque, utrŭmque, *either, both;* dux ŭterquĕ (*sing.*) *both leaders*
ūtĭlis, -e, *useful*
ūtĭlĭtās, -ātis, *f. utility, service*
ŭtĭnam ! *conj. O that, would that !* (*g. subj., see* Par. 330)
ūtor, ūsus, 3, *v. dep. I use* (207)
utrimque, *adv. on both sides*
utrum, *conj. whether* (171, 174)
uxor, -ōris, *f. a wife*

**Văcŭus**, -a, -um, *empty of* (*g. abl.*)
valdē (*i.e.* validē) *adv. strongly, exceedingly*
vălĕo, -ŭi, -ĭtum, 2, *I am in good health;* vălēte, *farewell !*
vălētūdo, -ĭnis, *f. health*
vălĭdus, -a, -um, *strong*
vallis, -is, *f. a valley*
vallum, -i, *n. the camp palisade composed of valli* (see vallus)

vallus, -i, *the stake borne by each Roman soldier for the formation of the* vallum [*hood*
vānĭtās, -ātis, *f. emptiness, false-*
vărĭus, -a, -um, *different, various*
vastus, -a, -um, *vast*
vasto, -āvi, -ātum, 1, *lay waste*
-vĕ, *conj. or (an enclitic form of* vĕl)
vectīgăl, -ālis, *n. a tax*
vĕhĕmens, -ntis, *vehement, warm*
vĕhĕmenter, *adv. vehemently, warmly;* -issĭmē, *very warmly*
vĕhĕmentĭa, -ae, *f. vehemence, passion* [*ride*)
vĕho, -xi, -ctum, 3, *carry* (pass.
vĕl, *or (if you like),* Par. 157a; hic discessus. vĕl pŏtĭus fŭga, *this departure or rather (if you will have strict correctness) flight;* even, hōc vĕl pŭĕro făcĭlē est, *this is easy even for a boy* (141a); (*with superl.*) *very,* Stoĭcōrum vĕl maxĭmus est, *he is the very greatest of the Stoics*
vēlōx, -ōcis, *adj. swift*
vēnātor, -ōris, *m. hunter*
vendo, -dĭdi, -dĭtum, 3, *sell*
vĕnēnātus, -a, -um, *poisoned*
vĕnēnum, -i, *n. poison*
vĕnĕror, -ātus, 1, *v. dep. reverence, worship*
vĕnĭa, -ae, *f. pardon,* dăre veniam ei, *to pardon him*
vĕnio, vēni, ventum, 4, *I come*
vēnor, -atus, 1, *v. dep. I hunt*
venter, -tris, *m. the stomach*
ventĭto, -āvi, 1, *v. freq. I come frequently*
ventus, -i, *m. the wind*
Vĕnŭs, -ĕris, *f. Venus*
vēr, vēris, *n. the spring*
verber, -ĕris, *n. lash, stripe*
verbum, -i, *n. word;* verbo tĕnus, *so far as words go*
vērē, *adv. truthfully, accurately*
vĕrĕor, -ĭtus, 2, *fear, reverence* (301)

Vergīlĭus, -i, m. *Virgil*
vĕrīsĭmĭlis, -e, *adj. likely, probable*
vĕrĭtās, -ātis, *f. truth*
vĕro, *conj. however, truly* (139a)
versus, -ūs, *m. line, verse*
versŭs, *prep. with acc. towards (only of place or direction)*
vertĕx, -ĭcis, *m. top*
verto, verti, versum, 3, *turn;* in fūgam vertĕre, *to put to flight*
vĕrus, -a, -um, *true* [*abl.*)
vescor, 3, *v. dep. feed on* (g.
vesper, -pĕri, *m. evening*
vespĕrascit, -āvit, -ascĕre, *v. impers. evening approaches*
Vesta, -ae, *f. Vesta, the goddess of fire and the hearth*
Vestālis, -e, *Vestal, belonging to Vesta*
vester, -tra, -trum, *your, yours*
vestīmentum, -i, *n. clothing*
vestĭo, -īvi *or* -ĭi; -ītum, 4, *clothe*
vestis, -is, *f. clothing, garment*
vestītus, -ūs, *m. clothing*
vĕtus, vĕtĕris, *old* (61)
vexo, -āvi, -ātum, 1, *I vex, harass*
vī, *see* vīs
vĭa, -ae, *f. way, road*
victor, -ōris, *m. conqueror*
victōrĭa, -ae, *f. victory*
victus, -a, -um, *pass. part. of* vinco
vīcus, -i, *m. village*
vĭdĕo, vīdi, vīsum, 2, *see* (*in passive*) *seem, appear;* quid tĭbĭ vĭdētur ? *What seems* (*good*) *to you,* i.e. *what do you think ?*
vĭgĭl, *gen.* -ĭlis, *watchful* (47)
vĭgĭlĭa, -ae, *f. night watch; the night from 6 P.M to 6 A.M. was divided into four "watches"*
vĭgĭlo, -āvi, -ātum, 1, *I watch, I am awake*
vīlis, -e, *adj. cheap, common*
vincĭo, -nxi, -nctum, 4, *bind*
vinco, vīci, victum, 3, *conquer*
vincŭlum, -i, *n. a chain, bond*

vīnētum, -i, *n. vineyard, vines*
vīnum, -i, *n. wine*
vĭŏla, -ae, *f. violet*
vĭŏlentĭa, -ae, *f. violence*
vīres, -īum, *f. pl. strength; see* vīs
Virgilĭus, -ii, *see* Vergīlĭus
virga, -ae, *f. rod, stick*
virgo, -ĭnis, *f. maiden*
vĭr, vĭri, *m. hero, man*
virga, -ae, *f. twig, rod, stick*
vĭrĭdis, -e, *green*
virtūs, -ūtis, *f. valour, virtue*
vīs, *irreg. see* Par. 311; *force, violence, power, efficacy; pl.* vīres, *strength; see also* vŏlo, p. 238
viso, -vīsi, 3, (*v. freq.*) *come to see, visit*
vīsus, -ūs, *m. sight*
vīta, -ae, *f. life*
vĭtĭōsus, -a, -um, *full of vice, vicious*
vītis, -is, *f. vine*
vĭtĭum, -i, *n. vice, fault;* dăre vĭtĭo, *to impute as a fault* (Par. 268)
vīto, -āvi, -ātum, 1, *avoid*
vĭtŭpĕro, -āvi, -ātum, *revile*
vīvo, vixi, victum, 3, *live*
vix, *adv. scarcely*
vŏlo, -āvi, -ātum, 1, *I fly*
vŏlo, vŏlŭi, vellĕ, *v. irreg. I wish, am willing;* ĭdem velle, *to wish for the same thing* (pp. 128–130)
vŏluntas, -ātis, *f. a wish, will*
vŏluptas, -tātis, *f. pleasure*
vŏro, -āvi, -ātum, 1, *devou*
vos, *see* p. 45.
vox, vōcis, *f. a voice*
Vulcānus, -i, *m. Vulcan*
vulnĕro, -āvi, -ātum, 1, *wound*
vulnus, -ĕris, *n. a wound*
vulpĕs, -is, *f. fox*
vultur, -ŭris, *m. a vulture*
vultus, -ūs, *m. countenance, looks*

Xĕnŏphŏn, -ontis, *m. Xenophon*
Xerxĕs, -is, *m. Xerxes*

# APPENDIX XI.

## VOCABULARY—II.

### ENGLISH INTO LATIN.[1]

**A** (i.e. *a certain*), quīdam, quaedam, quoddam (*pron. neut.* quiddam); *a man said to me,* quīdam mĭhī dixit; *he had a wonderful power of speaking,* erat hŏmĭni mīra quaedam dīcendi făcultas
*ability* (*mental*), ingĕnium, -i, n.
*able, to be,* possum, pŏtui, posse; *see* Par. 229
*abode,* sēdēs, -is, f.
*abound,* ăbundo, 1
*about* (*around*), circum (*g. acc.*; *also adv.*); (*concerning*) dē (*g. abl.*); (*nearly*) fĕrē
*above,* sŭper (*g. acc. and abl.*); *from above,* dēsŭper, *adv.*
*abroad* (*rest*) fŏris; (*motion*) fŏrās
*absent, to be,* absum, āfui, ăbesse; *absent,* adj. absens, -ntis
*abstain from,* abstĭneo, -ui, -tentum, 2 (*g. abl.*)
*abundantly,* ăbundanter
*accept,* accĭpio, -cēpi, -ceptum, 3
*acceptable,* grātus, -a, -um
*accident,* cāsus, -ūs, m.; *by accident,* cāsu; fortĕ (*adv.*)
*accompany,* cŏmĭtor, 1, dep.

*accomplish,* perfĭcio, -fēci, -fectum, 3; *without accomplishing anything,* rē infectā
*accord, of his, my own accord,* sponte suā, meā, &c.
*accordingly,* ĭtăque, ĭgĭtur (*adv.*). N.B. *ĭgĭtur should not stand first in a clause*
*account, on account of,* propter, *or* ŏb, *prep. g. acc.; on that account,* ŏb ĭd, ĭdeo
*accurate* (of things, not persons), accūrātus, -a, -um
*accusation,* crīmen, -inis, n.
*accuse,* accūso, 1
*accused* (*man*), *the,* reus, -i, m.
*accuser,* accūsātor, -oris, m. [dep.
*accustomed, to be,* sŏleo, sŏlĭtus, 2,
*Achilles,* Ăchillēs, -is, m.
*acknowledge,* agnosco, -nōvi, -nĭtum, 3
*acquainted with, to be,* see *to know*
*acquire, to,* ădĭpiscor, ădeptus, 3, dep.
*acquit,* absolvo, -vi, -ūtum, 3; (*with g. of charge,* Par. 290)
*acre,* jŭger, -eris, n.
*across,* trans (*g. acc.*)

---

[1] In this Vocabulary it has not been thought necessary to write the terminations of the regular Conjugations 1, 2, and 4, *i.e.* -āvi, -ātum; -ui, -itum; -īvi, Itum.

*act, an,* factum, -i, n.; *act, to,* ăgo, ēgi, actum, 3
*Actium,* Actium, -i, n.
*active,* strēnuus, -a, -um
*actor, an,* mīmus, -i, m.
*adapted,* aptus, -a, um
*add,* addo, -dĭdi, -dĭtum, 3
*address,* allŏquor, -cūtus, 3, dep.
*admire,* admīror, 1, dep.
*admiration,* admīrātio, -onis, f.
*admit,* admitto, -mīsi, -missum, 3; *(confess)* confĭteor, -fessus, 2, dep.
*admonish,* admŏneo, -ui, -ĭtum, 2
*adorn,* orno, 1
*advance, to,* prōgrĕdior, -gressus, 3, dep.; prōcēdo, -cessi, -cessum, 3
*advantage,* commŏdum, -i, n.
*adverse,* adversus, -a, -um; inīquus, -a, -um
*adversity,* rēs adversae
*advice,* consĭlium, -i, n.; *by my, his, advice,* mē, eo, auctōre (197)
*advise,* admŏneo, -ui, -ĭtum, 2 (143)
*Aetna,* Aetna, -ae, f.
*affair,* rēs, rei, f.
*affection,* cārĭtās, -ātis, f.; *filial affection,* pĭĕtās, -ātis, f.
*affectionate,* cārus, -a, -um; pius, -a, -um
*affirm,* assĕvēro, 1; affirmo, 1
*afflict,* ango, 3; vexo, 1
*afford,* praebeo, -ui, -ĭtum, 2
*afraid, to be,* tĭmeo, 2; vereor, vĕrĭtus, 2, dep. *(constr.* Par. 301)
*Africa,* Afrĭca, -ae, f.
*after,* post *(g. acc.); after (conj.),* postquam, (1) *foll. by perf., except where* (2) *the interval is defined;* (1) *after he had come,* postquam vēnit; (2) *ten days after he had come,* decimo die postquam vēnerat
*afterwards,* posteā; *a few days afterwards,* paucis post diēbus (313)
*again,* rursus, (ĭtĕrum, *a second time*); *again and again,* ĭtĕrum atque ĭtĕrum
*against,* contrā, adversus, in *(all g. acc.); he was sent against the enemy,* missus est adversus hostes; *against the laws,* contrā jūs; *against one's will,* invītus, -a, um; *she came a.* &c. invīta vēnit
*Agamemnon,* Ăgămemnon, -ŏnis, m.
*age.* aetās, ātis, f.; *old age,* sĕnectūs, -ūtis, f.; *age, an,* saecŭlum, -i, n.
*Agesilaus,* Ăgēsĭlāus, -i, m.
*ago,* ăbhinc *(with acc. or abl.); two years ago,* ăbhinc bĭennio, *or* biennium
*agree,* consentio, -sensi, -sensum, 4 *(foll. by dat., or* cum)
*agreeable,* jūcundus, -a, -um
*agreement,* consensus, -ūs, m.
*Ah!* interject. O! *foll. by acc.; Ah, the lucky fellow!* O felicem hominem!
*aid,* auxĭlium, -ii, n.; *aid, to,* subvĕnio, -vēni, -ventum, 4
*air,* aër, aëris, m.
*Ajax,* Ajax, -jācis, m.
*alas!* heu! *or* ēheu!
*Alban,* Albānus, -a, -um
*Alexander,* Alexander, -dri, m.
*alliance,* sociĕtās, -ātis, f.
*alien,* ălĭēnus, -a, -um
*alike,* părĭter
*alive,* vīvus, -a, -um
*all,* omnis, -e; *(all) men,* omnes; *from all sides,* undīque; *all the best citizens,* optĭmus quisquĕ civium; *all the food we had, was consumed,* quidquid cĭbi nōbīs fuĕrat, consumptum est
*allow,* sino, sīvi, sĭtum, 3
*allure,* allĭcio, -lexi, -lectum, 3
*ally,* sŏcius, -i, m.
*almost,* paenĕ, fĕrē
*alone,* sōlus, -a, -um; ūnus, -a, -um (85); *Cato alone thought otherwise,* Catōni ūni ălĭter vīsum est

*along* (*prep.*), per (*g. acc.*)
*Alps*, Alpes, -ium, f. pl.
*already*, jam
*also*, (1) ětiam, *mostly before*, (2) quŏquĕ, *always after, the word modified; not only...but also*, nōn sōlum...sĕd ětiam, *or*, cum ...tum
*altar*, āra, -ae, f.
*altogether*, omnīno
*always*, semper
*ambassador*, lēgātus, -i, m.
*ambush*, insĭdiae, -ārum, f.
*amiss, something amiss has happened to him*, ălĭquid ei hūmānĭtus accĭdit
*among*, inter (*g. acc.*); *among the Romans*, apud Rŏmanos; *they are fighting amongst one another*, inter sē pugnant
*ancestors*, mājores, -um, m. pl.
*ancient*, antīquus, -a, -um; priscus, -a, -um; vĕtus, -ĕris; *among the ancients*, ăpud antīquos
*and*, et; atquĕ; -quĕ (Par. 37); *and no one, never, nothing, &c.*, nec quisquam, unquam, quidquam, &c.
*anger*, īra, -ae, f.; *in* or *with a.*, īrācundē, summā īrā, *or* cum īrā (Par. 276)
*angry, to be*, īrascor, īrātus, 3, dep.; *angry*, īrātus, -a, -um
*animal*, ănĭmal, -ālis, n.; *wild animal*, fĕra, -ae, f.
*announce*, nuntio, 1
*annually*, quŏtannīs
*another*, ălius, -a, -ud; *the other*, alter, -ĕra, -ĕrum, (Par. 86)
*answer, to*, respondeo, -di, -nsum, 2 (*g. dat. of pers.*); *answer, an*, responsum, -i, n.; *to make answer*, respondēre; *I was answered*, respōnsum est mĭhī
*Antonius*, Antōnius, -i, m.
*any, any one* (*in neg. compar. and interrog. sentences*), quisquam *or* ullus (309); (*with* num, sī, nĕ) quĭs (294); *any* (*you please*), quilĭbet, quaelĭbet, quodlĭbet, (*pron. neut.* quidlĭbet); *the enemy can attack us at any time* (*they please*), quōlĭbet tempŏre
*anywhere*, usquam
*apiece*, (*trans. by distributive numeral, see* Par. 77), *he gave us three denarii apiece*, nōbīs ternos dēnārios dĕdit
*Apollo*, Apollo, -ĭnis, m. [-ui, 2
*appear*, vĭdeor, vīsus, 2; appāreo,
*appearance*, spĕcies, -ei, f.
*appease*, plāco, 1
*apple*, pōmum, -i, n.; mālum, -i, n.
*appoint*, constĭtuo, -ui, -ūtum, 3
*approach, to*, ădeo, -ii, -ĭtum, (*foll. by acc.*); accēdo, -cessi, -cessum, 3, (*foll. by* ad); *an*, ădĭtus, -ūs, m.
*approve*, prŏbo, 1; *a man of approved excellence*, vir spectātae (*or, more often*, -ā) virtūtis (*or* -ĕ)
*apt*, aptus, -a, -um
*Archimedes*, Archĭmēdēs, -is, m.
*ardour*, ardor, -ōris, m.
*Argos*, Argi, -ōrum, m.
*Arion*, Arīon, -ŏnis, m.
*Ariovistus*, Ariovistus, -i, m.
*arise*, ŏrior, ortus, 4, dep.; (*from bed, seat, &c.*) surgo, surrexi, surrectum, 3
*Aristippus*, Ărĭstippus, -i, m.
*arm, an*, brăchium, -i, n.; *arm, to*, armo, 1
*armed*, armātus, -a, -um
*arms* (*military*), arma, -ōrum, n.
*army*, exercĭtus, -ūs, m. [*adv.*)
*around*, circum (*prep. g. acc., and Arpinum*, Arpīnum, -i, n.
*arrange*, dīgero, -gessi, -gestum, 3
*arrival*, adventus, -ūs, m.
*arrive*, pervĕnio, -vēni, -ventum, 4 (*foll. by* ad); *we arrived at Rome*, Rōmam pervēnĭmus (249)

*arrow*, săgitta, -ae, f.
*art*, ars, -tis, f.
*as*, ut ; *as if*, tanquam, quăsi ; *as long as*, dōnĕc ; *as far as*, tēnus (*g. abl.*); *as*, (*often trans. by Apposition*), *you do many things, as a boy, which you will not do, as an old man*, multa, puer, făcis, quae, sĕnex, non făcies ; *as quickly as possible*, quam cĕlerrĭmē ; (*sometimes rel. pron.*) *he is the same as he always was*, īdem est qui (*or* ac) semper fuit ; *for the same price as*, i.e., *for which*, ĕodem prĕtio quo ; ( "*as*" *is sometimes rend. by the dat. of purpose*) *he sent a legion as a reinforcement*, mīsit lĕgĭōnem subsĭdĭo (266) ; *as much money as*, tantum pĕcūniae quantum
*ascend*, ascendo, -ndi, -nsum, 3
*ascertain*, cognosco, cognōvi, cognĭtum, 3 ; compĕrio, compĕri, compertum, 4
*ashamed, to be*, pŭdet, -uit, 2 (*impers.*) ; *I am ashamed of doing, having done*, pŭdet me făcĕre, fēcisse (219)
*Asia*, Ăsia, -ae, f.
*ask, to*, (1) *meaning question*, rŏgo, 1 ; interrŏgo, 1 ; quaero, -sīvi, sītum, 3 (*with* ex,dē, *or* ā) ; (2) *meaning beg*, rŏgo, 1 ; ōro, 1 (143) ; (*peace*) pācem pĕtere ; *he was asked his opinion*, sententiam rŏgātus est
*ass*, ăsĭnus, -i, m.
*assassin*, sĭcărius, -i, m.
*assault, to*, oppugno, 1 ; *assault, an*, impĕtus, -us, m.
*assemble*, convĕnio, -vēni, -ventum, 4 (*intrans.*) ; convŏco, 1 (*trans.*)
*assembly*, concĭlium, -ii, n ; conventus, -us, m.
*assist*, subvĕnio, -vēni, -ventum, 4 (*g. dat.*)
*assistance*, auxĭlium, -i, n.

*assume* (*take*), sumo, sumpsi, sumptum, 3
*astonishment*, admīrātio, -ōnis, f.
*at*, ăpud (*g. acc.*) ; ăd (*g. acc.*) ; *at all*, omnīno ; *at least*, saltem ; *at last, at length*, tandem, ălĭquando ; *at once*, sĭmul, stătim
*Athens*, Ăthēnae, -ārum, f. pl.
*Athenian*, Ăthēniensis, -e
*attack, to*, aggrĕdior, gressus, 3, dep.; oppugno, 1 (*to attack a town*); *attack, an*, impĕtus,-ūs, m.
*attempt, to*, cōnor, 1, dep. (*this v. is an exc. to the rule* (143) *about v. of "striving" ; it is foll. by inf.*); *attempt, an*, cōnātus, -ūs, m. [dat.
*attention, to pay*, ŏpĕram dăre, *g.*
*Attica*, Attĭca, -ae, f.
*attract*, trăho, -xi, -ctum, 3
*audacity*, audācia, -ae, f.
*augur*, augur, -ŭris, m.
*augury*, augŭrium, -i, n ; ōmĕn, -ĭnis, n.
*Augustus*, Augustus, -i, m.
*auspice*, auspĭcium, -i, n.
*author*, auctor, -ōris, m.
*authority*, auctōrĭtās, -ātis, f.
*autumn*, auctumnus, -i, m.
*auxiliaries*, auxĭlia, -ōrum, n.
*avail*, văleo, -ui, 2 ; *threats ? what avail*, quid vălent mĭnae ?
*avarice*, ăvārĭtia, -ae, f.
*avaricious*, ăvārus, -a, -um
*avenge*, ulciscor, -ultus, 3, dep.
*avoid*, vīto, 1 ; fŭgio, fūgi, 3
*await, I*, expecto, 1 ; *death awaits us*, mors nōs mănet
*awake*, expergiscor, -perrectus, 3, dep.
*aware of*, gnārus, -a, -um (*g. gen.*)
*awful*, dīrus, -a, -um
*axe*, secūris, -is, f. ; *acc.* -em *or* -im, *abl.* -i

**Bacchus**, Bacchus, -i, m.
*back*, tergum, -i, n. ; *the enemy*

*turn their backs, i.e. flee*, terga dant ; *drive back*, see *drive*
**bad**, mălus, -a, -um ; *badly*, mălĕ ; *bad men*, imprŏbi
**baggage**, impĕdīmenta, -ōrum, n.
**Balbus**, Balbus, -i, m.
**banish**, pello, pepŭli, pulsum, 3 ; expello, -pŭli, -pulsum, 3
**bankrupt**, impar solvendo, i.e. *unequal to paying*
**banquet**, ĕpŭlum, -i, n. ; pl. epulae, ārum, f. (the sing. mostly means *a public banquet*)
**barbarian**, barbărus, -a, -um
**barbarous**, fĕrus, -a, -um
**barber**, tonsor, -ōris, m.
**bargain**, *to make a*, păciscor, pactus, 3, dep.
**barn**, horreum, -i, n.
**barren**, stĕrĭlis, -e
**base**, turpis, -e
**baseness**, turpĭtūdo, -ĭnis, f.
**battle**, proelium, -i, n. ; pugna, -ae, f. ; *see* Cannae
**beak**, rostrum, -i, n.
**bear**, *to*, fĕro, -tŭli, -lātum, ferre
**beard**, barba, -ae, f.
**beast**, bestia, -ae, f. ; *of burden*, jūmentum, -i, n.
**beat**, caedo, cĕcĭdi, caesum, 3
**beaten**, *to be*, vāpŭlo, 1
**beautiful**, pulcher, -chra, -chrum
**beauty**, forma, -ae, f. ; pulchritūdo, -ĭnis, f.
**because**, quia, quod
**become**, fio, factus, fiĕri (258) ; *it becomes me*, dĕcet mĕ (220)
**bed**, lectus, -ĭ, m.
**beech-tree**, fāgus, -i, f.
**befall** (*amiss*), accĭdo, -ĭdi, 3 ; (*good*) contingo, -tigi, -tactum, 3 (*both g. dat.*)
**befit**, dĕcet, -uit, 2, impers.
**before**, (*prep.*) antĕ (*g. acc.*) ; *in the presence of*, cōram, (*g. abl.*) ; (*conj.*) priusquam, antĕquam ; *beforehand*, (*adv.*) anteā, antĕ ; *a few* 

*years before*, paucis antĕ annis ; *the day before*, see "*day*" ; *before the last*, extrēmis prior
**beg**, ōro, 1 ; *beggar*, mendīcus, -i, m.
**begin**, incĭpio, -cēpi, -ceptum, 3 ; (*a battle*), ĭneo, ĭnii, ĭnĭtum, ĭnīre ; *before a pass. inf.* use coepi, coeptus sum, coepisse, v. def. ; *the city began to be besieged*, urbs coepit (*or* coepta est) obsidēri
**beginning**, ĭnĭtium, -i, n.
**behind**, post (*g. acc.*)
**behold**, aspĭcio, -exi, -ectum, 3 ; vĭdeo, vīdi, visum, 2
**behoves**, *it*, ŏportet, -uit, 2
**believe**, crēdo, -dĭdi, -dĭtum, 3 (*g. dat. of person*) ; *I believe that he will come*, crēdo eum ventūrum esse ; *I believe him*, crēdo ei
**Belgae**, Belgae, -ārum, m.
**belly**, venter, -tris, m.
**below**, infrā (*g. acc.*)
**benefactor**, bĕnĕfactor, -ōris, m.
**benefit**, *to*, bĕnĕfăcio, -fēci, -factum, 3 ; prōsum, -fui, esse (*dat.*) ; *benefit*, *a*, bĕnĕfactum, -i, n.
**benevolence**, bĕnĕvŏlentia, -ae, f.
**benevolent**, benevolus, -a, -um (68a)
**beseech**, ōro, 1 (143)
**beside**, iuxtā (*g. acc.*) ; praeter (*g. acc.*) ; *besides* (*prep.*) praeter (*g. acc.*) (183) ; (*adv.*) praetĕreā
**besiege**, obsĭdeo, -sēdi, -sessum, 2
**best**, optĭmus, -a, -um ; *I do my best to write*, id ăgo ŭt scrībam
**betake**, confĕro, -tŭli, -ferre, collātum ; rĕcĭpio, -cēpi, -ceptum, 3 ; *he betook himself to Corinth*, Cŏrinthum se contŭlit
**betray**, prōdo, -dĭdi, -dĭtum, 3
**betroth**, spondeo, spŏpondi, sponsum, 3
**better**, mĕlior, -us
**between**, inter (*g. acc.*)
**bewail**, plōro, 1
**beware**, căveo, cāvi, cautum, 2

*beyond*, ultrā (*g. acc.*); praeter (*g. acc.*)
*big*, see *large*
*bind*, vincio, vinxi, vinctum, 4; (*by oath*) jūre-jūrando obstringo, -strinxi, -strictum, 3
*bird*, ăvis, -is, f.
*birth*, partus, -ūs, m.; *noble birth*, nōbĭlĭtās, -ātis, f.
*bite, a*, morsus, -ūs, m.; *to bite*, mordeo, mŏmordi, morsum, 2 [-a, -um
*bitter*, ăcerbus, -a, -um: āmārus,
*black*, nīger, -gra, -grum; *gloomy*, āter, -tra, -trum [po, 1
*blame*, culpa, -ae, f.; *to blame*, cul-
*blind*, caecus, -a, -um
*blindness*, caecĭtās, -ātis, f.
*blood*, sanguis, -ĭnis, m.
*blot out*, dēleo, -ēvi, -ētum, 2
*blow*, ictus, -ūs, m.; *to blow, v. intr.* flo, flāvi, flātum, 1
*blush*, ĕrŭbesco, -ui, 3
*boar*, ăper, -pri, m.
*boast*, glōrior, 1, dep.; jacto, 1
*boasting*, jactātio
*body*, corpus, -ŏris, n.; *dead body*, cădāver, -ĕris, n.
*Boeotia*, Boeōtia, -ae, f.
*bold*, audax, -ācis; fortis, -e
*bone*, ŏs, ossis, n.
*book*, lĭber, -bri, m.
*booty*, praeda, -ae, f.
*border*, fīnis, -is, m.
*bordering-on*, fīnĭtĭmus, -a, -um (112)
*born, to be*, nascor, nātus, 3, dep.; *born of low parentage*, hŭmĭlĭbus părentĭbus nātus. N.B. nascor means, *I am being born*, nātus sum, *I am born*
*bosom*, sīnus, -ūs, m.
*both*, (*adj.*) ambo, -ae, -o, ŭterque, -traque,-trumque; *both of us*, nōs ambo or ŭterque nostrum; (*conj.*) *both...and*, ĕt...ĕt, (12) or cum... tum, (317)
*bottom*, ĭmus, -a, -um, *adj.*

*bound, boundary*, fīnis, -is, m.; termĭnus, -i, m.
*bow*, arcus, -ūs, m. (53)
*boy*, puer, -ĕri, m; *boyhood*, puĕrĭtia, -ae, f.; *from his b., from a boy*, indĕ ā puĕrĭtiā, or puĕro
*branch*, rāmus, -i, m.
*brave*, fortis, -e; *bravely*, fortĭter
*bravery*, virtūs, -ūtis, f.
*bread*, pānis, -is, m.
*break*, frango, frēgi, fractum, 3; rumpo, rūpi, ruptum, 3; *break out*, ērumpo, -rūpi, -ruptum, 3; *break down* (*a bridge*), interrumpo, -rūpi, -ruptum, 3
*breast*, pectus, -ŏris, n. [m.
*breath*, ănĭma, -ae, f.; hālĭtus, -ūs,
*breed, to*, ălo, -ui, altum, 3
*bribery*, ambĭtus, -ūs, m.
*bridge*, pons, -ntis, m.; *to bridge*, (*a river*), flŭvium ponte jungĕre
*bright*, clārus, -a, -um; splendĭdus, -a, -um
*bring*, affĕro, attŭli, allātum, afferre; *I will bring you help*, fĕram tĭbi auxĭlium; *bring back*, rĕdūco, -duxi, -ductum, 3; *bring in*, infĕro, -tŭli, -illātum, inferre; intrōdūco, -xi, -ctum, 3; *bring up* (*educate*), ēdūco, 1; *bring back word*, rĕnuntio, 1
*briskly*, ălacrĭter
*Britain*, Brĭtannia, -ae, f.
*Briton, a*, Brĭtannus, -i, m.
*brother*, frāter, -tris, m.
*brow*, frons, -ntis, f.
*Brutus*, Brūtus, -i, m.
*build*, aedĭfĭco, 1; *building*, aedĭfĭcium, -i, n.; *to see to the building of a temple*, cūrāre templum aedĭfĭcandum
*bulk*, magnĭtūdo, -ĭnis, f.
*bull*, taurus, -i, m.
*burden*, ŏnus, -ĕris, n.
*burn*, ūro, ussi, ustum, 3 (*trans.*): (*a house, city, &c.*) incendo,

incendi, incensum, 3 (*trans.*);
ardeo, arsi, arsum, 2 (*intrans.*);
*a burning*, incendium, -i, n.
*burst into*, irrumpo, -rūpi, -ruptum,
3, *foll. by* in *and acc.*
*bury*, sĕpĕlio, -ivi, sĕpultum, 4
*bush*, dūmus, -i, m.
*bushel*, mŏdius, -ii, m. [n.
*business*, rēs, rei, f. ; nĕgōtium, -i,
*but*, (i) *coord. conj.* sĕd (comes first in a clause, means *on the other hand*; *but still*; *but yet*) ; autem (never comes first in a clause, means *in the second place*), vēro (139*a*); (ii) *subord. conj.* quīn ; *I doubt not but he will come*, nōn dūbĭto quīn ventūrus sit
*but* (*prep.*), praetĕr ; *no one but Tullius was present*, praetĕr Tullium nēmo ădĕrat ; *but sometimes, in negatives and questions that expect a neg. answer*, nĭsĭ (*coupling nouns in the same case, like* quam, 62) ; *what is filial affection but gratitude towards parents?* quĭd est pĭĕtās nĭsĭ grāta ergā părentes vŏluntās ?
*but* (a neg. rel. pron., *that not*), (i) nom., *there was no one but hated you*, nēmo ĕrat quīn tē ōdisset ; (2) abl., *not a day passed but I wept*, dies fĕrē nullus fuit quīn (*i.e.* quo nōn) flērem
*butterfly*, pāpĭlio, -ōnis, m.
*buy*, ĕmo, ēmi, emptum, 3
*buyer*, emptor, -ōris, m.
*by*, ā, ăb (Par. 178); *by this time*, jam

**Caesar**, Caesar, -ăris, m.
*calamity*, călămĭtās, -ātis, f.
*call*, vŏco, 1; *call together*, convŏco, 1 ; (*address*) appello, 1 ; *do you call me an enemy ?* num mē inĭmīcum appellas ?
*calm*, plăcĭdus, -a, -um
*Camillus*, Cămillus, -i, m.

*camp*, castra, -ōrum, n. pl.
*Campania*, Campānia, -ae, f. N.B. *a district, not a city.*
*can* (see *able*) *you can come*, vĕnīre pŏtĕs ; *it cannot be that you would venture on this*, fĭĕri nōn pŏtest ŭt hōc audeās
*Cannae*, Cannae, -ārum, f. ; *of Cannae*, Cannensis, -e, adj.; *the battle of C.*, proelium Cannense, or p. Cannis pugnātum
*capital*, căput, -ĭtis, n.
*Capitol*, Căpĭtōlium, -i, n.
*captive*, *adj.* captīvus, -a, -um
*captive, a*, captivus, -i, m.
*capture, to*, căpio, cēpi, captum, 3
*Capua*, Căpua, -ae, f.
*carcass*, cădāver, -ĕris, n.
*care*, cūra, -ae, f. ; *take care of* cūro, 1, *g acc.* ; *take care to*, cūrā ut
*carefully*, dīlĭgenter
*careless*, neglĕgens, -ntis
*carelessness*, incūria, -ae, f. ; neglĕgentia, -ae, f.
*carry*, porto, 1 (*on one's shoulders*); vĕho, vexi, vectum, 3 (*of horses*); ferre, tŭli, lātum (*a letter*)
*carry off*, aufĕro, abstŭli, ablātum, auferre ; (*a victory*) rĕporto, 1
*carry on, to, a war*, bellum gĕrĕre, gessi, gestum, 3
*Carthage*, Carthāgo, -ĭnis, f.
*Carthaginian*, Poenus, -a, -um
*cast*, jăcio, jēci, jactum, 3
*cast away*, abjicio, abjēci, abjectum, 3 ; *cast down*, dēmitto, -mīsi, -missum, 3
*cat*, fĕlis, -is, f.
*catch*, căpio, cēpi, captum, 3
*Catiline*, Catĭlīna, -ae, m.
*Cato*, Căto, -ōnis, m.
*cattle*, armenta, -ōrum, n. pl.
*cause*, causa, -ae, f.
*cause, to*, effĭcio, fēci, fectum, 3 ; *you caused me sorrow*, tristĭtiam mĭhĭ attŭlisti
*cautiously*, cautō

*cavalry*, ĕquĭtes, -um, m. pl.; ĕquĭtātus, -ūs, m.
*cease*, dēsĭno, -sīvi *or* -sii, 3
*celebrated*, praeclārus, -a, -um
*centurion*, centŭrio, -ōnis, m.
*century*, centŭria, -ae, f.
*Ceres*, Cĕrēs, Cĕrĕris, f.
*certain*, certus, -a, -um (*g. gen.*); *a certain person*, quĭdam; *a c. fixed day*, certus quĭdam dies; (*meaning "kind of"*) quĭdam; *there is a c. pleasure*, est quaedam vŏluptas (310a)
*certainly*, certĕ, prŏfecto       [-i, n.
*chain*, cătēna, -ae, f.; vincŭlum,
*challenge, to*, prŏvŏco, 1
*chance*, cāsus, -ūs, m.; *by c.*, fortĕ
*change, to*, mūto, 1
*charge, (accusation)*, crīmen, -ĭnis, n.; *(onset)* impĕtus, -ūs, m.; *let us charge the enemy*, impĕtum făciāmus in hostem       [-i, n.
*chariot*, currus, -ūs, m.; essĕdum,
*charioteer*, aurīga, -ae, m.
*charm, to*, dēlecto, 1
*chastise, to*, castīgo, 1
*cheap*, vīlis, -e
*cheer, be of good cheer*, ĕrĭgīte (ĕrĭgo, -rexi, -rectum, 3) ănĭmos; ădeste ănĭmis
*cheese*, cāseus, -i, m.
*cherish*, fŏveo, fōvi, fōtum, 2; cŏlo, cŏlui, cultum, 3
*cherry*, cĕrăsum, -i, n.
*chew*, mando, -di, -sum, 3
*chicken*, pullus, -i, m.
*chide*, culpo, 1
*chief*, dux, dŭcis, m.; princeps,       [-ĭpis, m.
*chief men*, primōres, -um, m. pl.
*chiefly*, maximē; imprīmīs
*child*, puer, -eri, m., *or* puella, -ae, f.
*children*, lībĕri, -ōrum, m.
*choice (of style)*, ēlĕgans, -ntis
*choiceness of style*, ēlĕgantia, -ae, f.
*choose*, ēlĭgo, -lēgi, -lectum, 3
*Christian, a*, Christiānus, -i, m.
*Cicero*, Cĭcĕro, -ōnis, m.

*Cincinnatus*, Cincinnātus, -i, m.
*circuit*, ambĭtus, -ūs, m.
*circumstance*, rēs, rei, f.
*citadel*, arx, -cis, f.; *gen. pl.* arcĭum (40)
*citizen*, cīvis, -is, m.
*city*, urbs, -bis, f.; *the city of Carthage*, Carthāgo urbs       [1
*claim*, posco, pŏposci, 3; vindĭco,
*clamour for*, postŭlo, 1
*claw*, unguis, -is, m.
*Claudius*, Claudius, -i, m.
*clear*, clārus, -a, -um; *to explain clearly*, lūcŭlenter explĭcāre
*clear, it is*, lĭquet, 2, impers. (222)
*clemency*, clēmentia, -ae, f.
*clerk*, scrība, -ae, m.
*climb*, scando, -di, -sum, 3
*close*, claudo, -si, -sum, 3
*close to*, prŏpe (*g. acc.*); *he is close at hand*, prŏpe ā nōbīs ăbest
*close quarters, at*, commĭnus
*clothe*, vestio, -īvi *or* -ii, -ītum, 4
*clothing*, vestītus, -ūs, m.
*cloud*, nūbēs, -is, f.
*Clytemnestra*, Clytemnestra, -ae, f.
*coast*, lĭtus, -ŏris, n.; ōra, -ae, f.
*cobbler*, sūtor, -ōris, m.
*Codrus*, Codrus, -i, m.
*cock*, gallus, -i, m.
*cohort*, cŏhors, -rtis, f.
*coin*, nummus, -i, m.
*cold*, frīgus, -ŏris, n.
*cold*, frīgĭdus, -a, -um
*colleague*, collēga, -ae, m.
*collect*, collĭgo, -lēgi, -lectum, 3
*colony*, cŏlōnia, ae, f.
*colour*, cŏlor, -ōris, m.
*column, (of men)* agmen, -ĭnis, n.
*come*, vĕnio, vēni, ventum, 4
*command, (military)* impĕrium, -i, n.; *commands*, jussa, -orum, n. pl.; *at the command of Tullius*, Tullio jŭbente (197)
*command, to*, impĕro, 1: praesum, -fui, -esse (*both g. dat. of person*); jŭbeo, jussi jussum, 2

u 2

*command of, to be in,* praesum, -fui, -esse (*g. dat.*)
*commander,* impĕrātor, -ōris, m.; dux, dŭcis, m. [3
*commit,* committo, -mīsi, -missum,
*common,* commūnis, -e.
*common-people,* plebs, plēbis, f.; vulgus, -i, n.
*commonwealth,* respublica, reipublicae, f.
*companion,* cŏmĕs, -ĭtis, m.
*compare,* compăro, 1; confĕro, contŭli, collātum, conferre
*compassion,* mĭsĕrĭcordia, -ae, f.
*compel,* cōgo, coēgi, coactum, 3 (inf-, *or* ut, *or* ad *with gerund.*)
*complain,* quĕror, questus, 3, dep.
*complaint,* quĕrēla, -ae, f. [3
*complete, to,* conficio, -fēci, -fectum,
*conceal,* cēlo, 1 (*g. two acc.,* 312)
*concede,* concēdo, -cessi, -cessum, 3
*conceive a hope,* vĕnīre in spem
*concerning,* dē (*g. abl.*)
*concerns, it,* see *"important*
*conciliate,* concĭlio, 1
*concord,* concordia, ae, f.
*concourse,* concursus, -ūs, m.
*condemn,* damno, 1; condemno, 1; *to condemn to death,* căpĭtĭs damnāre
*condition,* condĭcio, -ōnis, f.
*conduct, to, a war,* bellum gĕrĕre
*conduct,* mōres, -um, m. pl.
*confer,* confĕro, contŭli, collātum, conferre; *to c. a benefit on you,* bĕnĕfĭcĭum in tē c.
*conference,* collŏquĭum, -i, n.
*confess,* fătĕor, fassus, 2, dep.; confĭteor, -fessus, 2, dep.
*confession,* confessio, -ōnis, f.
*confidence,* fĭdēs, -ei, f.
*confirm,* confirmo, 1
*conflagration,* incendium, -i, n.
*congratulate,* grātŭlor, 1, dep. (*g. dat.*); *I c. you that, g.* tĭbi quod
*conquer,* vinco, vīci, victum, 3; sŭpĕro, 1

*conquered,* victus, -a, -um; *the conquered,* victi m. pl.
*conqueror,* victor, -ōris, m.
*conquest,* victōria, -ae, f. [*gen.*)
*conscious,* conscius, -a, -um (*g.*
*consciousness,* conscientia, -ae, f.
*consecrate,* consecro, 1
*consent, to,* consentio, -sensi, -sensum, 4 (*dat., or* cum)
*consent,* consensus, -ūs, m.
*consider,* pŭto, 1
*consist,* consto, -stĭti, -stătum, 1; *foll. by* ex *or* ē, *the legions consisted of ten cohorts each,* lĕgiōnes ē dĕnis cŏhortĭbus constĭtērunt
*consolation,* sŏlātium, -i, n.
*console,* sōlor, 1, dep.
*conspiracy,* conjŭrātio, -ōnis, f.
*conspire,* conjūro, 1
*conspirator,* conjūrātus, -a, -um, *used as a noun*
*constancy,* constantia, -ae f.
*consul,* consŭl, -ŭlis, m.
*consulate,* consŭlātus, -ūs, m.
*consult,* consŭlo, -sului, -sultum, 3; *to c. Tullius,* consŭlĕre Tullium, *to c. T.'s interests,* consŭlĕre Tullio
*consume,* consūmo, -sumpsi, -sumptum, 3
*contemplate,* contemplor, -ātus sum, 1
*contend,* contendo, -di, -tum, 3
*content,* contentus, -a, -um (*g. abl.*)
*contest,* certāmen, -ĭnis, n.
*contradict,* contrādīco, -dixi, -dictum, 3 (*g. dat.*)
*contrary,* contrārius, -a, -um (189)
*contrary, on the,* contrā (*adv.*)
*contrary-to,* contrā (*g. acc.*)
*conversation,* sermo, -ōnis, m.; collŏquium, -i, n. [3, dep.
*converse, to,* collŏquor, collŏcūtus,
*convey,* vĕho, vexi, vectum, 3
*cook,* cŏquus, -i, m.
*cook, to,* cŏquo, coxi, coctum, 3
*copper,* aes, aeris, n.

*Corinth*, Cŏrinthus, -i, f.
*Corinthian*, Cŏrinthius, -a, -um
*Coriolanus*, Cŏrĭōlānus, -i, m.
*Corioli*, Cŏrĭŏli, -ōrum, m. pl. *the small town of Corioli was burned*, C., oppĭdum parvum, incensum est
*corn*, (*harvested*) frūmentum, -i, n. ; *to sow corn*, frūmenta sĕrĕre
*Cornelia*, Cornēlia, -ae, f.
*corpse*, cădāver, -ĕris, n.
*correct*, corrĭgo, -rexi, -rectum, 3
*corrupt*, corrumpo, -rūpi, -ruptum, 3
*cost*, prĕtium, -i, n. ; *expense*, sumptus, -ūs, m.
*cost, to*, sto, stĕti, stătum, 1, consto, -stĭti, -stătum, 1, (*both g. abl. of definite, gen. of indef. price*) *this cost me more*, hōc mĭhi plūris constĭtit ; *this will cost you much blood*, hōc vōbis multo sanguĭne stābit
*costly*, sumptuōsus, -a, -um
*cottage*, căsa, -ae, f.
*cover*, tĕgo, texi, tectum, 3
*covet*, cŭpio, -īvi, -ītum, 3
*covetous*, cŭpĭdus, -a, -um (*g. gen.*)
*couch*, lectus, -i, m., cŭbīle, -is, n.
*could* (see *able*), *you could have come*, vĕnīre pŏtŭisti
*council*, concĭlium, -i, n.
*counsel*, consĭlium, -i, n.
*count*, nŭmĕro, 1
*countenance*, vultus, -ūs, m.
*country*, terra, -ae, f. ; *the country* (*as distinct from the city*), rūs, rūris, n. see Par. 265 and 249 ; *one's own, his, my, your, country*, patria, -ae, f. ; *let us die for our country*, prō patriā mŏriămur ; *this is for the good of the country*, hōc est ē rē-publicā ; *a rough country*, i.e. *district*, rēgio aspĕra
*countrymen*, cīves, -ium, m. pl.
*courage*, virtūs, -ūtis, f.
*course*, cursus, -ūs, m.

*courtesy*, hūmānĭtas, -ātis, f.
*cover*, tĕgo, -xi, -ctum, 3
*coward, cowardly*, ignāvus, -a, -um
*cowardice*, ignāvia, -ae, f.
*crafty*, callĭdus, -a, -um
*crane*, grus, gruis, c. ; *mostly* f.
*Crassus*, Crassus, -i, m.
*create*, creo, 1
*creature*, ănĭmal, -ālis, n.
*credible*, credĭbĭlis, -e.
*credit*, fĭdēs, -ei, f.
*Crete*, Crēta, -ae, f.
*crime*, scĕlus, -ĕris, n.; *monstrous*, c. flāgĭtium, -i, n.
*crocodile*, crŏcŏdīlus. -i, m.
*Croesus*, Croesus, -i. m.
*cross*, crux, crūcis, f.
*cross, to*, trājĭcio, -jēci, -jectum, 3 ; transeo, -īvi *or* -ii, ītum, 4
*crowd*, turba, -ae, f.
*crown*, cŏrōna, -ae, f.
*cruel*, crūdēlis, -e. ; saevus, -a, -um
*cruelty*, crūdēlĭtas, -ātis, f.      [3
*crush*, opprĭmo, -pressi, -pressum,
*cry*, (*shout*) clāmo, 1
*cry, a*, clāmor, -ōris, m.
*cultivate*, cŏlo, cŏlui, cultum, 3
*cunning*, callĭdus, -a, -um
*cup*, călix, -ĭcis, m.
*cure*, rĕmĕdium, -i, n.
*cure, to*, sāno, 1 (*acc.*) ; mĕdeor, 2 r. dep. (*dat.*)
*custom*, mōs, mōris, m.
*cut*, caedo, cĕcīdi, caesum, 3 : *cut off, to, the enemy from supplies*, interclūdĕre, (-clūsi, -clūsum, 3) hostes commeātū (*or* -ĭbus)
*cut to pieces*, concīdo, -di, -sum, 3
*Cyclops, the*, Cyclōpes, -um, m. pl.
*Cyprus*, Cyprus, -i, f.
*Cyrus*, Cȳrus, -i, m.

**Dagger**, pūgio, -ōnis, m.
*daily, adv.* quŏtĭdiē (*better spelt* cōtīdiē)
*dance*, salto, 1
*danger*, pĕrīcŭlum, -i, n.

*dangerous*, pĕrīcŭlōsus, -a, -um
*Danube*, Ister, -tri, m.
*Daphne*, Daphnē, -ēs, f.
*dare*, audeo, ausus sum, 2, dep.
*Darius*, Dārīus, -i, m.
*dark*, obscūrus, -a, -um ; pullus, -a, -um
*darken*, obscūro, 1
*darkness*, cālīgo, -inis, f. ; tĕnebrae, -ārum, f.
*dart*, tēlum, -i, n.; jăcŭlum, -i, n.
*daughter*, fīlia, -ae, f.
*dawn*, prīma lux ; māne, indecl. ; *before dawn*, antĕ lūcem
*dawn, to*, illūcesco, illuxi, 3
*day*, dies, -iēi m.; *by day*, dīē ; *daybreak*, prīma lux ; *the-day-before* (*adv. used as a prep.*) prīdiē Kălendas ; (*used as a conj. with* quam) *the day before I came*, prīdiē quam vēni ; *two days*, bīduum, -i, n.; *three days*, trīduum, -i, n.
*dead*, mortuus, -a, -um
*dead body*, cădāver, -ĕris, n.
*deaf*, surdus, -a, -um
*dear*, cārus, -a, -um
*death*, mors, mortis, f. ; *he was put to death*, morte affectus est ; *he was condemned to death*, căpĭtis damnātus est
*debt*, aes ăliēnum
*deceit*, dŏlus, -i, m. ; fallācia, -ae, f.
*deceitful*, fallāx, -ācis
*deceive*, dēcipio, -cēpi, -ceptum, 3 ; fallo, fĕfelli, falsum, 3
*decide, to*, (*judge*) jūdĭco, 1 ; *they decided to return*, constĭtuērunt redīre
*declare*, dīco, dixi, dictum, 3 ; *to declare war against*, bellum indīcĕre, *g. dat.*
*decree, to*, dēcerno, -crēvi, -crētum, 3
*decree, a*, dēcrētum, -i, n. ; ēdictum, -i, n.
*deed*, factum, -i, n. ; făcĭnŭs, ŏris, n.
*deem worthy*, dignor, 1, dep.

*deep*, altus, -a, -um
*deer*, dāma, -ae, f.
*defeat, a*, clādēs, -is, f.
*defeat, to*, vinco, vīci, victum, 3
*defence*, praesĭdium, -i, n.
*defend*, dēfendo, -di, -sum, 3
*defendant*, reus, -i, m.
*defile*, polluo, -ui, ūtum, 3
*deity*, nūmen, -ĭnis, n.
*delay*, mŏra, -ae, f.
*delay, to*, mŏror, 1, dep. ; cunctor, 1. dep.
*deliberate*, dēlībĕro, 1
*delight*, gaudium, -i, n. ; *to delight*, dēlecto, 1, *v. tr.* (*g. acc.*)
*deliver* (*hand over*), trādo, -dĭdi, -dĭtum, 3 ; (*free*) lībĕro, 1 (*g. acc. of pers. and abl. of thing*)
*Delos*, Dēlos, -i, f.
*demand*, posco, pŏposci, 3
*Demosthenes*, Dēmosthĕnēs, -is, m.
*denarius*, dēnārius, -ii, m.
*deny*, nĕgo, 1
*depart*, discēdo, -cessi, -cessum, 3
*departure*, discessus, -ūs, m.
*deplore*, plōro, 1
*depraved*, prāvus, -a, um
*deprive*, spŏlio, 1 ; prīvo, 1 (279)
*descend*, descendo, -di, -sum, 3 ; *he was descended from kings*, ā rēgĭbus ortus ĕrat
*desert*, dēsĕro, -rui, -rtum, 3 ; rĕlinquo, -līqui, -lictum, 3
*deserter*, transfŭga, -ae, m.
*deserve*, mĕreor, mĕrĭtus, 2, dep.
*design*, consĭlium, -i, n.
*desire*, cŭpīdo, -ĭnis, f. ; *to desire*, cŭpio, -īvi, -ītum, 3 ; opto, 1 ; vŏlo (*all generally foll. by Infinitive*)
*desirous*, cŭpĭdus, -a, -um ; stŭdĭōsus, -a, -um (*both g. gen.*) sometimes *with gerundive*
*desist from*, dēsisto, -stīti, -stītum, 3
*despair, to*, despēro, 1 ; *despair*, despērātio, -ōnis, f. [tum, 3
*despise*, contemno, -tempsi, temp-

*despoil*, spŏlio, 1 ; *I despoil you of liberty*, s. tĕ lībertāte
*destroy*, dēleo, -ēvi, -ētum ; perdo, -dĭdi, -dĭtum, 3
*destructive*, pernĭciōsus, -a, -um
*detain*, dētĭneo, -ui, -tentum, 2
*determine*, stătuo, -ui, -ūtum, 3
*devastate*, vasto, 1
*devoid of*, expers, -rtis, *adj.* (*g. gen.*)
*devote*, dĕvŏveo, -vŏvi, -vōtum, 2
*devour*, dĕvŏro, 1
*Diana*, Diāna, -ae, f.
*dictator*, dictātor, -ōris, m.
*dictatorship*, dictatūra, -ae, f.
*die*, mŏrior, mortnus, 3, dep. ; *he died*, ŏbiit (mortem)
*difference*, discrīmen, -ĭnis, n. ; *it makes a great difference*, multum intĕrest ; *how great a difference there is !* quantum intĕrest !
*difficult*, diffĭcĭlis, -e (60)
*difficulty*, diffĭcultas, -atis, f. ; *with difficulty*, vix ; *with very great difficulty*, difficillimē
*dig*, fŏdio, fōdi, fossum, 3 ; *dig up*, effŏdio, -fōdi, -fossum, 3
*dignity*, dignĭtās, -ātis, f.
*diligent*, strēnuus, -a, -um ; dīlĭgens, -ntis
*diminish*, mĭnuo, -ui, -ūtum, 3
*dine*, cēno, 1, *dep. particip.* cēnatus (*less correctly* coeno)
*Dionysius*, Diŏnȳsius, -i, m.
*direction ; in - the - direction - of the Rhine*, Rhēnum versūs
*disagreeable*, injūcundus, -a, -um
*disappear*, ēvānesco, -ui, 3 [-is, f.
*disaster*, damnum, -i, n. ; clādes,
*discern*, cerno, 3
*discharge (duty)*, fungor, functus, 3 *dep.* (*abl.*) ; (*darts*), conjĭcio, -jēci, -jectum, 3
*disciple*, discĭpŭlus, -i, m.
*discipline*, disciplīna, -ae, f.
*disclose*, dētĕgo, -texi, -tectum, 3
*discord*, discordia, -ae, f.

*discourse*, sermo, -ōnis, m.
*discover*, invĕnio, -vēni, -ventum, 4 ; rĕperio, repperi, repertum, 4
*disease*, morbus, -i, m.
*disembark*, (*trans. v.*) expōno, -pŏsui, -pŏsĭtum, 3
*disgrace*, dēdĕcus, -ŏris, n. ; *to disgrace*, foedo, 1
*disgraceful*, turpis, -e
*dishevelled*, passus, -a, -um
*dismiss*, dīmitto, -mīsi, -missum, 3
*displease*, displĭceo, -ui, ĭtum, 2 (*q. dat.*)
*displeasing*, ingrātus, -a, -um
*disposition*, indŏlēs, -is, f. ; ingĕnium, -i, n. [-ōnis, f.
*dispute, a*, rixa, -ae, f. ; contentio,
*dissemble*, dissĭmŭlo, 1
*dissembler*, dissĭmŭlātor, -ōris, m.
*dissension*, dissensio, -ōnis, f.
*distant, to be*, absum, ăfui, ăbesse
*distasteful, to become*, displĭceo, 2
*distinguished*, insignis, -e ; clārus, -a, -um
*distribute*, distrĭbuo, -ui, -ūtum, 3
*district*, rĕgio, -ōnis, f.
*distrust*, diffīdo, -fīsus, 3, *or* parum crēdere, confīdere (*dat.*)
*disturb*, turbo, 1
*disturbance*, mōtus, -ūs, m.
*ditch*, fossa, -ae, f.
*divide*, dīvĭdo, -vīsi, -vīsum, 3
*divine*, dīvīnus, -a, -um
*do*, făcio, fēci, factum, 3 : *I (can) easily do without wine*, vīno făcĭle căreo
*dog*, cănis, -is, c.
*dolphin*, delphīn, -īnis, m.
*domestic*, dŏmestĭcus, -a, -um
*door*, jānua, ae, f. ; fŏres, -um, f. pl. ; *out of doors* (i) (*rest*) fŏris, (*motion towards*) fŏras
*doubt, to*, dŭbĭto, 1 ; *there is no doubt that*, nōn dŭbium est quīn, Par. 145 ; *I have no doubt that*, non dŭbĭto quīn ; *without doubt*, sīnĕ dŭbio

*doubtful,* incertus, -a, -um ; dŭbius, -a, -um.
*dove,* cŏlumba, -ae, f.
*downcast,* dēmissus, -a, -um
*down from,* dē (*g. abl.*)
*drachma,* drachma, -ae, f.
*drag,* trăho, traxi, tractum, 3
*draw* (*a sword*), stringo, -nxi, ictum, 3 ; *draw along,* dūco, -xi, -ctum, 3 ; *draw back,* reduco, -xi, -ctum, 3 ; *draw up* (*an army*), instruo, -struxi, -structum, 3 ; *draw lots,* sortior, -tītus, 4, dep. ; *draw water,* I, aquam haurio, hausi, haustum, 4 ; *draw together,* contrăho, -traxi, -tractum, 3
*dread, to,* formīdo, 1
*dreadful,* dīrus, -a, -um
*dream, a,* somnium, -i, n. ; *dream, to,* somnio, 1
*dress,* vestītus, -ūs, m. ; vestis, -is, f.
*drink,* bibo, bībi, bibītum, 3 ; pōto, 1
*drive,* ăgo, ēgi, actum, 3 ; pello, pĕpŭli, pulsum, 3 ; *to drive into exile,* pellĕre ĭn exĭlĭum ; *drive back,* rĕpello, reppŭli, rĕpulsum, 3 ; *drive out,* expello, expŭli, expulsum, 3 ; *drive down,* dēpello, dĕpŭli, dēpulsum, 3
*drop, a,* gutta, -ae, f.
*drown,* mergo, mersi, mersum, 3
*Druids,* Druĭdes, -um, m. pl.
*drunk,* ēbrius, -a, -um
*dry,* siccus, -a, -um ; ārĭdus, -a, -um
*duck,* ănas, -ătis, c.
*duly,* rītĕ
*dutiful conduct,* pĭĕtās, -ātis, f.
*duty,* offĭcium, -ii, n.
*dwell, to,* hăbĭto, 1
*dwelling,* dŏmus, -ūs, f.
*dye, to,* tingo, tinxi, tinctum, 3

**Each,** quisquĕ, quaequĕ, quodquĕ, *or, when used as n.*, quicquĕ, ; *foll. superl.*, suus., &c., (140, 165) ; (*of two*) ŭterquĕ (both are used in sing.)
*eager,* cŭpĭdus, -a, -um
*eagle,* ăquĭla, -ae, f.
*ear,* auris, -is, f.
*early,* matūrē
*earth,* terra, -ae, f. ; tellūs, -ūris, f.
*ease,* ōtium, -i, n.
*easily,* făcĭlĕ ; *more e.*, făcĭlĭŭs
*east, the,* ŏriens, -entis, m.
*easy,* făcĭlis, -e (60)
*eat,* vescor, 3, dep. (*g. abl.*) ; ĕdi, ēdi, ēsum, 3
*educate,* ēdŭco, 1
*effect,* mŏdus, -i, m ; *he spoke to this effect,* in hunc mŏdum ōrātiōnem hăbuit ; *effect, to,* effĭcio -fēci, -fectum, 3
*egg,* ōvum, -i, n.
*Egypt,* Aegyptus, -i, f.
*Egyptian,* Aegyptius, -a, -um
*eight,* octō, indcl.
*eighth,* octāvus, -a, -um
*eighty,* octōgintā, indcl.
*either,* (*conj.*) aut, vĕl (157a)
*elder,* sĕnior, -ōris, *adj. used as n.* ; *also* mājor nātū (71)
*elect,* ēlĭgo, -lēgi, -lectum, 3
*elephant,* ŏlĕphantus, -i, m ; ĕlĕphās, -antis, m.
*eloquence,* făcundia, -ae, f.
*eloquent,* făcundus, -a, um
*else,* (*when adj.*) ălius, -a, ŭd ; *or else* aut ; *elsewhere,* ălĭbī
*embrace, to,* amplector, -plexus, 3, dep. ; *embrace,* amplexus, -ūs, m.
*emperor,* princeps, -ĭpis, m.
*empire,* impĕrium, -i, n.
*empty,* văcuus, -a, -um
*enact,* sancio, -xi, -ctum, 4 ; ("*shall* and "*should,*" *after this v., must be rend. by pres. and imperf. subj.*) *it has been enacted that no one shall ride in a carriage,* sanctum est nē quis currū vĕhātur

*encourage*, hortor, 1, dep.; stĭmŭlo, 1
*end, to*, fīnio, 4
*end*, fīnis, -is, m.
*endeavour*, cōnor, 1, dep. (*foll. by inf.*)
*endowed with*, praedĭtus, -a, -um (*g. abl.*)
*endurance*, pătientia, -ae, f.
*endure*, perfĕro, -tuli, -lātum, -ferre
*enemy*, hostis, -is, m.; (*in war, mostly pl.*) *the enemy's camp*, hostium (*not* hostis) castra; *a private enemy*, ĭnĭmīcus, -a, -um
*energetic*, strĕnuus, -a, -um
*engagement*, certāmen, -ĭnis, n.; pugna, -ae, f.
*England*, Anglia, -ae, f.
*enjoy*, fruor, fruitus, 3, dep. (*g. abl.*)
*enormous*, ingens, -ntis
*enough*, sătĭs
*enraged*, īrātus, -a, -um
*enter*, intro, 1; ineo, -īvi *or* -ii, ītum, 4
*enterprise*, cōnātus, -ūs, m.
*enticements*, illĕcebrae, -arum, f. pl.
*entirely*, omnīno
*entrails*, viscĕra, -um, n.
*entreat*, ōro, 1 (143)
*entrust*, crēdo, -dĭdi, -dĭtum, 3
*envious*, invĭdus, -a, -um
*envy*, invĭdia, -ae, f.; *envy, to*, invĭdeo, -vīdi, vīsum, 3 (*g. dat.*)
*Epaminondas*, Epămĭnondās, -ae, m.
*Ephesus*, Ephĕsus, -i, f.
*Epicurus*, Epīcūrus, -i, m.
*equal*, păr, păris
*equally*, părĭter
*equipped*, instructus, -a, -um, *part. of* instruo
*erect* (*build*), exstruo, -struxi, -structum, 3; erĭgo, -rexi, -rectum, 3
*err*, erro, 1
*error*, error, -ōris, m.

*escape*, fŭga, -ae, f.; *escape, to*, ēvādo, -vāsi, -vāsum, 3; effŭgio, -fūgi, 3; *escape the notice of*, fallo, fĕfelli, falsum, 3 (*g. acc.*)
*escort*, dēdūco, -duxi, -ductum, 3
*especially*, maxĭmē; praesertim
*estimate*, aestĭmo, 1
*eternal*, aeternus, -a, -um
*Europe*, Eurōpa, -ae, f.
*even*, ĕtiam; vĕl (141 *a*); *not even*, nē—quidem (141); *even a boy*, vĕl puer; *even now*, ĕtiam nunc; *even if*, ĕtiam sī
*evening*, vesper, -ĕris *and* -ĕri, m.; *in the evening*, vespĕrĕ, *or adv.* vespĕri (*not* vespĕro)
*event*, ēventus, -ūs, m.
*ever*, unquam; (*always*) semper; *if you ever come*, sī quando vĕneris; *did you e. come?* num quando (*or* ecquando) vēnisti?
*every, every good man*, omnes bŏni, *or* optĭmus quisquĕ (140); *every day*, quŏtīdiē (*or* cŏtīdiē)
*everywhere*, passim
*evil*, mălus, -a, -um; *an evil*, [mălum, -i, n.
*examine*, investīgo, 1
*example*, exemplum, -i, n.
*exceedingly*, valdē
*excellence*, virtūs, -ūtis, f.
*excellent*, ēgrĕgius, -a, -um (68*b*); praestans, -ntis; optĭmus, -a, -um
*except*, prep. praetĕr (*g. acc.*); conj. nĭsī; *why do you fight except to conquer?* cur pugnas nĭsī ūt vincās?
*excessive*, nĭmius, -a, -um
*exchange*, mūto, 1 [-ōnis, f.
*excuse*, excūso, 1; *an e.*, excūsātio,
*exercise, to*, exerceo, -ui, -ĭtum, 2
*exhort*, cōhortor, -ātus, 1, dep.
*exile*, exĭlium, -i, n.; *exile, an*, exsul, -ŭlis, m.
*expectation*, expectātio, -ōnis, f.; spēs, spei, f.
*expediency*, ūtĭlĭtas, -ātis, f.

*expedient,* ūtĭlis, -e
*expense,* sumptus, -ūs, m.
*experience,* expĕrientia, -ae, f.;
  ūsus, -ūs, m.; *experience, to,*
  expĕrior, -pertus, 4, dep.
*explain,* explĭco, 1
*explore,* explōro, 1
*extend,* păteo, -ui, 2 (*intrans.*);
  pando, pandi, passum, 3 (*trans.*)
*extent,* spătium, -i, n.  [3
*extinguish,* exstinguo, -nxi, -nctum,
*extraordinary,* mīrus, -a, -um
*extreme,* extrēmus, -a, -um
*extremely,* valdē
*exult,* exulto, 1
*eye,* ŏcŭlus, -i, m.

**Fabius,** Făbius, -i, m.
*fable,* fābŭla, -ae, f.
*face,* făcies, -ei, f.; ōs, ōris, n.;
  vultus, -ūs, m.
*factions,* partes, -ium, f.
*fact,* rēs, rei, f.; *facts must be
  clearly arranged,* rēs lūculenter
  sunt dīgĕrendae
*fail* (*fall short*), dēsum, -fui,
  esse, (*g. dat*); (*forsake*), dēfĭcio, -fēci, -fectum, 3; *time
  fails me,* tempus mē dēfĭcit
*faith,* fĭdēs, -ei, f.  [-um
*faithful,* fĭdēlis, -e; fīdus, -a,
*fall, to,* cădo, cĕcĭdi, cāsum, 3;
  (*in battle*) occĭdo, -cĭdi, -cāsum,
  3
*fall asleep, to,* obdormio, -ii *or*
  -īvi, -ītum, 4
*false* (*things*), falsus, -a, -um;
  (*persons*), mendax, -ācis
*falsehood,* mendācium, -ii, n.
*fame,* fāma, -ae, f.
*family,* fămĭlia, -ae, f.; dŏmus,
  -ūs, f.
*famine,* fămēs, -is, f.
*far,* prŏcŭl; longē; *as far as,*
  tĕnŭs (*g. abl. or gen.,* 178)
*farm,* praedium, -i, n.
*farthing,* as, assis, m.; *I do not
  care a farthing for you,* nōn
  assis tē făcio
*"fasces," the,* fascēs, -ium, m. pl.
  *the rods which were the signs
  of the consul's power*
*fat,* pinguis, -e
*fate,* fātum, -i, n.
*father,* păter, -tris, m.
*fault,* culpa, -ae, f.
*favour,* grātia, -ae, f.; *favour, to,*
  făveo, făvi, fautum, 2 (*g. dat.*)
*fear,* tĭmor, -oris, m.; mĕtus, -ūs,
  m.
*fearful,* păvĭdus, -a, -um
*fear, to,* tĭmeo, -ui, 2; mĕtuo, -ui,
  3; vĕreor, vĕrĭtus, dep. 2
*fearless,* impăvĭdus, -a, -um
*feast,* ĕpŭlae, -ārum, f.  [f.
*feather,* penna, -ae, f.; plūma, -ae,
*features,* vultus, -ūs, m.
*feeble,* infirmus, -a, -um
*feed,* (*trans.*) pasco, pāvi, pastum,
  3; (*intrans.*) pascor, *pass.*
*feed on,* vescor, 3 dep. (*g. abl.*)
*feel,* sentio, sensi, sensum, 4
*feign,* fingo, finxi, fictum, 3
*fellow,* hŏmo, -ĭnis, m.: *that
  fellow,* istĕ
*fertile,* fertĭlis, -e
*fetch,* see *bring*
*fetter,* compēs, -ĕdis, f.  [-ŏ
*fever,* febris, -is f. (-im *or* -em, -I *or*
*few,* paucus, -a, -um, (*mostly pl.*);
  *very few,* perpauci
*field,* ăger, -gri, m.
*fierce,* fĕrox, -ōcis
*fifth, fifty,* see Par. 81
*fig, fig-tree,* fīcus, -i, *and* -ūs, f.
*fight,* pugna, -ae, f.
*fight, to,* pugno, 1
*fill,* complĕo, -plēvi, -pletum, 2
*finally,* dēnīquē (*not to stand first
  in a clause*)
*find,* invĕnio, -vēni, -ventum, 4; *he
  was found guilty of,* damnātus
  est (*g. gen.*)
*fine,* multa, -ae, f.

*fine, to*, multo, 1
*finger*, dĭgĭtus, -i, m.
*finish*, confĭcio, -fēci, -fectum, 3 ; pĕrăgo, -ēgi, -actnm, 3
*fire*, ignis, -is, -m., *abl.* ignī ; *under fire*, sub jactu, *or* jactum, tēli, (180)
*firm*, firmus, -a, -um
*first*, prīmus, -a, -um ; *at f.* ; prīmo (*adv.*) ; *T. was the first to come* (*or who came*), Tallius prīmus vēnit
*fish*, piscis, -is, m.
*fisherman*, piscātor, -ōris, m.
*fit*, aptus, -a, -um ; ĭdōneus, -a, -um ; *for running*, aptus ad currendum (186)
*five*, quinquĕ, indcl. ; *five hundred*, quingenti, -ae, -a
*fix*, fīgo, -xi, -xum, 3
*fixed*, certus, -a, -um ; *a certain fixed day*, certus quīdam diēs
*flame*, flamma, -ae, f.
*flatter*, ădŭlor, 1, dep.
*flee*, fŭgio, fūgi, 3
*fleet*, classis, -is, f.
*flesh*, căro, carnis, f.
*flight*, fŭga, -ae, f. ; *of a bird*, vŏlātus, -us, m.
*flight, put to*, fŭgo, 1
*flourish*, flōreo, -ui, 2
*flow*, fluo, -xi, 3, *fut. part.* fluxūrus
*flower*, flōs, -ōris, m.
*fly, a*, musca, -ae, f.
*fly, to*, see *flee* ; (*of a bird*) vŏlo, 1
*foe*, hostis, -is, m.
*follow*, sĕquor, sĕcūtus, 3, dep.
*follower*, cŏmĕs, -ĭtis, m.
*folly*, stultĭtia, -ae, f.
*food*, cĭbus, -i, m.
*fond of*, studiōsus, -a, -um, (*g. gen.*)
*fool, foolish*, stultus, -a, -um
*foolishly*, stultē
*foot*, pēs, pĕdis, m.
*foot-soldier*, pĕdĕs, -ĭtis. m.
*for* (*conj.*) nam (*at the beginning of a clause*) ; ĕnim (*after the first word in a clause*) ; (*prep.*) pro, prae, (*g. abl.*) ; ob, (*g. acc.*) Par. 178 ; (*born, fit, useful*, &c.) *for acting*, ăd ăgendum ; *for a few days*, paucos diēs (262)
*forbid*, vĕto, -ui, -ĭtum, 1 ; prŏhĭbeo, -ui, -ĭtum, 2
*force*, vīs, *acc.* vim, *abl.* vi, f.
*forced marches*, magna ĭtĭnĕra
*forces*, cōpĭae, -ārum, f.
*forehead*, frons, -ntis, f.
*foreign*, externus, -a, -um ; pĕregrīnus, -a, -um
*foresee*, prōvĭdeo, -vīdi, -vīsum, 2
*forest*, silva, -ae, f.
*forget*, oblīviscor, oblĭtus, 3, dep. (*g. gen.*)
*forgetful*, immĕmor, -ōris (*g. gen.*)
*form*, forma, -ae, f.
*former*, prior, prius ; *the former... the latter*, ille...hic
*formerly*, quondam, ōlim
*fort*, castrum, -i, -n. ; castellum, -i, n.
*fortify*, mūnio, -ivi *or* -ii ,-itum 4,
*fortitude*, fortĭtūdo, -ĭnis, f. ; *with fortitude*, fortĭter
*fortunate*, fēlix, -īcis
*fortune*, fortūna, -ae, f.
*fortunes, they distrusted their f.*, rēbus suis diffīsi sunt
*forty*, quadrāgintā, indcl.
*forum*, fŏrum, -i, n.
*found*, condo, -ĭdi, -ditum, 3
*founder*, condĭtor, -ōris, m.
*fountain*, fons, fontis, m.
*four, fourteen, &c.* see Par. 81
*four times*, quăter
*fourth*, quartus, -a, -um
*free*, lĭber, -ĕra, -ĕrum : *f. from fault*, culpā văcuus (279)
*free, to*, lībĕro, 1, (*acc. & abl.*)
*freed from debt*, aere ăliēno lībĕrātus
*freedom*, lībertās, -ātis, f.
*frequent*, crēber, -bra, -brum
*frequently*, saepĕ

*fresh*, rĕcens, -ntis; nŏvus, -a, -um
*friend*, ămīcus, -i, m.
*friendly*, ămīcus, -a, -um
*friendship*, ămīcĭtĭa, -ae, f.
*frighten*, terreo, -ui, 2
*frog*, rāna, -ae, f.
*from*, ā, ē, or ex, dē (*g. abl.*); *from boyhood*, indĕ a puĕro
*from a distance*, ēmĭnŭs
*front, in*, adversus, -a, -um
*frost*, gĕlū, *indel.* n.
*frugality*, parsĭmōnĭa, -ae, f.
*fruit*, fructus, -ūs, m.; *the fruits (of the earth)*, frūges, -um, f. pl.
*fruitful*, fertĭlis, -e; fērax, -ācis
*fulfil*, perfĭcio, -fēci, -fectum, 3; explco, -plēvi, -plētum, 2
*full*, plēnus, -a, -um (*g. gen.* or *abl.*)
*funeral*, fūnus, -ĕris, n.; *funeral rites*, infĕriae, -arum, f.
*furrow*, sulcus, -i, m.
*fury*, fūror, -ōris, m.
*future*, fŭtūrus, -a, -um

**Găbii**, Găbii, -ōrum, m. pl.
*gain*, quaestus, -ūs, m.; lucrum, -i, n.
*gain, to*, (*a victory*) rĕportāre, 1; acquīro, quīsīvi, quīsītum, 3; păro, 1
*gain possession of*, pŏtior, -ītus, 4, dep. (*g. abl.*) See Par. 207.
*Gallic*, Gallĭcus, -a, -um
*gallows*, crux, crŭcis, f.
*game*, lūdus, -i, m.
*garden*, hortus, -i, m.
*garland*, sertum, -i, n.
*garment*, vestis, -is, f.
*garrison*, praesĭdium, -i, n.
*gate*, porta, -ae, f.
*gather*, lĕgo, lĕgi, lectum, 3; collĭgo, lĕgi, lectum, 3
*Gaul*, Gallia, -ae, f.
*Gaul, a*, Gallus, -i, m.
*gem*, gemma, -ae, f.
*general*, dux, dŭcis, m.; impĕrātor, -ōris, m.

*generally*, plērumque
*gentleness*, cōmĭtas, -ātis, f.
*gently*, lēnĭter
*German*, Germānus, -a, -um
*Germany*, Germānia, -ae, f.
*get*, păro, 1; ădĭpiscor, ădeptus, 3
*giant*, gīgās, -antis, m.
*gift*, dōnum, -i, n.
*gird*, cingo, -nxi, -nctum, 3
*girl*, puella, -ae, f.
*give*, do, dĕdi, dătum, 1
*give back*, reddo, -dĭdi, -dĭtum, 3
*give birth to*, părio, pepĕri, partum, 3 (*g. acc.*)
*give orders to*, impĕro, 1 (*g. dat.*)
*give up*, trādo, -dĭdi, -dĭtum, 3
*glad*, laetus, -a, -um
*Glaucus*, Glaucus, -i, m.
*glitter*, mĭco, -ui, 1
*gloomy*, tristis, e
*glorious*, praeclārus, -a, -um
*glory*, glōria, -ae, f.
*go*, eo, -īvi or -ii, -ĭtum, 4; *I am going-to-die*, mŏrĭtūrus sum
*go away*, ăbeo, -ii, -ĭtum, 4
*go by*, praetĕreo, īvi or -ii, -ītum, 4
*go forth, or out*, exeo, -ii, -ĭtum, 4
*go on*, prōcēdo, -cessi, -cessum, 3
*go under*, sŭbeo, -ii, -ĭtum, 4
*goat*, căper, -pri, m.
*god*, deus, dei, m.; nom. pl. *often* dii, or di
*goddess*, dea, -ae, f. Par. 311
*gold*, aurum, -i, n.
*golden*, aureus, -a, -um
*good*, bŏnus, -a, -um
*goodwill*, bĕnĕvŏlentia, -ae, f.
*goose*, anser, -ĕris, m.
*govern*, rĕgo, rexi, rectum, 3
*government*, impĕrium, -i, n.
*grace*, grātia, -ae, f.
*grandfather*, ăvus, -i, m.
*grandson*, nĕpōs, -ōtis, m.
*grant* (see *give*); *I grant him pardon*, do ei vĕniam
*grape*, ūva, -ae, f.
*grass*, herba, -ae, f.

*grateful,* grātus, -a, -um
*gray,* cānus, -a, -um
*great,* magnus, -a, -um ; *very great,* permagnus ; *with "this,"* tantus; *this great slaughter,* haec tanta caedēs
*greatly,* magnŏpĕre, valdē
*greatness,* magnĭtūdo, -ĭnis, f.
*Grecian, Greek,* Graecus, -a, -um
*Greece,* Graecia, -ae, f.
*greedy,* ăvĭdus, -a, -um, ăvārus, -a, -um (*both g. gen.*)
*green,* vĭrĭdis, -e
*green, to grow,* vĭresco, 3 [m.
*grief,* dŏlor, -ōris, m. ; luctus, -ūs,
*grieve,* dŏleo, -ui, 2 (*intrans.*); ango, 3 (*trans.*)
*groan,* gēmĭtus, -ūs, m.
*groan, to,* gĕmo, -ui, 3
*ground,* hŭmus, -i, f. ; *on the ground,* hŭmi
*grove,* lūcus, -i, m.
*grow,* cresco, crēvi, cretum, 3
*guard,* (*a single person*) custōs, -ōdis, m. ; (*a garrison*) praesĭdium, -i, n.
*guard, to,* custōdio, -īvi or -ii, -ītum, 4 ; *guard strongly,* firmāre praesĭdiō
*guest,* hospĕs, -ĭtis, m.
*guide,* dux, dŭcis, m.
*guide, to,* dūco, duxi, ductum, 3
*guile,* dŏlus, -i, m.
*guilt,* culpa, -ae, f. ; scĕlus, -ĕris, n.
*guilty,* sons, sontis ; *to be found guilty of,* damnāri (*g. gen.*)

**Habit,** mōs, mōris, m.
*hail,* grando, -ĭnis, f.
*hair,* crīnis, -is, m. ; *not even a hair's breadth,* ne transversum quidem unguem, lit. *a nail's breadth*
*half,* dīmĭdium, -i, n.
*halt,* consisto, -stĭti, -stĭtum, 3
*hand,* mănus, -ūs, f. ; *right hand,* dextra ; *left hand,* sĭnistra ; *I am at hand,* adsum, -fui, -esse ; *it is in your hands,* pĕnes tē est (183)
*hand down,* trādo, -dĭdi, -dĭtum, 3
*handsome,* pulcher, -chra, -chrum
*hang,* pendeo, pĕpendi, 2 (*intrans.*); pendo, pĕpendi, pensum, 3 (*trans.*)
*Hannibal,* Hannĭbal, -ălis, m.
*happen,* (*of ill fortune*) accĭdo, -cĭdi, 3 (*mostly foll. by* ŭt ; (*of good*) contingo, -tĭgi, 3
*happy,* (*fortunate*) fēlix, -īcis ; (*joyful*) laetus, -a, -um ; (*blessed*) bĕātus, -a, -um
*harbour,* portus, -ūs, m.
*hard,* dūrus, -a, -um
*hare,* lĕpus, -ŏris, m.
*harm,* detrīmentum, -i, n.
*harmful,* noxius, -a, -um
*harp,* cĭthăra, -ae, f.
*harvest,* messis, -is, f.
*Hasdrubal,* Hasdrŭbal, -ălis, m.
*haste,* cĕlĕrĭtās, -ātis, f. ; *in haste,* cum cĕlĕrĭtāte, *or* cĕlĕrīter, *or* summā cĕlĕrĭtāte (181) ; *make haste,* see *hasten*
*hasten,* festīno, 1 ; prŏpĕro, 1
*hastily,* i.e. *rashly,* tĕmĕrē
*hate,* ŏdium, -i, n.
*hate, to,* ōdi, def. 3 ; *see* App. II., page 215
*hatred,* see *hate*
*have,* hăbeo, -ui, -ĭtum, 2
*hawk,* accĭpĭter, -tris, m.
*he,* ille, -a, -ud ; is, ea, ĭd ; *he who,* qui (*is being often omitted, or placed after* qui, Par. 107)
*head,* căput, -ĭtis, n.
*headlong,* praeceps, -cĭpĭtis
*health,* sălūs, -ūtis, f.
*healthy,* sānus, -a, -um ; *healthful,* sălūber, -bris, -bre
*heap,* ăcervus, -i, m.
*hear,* audio, -īvi or -ii, -ītum, 4
*hearer,* audĭtor, -ōris, m.
*heart,* cŏr, -dis, n.

*hearth*, fŏcus, -i, m.
*heat*, călor, -ōris, m.
*heaven*, caelum, -i, m.
*heavy*, grăvis, -e
*Hector*, Hectŏr, Hectŏris, m.
*hedge round, to,* saepio, saepsi, saeptum, 4
*heir*, hērēs, -ēdis, m.
*Helena*, Hĕlĕna, -ae, f.
*helmet*, gălea, -ae, f.
*help*, auxĭlium, -ĭ, n.
*help, to,* subvĕnio, -vēni, -ventum, 4 (*g. dat.*)
*Helvetii, the,* Helvĕtii,-ōrum, -ĭ, m.
*hemlock*, cĭcūta, -ae, f.
*hence*, hinc
*herb*, herba, -ae, f.
*Hercules*, Hercŭlēs, -is, m.
*herd*, pĕcŭs, -ŏris, n.
*here*, hīc ; *often used for "hither" and then to be trans. by* hūc
*hero*, hēros, -ŏĭs, m. (*acc. pl.* -ŏas)
*hesitate*, dŭbĭto, 1
*hide, to,* condo, -dĭdi, dĭtum, 3 ; abdo, -dĭdi, -dĭtum, 3
*hiding place*, lătebra, -ae, f.
*high*, altus, -a, -um ; *to buy at a very high price,* permagnō ĕmĕre
*highest*, summus, -a, -um
*hill*, collis, -is, m.
*himself*, sē, suī, &c. See Par. 94
*hinder*, prŏhĭbeo, 2, *I hindered you from coming,* prŏhĭbui quomĭnŭs vĕnīrēs
*hinge*, cardo, -dĭnis, m.
*hire*, condūco, -duxi, -ductum, 3
*his*, Par. 98, 218, 306, *and p.* 328
*historian*, auctor, -ōris, m.
*hither*, hūc ; *hitherto,* ădhūc
*hold*, tĕneo, -ui, 2 ; hăbeo, -ui, -ĭtum, 2
*holiday*, fēriae, -ārum, f.
*hollow*, căvus, -a, -um ; *to hollow,* căvāre
*holy*, săcer, -cra, -crum
*home*, dŏmus, -ūs, f. (Ex. LXXXIV.) ; *at home,* dŏmi (265)

*Homer*, Hŏmērus, -i, m.
*honest*, prŏbus, -a, -um
*honesty*, prŏbĭtas, -ātis, f.
*honey*, mĕl, mellis, n.
*honour*, hŏnor, -ōris, m.; *to be in great honour with the Romans,* in magno hŏnōre esse ăpŭd Rōmānos
*honourable*, hŏnestus, -a, -um
*hoof*, ungŭla, -ae, f.
*hook*, hāmus, -i, m.
*hope*, spēs, spei, f.
*hope, to,* spēro, 1 ; *do you hope to take the city?* spērasne tē urbem captūrum esse ?
*Horace*, Hŏrātius, -ii, m.
*Horatii, the,* Hŏrātii, -ōrum, m.
*horn*, cornū, -ūs, n.
*horrible*, dīrus, -a, -um ; nĕfandus, -a, -um ; *h. to relate!* nĕfās dictū ! (246)
*horse*, ĕquus, -i, m.
*horseman*, ĕquĕs, -ĭtis, m.
*hospitality*, hospĭtium, -i, n.
*host*, hospĕs, -ĭtis, m.
*hostage*, obses, -ĭdis, m.
*hostile*, infestus, -a, -um
*Hostilius*, Hostīlius, -i, m.
*hound*, cănis, -is, c.
*hour*, hōra, -ae, f.
*house*, dŏmus, -ūs, f. (311); aedes, -ium, f. pl. ; *household,* fămĭlia, -ae, f.
*how? in what way?* quōmŏdo ? *to how great an extent,* quam, quantum ; *how great or much,* quantus, -a, -um ; *how many?* quot ? *how often?* quŏtiens ? *how long?* quamdiu ? *how good, bad, &c.,* quam bŏnus, mălus, &c. ; *how few there are who use riches well!* quŏtus quisque est qui dīvĭtiis bĕnĕ ūtātur! *for how much did you buy it?* quanti id ēmisti ? *how important it is!* quantum intĕrest *or* rēfert (329)
*however*, tămen

*huge*, ingens, -tis
*human*, hūmānus, -a, -um
*hundred*, centum, *indecl.* (81)
*hunger*, fāmes, -is, f.
*hungry, to be*, ēsŭrio, 4
*hunt*, vēnor, -atus, 1, dep.
*hunter, huntsman*, vēnātor, -ōris, m.
*hunting*, vēnātio, -ōnis, f.
*hurl*, conjĭcio, -jēci, -jectum, 3
*hurt, to*, nŏceo, 2 (*g. dat.*); laedo, -si, -sum, (*g. acc.*)
*hurtful*, noxius, -a, um
*husband*, mărītus, -i, m.
*husbandman*, agrĭcŏla, -ae, m.

*I*, ĕgo; *see page* 45
*Ida*, Ĭda, -ae, f.
*idle*, ignāvus, -a, -um
*idleness*, ignāvia, -ae, f.
*if*, sī; *if...not*, nĭsĭ (125, 295)
*ignorant*, ignārus, -a, -um (*g. gen.*); *ignorant of, to be*, ignōro, 1; nescio, -ii, 4 (*both g. acc.*); *are you ignorant that the man is here?* nescīsnĕ hŏmĭnem ădesse? *are you ignorant how*, &c., nescīsnĕ quōmŏdo, *foll. by subjunct.*
*ill* (*sick*), aeger, -gra, -grum; (*subst.*) mălum, -i, n.; *ill* (*adv.*), i.e. *badly*, mălĕ
*illness*, morbus, -i, m. [nis, -e
*illustrious*, clārus, -a, -um; insig-
*image*, ĭmāgo, -ĭnis, f.
*imagine*, pŭto, 1
*imitate*, ĭmĭtor, 1, dep.
*immediately*, stătim
*immense*, ingens, -ntis
*immortal*, -immortālis, e
*immortality*, immortālitas, -ātis, f.
*impatient*, impătiens, -tis
*impede*, impĕdio, -īvi *or* ii, ītum, 4
*impel*, impello, -pŭli, -pulsum, 3
*impious*, impĭus, -a, -um
*implore*, ōro, 1
*important. It is important for Balbus*, Balbi intĕrest; ("*should*," *after this v., is often rendered by pres. inf.*) *it is imp. that Catiline should perish*, intĕrest Cătĭlīnam pĕrīre; *it is i. for me*, meā intĕrest; *see Par.* 329
*importune*, fătīgo, 1
*impose*, impōno, -pŏsui, -pŏsĭtum, 3; *I impose tribute on a nation*, trĭbūtum genti impōno
*improve, to*, ēmendo, 1 [er
*impudent*, impŭdens, -tis; -*ly*, -ent-
*impunity, with*, impūnē
*impute, he i. this to me as a fault*, hōc mĭhi vĭtĭo dat, *or* vertit
*in*, in (*g. abl.*); *in the direction of*, versŭs (*foll. acc.*); *in the pages of*, ăpŭd (*g. acc.*); *in the power of*, pĕnes (*g. acc.*); *in the presence of*, cōram (*g. abl.*), *see Par.* 178-180; *in order to*, ŭt; *in three days, Par.* 263; *in Gabii, Par.* 265; *in haste, Par.* 181.
*increase*, augeo, auxi, auctum, 2 (*trans.*); cresco, crēvi, crētum, 3 (*intrans.*)
*incredible*, incrēdĭbĭlis, -e
*incursion*, incursio, -ōnis, f.
*indeed*, quĭdem; *you i....but I*, tū quĭdem...ĕgo autem, (*or* vērō)
*India*, India, -ae, f.
*indignation, see anger*
*indolence*, ignāvia, -ae, f. [(*dat.*)
*indulge*, indulgeo, -lsi, -ltum, 2
*industrious*, dīlĭgens, -ntis
*infantry*, pĕdĭtes, m. pl.; pĕdĭtātus, -ūs, m.
*infirm*, infirmus, -a, -um, -um
*influence*, mŏveo, mōvi, mōtum, 2
*inform, I informed him*, certiorem eum fēci (*gen. or de.*)
*in front*, adversus, -a, -um, *adj.*
*inglorious*, ĭnhŏnestus, -a, -um
*inhabit*, incŏlo, -colui, -cultum, 3; hăbĭto, 1
*inhabitant*, incŏla, -ae, m.
*injure*, nŏceo, -ui, 2 (*g. dat.*)
*injury*, injūria, -ae, f.
*injustice, see* (34) *unjust* (*things.*)

*innocence,* innŏcentia, -ae, f.
*innocent,* innŏcens, -tis; insons, -ntis; *innocent of all fault,* omni culpā văcuus (279)
*innumerable,* innŭmĕrābĭlis, -e
*inquire,* quaero, quaesīvi, quaesītum, 3; rŏgo, 1
*inquiry,* quaestio, ōnis, f.
*insolence,* insŏlentia, -ae, f. [3
*inspect,* inspĭcio, -spexi, -spectum,
*insolent,* insŏlens, -tis
*instance,* exemplum, -i, n.
*instead of,* prō (*g. abl.*)
*instruct,* ĕrŭdio, 4
*instrument,* instrūmentum, -i, n.
*insufficient,* impar, *gen.* impăris
*insult,* contŭmĕlia, -ae, f.
*insurrection,* sēdĭtĭo, -ĭōnis, f.
*integrity,* prŏbĭtas, ātis, f.
*intellect,* ingĕnium, -i, n.
*intention,* consĭlium, -i, n.
*inter,* sĕpĕlio, -īvi *or* -ii, -pultum, 4
*intercept,* interclūdo, -si, -sum, 3
*intercourse,* consuētūdo, -inis, f.
*interest, it is my i.,* meā intĕrest; *it is the i. of Tullius,* Tullii intĕrest (*see* Ex. XCII.); (*interests*) *to consult my, Tullius's, i.,* mihi, Tullio, consŭlere
*into,* in (*g. acc.*) Par. 55. [3
*introduce,* indūco, -duxi, -ductum,
*invade,* invādo, -si, -sum, 3
*in turn,* invĭcem
*in vain,* frustrā
*inventor,* inventor, -ōris, m.
*investigate,* explōro, 1
*invite,* invīto, 1
*invoke,* invŏco, 1
*Ireland,* Hībernia, -ae, f.
*iron,* (*subst.*) ferrum, -i, n.; (*adj.*) ferreus, -a, -um
*island,* insŭla, -ae, f.
*it, see* page 46, Par. 219-226
*Italy,* Ĭtălia, -ae, f.
*ivory* (*subst.*), ĕbur, -ŏris, n.; (*adj.*) ĕburnus, -a, -um
*ivy,* hĕdĕra, -ae, f.

**Javelin,** jăcŭlum, -i, n.
*jaw,* māla, -ae, f.
*jest,* jŏcus, -i, m.; pl. -i *and* -a
*join,* jungo, -nxi, -nctum, 3
*journey,* ĭtĕr, itĭnĕris, n.; *to journey,* ĭter făcĕre; *we shall have to journey,* ĭter nōbīs făcĭendum ĕrit
*joy,* gaudium, -i, n.
*joyful,* laetus, -a, -um
*joyfully,* laetē
*judge,* jūdex, -ĭcis, m.; *judge, to,* jūdĭco, 1
*judgment,* jūdĭcium, -i, n.; *in my judgment,* mē jūdĭcĕ
*juice,* jūs, jūris, n.
*jump, to,* salto, 1
*juniper,* saltātor, -ōris, m.
*Juno,* Jūno, -ōnis, f.
*Jupiter,* Juppĭter, Jŏvis, m.; *dat., acc., abl.,* Jŏvi, -em, -ĕ
*just,* justus, -a, -um
*justice,* justĭtia, -ae, f.; jūs, jūris, n.

**Keen,** ācer, -crĭs, -crĕ (44, 61)
*keep,* tĕneo, -ui, 2; servo, 1; *I keep my word,* fĭdem praesto, -stĭtī, -stātum & -stĭtum, 1; *keep off,* arceo, -ui, 2
*keeper,* custōs, -ōdis, m.
*key,* clāvis, -is, f.
*kill,* interfĭcio, -fēci, -fectum, 3
*kind,* bĕnignus, -a, -um
*kind,* gĕnus, -ĕris, n.; *a barren kind of style,* jējūna quaedam ōrātio; *see* Ex. LXXXIII. note 310a
*kindness,* bĕnignĭtas, -ātis, f.
*kindle,* incendo, -di, -sum, 3
*kindly,* bĕnignē
*kindness, a,* bĕnĕfĭcium, -i, n.
*king,* rex, rēgis, m.
*kingdom,* regnum, -i, n.
*kiss,* oscŭlor, 1, dep.
*knee,* gĕnū, -ūs, n.
*knife,* culter, -tri, m.

**LET**

*knight*, ĕquĕs, -ĭtis, m.
*know*, scio, -īvi *or* -ii, -ītum, 4; nŏvi, *see* nosco; *I do-not-know*, nescio, -scīvi -scītum, 4
*knowledge*, scientia, -ae, f.; *without his knowledge*, clam eo
*known*, nōtus, -a, -um; *it is well known*, constat

**Labienus**, Lăbiēnus, -i, m.
*labour*, lăbor, -ōris, m.
*lady*, mŭlier, -ĕris, f.
*lake*, lăcus, -ûs, m.
*lamb*, agnus, -i, m.
*lame*, claudus, -a, -um
*lament*, lūgeo, -xi, -ctum, 2 (*trans.*): dŏleo, -ui, 2 (*intrans.*) [*grief*
*lamentation*, maeror, -ōris, m., sec
*lance*, hasta, ae, f.
*land*, terra, -ae, f.; *lands* (*as possessions*), ăger, -gri, m.; fines, -ium, m. pl.; *land* (*adj.*) terrestris, -e
*large*, magnus, -a, -um (*for comp. and superl. see* Par. 68); *a l. sum of money*, grandis pĕcūnia
*lashes*, verbĕra, -um, n. pl.
*last* (*as opp. to first in a race*), extrēmus, see Par. 69; *at last*, tandem
*lasting*, pĕrennis, -e
*late*, sērus, -a, -um; *late*, adv. sērō; *rather late, too late*, sērius
*lately*, nūper
*Latin*, Latīnus, -a, -um
*latter*, hic; *the former...the latter*, ille...hic
*Latona*, Lătōna, -ae, f.
*laugh*, rīdeo, rīsi, rīsum, 2; *laugh at, mock* (*a person*), irrīdeo, -si, -sum, 2 (*g. dat.*); (*a thing*) rīdeo (*g. acc.*), *gentler than* irrīdeo
*laughing-stock*, lūdibrium, -i, n.
*laurel*, laurus, -i, f.
*law*, (*a statute*), lĕx, lēgis, f.; (*the laws*) jūs, jūris, n.; *the laws of men and God*, jūs et fās; *against the laws*, contrā jūs [*pers.*
*lawful, it is*, lĭcet, -uit, 2, im-
*lay aside*, pōno, pŏsui, pŏsĭtum, 3; *lay down*, dēpōno, -pŏsui, -pŏsĭtum, 3; *lay waste*, vasto, 1
*laziness*, ĭnertia, -ae, f.
*lazy*, segnis, -e; ĭners, -tis
*lead*, dūco, -xi, -ctum, 3; *lead out*, ēdūco, -xi, -ctum, 3
*leader*, dux, dŭcis, m.
*leaf*, frons, -dis, f.
*lean, adj.*, măcer, -cra, crum
*leap, to*, sălio, -ii *or* -ŭi, -saltum, 4; *leap across*, transĭlio, -ui, -sultum, 4; *leap down*, dēsĭlio, -sĭlui, -sultum, 4; *leap out*, exsĭlio, -sĭlui, -sultum, 4, *foll. by* dē *or* ē
*learn*, disco, dĭdĭci, 3
*learned*, doctus, -a, -um; *learned in the law*, jūris perītus (287)
*learning*, doctrīna, -ae, f. ["*at*"
*least*, mĭnĭmus, -a, -um; *at l.*, see
*leave, to*, linquo, -līqui, -lictum, 3; rĕlinquo, -līqui, -lictum, 3; *I leave* (*by will*), lēgo, 1; *leave*, pŏtestās, -ātis, f.
*left*, rĕlĭquus, -a, -um; *left* (*hand*), sĭnister, -tra, -trum
*leg*, crūs, crūris, n.
*legion*, lĕgio, -ōnis, f.
*leisure*, ōtium, -i, n.; *leisure, to have*, văco, 1
*Lemnos*, Lemnos, -i, f.
*lend*, crēdo, -dĭdi, -dĭtum, 3
*length*, longĭtūdo, -ĭnis, f.; *at length*, tandem
*Lentulus*, Lentŭlus, -i, m.
*Leonidas*, Leōnĭdas, -ae, m.
*less*, mĭnor, -is; *it was sold for less* (Ex. LXX.), mĭnōris vendĭtum est; *it is less honourable*, mĭnus hŏnestum est
*lest*, nē
*let*; (*oft. rend. by subjunct.*) *let them love, hate*, &c., āment,

x

ōdĕrint ; *let this be an example to you*, sĭt tĭbĭ hōc exemplo ; (*or by* făc ut, cūrā ut) *let your conduct be improved*, făc ut mōres tui ēmendentur ; *let them murmur*, lĭcet frĕmant (227)
letter, littĕrae, -arum, f. pl. ; *letter of the alphabet*, littĕra, -ae, f.; ĕpistŏla (*or* ĕpistŭla) -ae, f.
level, aequus, -a, -um ; *level, to*, aequo, 1
levy, a, dēlectus, -ūs, m.; *levy, to*, conscrībo, -psi, -ptum, 3
liar, mendāx, -ācis
liberate, lībĕro, 1 (*g. abl. of thing*)
liberty, libertās, -ātis, f.
lictor, lictor, -ōris, m.
lie (*to tell lies*), mentior, -ītus, 4, dep.; *lie down*, jăceo, -ui, 2 ; *lie hid*, lăteo, -ui, 2 ; *lie in ambush, in wait for*, insĭdior, 1, (*g. dat.*)
life, vīta, -ae, f.
light, lūx, lūcis, f.; lūmen, -ĭnis, n.; *light*, lĕvis, -e [-ĭnis, n.
lightning, fulgŭr, -ŭris, n.; fulmen,
like, sĭmĭlis, -e ; *I like to walk*, me jŭvat, *or* mĭhĭ plăcet, ambŭlāre
likeness, sĭmĭlĭtūdo, -ĭnis, f.
limb, membrum, -i, n.
limit, fīnis, -is, m.; līmĕs, -ĭtis, m.
line (*of battle*), ăcies, -ēi, f.
lion, leo, -ōnis, m.
lip, labrum, -i, n.
listen to, audio, -īvi *or* -ii, -ītum, 4
little, parvus, -a, -um ; *I have too l. strength*, părum vīrium hăbeo ; *it matters l.* paulum rēfert
live, to, vīvo, vixi, victum, 3 ; (*dwell*) habitāre *or* vītam ăgĕre ; *I live on bread*, vescor, (3, dep.) pāne (207)
load, ŏnus, -ĕris, n.
lofty, altus, -a, -um
log, lignum, -i, n.
long, longus, -a, -um ; *long*, adv. diu ; *longer*, adv. diūtius; *how long?* quamdiu ? *I have long been desiring*, jamprīdem (*or* jamdūdum) cŭpio ; *no longer*, non jam
look, *look at*, aspĭcio, -spexi, -spectum, 3 ; *look for*, quaero, quaesīvi, quaesītum, 3 ; *look, a* (*of the human countenance*), vultus, -ūs, m.; *look round*, circumspicio, -spexi, -spectum, 3
lord, dŏmĭnus, -i, m.
lose, āmitto, -mīsi, -missum, 3 ; perdo, -dĭdi, -dĭtum, 3
loss, damnum, -i, n.
lot, sors, -tis, f. ; *to draw lots about*, sortīri dē
lovable, ămābĭlis, -e
love, ămor, -ōris, m.; *love, to*, ămo, 1 ; dīlĭgo, -lexi, -lectum, 3
loving, ămans, -tis
low, *lowly*, hŭmĭlis, -e
lower, infĕrior, -us ; *the lowest of the citizens*, cīvium infīmi
luck, fortūna, -ae, f.
lucky, fēlīx, -īcis ; faustus, -a, -um
luxury, luxŭria, -ae, f.
Lydia, Lydia, -ae, f.
lying, mendāx, -ācis
lyre, lyra, -ae, f.

Macedonians, *the*, Măcĕdŏnes, -ŏnum, m.
machine, māchĭna, -ae, f.
mad, insānus, -a, -um ; āmens, -tis ; *mad, to be*, fŭro, 3 ; insānio, -īvi *or* -ii, 4 [-ae, f.
madness, insānia, -ae, f.; āmentia,
magic, măgĭcus, -a, -um
magistrate, măgistrātus, -ūs, m.
maiden, virgo, -ĭnis, f.
make, făcio, fēci, factum, 3 ; *make peace*, pācem ferīre; *make haste*, see *hasten*
man, (*hero*, &c.), vir, -i, m. ; (*human being*) hŏmo, -ĭnis, m. ; *all to a man*, omnes ăd ūnum
manage, admĭnistro, 1

*manifest*, mănĭfestus, -a, -um
*manner*, mōs, mōris, m.; mŏdus, -i, m.
*many*, multus, -a, -um, *very m.* permulti, *or* plūrimi ; *so m.* tot
*marble*, marmor, -ŏris, n.; (*adj.*) marmŏreus, -a, -um
*march, to*, (*set out*) prŏfīciscor, -fectus, 3, dep.; contendo, -di, -tum, 3; *march, a*, ĭter, ĭtĭnĕris, n.
*Marcius*, Marcius, -i, m.
*Marcus*, Marcus, -i, m.
*mark*, signum, -i, n.; nŏta, -ae, f.; *it is the m. of*, est (*foll. by gen.*); *see* Par. 289.
*Maro*, Măro, -ōnis, m., Publius Vergĭlius Măro, *commonly called Virgil*
*marriage*, mātrĭmōnium, -ii, n.
*marry* (*of men*), dūco, duxi, ductum, 3; (*of women*), nūbo, nupsi, nuptum, 3 (*g. dat.*); *he married Tullia*, Tulliam duxit; *she married Tullius*, Tullio nupsit
*Mars*, Mars, Martis, m.
*marsh*, pălūs, -ūdis, f.
*master*, dŏmĭnus,-i, m.; *of a school*, măgister, -tri, m.
*matter*, rēs, rei, f.
*matters, it*, rēfert, *impers.* (Ex. XCII.); *what does it matter?* quid rēfert? *it matters little what you think*, paulum rēfert quĭd (240a) sentīas
*may, he may come, to be rendered by* lĭcet, possum, fĭeri potest ut, &c., *according to the sense; someone may* (*be inclined to*) *say*, dixĕrit ăˈlĭquīs
*meadow*, prātum, -i, n.
*means*, ŏpes, -um, f. pl.; cōpia, -ae, f.
*meanwhile*, intĕreă, intĕrim
*measure*, mŏdus, -i, m.; *beyond measure*, praeter mŏdum; *to measure*, mētior, mensus, 4, dep.

*meat*, căro, carnis, f.
*medicine*, mĕdīcīna, -ae, f.
*meditate*, mĕdĭtor, -ātus, *v. dep.*
*meet, to*, occurro, -curri, -cursum, 3 (*dat.*); *to meet death*, ŏbīre mortem; (*adv.*) obviam (*dat.*); *he met me*, obviam mĭhĭ factus est
*memorable*, insignis, -e
*memory*, mĕmŏria, -ae, f.
*Menenius*, Mĕnēnius, -i, m.
*mention*, mentio, -ōnis, f.
*merchant*, mercātor, -ōris, m
*mercy*, clēmentia, -ae, f.
*merited*, mĕrĭtus, -a, -um
*message*, nuntius, -i, m.
*messenger*, nuntius, -i, m.
*metal*, mĕtallum, -i, n.
*Metellus*, Mĕtellus, -i, m.
*middle, midst*, mĕdius, -a, -um; *the middle of the night*, mĕdia nox; *he rushed into the midst of the foe*, in mĕdios hostes ruit
*might* (i.e. *had the right to*) lĭcuit: *you m. have come*, l. tibi vĕnīre; (*had the ability to*) pŏtuisti vĕnīre
*mighty*, pŏtens, -tis; ingens, -tis
*migrate*, mĭgro, 1
*mildness*, lēnĭtas, -ātis, f.
*mile, a*, mille passus; *three miles*, tria mīˈlia passuum
*Miletus*, Mīlētus, -i, f.
*military*, mīlĭtāris, -e
*milk*, lāc, -tis, n.
*Milo*, Mĭlo, -ōnis, m.
*mind*, mens, -tis, f., ănĭmus, -i, m.
*mindful*, mĕmor, -ōris (*g. gen.*)
*mine*, meus, -a, -um
*mine, a*, mĕtallum, -i, n.: *he was condemned to the mines*, in mĕtalla damnātus est
*mingle*, misceo, -ui, -xtum, 2
*mirth*, laetĭtia, -ae, f.
*misbecome, it misbecomes*, dĕdĕcet, -uit, 2, impers. (220)
*miserable*, mĭser, -ĕra, -ĕrum

x 2

*misfortune,* mălum, -i, n. ; călămĭtās, -ātis, f.
*mistake,* error, -ōris, m.
*mix,* see *mingle*
*mob,* turba, -ae, f.
*mock,* lūdo, -si, -sum, 3
*mockery,* lūdibrium, -i, n.
*modest,* mŏdestus, -a, -um
*modesty,* mŏdestia, -ae, f.
*moist,* hūmĭdus, -a, -um
*moisture,* hūmor, -ōris, m.
*money, sum of money,* pĕcūnia, -ae, f.
*monster,* monstrum, -i, n.
*monstrous,* nĕfās (*indecl.*); (*used in apposition to statements*) *the woman (monstrous to relate!) slew her son,* mŭlier (nefās dictu) fīlīum suum interfēcit
*month,* mensis, -is, m.
*monument,* mŏnŭmentum, -i, n.
*moon,* lūna, -ae, f.
*morals,* mōres, -um, m. pl.
*more,* (*adj.*) plūs, plūris (72); *he said no more,* nec plūra dixit ; (*adv.*) măgis *with adj.* (*to a greater degree*), plūs *with verbs* (*to a greater extent*) ; *more than,* plūsquam (*adv.*) ; *it was not divided into more than three parts,* non plusquam in tres partes dīvīsum est ; *let no ship have more than thirty oars,* nulla nāvis plusquam trīginta rēmis ăgātur ; suprā (*prep.*) ; *more than twenty thousand fell that day,* caesa eo die suprā mīlia vīginti
*moreover,* praetĕreā
*morning, in the,* mānĕ, (*adv. indecl.*)
*mortal,* mortālis, -e.
*most, most men,* plērique ; *most of the sheep,* plēraeque ŏvium
*mother,* māter, -tris, f.
*motion,* mōtus, -ūs, m.
*mound,* agger, -ĕris, m.
*mount,* ascendo, -di, -sum, 3 ; conscendo, -di, -sum, 3
*mountain,* mons, -tis, m.

*mourn,* lūgeo, -xi, -ctum, 2
*mournful,* maestus, -a, -m.
*mourning,* luctus, -ūs, m.
*mouse,* mus, mūris, c.
*mouth,* ōs, ōris, n.
*move,* mŏveo, mōvi, mōtum, 2
*much,* multus, -a, -um ; (*adv.*) multum, *sometimes used as a noun,* Par. 71 ; *much, very much, as* (or *so) much, money,* multum, plūrĭmum, tantum, pĕcūniae ; *for how much did you buy it?* quanti id ēmisti? *with comp.* e.g. (*by*) *much better,* multo mĕlior (274)
*Mucius,* Mūcius, -i, m.
*multitude,* multĭtūdo, -ĭnis, f.
*Mummius,* Mummius, -i, m.
*munificence,* mūnĭfĭcentia, -ae, f.
*murder,* caedēs, -is, f. ; *to murder,* interfĭcio, -fēci, -fectum, 3 ; trucīdo, 1
*murmur,* murmur, -ŭris, n. ; *to murmur,* frĕmo, -ui, -ĭtum, 3 ; *let them murmur,* lĭcet frĕmant
*music,* mūsĭca, -ae, f.
*must* (163), and *see* nĕcessĕ, ŏportet
*my,* meus, -a, -um ; *voc.* mi
*myrrh,* myrrha, -ae, f.
*myrtle,* myrtus, -i, f.

**Naked,** nūdus, -a, -um
*name,* nōmen, -ĭnis, n. ; *to name,* nōmĭno, 1 ; vŏco, 1
*narrate,* narro, 1
*narrow,* angustus, -a, -um
*nation,* gens, -tis, f. ; pŏpŭlus, -i, m.
*native, a,* incŏla, -ae, m. ; *nativeland,* patria, -ae, f.
*nature,* nātūra, -ae, f.
*naval,* nāvālis, -e
*near,* prŏpinquus, -a, -um ; (*prep.*) prŏpĕ (*g. acc.*) ; ăd (*g. acc.*) ; *nearer, nearest, see* Par. 69
*nearly,* fĕrĕ, paenĕ
*necessary,* nĕcessārius, -a, -um ; *it is n. see* nĕcesse *and* ŏpus

*necessity*, nĕcessĭtas, -ātis, f.
*neck*, collum, -i, n.
*need, to*, ĕgeo, -ui, 2 (*abl.*); *there is no need of words*, non ŏpus est verbis
*needle*, ăcus, -ūs, f.
*neglect*, neglĕgo, -lexi, -lectum, 3
*negligence*, incūria, -ae, f.
*neighbour, neighbouring*, vīcīnus, -a, -um; fīnĭtĭmus, -a, -um
*neither*, (*pron.*) neuter, -tra, -trum, Par. 85; (*conj.*) nĕc, nĕque
*nephew*, nĕpōs, -ōtis, m.
*Neptune*, Neptūnus, -i, m.
*Nero*, Nĕro, -ōnis, m.
*nest*, nīdus, -i, m.
*net*, rēte, -is, n.
*never*, nunquam; *nevertheless*, tămen (*at the beginning of a clause, or after an emphatic word*).
*new*, nŏvus, -a, -um; *news*, nuntius, -i, m.
*next*, proxĭmus, -a, -um; *on the next day*, postĕro (*more rarely* proxĭmo) dĭe; *we shall know all within the next five hours*, his quinquĕ hōris omnia comperta habēbĭmus
*night*, nox, nŏctis, f.; *by n.* noctu
*nightingale*, phĭlŏmēla, -ae, f.
*Nile*, Nīlus, -i, m.
*nine*, nŏvem, indcl.
*no* (*adj.*), (*with things*) nullus, -a, -um; (*with persons*) nēmo; *no poet*, nēmo pŏēta; *no one*, nēmo (Par. 92); *and no... neque ullus; and no one*, nĕc quisquam; *there is no need of words*, nōn ŏpus est verbis; *by no means all came*, nēquăquam omnes vēnērunt
*no* (*adv.*), *no longer*, nōn jam; *no better i.e. better by nothing*, nĭhilo, *or* nēquăquam melior; *he said no more*, nĕc plūra dixit
*nobility*, nōbĭlĭtas, -ātis, f.
*noble*, nōbĭlis, -e
*noise*, sŏnus, -i, m.; clāmor, -ōris, m.
*nor*, nĕquĕ, nĕc
*nose*, nāsus, -i, m.
*not*, nōn; *not even*, (141); *see also* 129, 143; *if... not*, nĭsĭ; *not yet*, nōndum
*nothing*, nĭhil *or* nīl, n. indcl.
*notice*, ănĭmadverto, -ti, -sum, 3
*notwithstanding*, tămen
*nourish*, nūtrio, -ĭvi and -ii, -ītum, 4
*novelty*, nŏvĭtās, -ātis, f.
*now*, nunc; *meaning already or by this time*, jam.
*nowhere*, nusquam
*Numa*, Nŭma, -ae, m.
*number*, nŭmĕrus, -i, m.
*nurse*, nūtrix, -īcis, f.
*nut*, nux, nŭcis, f.
*nymph*, nympha, -ae, f.

*O! O!* (*foll. by Acc.*, 205); *O that!* ŭtĭnam (330)
*oak*, quercus, -ūs, f.
*oar*, rēmus, -i, m.
*oath*, jusjūrandum, jūrisjūrandi, n.; (*military*) sacrămentum, -i, n.
*obedient*, ōbēdiens, -tis (*g. dat.*)
*obey*, pāreo, -ui, 2, (*g. dat.*)
*obtain*, păro, 1; compăro. 1; ădĭpiscor, ădeptus, 3, (*by entreaty*), impetro, 1; (*by lot*), sortior, -ītus, 4.
*occasion*, tempus, -ŏris, n.
*ocean*, ŏcĕănus, -i, m.
*odour*, ŏdor, ŏris, m.
*of* (282-90); *the town* (*of*) *Corioli*, Cŏriŏli oppĭdum; *both of us wept*, ambo flēvĭmus; *the top of the mountain*, summus mons
*offer*, offĕro, obtŭli, oblātum, offerre (238); *offering*, dōnum, -i, n.
*office*, mūnus, -ĕris, n.
*offspring*, prōlēs, -is, f.
*often*, saepĕ; *how often*, quŏtĭēns
*old*, antīquus, -a, -um; vĕtus, -ĕris; *an old soldier*, vĕtus mīlĕs (61);

**old age,** sĕnectūs, -ūtis, f. ; *old man,* sĕnex, sĕnis, m.; *old woman,* ănus, -ūs, f. ; *older men,* sĕnīōres, *or* mājōres nātu ; *older, oldest,* mājor, maxĭmus nātu
**omen,** ōmen, -ĭnis, n.
**omit,** ŏmitto, -mīsi, -missum, 3
**on,** ĭn (*g. abl.*) ; (*upon*) sŭper ; *on account of,* ŏb, prŏpter (*g. acc.*)
**once,** (*meaning "once for all"*) sĕmel ; (*formerly*) ōlim, quondam ; (*once upon a time*) fortĕ ; *at once,* stătim
**one** (*only one*), ūnus, -a, -um ; *one by one,* singŭli, -ae, -a ; *a certain one,* quidam (310*a*) ; *one...another,* ălius...ălius ; *the one...the other,* alter...alter (86)
**only,** (*adj.*) sōlus, -a, -um ; *only Tullius dissented,* ūni Tullio ăliter vīsum est ; *not only...but also,* non sōlum...sed ĕtiam, *or* cum...tum ; *he lived only ten years,* sōlos dĕcem annos vixit ; *if only,* sī mŏdo
**onset,** impĕtus, -ūs, m.
**open,** *to,* ăpĕrio, -ui, -rtum, 4
**opinion,** sententia, -ae, f.
**opponent,** adversārius, -i, m.
**opportunity,** occāsio, -ōnis, f.
**oppose,** obsisto, -stĭti, -stĭtum, 3 (*g. dat.*) ; *if* oppōno *is used, note that it means "I place against" ; he opposed the enemy,* oppōsuit sēsĕ hosti [sum, 3
**oppress,** opprĭmo, -pressi, -pres-
**or,** (i) *in statements and commands,* vĕl, aut (157*a*) ; (ii) *in alternative questions* (171), ăn, *preceded by* utrum *or* -nĕ ; (*a*) (*Whether*) *do you prefer this or that?* Utrum hoc (*or* hocnĕ) ăn illud mavultis? (*b*) *I asked whether...or,* interrŏgāvi utrum...ăn ; *whether ... or not ...* annōn, *or* necnĕ
**orator,** ōrātor, -ōris, m.
**order** (*a command*), mandatum, -i, n. ; jussum, -i, n.; *to give orders* (*in war*), impĕro, 1, *with dat.,* ut, *and subjunctive; to order,* jŭbeo, jussi, jussum, 2 (*acc. and inf.*) ; impĕro, 1 (*g. dat. and ut.*) ; *order* (*a rank*), ordo, -ĭnis, m. ; *the order of the knights,* ĕquestris ordo ; *in order to,* ŭt
**ornament,** ornātus, -ūs, m.
**other,** ălius, -a, -ud ; *the other,* alter (86) ; *the wealth of-others,* ăliēnae dīvĭtiae
**ought,** dēbeo, -ui, -ĭtum, 2 ; *you ought to fight,* pugnāre dēbes ; *you ought to have fought,* pugnāre dēbuisti (223)
**our** (87) noster ; *our men* (34) nostri
**out of,** ē, ex (*g. abl.*); (*meaning "outside"*) extrā; *out of shot,* extrā jactum; *outer, adj.* extĕrior, *neut.* -ius (69) ; *outside, prep.* extrā (*g. acc.*)
**over,** sŭper ; *across,* trans (*g. acc.*)
**overcome,** sŭpero, 1
**overthrow,** see **overcome**
**overturn,** subverto, -verti, -versum, 3 [sum, 3
**overwhelm,** opprĭmo, -pressi, -pres-
**owe,** dēbeo, -ui, -itum, 2
**own** (see Par. 98) ; *your or my own name,* tuum *or* meum, ipsius, nōmen (*where* ipsius *agrees with the gen.* tui *or* mei *implied in* tuum *or* meum)
**owner,** dŏmĭnus, -i, m.
**ox,** bōs, bŏvis, c. See Par. 311

**Pace,** passus, -ūs, m.
**pain,** dŏlor, -ōris, m.
**paint,** pingo, -nxi, -ctum, 3
**painter,** pictor, -ōris, m.
**painting,** pictūra, -ae, f
**palace,** pălātium, -i, n.
**Pallas,** Pallăs, -ădis, f.
**palm,** palma, -ae, f.; *to carry off the palm,* palmam ferre

*panic*, păvor, -ōris, m.
*parched*, ārĭdus, -a, -um; tostus, -a, -um
*pardon*, vĕnia, -ae, f.; *I grant him pardon*, do ei veniam; *to pardon*, ignosco, -nōvi, -nōtum, 3, g. dat.
*parent*, părens, -tis, c.
*Paris (of Troy)*, Păris, -ĭdis, m.
*parricide*, parrĭcīda, -ae, m.
*part*, pars, -tis, f.; *it is the p. of an orator*, ōrātōris est (289); *to take part in a battle*, intercsse praelio; *for my part*, ĕquidem (139)
*partner*, sŏcius, -i, m.
*pass, pass by, pass on*, praetĕreo, -īvi *or* -ii, -ĭtum, 4
*path*, callis, -is, m.
*past*, praetĕrĭtus, -a, -um
*patience*, pătĭentĭa, -ae, f.
*patient*, pătĭens, -ntis (g. gen.)
*patiently*, pătĭenter
*patrician*, patrĭcius, -a, -um
*pay*, stīpendium, -i, n.; *to pay*, solvo, -vi, -ūtum, 3; pendo, pĕpendi, pensum, 3; *pay attention*, ŏperam dare; *pay penalty*, poenas dare; *pay tribute*, trĭbūtum penděre; *able to pay*, par (*gen.* păris) solvendo, i.e. equal to paying
*peace*, pāx, pācis, f.
*penalty*, poena, -ae, f.; *to pay penalty*, poenas dāre
*penetrate*, pĕnetro, 1
*penitence*, poenĭtentia, -ae, f. [m.
*penny*, dēnārius, -i, m.; as, assis,
*people*, pŏpŭlus, -i, m.
*perfidy*, perfĭdia, -ae, f.
*perform*, perfĭcio, -fēci, -fectum, 3
*perfume*, ŏdor, -ōris, m.
*perhaps*, fortasse, forsĭtan (forsĭtan *gen. takes the subjunctive*)
*peril*, pĕrīcŭlum, -i, n.
*perish*, pĕreo, -ivi *or* -ii, 4
*permission*, pŏtestas, -ātis, f.

*permit*, pătior, passus, 3, dep.
*perseverance*, persĕvērantia, -ae, f.
*persevere*, persĕvēro, 1
*Persian*, Persa, -ae, m.
*person*, hŏmo, -ĭnis, m.
*persuade*, persuādeo, -si, -sum (g. dat. of person) (i) *I p. him to come*, p. ei ut vĕniat; (ii) *I p. him (or am persuaded) that this is true*, p. ei (*or* persuāsum est mĭhi) hōc vērum esse
*Philip*, Phĭlippus, -i, m.
*Philoctetes*, Phĭloctētes, -ae, m.
*philosopher*, phĭlŏsŏphus, -i, m.
*philosophy*, phĭlŏsŏphia, ae, f.
*physician*, mĕdĭcus, -i, m.
*picture*, tăbŭla, -ae, f.
*pierce*, transfīgo, -xi, -xum, 3
*pig*, porcus, -i, m.
*pigeon*, cŏlumba, -ae, f.
*pile up*, exstruo, -struxi, -structum, 3
*pilot*, gŭbernātor, -ōris, m.
*pine tree*, pīnus, -ūs, f.
*pious*, pius, -a, -um, *no superl.*
*pirate*, praedo, -ōnis, m.
*pitch (a camp)*, pōno, pŏsui, pŏsĭtum, 3
*pitiful*, mīserĭcors, -cordis
*pity*, mĭsericordia, -ae, f.; *feel pity for*, mĭsĕreor, -sĕrĭtus *or* -sertus, 2, dep. (g. gen.); *shew pity to*, mĭsĕror, 1 (g. acc.)
*place*, lŏcus, -i, m.; *plural*, loca, n. pl.; *place, to*, pōno, pŏsui, pŏsĭtum, 3; *place before*, antĕpono, -pŏsui, -pŏsĭtum, 3; virtūtem vŏluptāti antĕpōno, *I p. virtue before pleasure*
*plain*, campus, -i, m.
*plan*, consĭlium, -i, n.
*plant*, planta, -ae, f.; *plant, to*, see *sow*
*Plataea*, Plătaeae, ārum, f. pl.
*Plato*, Plăto, -ōnis, m.
*play*, lūdus, -i, m.; *play, to*, lūdo, -si, -sum, 3

*plead, a cause,* ăgĕre causam
*pleasant* or *pleasing,* grātus,-a, -um; jūcundus, -a, -um ; dulcis, -e
*please,* plăceo, -ui, -ītum 2 (*g. dat.*)
*pleasure,* vŏluptas, -ātis, f.
*pledge oneself, to, I p. myself to pay,* spondeo (spŏpondi, sponsum, 2) me solūturum esse
*plot,* dŏlus, -i, m.
*plough,* ărātrum, -i, n.; *plough, to,* ăro, 1
*ploughman,* ărātor, -ōris, m.
*ploughshare,* vōmer, -ĕris, m.
*pluck,* carpo, -psi, -ptum, 3
*plunder,* praeda, -ae, f.; *plunder, to,* dīrĭpio, -rĭpui, -reptum, 3
*plunge, v. trans.* mergo, -si, -sum, 3 ; *he plunged into the water,* in ăquam (*or* aquā) sē mersit
*Pluto,* Plūto, -ōnis, m.
*poem,* carmen, -ĭnis, n.
*poet,* pŏēta, -ae, m.
*point, on the point of,* in eo ŭt, see Par. 166
*point out,* monstro, 1
*poison,* vĕnēnum, -i, n.
*pollute,* polluo, -ui, -ūtum, 3
*pomp,* pompa, -ae, f.
*Pompeius,* Pompeius, -i, m.
*Pontius,* Pontius, -i, m.
*poor,* (i.e. *not rich*) pauper, -ĕris (61)
*poppy,* păpāver, -ĕris, n.
*populace,* vulgus, -i, n. *or* m.
*populous,* frĕquens, -tis
*porch,* portĭcus, -ūs, f.
*Porsena,* Porsĕna, -ae, m.
*port,* portus, -ūs, m.
*portent,* prōdĭgium, -i, n.
*portion,* pars, -tis, f.
*portrait,* effĭgĭes, -ĕi, f.
*Porus,* Pōrus, -i, m.
*position,* lŏcus, -i, m.
*possess,* hăbeo, -ui, -ītum, 2; (*land*) possĭdeo, possēdi, possessum, 2
*possession of, to take,* occŭpo, 1 ; *to gain possession of,* pŏtior, pŏtītus, 4, dep. (*g. abl.*) see Par. 207

*possible, it is p. that,* fĭeri pŏtest ut (299); *as great as possible,* quam maxĭmus ; *as well as possible;* quam optĭmē
*posterity,* postĕri, -ōrum, m. pl.
*pour,* fundo, fūdi, fūsum, 3
*poverty,* paupertas, -ātis, f.
*power,* pŏtestas, -ātis, f.; *in the power of,* pĕnĕs (*g. acc.*)
*powerful,* pŏtens, -tis
*practice,* usus, -ūs, m.
*practise,* exerceo, -ui, -ĭtum, 2
*praetor,* praetor, -ōris, m.
*praise,* laus, -dis, f.; *praise, to,* laudo, 1
*pray,* ōro, 1 ; prĕcor, 1, dep. (*foll. by* ut)
*prayers,* prĕces, -um, f.
*precept,* praeceptum, -i, n.
*precious,* prĕtĭōsus, -a, -um
*predict,* praedīco, -dixi, -dictum, 3
*prefer,* mālo, -ui, -malle, *foll. by* quam, page 230 ; antĕpono, -pŏsui, -pŏsĭtum, 3 (*g. acc. and dat.*)
*preparation ; I have made every p.,* omnia părāvi
*prepare,* păro, 1
*presence of, in the,* cōram (*g. abl.*)
*present, to be,* adsum, -fui, -esse (*g. dat.*)
*present, a,* dōnum, -i, n.; mūnus, -ĕris, n.; *present, to,* dōno, 1 (*g. acc. and dat. or abl. and acc.*); *I p. you with a horse,* ĕquo tē dōno
*preserve,* servo, 1
*press,* prĕmo, pressi, pressum, 3
*pretence,* spĕcies, -ei, f.; sĭmŭlātio, -ōnis, f.
*pretend,* sĭmŭlo, 1
*prevent,* prŏhĭbeo, -ui, -ĭtum, 2; impĕdio, -īvi *or* -ii, ĭtum, 4 ; obsto, -stāre, -stĭti, -stātum, *g. dat.*; *what prevents you from coming?* quĭd obstat (*or* prŏhĭbet) quōmĭnus vĕnĭas ?

*previously*, antĕ, anteā
*prey*, praeda, -ae, f.
*Priam*, Priămus, -i, m.
*price*, prĕtium, -i, n.; *at a great, small price*, &c., *see* Par. 284
*pride*, sŭperbia, -ae, f.
*priest, priestess*, săcerdōs, -ōtis, c.
*prison*, carcer, -ĕris, m.
*prisoner*, captīvus, -i, m.
*private*, prīvātus, -a, -um
*prize*, praemium, -i, n.
*proceed*, prōgredior, -gressus, 3, dep.
*proclaim*, prōnuntio, 1; ēdīco, -dixi, -dictum, 3
*proconsul*, prōconsul, -ŭlis, m.
*procure*, păro, 1
*prodigal*, prōdĭgus, -a, -um
*produce*, părio, pĕpĕri, partum, 3
*profit*, quaestus, -ūs, m.
*profuse, see prodigal*
*promise*, prōmissum, -i, n.; *to make many, large, false*, &c., *promises*, multa, magna, falsa, &c., prō-mittere; *promise, to*, pollĭceor, -cītus, 2, dep.; prōmitto, -mīsi, -missum, 3; *I p. to come*, p. me ventūrum esse (280); *I promise (in marriage)*, spondeo, spŏpondi, sponsum, 2
*prone*, prōnus, -a, -um
*property*, rēs, rei, f.; bŏna, -ōrum, n. pl.
*prophet*, vātēs, -is, m.
*propitious*, prŏpĭtius, -a, -um
*propose, (a law)* rŏgo, 1   [3
*proscribe*, proscrībo, -psi, -ptum,
*prosperity*, rēs sĕcundae
*prosperous, (of winds*, &c.) sĕcundus, -a, -um; *a prosperous city*, urbs florentissĭma
*prosperously*, fēlīcĭter; *very prosperously*, fēlīcissĭmē
*protection*, praesĭdium, -i, n.
*protest, to*, rĕclāmo, 1
*proud*, sŭperbus, -a, -um
*prove*, dēmonstro, 1

*provided that*, dum mŏdo, *or* dummŏdo (*all g. subj.*)
*province*, prōvincia, -ae, f.
*provisions*, commeātus, -ūs, m.
*provoke*, lăcesso, -īvi, -ītum, 3
*prudence*, prudentia, -ae, f.
*prudent*, prūdens, -tis
*public*, publĭcus, -a, -um
*Publius*, Publius, -i, m.
*pull*, trăho, -xi, -ctum, 3
*punish*, castĭgo, 1; pūnio, -īvi *or* -ii, ītum, 4; *punishment*, supplĭcium, -i. n.; poena, -ae, f.
*pure*, pūrus, -a, -um
*purple*, purpŭreus, -a, -um
*purpose, to*, habēre in animo
*pursue*, sĕquor, -cūtus, 3, dep.
*push down*, dētrūdo, -si, -sum, 3
*put*, pōno, pŏsui, pŏsĭtum, 3; *put over*, praefĭcio, -fēci, -fectum, 3 (*g. dat.*); *put to death*, interfĭcere, morte afficĕre; *put to flight*, fŭgo, 1; in fŭgam verto, *see* verto
*Pyrrhus*, Pyrrhus, -i, m.

**Quaestor**, quaestor, -ōris, m.
*quantity*, cōpia, -ae, f.; vīs, vim, vī, f.   [n.
*quarters, winter*, bīberna, -ōrum,
*queen*, rēgīna, -ae, f.
*quench (thirst)*, restinguo, -stinxi, -stinctum, 3
*question, to*, interrŏgo, 1; rŏgo, 1
*quick*, cĕler, -ĕris, -e; *quickly*, cĕlĕrĭter; *very quickly*, cĕlerrĭmē; *quickness*, cĕlĕrĭtās, -ātis, f.
*quiet*, tranquillus, -a, -um; quiētus, -a, -um
*quite*, omnīno
*Quirinus*, Quirīnus, -i, m.

**Race**, gĕnus, ĕris, n.
*rage*, īra, -ae, f.; fŭror, -ōris, m.; *rage, to*, saevio, -ii, -ītum, 4
*rain*, imber, -bris, m.; plŭvia, -ae, f.

*raise*, tollo, sustŭli, sublātum, 3
*rampart*, vallum, -i, n.
*rank*, ordo, -ĭnis, m.
*rapacious*, răpāx, -ācis [-is, -e
*rapid*, răpĭdus, -a, -um; cĕler,
*rapidity*, cĕlĕrĭtās, -ātis, f.
*rare*, rārus, -a, -um
*rashly*, tĕmĕrē
*rashness*, tĕmĕrĭtas, -ātis, f.
*rate, to value at a very high rate*, permagni aestĭmāre
*rather*, pŏtĭus; *rather slow, quick*, &c., tardior, cĕlĕrior; (Par. 65)
*ravage*, vasto, 1
*raven*, corvus, -i, m.
*raw*, crūdus, -a, -um
*ray*, rădius, -i, m.
*reach*, attingo, -tĭgi, -tactum, 3 (*g. acc.*); pervĕnio, -vēni, -ventum, 4 (*foll. by* ad)
*read*, lĕgo, lēgi, lectum, 3
*readily*, lĭbenter
*ready*, părātus, -a, -um; *ready to fight*, ad pugnandum; *I am ready to die*, nōn rĕcūso mŏri
*real*, vĕrus, -a, -um
*reality*, vĕrĭtās, -ātis, f.
*really*, vērē
*reap*, mĕto, messui, messum, 3
*rear*, ălo, ălui, altum, 3
*reason* (*cause*), causa, -ae, f.; *by reason of*, ŏb, propter (*both g. acc.*)
*rebuke*, incrĕpo, -ui, -ĭtum, 1
*recall*, rĕvŏco, 1
*receive*, accĭpio, -cēpi, -ceptum, 3 [*not* rĕcĭpio]
*recent*, rĕcens, -tis; nŏvus, -a, -um
*recently*, nūper
*reckon*, nŭmĕro, 1
*recline*, (*at meals*) discumbo, -cŭbui, -cŭbitum, 3 [3
*recognise*, agnosco, -nōvi, -nĭtum,
*recollect*, rĕcordor, rĕcordātus, 1, dep.; mĕmĭni, see Appendix II., p. 215

*recollection*, mĕmŏria, -ae, f.
*recover*, rĕcŭpĕro, 1; recĭpio, -cēpi, -ceptum, 3
*recount*, narro, 1
*refrain* (*oneself*) *from*, abstĭneo, -ui, -tentum, 2; *I abstained from food*, cĭbo mē abstĭnēbam
*refer*, rĕfĕro, rettuli, rĕlātum (238); *I referred the subject of the hostages to the senate*, de obsĭdĭbus ad Patres rettŭli
*refuge*, perfŭgium, -i, n.
*refuse*, rĕcūso, 1; *g. acc.; or inf.; or foll. by* quin *with subjunctive*
*regard, have regard to*, respĭcio, -spexi, -spectum, 3 (*g. acc.*)
*region*, rĕgio, -ōnis, f.
*regret*, dēsĭdĕrium, -i, n.; *regret, to*, dēsĭdĕro, 1
*Regulus*, Rĕgŭlus, -i, m.
*reign*, regnum, -i, n.; *during his reign*, eo regnante *or* rēge (197); *reign, to*, regno, 1 (*intr.*); impĕro (*g. dat.*)
*rein*, hăbēna, -ae, f.
*reinforcement*, subsĭdium, -i, n.
*reject*, rējĭcio, rējēci, rējectum, 3
*rejoice*, gaudeo, gāvīsus, 2, dep.
*relate*, narro, 1; *horrible to relate!* nĕfās dictu!
*relation*, prŏpinquus, -i, m.
*relieve, the city was relieved from the siege*, obsĭdĭōne urbs lĕvāta est (279)
*religion*, rĕlĭgio, -ōnis, f.
*relying*, frētus, -a, -um (*g. abl.*)
*remain*, mǎneo, -mansi, -nsum, 2; *remain over*, sŭpersum, -fui, -esse
*remaining*, rĕlĭquus, -a, -um
*remarkable*, insignis, -e; *to a r. degree*, ūnĭcē
*remedy*, rĕmĕdium, -i, n.
*remember*, (1) rĕcordor, -ātus, 1, dep.; reminiscor, -i (*g. acc., but sometimes gen.*); (2) mĕmĭni (*def.*), see p. 215
*remembrance*, mĕmŏria, -ae, f.

*remind*, admŏneo, -ui, -ītum, 2
*remove*, āmŏveo, -mōvi, -mōtum, 2
*remorse*, dŏlor, -ōris, m.; poenĭtentia, -ae, f.
*render*, reddo, -dĭdi, -dĭtum, 3
*renew*, rĕnŏvo, 1
*renown*, fāma, -ae, f.
*renowned*, clārus, -a, -um
*repair*, rĕfĭcio, -fēci, -fectum, 3
*repeat*, ĭtero, 1
*repel*, repello, -pulsum, reppŭli, 3
*repent*, poenĭtet, -uit, 2, impers. (see Par. 219 and foll.)
*repentance*, poenĭtentia, -ae, f.
*reply*, responsum, -i, n.; *reply, to,* respondeo, -di, -sum, 2
*report*, fāma, -ae, f.; rūmor, -ōris, m.; *report, to,* nuntio, 1; *it is reported that Tullius said,* fertur Tullius dixisse
*repose*, quiēs, -ētis, f.
*republic*, rēspublĭca, reipublĭcae, f.
*repulse*, prōpulso, 1
*reputation*, fāma, -ae, f. [dat.]
*resist*, rēsisto, -stĭti, -stĭtum, 3 (*g.*
*resolve*, constituo, -ui, -ūtum, 3
*resources*, ŏpes, -um, f.
*response*, responsum, -i, n.
*rest*, quiēs, -ētis, f.; *rest, the,* [cēter] -ĕra, -ĕrum, *mostly pl.*; (*residue*) rĕlĭquus, -a, -um; *rest, to,* quiesco, -evi, -ētum, 3
*restore*, reddo, -dĭdi, -dĭtum, 3; restĭtuo, -ui, -ūtum, 3
*restrain*, coerceo, 2
*result*, ēventus, -ûs, m.
*retain*, rĕtĭneo, -ui, -tentum, 2
*retake*, rĕcĭpio, -cēpi, -ceptum, 3
*retire*, rĕcēdo, -cessi, -cessum, 3; *the soldiers retire,* milĭtēs sē rĕcĭpĭunt
*retreat*, rĕceptus, -ûs, m.; *retreat, to,* cēdo, cessi, cessum, 3
*return*, rĕdĭtus, -ûs, m.; *return, to,* rĕdeo, -ii, -ĭtum, 4; rĕvertor, -versus, 3, dep.; *to return thanks,* grātĭās ăgĕre

*reveal*, pătĕfăcio, -fēci, -factum, 3
*revenge*, ultio, -ōnis, f.; *revenge, to,* ulciscor, ultus, 3, dep.
*revenue*, vectīgal, -ālis, n.
*reverence*, rĕvĕrentia, -ae, f.
*revere, reverence,* vĕnĕror, -atus, 1, dep.; vĕreor, -ĭtus, 2, dep.
*revolt*, sēdĭtio, -ōnis, f.; *revolt, to,* dēfĭcio, -fēci, -fectum, 3
*reward*, praemĭum, -i, n.; mercēs, -ēdis, f.
*Rhodes* (island), Rhŏdus, -i, f. (265)
*rich*, dīvĕs, -ĭtis, *reg. comp.* (*not* dītior, dītissimus, *except in poetry*)
*riches*, dīvĭtiae, -arum, f.; ŏpes, -um, f.
*ride*, ĕquĭto, 1; vĕhor, vectus, 3
*rider*, ĕquĕs, -ĭtis, m.
*ridiculous*, rĭdĭcŭlus, -a, -um
*right*, rectus, -a, -um; *right,* jūs, jūris, n.; fās, indcl.
*right-hand*, dexter, -tra, -trum, (*noun*), dextra *or* dextĕra, -ae, f.
*rightly*, jūre (Par. 182)
*ring*, ānŭlus, -i, m.
*ripe*, mātūrus, -a, -um
*rise* (*from bed*), surgo, surrexi, -rectum, 3; ŏrĭor, ortus, 4 dep.
*risk*, pĕrīcŭlum, -i, n.
*rite*, rītŭs, -ûs, m.
*rival*, aemŭlus, -a, -um (*used as a n.*); *he had many rivals,* multos sĭbi aemŭlos hăbuit
*rivalry*, aemŭlātio, -ōnis, f.
*river*, flūmen, -ĭnis, n.; amnis, -is, m.; flūvius, -i, m.
*road*, via, -ae, f.; ĭter, itĭnĕris, n.
*rob*, spŏlio, 1 (*acc. of pers., abl. of thing*)
*robber*, latro, -ōnis, m.
*rock*, scŏpŭlus, -i, m.; rūpĕs, -is, f.
*roll*, volvo, -vi, volūtum, 3 (*trans.*); *the stone is rolling,* lăpis volvītur
*Rome*, Rōma, -ae, f.
*Roman*, Rōmānus, -a, -um
*Romulus*, Rŏmŭlus, -i, m.

*roof,* tectum, -i, n.
*root,* rādīx, -īcis, f.
*rope,* fūnis, -is, m.
*rose,* rŏsa, -ae, f.
*rough,* asper, -ĕra, -ĕrum
*round,* rŏtundus, -a, -um; tĕrĕs, -ĕtis
*round (prep.),* circum *(g. acc.)*
*rouse,* excito, 1
*rout,* fŭgo, 1; fundo, fūdi, fusum, 3
*royal,* rēgālis, -e; rēgius, -a, -um
*rude,* rŭdis, -e; incultus, -a, um
*rugged,* asper, -ĕra, -ĕrum
*ruin (destruction),* exĭtium, -i, n.
*rule, to,* rĕgo, -xi, -ctum *(g. acc.);* impĕro, 1 *(g. dat.)*
*rule,* impĕrium, -i, n.
*rumour,* fāma, -ae, f.; rūmor, -ōris, m.
*run,* curro, cŭcurri, cursum, 3
*run up,* accurro, -curri, -cursum, 3
*run away,* aufŭgio, -fūgi, 3
*running,* cursus, -ūs, m.
*rush,* impĕtus, -ūs, m.
*rush, to,* rŭo, -ui, 3          [3
*rush forth,* ērumpo, -rūpi, -ruptum,
*rustic,* rustĭcus, -a, -um

**Sabine,** Săbīnus, -a, -um
*sacred,* săcer, -cra, -crum
*sacrifice,* săcrĭfĭcium, -i, n.
*sacrifice, to,* sacrĭfĭco, 1
*sad,* tristis, -e
*safe,* tūtūs, -a, -um; salvus, -a, -um; incŏlŭmis, -e
*safely,* tūto
*safety,* sălūs, -ūtis, f.
*sagacious,* săgax, -ācis
*sail, a,* vēlum, -i, n.
*sail, to,* nāvĭgo, 1
*sailor,* nauta, -ae, m.
*sake, for the,* causā *(adverbial abl. foll. by gen. of gerundive)*
*salt,* sal, sălis, m.
*salutation,* sălūtātio, -ōnis, f.
*salute,* sălūto, 1

*same,* īdem, ĕādem, īdem (103)
*Samos,* Sāmos, -i, f.
*Samnites,* Samnītes, -ium, m.
*sand,* ărēna, -ae, f.
*sate, satiate,* sătio, 1; expleo, -plēvi, -pletum, 2
*satisfy,* sătisfăcio, -fēci, -factum, 3 *(g. dat.)*
*savage,* saevus, -a, -um; fĕrus, -a, -um
*savageness,* fĕrĭtās, -ātis, f.
*save* (i.e. *preserve),* servo, 1
*say,* dīco, -xi, -ctum, 3; *say...not,* nĕgo, 1; *do you say it is not so?* nĕgasnĕ ita esse? *I say I cannot come,* nĕgo mē venīre posse; *said he, I say* (*used parenthetically*) inquit, inquam; *see page* 315; *it is said that Balbus lies,* dīcĭtur Balbus mentīri (Par. 177).
*saying,* dictum, -i, -n
*scanty,* exĭguus, -a, -um
*scarcely,* vix
*scarcity,* inŏpia, -ae, f.
*scatter,* spargo, -rsi, -rsum, 3; fundo, fūdi, fusum, 3
*scent,* ŏdor, -ōris, m.
*science,* scientia, -ae, f.
*Scipio,* Scīpio, -ōnis, m.
*scorch,* adūro, -ussi, -ustum, 3; torreo, -ui, tostum, 2
*scorn,* aspernor, 1, *dep.*; sperno, sprēvi, sprētum, 3
*scourge, to,* virgis caedĕre, lit. *to strike with rods;* (virga, -ae, f.)
*scout,* explōrātor, -ōris, m.
*sculptor,* sculptor, -ōris, m.
*sculpture,* sculptūra, -ae, f.
*Scythian,* Scy̆tha, -ae, m.
*sea,* măre, -is, n.; pĕlăgus, -i, -n. *(adj.)* mărīnus, -a, -um; nāvālis, -e
*search,* explōro, 1; quaero, -sīvi, -sītum, 3
*season,* tempus, -ŏris, n.; tempestās, -ātis, f.

**seasonable**, opportūnus, -a, -um
**seat**, sēdēs, -is, f.
**second** (*in ordinary numeration*), sĕcundus, -a, -um; (*a, or the second, where only two are contemplated*), alter, -ĕra, -ĕrum; *a second time*, ĭtĕrum; *a friend is a second self*, ămīcus est alter ĕgo
**secret**, secrētus, -a, -um
**secretary**, scrība, -ae, m.
**secretly**, clam
**secure**, sēcūrus, -a, -um; see *safe*
**security**, see *safety*
**sedition**, sēdītio, -ōnis, f.
**see**, vĭdeo, vīdi, visum, 2; *to see-to this being done*, cūrāre hōc făciendum
**seed**, sēmen, -ĭnis, n.
**seek**, quaero, quaesīvi, quaesītum, 3; (*peace*) pĕto, -īvi *or* -ii, -ītum, 3
**seem**, vĭdeor, vīsus, 2 dep.
**seize**, occŭpo, 1; corrĭpio, -rĭpui, -reptum, 3
**seldom**, rāro
**self**, ipsĕ, -a, -um, (105, 308); sŭ (94, 218, 305–8)
**sell**, vendo, -dĭdi, -dĭtum, 3
**seller**, vendĭtor, -ōris, m.
**senate**, sĕnātus, -ūs, m.; *also* Patres, -rum; *it was referred to the s.*, ad Patres rēlātum est
**senate-house**, cūria, -ae, f.
**senator**, sĕnātor, -ōris, m.
**send**, mitto, mīsi, missum, 3 (*to*, ăd)
**send away**, dīmitto, mīsi, missum, 3
**send for**, arcesso, -īvi, -ītum, 3
**send on**, praemitto, -mīsi, -missum,
**sentinel**, vĭgil, -ĭlis, m.
**separate**, sēpăro, 1
**serious**, grăvis, -e
**serpent**, serpens, -tis, c.
**servant** (*slave*), servus, -i, m.; (*attendant*) mĭnister, -ri, m.
**serve**, servio, -ivi *or* -ii, -ītum, 4

(*g. dat.*); *to s.* (*as a soldier*), stīpendium mĕrēre
**service**, (*benefit*), bĕnĕfĭcium, -i, n.; *to perform military service*, stīpendium merēre
**servile**, servīlis, -e
**servitude**, servĭtium, -i, n.; (*but in Cicero*) servĭtūs, -ūtis, f.
**set**, (*of the sun*) occĭdo, -cīdi, -cāsum, 3; *set out*, prŏficiscor, -fectus, 3, dep. ("*for*" *after this v. must be rendered* ad; *but see* Par. 249); *set an example*, exemplum praebēre; *set on fire*, incendo, -cendi, -censum, 3
**setting**, occāsus, -ūs, m.
**seven**, septem, *indecl.*; see Par. 81
**several**, plūres, -a (72)
**severe**, grăvis, -e; **severely**, grăvĭter
**severity**, sĕvĕrĭtās, -ātis, f.
**shade, shadow**, umbra, -ae, f.
**shady**, umbrōsus, -a, -um
**shake**, quătio, quassum, 3; *I shake off sleep*, somnum excŭtio, -cussi, -cussum, 3
**shame**, pŭdor, -ōris, m.
**shameful**, turpis, -e
**shameless**, impŭdens, -tis
**shamelessness**, impŭdentia, -ae, f.
**shape**, forma, -ae, f.
**share**, pars, -tis, f.
**share, to**, dīvĭdo, -si, -sum, 3
**sharp**, ăcūtus, -a, -um; ācer, acris, acre
**sharpen**, ăcuo, -ui, -ūtum, 3
**shave**, rādo, -si, -sum, 3
**she**, see *he*
**shear**, tondeo, tŏtondi, tonsum, 2
**sheep**, ŏvis, -is, f.
**shepherd**, pastor, -ōris, m.
**shield**, scūtum, -i, n.; clĭpĕus, -i, m.
**shine**, lūceo, -xi, 2; (*of a meadow*) nĭteo, -ui, 2
**ship**, nāvis, -is, f.; (*of war*) n. longa
**shipwreck**, naufrăgium, -i, n.
**shirt**, tŭnĭca, -ae, f.
**shock**, impĕtus, -ūs, m.

*shore,* lītus, -ōris, n.; ōra, -ae, f.
*short,* brĕvis, -e; *for a short time* paulisper
*shoulder,* (h)ŭmĕrus, -i, m.
*shout,* clāmor, -ōris, m.
*shout, to,* clāmo, 1
*show, to,* monstro, 1
*shower,* imber, -bris, m.
*shrub,* frŭtex, -ĭcis, m.
*shun,* fŭgio, fŭgi, 3; vīto, 1
*shut, shut in,* claudo, -si, -sum, 3
*Sicily,* Sĭcĭlia, -ae, f.
*sick, sickly,* aeger, -gra, -grum; infirmus, -a, -um
*side,* lătus, -ĕris, n.; *on this side,* citrā, cis (*g. acc.*); *on one side... on the other side,* hinc...illinc; *sides, on all,* passim; *sides, from all,* undĭque
*sight,* vīsus, -ūs, m.; conspectus, -ūs, m.; *in the sight of the people,* pălam pŏpŭlo
*sign, signal,* signum, -i, n.
*silence,* sĭlentium, -i, n.
*silent,* sĭlens, -tis; tăcĭtus, -a, -um; *silently,* tăcĭtē
*silent, to be,* tăceo, -uī, -ĭtum, 2; sīleo, -ui, 2
*silver,* argentum, -i, n.; (*adj.*) argenteus, -a, -um
*simple,* simplex, -ĭcis
*sin,* peccātum, -i, n.; scĕlus, -ĕris, n.
*sin, to,* pecco, 1
*since,* quŏniam (*with indic.*); cum (*with subj.*); *since this is so,* quae cum ĭtă sint (151)
*sing,* canto, 1; căno, cecĭni, cantum, 3
*single,* ūnus, -a, -um
*sink,* mergo, -rsi, -rsum, 3 (*trans.*); mergor (*intrans.*)
*sister,* sŏror, -ōris, f.
*sit,* sĕdeo, sēdi, sessum, 3
*sit down,* consīdo, -sēdi, -sessum, 3
*six, sixty, &c.* See Par. 81
*size,* magnĭtūdo, -ĭnis, f.
*skilful, skilled,* pĕrītus, -a, -um

*skill,* pĕrītia, -ae, f.
*skin,* cŭtis, -is, f.; pellis, -is, f.
*sky,* caelum, -i, n.
*slander,* mălĕdīco, -xi, -ctum, 3 (*g. dat.*)
*slaughter,* caedēs, -is, f.
*slave,* servus, -i, m.; *to be a slave,* servīre
*slavery,* servĭtūs, -ūtis, f.
*slay,* interfĭcio, -fēci, -fectum, 3; occīdo, -cīdi, -cīsum, 3
*sleep,* somnus, -i, m. [4
*sleep, to,* dormio, -ivi *or* -ii, -ītum,
*slender,* grăcĭlis, -e (60); tĕnuis, -e
*slight,* lĕvis, -e
*slip,* lābor, lapsus, 3 dep.
*slip down,* dēlābor, -lapsus, 3, dep.
*sloth,* ignāvia, -ae, f.
*slow,* tardus, -a, -um
*slowly,* tardē
*slumber,* somnus, -i, m.
*small,* parvus, -a, -um
*smear,* oblīno, -lēvi, -lītum, 3
*smell,* ŏdor, -ōris, m.
*smile,* rīdeo, -si, -sum, 2
*snake,* cŏlŭber, -bri, m. (*rare*); anguis, -is, m.
*snare,* insĭdiae, -ārum, f.
*snatch,* răpio, -ui, -ptum, 3; *snatch from,* erĭpio, -rĭpui, -eptum, *g. dat. of pers.* (192) [3
*snatch away,* abrĭpio, -ui, -reptum,
*snow,* nix, nīvis, f.
*so,* (*with adj.*) tam; *so good,* tam bŏnus; ĭtā; *and so,* i.e. thereupon, ĭtăquĕ; (*in this way*) sīc (*to such an extent*) tam
*so great, large,* tantus, -a, -um
*so many,* tŏt, indcl.
*so much* (*money, &c.*), tantum (pĕcūniae, &c.).
*Socrates,* Sŏcrătēs, -is, m.
*soft,* mollis, -e
*soften,* mollio, -ivi *or* -ii, -ītum, 4
*soil,* sŏlum, -i, n.; hŭmus, -i, f.
*soldier,* mīlĕs, -ĭtis, m.
*sole,* ūnus, -a, -um; ūnĭcus, -a, -um

*some*, nonnullus, -a, -um ; *some... others*, ălii...alii ; *there is something after death*, est ălĭquĭd post mortem ; *I fear something has happened*, vĕreor nē quĭd accĭdĕrit ; *some poet says*, pŏēta quĭdam dīcit ; *there is some* (i.e. *something of*) *art in writing*, est ălĭquĭd artis in scrībendo ; *there are (some) who say*, sunt qui dīcant
*sometimes*, interdum, aliquando
*somewhat* (*with adj.*) see Par. 65
*son*, fīlius, -i, m. ; *listen, my son*, audi, mi fili (13)
*son-in-law*, gĕner, -ĕri, m.
*song*, carmen, -ĭnis, n.; cantus, -ûs, m.
*soon*, mox
*soothsayer*, hăruspex, -icis, m.
*sorrow*, dŏlor, -ōris, m.
*sort*, gĕnus, -ĕris, n.
*soul*, ănĭma, -ae, f.
*sound, a*, sŏnus, -i, m ; sŏnĭtus, -ûs, m.
*sound, to*, sŏno, -ui, -ĭtum, 1 ; *the trumpet sounds*, tūba cănit
*sour*, ăcerbus, -a, -um
*source*, fons, -ntis, m.
*sow*, sĕro, sĕvi, sătum, 3.
*space*, spătium, -i, n.
*Spain*, Hispānia, -ae, f.
*spare*, parco, pĕperci, parsum, 3 (*g. dat.*)
*Sparta*, Sparta, -ae, f.
*speak*, dīco, -xi, -ctum, 3 ; lŏquor, -cūtus, 3 dep.
*spear*, hasta, -ae, f.
*spectacle*, spectācŭlum, -i, n.
*spectre*, spectrum, -i, n. [-ōnis, f.
*speech*, ōrātio. -ōnis, f. ; contio,
*speed*, cĕlĕrĭtās, -ātis, f.; *with speed, speedily*, cĕlĕrĭter
*spend*, consūmo, -sumpsi, -sumptum, 3 [m.
*spirit*, spīrĭtus, -ûs, m.; ănĭmus, -i,
*splendid*, splendĭdus, -a, -um

*splendour*, splendor, -ōris, m.
*spoil*, spŏlio, 1 (*acc. of pers., abl. of thing*)
*spoils*, spŏlia, -ōrum, n.
*sport*, lūdus, -i, m.
*spot*, lŏcus, -i, m.; plur. lŏca
*spring*, vĕr, vĕris, n.
*spring forward*, prōsĭlio, -sĭlui, -sultum, 4
*spur*, calcar, -āris, n. (39)
*spurn*, sperno, sprēvi, sprētum, 3
*spy*, explōrātor, -ōris, m.
*squander*, dissĭpo, 1.
*stab*, confŏdio, -fōdi, -fossum, 3
*stag*, cervus, -i, m.
*stand*, sto, stĕti, statum, 1
*stand up*, consurgo, -surrexi, 3
*standard*, signum, -i, n.
*star*, stella, -ae, f. ; sīdus, -ĕris. n.
*state*, cīvĭtās, -ātis, f. ; respublica, reipublicae, f.
*station, to*, lŏco, 1
*statue*, stătua, -ae, f.
*stay*, mănĕo, -nsi, -nsum, 2 ; mŏror, -ātus, 1 dep.
*steadily*, constanter [-ōcis
*stern*, sĕvĕrus, -a, -um ; atrox,
*sternness*, sĕvĕrĭtās, -ātis, f.
*stick*, băcŭlus, -i, m.
*still* (i. e. *yet*), adhūc
*stir*, mŏveo, mōvi, mōtum, 2
*stomach*, venter, -tris, m.
*stone*, lăpĭs, -ĭdis, m. ; saxum, -i, n.
*stop*, consisto, -stĭti, -stĭtum, 3
*stop*, (*trans.*) mŏror, 1, dep.
*storm*, prŏcella, -ae, f. ; tempestās, -ātis, f.
*storm, to*, expugno, 1
*story*, fābŭla, -ae, f.
*straight*, rectus, -a, -um
*strange*, mīrus, -a, -um
*stranger*, hospĕs, -ĭtis, m. ; advĕna, -ae, m.
*stratagem*, dŏlus, -i. m.
*stream*, flūmen, -ĭnis, n. ; rīvus, -i, m.

*street*, vīcus, -i, m.
*strength*, vīres, -ium, f. pl.
*strengthen*, firmo, 1
*stretch out*, extendo, -di, -sum, 3
*strew*, sterno, strāvi, strātum, 3
*strike*, *strike down*, caedo, cĕcĭdi, caesum, 3 ; *having been struck by lightning*, fulmĭne ictus (-a, -um)
*strive*, (i.e. *endeavour*) nītor, nīsus or nixus, 3, dep. (*with* ut *and subjunctive*); (i.e. *fight*) certo, 1 ; *we strive for mastery with the Roman people*, de impĕrio cum pŏpŭlo Rōmāno armis certāmus (*constr. with inf., and with dat. for* cum, *is mostly poetical*)
*strong*, vălĭdus, -a, -um
*struggle*, certāmen, -ĭnis, n.
*struggle, to*, luctor, 1 dep.
*study*, stŭdium, -i, n.
*study, to*, stŭdeo, -ui, 2 (*g. dat.*)
*stuff, to*, farcio, farsi, fartum, 4
*stupid*, stultus, -a, -um
*subdue*, *subjugate*, sŭbĭgo, -ēgi, -actum, 3
*subtle*, callĭdus, -a, -um .
*subtract*, dēmo, dempsi, demptum, 3 (*foll. by* de ; *or dat. of pers., acc. of thing*)
*succeed, I succeed*, i.e. *I prosper*, rēs mĭhĭ bĕnĕ succēdit, *or* rem bĕnĕ gĕro. N.B. *not, in this sense*, succēdo, -ssi, -ssum, 3, *which is only used for "take the place of," and g. dat.; fresh men succeeded the wearied*, integri dēfătīgātis successērunt
*success*, victōria, -ae, f. ; *they returned without s.*, rē infectā rĕdĭērunt
*successfully*, fēlīcĭter ; *more successfully*, fēlīcius
*succumb*, succumbo, succŭbui, succŭbĭtum, 3 (*g. dat.*)
*such*, tālis, -e
*sudden*, sŭbĭtus, -a, -um

*suddenly*, rĕpentē, sŭbĭto, stătim
*Suevi*, Suēvi, -ōrum, m.
*suffer*, pătior, passus, 3 dep.
*sufficient*, sătis, *indcl.* ; ĭdōneus, -a, -um ; *sufficiently good*, sătĭs bŏnus
*suited for*, *suitable*, aptus, -a, -um, ĭdōneus, -a, -um (*with dat. or* ad ; aptus, *with persons, dat.*)
*sum of money*, pĕcūnia, -ae, f.
*summer*, aestas, -ātis, f.
*summit*, culmen, -ĭnis, n.
*summon*, vŏco, 1 ; convŏco, 1
*sun*, sōl, sōlis, m.
*sunrise*, lūx, lūcis, f. ; sōlis ortus
*sunset*, sōlis occāsus
*sup*, cēno, 1
*superstition*, sŭperstĭtio, -ōnis, f.
*supper*, cēna, -ae, f.
*suppliant*, supplex, -ĭcis
*supplies*, commeātus, -ūs, m. ; *we are hindered from getting s.*, prŏhĭbēmur commeātu
*support* (*nourish*), nūtrio, -īvi, -ītum, 4 ; sustĭneo, -ui, -tentum, 2 ; sustento, 1
*suppose*, pŭto, 1
*supreme*, suprēmus, -a, -um ; summus, -a, -um
*sure*, certus, -a, -um
*surname*, cognōmen, -ĭnis, n.
*surrender*, trādo, -dĭdi, -dĭtum, 3 ; *also* (*but most frequ. of s. persons*) dēdo, dēdĭdi, dēdĭtum, 3
*surround*, circumdo, -dĕdi, -dătum, dăre (*acc. and abl. or acc. and dat.* ; *see Ex. LXII.*) [*dat.*)
*survive*, sŭpersum, -fui, -esse (*g. suspicion*, suspĭcio, -ōnis, f.
*sustain*, sustĭneo, 2 ; (*nourish*), nutrio, -īvi, -ītum, 4
*swallow*, hĭrundo, -ĭnis, f.
*swan*, cycnus, -i, m.
*swear*, jūro, 1 ; *I swear to come*, j. me ventūrum esse ; *I s. to obey a law*, j. in lēgem.
*sweat*, sūdor, -ōris, m.

*sweet*, dulcis, -e ; suāvis, -e
*swift*, cĕler, -is, -e
*swiftly*, celĕrīter
*swiftness*, celĕrĭtās, -ātis, f.
*swim, to*, no, nāvi, nātum, 1
*sword*, glădius, -i, m. ; *with fire and sword*, ferro atque igni
*Syracuse*, Sўrācūsae, -ārum, f. pl.
*Syria*, Sўria, -ae, f.

**Table**, mensa, -ae, f.
*tail*, cauda, -ae, f.
*take*, căpio, cēpi, captum, 3 ; *take away*, adĭmo, -ēmi, -emptum, 3 ; aufĕro, abstŭli, ablātum, auferre; *take by storm*, expugno, 1 ; *take care of*, cūro, 1 (*g. acc.*); *take care to*, cūrā ut ; *take place*, see *happen*
*talk*, lŏquor, lŏcūtus, 3 dep.
*talkative*, lŏquāx, -ācis
*tall*, prōcērus, -a, -um ; altus, -a, [-um
*tame*, mansuētus, -a, -um ; *to tame*, dŏmo, -ui, -ĭtum, 1
*Tarquin*, Tarquīnius, -i, m.
*task*, ŏpus, -ĕris, n.
*taste*, gusto, 1
*tasteful*, ēlĕgans, -ntis ; *tastefully*, ĕlĕganter
*Tatius*, Tătius, -i, m.
*Taurus, mount*, Taurus, -i, m.
*tax*, trĭbūtum, -i, n. ; vectīgal, -ālis, n.
*teach*, dŏceo, -ui, -ctum, 2 (*g. two acc.*) See Par. 312
*teacher*, măgister, -tri, m.
*tear*, lăcrĭma, -ae, f.
*tear, to*, scindo, scĭdi, scissum, 3 ; *tear away*, āvello, -velli, -vulsum, 3 ; *tear out*, ēvello, -velli, -vulsum, 3 ; *to tear away from one's embrace*, āvellĕre de amplexu
*tell*, dīco, -xi, -ctum, 3, *dat. & acc.*
*temerity*, tĕmĕrĭtās, -ātis, f.
*temper*, ănĭmus, -i, m.
*tempest*, tempestās, -ātis, f. ; prōcella, -ae, f.

*temple*, templum, -i, n. ; aedes, -is f.
*ten*, dĕcem, *indecl.* : (*distr.*) dēnus -a, -um ; *see* Par. 314
*tender*, tĕner, -ĕra, ĕrum (61)
*tent*, tentōrium, -i, n.
*tenth*, dĕcĭmus, -a, -um
*terminate*, finio, 4
*terrible*, dīrus, -a, -um
*terrify*, terreo, -ui, -ĭtum, 2
*territories*, fīnes, -ium, m.
*terror*, terror, -ōris, m.
*Thames*, Tămĕsis, -is, m.
*than*, (62, 63) quam
*thanks*, grātiae, -ārum, f.; *I return t.*, grātias ăgo
*that (dem. pron.)*, illĕ, -a, -ud ; īs, ĕa, ĭd ; *that of yours*, istĕ, -a, -ud (*if used with adj. and nouns the position of* illĕ, ĭs, istĕ *is like that of* hic ; *see* "*this*")
*that (rel. pron.)* qui ; *that (nom. or abl.)* . . . *not*, quīn (145, 300) ; *there was no one that did not hate you*, nēmo ĕrat quīn tē ōdisset
*that (conj.)* ut ; *that not*, nē (131); (*with comp.*) quo (303) ; *that they might the more easily go*, quo făcĭlius īrent. N.B. *Unless* "*that*" *denotes purpose or consequence, it must not be rendered by* ut
*theatre*, theātrum, -i, n.
*Theban*, Thēbānus, -ī, m.
*Thebes*, Thēbae, -ārum, f.
*theft*, furtum, -i, n.
*their*, eōrum, eārum, eōrum ; (*own*) suus, -a, -um
*Themistocles*, Thĕmistŏclēs, -is, m.
*then*, tum ; tunc ; deinde ; *see* tum, tunc *in L. Vocab.*
*thence*, inde
*there*, ĭbi, illīc ; *often not trans. in Lat., e.g. there are some who say* sunt qui dīcant [*Vocab.*
*therefore*, ĭgĭtur, ĭtăquĕ ; *see Lat.*
*Thermopylae*, Thermŏpўlae, -ārum, f.

Y

*Thetis*, Thětis, -ĭdis, f.
*thick*, (*of garments*) crassus, -a, um ; densus, -a, -um
*thicket*, dūmētūm, -i, n.
*thief*, fūr, -is, m.
*thin*, măcer, -cra, -crum ; tenuis, -e
*thing*, rēs, rei, f.
*think*, pŭto, 1 ; existĭmo, 1 ; cōgito, 1 ; reor, rătus, rēri ; *thinking that the enemy were at hand*, rătus hostes ădesse ; *I thought to myself*, mēcum cōgĭtābam
*third*, tertius, -a, -um
*thirst*, sĭtis, -is, f. *acc.* -im, *abl.* -i ; *to die of thirst*, sĭtī mŏri
*thirteen*, trĕdĕcim, *indecl.*
*thirty*, trīgintā, *indecl.*
*this*, hic, haec, hōc (*if used with Adj. and Noun, mostly comes between the two ; this sad calamity*, tristis haec călămĭtās ; *or else* tam, "*so*" *is inserted*, haec tam tristis c. ; *this great army*, hic tantus exercĭtus). N.B. *the same rule applies to the pron. adj. generally*, illĕ, istĕ, meus, tuus, &c.
*thither*, eo, illūc
*thou*, tū, see p. 45
*though*, quamvis (*g. subj.*) ; quamquam (*g. ind.*), *see* Par. 323
*thousand, see* Par. 80
*threat*, mĭna, -ae, f.
*threaten*, mĭnor, 1, dep. (*g. acc. of thing and dat. of person*) ; *I threaten you with death*, mĭnor tĭbĭ mortem
*three*, trēs, trīa (78) ; *three hundred*, trĕcenti, -ae, -a ; *three hundred apiece*, trĕcēni, -ae, -a (314) ; *three times*, *thrice*, ter ; *three days*, trĭdŭum, -i, n. ; *three years*, triennium, -i, n.
*thrifty*, parcus, -a, -um
*throat*, guttur, -ŭris, n.
*throne*, sŏlium, -i, n.

*through*, pĕr (*g. acc.*)
*throw*, conjĭcio, -jēci, -jectum, 3
*thrush*, turdus, -i, m.
*thumb*, pollex, -ĭcis, m.
*thunder, to*, tŏno, -ui, -ĭtum, 1
*thunderbolt*, fulmen, -ĭnis, n.
*thus*, sīc, ĭtā
*thy*, tuus, -a, -um
*Tiber*, Tībĕris, -is, m.
*tide*, aestus, -ūs, m.
*tiger*, tigris, -is *or* -ĭdis, c.
*till*, dōnec, dum, quoad ; *to till*, cŏlo, -ui, cultum, 3
*time*, tempus, -ŏris, n. ; *a second time*, ĭtĕrum ; *by this time*, jam ; *four times*, see "*four*"
*timely*, opportūnus, -a, -um
*timid*, tĭmĭdus, -a, -um
*Titus*, Tītus, -i, m.
*to*, ĭn, ăd (*g. acc.*). N.B. (1) "*to*" *before a verb is never to be rend. by the Lat. inf. unless the inf. is the subj. or obj. of another verb ;* (2) *nor by the supine except after a verb of motion ;* (3) *it is rendered by the subjunctive when meaning* "*in order to,*" *and also after verbs of asking, &c.* (143) ; (4) *see also* ăd *and gerundive* (186)
*to-day*, hŏdiē
*together*, sĭmul, ūna ; *having conversed*, inter sēsē collŏcūti
*toil*, lăbor, -ōris, m.
*token*, indĭcium ; -i, n. ; *pledge*, pignus, -ŏris, n.
*tolerate*, pătior, passus, 3 dep.
*tomb*, sĕpulcrum, -i, n. ; tŭmŭlus, -i, m.
*to-morrow*, cras
*tongue*, lingua, -ae, f.
*too, too much*, (*adv.*) nĭmis, nĭmium ; *too little*, părum (*adv.* used also as a *noun*) ; *he has too little strength*, părum vīrium hăbet ; *this task is too difficult for you to accomplish*, hōc ŏpus difficĭlius est quam quod (*or* ut

hŏc) perfĭcĭās; *see also* Par. 64, 149
**tooth**, dens, -tis, m.
**top**, vertex, -ĭcis, m.; *the top of the mountain*, mons summus
**torch**, taeda, -ae, f.; fax, fācis, f.
**turn**, lacer, -ĕra, -ĕrum
**torture**, crŭciātus, -ūs, m.
**touch**, tango, tetĭgi, tactum, 3
**towards**, versus (*of places*); ergā (*of conduct towards persons*); ad (*all g. acc.*), *see* Par. 183
**tower**, turris, -is, f.
**town**, oppĭdum, -i, n.
**trace**, vestīgium -i, n.
**train**, exerceo, -ui, -ītum, 2; (*educate*) ērŭdio, -ivi, -ītum, 4
**traitor**, prodĭtor, -ōris, m.
**tranquil**, tranquillus, -a, -um
**tranquillity**, tranquillĭtas, -ātis, f.
**transact**, ago, ēgi, actum, 3
**transfer, transport**, transfĕro, -tŭli, -lātum, -ferre
**travel**, ĭter facĕre
**traveller**, viātor, -ōris; m.
**treacherous**, perfĭdus, -a, -um; **treacherously**, per dŏlum
**treachery**, perfĭdia, -ae, f.; dŏlus, -i, m.
**treason**, (*military*) prodĭtio, -ōnis, f.; (*civil*) mājestas, -atis, f.
**treasure**, thēsaurus, -i, m.
**treasury**, aerārium, -i, n.
**treaty**, foedus, -ĕris, n.
**tree**, arbor, -ŏris, f.
**tremble**, trĕmo, -ui, 3; (*from top to toe*) contrĕmo, -ui, 3
**tribe**, trĭbus, -ūs, f.
**tribunal**, trĭbūnal, -ālis, n.
**tribune**, trĭbūnus, -i, m.
**tribuneship**, trĭbūnātus, -ūs, m.
**tribute**, trĭbūtum, -i, n.
**trick**, dŏlus, -i, m.
**trifles**, nūgae, -ārum, f. pl.
**triumph**, triumphus, -i, m.; *to triumph*, triumpho, 1
**Trojan**, Trojānus, -i, m.

**troop** (*of horse*), turma, -ae, f.
**troops**, cōpiae, -ārum, f.
**trophy**, trŏpaeum, -i, n.
**trouble**, ŏpĕra, -ae, f.; *to trouble*, turbo, 1
**troublesome**, mŏlestus, -a, -um
**Troy**, Troja, -ae, f.
**true**, vērus, -a, -um; *truly*, i.e. *truthfully*, vērē
**trumpet**, tŭba, -ae, f.
**trunk**, truncus, -i, m.;
**trust, to**, crēdo, -dĭdi, -dĭtum, 3 (*dat.*); confīdo, -fīsus sum, 3 (*dat of pers., abl. of thing*); *trusting in the nature of their position*, naturā lŏci confīsi; **trust**, fĭdes, -ei, f.
**trusty**, fĭdēlis, -e; fĭdus, -a, -um
**truth**, (*abstract*) vērĭtās, -ātis, f.; (*what is true, fact*) vērum, -i, n.; *if you will have the truth*, si vērum audīre vis; *you have spoken the truth*, vēra dixisti
**try**, cōnor, 1, dep. (*with inf.*); *make proof of*, tento, 1; *we have tried this danger*, tentāvĭmus hoc pĕrĭcŭlum
*Tullius*, Tullius, -i, m. (13)
*Tullia*, Tullia, -ae, f.
*Tulliola*, Tulliola, -ae, f., i.e. *the little Tullia* (*a child's name*)
*Tullus*, Tullus, -i, m.
**tumult**, tŭmultus, -ūs, m.
**turn**, verto, -ti, -sum, 3; *he turned to* (*in speaking*), se convertit ad; *the enemy turned their backs*, i.e. *fled*, terga dĕdĕrunt; *turn out*, ēvĕnio, -vēni, -ventum, 4; *in turn*, invĭcem
**twelve**, see Par. 81; distrib. 314
**twenty, twentieth**, see Pars. 81, 314
**twice**, bis
**twist**, torqueo, -si, -tum, 2
**two**, duo, -ae, -o (78, 314); *two hundred*, dŭcenti, -ae, -a; *two days*, bĭduum, -i, n.
**tyrant**, tўrannus, -i, n.

**Ugliness**, dēformĭtas, -ātis, f.
*ugly*, turpis, -e
*Ulysses*, Ŭlysses, -is, m.
*unable, I am*, nĕqueo, -quīvi, 4; *imperf.* nequībam; *see* L. Vocab.
*unaccustomed*, insŏlĭtus, -a, -um
*unarmed*, ĭnermis, -e
*uncertain*, incertus, -a, -um (*g. gen.*)
*uncultivated*, incultus, -a, -um
*under*, sŭb, Par. 180 (*g. abl. or acc.*); *under Caesar (as general)*, Caesăre dūce (197)
*undergo*, sŭbeo, -īvi *or* -ii, 4
*understand*, intellĕgo, -lexi, -lectum, 3
*undertake*, suscĭpio, -cēpi, -ceptum, 3; *to undertake politics*, căpēssere rem-publĭcam
*undeserving*, indignus, -a, -um (*g. abl.*)
*unequal*, impăr, -păris
*unfair*, ĭnīquus, -a, -um
*unfortunate*, infēlīx, -īcis
*unfriendly*, ĭnĭmīcus, -a, -um
*ungrateful*, ingrātus, -a, -um
*unhappy*, infēlix, -īcis
*unity*, concordia, -ae, f.
*universal*, ūnĭversus, -a, -um
*unjust*, injustus, -a, -um
*unknown*, ignōtus, -a, -um
*unlearned*, indoctus, -a, -um
*unless*, nĭsĭ (*same construction as sī, see Par.* 125, 295)
*unlike*, dissĭmĭlis, -e
*unlucky*, infēlīx, -īcis; infaustus, -a, um [*gen.*]
*unmindful*, immĕmor, -ŏris, (*g.*)
*unpleasant*, ingrātus, -a, -um
*unseasonable*, ĭnopportūnus, -a, -um
*unsuccessfully*, infēlīcĭter
*until*, dum; dōnĕc; quoad; *not until*, nōn antĕquam; *he did not answer until I twice questioned him*, nōn antĕ respondit quam bīs eum interrŏgāvi

*unwarlike*, imbellis, -e
*unwilling, I am v. to come*, nōlo (nōlui, nolle, 234) vĕnīre; *she came unwillingly*, invīta (-a, -um) vĕnit. N.B. *This adj. agrees with its noun, but is only used adverbially;* invītus est *is not Latin* [*abl.*)
*unworthy*, indignus, -a, -um (*g.*)
*uphold*, sustĭneo, -ui, -tentum, 2
*upon*, sŭper (180)
*uprightness*, prŏbĭtās, -ātis, f.
*up to*, tĕnus (178)
*urge*, urgeo, ursi, 2
*us, see* Par. 90, 93
*use, to*, ūtor, usus, 3, dep. (*g. abl.*)
*used, he, they, used to*, &c. (*turn by imperf. indic. or by* sŏleo, sŏlĭtus, 2, *dep.*)
*useful*, ūtĭlis, -e
*useless*, ĭnūtĭlis, e
*usual*, sŏlĭtus, -a, -um
*usually*, fĕrē, plērumquĕ
*utter*, ēdo, -dĭdi, -dĭtum, 3
*utterly*, omnīno; *utterly destroy*, dēleo, -ēvi, -ētum, 2 (*for other verbs used with "utterly," see the verbs themselves*)

**Vain**, vānus, -a, -um; ĭnānis, -e
*vainly, in vain*, frustrā; nēquīquam
*valley*, vallis, -is, f.
*valour*, virtūs, -ūtis, f.
*value*, prĕtium, -i, n.; *to estimate at a high value*, magni aestĭmāre; *to value*, aestĭmo, 1 (283, 284)
*valuable*, prĕtiōsus, -a, -um
*vanish*, ēvānesco, ēvānui, 3
*vanquish*, vinco, vīci, victum, 3
*variety*, vărĭĕtās, -ātis, f.
*various, varying*, vărius, -a, -um
*vast*, ingens, -tis
*venerate (worship)*, vĕnĕror, 1, dep.
*venom*, vīrus, -i, n.
*venture*, audeo, ausus, 2, dep.
*Venus*, Vĕnus, -ĕris, f.

*verse*, versus, -ūs, m.
*very*, ipse, -a, -um ; *your very life*, vīta tua ipsa ; *very small*, parvŭlus, -a, -um ; *very great, very many*, &c., permagnus, permulti, &c.
*vessel*, nāvis, -is, f. ; nāvĭgium, -i, n.
*Vesta*, Vesta, -ae, f.
*vice*, vĭtium, -i, n.
*vicious*, prăvus, -a, -um
*victim*, victīma, -ae, f.
*victor*, victor, -ōris, m.
*victorious*, victor, -ōris, m. ; victrīx, -īcis, f.
*victory*, victōria, -ae, f.
*vigour*, vĭgor, -ōris, m. ; vīres, -ium, f.
*village*, vīcus, -i, m.
*villain*, scĕlestus, -a, -um
*vine*, vītis, -is, f.
*vineyard*, vīnea, -ae, f.
*violate*, vĭŏlo, 1
*violence*, vīs, *acc.* vim, *abl.* vī, f. ; *by v.*, per vim, *or* vī
*violent*, vĭŏlentus, -a, -um
*violently*, vĭŏlenter, *or* vī
*Virgil*, Vergĭlius, -i, m.
*virgin*, virgo, -ĭnis, f.
*virtue*, virtūs, -ūtis, f.
*virtuous*, prŏbus, -a, -um
*vision*, vīsus, -ūs, m. ; *dream*, somnium, -i, n.
*visit*, vīso, -si, 3 ; *visit* (*with punishment*), afficio, -fēci, -fectum, 3
*voice*, vōx, vōcis, f.
*void*, expers, -tis
*vomit forth*, ēvŏmo, -ui, -ĭtum, 3 ; (*against any one*, in *with acc.*)
*vow*, vōtum, -i, n. ; *vow, to*, vŏveo, vōvi, vōtum, 2
*Vulcan*, Vulcānus, -i, m.
*vulture*, vultur, -ūris, m.

**Wage**, gĕro, gessi, gestum, 3 ; *I wage war*, bellum gĕro

*wait*, mǎneo, -nsi, -nsum, 2 ; *wait for*, expecto, 1
*walk*, ambŭlo, 1
*wall*, mūrus, -i, m. ; *town walls*, moenia, -ium, n. pl.
*wander*, erro, 1 ; văgor, pălor, 1, dep.
*wandering*, error, -ōris, m.
*want*, inŏpia, -ae, f.
*wanting, to be*, dēsum, -fui, -esse
*war*, bellum, -i, n. ; *in war and in peace*, dŏmi bellīque, *or* (*more commonly*) mīlĭtĭaeque (265) ; *a ship of war*, nāvis longa
*warlike*, bellĭcōsus, -a, -um
*warm*, călĭdus, -a, -um ; *warm, to grow*, călesco, 3
*warmth*, călor, -ōris, m.
*warn*, mŏneo, -ui, -ĭtum, 2 (143)
*wash*, lăvo, lāvi, lōtum, 1
*waste, lay waste*, vasto, 1 ; *to waste time*, tempus tĕrĕre, -trīvi, -trītum, 3 ; *waste* (*adj.*), *a w. district*, rĕgio inculta
*watch*, vĭgĭlia, -ae, f. ; *watch, to*, vĭgĭlo, 1
*water*, ăqua, -ae, f. ; *water, to*, rĭgo, 1 ; *a river waters this valley*, amnis hanc vallem rĭgat
*wave*, fluctus, -ūs, m.
*way*, via, -ae, f. ; ĭter, itinĕris, n.: *manner*, mŏdus, -i, m. ; *in what way?* quōmŏdo?
*we*, see page 45
*weak*, infirmus, -a, -um
*weaken*, mĭnuo, -ui, ūtum, 3
*weakness*, dēbĭlĭtās, -ātis, f.
*wealth*, dīvĭtiae, -ārum, f. ; ŏpes, -um, f.
*wealthy*, dīvĕs, -ĭtis
*weapon*, tēlum, -i, n.
*weary*, fessus, -a, -um ; *I am weary of*, taedet mē (*g. gen.*) Par. 222 and foll.
*weave*, texo, -ui, -xtum, 3
*web*, tēla, -ae, f.
*weep*, fleo, flēvi, flētum, 2

*weight*, pondus, -ĕris, n.
*weighty*, grăvis, -e
*well, a,* pŭteus, -i, m.; (*adv.*) bĕnĕ; *well, to be,* vălĕo, -ui, 2; *well known, it is,* constat, 1, impers.
*west,* occĭdens, -tis, m.
*wet,* mădĭdus, -a, -um
*whale,* bālaena, -ae, f.
*what?* quĭd? (*that which*) quod; *what was good for one was bad for another,* quod ălii prōfuit, ălii obfuit; *what deed? see* Par. 111
*what* (*in order of number*)? quŏtus, -a, -um? *what o'clock?* quŏta hōra?
*whatever,* quisquis, quīcumquĕ; *w. he said, was false,* quodcumquĕ dixit, falsum ĕrat; (*oft. used partitively*) *whatever arms we had, were given up to the enemy,* quidquid (*or* quodcumquĕ) armōrum hăbuĭmus, hostĭbus trādĭtum est
*when,* (1) cum,[1] ŭbi; (2) (*interrogative*), quando? (*also used dependently*); *tell me when you will come,* dīc mĭhĭ quando ventūrus sīs
*whence,* undĕ [ŭbi?
*where,* quā, ŭbi; (*interrogative*)
*whether,* conj. (1) (*in dep. quest.*) num, nōnnĕ (135); *whether...or,* (a) utrum...ăn, (b) -nĕ...ăn (171); *I do not know w.,* nescio ăn (302)
*whether,* conj. (2) (*in alternative suppositions*), *whether...or* (a) sīve... sīve, (b) seu...seu; *whether this is true or false, I shall go to Rome,* ĕquĭdem, sīve haec vēra sunt, sīve falsa, Rōmam ībo

*whether* (*archaic pron.*) *whether of the two?* ŭter? utra? utrum?
*which,* qui, quae, quod; (*of the two*) ŭter, utra, utrum, see Par. 85
*while,* dum (272), *foll. by indic.*
*white,* candĭdus, -a, -um
*whither,* quō; *whither in the world?* quonam terrārum?
*who,* qui, quae, quod; *T. was the first who did this,* T. prīmus hōc fēcit; (*interrogative*) quĭs, quĭd
*whole,* tōtus, -a, -um (85); *the whole of the valley,* vallis tōta
*why,* cūr?
*wicked,* imprŏbus, -a, -um
*wickedness,* scĕlus, -ĕris, n.
*wide,* lātus, -a, -um
*wife,* uxor, -ōris, f.
*wild,* fĕrus, -a, -um; *w. beast,* fĕra, -ae, f.; *wild boar,* ăper, -pri, m.
*will,* vŏluntas, -ātis, f.
*willing, to be,* vŏlo, vŏlui, velle
*willingly,* lībenter
*wind,* ventus, -i, m.
*wine,* vīnum, -i, n.
*wing,* āla, -ae, f.; *of an army,* cornū, -ūs, n.
*winter,* hiemps, -ĕmis, f.; *winter quarters,* hīberna, -ōrum, n.
*wisdom,* săpientia, -ae, f.; (*military*) *as distinct from "valour,"* consĭlium, -i, n.
*wise,* săpiens, -tis
*wish,* vŏluntas, -ātis, f.; stŭdium, -i, n.; *wish, to, or wish for,* vŏlo, velle, vŏlui; pp. 128, 129
*with,* cum (g. abl.); (*in-the-house-of*) ăpŭd (178)
*withdraw* (*trans.*), dētrăho, -traxi, -tractum, 3; (*intrans.*) recēdo, -cessi, -cessum, 3

---

[1] The form **quum**, which is still erroneously retained in some modern editions of classical authors, has no authority. It is "of the rarest possible occurrence even in late MSS." and was long ago described by an eminent grammarian as "dead and buried."

*within*, intrā (*g. acc.*); (*adv.*) intus; *w. three days*, tribus his diēbus (263a)
*without*, sĭnĕ (*g. abl.*); (*outside*), extrā (*g. acc.*), (*adv.*) extrā; *without accomplishing anything*, rē infectā; *without the knowledge of*, clam (*g. abl.*)
*withstand*, rĕsisto, -stĭti, -stĭtum, 3 (*g. dat.*)
*witness*, testis, -is, m.; *witness, call to*, testor, 1, dep.
*witty*, lĕpĭdus, -a, -um
*woe!* vae! (*interjection*)
*wolf*, lŭpus, -i, m.
*woman*, mŭlier, -ĕris, f.; fēmina, -ae, f.
*womanish*, mŭliebris, -e
*wonder, wonder at*, mīror, 1; dep.
*wonderful*, mīrus, -a, -um
*wont, to be*, sŏleo, sŏlĭtus, 2; (*also rend. by imperf. indic.*) *the land was wont to be laid waste*; ăger vastābātur
*wood, a*, silva, -ae, f.; *wood*, mătĕries, ēi, f.
*wooden*, ligneus, -a, -um
*wool*, lāna, -ae, f.
*word*, verbum, -i, n.; *to keep one's word*, fīdem praestāre; *to bring word*, rēnuntiāre
*work*, ŏpus, -ĕris, n.
*workman*, făber, -ri, m.
*world, where, whither, &c., in the world?* ŭbī, quonam, *&c.*, terrārum? *the world*, (terrarum) orbis, -is, m.; N.B. mundus, -i, m. *means "universe" incl. the stars; the Campanian country is the most beautiful in the world*, ăger Campānus orbis (*gen.*) terrārum pulcherrĭmus est
*worm*, vermis, -is, m.
*worn out*, confectus, -a, -um
*worse*, pĕjor, -ōris (68)
*worship*, cŏlo, -ui, -cultum, 3
*worst*, pessĭmus, -a, -um (69)

*worth, to be*, văleo, -ui, 2
*worthless (of men)*, nēquam, *indecl.*; *more w., most w.*, see Par. 68
*worthy*, dignus, -a, -um (*g. abl.*); *the worthy Tullius*, T., vīr optĭmus; *worthy, to deem*, dignor, 1, dep. (*g. abl.*)
*would, he would not* (i.e. *wished not to*) *come*, nōluit venīre; *he would* (i.e. *he was determined to*) *come*, vŏluit vĕnīre
*would that*, ūtĭnam (*g. pres. subj. of possible, imperf. subj. of impossible wishes*; see Par. 295)
*wound*, vulnus, -ĕris, n.; *wound, to*, vulnĕro, 1
*wrath*, īra, -ae, f.
*wreck*, naufrăgium, -i, n.
*wreath*, sertum, -i, n.
*wrest, to*, extorqueo, -torsi, -tortum, 2 (*dat. of pers. or abl. with* a)
*wretched*, mĭser, -ĕra, -ĕrum
*write*, scrībo, scripsi, scriptum, 3
*writer*, scriptor, -ōris, m.
*wrong, a*, iniūria, -ae, f.

**Xenophon**, Xĕnŏphon, -phontis, m.
*Xerxes*, Xerxēs, -is, m.

**Year**, annus, -i, m.
*yearly, every year*, quŏtannīs
*yesterday*, hĕri; *yesterday night*, nox hesterna
*yet, as yet*, ădhūc; *nevertheless*, tămen (*at the beginning of a clause, or after an emphatic word*); *not yet*, nōndum
*yield*, cēdo, cessi, cessum, 3 (*g. dat.*)
*yoke*, iŭgum, -i, n; *to send under the yoke*, sub jŭgum mittĕre
*you*, vōs; see page 45
*young (man)*, jŭvĕnis, -is, -m.; ădūlescens, -tis, m.; (*boys*), pŭĕri

parvŭli; *young (ones)*, pulli, -ōrum, m. ; '*the young*' *may be transl.* jūniōres, *or* pŭĕri
*younger*, jūnior, -iōris (69) ; *youngest*, mĭnĭmus nātu
*your*, vester, -tra, -trum

*yourself*, see Par. 105 (*not* sē)
*youth*, iŭvēntūs, -ūtis, f.; *youth, a juvĕnis*, -is, m.

**Zeal**, stŭdium, -i, n. ; *with zeal*, cum (*or* summo) stŭdio, 181

### Note on se, suus, &c.

**Sē, suus** are used (not **eum, eius**) only when the Pronoun (1) refers to the Principal Subject; (2) is in a Subordinate Clause. Unless *both* these conditions are satisfied, **sē, suus** must not be used.

I. In the following examples condition (1) is satisfied, but (2) is not : (*a*) *T. thanks me, for I helped him*, T. grātias mĭhi ăgit, nam **ei** subvēni; (*b*) *T. loves me, and I forgive him*, T. mē ămat, ĕt **ei** ignosco ; (*c*) *T. and his brother came*, T. et frāter **eius** vēnērunt.

II. In the following, (2) is satisfied, but (1) is not : (*a*) *I know that he rejoices ;* Scio **eum** gaudēre; (*b*) *I said that his brother had come*, Dixi frātrem **eius** vēnīsse.

III. In the following, *both* conditions are satisfied : (*a*) *He begs me to pardon him* (i.e. *himself*), Ōrat ŭt **sĭbi** ignoscam ; (*b*) *He asks whether you saw his brother*, Quaerit num frātrem **suum** vīdĕris.

www.ingramcontent.com/pod-product-compliance
Lightning Source LLC
Chambersburg PA
CBHW030745250426

**43672CB00028B/789**